T0184709

Lecture Notes in Computer Science 12652

Advanced Research in Computing and Software Science
Subline of Lecture Notes in Computer Science

More information about this subseries at http://www.springer.com/series/7407

Jan Friso Groote · Kim Guldstrand Larsen (Eds.)

Tools and Algorithms for the Construction and Analysis of Systems

27th International Conference, TACAS 2021
Held as Part of the European Joint Conferences
on Theory and Practice of Software, ETAPS 2021
Luxembourg City, Luxembourg, March 27 – April 1, 2021
Proceedings, Part II

 Springer

Editors
Jan Friso Groote
Eindhoven University of Technology
Eindhoven, The Netherlands

Kim Guldstrand Larsen
Aalborg University
Aalborg East, Denmark

ISSN 0302-9743   ISSN 1611-3349   (electronic)
Lecture Notes in Computer Science
ISBN 978-3-030-72012-4   ISBN 978-3-030-72013-1   (eBook)
https://doi.org/10.1007/978-3-030-72013-1

LNCS Sublibrary: SL1 – Theoretical Computer Science and General Issues

This Springer imprint is published by the registered company Springer Nature Switzerland AG
The registered company address is: Gewerbestrasse 11, 6330 Cham, Switzerland

ETAPS Foreword

Welcome to the 24th ETAPS! ETAPS 2021 was originally planned to take place in Luxembourg in its beautiful capital Luxembourg City. Because of the Covid-19 pandemic, this was changed to an online event.

ETAPS 2021 was the 24th instance of the European Joint Conferences on Theory and Practice of Software. ETAPS is an annual federated conference established in 1998, and consists of four conferences: ESOP, FASE, FoSSaCS, and TACAS. Each conference has its own Program Committee (PC) and its own Steering Committee (SC). The conferences cover various aspects of software systems, ranging from theoretical computer science to foundations of programming languages, analysis tools, and formal approaches to software engineering. Organising these conferences in a coherent, highly synchronised conference programme enables researchers to participate in an exciting event, having the possibility to meet many colleagues working in different directions in the field, and to easily attend talks of different conferences. On the weekend before the main conference, numerous satellite workshops take place that attract many researchers from all over the globe.

ETAPS 2021 received 260 submissions in total, 115 of which were accepted, yielding an overall acceptance rate of 44.2%. I thank all the authors for their interest in ETAPS, all the reviewers for their reviewing efforts, the PC members for their contributions, and in particular the PC (co-)chairs for their hard work in running this entire intensive process. Last but not least, my congratulations to all authors of the accepted papers!

ETAPS 2021 featured the unifying invited speakers Scott Smolka (Stony Brook University) and Jane Hillston (University of Edinburgh) and the conference-specific invited speakers Işil Dillig (University of Texas at Austin) for ESOP and Willem Visser (Stellenbosch University) for FASE. Inivited tutorials were provided by Erika Ábrahám (RWTH Aachen University) on analysis of hybrid systems and Madhusudan Parthasararathy (University of Illinois at Urbana-Champaign) on combining machine learning and formal methods.

ETAPS 2021 was originally supposed to take place in Luxembourg City, Luxembourg organized by the SnT - Interdisciplinary Centre for Security, Reliability and Trust, University of Luxembourg. University of Luxembourg was founded in 2003. The university is one of the best and most international young universities with 6,700 students from 129 countries and 1,331 academics from all over the globe. The local organisation team consisted of Peter Y.A. Ryan (general chair), Peter B. Roenne (organisation chair), Joaquin Garcia-Alfaro (workshop chair), Magali Martin (event manager), David Mestel (publicity chair), and Alfredo Rial (local proceedings chair).

ETAPS 2021 was further supported by the following associations and societies: ETAPS e.V., EATCS (European Association for Theoretical Computer Science), EAPLS (European Association for Programming Languages and Systems), and EASST (European Association of Software Science and Technology).

The ETAPS Steering Committee consists of an Executive Board, and representatives of the individual ETAPS conferences, as well as representatives of EATCS, EAPLS, and EASST. The Executive Board consists of Holger Hermanns (Saarbrücken), Marieke Huisman (Twente, chair), Jan Kofron (Prague), Barbara König (Duisburg), Gerald Lüttgen (Bamberg), Caterina Urban (INRIA), Tarmo Uustalu (Reykjavik and Tallinn), and Lenore Zuck (Chicago).

Other members of the steering committee are: Patricia Bouyer (Paris), Einar Broch Johnsen (Oslo), Dana Fisman (Be'er Sheva), Jan Friso Groote (Eindhoven), Esther Guerra (Madrid), Reiko Heckel (Leicester), Joost-Pieter Katoen (Aachen and Twente), Stefan Kiefer (Oxford), Fabrice Kordon (Paris), Jan Křetínský (Munich), Kim G. Larsen (Aalborg), Tiziana Margaria (Limerick), Andrew M. Pitts (Cambridge), Grigore Roşu (Illinois), Peter Ryan (Luxembourg), Don Sannella (Edinburgh), Lutz Schröder (Erlangen), Ilya Sergey (Singapore), Mariëlle Stoelinga (Twente), Gabriele Taentzer (Marburg), Christine Tasson (Paris), Peter Thiemann (Freiburg), Jan Vitek (Prague), Anton Wijs (Eindhoven), Manuel Wimmer (Linz), and Nobuko Yoshida (London).

I'd like to take this opportunity to thank all the authors, attendees, organizers of the satellite workshops, and Springer-Verlag GmbH for their support. I hope you all enjoyed ETAPS 2021.

Finally, a big thanks to Peter, Peter, Magali and their local organisation team for all their enormous efforts to make ETAPS a fantastic online event. I hope there will be a next opportunity to host ETAPS in Luxembourg.

February 2021

Marieke Huisman
ETAPS SC Chair
ETAPS e.V. President

Preface

TACAS 2021 was the 27th edition of the International Conference on Tools and Algorithms for the Construction and Analysis of Systems conference series. TACAS 2021 was part of the 24th European Joint Conferences on Theory and Practice of Software (ETAPS 2021), which although originally planned to take place in Luxembourg City, was held as an online event on March 27 to April 1 due the the COVID-19 pandemic.

TACAS is a forum for researchers, developers, and users interested in rigorously based tools and algorithms for the construction and analysis of systems. The conference aims to bridge the gaps between different communities with this common interest and to support them in their quest to improve the utility, reliability, flexibility, and efficiency of tools and algorithms for building computer-controlled systems. There were four types of submissions for TACAS:

- Research papers advancing the theoretical foundations for the construction and analysis of systems.
- Case study papers with an emphasis on a real-world setting.
- Regular tool papers presenting a new tool, a new tool component, or novel extensions to an existing tool and requiring an artifact submission.
- Tool demonstration papers focusing on the usage aspects of tools, also subject to the artifact submission requirement.

This year 141 papers were submitted to TACAS, consisting of 90 research papers, 29 regular tool papers, 16 tool demo papers, and 6 case study papers. Authors were allowed to submit up to four papers. Each paper was reviewed by three Program Committee (PC) members, who made extensive use of subreviewers.

Similarly to previous years, it was possible to submit an artifact alongside a paper, which was mandatory for regular tool and tool demo papers. An artifact might consist of a tool, models, proofs, or other data required for validation of the results of the paper. The Artifact Evaluation Committee (AEC) was tasked with reviewing the artifacts, based on their documentation, ease of use, and, most importantly, whether the results presented in the corresponding paper could be accurately reproduced. Most of the evaluation was carried out using a standardised virtual machine to ensure consistency of the results, except for those artifacts that had special hardware requirements.

The evaluation consisted of two rounds. The first round was carried out in parallel with the work of the PC. The judgment of the AEC was communicated to the PC and weighed in their discussion. The second round took place after paper acceptance notifications were sent out; authors of accepted research papers who did not submit an artifact in the first round could submit their artifact here. In total, 72 artifacts were submitted (63 in the first round and 9 in the second), of which 57 were accepted and 15 rejected. This corresponds to an acceptance rate of 79 percent. Papers with an accepted artifact include a badge on the first page.

Selected authors were requested to provide a rebuttal for both papers and artifacts in case a review gave rise to questions. In total 166 rebuttals were provided. Using the review reports and rebuttals the Programme and the Artifact Evaluation Committees extensively discussed the papers and artifacts and ultimately decided to accept 32 research papers, 7 tool papers, 6 tool demos, and 2 case studies.

Besides the regular conference papers, this two-volume proceedings also contains 8 short papers that describe the participating verification systems and a competition report presenting the results of the 10th SV-COMP, the competition on automatic software verifiers for C and Java programs. These papers were reviewed by a separate program committee (PC); each of the papers was assessed by at least three reviewers. A total of 30 verification systems with developers from 11 countries entered the systematic comparative evaluation, including four submissions from industry. Two sessions in the TACAS program were reserved for the presentation of the results: (1) a summary by the competition chair and of the participating tools by the developer teams in the first session, and (2) an open community meeting in the second session.

March/April 2021

Jan Friso Groote
Kim Guldstrand Larsen
Frédéric Lang
Thierry Lecomte
Thomas Neele
Peter Gjøl Jensen
Dirk Beyer
Alfredo Rial

Organization

Program Committee (TACAS)

Christel Baier	TU Dresden, Germany
Dirk Beyer	LMU Munich, Germany
Armin Biere	Johannes Kepler University Linz, Austria
Valentina Castiglioni	Reykjavik University, Iceland
Alessandro Cimatti	Fondazione Bruno Kessler, Italy
Rance Cleaveland	University of Maryland, USA
Pedro R. D'Argenio	Universidad Nacional de Córdoba - CONICET, Argentina
Yuxin Deng	East China Normal University, China
Carla Ferreira	Universidade NOVA de Lisboa, Portugal
Goran Frehse	ENSTA Paris, France
Susanne Graf	Université Grenoble Alpes/CNRS/VERIMAG, France
Jan Friso Groote (Chair)	Eindhoven University of Technology, Netherlands
Orna Grumberg	Technion - Israel Institute of Technology, Israel
Kim Guldstrand Larsen (Chair)	Aalborg University, Denmark
Klaus Havelund	Jet Propulsion Laboratory, USA
Holger Hermanns	Saarland University, Germany
Peter Höfner	Australian National University, Australia
Hossein Hojjat	Rochester Institute of Technology, USA
Falk Howar	TU Dortmund, Germany
David N. Jansen	Institute of Software, Chinese Academy of Sciences, China
Marcin Jurdziński	The University of Warwick, Great Britain
Joost-Pieter Katoen	RWTH Aachen/Universiteit Twente, Germany/Netherlands
Jeroen J. A. Keiren	Eindhoven University of Technology, Netherlands
Sophia Knight	University of Minnesota, USA
Laura Kovács	Vienna University of Technology, Austria
Jan Křetínský	Technical University of Munich, Germany
Alfons Laarman	Leiden University, Netherlands
Frédéric Lang	Inria Grenoble - Rhône-Alpes/CONVECS, France
Thierry Lecomte	ClearSy Systems Engineering, France
Xinxin Liu	Institute of Software, Chinese Academy of Sciences, China
Mieke Massink	CNR-ISTI, Italy
Radu Mateescu	Inria, France
Jun Pang	University of Luxembourg, Luxembourg

Dave Parker	University of Birmingham, Great Britain
Jaco van de Pol	Aarhus University, Denmark
Natasha Sharygina	Università della Svizzera Italiana, Switzerland
Jan Strejček	Masaryk University, Czech Republic
Antti Valmari	University of Jyväskylä, Finland
Björn Victor	Uppsala University, Sweden
Sarah Winkler	Free University of Bozen-Bolzano, Italy

Artifact Evaluation Committee – AEC

Elvio Gilberto Amparore	University of Turin, Italy
Haniel Barbosa	Universidade Federal de Minas Gerais, France
František Blahoudek	University of Texas at Austin, USA
Olav Bunte	Eindhoven University of Technology, Netherlands
Damien Busatto-Gaston	Université Libre de Bruxelles, Belgium
Nathalie Cauchi	University of Oxford, Great Britain
Jesús Mauricio Chimento	KTH, Sweden
Joshua Dawes	University of Luxembourg, Luxembourg
Mathias Fleury	Johannes Kepler University Linz, Austria
Daniel J. Fremont	University of California, Santa Cruz, USA
Manuel Gieseking	University of Oldenburg, Germany
Peter Gjøl Jensen (Chair)	Aalborg University, Denmark
Kush Grover	Technical University of Munich, Germany
Hans-Dieter Hiep	CWI, Netherlands
Daniela Kaufmann	Johannes Kepler University Linz, Austria
Mitja Kulczynski	Kiel University, Germany
Alfons Laarman	Leiden University, Netherlands
Luca Laurenti	University of Oxford, Great Britain
Maurice Laveaux	Eindhoven University of Technology, Netherlands
Yong Li	Institute of Software, Chinese Academy of Sciences, China
Debasmita Lohar	Max Planck Institute for Software Systems, Germany
Viktor Malík	Brno University of Technology, Czech Republic
Joshua Moerman	RWTH Aachen University, Germany
Stefanie Mohr	Technische Universität München, Germany
Marco Muñiz	Aalborg University, Denmark
Thomas Neele (Chair)	Royal Holloway University of London, Great Britain
Wytse Oortwijn	University of Twente, Netherlands
Elizabeth Polgreen	University of Edinburgh, Great Britain
José Proença	CISTER-ISEP and HASLab-INESC TEC, Portugal
Etienne Renault	LRDE, France
Alceste Scalas	Technical University of Denmark, Denmark
Morten Konggaard Schou	Aalborg University, Denmark
Veronika Šoková	Brno University of Technology, Czech Republic
Yoni Zohar	Stanford University, USA

Program Committee and Jury – SV-COMP

Pavel Andrianov (CPALockator)	ISP RAS, Russia
Philipp Berger (NITWIT)	RWTH Aachen, Germany
Dirk Beyer (Chair)	LMU Munich, Germany
Marek Chalupa (Symbiotic)	Masaryk University, Brno, Czech Republic
Lucas Cordeiro (ESBMC-kind)	University of Manchester, Great Britain
Priyanka Darke (VeriAbs)	Tata Consultancy Services, India
Daniel Dietsch (UTaipan)	University of Freiburg, Germany
Gidon Ernst (Korn)	LMU Munich, Germany
Ákos Hajdu (Gazer-Theta)	BME, Hungary
Matthias Heizmann (UAutomizer)	University of Freiburg, Germany
Hossein Hojjat (JayHorn)	Rochester Institute of Technology, USA
Stephan Holzner (CPA-Seq)	LMU Munich, Germany
Falk Howar (JDart)	TU Dortmund, Germany
Soha Hussein (Java Ranger)	University of Minnesota, USA
Omar Inverso (Lazy-CSeq)	Gran Sasso Science Institute, Italy
Saurabh Joshi (Pinaka)	IIT Hyderabad, India
Dominik Klumpp (UKojak)	University of Freiburg, Germany
Henrich Lauko (DIVINE)	Masaryk University, Brno, Czech Republic
Viktor Malík (2LS)	Brno University of Technology, Czech Republic
Felipe R. Monteiro (ESBMC-incr)	Amazon Web Services, USA
Vadim Mutilin (CPA-BAM-BnB)	ISP RAS, Russia
Hernán Ponce de León (Dartagnan)	Bundeswehr University Munich, Germany
Zvonimir Rakamaric (SMACK)	University of Utah, USA
Cedric Richter (PeSCo)	Paderborn University, Germany
Simmo Saan (rGoblint)	University of Tartu, Estonia
Peter Schrammel (JBMC)	University of Sussex/Diffblue, Great Britain
Martin Spiessl (Frama-C)	LMU Munich, Germany
Michael Tautschnig (CBMC)	Amazon Web Services, USA

Steering Committee

Dirk Beyer	LMU Munich, Germany
Rance Cleaveland	University of Maryland, USA
Holger Hermanns	Saarland University, Germany

Joost-Pieter Katoen (Chair)   RWTH Aachen/Universiteit Twente,
                                Germany/Netherlands
Kim Guldstrand Larsen   Aalborg University, Denmark
Bernhard Steffen   Technische Universität Dortmund, Germany

Additional Reviewers

Abate, Carmine
Achilleos, Antonis
Akshay, S.
Andriushchenko, Roman
André, Étienne
Asadi, Sepideh
Ashok, Pranav
Azeem, Muqsit
Bannister, Callum
Barnett, Lee
Basile, Davide
Batz, Kevin
Baumgartner, Peter
Becchi, Anna
ter Beek, Maurice H.
Bendík, Jaroslav
Bensalem, Saddek
van der Berg, Freark
Berg, Jeremias
Berger, Philipp
Bernardo, Marco
Biewer, Sebastian
Bischopink, Christopher
Blicha, Martin
Bønneland, Frederik M.
Bouvier, Pierre
Bozzano, Marco
Brellmann, David
Broccia, Giovanna
Budde, Carlos E.
Bursuc, Sergiu
Cassel, Sofia
Castro, Pablo
Chalupa, Marek
Chen, Mingshuai
Chiang, James
Ciancia, Vincenzo
Ciesielski, Maciej

Clement, Bradley
Coenen, Norine
Cubuktepe, Murat
Degiovanni, Renzo
Demasi, Ramiro
Dierl, Simon
Dixon, Alex
van Dijk, Tom
Donatelli, Susanna
Dongol, Brijesh
Edera, Alejandro
Eisentraut, Julia
Emmi, Michael
Evangelidis, Alexandros
Fedotov, Alexander
Fedyukovich, Grigory
Fehnker, Ansgar
Feng, Weizhi
Ferreira, Francisco
Fleury, Mathias
Freiberger, Felix
Frenkel, Hadar
Friedberger, Karlheinz
Fränzle, Martin
Funke, Florian
Gallá, Francesco
Garavel, Hubert
Geatti, Luca
Gengelbach, Arve
Goodloe, Alwyn
Goorden, Martijn
Goudsmid, Ohad
Griggio, Alberto
Groce, Alex
Grover, Kush
Hafidi, Yousra
Hallé, Sylvain
Hecking-Harbusch, Jesko

Heizmann, Matthias
Holzner, Stephan
Holík, Lukáš
Hyvärinen, Antti
Irfan, Ahmed
Javed, Omar
Jensen, Mathias Claus
Jonas, Martin
Junges, Sebastian
Käfer, Nikolai
Kanav, Sudeep
Kapus, Timotej
Kauffman, Sean
Khamespanah, Ehsan
Kheireddine, Anissa
Kiviriga, Andrej
Klauck, Michaela
Kobayashi, Naoki
Köhl, Maximilian Alexander
Kozachinskiy, Alexander
Kutsia, Temur
Lahkim Bennani, Ismail
Lammich, Peter
Lang, Frédéric
Lanotte, Ruggero
Latella, Diego
Laurenti, Luca
Ledent, Philippe
Lehtinen, Karoliina
Lemberger, Thomas
Li, Jianlin
Li, Qin
Li, Xie
Li, Xin
Lin, Shaokai
Lion, Benjamin
Liu, Jiaxiang
Liu, Wanwei
Loreti, Michele
Magnago, Enrico
Major, Juraj
Marché, Claude
Mariegaard, Anders
Marsso, Lina
Mauritz, Malte
McClurg, Jedidiah

Meggendorfer, Tobias
Metzger, Niklas
Meyer, Roland
Micheli, Andrea
Mittelmann, Munyque
Mizera, Andrzej
Moerman, Joshua
Mohr, Stefanie
Mora, Federico
Mover, Sergio
Mues, Malte
Muller, Lucie
Muroor-Nadumane, Ajay
Möhle, Sibylle
Neele, Thomas
Noll, Thomas
Norman, Gethin
Otoni, Rodrigo
Parys, Paweł
Pattinson, Dirk
Pavela, Jiří
Pena, Lucas
Pinault, Laureline
Piribauer, Jakob
Pirogov, Anton
Pommellet, Adrien
Quatmann, Tim
Rappoport, Omer
Raskin, Jean-François
Rothenberg, Bat-Chen
Rouquette, Nicolas
Rümmer, Philipp
S., Krishna
Šafránek, David
Sankaranarayanan, Sriram
Schallau, Till
Schupp, Stefan
Serwe, Wendelin
Shafiei, Nastaran
Shi, Xiaomu
Síč, Juraj
Sickert, Salomon
Singh, Gagandeep
Slivovsky, Friedrich
Sølvsten, Steffen
Song, Fu

Spel, Jip
Srivathsan, B.
Stankovic, Miroslav
Stock, Gregory
Strejček, Jan
Su, Cui
Suda, Martin
Sun, Jun
Svozil, Alexander
Tian, Chun
Tibo, Alessandro
Tini, Simone
Tonetta, Stefano
Trtík, Marek
Turrini, Andrea

Vandin, Andrea
Weber, Tjark
Weininger, Maximilian
Wendler, Philipp
Wolf, Karsten
Wolovick, Nicolás
Wu, Zhilin
Xu, Ming
Yang, Pengfei
Yang, Xiaoxiao
Zhan, Naijun
Zhang, Min
Zhang, Wenbo
Zhang, Wenhui
Zhao, Hengjun

Contents – Part II

Tool Papers

Tool Demo Papers

Contents – Part I

Verification Techniques (not SMT)

Directed Reachability for Infinite-State Systems*

Michael Blondin[1], Christoph Haase[2], and Philip Offtermatt[1,3] (✉)

[1] Université de Sherbrooke, Sherbrooke, Canada
{michael.blondin, philip.offtermatt}@usherbrooke.ca
[2] University of Oxford, Oxford, United Kingdom
christoph.haase@cs.ox.ac.uk
[3] Max Planck Institute for Software Systems, Saarbrücken, Germany

Abstract. Numerous tasks in program analysis and synthesis reduce to deciding reachability in possibly infinite graphs such as those induced by Petri nets. However, the Petri net reachability problem has recently been shown to require non-elementary time, which raises questions about the practical applicability of Petri nets as target models. In this paper, we introduce a novel approach for efficiently semi-deciding the reachability problem for Petri nets in practice. Our key insight is that computationally lightweight over-approximations of Petri nets can be used as distance oracles in classical graph exploration algorithms such as A* and greedy best-first search. We provide and evaluate a prototype implementation of our approach that outperforms existing state-of-the-art tools, sometimes by orders of magnitude, and which is also competitive with domain-specific tools on benchmarks coming from program synthesis and concurrent program analysis.

Keywords: Petri nets · reachability · shortest paths · model checking

1 Introduction

Many problems in program analysis, synthesis and verification reduce to deciding reachability of a vertex or a set of vertices in infinite graphs, *e.g.*, when reasoning about concurrent programs with an unbounded number of threads, or when arbitrarily many components can be used in a synthesis task. For automated reasoning tasks, those infinite graphs are finitely represented by some mathematical model. Finding the right such model requires a trade-off between the two conflicting goals of maximal expressive power and computational feasibility of the relevant decision problems. Petri nets are a ubiquitous mathematical model that provides a good compromise between those two goals. They are

---

* An extended version containing full proofs as well as a primer on applications of the Petri net reachability problem can be obtained from: arxiv.org/abs/2010.07912. This work is part of a project that has received funding from the European Research Council (ERC) under the European Union's Horizon 2020 research and innovation programme (Grant agreement No. 852769, ARiAT). It is also supported by a Discovery Grant from the Natural Sciences and Engineering Research Council of Canada (NSERC). Parts of this research were carried out while the second author was affiliated with the Department of Computer Science, University College London, UK.

J. F. Groote and K. G. Larsen (Eds.): TACAS 2021, LNCS 12652, pp. 3–23, 2021.
https://doi.org/10.1007/978-3-030-72013-1_1

expressive enough to find a plethora of applications in computer science, in particular in the analysis of concurrent processes, yet the reachability problem for Petri nets is decidable [47,40,41,43]. *Counter abstraction* has evolved as a generic abstraction paradigm that reduces a variety of program analysis tasks to problems in Petri nets or variants thereof such as well-structured transition systems, see *e.g.* [30,39,61,5]. Due to their generality and versatility, Petri nets and their extensions find numerous applications also in other areas, including the design and analysis of protocols [22], business processes [57], biological systems [33,11] and chemical systems [2]. The goal of this paper is to introduce and evaluate an efficient generic approach to deciding the Petri net reachability problem on instances arising from applications in program verification and synthesis.

A Petri net comprises a finite set of *places* with a finite number of *transitions*. Places carry a finite yet unbounded number of *tokens* and transitions can remove and add tokens to places. A *marking* specifies how many tokens each place carries. An example of a Petri net is given on the left-hand side of Figure 1, where the two places $\{p_1, p_2\}$ are depicted as circles and transitions $\{t_1, t_2, t_3\}$ as squares. Places carry tokens depicted as filled circles; thus p_1 carries one token and p_2 carries none. We write this as $[p_1: 1, p_2: 0]$, or $(1,0)$ if there is a clear ordering on the places. Transition t_1 can add a single token to place p_1 at any moment. As soon as a token is present in p_1, it can be consumed by transition t_2, which then adds a token to place p_2 and puts back one token to place p_1. Finally, transition t_3 consumes tokens from p_1 without adding any token at all.

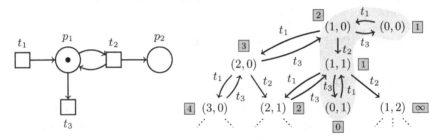

Fig. 1. *Left:* A Petri net $\mathcal{N}$. *Right:* Search of the forthcoming Algorithm 1 over the graph $G_{\mathbb{N}}(\mathcal{N})$ from $(0,0)$ to $(0,1)$, where (x, y) denotes $[p_1: x, p_2: y]$ and each number in a box next to a marking is its heuristic value. Only the blue region is expanded.

A Petri net induces a possibly infinite directed graph whose vertices are markings, and whose edges are determined by the transitions of the Petri net, *cf.* the right side of Figure 1. Given two markings, the *reachability problem* asks whether they are connected in this graph. In Figure 1, the marking $(0,1)$ is reachable from $(0,0)$, *e.g.*, via paths of lengths 3 and 5: $(0,0) \xrightarrow{t_1} (1,0) \xrightarrow{t_2} (1,1) \xrightarrow{t_3} (0,1)$ and $(0,0) \xrightarrow{t_1} (1,0) \xrightarrow{t_1} (2,0) \xrightarrow{t_2} (2,1) \xrightarrow{t_3} (1,1) \xrightarrow{t_3} (0,1)$.

In practice, the Petri net reachability problem is a challenging decision problem due to its horrendous worst-case complexity: an exponential-space lower bound was established in the 1970s [45], and a non-elementary time lower bound has only recently been established [13]. One may thus question whether a problem with such high worst-case complexity is of any practical relevance, and whether reducing program analysis tasks to Petri net reachability is anything else than merely an intellectual exercise. We debunk those concerns and present a technique which decides most reachability instances appearing in the wild. When evaluated on large-scale instances involving Petri nets with thousands of places and tens of thousands of transitions, our prototype implementation is most of the time faster, even up to several orders of magnitude on large-scale instances, and solves more instances than existing state-of-the-art tools. Our implementation is also competitive with specialized domain-specific tools. One of the biggest advantages of our approach is that it is extremely simple to describe and implement, and it readily generalizes to many extensions of Petri nets. In fact, it was surprising to us that our approach has not yet been discovered. We now describe the main observations and techniques underlying our approach.

Ever since the early days of research in Petri nets, state-space over-approximations have been studied to attenuate the high computational complexity of their decision problems. One such over-approximation is, informally speaking, to allow places to carry a negative number of tokens. Deciding reachability then reduces to solving the so-called *state equation*, a system of linear equations associated to a Petri net. Another over-approximation are *continuous Petri nets*, a variant where places carry fractional tokens and "fractions of transitions" can be applied [14]. The benefit is that deciding reachability drops down to polynomial time [25]. While those approximations have been applied for pruning search spaces, see *e.g.* [23,4,8,29], we make the following simple key observation:

> If a marking m is reachable from an initial marking in an over-approximation, then the length of a shortest witnessing path in the over-approximation lower bounds the length of a shortest path reaching m.

The availability of an oracle providing lower bounds on the length of shortest paths between markings enables us to appeal to classical graph traversal algorithms which have been highly successful in artificial intelligence and require such oracles, namely A^* and greedy best-first search, see *e.g.* [52]. In particular, determining the length of shortest paths in the over-approximations described above can be phrased as optimization problems in (integer) linear programming and optimization modulo theories, for which efficient off-the-shelf solvers are available [32,7]. Thus, oracle calls can be made at comparably modest computational cost, which is crucial for the applicability of those algorithms. As a result, a large class of existing state-space over-approximations can be applied to obtain a highly efficient forward-analysis semi-decision procedure for the reachability problem. For example, in Figure 1, using the state equation as distance oracle, A^* only explores the four vertices in the blue region and directly reaches the target vertex, whereas a breadth-first search may need to explore all vertices of the figure and a depth-first search may even not terminate.

In theory, our approach could be turned into a decision procedure by applying bounds on the length of shortest paths in Petri nets [44]. However, such lengths can grow non-elementarily in the number of places [13], and just computing the cut-off length will already be infeasible for any Petri net of practical relevance. It is worth mentioning that, in practice, it has been observed that the over-approximations we employ also often witness non-reachability though, see *e.g.* [23]. Still, when dealing with finite state spaces, our procedure is complete.

A noteworthy benefit of our approach is that it enables finding *shortest* paths when A* is used as the underlying algorithm. In program analysis, paths usually correspond to traces reaching an erroneous configuration. In this setting, shorter error traces are preferred as they help understanding why a certain error occurs. Furthermore, in program synthesis, paths correspond to synthesis plans. Again, shorter paths are preferred as they yield shorter synthesized programs. In fact, we develop our algorithmic framework for *weighted* Petri nets in which transitions are weighted with positive integers. Classical Petri nets correspond to the special instance where all weights are equal to one. Weighted Petri nets are useful to reflect cost or preferences in synthesis tasks. For example, there are program synthesis approaches where software projects are mined to determine how often API methods are called to guide a procedure by preferring more frequent methods [27,26,46]. Similarity metrics can also be used to obtain costs estimating the relevance of invoking methods [24]. It has further been argued that weighted Petri nets are a good model for synthesis tasks of chemical reactions as they can reflect costs of various chemical compounds [58]. Finally, weights can be viewed as representing an amount of time it takes to fire a transition, see *e.g.* [50].

Related work. Our approach falls under the umbrella term *directed model checking* coined in the early 2000s, which refers to a set of techniques to tackle the state-explosion problem via guided state-space exploration. It primarily targets disproving safety properties by quickly finding a path to an error state without the need to explicitly construct the whole state space. As such, directed model checking is useful for bug-finding since, in the words of Yang and Dill [60], *in practice, model checkers are most useful when they find bugs, not when they prove a property.* The survey paper [20] gives an overview over various directed model checking techniques for finite-state systems.

For Petri nets, directed reachability algorithms based on over-approximations as developed in this work have not been described. In [56], it is argued that exploration heuristics, like A*, can be useful for Petri nets, but they do not consider over-approximations for the underlying heuristic functions. The authors of [36] use Petri nets for scheduling problems and employ the state equation, viewed as a system of linear equations over $\mathbb{Q}$, in order to explore and prune reachability graphs. This approach is, however, not guaranteed to discover shortest paths. There has been further work on using A* for exploring the reachability graph of Petri nets for scheduling problems, see, *e.g.*, [42,48] and the references therein.

2   Preliminaries

Let $\mathbb{N} := \{0, 1, \ldots\}$. For all $\mathbb{D} \subseteq \mathbb{Q}$ and $\succ \in \{\geq, >\}$, let $\mathbb{D}_{\succ 0} := \{a \in \mathbb{D} : a \succ 0\}$, and for every set X, let $\mathbb{D}^X$ denote the set of vectors $\mathbb{D}^X := \{v \mid v \colon X \to \mathbb{D}\}$.

We naturally extend operations componentwise. In particular, $(\boldsymbol{u} + \boldsymbol{v})(x) :=$ $\boldsymbol{u}(x) + \boldsymbol{v}(x)$ for every $x \in X$, and $\boldsymbol{u} \geq \boldsymbol{v}$ iff $\boldsymbol{u}(x) \geq \boldsymbol{v}(x)$ for every $x \in X$.

Graphs. A *(labeled directed) graph* is a triple $G = (V, E, A)$, where V is a set of *nodes*, A is a finite set of elements called *actions*, and $E \subseteq V \times A \times V$ is the set of *edges* labeled by actions. We say that G has *finite out-degree* if the set of outgoing edges $\{(w, a, w') \in E : w = v\}$ is finite for every $v \in V$. Similarly, it has *finite in-degree* if the set of ingoing edges is finite for every $v \in V$. If G has both finite out- and in-degree, then we say that G is *locally finite*. A *path* π is a finite sequence of nodes $(v_i)_{1 \leq i \leq n}$ and actions $(a_i)_{1 \leq i < n}$ such that $(v_i, a_i, v_{i+1}) \in E$ for all $1 \leq i < n$. We say that π is a *path from v to w* (or a *v-w path*) if $v = v_1$ and $w = v_n$, and its *label* is $a_1 a_2 \cdots a_{n-1}$, where ε denotes the empty sequence.

A *weighted* graph is a tuple $G = (V, E, A, \mu)$ where (V, E, A) is a graph with a *weight function* $\mu \colon E \to \mathbb{Q}_{>0}$. The *weight* of path π is the weight of its edges, *i.e.* $\mu(\pi) := \sum_{1 \leq i < n} \mu(v_i, a_i, v_{i+1})$. A *shortest path from v to w* is a v-w path π minimizing $\mu(\pi)$. We define $\mathrm{dist}_G \colon V \times V \to \mathbb{Q}_{\geq 0} \cup \{\infty\}$ as the *distance function* where $\mathrm{dist}_G(v, w)$ is the weight of a shortest path from v to w, with $\mathrm{dist}_G(v, w) := \infty$ if there is none. We assume throughout the paper that weighted graphs have a *minimal weight*, *i.e.* that $\min\{\mu(e) : e \in E\}$ exists. For graphs with finite out-degree, this ensures that if a path exists between two nodes, then a shortest one exists.[4] This mild assumption always holds in our setting.

Petri nets. A *weighted Petri net* is a tuple $\mathcal{N} = (P, T, f, \lambda)$ where

- P is a finite set whose elements are called *places*,
- T is a finite set, disjoint from P, whose elements are called *transitions*,
- $f \colon (P \times T) \cup (T \times P) \to \mathbb{N}$ is the *flow function* assigning multiplicities to arcs connecting places and transitions, and
- $\lambda \colon T \to \mathbb{Q}_{>0}$ is the *weight function* assigning weights to transitions.

A *marking* is a vector $\boldsymbol{m} \in \mathbb{N}^P$ which indicates that place p holds $\boldsymbol{m}(p)$ *tokens*. A weighted Petri net with $\lambda(t) = 1$ for each $t \in T$ is called a *Petri net*. For example, Figure 1 depicts a Petri net $\mathcal{N}$ with $P = \{p_1, p_2\}$, $T = \{t_1, t_2, t_3\}$, $f(p_1, t_3) = f(p_1, t_2) = f(t_1, p_1) = f(t_2, p_1) = f(t_2, p_2) = 1$ (multiplicity omitted on arcs) and $f(-, -) = 0$ elsewhere (no arc). Moreover, $\mathcal{N}$ is marked with $[p_1 \colon 1, p_2 \colon 0]$.

The *guard* and *effect* of a transition $t \in T$ are vectors $\boldsymbol{g}_t \in \mathbb{N}^P$ and $\boldsymbol{\Delta}_t \in \mathbb{Z}^P$ where $\boldsymbol{g}_t(p) := f(p, t)$ and $\boldsymbol{\Delta}_t(p) := f(t, p) - f(p, t)$. We say that t is *firable* from marking $\boldsymbol{m}$ if $\boldsymbol{m} \geq \boldsymbol{g}_t$. If t is firable from $\boldsymbol{m}$, then it may be *fired*, which leads to marking $\boldsymbol{m}' := \boldsymbol{m} + \boldsymbol{\Delta}_t$. We write this as $\boldsymbol{m} \xrightarrow{t}_\mathbb{N} \boldsymbol{m}'$. These notions naturally extend to sequences of transitions, *i.e.* $\xrightarrow{\varepsilon}_\mathbb{N}$ denotes the identity relation over $\mathbb{N}^P$, $\boldsymbol{\Delta}_\varepsilon := \boldsymbol{0}$, $\lambda(\varepsilon) := 0$, and for every $t_1, t_2, \ldots, t_k \in T$: $\boldsymbol{\Delta}_{t_1 t_2 \cdots t_k} := \boldsymbol{\Delta}_{t_1} + \boldsymbol{\Delta}_{t_2} + \cdots + \boldsymbol{\Delta}_{t_k}$, $\lambda(t_1 t_2 \cdots t_k) := \lambda(t_1) + \lambda(t_2) + \cdots + \lambda(t_k)$, and

$$\xrightarrow{t_1 t_2 \cdots t_k}_\mathbb{N} := \xrightarrow{t_k}_\mathbb{N} \circ \cdots \circ \xrightarrow{t_2}_\mathbb{N} \circ \xrightarrow{t_1}_\mathbb{N}.$$

---

[4] Otherwise, there could be increasingly better paths, *e.g.* of weights $1, 1/2, 1/4, \ldots$.

We say that $\rightarrow_\mathbb{N} := \cup_{t \in T} \xrightarrow{t}_\mathbb{N}$ and $\xrightarrow{*}_\mathbb{N} := \cup_{\sigma \in T^*} \xrightarrow{\sigma}_\mathbb{N}$ are the *step* and *reachability* relations. Note that the latter is the reflexive transitive closure of $\rightarrow_\mathbb{N}$.

For example, $\boldsymbol{m} \xrightarrow{t_2 t_3}_\mathbb{N} \boldsymbol{m}'$ and $\boldsymbol{m} \xrightarrow{t_1 t_2 t_3 t_3}_\mathbb{N} \boldsymbol{m}'$ in Figure 1, where $\boldsymbol{m} := [p_1\colon 1, p_2\colon 0]$ and $\boldsymbol{m}' := [p_1\colon 0, p_2\colon 1]$. Moreover, t_2 is not firable in $\boldsymbol{m}'$.

Given a sequence $\sigma \in T^*$, denote by $|\sigma|_t \in \mathbb{N}$ the number of times transition t occurs in σ. The *Parikh image* of σ is the vector $\boldsymbol{\sigma} \in \mathbb{N}^T$ that captures the number of occurrences of transitions appearing in σ, i.e. $\boldsymbol{\sigma}(t) := |\sigma|_t$ for all $t \in T$.

Each weighted Petri net $\mathcal{N} = (P, T, f, \lambda)$ induces a locally finite weighted graph $G_\mathbb{N}(\mathcal{N}) := (V, E, T, \mu)$, called its *reachability graph*, where $V := \mathbb{N}^P$, $E := \{(\boldsymbol{m}, t, \boldsymbol{m}') : \boldsymbol{m} \xrightarrow{t}_\mathbb{N} \boldsymbol{m}'\}$ and $\mu(\boldsymbol{m}, t, \boldsymbol{m}') := \lambda(t)$ for each $(\boldsymbol{m}, t, \boldsymbol{m}') \in E$. An example of a reachability graph is given on the right of Figure 1. We write $\mathrm{dist}_\mathcal{N}$ to denote $\mathrm{dist}_{G_\mathbb{N}(\mathcal{N})}$. We have $\mathrm{dist}_\mathcal{N}(\boldsymbol{m}, \boldsymbol{m}') \neq \infty$ iff $\boldsymbol{m} \xrightarrow{\sigma}_\mathbb{N} \boldsymbol{m}'$ for some $\sigma \in T^*$, and if the latter holds, then $\mathrm{dist}_\mathcal{N}(\boldsymbol{m}, \boldsymbol{m}')$ is the minimal weight among such firing sequences σ. Moreover, for (unweighted) Petri nets, $\mathrm{dist}_\mathcal{N}(\boldsymbol{m}, \boldsymbol{m}')$ is the minimal number of transitions to fire to reach $\boldsymbol{m}'$ from $\boldsymbol{m}$.

3   Directed Search Algorithms

Our approach relies on classical pathfinding procedures guided by node selection strategies. Their generic scheme is described in Algorithm 1. Its termination with a value $d \neq \infty$ indicates that the weighted graph $G = (V, E, A, \mu)$ has a path from s to t of weight d, whereas termination with $d = \infty$ signals that $\mathrm{dist}_G(s, t) = \infty$.

Algorithm 1 maintains a set of *frontier nodes* C and a mapping $g\colon V \to \mathbb{Q}_{\geq 0} \cup \{\infty\}$ such that $g(w)$ is the weight of the best known path from s to w. In Line 4, a *selection strategy* S determines which node v to *expand* next. Starting from Line 6, a successor w of v is added to the frontier if its distance improves.

1   $g := [s \mapsto 0, v \mapsto \infty : v \neq s]$
2   $C := \{s\}$
3   **while** $C \neq \emptyset$ **do**
4        $v := \arg\min_{v \in C} S(g, v)$
5   **if** $v = t$ **then return** $g(t)$
6   **for** $(v, a, w) \in E$ **do**
7   **if** $g(v) + \mu(v, a, w) < g(w)$ **then**
8                  $g(w) := g(v) + \mu(v, a, w)$
9                  $C := C \cup \{w\}$
10       $C := C \setminus \{v\}$
11 **return** ∞

Algorithm 1: Directed search algorithm.

Let $h\colon V \to \mathbb{Q}_{\geq 0} \cup \{\infty\}$ estimate the distance from all nodes to a target $t \in V$. The selection strategies sending (g, v) respectively to $g(v)$, $g(v) + h(v)$ or $h(v)$ yield the classical Dijkstra's, A^* and greedy best-first search (*GBFS*) algorithms.

When instantiating S with Dijkstra's selection strategy, a return value $d \neq \infty$ is guaranteed to equal $\mathrm{dist}_G(s, t)$. This is not true for A^* and GBFS. However, if h fulfills the following *consistency* properties, then A^* also has this guarantee: $h(t) = 0$ and $h(v) \leq \mu(v, a, w) + h(w)$ for every $(v, a, w) \in E$ (see, e.g., [52]).

In the setting of infinite graphs, unlike GBFS, A^* and Dijkstra's selection strategies guarantee termination if $\mathrm{dist}_G(s, t) \neq \infty$. Yet, we introduce *unbounded heuristics* for which termination is also guaranteed for GBFS. Note that these guarantees would vanish in the presence of zero weights. An *infinite path* π is a sequence of nodes $(v_i)_{i \in \mathbb{N}}$ and actions $(a_i)_{i \in \mathbb{N}}$ such that $(v_i, a_i, v_{i+1}) \in E$ for all $i \in \mathbb{N}$. We say that heuristic h is *unbounded* (w.r.t. G) if for every infinite simple path $v_0, v_1, v_2, \ldots$ of G and for every $b \in \mathbb{Q}_{\geq 0}$, there exists an index i s.t. $h(v_i) \geq b$. In other words, unboundedness forbids an infinite simple path of G to "cap" at some distance estimate b. The following technical lemma enables to prove termination of GFBS in the presence of unbounded heuristics.

Lemma 1. *If G is locally finite, then the following holds:*

1. *The set of paths of weight at most $c \in \mathbb{Q}_{\geq 0}$ starting from node s is finite.*
2. *Let $W \subseteq V$. The set $\mathrm{dist}_G(W, t) := \{\mathrm{dist}_G(w, t) : w \in W\}$ has a minimum.*
3. *No node is expanded infinitely often by Algorithm 1.*

Theorem 1. *Algorithm 1 with the greedy best-first search selection strategy always finds reachable targets for locally finite graphs and unbounded heuristics.*

Proof. First observe that Algorithm 1 satisfies this invariant:

$$\text{if } g(v) \neq \infty, \text{ then } g(v) \text{ is the weight of a path from } s \text{ to } v \text{ in } G$$
$$\text{whose nodes were all expanded, except possibly } v. \quad (*)$$

Assume $\mathrm{dist}_G(s, t) \neq \infty$. For the sake of contradiction, suppose t is never expanded. Let K_i be the subgraph of G induced by nodes expanded at least once within the first i iterations of the **while** loop. In particular, K_1 is the graph made only of node s. Let $K = K_1 \cup K_2 \cup \cdots$. By Lemma 1 (3), no node is expanded infinitely often, hence K is infinite. Moreover, K has finite out-degree, and each node of K is reachable from s in K by $(*)$. Thus, by König's lemma, K contains an infinite path $v_0, v_1, \ldots \in V$ of pairwise distinct nodes.

Let w be a node of K minimizing $\mathrm{dist}_G(w, t)$. That minimum is well-defined by Lemma 1 (2). Since $s \in K_1 \subseteq K$ and t is reachable from s, we have $\mathrm{dist}_G(w, t) \leq \mathrm{dist}_G(s, t) < \infty$. By minimality of $w \neq t$, there exists an edge (w, a, w') of G such that $\mathrm{dist}_G(w', t) < \mathrm{dist}_G(w, t)$ and w' does not appear in K. Note that w' is added to C at some point, but is never expanded as it would otherwise belong to K. Let i be the smallest index such that w belongs to K_i. Since h is unbounded, there exists j such that $h(v_j) > h(w')$ and v_j is expanded after iteration i of the while loop. This is a contradiction as w' would have been expanded instead of v_j. □

4   Directed Reachability

In this section, we explain how to instantiate Algorithm 1 for finding short(est) firing sequences witnessing reachability in weighted Petri nets. Since Dijkstra's selection strategy does not require any heuristic, we focus on A* and greedy best-first search which require consistent and unbounded heuristics. More precisely, we introduce distance under-approximations (Section 4.1); present relevant concrete distance under-approximations (Section 4.2); and put everything together into our framework (Section 4.3).

4.1   Distance Under-approximations

A *distance under-approximation* of a weighted Petri net $\mathcal{N} = (P, T, f, \lambda)$ is a function $d\colon \mathbb{N}^P \times \mathbb{N}^P \to \mathbb{Q}_{\geq 0} \cup \{\infty\}$ such that for all $\boldsymbol{m}, \boldsymbol{m}', \boldsymbol{m}'' \in \mathbb{N}^P$:

- $d(\boldsymbol{m}, \boldsymbol{m}') \leq \mathrm{dist}_{\mathcal{N}}(\boldsymbol{m}, \boldsymbol{m}')$,
- $d(\boldsymbol{m}, \boldsymbol{m}'') \leq d(\boldsymbol{m}, \boldsymbol{m}') + d(\boldsymbol{m}', \boldsymbol{m}'')$ (*triangle inequality*), and
- d is effective, *i.e.* there is an algorithm that evaluates d on all inputs.

We naturally obtain a heuristic from d for a directed search towards marking $\boldsymbol{m}_{\mathrm{target}}$. Indeed, let $h\colon \mathbb{N}^P \to \mathbb{Q}_{\geq 0} \cup \{\infty\}$ be defined by $h(\boldsymbol{m}) := d(\boldsymbol{m}, \boldsymbol{m}_{\mathrm{target}})$. The following proposition shows that h is a suitable heuristic for A^*:

Proposition 1. *Mapping h is a consistent heuristic.*

Proof. Let $\boldsymbol{m}, \boldsymbol{m}' \in \mathbb{N}^P$ and $t \in T$ be such that $\boldsymbol{m} \xrightarrow{t}_{\mathbb{N}} \boldsymbol{m}'$. We have:

$$
\begin{aligned}
h(\boldsymbol{m}) &= d(\boldsymbol{m}, \boldsymbol{m}_{\mathrm{target}}) && \text{(by def. of } h) \\
&\leq d(\boldsymbol{m}, \boldsymbol{m}') + d(\boldsymbol{m}', \boldsymbol{m}_{\mathrm{target}}) && \text{(by the triangle inequality)} \\
&\leq \mathrm{dist}_{\mathcal{N}}(\boldsymbol{m}, \boldsymbol{m}') + d(\boldsymbol{m}', \boldsymbol{m}_{\mathrm{target}}) && \text{(by distance under-approximation)} \\
&\leq \lambda(t) + d(\boldsymbol{m}', \boldsymbol{m}_{\mathrm{target}}) && \text{(since } \boldsymbol{m} \xrightarrow{t}_{\mathbb{N}} \boldsymbol{m}') \\
&= \lambda(t) + h(\boldsymbol{m}') && \text{(by def. of } h).
\end{aligned}
$$

Moreover, $h(\boldsymbol{m}_{\mathrm{target}}) = d(\boldsymbol{m}_{\mathrm{target}}, \boldsymbol{m}_{\mathrm{target}}) \leq \mathrm{dist}_{\mathcal{N}}(\boldsymbol{m}_{\mathrm{target}}, \boldsymbol{m}_{\mathrm{target}}) = 0$, where the last equality follows from the fact that weights are positive. □

4.2   From Petri Net Relaxations to Distance Under-approximations

We now introduce classical relaxations of Petri nets which over-approximate reachability and consequently give rise to distance under-approximations. The main source of hardness of the reachability problem stems from the fact that places are required to hold a non-negative number of tokens. If we relax this requirement and allow negative numbers of tokens, we obtain a more tractable relation. More precisely, we write $\boldsymbol{m} \xrightarrow{t}_{\mathbb{Z}} \boldsymbol{m}'$ iff $\boldsymbol{m}' = \boldsymbol{m} + \boldsymbol{\Delta}_t$. Note that transitions are always firable under this semantics. Moreover, they may lead to "markings" with negative components.

Another source of hardness comes from the fact that markings are discrete. Hence, we can further relax $\to_{\mathbb{Z}}$ into $\to_{\mathbb{Q}}$ where transitions may be scaled down:

$$
\boldsymbol{m} \xrightarrow{t}_{\mathbb{Q}} \boldsymbol{m}' \iff \boldsymbol{m}' = \boldsymbol{m} + \delta \cdot \boldsymbol{\Delta}_t \text{ for some } 0 < \delta \leq 1.
$$

One gets a less crude relaxation from considering *nonnegative* "markings" only:

$$
\boldsymbol{m} \xrightarrow{t}_{\mathbb{Q}_{\geq 0}} \boldsymbol{m}' \iff (\boldsymbol{m} \geq \delta \cdot \boldsymbol{g}_t) \text{ and } (\boldsymbol{m}' = \boldsymbol{m} + \delta \cdot \boldsymbol{\Delta}_t) \text{ for some } 0 < \delta \leq 1.
$$

Under these, we obtain "markings" from $\mathbb{Q}^P$ and $\mathbb{Q}_{\geq 0}^P$ respectively. Petri nets equipped with relation $\to_{\mathbb{Q}_{\geq 0}}$ are known as *continuous Petri nets* [14,15].

To unify all three relaxations, we sometimes write $m \xrightarrow{\delta t}_{\mathbb{G}} m'$ to emphasize the scaling factor δ, where $\delta = 1$ whenever $\mathbb{G} = \mathbb{Z}$. Let $d_{\mathbb{G}} : \mathbb{N}^P \times \mathbb{N}^P \to \mathbb{Q}_{\geq 0} \cup \{\infty\}$ be defined as $d_{\mathbb{G}}(m, m') := \infty$ if $m \not\to_{\mathbb{G}} m'$, and otherwise:

$$d_{\mathbb{G}}(m, m') := \min \left\{ \sum_{i=1}^{n} \delta_i \cdot \lambda(t_i) : m \xrightarrow{\delta_1 t_1 \cdots \delta_n t_n}_{\mathbb{G}} m' \right\}.$$

In words, $d_{\mathbb{G}}(m, m')$ is the weight of a shortest path from m to m' in the graph induced by the relaxed step relation $\to_{\mathbb{G}}$, where weights are scaled accordingly.

We now show that any $d_{\mathbb{G}}$, which we call the $\mathbb{G}$-*distance*, is a distance under-approximation, and first show effectiveness of all $d_{\mathbb{G}}$. It is well-known and readily seen that reachability over $\mathbb{G} \in \{\mathbb{Z}, \mathbb{Q}\}$ is characterized by the following *state equation*, since transitions are always firable due to the absence of guards:

$$m \xrightarrow{*}_{\mathbb{G}} m' \iff \exists \sigma \in \mathbb{G}_{\geq 0}^T : m' = m + \sum_{t \in T} \sigma(t) \cdot \Delta_t.$$

Here, σ can be seen as the Parikh image of a sequence σ leading from m to m'.

Proposition 2. *The functions $d_{\mathbb{Z}}$, $d_{\mathbb{Q}}$, $d_{\mathbb{Q}_{\geq 0}}$ are effective.*

Proof. By the state equation, we have:

$$d_{\mathbb{G}}(m, m') = \min \left\{ \sum_{t \in T} \lambda(t) \cdot \sigma(t) : \sigma \in \mathbb{G}_{\geq 0}^T, m' = m + \sum_{t \in T} \sigma(t) \cdot \Delta_t \right\}.$$

Therefore, $d_{\mathbb{Q}}(m, m')$ (resp. $d_{\mathbb{Z}}(m, m')$) are computable by (resp. integer) linear programming, which is complete for P (resp. NP), in its variant where one must check whether the minimal solution is at most some bound.

For $d_{\mathbb{Q}_{\geq 0}}$, note that the reachability relation of a continuous Petri net can be expressed in the existential fragment of linear real arithmetic [8]. Hence, effectiveness follows from the decidability of linear real arithmetic. □

Altogether, we conclude that $d_{\mathbb{G}}$ is a distance under-approximation. Furthermore, we can show that $d_{\mathbb{G}}$ yields *unbounded* heuristics, which, by Theorem 1, ensure termination of GBFS on reachable instances:

Theorem 2. *Let $\mathbb{G} \in \{\mathbb{Z}, \mathbb{Q}, \mathbb{Q}_{\geq 0}\}$, then $d_{\mathbb{G}}$ is a distance under-approximation. Moreover, the heuristics arising from it are unbounded.*

Proof. Let $\mathcal{N} = (P, T, f, \lambda)$ be a weighted Petri net. Effectiveness of $d_{\mathbb{G}}$ follows from Proposition 2. By definitions and a simple induction, $\xrightarrow{\sigma}_{\mathbb{N}} \subseteq \xrightarrow{\sigma}_{\mathbb{G}}$ for any sequence $\sigma \in T^*$, with weights left unchanged for unscaled transitions. This implies that $d_{\mathbb{G}}(m, m') \leq \text{dist}_{\mathcal{N}}(m, m')$ for every $m, m' \in \mathbb{G}^P$. Moreover, the triangle inequality holds since for every $m, m', m'' \in \mathbb{G}^P$ and sequences σ, σ':

$$m \xrightarrow{\sigma}_{\mathbb{G}} m' \xrightarrow{\sigma'}_{\mathbb{G}} m'' \text{ implies } m \xrightarrow{\sigma \sigma'}_{\mathbb{G}} m''.$$

Let us sketch the proof of the second part. Let m_{target} be a marking and let h_G be the heuristic obtained from d_G for m_{target}. Since $h_{\mathbb{Q}}(m) \leq h_G(m)$ for all m and $G \in \{\mathbb{Z}, \mathbb{Q}_{\geq 0}\}$, it suffices to prove that $d_{\mathbb{Q}}$ is unbounded. Suppose it is not. There exist $b \in \mathbb{Q}_{\geq 0}$ and pairwise distinct markings $m_0, m_1, \dots$ each with $h_{\mathbb{Q}}(m_i) \leq b$. Let x_i be a solution to the state equation that gives $h_{\mathbb{Q}}(m_i)$. By well-quasi-ordering and pairwise distinctness, there is a subsequence such that $m_{i_0}(p) < m_{i_1}(p) < \cdots$ for some $p \in P$. Thus, $\lim_{j\to\infty} m_{target}(p) - m_{i_j}(p) = -\infty$, and hence $\lim_{j\to\infty} x_{i_j}(s) = \infty$ for some $s \in T$ with $\Delta_s(p) < 0$. This means that $b \geq h_{\mathbb{Q}}(m_{i_j}) = \sum_{t \in T} \lambda(t) \cdot x_{i_j}(t) > b$ for a sufficiently large j. $\square$

4.3   Directed Reachability Based on Distance Under-approximations

We have all the ingredients to use Algorithm 1 for answering reachability queries.

A *distance under-approximation scheme* is a mapping $\mathcal{D}$ that associates a distance under-approximation $\mathcal{D}(\mathcal{N})$ to each weighted Petri net $\mathcal{N}$. Let $h_{\mathcal{D}(\mathcal{N}),m_{target}}$ be the heuristic obtained from $\mathcal{D}(\mathcal{N})$ for marking m_{target}. By instantiating Algorithm 1 with this heuristic, we can search for a short(est) firing sequence witnessing that m_{target} is reachable. Of course, constructing the reachability graph of $\mathcal{N}$ would be at least as difficult as answering this query, or impossible if it is infinite. Hence, we provide $G_{\mathbb{N}}(\mathcal{N})$ *symbolically* through $\mathcal{N}$ and let Algorithm 1 explore it on-the-fly by progressively firing its transitions.

For each $G \in \{\mathbb{Z}, \mathbb{Q}, \mathbb{Q}_{\geq 0}\}$, the function $\mathcal{D}_G$ mapping a weighted Petri net $\mathcal{N}$ to its G-distance d_G is a distance under-approximation scheme with consistent and unbounded heuristics by Proposition 1, Theorem 1 and Theorem 2. Although Algorithm 1 is geared towards finding paths, it can prove *non*-reachability even for infinite reachability graphs. Indeed, at some point, every candidate marking $m \in C$ may be such that $h_{\mathcal{D}(\mathcal{N}),m_{target}}(m) = \infty$, which halts with ∞. There is no guarantee that this happens, but, as reported *e.g.* by [23,8], the G-distance for domains $G \in \{\mathbb{Z}, \mathbb{Q}, \mathbb{Q}_{\geq 0}\}$ does well for witnessing non-reachability in practice, often from the very first marking m_{init}.

An example. We illustrate our approach with a toy example and $\mathcal{D}_{\mathbb{Q}}$ (the scheme based on the state equation over $\mathbb{Q}_{\geq 0}^T$). Consider the Petri net $\mathcal{N}$ illustrated on the left of Figure 1, but marked with $m_{init} := [p_1 \colon 0, p_2 \colon 0]$. Suppose we wish to determine whether m_{init} can reach marking $m_{target} := [p_1 \colon 0, p_2 \colon 1]$ in $\mathcal{N}$.

We consider the case where Algorithm 1 follows a greedy best-first search, but the markings would be expanded in the same way with A*. Let us abbreviate a marking $[p_1 \colon x, p_2 \colon y]$ as (x, y). Since $\Delta_{t_2} = (0, 1)$, the heuristic considers that m_{init} can reach m_{target} in a single step using transition t_2 (it is unaware of the guard). Marking $(1, 0)$ is expanded and its heuristic value increases to 2 as the state equation considers that both t_2 and t_3 must be fired (in some unknown order). Markings $(2, 0)$ and $(1, 1)$ are both discovered with respective heuristic values 3 and 1. The latter is more promising, so it is expanded and target $(0, 1)$ is discovered. Since its heuristic value is 0, it is immediately expanded and the correct distance $dist_{\mathcal{N}}(m_{init}, m_{target}) = 3$ is returned. Note that, in this example, the only markings expanded are precisely those occurring on the shortest path.

Handling multiple targets. Algorithm 1 can be adapted to search for *some* marking from a given target set $X \subseteq \mathbb{N}^P$. The idea consists simply in using a heuristic $h_X \colon \mathbb{N}^P \to \mathbb{Q}_{\geq 0} \cup \{\infty\}$ estimating the weight of a shortest path to *any* target:

$$h_X(\boldsymbol{m}) := \min\{h_{\mathcal{D}(\mathcal{N}), \boldsymbol{m}_{\text{target}}}(\boldsymbol{m}) : \boldsymbol{m}_{\text{target}} \in X\}.$$

This is convenient for partial reachability instances occurring in practice, *i.e.*

$$X := \{\boldsymbol{m}_{\text{target}} \in \mathbb{N}^P : \boldsymbol{m}_{\text{target}}(p) \sim_p \boldsymbol{c}(p)\} \text{ where } \boldsymbol{c} \in \mathbb{N}^P \text{ and } each \sim_p \in \{=, \geq\}.$$

5   Experimental Results

We implemented Algorithm 1 in a prototype called FASTFORWARD [10], which supports all presented selection strategies and distance under-approximations. We evaluate FASTFORWARD empirically with three main goals in mind. First, we show that our approach is competitive with established tools and can even vastly outperform them, and we also give insights on its performance w.r.t. its parameterizations. Second, we compare the length of the witnesses reported by the different tools. Third, we briefly discuss the quality of the heuristics.

Technical details. Our tool is written in C# and uses GUROBI [32], a state-of-the-art MILP solver, for distance under-approximations. Benchmarks were run on an machine with an 8-Core Intel® Core™ i7-7700 CPU @ 3.60GHz running Ubuntu 18.04 and with memory constrained to ~8GB. We used a timeout of 60 seconds per instance, and all tools were invoked from a PYTHON script using the `time` module for time measurements.

A minor challenge arises from the fact that many instances specify an upward-closed set of initial markings rather than a single one. For example, $\boldsymbol{m}_{\text{init}}(p) \geq 1$ to specify, *e.g.*, an arbitrary number of threads. We handle this by setting $\boldsymbol{m}_{\text{init}}(p) = 1$ and adding a transition t_p producing a token into p.

As a preprocessing step, we implemented *sign analysis* [29]. It is a general pruning technique running in polynomial time that has been shown beneficial for reducing the size of the state-space of Petri nets. Initially, places that carry tokens are viewed as marked. For each transition whose input places are marked, the output places also become marked. When a fixpoint is reached, places left unmarked cannot carry tokens in any reachable marking, so they are discarded.

Benchmarks. Due to the lack of tools handling reachability for *unbounded* state spaces, benchmarks arising in the literature are primarily *coverability* instances[5], *i.e.* reachability towards an upward closed set of target markings. We gathered 61 positive and 115 negative coverability instances originating from five suites [39,28,6,35,18] previously used for benchmarking [23,8,29]. They arise from the analysis of multi-threaded C programs with shared-memory; mutual

---

[5] The Model Checking Contest focuses on reachability for *finite* state spaces.

exclusion algorithms; communication protocols; provenance analysis in the context of a medical messaging and a bug-tracking system; and the verification of ERLANG concurrent programs. We further extracted the *sypet* suite made of 30 positive (standard) reachability instances arising from queries encountered in type-directed program synthesis [24]. The overall goal of this work is to enable a vast range of untapped applications requiring reachability over unbounded state-spaces, rather than just coverability. To obtain further (positive) instances of the Petri net reachability problem, we performed random walks on the Petri nets from the aforementioned coverability benchmarks. To this end, we used the largest quarter of distinct Petri nets from each coverability suite, for a total of 33. We performed one random walk each of lengths 20, 25, 30, 35, 40, 50, 60, 75, 90 and 100, and we saved the resulting marking as the target. For nets with an upward-closed initial marking, we randomly chose to start with a number of tokens between 1 and 20% of the length of the walk. It is important to note that even with long random walks, instances can (and in fact tend to) have short witnesses. To remove trivial instances and only keep the most challenging ones, we removed those instances where any considered tool reported a witness of length at most 20, disregarding the transitions used to generate the initial marking. This leaves us with 127 challenging instances on which the shortest witness is either unknown or has length more than 20. Moreover, this yields real-world Petri nets with no bias towards any specific kind of targets.

This table summarizes the characteristics of the various benchmarks:

Suite	Size	Number of places				Number of transitions			
		min.	med.	mean	max.	min.	med.	mean	max.
COVERABILITY	61	16	87	226	2826	14	181	1519	27370
SYPET	30	65	251	320	1199	537	2307	2646	8340
RANDOM WALKS	127	52	306	531	2826	60	3137	5885	27370

Tool comparison. To evaluate our approach on reachability instances, we compare FASTFORWARD to LoLA [53], a tool developed for two decades that wins several categories of the Model Checking Contest every year. LoLA is geared towards model checking of finite state spaces, but it implements semi-decision procedures for the unbounded case. We further compare the three selection strategies of Algorithm 1: A^*, GBFS and Dijkstra; the two first with the distance under-approximation scheme $\mathcal{D}_{\mathbb{Q}}$, which provides the best trade-off between estimate quality and efficiency. In fact, the other heuristics perform strictly worse on almost all instances. We also considered comparing with KREACH [17], a tool showcased at TACAS'20 that implements an exact non-elementary algorithm. However, it timed out on all instances with a larger time limit of 10 minutes.

Figure 2 depicts the number of reachability instances decided by the tools within the time limit. As shown, all approaches outperform LoLA, with GBFS as the clear winner on the RANDOM-WALK suite and A^* slightly better on the SYPET suite. Note that Dijkstra's selection strategy sometimes competes due

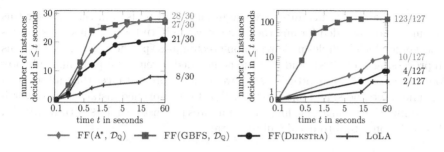

Fig. 2. Cumulative number of reachability instances decided over time. *Left*: SYPET suite (semi-log scale). *Right*: RANDOM-WALK suite (log scale).

to its locally very cheap computational cost (no heuristic evaluation), but its performance generally decreases as the distance increases.

To show the versatility of our approach, we also benchmarked FASTFOR-WARD on the original coverability instances. Recall that coverability EXPSPACE-complete and reduces to reachability in linear time [45,51]. While exceeding the PSPACE-completeness of reachability for finite state-spaces [38,21], coverability is much more tame than the non-elementary complexity of (unbounded) reachability. We compare FASTFORWARD to four tools implementing algorithms tailored, some of which are specifically to the coverability problem: LoLA, BFC [39], ICOVER [29] and the backward algorithm (based on [1]) of MIST [28]. We did not test PETRINIZER [23] since it only handles negative instances, while we focus on positive ones; likewise for QCOVER [8] since it is superseded by ICOVER.

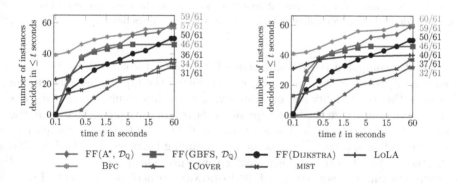

Fig. 3. Cumulative number of (positive) coverability instances decided over time. *Left*: Evaluation on the original instances. *Right*: Evaluation on the pre-pruned instances.

Figure 3 illustrates the number of coverability instances decided within the time limit. The left side corresponds to an evaluation on the original instances where FASTFORWARD performs pruning (included in its runtime). On the right-hand side the pruned instances are the input for all tools, and the time for this pruning is not included for any tool. As a caveat, ICOVER performs its own pre-processing which includes pruning among techniques specific to coverability. This preprocessing is enabled (and its time is included) even when pruning is already done. Using FASTFORWARD(A^*, $\mathcal{D}_\mathbb{Q}$), we decide more instances than all tools on unpruned Petri nets, and one less than BFC for pre-pruned instances. It is worth mentioning that with a time limit of 10 minutes per instance, FASTFORWARD(A^*, $\mathcal{D}_\mathbb{Q}$) is the only tool to decide all 61 instances.

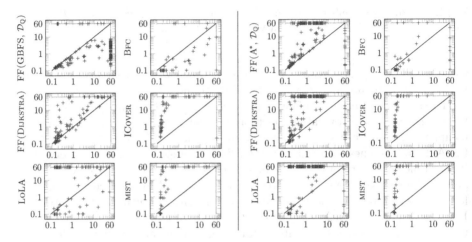

Fig. 4. Runtime comparison against FF(A^*, $\mathcal{D}_\mathbb{Q}$) (*left*) and FF(GBFS, $\mathcal{D}_\mathbb{Q}$) (*right*), in seconds, for individual instances without pre-pruning. Tools on the first column of each side include coverability and reachability instances, while those on the second column of each side include coverability only. Marks on the green lines denote timeouts (60 s).

We also compared the running time of A^* and GBFS with $\mathcal{D}_\mathbb{Q}$ to the other tools and approaches. For each tool, we considered the type of instances it can handle: either reachability and coverability, or coverability only. Figure 4 depicts this comparison, where the base approach is faster for data points that lie in the upper-left half of the graph. The axes start at 0.1 second to avoid a comparison based on technical aspects such as the programming language. Yet, LoLA, BFC and MIST regularly solve instances faster than this, which speaks to their level of optimization. We can see that FASTFORWARD outperforms ICOVER, LoLA and MIST overall. We cannot compete with BFC in execution time as it is a highly optimized tool specifically tailored to only the coverability problem that can employ optimization techniques such as Karp-Miller trees that do not work for reachability queries.

Length of the witnesses. Since our approach is also geared towards the identification of short(est) reachability witnesses, we compared the different tools with respect to length of the reported one, depicted in Figure 5. Positive values on the y-axis mean the witness was not minimal, while $y = 0$ means it was. Note that the points for BFC must be taken with a grain of salt: it uses a different file format, and its translation utility can introduce additional transitions. This means that even if BFC found a shortest witness, it could be longer than a shortest one of the original instance.

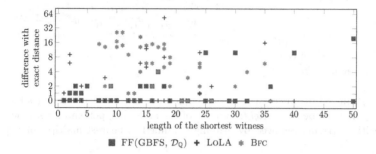

Fig. 5. Length of the returned witness, per tool, compared to the length of a shortest witness. ICOVER is left out as it does not return witnesses. FF(A^*, $\mathcal{D}_{\mathbb{Q}}$), FF(DIJKSTRA) and MIST are left out as they are guaranteed to return shortest witnesses.

Still, the graph shows that reported witnesses can be far from minimal. For example, on one instance LoLA returns a witness that is 53 transitions longer than the one of FASTFORWARD(A^*, $\mathcal{D}_{\mathbb{Q}}$). Still, LoLA returns a shortest witness on 28 out of 43 instances. Similarly, FASTFORWARD(GBFS, $\mathcal{D}_{\mathbb{Q}}$) finds a shortest path on 60 out of 83 instances[6]. In contrast, MIST finds a shortest witness on all instances since its backward algorithm is guaranteed to do so on unweighted Petri nets, which constitute all of our instances. Again, this approach is tailored to coverability and cannot be lifted to reachability.

Heuristics and pruning. We briefly discuss the quality of the heuristics and the impact of pruning. The left-hand side of Figure 6 compares the exact distance to the estimated distance from the initial marking.[7] It shows that it is incredibly accurate for all $\mathbb{G}$-distances, but even more so for $\mathbb{G} = \mathbb{Q}_{\geq 0}$. We experimented with this distance using the logical translation of [8] and Z3 [49] as the optimization modulo theories solver. At present, it appears that the gain in estimate quality does not compensate for the extra computational cost.

As depicted on the right-hand side of Figure 6, pruning can make some instances trivial, but in general, many challenging instances remain so. On average, around 50% of places and 40% of transitions were pruned.

---

[6] These numbers disregard instances where the tool did not finish or where a shortest witness is not known, *i.e.* no method guaranteeing one finished in time.

[7] Z3 reported two non optimal solutions which explains the two points above the line.

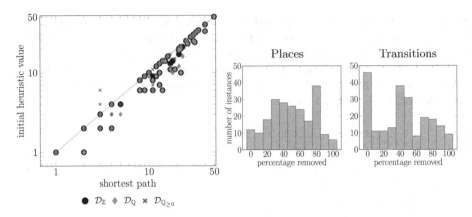

Fig. 6. *Left*: initial distance estimation compared to the exact distance (points closer to the diagonal are better). *Right*: number of instances per percentage of places (left) and transitions (right) removed by pruning (rounded to nearest multiple of 10).

6   Conclusion

We presented an efficient approach to the Petri net reachability problem that uses state-space over-approximations as distance oracles in the classical graph traversal algorithms A^* and greedy best-first search. Our experiments have shown that using the state equation over $\mathbb{Q}_{\geq 0}^T$ provides the best trade-off between computational feasibility and the accuracy of the oracle. However, we expect that further advances in optimization modulo theories solvers may enable employing stronger over-approximations such as continuous Petri nets in the future.

Moreover, non-algebraic distance under-approximations also fit naturally in our framework, *e.g.* the syntactic distance of [55] and "α-graphs" of [24]. These are crude approximations with low computational cost. Our preliminary tests show that, although they could not compete with our distances, they can provide early speed-ups on instances with large branching factors. An interesting line of research consists in identifying cheap approximations with better estimates.

We wish to emphasize that our approach to the reachability problem has the potential to also be naturally used for semi-deciding reachability in extensions of Petri nets with a recursively enumerable reachability problem, such as Petri nets with resets and transfers [3,19] as well as colored Petri nets [37]. These extensions have, for instance, been used for the generation of program loop invariants [54], the validation of business processes [59] and the verification of multi-threaded C and JAVA program skeletons with communication primitives [16,39]. Linear rational and integer arithmetic over-approximations for such extended Petri nets exist [12,9,34,31] and could smoothly be used inside our framework.

Acknowledgments

We thank Juliette Fournis d'Albiat for her help with extracting the SYPET suite.

References

1. Abdulla, P.A., Cerans, K., Jonsson, B., Tsay, Y.: General decidability theorems for infinite-state systems. In: Proc. 11th Annual IEEE Symposium on Logic in Computer Science (LICS). pp. 313–321. IEEE Computer Society (1996). https://doi.org/10.1109/LICS.1996.561359
2. Angeli, D., De Leenheer, P., Sontag, E.D.: A Petri net approach to the study of persistence in chemical reaction networks. Mathematical Biosciences **210**(2), 598–618 (2007). https://doi.org/10.1016/j.mbs.2007.07.003
3. Araki, T., Kasami, T.: Some decision problems related to the reachability problem for Petri nets. Theoretical Computer Science **3**(1), 85–104 (1976). https://doi.org/10.1016/0304-3975(76)90067-0
4. Athanasiou, K., Liu, P., Wahl, T.: Unbounded-thread program verification using thread-state equations. In: Proc. 8th International Joint Conference on Automated Reasoning (IJCAR). pp. 516–531. Springer (2016). https://doi.org/10.1007/978-3-319-40229-1_35
5. Bansal, K., Koskinen, E., Wies, T., Zufferey, D.: Structural counter abstraction. In: Proc. 19th International Conference on Tools and Algorithms for the Construction and Analysis of Systems (TACAS). pp. 62–77. Springer (2013). https://doi.org/10.1007/978-3-642-36742-7_5
6. Barth, A., Mitchell, J.C., Datta, A., Sundaram, S.: Privacy and utility in business processes. In: Proc. 20th IEEE Computer Security Foundations Symposium (CSF). pp. 279–294. IEEE Computer Society (2007). https://doi.org/10.1109/CSF.2007.26
7. Bjørner, N., Phan, A., Fleckenstein, L.: νZ - an optimizing SMT solver. In: Proc. 21st International Conference on Tools and Algorithms for the Construction and Analysis of Systems (TACAS). pp. 194–199. Springer (2015). https://doi.org/10.1007/978-3-662-46681-0_14
8. Blondin, M., Finkel, A., Haase, C., Haddad, S.: The logical view on continuous Petri nets. ACM Transactions on Computational Logic (TOCL) **18**(3), 24:1–24:28 (2017). https://doi.org/10.1145/3105908
9. Blondin, M., Haase, C., Mazowiecki, F.: Affine extensions of integer vector addition systems with states. In: Proc. 29th International Conference on Concurrency Theory (CONCUR). pp. 14:1–14:17. Schloss Dagstuhl - Leibniz-Zentrum für Informatik (2018). https://doi.org/10.4230/LIPIcs.CONCUR.2018.14
10. Blondin, M., Haase, C., Offtermatt, P.: Fastforward: A tool for reachability in Petri nets with infinite state spaces. Artifact for the TACAS21 contribution "Directed Reachability for Infinite-State Systems" (2021). https://doi.org/10.6084/m9.figshare.13573592
11. Chaouiya, C.: Petri net modelling of biological networks. Briefings in Bioinformatics **8**(4), 210–219 (2007). https://doi.org/10.1093/bib/bbm029
12. Chistikov, D., Haase, C., Halfon, S.: Context-free commutative grammars with integer counters and resets. Theoretical Computer Science **735**, 147–161 (2018). https://doi.org/10.1016/j.tcs.2016.06.017
13. Czerwiński, W., Lasota, S., Lazić, R., Leroux, J., Mazowiecki, F.: The reachability problem for Petri nets is not elementary. In: Proc. 51st Annual ACM SIGACT Symposium on Theory of Computing (STOC). pp. 24–33. ACM (2019). https://doi.org/10.1145/3313276.3316369
14. David, R., Alla, H.: Continuous Petri nets. In: Proc. 8th European Workshop on Application and Theory of Petri nets. vol. 340, pp. 275–294 (1987)

15. David, R., Alla, H.: Discrete, Continuous, and Hybrid Petri nets. Springer, 2nd edn. (2010)
16. Delzanno, G., Raskin, J., Van Begin, L.: Towards the automated verification of multithreaded Java programs. In: Proc. 8th International Conference on Tools and Algorithms for the Construction and Analysis of Systems (TACAS). pp. 173–187. Springer (2002). https://doi.org/10.1007/3-540-46002-0_13
17. Dixon, A., Lazić, R.: Kreach: A tool for reachability in Petri nets. In: Proc. 26th International Conference on Tools and Algorithms for the Construction and Analysis of Systems (TACAS). pp. 405–412. Springer (2020). https://doi.org/10.1007/978-3-030-45190-5_22
18. D'Osualdo, E., Kochems, J., Ong, C.L.: Automatic verification of erlang-style concurrency. In: Proc. 20th International Symposium on Static Analysis (SAS). pp. 454–476. Springer (2013). https://doi.org/10.1007/978-3-642-38856-9_24
19. Dufourd, C., Finkel, A., Schnoebelen, P.: Reset nets between decidability and undecidability. In: Proc. 25th International Colloquium on Automata, Languages and Programming (ICALP). pp. 103–115. Springer (1998). https://doi.org/10.1007/BFb0055044
20. Edelkamp, S., Schuppan, V., Bosnacki, D., Wijs, A., Fehnker, A., Aljazzar, H.: Survey on directed model checking. In: Proc. 5th International Workshop on Model Checking and Artificial Intelligence (MoChArt). pp. 65–89. Springer (2008). https://doi.org/10.1007/978-3-642-00431-5_5
21. Esparza, J.: Decidability and complexity of Petri net problems — An introduction, pp. 374–428. Springer (1998). https://doi.org/10.1007/3-540-65306-6_20
22. Esparza, J., Ganty, P., Leroux, J., Majumdar, R.: Verification of population protocols. Acta Informatica **54**(2), 191–215 (2017). https://doi.org/10.1007/s00236-016-0272-3
23. Esparza, J., Ledesma-Garza, R., Majumdar, R., Meyer, P.J., Nikšić, F.: An SMT-based approach to coverability analysis. In: Proc. 26th International Conference on Computer Aided Verification (CAV). pp. 603–619. Springer (2014). https://doi.org/10.1007/978-3-319-08867-9_40
24. Feng, Y., Martins, R., Wang, Y., Dillig, I., Reps, T.W.: Component-based synthesis for complex APIs. In: Proc. 44th ACM SIGPLAN Symposium on Principles of Programming Languages (POPL). pp. 599–612. ACM (2017). https://doi.org/10.1145/3009837.3009851
25. Fraca, E., Haddad, S.: Complexity analysis of continuous Petri nets. Fundamenta Informaticae **137**(1), 1–28 (2015). https://doi.org/10.3233/FI-2015-1168
26. Galenson, J.: Dynamic and Interactive Synthesis of Code Snippets. Ph.D. thesis, University of California (2014)
27. Galenson, J., Reames, P., Bodík, R., Hartmann, B., Sen, K.: Codehint: dynamic and interactive synthesis of code snippets. In: Proc. 36th International Conference on Software Engineering (ICSE). pp. 653–663. ACM (2014). https://doi.org/10.1145/2568225.2568250
28. Ganty, P.: Algorithmes et structures de données efficaces pour la manipulation de contraintes sur les intervalles. Master's thesis, Université Libre de Bruxelles (2002), (In French)
29. Geffroy, T., Leroux, J., Sutre, G.: Occam's razor applied to the Petri net coverability problem. Theoretical Computer Science **750**, 38–52 (2018). https://doi.org/10.1016/j.tcs.2018.04.014
30. German, S.M., Sistla, A.P.: Reasoning about systems with many processes. Journal of the ACM **39**(3), 675–735 (1992). https://doi.org/10.1145/146637.146681

31. Gupta, U., Shah, P., Akshay, S., Hofman, P.: Continuous reachability for unordered data Petri nets is in PTime. In: Proc. 22nd International Conference on Foundations of Software Science and Computation Structures (FoSSaCS). pp. 260–276. Springer (2019). https://doi.org/10.1007/978-3-030-17127-8_15
32. Gurobi Optimization, L.: Gurobi optimizer reference manual (2020), http://www.gurobi.com
33. Heiner, M., Gilbert, D.R., Donaldson, R.: Petri nets for systems and synthetic biology. In: Formal Methods for Computational Systems Biology. pp. 215–264. Springer (2008). https://doi.org/10.1007/978-3-540-68894-5_7
34. Hofman, P., Leroux, J., Totzke, P.: Linear combinations of unordered data vectors. In: Proc. 32nd Annual ACM/IEEE Symposium on Logic in Computer Science (LICS). pp. 1–11. IEEE Computer Society (2017). https://doi.org/10.1109/LICS.2017.8005065
35. Janák, J.: Issue Tracking Systems. Master's thesis, Masaryk University (2009)
36. Jeng, M.D., Chen, S.C.: A heuristic search approach using approximate solutions to Petri net state equations for scheduling flexible manufacturing systems. International Journal of Flexible Manufacturing Systems 10(2), 139–162 (1998). https://doi.org/10.1023/A:1008097430956
37. Jensen, K.: Coloured Petri nets: basic concepts, analysis methods and practical use, vol. 1. Springer Science & Business Media (2013)
38. Jones, N.D., Landweber, L.H., Lien, Y.E.: Complexity of some problems in Petri nets. Theoretical Computer Science 4(3), 277–299 (1977). https://doi.org/10.1016/0304-3975(77)90014-7
39. Kaiser, A., Kroening, D., Wahl, T.: A widening approach to multithreaded program verification. ACM Transactions on Programming Languages and Systems (TOPLAS) 36(4), 14:1–14:29 (2014). https://doi.org/10.1145/2629608
40. Kosaraju, S.R.: Decidability of reachability in vector addition systems (preliminary version). In: Proc. 14th Symposium on Theory of Computing (STOC). pp. 267–281. ACM (1982). https://doi.org/10.1145/800070.802201
41. Lambert, J.: A structure to decide reachability in Petri nets. Theoretical Computer Science 99(1), 79–104 (1992). https://doi.org/10.1016/0304-3975(92)90173-D
42. Lee, D.Y., DiCesare, F.: Scheduling flexible manufacturing systems using Petri nets and heuristic search. IEEE Transactions on robotics and automation 10(2), 123–132 (1994). https://doi.org/10.1109/70.282537
43. Leroux, J.: Vector addition systems reachability problem (A simpler solution). In: Turing-100 – The Alan Turing Centenary. pp. 214–228. EasyChair (2012)
44. Leroux, J., Schmitz, S.: Demystifying reachability in vector addition systems. In: Proc. 30th Annual ACM/IEEE Symposium on Logic in Computer Science (LICS). pp. 56–67. IEEE Computer Society (2015). https://doi.org/10.1109/LICS.2015.16
45. Lipton, R.J.: The reachability problem requires exponential space. Tech. rep., Yale University (1976)
46. Liu, B., Dong, W., Zhang, Y.: Accelerating API-based program synthesis via API usage pattern mining. IEEE Access 7, 159162–159176 (2019). https://doi.org/10.1109/ACCESS.2019.2950232
47. Mayr, E.W.: An algorithm for the general Petri net reachability problem. In: Proc. 13th Symposium on Theory of Computing (STOC). pp. 238–246. ACM (1981). https://doi.org/10.1145/800076.802477
48. Mejía, G., Odrey, N.G.: An approach using Petri nets and improved heuristic search for manufacturing system scheduling. Journal of Manufacturing Systems 24(2), 79–92 (2005). https://doi.org/10.1016/S0278-6125(05)80009-3

49. de Moura, L.M., Bjørner, N.: Z3: an efficient SMT solver. In: Proc. 14th International Conference on Tools and Algorithms for the Construction and Analysis of Systems (TACAS). pp. 337–340. Springer (2008). https://doi.org/10.1007/978-3-540-78800-3_24, tool available at https://github.com/Z3Prover/z3.

50. Murata, T.: Petri nets: Properties, analysis and applications. Proceedings of the IEEE **77**(4), 541–580 (1989). https://doi.org/10.1109/5.24143

51. Rackoff, C.: The covering and boundedness problems for vector addition systems. Theoretical Computer Science **6**, 223–231 (1978). https://doi.org/10.1016/0304-3975(78)90036-1

52. Russell, S., Norvig, P.: Artificial Intelligence: A Modern Approach. Prentice Hall Press, 3rd edn. (2009)

53. Schmidt, K.: LoLA: A low level analyser. In: Proc. International Conference on Application and Theory of Petri Nets (ICATPN). pp. 465–474. Springer (2000). https://doi.org/10.1007/3-540-44988-4_27

54. Silverman, J., Kincaid, Z.: Loop summarization with rational vector addition systems. In: Proc. 31st International Conference on Computer Aided Verification (CAV). pp. 97–115. Springer (2019). https://doi.org/10.1007/978-3-030-25543-5_7

55. Strazny, T.: An algorithmic framework for checking coverability in well-structured transition systems. Ph.D. thesis, Universität Oldenburg (2014), http://csd.informatik.uni-oldenburg.de/~skript/pub/diss/strazny-phdthesis-roterbericht.pdf

56. Uma, G., Prasad, B.: Reachability trees for Petri nets: a heuristic approach. Knowledge-Based Systems **6**(3), 174 – 177 (1993). https://doi.org/10.1016/0950-7051(93)90042-R

57. van der Aalst, W.: The application of Petri nets to workflow management. Journal of Circuits, Systems, and Computers **8**(1), 21–66 (1998). https://doi.org/10.1142/S0218126698000043

58. Watel, D., Weisser, M., Barth, D.: Parameterized complexity and approximability of coverability problems in weighted Petri nets. In: Proc. 38th International Conference on Application and Theory of Petri Nets and Concurrency (PETRI NETS). pp. 330–349. Springer (2017). https://doi.org/10.1007/978-3-319-57861-3_19

59. Wynn, M.T., van der Aalst, W.M.P., ter Hofstede, A.H.M., Edmond, D.: Synchronization and cancelation in workflows based on reset nets. International Journal of Cooperative Information Systems **18**(1), 63–114 (2009). https://doi.org/10.1142/S0218843009002002

60. Yang, C.H., Dill, D.L.: Validation with guided search of the state space. In: Proc. 35th Conference on Design Automation (DAC). pp. 599–604. ACM (1998). https://doi.org/10.1145/277044.277201

61. Zuck, L.D., Pnueli, A.: Model checking and abstraction to the aid of parameterized systems (a survey). Computer Languages, Systems & Structures **30**(3-4), 139–169 (2004). https://doi.org/10.1016/j.cl.2004.02.006

Bridging Arrays and ADTs in Recursive Proofs

Grigory Fedyukovich[1]([✉])[ID] and Gidon Ernst[2][ID]

[1] Florida State University, Tallahassee, USA, grigory@cs.fsu.edu
[2] Ludwig-Maximilians-University, Munich, Germany, gidon.ernst@lmu.de

Abstract. We present an approach to synthesize relational invariants to prove equivalences between object-oriented programs. The approach bridges the gap between recursive data types and arrays that serve to represent internal states. Our relational invariants are recursively-defined, and thus are valid for data structures of unbounded size. Based on introducing recursion into the proofs by observing and lifting the constraints from joint methods of the two objects, our approach is fully automatic and can be seen as an algorithm for solving Constrained Horn Clauses (CHC) of a specific sort. It has been implemented on top of the SMT-based CHC solver ADTCHC and evaluated on a range of benchmarks.

1 Introduction

Relational verification is widely applicable during an iterative process of software development, when a high-level specification, a prototype implementation, or even an arbitrary previous version is compared to the current version and verified for the absence of newly introduced bugs. As software grows large, *compositionality* becomes a crucial factor to achieve scalability of relational verification tasks: reasoning about pairs of entire programs is reduced to reasoning about pairs of modules or isolated components of code. Proofs found for one component can be reused while reasoning about another component, or even the system in a whole. Successful examples in large-scale verification projects include a step-wise refinement in seL4 [30] and the integration of model checking to software development workflow in AWS C Common [11].

In this work, we represent relational verification problems over *object-oriented programs* as Constrained Horn Clauses (CHC). A CHC is an implication in first-order logic that involves a set of unknown predicates. For a system of CHCs, we wish to find an interpretation for all predicates that validates all implications. CHCs are used in various tasks appearing in verification, e.g., finding loop invariants or function summaries. For relational verification, a system of CHCs can be constructed by pairing components of code of two versions in lockstep and supplying it with relational pre- and post-conditions [14,39,44,53]. State-of-the-art tools for solving CHC, e.g., [9,19,21,27,32], are based on Satisfiability Modulo Theories (SMT), e.g., [40,47], they gradually become more robust, as long as the programs under analysis do not have a *mixed use of data structures*.

Verification conditions of real-world problems involve data structures such as arrays and Algebraic Data Types (ADTs) of unknown size, expecting the

J. F. Groote and K. G. Larsen (Eds.): TACAS 2021, LNCS 12652, pp. 24–42, 2021.
https://doi.org/10.1007/978-3-030-72013-1_2

proofs to capture (quantified or recursive) properties over countably infinite sets of elements. Arrays are being handled in loops and often require finding universally-quantified loop invariants [21]. ADTs, such as lists, maps, and sets, require reasoning by structural induction [47] and often rely on additional helper lemmas which are difficult to be synthesized automatically. For relational verification tasks, where one program is over arrays, and another is over ADTs, the solvers should likely reason over quantified formulas and induction *at the same time*, which is currently challenging for most of the automated tools.

We propose a set of new algorithms for solving CHCs constructed by pairing programs over arrays and ADTs. Because we deal with object-oriented programs, the data structures might be accessed and modified in any given method, and our pairing is done for each method separately. Relational proofs are synthesized over the data structures – they describe a relation that holds while *simultaneously traversing pairs of elements* by any of the methods. Our key idea is that not all methods may be needed for the actual synthesis. In fact, our algorithm generates a candidate proof by bridging a single pair of methods and then validates/repairs it on all others. In essence, we observe how pairs of inputs (or pairs of outputs) change the states, guess a candidate relation between elements of states, and (dis-)prove it on all other methods using an SMT-based theorem prover.

Our synthesis strategy is customized for different classes of benchmarks via so called *recipes*. We present two recipes for the list ADT that are applicable, respectively, for (1) stacks and queues, and (2) sets, multisets, and maps. They both discover nontrivial invariants that need a *recursive interpretation*. We independently generate its base and recursive cases. The key point in determining the relations is to automatically investigate how an input or an output affects the state. Finally, we discover auxiliary lemmas that provide additional properties about objects in isolation and help proving the inferred invariants are valid.

Importantly, in contrast to a more lightweight CHC setting over numerical theories (and even arrays) that can rely on an SMT solver to validate its recursion-free solutions, the validation of our *recursive solutions* is conducted by structural induction. We thus rely on recent advances in SMT-based *fully automated* theorem proving [55] that (since recently) supports arrays. The experiments have shown that the approach is reasonably fast in practice. Our contribution, while presented in the CHC context, can be lifted on the program analysis context and implemented in a range of robust verification tools that are designed to support compositionality [7,24].

The rest of the paper is structured as follows. A short outline on background and notation is given in Sect. 2. In Sect. 3, we give an overview of the approach. Then, Sect. 4 and Sect. 5 present our recipes. Finally, we give the evaluation details in Sect. 6, related work in Sect. 7, and conclude the paper in Sect. 8.

2   Preliminaries

An *object* $O = (St, Init, (Op_n)_{n \in [1,N]})$ is defined over internal states St, with initialization $Init(s)$ denoting initial states s, and methods Op_n, also called operations, for some identifier n (which for simplicity is treated as a natural number in some finite interval, but later sections liberally refer to Op_n by their name). Each operation $Op_n(in, s, s', out)$ defines transitions between a pair of states s and s' for a given input in, producing an output out. Moreover, each operation has an associated precondition $pre_n(in, s)$, ranging over the input and pre-state.

In this paper, we take a syntactic approach by representing states as tuples of variables. Specifically, we assume that $Init(s)$ and each operation $Op(in, s, s', out)$ is given as a predicate, i.e., as a characteristic formula, over the specified parameters, that holds for initial states, respectively, when the program can take a particular transition. Such a formula can be obtained from the source code by symbolic execution, and we assume that effect of loops inside operations is captured by quantified formulas, creation of which is an orthogonal problem. Hence, our approach is language agnostic.

We assume that the programs under consideration are deterministic, and we assume that $pre(in, s) \implies \exists s', out.\ Op_n(in, s, s', out)$. Note that for deterministic programs, the existential quantifier in $\exists s', out.\ Op_n(in, s, s', out)$ can be eliminated if $pre(in, s)$ holds as s', out are functionally determined by in, s.

We aim at solving a *relational verification problem* over two objects and reduce it to *inductive invariant* inference over a *composition* of two objects.

Definition 1. *Two objects A and C are* equivalent *if there exists an inductive invariant $\mathbf{R}$ over a* composition *of these objects, which satisfies all clauses below. It connects two states St^A and St^C before and after each pair of operations $(Op_n^A, Op_n^C)_{n \in [1, N]}$.*

$\left\{\begin{array}{l}
\textbf{initialization:}\\[4pt]
\qquad\qquad\qquad\qquad Init^A(as) \land Init^C(cs) \implies \mathbf{R}(as, cs)\\[6pt]
\textbf{consecution:}\\[4pt]
\mathbf{R}(as, cs) \land Op_1^A(in, as, as', out^A) \land Op_1^C(in, cs, cs', out^C) \implies \mathbf{R}(as', cs')\\[4pt]
\qquad\qquad\qquad\qquad\qquad\cdots\\[4pt]
\mathbf{R}(as, cs) \land Op_N^A(in, as, as', out^A) \land Op_N^C(in, cs, cs', out^C) \implies \mathbf{R}(as', cs')\\[4pt]
\textbf{safety: applicability:}\\[4pt]
\qquad\qquad \mathbf{R}(as, cs) \land pre_1^A(in, as) \implies pre_1^C(in, cs)\\[4pt]
\qquad\qquad \mathbf{R}(as, cs) \land pre_1^C(in, as) \implies pre_1^A(in, cs)\\[4pt]
\qquad\qquad\qquad\qquad\cdots\\[4pt]
\qquad\qquad \mathbf{R}(as, cs) \land pre_N^A(in, as) \implies pre_N^C(in, cs)\\[4pt]
\qquad\qquad \mathbf{R}(as, cs) \land pre_N^C(in, as) \implies pre_N^A(in, cs)\\[4pt]
\textbf{safety: outputs:}\\[4pt]
\mathbf{R}(as, cs) \land Op_1^A(in, as, as', out^A) \land Op_1^C(in, cs, cs', out^C) \implies out^A = out^C\\[4pt]
\qquad\qquad\qquad\qquad\qquad\cdots\\[4pt]
\mathbf{R}(as, cs) \land Op_N^A(in, as, as', out^A) \land Op_N^C(in, cs, cs', out^C) \implies out^A = out^C
\end{array}\right.$

Implications in Def. 1 define a set of Constrained Horn Clauses (CHC) over an uninterpreted relation symbol R. There are three types of constraints: (1) initialization, (2) consecution, and (3) safety. The third, safety, reflects the actual relational specification, i.e., the correspondence between the programs under analysis, in terms of the user-visible variables, namely the input in, and the respective outputs, out and out'. Here, safety is divided into applicability (coincidence of preconditions) and equivalence of outputs, which together ensure that the two programs are observationally equivalent. To prove that this equivalence holds, one needs to infer a more complicated invariant R over the internal state. For this reason, we need the initiation and the consecution constraints: whatever happens due to each operation, the invariant is maintained, and by safety, the programs remain observationally equivalent indefinitely.

Problem Statement: We seek an interpretation of R that satisfies all constraints in Def. 1 simultaneously. This conventional formulation of a CHC task lets us to use any off-the-shelf CHC solver. However, the problem is undecidable in general, thus no solver guarantees to handle our specific tasks. Furthermore, existing solvers mainly support the lightweight arithmetic theories, and a few exceptions support also ADTs [27] and arrays [21,32]. To the best of our knowledge, there is no CHC solver that supports ADTs and arrays *at the same time*, and there is no CHC solver that synthesizes recursive solutions.

Context: The system of CHCs ensures that A and C can be substituted interchangeably in any calling context, and it is applicable to a wide range of techniques for formal program development. The focus on equivalence instead of subsumption is not essential for our work, and the presented approach works for the asymmetric case just the same. Specifically, Liskov and Wing's substitution principle [36] follows (precondition strengthening is reflected by the applicability constraints from pre^A to pre^C, and all postconditions with respect to the outputs are equivalent). Data Refinement [15,25] follows similarly (Def. 1 characterizes that R is a forward simulation [37]). See Sect. 7 for more details.

3   Synthesis of Recursive Relational Invariants

In this section, we present the fundamentals of the approach to synthesize recursive relational invariants for systems over arrays and ADTs that we instantiate and illustrate on examples in the subsequent sections.

3.1   Overview

Our approach is purely symbolic and fully automatic in both stages: generating a candidate relational invariant, and proving it correct (i.e., validating). The key insight is an analysis of the operations joint in the constraints of Def. 1. We follow a strategy of introducing recursion into the interpretation based on ADTs, and by aligning the base case to initialization and the recurrence conditions to joint operations. In particular, a relational invariant R that bridges an algebraic list xs

---

Algorithm 1: Automated synthesis of recursive relational invariants

---

Input: Objects $A = (as, Init^A, (Op_n^A)_{n \in N})$ and $C = (cs, Init^C, (Op_n^C)_{n \in N})$,
    where as, cs are the state variables, and xs is a list variable of as

Output: relational invariant R between A and C

1 $R(\text{nil}, cs) \leftarrow Init^A(as[xs := \text{nil}]) \wedge Init^C(cs)$;

2 $\phi_r \leftarrow true$;

3 let y and ys be fresh variables;

4 **while** $true$ **do**

5      $cs_r \leftarrow \text{UPDATE}(Op_n^A, Op_n^C, as[xs := \text{cons}(y, ys)], cs)$ for some $n \in N$;

6      $\phi_r \leftarrow \phi_r \wedge \text{MATCH}(Op_m^A, Op_m^C, as[xs := \text{cons}(y, ys)], cs, cs_r)$ for some $m \in N$;

7      $R(as[xs := \text{cons}(y, ys)], cs) \leftarrow \phi_r \wedge R(as[xs := ys], cs_r)$;

8   **if** $\text{VALIDATE}(R, A, C)$ **then return** R;

---

and an array (with auxiliary variables, such as *index*) cs is defined recursively over the structure of xs, which produces this general schema:

$$R(xs, cs) = \begin{cases} \phi_b(cs) & \text{if } xs = \text{nil} \\ \exists \ cs_r. \ \phi_r(y, ys, cs, cs_r) \wedge R(ys, cs_r) & \text{if } xs = \text{cons}(y, ys) \end{cases} \tag{1}$$

This schema has two placeholders for constraints, ϕ_b in the base case and ϕ_r in the recursive case, that may refer to the variables in scope (as indicated by their respective parameter lists). Moreover, we seek a Skolem function to eliminate the existentially-quantified state variable cs_r in the recursive position. Intuitively the desired Skolem function captures the delta between two array states that corresponds to the delta between xs and ys.

Alg. 1 gives our top-level synthesis procedure for interpretations of R. It takes as input two objects, A and C, where as and cs are tuples variables that represent their respective states. We refer to primed versions of these state variables to as as' and cs', assuming that all as, cs, as', and cs' are distinct. The algorithm works with algebraic lists specifically and thus as is assumed to have such a component given by the state variable xs. We denote by $as[xs := e]$ the updated vector of variables such that xs is replaced in as by symbolic expression e.

The base case of the interpretation of R is straightforward (line 1): the algorithm uses a predicate $Init^C$ and a predicate $Init^A$ in which the xs variable is instantiated to nil. The inductive case of the interpretation of R is trickier (line 7). Because several different operations that *produce* state, *consume* state, or *do nothing* with a state are possible (see Def. 2 later in the section), some of them might contribute to different parts of the interpretation being synthesized. In particular, methods MATCH and UPDATE are responsible for generating a body of R. They are instantiated differently for our two recipes in Sect. 4 (applicable for stacks and queues) and Sect. 5 (applicable for (multi)sets and maps).

The first method, UPDATE, synthesizes an updated symbolic state cs_r, a tuple of symbolic expressions, to be used in the nested inductive call of R. It can therefore be understood to compute a witness (or Skolem function) to existential quantifier in Eq. (1) as an expression of the remaining variables in scope, y, ys, as, cs. The second method, MATCH then collects constraints ϕ_r from suitable transitions w.r.t. this cs_r.

In a loop for each candidate interpretation of R, our algorithm runs an automated SMT-based theorem prover [55] to validate it (line 8). The algorithm can iterate several times and converges after a successful theorem-prover run.

A noteworthy feature of our framework is that UPDATE and MATCH should not necessarily be synchronized in pairs. Although cs_r and the result of MATCH are going to be eventually combined and used in a single formula, the nondeterministic nature of our synthesis procedure suggests that the two ingredients may originate from potentially non-joint operations, thereby enlarging the search space of possible relational invariants.

3.2   Classifying Operations

Our particular strategies for choosing ingredients for the inductive interpretation of R are based on the classification of the operations of the abstract object.

We define a partial ordering "$\preceq$" on ADT states that connects constructors discerned by the recurrence in R to the transitions of operations. With respect to this ordering, we can for example recognize operations that leave the ADT unchanged ("noops", which play a special role in Sect. 5), operations that "produce" constructors and thereby enlarge the internal state by additional elements and conversely operations that "consume" constructors. A natural choice for $\preceq$ is the reflexive closure of the subterm ordering, where $xs \preceq ys$ for lists specifies that xs is a suffix of ys. In general, this ordering can be used to control the result of the synthesis for specific applications, and is a heuristic choice. A choice which works well for our examples is that xs is a non-strict subsequence of ys.

The $\preceq$ ordering naturally extends to tuples of variables (and thus, states), and lets us classify operations into the following three kinds.

Definition 2. *Let Op be an operation of an abstract object. Then,*

$$\text{ISNO}(Op) \overset{\text{def}}{=} \forall i, s, s', o \,.\, Op(i, s, s', o) \implies s = s'$$

$$\text{ISPROD}(Op) \overset{\text{def}}{=} \forall i, s, s', o \,.\, Op(i, s, s', o) \implies s \preceq s' \wedge \neg\text{ISNO}(Op)$$

$$\text{ISCONSM}(Op) \overset{\text{def}}{=} \forall i, s, s', o \,.\, Op(i, s, s', o) \implies s' \preceq s \wedge \neg\text{ISNO}(Op)$$

Example 1. The class of an operation can often be identified by a cheap syntactic check to recognize when cons is applied to a current state or a next state variable. In the upcoming stack example in Fig. 1, from xs' = cons(in, xs) we have that push is a producer operation, and from cons(out, xs') = xs we classify pop as consumer operation. A top operation, not shown in Fig. 1, would be recognized as a noop (see also hasElement in the upcoming example in Fig. 3).

In the next two subsections, we introduce our particular strategies for the implementations of UPDATE and MATCH of Alg. 1, in reference to Def. 2. Some operations fall into neither of the classes; or it may be hard to determine so if they do, given that Def. 2 is semantic; and different operations may contribute different ingredients for a correct definition of R. To make use of as many operations as possible, we suggest strategies for all three classes of operations, to be able to synthesize a relational invariant in complex cases, even when complete information about the system is difficult to obtain.

4   Recipe 1: Linear Scan

We identify a class of problems that require *scanning* the arrays in implementations of stacks and queues *linearly*. A distinguishing feature in this class is the presence of a numeric variable in cs through which array cells are accessed (denoted *index* in the rest of the section). We first illustrate the synthesis process on the following example and then present the algorithmic details.

4.1   Motivating Example

Two realizations of a FIFO stack are shown in Fig. 1: one is based on linked lists, and another is based on arrays. They share a common interface of initialization and the two operations push and pop. For example, the encodings of pop of ListStack and ArrStack are respectively:

$$Op_{\text{pop}}^{\text{ListStack}}(xs, xs', out)$$
$$= (xs \neq \text{nil} \wedge xs' = xs.\text{tail} \wedge out = xs.\text{head})$$
$$= (xs = \text{cons}(out, xs')) \qquad \text{(after simplification)}$$
$$Op_{\text{pop}}^{\text{ArrStack}}(a, n, a', n', out)$$
$$= (n > 0 \wedge a' = a \wedge n = n - 1 \wedge out = a[n'])$$

where $xs \neq \text{nil}$ and $n > 0$ are the preconditions, and out captures the return value. As an illustration, formula $Op_{\text{pop}}^{\text{ListStack}}(s, \_, 7)$ holds for all states s in which pop terminates and returns 7 (by convention we use $\_$ to denote terms that are irrelevant in a particular context). Note also that in the implementation of ArrStack, the popped value is not erased from the array – in order for $a[n]$ to be considered in the future, it has to be rewritten by some push operator. In general, the array always contains infinitely many unknown values outside the range of cells $a[0], \ldots, a[n-1]$ which are never accessed.

A possible relational invariant $R(xs, n, a)$ bridging ListStack and ArrStack is defined as follows:

$$R(xs, n, a) = \begin{cases} n = 0 & \text{if } xs = \text{nil} \\ n > 0 \wedge y = a[n-1] \wedge R(ys, n-1, a) & \text{if } xs = \text{cons}(y, ys) \end{cases} \qquad (2)$$

Intuitively, this R captures that a list xs has the same content as the portion of an array a between indexes 0 (including) and n (excluding). When xs is empty, then the portion of a should be empty too, thus $n = 0$. Otherwise, xs is created by cons-ing some other list ys and an element y then (1) n should be strictly positive, and (2) y should belong to the designated portion of a.

```
class ListStack:                    class ArrStack:
  def init():                         def init():
    xs = nil                            n = 0
                                        a = [...]

  def push(in):                       def push(in):
    xs = cons(in, xs)                   a[n] = in
                                        n = n + 1
  def pop():
    assert xs != nil                  def pop():
    out = xs.head                       assert n > 0
    xs = xs.tail                        n = n - 1
    return out                          return a[n]
```

Fig. 1: Two implementations of a FIFO stack.

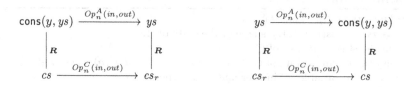

Fig. 2: Transitions of consumer operations (left) and producer operations (right) used to instantiate Eq. (1).

The schema in Sect. 3.1 has two placeholders for constraints, ϕ_b in the base case and ϕ_r in the recursive case, that may refer to the variables in scope (as indicated by their respective parameter lists). Moreover, we seek a state cs_r in the recursive position. Placeholder ϕ_b is instantiated by constraints from the initialization operations, such as $n = 0$ from ArrStack. This alignment of base case and initialization is not just a coincidence: many data structures start initially empty and are gradually populated by calling operations (e.g., collections).

The purpose of ϕ_r in the recursive case of Eq. (1) is twofold. First, it connects a portion of the ADT state (specifically y) to the array state cs, in the example via $a[n-1] = y$, and it determines a suitable array state cs_r as an argument of the recursive occurrence of R. For instance, we take $n - 1$ for the recursive call but leave a unchanged. This is motivated by the observation that a state where $xs = \text{cons}(y, ys)$ for some y, ys is *consumed* by pop. Using this information, the recurrence of R must align with the corresponding array transitions, too, as shown in Fig. 2 on the left. The constraint $n > 0$ is the precondition of the array operation, whereas $y = a[n-1]$ follows from comparing the outputs. As shown in Fig. 2 on the right, we can dually base the recurrence on push, which *produces* a cons, i.e., a transition from ys to $xs = \text{cons}(y, ys)$ for some y. In this case, both transitions need to be viewed *in reverse* such that the respective successor states of push now match the left side $R(xs, cs)$ of the schema. Then, the assignment n = n + 1 can be rewritten to yield the equation $n_r = n - 1$.

Algorithm 2: UPDATE (recipe 1)

Input: Operations Op^A and Op^C,
 $\quad as[xs := \mathsf{cons}(y, ys)]$ the shape of the state of A,
 $\quad cs$ the state variables of C, assuming $cs = (\_, index, a)$ where $index$
 $\quad$ and a are variables of integer and array types, resp.
Output: Updated arguments cs_r
1 **if** ISPROD(Op^A) **then**
2 $\quad$ let $cs_r = (\_, index', a')$ be s.t. $\forall in, \exists out . Op^C(in, cs_r, cs, out)$;
3 $\quad$ **return** $(\_, index', a)$;
4 **if** ISCONSM(Op^A) **then**
5 $\quad$ let $cs_r = (\_, index', a')$ be s.t. $\forall in, \exists out . Op^C(in, cs, cs_r, out)$;
6 $\quad$ **return** $(\_, index', a)$;

Algorithm 3: MATCH (recipe 1)

Input: Operations Op^A and Op^C,
 $\quad as[xs := \mathsf{cons}(y, ys)]$ the shape of the state of A,
 $\quad cs$ the state variables of C,
 $\quad cs_r$ the updated state of C, assuming $cs_r = (\_, index', a)$ where $index'$
 $\quad$ and a are variables of integer and array types, resp.
Output: Formula ϕ_r
1 **if** ISPROD(Op^A) **then**
2 $\quad inv \leftarrow$ GETLOOPINVARIANT($index', Op^C$);
3 $\quad$ **return** $inv \wedge \neg Init^C(cs) \wedge y = a[index']$;
4 **if** ISCONSM(Op^A) **then**
5 $\quad$ **return** $pre_n^A \wedge pre_n^C \wedge y = a[index']$;
6 **return** $true$;

To make this intuition practical, our approach suggests a particular strategy for picking operations to take constraints from, recognizing consumers and producers more generally, and validating the guessed relational invariants using induction and lemmas.

4.2   Algorithm Description

Alg. 2 and Alg. 3 show the implementations of UPDATE and MATCH, respectively, that suit stacks and queues. Recall that these algorithms are called from Alg. 1 and take as input pairs of nondeterministically chosen joint operations of A and C; state variables cs of C; current version of state variables cs_r to be used in the recursive call of $\boldsymbol{R}$; and fresh variables y and ys introduced in Alg. 1 to define the inductive rule of $\boldsymbol{R}$. Outputs of UPDATE and MATCH are respectively an updated tuple of variables cs_r and a subformula ψ to be conjoined with the inductive definition of $\boldsymbol{R}$.

If the producing operator is picked (line 1 of Alg. 2), then we have to find a term $index'$, such that it would be transitioned by Op^C to $index$. In particular, after assigning a new value to an array cell, *index* is monotonically updated (i.e., incremented like in the example in Fig. 1, or decremented). Thus, to access the array cell containing a new value using an updated value of *index*, we have to invert the arithmetic operation and obtain $index - 1$ (for Fig. 1) or $index + 1$ (in the case of decrementation). Technically, in Alg. 2, it is realized by taking the *index* variable from cs, through which cells of the array can be observed (e.g., n in example in Fig. 1) and finding such a term $index'$, that would be transitioned by Op^C to *index*. Thus, the resulting cs_r is composed from the same ingredients as cs where $index'$ replaces *index*.

If the consuming operation is picked (line 4), then we proceed in the reverse direction and find $index'$ that is a result of transitioning of *index* through Op^C.

Alg. 3 for this recipe relies on the output of Alg. 2. Interestingly, it is supported even if cs_r is computed using the producer, but ψ in Alg. 3 is computed using the consumer. Our particular strategy for the consumers in this recipe is 1) to use the precondition for Op^C, and 2) to bridge the outputs of Op^A and Op^C via an equality. Alternatively, the inference via producer in line 1, in comparison, misses important constraint in the example, as the precondition of push is trivial. Such a situation can be mitigated by the discovery of a loop invariant (line 2) over *index*, i.e., usually just using Linear Integer Arithmetic (LIA), adding it, and blocking the initial state (to distinguish from the base case of the definition of $\boldsymbol{R}$) in the inductive case of the interpretation of R being synthesized. Loop invariants are generated as follows as interpretations of predicate *inv* satisfying the following two implications:

$$Init^C(cs) \implies inv(cs)$$

$$inv(cs) \wedge \left(\bigvee_{n \in N} Op_n^C(in, cs, cs', out) \right) \implies inv(cs')$$

Note that these CHCs (over LIA) can be solved by numerous existing approaches. Without a query, ideally *the strongest* loop invariant is desirable; however in practice it suffices to apply lightweight techniques based on forward-propagation of initial states using quantifier elimination, followed by its inductive subset computation [20]. This often finds an *adequately-strong* invariant.

Example 2. Recall the stack example in Fig. 1. Let the $index'$ term be computed by Alg. 2 via inverting the increment operation in push. Thus, it is used as an argument of the nested call to $\boldsymbol{R}$ in the inductive case of the definition of $\boldsymbol{R}$. By construction, the $a[index']$ cell contains a value of in, i.e., the argument of push. At the same time, in is the argument of cons in Op^A representing push, which lets us bridge the array and ADT in the proof. To allow this, Alg. 3 takes argument y of cons from the inductive definition of $\boldsymbol{R}$, and equates it with $a[index']$, producing $y = a[n - 1]$. Combining it all together, we get the final solution, as shown in (2).

```
class ListSet:                          class ArraySet:
    def init():                             def init():
        xs = nil                                a = [false, false, ...]

    def hasElement(in):                     def hasElement(in):
        return contains(xs, in)                 return a[in]

    def insert(in):                         def insert(in):
        xs = cons(in, xs)                       a[in] = true

    def erase(in):                          def erase(in):
        xs = removeall(xs, in)                  a[in] = false
```

Fig. 3: Two implementations of a set, where the list is not necessarily duplicate-free.

5   Recipe 2: Noop-based synthesis

In this subsection we present a recipe that suits sets, multisets, and maps, that are in some sense *non-linear*. That is, data structures do not maintain any *index* variable, which is usually used to access elements. Instead, arrays are viewed as maps, and the corresponding ADTs are equipped with recursive functions that traverse the data structure over and over again for each input. Oftentimes, these objects have noop operations, and our synthesis procedure makes use of them.

5.1   Motivating Example

Fig. 3 shows two implementations of a set. The list-based implementation stores elements in the order of their insert-ions. The elements are not removed unless erase is called explicitly. Thus, duplicate entries of the same elements are allowed. The implementation uses the recursive contains and removeall functions that both traverse the list and search for a specific element:

$$\text{contains}(xs, a) = \begin{cases} false & \text{if } xs = \text{nil} \\ (a = y) \vee \text{contains}(ys, a), & \text{if } xs = \text{cons}(y, ys) \end{cases}$$

$$\text{removeall}(xs, a) = \begin{cases} \text{nil} & \text{if } xs = \text{nil} \\ ite(a = y, \text{removeall}(ys, a), \\ \quad \text{cons}(y, \text{removeall}(ys, a))) & \text{if } xs = \text{cons}(y, ys) \end{cases}$$

The array-based implementation handles a map a from elements to Booleans. Initially, all cells in a are false. Inserting and removing an element is implemented by storing true and false to the corresponding cell respectively. The difficulty here is to support the shown implementation of insert and erase in Fig. 3, as well as possible variants that e.g., eagerly prune duplicate entries in the list-based implementation (see Sect. 6).

The expected output of our synthesis procedure is as follows:

$$\boldsymbol{R}(xs, a) = \begin{cases} \forall z. \ \neg a[z] & \text{if } xs = \text{nil} \\ a[y] \wedge \boldsymbol{R}(ys, a[y := \text{contains}(ys, x)]), & \text{if } xs = \text{cons}(y, ys) \end{cases} \quad (3)$$

Algorithm 4: UPDATE (recipe 2)

Input: Operations Op^A and Op^C such that $\text{ISNO}(Op^A)$ holds,
   $as[xs := \text{cons}(y, ys)]$ the shape of the state of A,
   cs the state variables of C
Output: Updated arguments cs_r
1 let cs' be fresh variables;
2 $\phi \leftarrow Op^A(y, as[xs := ys], as[xs := ys], out) \wedge Op^C(y, cs', \_, out)$;
3 $\psi \leftarrow \forall z . z \neq y \implies \exists out' . Op^C(z, cs, \_, out') \wedge Op^C(z, cs', \_, out')$;
4 assume $\text{QE}(\exists out . \phi \wedge \psi)$ simplifies to $(cs' = cs_r)$;
5 **return** cs_r;

Algorithm 5: MATCH (recipe 2)

Input: Operations Op^A and Op^C such that $\text{ISNO}(Op^A)$ holds,
   $as[xs := \text{cons}(y, ys)]$ the shape of the state of A, denoted as_0 below,
   cs the state variables of C,
   cs_r the updated state of C
Output: Formula ϕ_r
1 $\phi \leftarrow Op^A(y, as_0, as_0, out) \wedge Op^C(y, cs, cs_r, out)$;
2 **return** SIMPLIFY$(\text{QE}(\exists out . \phi))$;

5.2 Algorithm details

Alg. 4 and Alg. 5 show the implementations of UPDATE and MATCH, respectively, for this recipe. The arguments cs_r of the nested call to $\boldsymbol{R}$ in the inductive case of the definition of $\boldsymbol{R}$ are computed in Alg. 4 using the symbolic encoding of *noop*. In the set example, *noop* is the `hasElement` operation, which allows observing the status of the internal state and does not modify it. We furthermore assume that the input of Op_n coincides with the type of elements stored in the list, i.e., it is meaningful to call $Op_n(y, \cdots)$ with the list head y from the recursive case of (1) where $xs = \text{cons}(y, ys)$.

The key idea behind Alg. 4 is to make necessary adjustments to cs to construct cs_r that mirror any changes that can be observed via Op^A when transitioning from list xs to ys in (1). This update is determined in terms of an auxiliary variables cs' that are constrained to satisfy certain input/output pairs for the corresponding Op^C, by case analysis whether the input is this particular y that is removed by the recurrence. The primary intention is to reassign $a[y]$ appropriately. We do this by collecting constraints ϕ such that the output observed for Op^C for y and cs' matches that of the corresponding Op^A on the smaller state with ys. This is also the key difference to Sect. 4, where we heuristically keep a unchanged in the recursive call in (1). The outputs for all other inputs z, however, are enforced to be unchanged w.r.t. the original cs, which is expressed by the constraint ψ. We then eliminate the quantifier for out (which is straightforward as the operations are deterministic) and rewrite the formula to closed expressions cs_r for variables cs' as result.

Example 3. Specifically for the example in Sect. 5.1, the algorithm proceeds by symbolic execution of `hasElement`, yielding formulas the following constituents:

$$Op^A = (out = \text{contains}(ys, y))$$
$$Op^C = (out = a[y])$$
$$\phi = (out = \text{contains}(ys, y) \land out = a'[y])$$
$$\psi = (\forall z . y \neq z \implies \exists out' . out' = a'[z] \land out' = a[z])$$

The result $\exists out . \phi \land \psi$ of Alg. 4 is now solved for a'. The only free variables refer to the states of the systems. Bound variables out and out' can be eliminated by merging equalities over out and out':

$$a'[y] = \text{contains}(ys, y) \land (\forall z . y \neq z \implies a'[z] = a[z])$$

The first conjunct therefore provides the update for $a'[y]$, whereas the second conjunct of ϕ states that $a'[z]$ should *not* be changed at indices other than y. After applying the axioms over the theory of arrays we get as result the following equality, which pattern matches the expected shape in line 4:

$$QE(\exists out . \phi) \iff (a' = a[x := \text{contains}(ys, x)])$$

This transformation requires to "reverse-apply" the axiom of extensionality, i.e., switch from the pointwise comparison of a and a' to an equality between the entire arrays. Note that while in general quantifier elimination is difficult, our current implementation has a limited, but often sufficient, support that can be extended by supplying rules to the underlying SMT-based theorem prover.

While Op^A Alg. 4 predict *future* outputs of Op^A for input y, Alg. 5 executes Op^A on the state where $xs = \text{cons}(y, ys)$ to obtain the *current* output of Op^A for the same y. The generated constraint simply expresses that the output of Op^C has to match. For `hasElement` we obtain the following formula:

$$\exists out . (\text{contains}(\text{cons}(y, ys), y) = out) \land (a[y] = out)$$

Unfolding the definition of `contains` and simplification produces $true = a[x]$, which is then used as the "*body*" of the inductive case of $\boldsymbol{R}$ in (3).

6   Evaluation

We have implemented the approach in a prototype CHC solver called ADTCHC[3], relying on ADTIND [55] as an inductive prover, which in turn uses the Z3 [40] SMT solver to quickly perform the satisfiability checks over uninterpreted functions and linear arithmetic that are needed at various solving stages. ADTCHC automatically determines the appropriate synthesis recipe through analyzing the

---

[3] The tool and benchmarks are available at https://github.com/grigoryfedyukovich/aeval/tree/adt-chc.

syntax of the program (i.e., presence of index variables) and is able to successfully find relational invariants and prove them valid for all considered benchmarks.

We have evaluated the approach from Sect. 3 on different realizations of text-book data structures. The evaluation aims at answering two questions. Is the approach effective in the first place to discover suitable relational invariants, and how well can the necessary induction proofs be automated? The latter is relevant since Alg. 1 crucially depends on VALIDATE in its refinement loop.

All our benchmarks require recursive invariants. They fall into two categories. First, stacks and queues from Sect. 4 (with variations that store values only to even indexes of the array) are solved based on linear scan. Second, sets, multisets, and maps, (that differ in whether, e.g., duplicate elements are stored in the respective lists) are solved with the approach in Sect. 5. We include such variations to reflect different trade-offs when designing specifications, and to demonstrate that our technique is reasonably flexible. The only user-provided lemma was required for the multiset benchmark (marked * in Table 1): $\forall\, a, xs.\ \mathsf{num}(a, xs) = 0 \implies \mathsf{remove}(a, xs) = xs$.

The results from the evaluation[4] of both groups of benchmarks (resp., recipes used) are shown in Table 1. The choice which recipe to use was made by the tool itself at synthesis time. Total time (in seconds wall-clock) is entirely dominated by proof search in ADTIND, and includes the time for SMT queries. We remark that the time to synthesize the relational invariant is negligible in comparison to the proof time (and the proof time is often proportional to the number of internal SMT calls).

Table 1: Invariant synthesis timings.

Benchmark	Variant	Time (s)
Stack	Fig. 1	2.81
Stack	even cells	2.79
Queue	ordinary	40.61
Queue	even cells	42.18
Set	Fig. 3	2.12
Set	no duplicates	19.24
Multiset*	with remove	32.62
Multiset	with clear	3.59
Map	duplicates	1.95
Map	no duplicates	5.83

Most proofs are found using the default proof strategy (the same for every benchmark) within 20s. This is caused by the large proof search space created by a combination of array simplification and forward rewriting. We have also tested our tool of buggy implementations, e.g., in which the consumer operations are correct (and can be used for correct guesses of relational invariants), but producers are not. Expectedly, the tool is unable to synthesize a relational invariant for the whole systems in these cases.

We have already presented the relational invariants found for the stack (2), for the stack variant that stores to even array indices only, counter n is decreased by 2 instead of 1 in the recursive call as expected. Relational invariant $\boldsymbol{R}(xs, m, n, a)$ for the queue benchmarks keeps two indices into the array a, depending on the variant, the first element of the list xs is found at $a[m]$ or $a[n]$

---

[4] The evaluation was conducted on MacBook Pro, Processor: 2 GHz Intel Core i5, Memory: 8 GB 1867 MHz LPDDR3, MacOS v10.14.6.

and the recursion either increases m or decreases n. The relational invariants for the multiset and map examples are analogous. All necessary lemmas are automatically discovered and proved by ADTIND, as an example for the set benchmarks: $\forall\ xs, s, x.\ R(xs, s) \implies \text{contains}(x, xs) = s[x]$.

7 Related Work

Although there exist automated techniques to synthesize relational invariants, nothing was proposed to deal simultaneously with ADTs and arrays. Conceptually, our approach is related to SIMABS, an SMT-based algorithm to simulation synthesis [18]. SIMABS exploits a space of possible simulations and (dis-)proves them using an off-the-shelf decision procedure. Guesses for simulation relation are obtained also from the source code, by matching variables from two programs. Alternatively, simulation relations can be inferred from test runs [49] or through translation validation [41]. Our approach allows dealing with objects (not just imperative code) and contributes several novel strategies for guessing and proving non-trivial simulation relations.

Discovery of invariants to relate the behaviors of two programs or other ways of establishing program equivalence is an active research area [5,14,22,23,39,44,51]. These approaches typically reduce the relational verification problem to a safety verification problem and rely on the existing tools—often, solvers for constrained Horn clauses (CHC). Currently, since ADTs and arrays are challenging for the underlying solvers, the applicability of the approaches to our tasks are also limited. There are decision procedures for abstraction of ADTs to lists, sets, and multisets [52], however, these apply to certain predefined abstractions only.

Our approach can be seen as an application of Syntax-Guided Synthesis (SyGuS) [2]. Strategies dependent on types of benchmarks essentially represent sets of syntactic templates filled iteratively and checked using an SMT solver. SyGuS is successfully used also in CHC solving [19,21] and in lemma synthesis [46,47,55]. There are only a few approaches [21,28,31,55] that apply SyGuS to synthesize formulas over ADTs or arrays/quantifier. Data-driven approaches are complementary to such syntax-based approaches, e.g., [38]. Neither deals with arrays, quantifiers, and ADTs at the same time.

Unno et al. [53] support recursive predicates, by taking the least solution of initialization and consecution as the definition of R, however, this may lead to rather cumbersome inductive cases (e.g., for pop in the stack). We avoid the problem by basing the recurrence scheme on the data structure, and infer constraints that are well aligned to that scheme from the operations. Jennisys [34] tackles the related problem of generating recursive implementations from an abstract model, where the simulation relation is given.

More generally, the problem addressed in this work relates to the idea of step-wise refinement, originally conceived by [16] and [54] as a guideline to organize software development and later studied extensively in a formal setting for rigorous assessment of functional correctness (e.g., [1,4,15,25,29,33,36]). The standard proof technique relies on simulation relations [37] that couple the two state spaces, which is directly reflected in the CHC system of Def. 1.

Many methods and tools support development using formal refinement [1, 4, 8, 17, 26, 29, 33, 45]. Large-scale verification projects that are based on refinement include seL4 [30], FSCQ [10], Flashix [48], and CompCert [35], with high human effort involved. Correct-by-construction correspondence between low-level code and high-level data types helps to some extent in, e.g., [13] and COGENT [3]. Recent work on "push-button" verification includes a verified TLS library [12], AWS C Common library [11], file system [50], a hyperkernel [42], network functions [56], where the high degree of proof automation is in part achieved by statically bounding the state space of the systems. The latter work [56] specifically notes how non-experts can formulate high-level correctness requirements (their specifications are written in Python), as evidence that refinement-based approaches may ultimately overcome the "specification bottleneck" [6, 43].

8 Conclusion and Outlook

We have demonstrated an approach that can fully automatically synthesize and prove relational invariants over recursive data types and arrays. The approach is based on introducing quantifiers and recursion into the definition of such relations in a systematic way, and by instantiating this schema with constraints from joint transitions of the two systems. A somewhat surprising insight was that it is useful to view such transitions both forward and in reverse, leading to the classification into producers and consumers as a guideline for the search.

We have presented a general synthesis algorithm and two concrete instantiations for different data structures of different sorts. The approach is fully automatic in guessing a relation and proving it correct. It relies on the recently developed CHC solver called ADTCHC which in turn is based on an SMT-based theorem prover ADTIND featuring a support for arrays, quantifiers and structural induction. The approach is modular and can be extended by further synthesis strategies in the future. In particular, since based on CHC techniques, it can be integrated with other existing CHC solvers tailored to non-ADT reasoning, and can be used in large-scale verification frameworks such as [24] that reduce the safety verification to CHC tasks.

Many more interesting benchmarks lend themselves for further investigation: positional insertion and removal of lists, amortized data structures, benchmarks based on trees or nested arrays, and ultimately some real-world software systems. With a growing search space, it becomes more important to quickly recognize incorrect simulation relations, e.g., by evaluation-based counter-examples (cf. [31]), to prevent costly proof attempts. Similarly, incorporating external tools for invariant generation is another topic for future work.

References

1. J.-R. Abrial. *Modeling in Event-B: System and Software engineering.* Cambridge University Press, 2010.
2. R. Alur, R. Bodík, G. Juniwal, M. M. K. Martin, M. Raghothaman, S. A. Seshia, R. Singh, A. Solar-Lezama, E. Torlak, and A. Udupa. Syntax-Guided Synthesis. In *FMCAD*, pages 1–17. IEEE, 2013.
3. S. Amani, A. Hixon, Z. Chen, C. Rizkallah, P. Chubb, L. O'Connor, J. Beeren, Y. Nagashima, J. Lim, T. Sewell, J. Tuong, G. Keller, T. Murray, G. Klein, and G. Heiserer. COGENT: Verifying high-assurance file system implementations. In *ASPLOS*, pages 175–188. ACM, 2016.
4. R.-J. Back and J. Wright. *Refinement calculus: a systematic introduction.* Springer Science & Business Media, 2012.
5. G. Barthe, J. M. Crespo, and C. Kunz. Relational verification using product programs. In *FM*, volume 6664 of *LNCS*, pages 200–214. Springer, 2011.
6. C. Baumann, B. Beckert, H. Blasum, and T. Bormer. Lessons learned from microkernel verification–specification is the new bottleneck. In *SSV*, volume 102 of *EPTCS*, pages 18–32. Elsevier, 2012.
7. D. Beyer and M. E. Keremoglu. CPAchecker: A Tool for Configurable Software Verification. In *CAV*, volume 6806 of *LNCS*, pages 184–190. Springer, 2011.
8. E. Börger. The ASM refinement method. *Formal Aspects of Computing*, 15(2-3):237–257, 2003.
9. A. Champion, N. Kobayashi, and R. Sato. HoIce: An ICE-Based Non-linear Horn Clause Solver. In *APLAS*, volume 11275 of *LNCS*, pages 146–156. Springer, 2018.
10. H. Chen, D. Ziegler, A. Chlipala, N. Zeldovich, and M. F. Kaashoek. Using Crash Hoare Logic for certifying the FSCQ file system. In *SOSP*. ACM, 2015.
11. N. Chong, B. Cook, K. Kallas, K. Khazem, F. R. Monteiro, D. Schwartz-Narbonne, S. Tasiran, M. Tautschnig, and M. R. Tuttle. Code-level model checking in the software development workflow. In G. Rothermel and D. Bae, editors, *ICSE-SEIP*, pages 11–20. ACM, 2020.
12. A. Chudnov, N. Collins, B. Cook, J. Dodds, B. Huffman, C. MacCárthaigh, S. Magill, E. Mertens, E. Mullen, S. Tasiran, et al. Continuous formal verification of Amazon s2n. In *CAV*, pages 430–446. Springer, 2018.
13. C. L. Conway and C. W. Barrett. Verifying low-level implementations of high-level datatypes. In *CAV*, volume 6174 of *LNCS*, pages 306–320. Springer, 2010.
14. E. De Angelis, F. Fioravanti, A. Pettorossi, and M. Proietti. Solving Horn Clauses on Inductive Data Types Without Induction. *TPLP*, 18(3-4):452–469, 2018.
15. W.-P. de Roever and K. Engelhardt. *Data refinement: Model-oriented proof methods and their comparison.* Cambridge University Press, 1998.
16. E. W. Dijkstra. A constructive approach to the problem of program correctness. *BIT Numerical Mathematics*, 8(3):174–186, 1968.
17. G. Ernst, J. Pfähler, G. Schellhorn, D. Haneberg, and W. Reif. KIV: Overview and VerifyThis competition. *Software Tools for Technology Transfer (STTT)*, 17(6):677–694, 2015.
18. G. Fedyukovich, A. Gurfinkel, and N. Sharygina. Automated discovery of simulation between programs. In *LPAR*, volume 9450 of *LNCS*, pages 606–621. Springer, 2015.
19. G. Fedyukovich, S. Kaufman, and R. Bodík. Sampling Invariants from Frequency Distributions. In *FMCAD*, pages 100–107. IEEE, 2017.

20. G. Fedyukovich, S. Prabhu, K. Madhukar, and A. Gupta. Solving Constrained Horn Clauses Using Syntax and Data. In *FMCAD*, pages 170–178. IEEE, 2018.
21. G. Fedyukovich, S. Prabhu, K. Madhukar, and A. Gupta. Quantified Invariants via Syntax-Guided Synthesis. In *CAV, Part I*, volume 11561 of *LNCS*, pages 259–277. Springer, 2019.
22. D. Felsing, S. Grebing, V. Klebanov, P. Rümmer, and M. Ulbrich. Automating regression verification. In *ASE*, pages 349–360. ACM, 2014.
23. B. Godlin and O. Strichman. Inference rules for proving the equivalence of recursive procedures. *Acta Informatica*, 45(6):403–439, 2008.
24. A. Gurfinkel, T. Kahsai, A. Komuravelli, and J. A. Navas. The SeaHorn Verification Framework. In *CAV*, volume 9206 of *LNCS*, pages 343–361. Springer, 2015.
25. J. He, C. A. R. Hoare, and J. W. Sanders. Data refinement refined. In *ESOP*, pages 187–196. Springer, 1986.
26. C. A. R. Hoare. Unified theories of programming. In *Mathematical methods in program development*, pages 313–367. Springer, 1997.
27. H. Hojjat and P. Rümmer. The ELDARICA Horn Solver. In *FMCAD*, pages 158–164. IEEE, 2018.
28. J. P. Inala, N. Polikarpova, X. Qiu, B. S. Lerner, and A. Solar-Lezama. Synthesis of recursive ADT transformations from reusable templates. In *TACAS, Part I*, volume 10205 of *LNCS*, pages 247–263, 2017.
29. C. B. Jones. *Systematic software development using VDM*, volume 2. Prentice Hall Englewood Cliffs, 1990.
30. G. Klein, J. Andronick, K. Elphinstone, G. Heiser, D. Cock, P. Derrin, D. Elkaduwe, K. Engelhardt, R. Kolanski, M. Norrish, T. Sewell, H. Tuch, and S. Winwood. seL4: Formal verification of an operating-system kernel. *Communications of the ACM*, 53(6):107–115, 2010.
31. E. Kneuss, I. Kuraj, V. Kuncak, and P. Suter. Synthesis modulo recursive functions. In *OOPSLA*, pages 407–426, 2013.
32. A. Komuravelli, A. Gurfinkel, and S. Chaki. SMT-Based Model Checking for Recursive Programs. In *CAV*, volume 8559 of *LNCS*, pages 17–34, 2014.
33. L. Lamport. *Specifying systems: the TLA$^+$ language and tools for hardware and software engineers*. Addison-Wesley, 2002.
34. K. R. M. Leino and A. Milicevic. Program extrapolation with Jennisys. In *OOPSLA*, pages 411–430, 2012.
35. X. Leroy. Formal verification of a realistic compiler. *Communications of the ACM*, 52(7):107–115, 2009.
36. B. H. Liskov and J. M. Wing. A behavioral notion of subtyping. *Transactions on Programming Languages and Systems*, 16(6):1811–1841, 1994.
37. R. Milner. An algebraic definition of simulation between programs. In *IJCAI*, pages 481–489, 1971.
38. A. Miltner, S. Padhi, T. Millstein, and D. Walker. Data-driven inference of representation invariants. In *PLDI*, pages 1–15, 2020.
39. D. Mordvinov and G. Fedyukovich. Property Directed Inference of Relational Invariants. In *FMCAD*, pages 152–160. IEEE, 2019.
40. L. D. Moura and N. Bjørner. Z3: An efficient SMT solver. In *TACAS*, volume 4963 of *LNCS*, pages 337–340. Springer, 2008.
41. K. S. Namjoshi and L. D. Zuck. Witnessing program transformations. In *SAS*, volume 7935 of *LNCS*, pages 304–323. Springer, 2013.
42. L. Nelson, H. Sigurbjarnarson, K. Zhang, D. Johnson, J. Bornholt, E. Torlak, and X. Wang. Hyperkernel: Push-button verification of an OS kernel. In *OSDI*, pages 252–269, 2017.

43. P. W. O'Hearn. Continuous reasoning: scaling the impact of formal methods. In *LICS*, pages 13–25. ACM, 2018.
44. L. Pick, G. Fedyukovich, and A. Gupta. Exploiting Synchrony and Symmetry in Relational Verification. In *CAV, Part I*, volume 10981 of *LNCS*, pages 164–182. Springer, 2018.
45. M.-L. Potet and Y. Rouzaud. Composition and refinement in the B-method. In *Proc. of the B Conference*, volume 1393 of *LNCS*, pages 46–65. Springer, 1998.
46. A. Reynolds, H. Barbosa, A. Nötzli, C. W. Barrett, and C. Tinelli. cvc4sy: Smart and Fast Term Enumeration for Syntax-Guided Synthesis. In *CAV, Part II*, volume 11562 of *LNCS*, pages 74–83. Springer, 2019.
47. A. Reynolds and V. Kuncak. Induction for SMT solvers. In *VMCAI*, volume 8931 of *LNCS*, pages 80–98. Springer, 2015.
48. G. Schellhorn, G. Ernst, J. Pfähler, D. Haneberg, and W. Reif. Development of a verified Flash file system. In *ABZ*, volume 8477 of *LNCS*, pages 9–24. Springer, 2014. Invited Paper.
49. R. Sharma, E. Schkufza, B. R. Churchill, and A. Aiken. Data-driven Equivalence Checking. In *OOPSLA*, pages 391–406. ACM, 2013.
50. H. Sigurbjarnarson, J. Bornholt, E. Torlak, and X. Wang. Push-button verification of file systems via crash refinement. In *OSDI*, pages 1–16, 2016.
51. O. Strichman and M. Veitsman. Regression verification for unbalanced recursive functions. In *FM*, pages 645–658. Springer, 2016.
52. P. Suter, M. Dotta, and V. Kuncak. Decision procedures for algebraic data types with abstractions. *SIGPLAN notices*, 45(1):199–210, 2010.
53. H. Unno, S. Torii, and H. Sakamoto. Automating Induction for Solving Horn Clauses. In *CAV*, volume 10427 of *LNCS*, pages 571–591. Springer, 2017.
54. N. Wirth. Program development by stepwise refinement. *Communications of the ACM*, 14(4):221–227, 1971.
55. W. Yang, G. Fedyukovich, and A. Gupta. Lemma Synthesis for Automating Induction over Algebraic Data Types. In *CP*, volume 11802 of *LNCS*, pages 600–617. Springer, 2019.
56. A. Zaostrovnykh, S. Pirelli, R. Iyer, M. Rizzo, L. Pedrosa, K. Argyraki, and G. Candea. Verifying software network functions with no verification expertise. In *OSDI*, pages 275–290, 2019.

A Two-Phase Approach for
Conditional Floating-Point Verification

Debasmita Lohar[1] (✉), Clothilde Jeangoudoux[1],
Joshua Sobel[2], Eva Darulova[1], and Maria Christakis[1]

[1] MPI-SWS, Saarland Informatics Campus, Saarbrücken and Kaiserslautern,
Germany, {dlohar,jeangoudoux,eva,maria}@mpi-sws.org
[2] University of Rochester, Rochester, USA, jsobel3@u.rochester.edu

Abstract. Tools that automatically prove the absence or detect the
presence of large floating-point roundoff errors or the special values NaN
and Infinity greatly help developers to reason about the unintuitive nature
of floating-point arithmetic. We show that state-of-the-art tools, however,
support or provide non-trivial results only for relatively short programs.
We propose a framework for combining different static and dynamic
analyses that allows to increase their reach beyond what they can do
individually. Furthermore, we show how adaptations of existing dynamic
and static techniques effectively trade some soundness guarantees for
increased scalability, providing conditional verification of floating-point
kernels in realistic programs.

1 Introduction

Floating-point arithmetic is widely used across many domains, including machine
learning, scientific computing, embedded systems, and the Internet of Things.
Floating-point computations resemble real-valued arithmetic, but provide only
finite precision, which commits roundoff errors at potentially every operation.
While these errors are individually small, they propagate through an application
and can make its results meaningless [47]. In addition, floating-point arithmetic
features special values such as not-a-number (NaN) and Infinity [48]. As a result,
these computations are very challenging for developers to reason about and
debug manually. There is, therefore, a clear need for automated verification and
debugging techniques for such computations.

Unfortunately, today's techniques do not handle realistic floating-point programs well. Consider for example a program that simulates the interaction of
several bodies under gravity. We took a C implementation of this N-body problem
from Rosetta Code [5], which takes as input the masses, positions and velocities
of—in our case—three bodies, and shows their evolution over a number of time-
steps. The entire program is moderately-sized with 108 lines of code. Suppose
that we want to verify the absence or presence of special floating values and
cancellation (i.e. large roundoff) errors in this program. None of the currently
available floating-point analysis tools is able to do this.

© The Author(s) 2021
J. F. Groote and K. G. Larsen (Eds.): TACAS 2021, LNCS 12652, pp. 43–63, 2021.
https://doi.org/10.1007/978-3-030-72013-1_3

```
1   int main(int argc, char* argv[]) {... // Reads masses, positions and velocities
2     for(int i=0; i<timeSteps; i++) { simulate(mass, pos, v); ...}
3   }
4   void simulate() { compute_accelerations(mass, pos); ...}
5   void compute_accelerations(double mass[], vector pos[]){
6     for(int i=0;i<bodies;i++){ ...
7       for(int j=0;j<bodies;j++) {if(i!=j) {
8         acc[i] = numerical_kernel(mass[j], pos[i], pos[j], acc[i]);}}}}
9   vector numerical_kernel(double mass, vector pos_i, vector pos_j, vector acc) {
10    return addVectors(acc, scaleVector(g*mass/pow(mod(subtractVectors(pos_i,pos_j)),3),
          subtractVectors(pos_j,pos_i))); // compute acceleration
11  }
```

Listing 1.1. Snippet of Rosetta code N-body simulation

State-of-the-art static roundoff-error analysis tools [33,31,30,60,65,72] are in principle capable of proving the absence of both special values and large roundoff errors by computing an abstraction of the possible behaviors. However, they work only on small programs, mostly consisting of a single function, and thus do not work for our N-body example. The static tools that do scale [11,63,43] suffer from large over-approximations due to abstractions and thus effectively cannot prove the absence of issues either. Bounded model checking [52] or SMT decision procedures [25] perform exact bit-precise reasoning, but do not scale enough due to the complexity of floating-point arithmetic.

On the other hand, there exist dynamic analyses that search for concrete inputs proving the presence of Infinities [38], NaNs or cancellation errors [10,21,78]. We could not apply any of these tools on our example, to a large part because they, too, have been designed for relatively small programs. More guided techniques such as symbolic execution [57] rely on a back-end SMT solver, for which floating-point theories have very limited scalability.

We evaluated representative available tools on a new collection of floating-point benchmarks and get similar results for most of them (Section 5).

We observed that often only a relatively small part of a program performs complex numerical computations—we call these parts the *numerical kernels*. Existing state-of-the-art floating-point analyzers can be applied to these kernels, provided that one can supply a precondition that bounds the kernel's input ranges (their minimum and maximum values). Obtaining such preconditions manually is challenging, since the kernels are usually nested in loops as functions. Listing 1.1 shows a subset of the N-body example; the numerical kernel that we identified is on line 9, nested behind several for-loops and function calls.

Based on this observation, we propose a two-phase analysis that combines different program analyses to conditionally verify the absence of special values and cancellation errors in numerical kernels 'concealed' in large programs. First, we employ a scalable program analysis to infer the ranges of a kernel's inputs in the context of the containing application. In the second phase a different program analysis assumes these ranges to verify the kernels.

The main insight behind this combination is that the first scalable analysis does not need to perform sophisticated floating-point reasoning; the domain specifications required for the second numerical analysis need to only capture input ranges of variables.

The main challenge in our two-phase analysis is the first phase where our objective is to infer the ranges of the kernel inputs automatically. We first attempt to verify the numerical kernels fully soundly. Hence, we utilize abstract interpretation to infer sound ranges of kernel inputs. In case it is unable to infer useful (finite) ranges for the kernels, we propose to adapt existing blackbox and greybox fuzzing techniques [12], and evaluate them in their ability to produce large kernel input ranges capturing as many feasible inputs as possible.

After inferring the kernel ranges, the second phase utilizes a slightly adapted existing static and sound roundoff error analysis [30] to verify the kernels. In case this analysis produces warnings for special values, we additionally utilize SMT-based bounded model-checking [52] to check for spurious warnings.

Although there is a large body of work on combining different program analyses, our goal of analyzing real-world applications to verify their numerical kernels is novel. Our combination is specifically tailored to this setting, by considering the intricacies of floating-point arithmetic and the limitations of today's analysis techniques in reasoning about them.

Using a dynamic analysis in the first phase means that we are only able to infer approximations of the kernel input ranges. Consequently, we can verify the kernels only *conditionally*, because the verification is performed under the assumption that the input-domain specifications precisely describe possible values of the kernel inputs. Thus, we take a practical standpoint and relax the soundness guarantees in favor of wider applicability of today's static floating-point roundoff-error verification techniques.

Our evaluation shows that for 16 out of 24 kernels, this approach is able to verify that no special floating-point values occur; for 3 of those kernels, verification is sound. For 14 kernels, we additionally show the absence of cancellation errors that are a main cause of large roundoff errors.

Contributions To summarize, our paper makes the following contributions:

a) a two-phase framework that combines dynamic and static analyses to conditionally verify the absence of floating-point special values and large roundoff errors in kernels,
b) a novel guided blackbox fuzzing technique to infer kernel ranges, implemented in an open-source prototype tool called Blossom, and
c) an evaluation on a new benchmark set of mid-size numerical programs.

Our benchmarks, the tool Blossom as well as scripts of all of our experiments are available at https://github.com/dlohar/blossom.

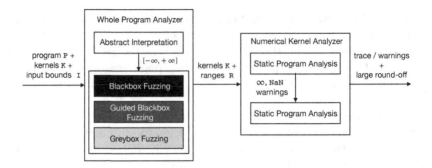

Fig. 1. Overview of our approach

2 A Two-Phase Approach

Figure 1 shows an overview of our two-phase approach that strives to increase the reach of existing floating-point analyses of floating-point numerical kernels. Our key observation is that such kernels appear in real-world applications from a variety of domains, but they are often 'hidden' behind several function calls and other non-numerical code that the round-off analyzers cannot handle. The first phase infers bounds on the input variables of a set of numerical kernels $\mathcal{K}$ that have been identified by a user in a program $\mathcal{P}$. In the second phase, we utilize these ranges to (conditionally) verify the kernels, i.e. to (conditionally) prove the absence of special values and large roundoff errors.

An alternative strategy would be to identify the largest kernel input ranges for which correctness can be guaranteed. However, even if one could infer such preconditions (we are not aware of a tool that performs such a backward analysis), our techniques for the first phase would still be needed to determine whether the program can execute the kernels on inputs outside of the safe ranges.

2.1 First Phase: Whole Program Analysis

In the first phase we have a whole program analyzer that, starting from the *program inputs* constrained by $\mathcal{I}$, infers bounds $\mathcal{R}$ on the *kernel inputs* automatically. These bounds are crucial, as the presence of cancellations and special values directly depends on the ranges of possible values; an unbounded input range will, in general, also lead to unbounded roundoff errors and special values.

To obtain the kernel ranges, we need to analyze the entire program. In general, it is infeasible to compute the exact ranges, so that we want to approximate them. We propose to first use a sound static analysis, which computes an over-approximation of the true ranges. They thus cover all feasible inputs, but additionally also spurious ones, so we want these ranges to be as tight (small) as possible. If the abstractions necessarily performed by the static analyzer become prohibitively large, we propose to use dynamic analysis to compute an unsound approximation of the kernel ranges. These ranges should be as wide as possible to capture as many concrete executions as possible.

Sound Static Analysis We choose abstract interpretation [26] and specifically the industry-strength analyzer Astrée [63] to infer a sound over-approximation of the kernel ranges, as Astrée scales for large programs with complex code and data structures and comes with a variety of abstract domains.

The choice of the abstract domain in Astrée is, in general, a trade-off between the amount of over-approximation and the analysis running time. The interval domain abstracts a set of concrete variable values by their lower and upper bounds: $[\underline{x}, \overline{x}] := \{x \mid \underline{x} \leq x \leq \overline{x}\}$. While operations on interval arithmetic [64] are efficient, intervals cannot capture correlations between variables and therefore over-approximate the real behavior (e.g. $x - x \neq 0$ in interval arithmetic). Nonetheless, for our benchmarks we have not observed any noticeable difference in the results with more sophisticated domains (e.g. octagon). This is likely due to our benchmarks having many nonlinear operations. Hence, we choose the interval domain as the numerical abstract domain for our purpose.

Dynamic Analysis Fuzzing finds inputs that demonstrate certain (unwanted) behavior. We propose to fuzz a program and at the same time monitor the kernel inputs to record the lower and upper bounds seen during concrete executions.

We instrument each user-specified kernel in the program with a kernel monitor that keeps track of the smallest and largest value seen for each kernel input. We repeatedly execute the instrumented program and report the minimum and maximum values seen for each kernel input over all executions. This approach crucially depends on the choice of program inputs that are used for fuzzing. We propose and experimentally compare blackbox, guided blackbox, and directed greybox fuzzing [12] as methods for input selection in Section 6.

Blackbox fuzzing is a naive but effective technique in many testing situations. In our setting, the blackbox fuzzer randomly draws inputs from the program ranges $\mathcal{I}$, i.e. without any reference to the internal structure of the program.

We further propose *guided blackbox* fuzzing that is guided toward enlarging the kernel input ranges. For this, the program input generator records those inputs that have widened the kernel ranges, and randomly generates new inputs that are within a certain (small) distance from these, in the hope that the new inputs would enlarge the monitored ranges even further.

While blackbox techniques are straightforward to implement, they do not take into account the program structure. We thus evaluate an adaptation of *directed greybox* fuzzing, implemented in the the state-of-the-art tool AFLGo [12] that can be directed toward specific program locations, while exploring as many different paths in the program as possible. We first fuzz the program to obtain an initial estimate for the kernel input ranges with AFLGo (targeting the kernel). Then, we employ AFLGo in a refinement loop that iteratively attempts to widen the currently seen kernel input ranges. We instrument the kernels with conditional statements that check whether a kernel input is outside of the current kernel range. We use this conditional statement as a target for AFLGo, effectively directing it to find kernel inputs that are outside of the current estimate. If AFLGo finds a program input that widens the current kernel input range, we update it accordingly and iterate the process until a user-defined timeout.

2.2 Second Phase: Numerical Kernel Analysis

With the ranges ($\mathcal{R}$) inferred in the first phase, we analyze the user-identified numerical kernels ($\mathcal{K}$) in the second phase with a static analyzer. Our objective in the second phase is to either show the absence of special floating-point values and large roundoff errors in a kernel or to generate warnings for the potential presence of such values.

We use the sound floating-point roundoff analysis tool Daisy [30], which automatically proves the absence of special values and computes an absolute error bound for each kernel output. When Daisy generates a warning that special values can potentially occur, we use a SAT/SMT-based model checker that performs exact floating-point reasoning and that can identify spurious warnings.

By itself, the error bound on the *kernel* output is not particularly helpful, however, since we do not know how this error propagates to the *end* of the program (although there exist scalable analyses that potentially can compute this information, e.g. [61]). That said, for many numerical applications the exact error bound is not important, since the algorithm itself is already approximate. For these applications, it is thus sufficient if we can show that the *roundoff errors are not too large*. We thus modify Daisy to report a warning when it detects a possible *cancellation*, i.e. when an arithmetic operation increases the relative error significantly (e.g. when two values that are close in magnitude get subtracted [42]). Additionally, Daisy includes an optimization procedure that can improve the accuracy of the kernels by rewriting the arithmetic expressions to commit smaller roundoff errors. We provide more details in Section 4.

2.3 Soundness Guarantees

To summarize, using the extended Daisy analysis, we can conditionally verify that kernels do not result in any NaN or Infinity, and that they do not commit cancellation errors, i.e. lead to large roundoff errors. When the kernel input ranges are computed soundly using abstract interpretation (e.g. Astrée), our verification is conditional in that we only verify the absence of cancellations for the kernels, but not for the rest of the program.

When the ranges are computed using dynamic analysis in the first phase, they include more concrete values than the fuzzer witnessed. Values between the lower and upper bound are not necessarily observed by the fuzzer, and are also not necessarily feasible. If one were to consider only values witnessed at runtime, then it would be possible to analyze kernels for individual traces, although this would be quite expensive [10]. However, if we can soundly show that no special values or large roundoff errors (cancellations) occur inside a kernel for a given input range, we have shown this for more executions than can be explored by dynamic testing in general (since there are usually too many floating-point values to explore exhaustively). Unlike for a NaN or Infinity that are obvious to detect, cancellation cannot, in general, be detected by inspecting the computed results and thus our combination is valuable.

3   First Phase: Whole Program Analysis

Abstract Interpretation with Astrée We utilize Astrée as it scales for large C programs with complex code and data structures. We add wrapper functions to provide bounds for global variables, since Astrée does not assume ranges for global variables directly. We further annotate the kernels $\mathcal{K}$ with Astrée's __ASTREE_log_vars() construct. This construct records the range information that Astrée logs about the kernel inputs at the entry of the kernels.

Note that the analysis of Astrée can be extensively parameterized with the knowledge of the program under analysis. Although this makes the analysis even more precise, it requires vast manual effort and knowledge of the intricacies of the program. To avoid this, we parameterize Astrée as generically as possible. We only use semantic loop unrolling until a defined loop bound to reduce the over-approximation in the analysis for all benchmarks.

Blackbox Fuzzing with Blossom We implement our novel blackbox fuzzing for kernel range computation in a tool we call Blossom. Blossom works by instrumenting the program to be analyzed. Blossom is implemented as an LLVM pass and works on C, C++, and Rust input programs with complex programming constructs and data types (and would work for any programming language that compiles to LLVM). Blossom takes as input the program $\mathcal{P}$, a configuration file that specifies the ranges of program inputs, the fuzzing technique that we want to execute (standard or guided blackbox), and a timeout. The LLVM pass automatically instruments $\mathcal{P}$ by inserting code that performs the indicated fuzzing process until the specified timeout, and records the ranges of kernel inputs.

In order to perform vanilla blackbox fuzzing, the code is instrumented with an input generator that utilizes the srand() function with distinctive seeds to randomly generate values of program inputs from the set of input bounds $\mathcal{I}$. This process is continued until the specified timeout.

Guided Blackbox Fuzzing with Blossom Algorithm 1 shows our guided blackbox fuzzing algorithm for generating program inputs to maximize kernel ranges. The algorithm is also implemented via LLVM-pass instrumentation in Blossom.

The inputs to Algorithm 1 are the program $\mathcal{P}$ with an identified set of kernels $\mathcal{K}$, a set of n program input ranges ($\mathcal{I}$), and a timeout ($\mathcal{T}$). The algorithm is also parameterized by the number of mutations m and a constant c that determines the neighborhood radii for all program inputs from which mutants (new program inputs) are drawn. The algorithm returns a set of kernel ranges $[\{\mathcal{R}_{lo}\}, \{\mathcal{R}_{hi}\}]$ (line 16). The goal is to compute the interval $[\{\mathcal{R}_{lo}\}, \{\mathcal{R}_{hi}\}]$ as wide as possible.

The algorithm keeps an input queue Q, which stores program inputs on which the program is to be executed. If Q is empty, m new random inputs taken from the program input ranges $\mathcal{I}$ are added to it (line 6–7). If Q is not empty, the algorithm first dequeues one valuation of all the program inputs $\{v_1, \cdots, v_n\}$ from Q (line 9), and executes the program $\mathcal{P}$ on these program inputs. During the execution of the program, the kernel monitor checks the kernel inputs and updates the kernel ranges as it is done in vanilla blackbox fuzzing (line 10). If the

---

Algorithm 1 Guided Blackbox Fuzzing

1: **procedure** GUIDED-BLACKBOX($\mathcal{P}$, $\mathcal{I}$, $\mathcal{K}$, T, m, c)
2:      $Q \leftarrow \phi$, $\{\mathcal{R}_{lo}\} =\{$DBL_MAX$\}$, $\{\mathcal{R}_{hi}\} =\{$DBL_MIN$\}$
3:      $\{r_1, \cdots, r_n\} \leftarrow$ computeRadii($\mathcal{I}$, c)   ▷ generates mutation radii
4:      **while** $T \neq 0$ **do**
5:          **if** $Q == \phi$ **then**
6:              **for** i from 1 to m **do**
7:                  $Q \leftarrow$ enqueue(generateRandomInput($\mathcal{I}$))   ▷ generates random inputs
8:          **else**
9:              $\{v_1, \cdots, v_n\} \leftarrow$ dequeue(Q)
10:             $[\{\mathcal{R}_{lo}\}, \{\mathcal{R}_{hi}\}] \leftarrow$ executeAndmonitorKernels($\mathcal{K}$)
11:             **if** $\big($kernelRangeUpdated($[\{\mathcal{R}_{lo}\}, \{\mathcal{R}_{hi}\}]$)$\big)$ **then**
12:                 **for** i from 1 to $m - 1$ **do**
13:                     $\{d_1, \cdots, d_n\} \leftarrow$ mutate($v_1 \mp r_1, \cdots, v_n \mp r_n$)
14:                     $Q \leftarrow$ enqueue($\{d_1, \cdots, d_n\}$)
15:             $Q \leftarrow$ enqueue(generateRandomInput($\mathcal{I}$))   ▷ avoids local max/min
16:     **return** $[\{\mathcal{R}_{lo}\}, \{\mathcal{R}_{hi}\}]$ ▷ returns kernel input ranges

---

kernel ranges were updated, i.e. we found an input that led to the kernel input being outside of the currently known range, we generate $m - 1$ mutants from a program input $\{v_1, \cdots, v_n\}$ by randomly drawing inputs from its neighborhood $v_1 \mp r_1, \cdots, v_n \mp r_n$ and add them to the queue (line 12–14). (We draw mutants randomly from the neighborhood to reduce the possibility of duplicate program inputs.) The neighborhood, i.e. maximal distance of a mutant to the original program input, is defined by the neighborhood radii $\{r_1, \cdots, r_n\}$ (computed once on line 3) that depend on the width of each input range. Effectively, if an input range is large, then we will draw mutants from a larger neighborhood as well. This step enables to search in the neighborhood of the inputs that enlarged the ranges of the kernels recently. Then, we generate one random input for all variables in the whole input range (line 15). This step ensures that we do not get stuck in a local maximum or minimum. The whole process is repeated until timeout T.

4 Second Phase: Static Analysis with Daisy and CBMC

Next, we use the computed kernel ranges $\mathcal{R}$ as kernel input specifications (preconditions) and adapt the state-of-the-art roundoff-error analyzer Daisy [30] to verify the absence of cancellation errors and special float values. The translation of kernels and the precondition annotation to Daisy's input language in Scala is currently done manually, but could be automated in the future.

Daisy's core roundoff-error analysis performs a forward dataflow analysis. It computes ranges and worst-case absolute error bounds for each intermediate arithmetic (abstract syntax tree) expression using the interval and affine arithmetic abstract domains. As part of this analysis, it checks for overflows and invalid expressions that could lead to NaN values, as their absence is a prerequisite for a meaningful roundoff-error computation.

We extend Daisy to check at every intermediate expression for a possible cancellation, using the ranges and absolute error bounds that Daisy computes by default. At each binary arithmetic operation, we compare the relative errors of the operands with the relative error of the binary operation result. If the relative error increases more than a given factor, we report an error. We compute the relative error for an intermediate expression x as the ratio of its worst-case absolute error bound divided by the smallest value that the range of x contains. When the range of x ($[x]$) contains zero, we divide instead by some small constant c, $\frac{\Delta_x}{\max(c, \min([x]))}$, to make relative errors always well-defined. While this does not compute a sound bound on the relative error, this is not needed for our purpose, since we are only interested in a relative comparison.

With this extension, we can prove for each kernel and the specified kernel input ranges, that cancellation and special values do not occur (but we cannot prove their presence). When Daisy cannot show this, it issues a warning with the possibly problematic intermediate expression. Spurious warnings for special values can be checked with a tool that performs exact reasoning, e.g. CBMC [52], and which reports a counterexample trace to the user who can use this trace to confirm whether the warning is genuine and if so, for debugging.

Optimizing the Kernels Daisy furthermore provides a rewriting optimization that finds an ordering of an arithmetic expression for which it can show a smaller (absolute) roundoff error [32]. The rewriting relies on the fact that floating-point arithmetic is not associative and distributive and hence different evaluation orders commit errors of different magnitudes. Daisy's algorithm uses real-valued identities such as associativity and distributivity to rewrite the expression. Using this optimization, we can thus locally improve the accuracy of the numerical kernels.

5   State of the Art on Real-World Programs

We collected a new set of real-world numerical programs from different application domains, as existing floating-point benchmark sets [29] cover kernels only. We first report on our experiments using existing representative state-of-the-art tools on these benchmarks, before evaluating our approach in Section 6.

Benchmarks All our benchmark programs are existing programs collected online from a variety of domains such as scientific computing simulations (nbody, pendulum, lulesh, reactor, molecular), physics algorithms (fbench, arclength), numerical methods (linpack) and machine learning (linearSVC). Table 1 provides an overview of the size and complexity of our benchmarks, as well as the number and arithmetic complexity of the kernels that we chose for verification. We also count the number of trigonometric operations (implemented in library functions) in the kernels, and the 'depth' column shows the number of function calls needed to reach the kernels from program entry.

benchmark	lang.	LOC	#in.	#func.	#loops	#	kernels #arith op.	#trig. op.	depth
arclength [68]	C	31	1	1	2	1	20	5	1
linearSVC [8]	C	32	4	1	3	1	7	-	1
raycasting [6]	C	94	2	4	3	1	4	-	4
nbody [5]	C	108	21	10	9	2	9, 22	-,-	2, 2
pendulum [2]	C	141	4	11	8	2	24, 42	2,11	4, 2
fbenchV2 [1]	C	215	8	2	5	2	6, 14	-,5	2, 2
molecular [4]	C++	323	3	8	13	3	8, 12, 11	-,-,3	1,1, 1
fbenchV1 [1]	C	380	8	10	8	4	19, 6, 14, 36	-,-,5,-	5, 2, 2, 3
reactor [7]	C++	467	4	11	2	3	14, 11, 13	-,2,2	2, 0, 1
linpack [3]	C	544	5	12	31	1	8	-	2
lulesh [51]	C++	2187	5	43	74	4	109, 77, 14, 41	-,-,-,-	6, 7, 6, 7

Table 1. Benchmark statistics

These benchmarks are single-threaded C or C++ floating-point programs with arrays, structures, branching, loops, and function calls (we translated the pendulum benchmark manually from Python to C). We modified the benchmarks by replacing dynamic memory allocation, pointer arithmetic, and I/O operations as appropriate, since these are challenging for most program analyses. We considered two versions of fbench: one with user-defined trigonometric functions (V1) and 380 LOC, and another with their library versions (V2). We specified bounds on the program inputs manually and identified a set of numerical kernels containing a large number of arithmetic operations.

State of the Art We first evaluate existing state-of-the-art tools on our benchmark set. For this, we choose CBMC, Astrée and AFLGo as representatives for model checking, abstract interpretation and directed greybox fuzzing, respectively. To the best of our knowledge, AFLGo was not used for floating-point debugging before. These tools check for assertion violations, so we have added assertions to our chosen kernels to check for absence of Infinity and NaN using the standard library functions isinf and isnan.

We do not include a deductive verifier (e.g. [24]) in this comparison, because it requires detailed user annotations of every function. None of the state-of-the-art static roundoff-error analysis tools [43,33,31,30,60,65,72] work on the whole applications in our benchmark set. Available dynamic analyses for finding large roundoff errors [10,21,77,21,78,44] or special values [38,57,9] also work only on smaller programs (often restricted to kernels). Only the dynamic-analysis tool FPDebug [10] has been shown to scale beyond numerical kernels, but unfortunately the code has not been actively maintained over the years.

All experiments are done for 64-bit precision and on a Debian server system with 2.67GHz and 50GB RAM. We have used CBMC version 5.12 with MiniSat 2.2.0 (we have observed in our preliminary experiments that CBMC performs better with MiniSat), Astrée's linux64_b5162300_release and AFLGo downloaded on June 9, 2020. We have set a 1-hour time budget for all experiments and unrolled all loops for 50 iterations for both CBMC and Astrée.

With CBMC and Astrée, we are able to prove the absence of special float values in linearSVC and rayCasting, two of the smallest benchmarks. Additionally, Astrée also proves the absence of special values in kernels 1 and 5 in fbenchV1. For all other C benchmarks (Astrée does not work on C++ programs), Astrée generates warnings for the potential existence of special values. With AFLGo, however, we do not find any special values within the time limit.

For the nbody and pendulum benchmarks, we originally had larger program input ranges. For these, AFLGo was able to show the presence of special values in the kernels, suggesting that greybox fuzzing is effective for detecting special values. For the subsequent experiments, we have used tighter program input ranges to avoid special values.

6   Evaluation of our Two-Phase Approach

We next evaluate our two-phase approach. For a fair comparison with the state-of-the-art tools, we designate a 1-hour time limit for the entire analysis, allocating 50 minutes for generating the kernel ranges and 10 minutes for the kernel analysis. We have empirically evaluated the effect of the time limit and observed that increasing the time does not affect the results of our benchmarks, but a smaller time limit led to worse results.

Computing Kernel Ranges The main step is the computation of the kernel ranges. We compare the kernel ranges obtained with blackbox fuzzing (BB), guided blackbox fuzzing (GBB) (both implemented in Blossom), AFLGo with our iterative widening (AFLGo), and a combination of BB and AFLGo iterative widening (BB+AFLGo). We have empirically determined that with 5 mutants GBB performs the best for all our benchmarks. For AFLGo, we first fuzz the program for 5 minutes and then run our iterative widening that employs the fuzzer in a refinement loop to widen the so-obtained ranges (see Section 2.1) for the next 45 minutes. For BB+AFLGo, we use Blossom's blackbox fuzzing for 25 minutes to generate the initial ranges. On these ranges, we use our range-widening technique with AFLGo for the next 25 minutes.

To compare the obtained kernel ranges, we first compute the width of each kernel range ($\overline{x} - \underline{x}$) and show in Table 2 the average width over all kernel inputs and over 5 runs with different random seeds. For our dynamic analyses, we want to maximize the kernel ranges to cover as many kernel inputs as possible.

We also add the sound over-approximated ranges computed by Astrée, whenever these are available. While Astrée produces a warning *inside* the arclength kernel, it still computes a finite range for the kernel *input*.

In 5 out of the 7 kernels where Astrée finds non-trivial ranges, our fuzzing techniques also compute ranges that are close to Astrée's. They are even equal in the case of rayCasting. In the other 2 cases, Astrée reports big ranges whereas

benchmark	kernel	#vars	avg range width					kernel analysis
			Astrée	BB	AFLGo	BB+AFLGo	GBB	
arclength	1	1	6.16e+4	**3.14**	**3.14**	**3.14**	**3.14**	✓
linearSVC	1	4	3.73	**3.73**	3.71	3.72	**3.73**	(✓)
rayCasting	1	5	12.20	**12.20**	**12.20**	**12.20**	**12.20**	✓
nbody	1	6	∞	1.09e+5	6.67e+4	1.21e+5	**1.02e+8**	✓
	2	9	∞	1.25e+4	8.45e+3	1.19e+4	**8.91e+6**	✗
pendulum	1	4	∞	14.80	12.86	**14.82**	14.56	✓
	2	5	∞	22.38	17.61	**22.39**	22.16	✓
fbenchV2	1	5	24.60	**20.46**	**20.46**	**20.46**	**20.46**	✗
	2	5	∞	**21.36**	**21.36**	**21.36**	**21.36**	✗
fbenchV1	1	1	403.00	**0.18**	**0.18**	**0.18**	**0.18**	✓
	2	5	20.50	**20.46**	**20.46**	**20.46**	**20.46**	✗
	3	5	∞	21.36	21.36	**24.76**	21.36	✗
	4	1	1.57	**1.54**	**1.54**	**1.54**	**1.54**	✓
linpack	1	8	∞	3.60e+6	4.44e+3	3.60e+6	**2.11e+269**	✗
molecular	1	4	✗	**9.04**	**9.04**	**9.04**	**9.04**	✗
	2	6	✗	**1.86**	**1.86**	**1.86**	**1.86**	✓
	3	7	✗	**12.88**	**12.88**	**12.88**	**12.88**	✓
reactor	1	1	✗	**1.00**	**1.00**	**1.00**	**1.00**	✓
	2	6	✗	1.43e+2	9.35e+1	1.43e+2	**1.46e+2**	✗
	3	1	✗	**2.50**	**2.50**	**2.50**	**2.50**	✓
lulesh	1	24	✗	**4.97**	4.80	**4.97**	4.95	(✓)
	2	18	✗	**6.09**	5.51	5.50	5.89	✓
	3	9	✗	**3.48**	3.09	3.42	3.25	✓
	4	12	✗	**5.95**	5.49	5.93	5.77	✓

Table 2. Comparison of kernel ranges generated by different techniques and settings

all fuzzing techniques compute smaller ranges with the same width, suggesting a possible large over-approximation of Astrée's ranges (or the inability of fuzzers to discover new kernel inputs within the time limit).

In the other cases, when Astrée finds unbounded ranges or does not work, we observe that for all but 3 kernels, all four fuzzing techniques compute very similar range widths. For 3 kernels, however, GBB finds significantly larger ranges, thus discovering kernel inputs that the other methods are not able to find. We thus conclude that guided blackbox fuzzing appears to be most suitable for computing kernel ranges in our benchmarks, as it can discover apparent outliers.

AFLGo often computes the smallest ranges. Our hypothesis is that because AFLGo aims to maximize the number of paths in the program to reach the target locations in the kernels, it focuses on generating values to find new paths rather than generating values exercising an already found path that may increase the width of the kernel ranges.

benchmark	kernel	#vars	BB	AFLGo	BB+AFLGo	GBB
linearSVC	1	4	-	2.21	-	-
nbody	1	6	121.05	312.93	144.86	181.26
	2	9	155.31	226.10	127.25	206.20
pendulum	1	4	0.69	51.77	0.57	5.25
	2	5	0.69	44.37	0.54	4.48
fbenchV2	1	5	-	-	1.99	-
	2	5	-	0.04	-	-
fbenchV1	1	1	-	0.03	-	-
	2	5	-	-	1.99	-
	3	5	-	0.04	8.85	-
linpack	1	8	0.01	100.15	-	114.58
molecular	2	6	0.25	8.0	0.15	0.33
reactor	1	1	-	0.01	-	-
	2	6	2.51	11.32	2.91	2.80
	3	1	-	0.01	-	-
lulesh	1	24	1.67	6.76	1.74	2.50
	2	18	4.28	19.73	15.59	6.96
	3	9	7.14	23.25	10.55	11.97
	4	12	3.91	16.13	3.49	5.88

Table 3. Variation of computed kernel range widths (from the average width) for our three fuzzing techniques (in %), '-' denotes no variation

Effect of Randomness All fuzzing techniques (BB, GBB, AFLGo) rely on randomness. To evaluate how the computed kernel ranges are affected by it, we calculate the variation of the range widths compared to the average range width (per variable) over 5 runs. For 7 kernels, we do not detect any variation at all for any of the methods; Table 3 shows the variations for the remaining kernels.

We observe that all methods have large variations for the benchmarks nbody and linpack, i.e. those for which GBB has found very large ranges. This suggests that there are a few corner-case inputs that lead to large kernel ranges (which only GBB was able to reliably find). Further, we see that AFLGo has a large range variation due to randomness for a few additional benchmarks, whereas BB and GBB have variations that are relatively small.

Conditional Kernel Verification We were able to (conditionally) prove the absence of special floating-point values for 16 out of the 24 kernels, and (conditionally) prove the absence of cancellation errors for 14 of those kernels. We show these results in the last column of Table 2: '✓' indicates that Daisy could prove both the absence of special values and cancellation in the kernel for the specified kernel ranges, '(✓)' indicates that only the absence of special values could be verified, and '✗' shows when Daisy reports a special-value warning. For the relatively small benchmarks arclength, linearSVC and rayCasting, our verification of the kernels is sound, i.e. unconditional, as we used ranges computed by Astrée.

When Daisy reports a warning, it is not guaranteed that a kernel can actually compute a special-value result, because of 1) Daisy's over-approximation of the concrete program semantics, and because 2) the range we compute may contain values that are not feasible in the actual program execution. To help developers debug warnings reported by the static analyzer, we use CBMC on those kernels.

CBMC reports counterexamples in all kernels for which Daisy reports warnings. Upon code inspection, however, we identified the counterexamples of nbody and fbench to be spurious for the particular program inputs we consider. In these cases, the true kernel input range was discontinuous, and the counterexamples were reported for the infeasible inputs. In particular, in kernel 2 of nbody, a NaN could be produced if the two bodies that are simulated collide, which would not happen for the initial conditions that we chose. Similarly, the kernels in the ray-tracing algorithm of fbench could produce Infinity, if the ray was chosen in a very particular way. With the program input ranges we have chosen, this was impossible.

For linpack, the arithmetic overflow reported is indeed genuine, since a division by zero can occur before the kernel if the input matrix contains a zero on the diagonal, which leads to undefined behavior and the huge range of the kernel inputs. Similarly, for molecular and reactor, arithmetic overflow can occur for a specific position of molecules and a specific value of the angle between particle's direction and the X-axis, respectively.

We note that given the counterexamples produced by CBMC, we could straight-forwardly identify the warnings as spurious or genuine. In future work, one could consider refining the kernel monitoring, such that it would not only track a single range per kernel but could detect discontinuous ranges.

Our extension of Daisy reports cancellation-error warnings for one kernel of linearSVC and one kernel of lulesh. We have used a threshold of 10^3 for reporting cancellation, i.e. if the relative errors of the operands and the result differ by more than three orders of magnitude, we report an error. We inspected the kernel code and confirmed that the cancellation warnings are genuine, i.e. there are indeed inputs that will result in a large roundoff error. The number of cancellations found may seem small. We suspect that this is the case, because our benchmarks were mostly written as reference or example programs (e.g. lulesh was developed to be a representative hydrodynamics simulation code), hence we expect them to be carefully developed and tested.

Kernel Optimization We have additionally applied Daisy's rewriting optimization on those kernels for which Daisy does not report possible special values. With this procedure, we could reduce the roundoff errors in 8 of the kernels out of which 6 cases are notable. We could reduce the error by 9.5% for linearSVC, 7.1% and 3.3% for two outputs of kernel 2 in pendulum, by 19.8%, 4.0%, 5.8%, and 5.8% for different kernel outputs of lulesh, and by 33.3% for one output of molecular. From these experimental results, we conclude that the ranges that we inferred in the first phase are actually useful for kernel analysis.

7   Related Work

Abstract interpretation-based techniques are in principle uniquely suitable for verifying the absence of special values and safety in floating-point programs. We have chosen Astrée [63] in this work because it is an industrial-strength tool, and as such, supports a wide range of C programs and is designed for scalability. Apron [50] is a library of numerical abstract domains that are sound w.r.t. floating-point arithmetic, and includes, for instance, the domain of polyhedra [19], which is, however, significantly more expensive than the interval arithmetic domain that we use. ELINA [71] provides performance-optimized implementations of many numerical abstract domains, but its polyhedra domain does not support floating-point arithmetic.

These domains only bound variable values; abstract domains [43,33,31,30] or optimization-based static analyses [60,65,72] for bounding roundoff errors provide nontrivial results only for relatively small kernels. For the second step in our framework, we could have in principle chosen any of these tools; we chose Daisy because we found it easy to modify for our needs, and because it already includes the rewriting optimization.

In the space of deductive verification, besides Frama-C [24], the Boogie intermediate verification language [53] also has support for floating-point arithmetic and discharges the verification conditions using the Z3 SMT solver. Similarly, bounded model checking [52] is limited by the performance of the underlying SAT/SMT solvers. While the floating-point support in today's SMT solvers [17,16] has improved significantly in recent years, it is still limited to relatively few arithmetic expressions.

Many interactive theorem provers have floating-point formalizations [49,15,37]. While these do allow to prove complex functional properties [13,14,46], the proofs are largely manual and require significant expertise.

Blackbox testing has been explored to find large roundoff errors by executing a higher-precision version of the program side-by-side [10,21,77]. Recently, whitebox testing has been used for detecting overflows [38], by phrasing the search as a mathematical optimization problem, and large roundoff errors [21,78], by adapting the notion of condition numbers. KLEE-Float [57], FPGen [44] and Ariadne [9] use symbolic execution for finding bugs in floating-point code, including overflows and large precision loss and cancellation. While KLEE-Float relies on the floating-point SMT decision procedures, Ariadne approximates the path constraints and uses the real-valued theory. FPGen injects specialized inaccuracy checks to find cancellations. Only FPDebug [10] has been shown to scale beyond numerical kernels and, to the best of our knowledge, none of the dynamic techniques have been used to obtain range information.

Once a large roundoff error has been identified, Herbgrind [69] can help to locate its root cause, which may be in a different instruction than where the error becomes significant. Herbgrind is thus complementary to our work and may be used to locate root causes of potential cancellation errors reported by Daisy.

Rewriting floating-point expressions in order to optimize roundoff errors has been explored in the tool Herbie [67] and others [74,76]. These approaches attempt to repair unstable code, checking accuracy using a dynamic analysis. They are alternatives to using Daisy for the second step in our framework. Alternative program optimizations that we have not explored in this work, but that also require range information, include mixed-precision tuning [32,20,68] and general non-semantics preserving approximation [70].

Apart from AFLGo [12], there is a wide range of targeted greybox fuzzers, such as those targeting specified program locations [18], rare branches [54], unexplored branches [55,73], or potential vulnerabilities [39,45,22,56]. In our setting, we require fuzzers like AFLGo to target the specific program locations of kernels.

There is a significant body of work on guiding program analyzers. In particular, test case generation is typically guided by a static analysis toward specific parts of the code (e.g., [27,35,66,41,40,58,62,28,59,23,36,34,75,44]). Our approach is similar to these techniques as it infers input ranges to guide verifiers of numerical kernels toward those kernel executions that are relevant in the context of the containing application.

8   Conclusion

Even though floating-point programs have received a lot of attention recently, their focus has been largely on verifying or debugging arithmetic kernels. Our review of existing techniques and tools has shown that few approaches with specific floating-point support are applicable to whole programs without significant user expertise. We have found, however, that standard greybox fuzzing proved to be effective in detecting overflows and NaNs. Meanwhile, static-analysis techniques to show the absence of special values and cancellation errors remain limited to programs with few bounded loops and numerical kernels, respectively.

Instead of trying to scale up existing roundoff-error analysis tools to whole programs, we *combine* them with more scalable analyses that compute the kernel preconditions needed for the roundoff analyses to work. We showed how relatively small adaptations to well-known techniques of directed blackbox and greybox fuzzing are enough to realize such a framework. Together with modifications to an existing roundoff-error analyzer, we are able to *conditionally verify* the absence of special values and cancellations in a number of numerical kernels in realistic floating-point programs that are out of reach for today's analyses. At the same time, our analysis is precise enough to identify several cases of cancellations. While our approach is not suitable and not intended for certification of safety-critical systems, we believe that it nonetheless provides valuable debugging feedback for many real-world applications.

Acknowledgements

This research was partially funded by the Deutsche Forschungsgemeinschaft (DFG, German Research Foundation) project 387674182 and project 389792660 as part of TRR 248 (see https://perspicuous-computing.science). We also thank Dr.-Ing. Jörg Herter from AbsInt for the training and assistance with Astrée.

References

1. FBench: Trigonometry Intense Floating Point Benchmark. https://www.fourmilab.ch/fbench/fbench.html, Accessed: 2020-10-05
2. Inverted-pendulum Control Problem. http://www.toddsifleet.com/projects/inverted-pendulum, Accessed: 2020-10-05
3. LINPACK Benchmark. https://people.sc.fsu.edu/~jburkardt/c_src/linpack_bench/linpack_bench.html, Accessed: 2020-10-05
4. Molecular Dynamics. https://people.math.sc.edu/Burkardt/cpp_src/md/md.html, Accessed: 2020-10-05
5. N-body Problem. https://rosettacode.org/wiki/N-body_problem#C, Accessed: 2020-10-05
6. Ray-casting Algorithm. https://rosettacode.org/wiki/Ray-casting_algorithm#C, Accessed: 2020-10-05
7. Simulated Test of Reactor Shielding. https://people.math.sc.edu/Burkardt/cpp_src/reactor_simulation/reactor_simulation.html, Accessed: 2020-10-05
8. Project Sklearn-porter. https://github.com/nok/sklearn-porter (2018)
9. Barr, E.T., Vo, T., Le, V., Su, Z.: Automatic Detection of Floating-Point Exceptions. In: ACM Sigplan Notices. No. 1, ACM (2013)
10. Benz, F., Hildebrandt, A., Hack, S.: A Dynamic Program Analysis to Find Floating-Point Accuracy Problems. In: Programming Language Design and Implementation (PLDI) (2012)
11. Blanchet, B., Cousot, P., Cousot, R., Feret, J., Mauborgne, L., Miné, A., Monniaux, D., Rival, X.: A Static Analyzer for Large Safety-Critical Software. In: Programming Language Design and Implementation (PLDI) (2003)
12. Böhme, M., Pham, V., Nguyen, M., Roychoudhury, A.: Directed Greybox Fuzzing. In: Computer and Communications Security (CCS) (2017)
13. Boldo, S., Clément, F., Filliâtre, J.C., Mayero, M., Melquiond, G., Weis, P.: Wave Equation Numerical Resolution: A Comprehensive Mechanized Proof of a C Program. Journal of Automated Reasoning **50**(4) (2013)
14. Boldo, S., Filliâtre, J., Melquiond, G.: Combining Coq and Gappa for Certifying Floating-Point Programs. In: Intelligent Computer Mathematics (2009)
15. Boldo, S., Melquiond, G.: Flocq: A Unified Library for Proving Floating-Point Algorithms in Coq. In: Computer Arithmetic (ARITH) (2011)
16. Brain, M., D'Silva, V., Griggio, A., Haller, L., Kroening, D.: Deciding Floating-Point Logic with Abstract Conflict Driven Clause Learning. Formal Methods Syst. Des. **45**(2) (2014)
17. Brain, M., Schanda, F., Sun, Y.: Building Better Bit-Blasting for Floating-Point Problems. In: Tools and Algorithms for the Construction and Analysis of Systems (TACAS) (2019)
18. Chen, H., Xue, Y., Li, Y., Chen, B., Xie, X., Wu, X., Liu, Y.: Hawkeye: Towards a Desired Directed Grey-box Fuzzer. In: Computer and Communications Security (CCS) (2018)
19. Chen, L., Miné, A., Cousot, P.: A Sound Floating-Point Polyhedra Abstract Domain. In: Asian Symposium on Programming Languages and Systems (APLAS) (2008)
20. Chiang, W.F., Baranowski, M., Briggs, I., Solovyev, A., Gopalakrishnan, G., Rakamarić, Z.: Rigorous Floating-point Mixed-precision Tuning. In: Principles of Programming Languages (POPL) (2017)
21. Chiang, W., Gopalakrishnan, G., Rakamaric, Z., Solovyev, A.: Efficient Search for Inputs Causing High Floating-Point Errors. In: Symposium on Principles and Practice of Parallel Programming (PPoPP) (2014)

22. Chowdhury, A.B., Medicherla, R.K., Venkatesh, R.: VeriFuzz: Program Aware Fuzzing—(Competition Contribution). In: Tools and Algorithms for the Construction and Analysis of Systems (TACAS) (2019)
23. Christakis, M., Müller, P., Wüstholz, V.: Guiding Dynamic Symbolic Execution Toward Unverified Program Executions. In: International Conference on Software Engineering (ICSE) (2016)
24. Claude, M., Moy, Y.: The Jessie plugin for Deductive Verification in Frama-C, Tutorial and Reference Manual. INRIA Saclay-Île-de-France & LRI, CNRS UMR 8623 (2018), http://krakatoa.lri.fr/jessie.html
25. Correnson, L., Cuoq, P., Kirchner, F., Prevosto, V., Puccetti, A., Signoles, J., Yakobowski, B.: Frama-C User Manual (2011), http://frama-c.com//support.html
26. Cousot, P., Cousot, R.: Abstract interpretation: a unified lattice model for static analysis of programs by construction or approximation of fixpoints. In: Principles of Programming Languages (POPL) (1977)
27. Csallner, C., Smaragdakis, Y.: Check 'n' Crash: Combining Static Checking and Testing. In: International Conference on Software Engineering (ICSE) (2005)
28. Czech, M., Jakobs, M.C., Wehrheim, H.: Just Test What You Cannot Verify! In: Fundamental Approaches to Software Engineering (FASE) (2015)
29. Damouche, N., Martel, M., Panchekha, P., Qiu, J., Sanchez-Stern, A., Tatlock, Z.: Toward a Standard Benchmark Format and Suite for Floating-Point Analysis. In: NSV (2016)
30. Darulova, E., Izycheva, A., Nasir, F., Ritter, F., Becker, H., Bastian, R.: Daisy - Framework for Analysis and Optimization of Numerical Programs. In: Tools and Algorithms for the Construction and Analysis of Systems (TACAS) (2018)
31. Darulova, E., Kuncak, V.: Towards a Compiler for Reals. TOPLAS 39(2) (2017)
32. Darulova, E., Horn, E., Sharma, S.: Sound Mixed-precision Optimization with Rewriting. In: International Conference on Cyber-Physical Systems (ICCPS) (2018)
33. De Dinechin, F., Lauter, C.Q., Melquiond, G.: Assisted Verification of Elementary Functions Using Gappa. In: ACM Symposium on Applied Computing (2006)
34. Devecsery, D., Chen, P.M., Flinn, J., Narayanasamy, S.: Optimistic Hybrid Analysis: Accelerating Dynamic Analysis Through Predicated Static Analysis. In: Architectural Support for Programming Languages and Operating Systems (ASPLOS) (2018)
35. Dwyer, M.B., Purandare, R.: Residual Dynamic Typestate Analysis Exploiting Static Analysis: Results to Reformulate and Reduce the Cost of Dynamic Analysis. In: ASE (2007)
36. Ferles, K., Wüstholz, V., Christakis, M., Dillig, I.: Failure-Directed Program Trimming. In: Foundations of Software Engineering (ESEC/FSE) (2017)
37. Fox, A., Harrison, J., Akbarpour, B.: A Formal Model of IEEE Floating Point Arithmetic. HOL4 Theorem Prover Library (2017)
38. Fu, Z., Su, Z.: Effective Floating-Point Analysis via Weak-Distance Minimization. In: Programming Language Design and Implementation (PLDI) (2019)
39. Ganesh, V., Leek, T., Rinard, M.C.: Taint-Based Directed Whitebox Fuzzing. In: International Conference on Software Engineering (ICSE) (2009)
40. Ge, X., Taneja, K., Xie, T., Tillmann, N.: DyTa: Dynamic Symbolic Execution Guided with Static Verification Results. In: International Conference on Software Engineering (ICSE) (2011)
41. Godefroid, P., Nori, A.V., Rajamani, S.K., Tetali, S.: Compositional May-Must Program Analysis: Unleashing the Power of Alternation. In: Principles of Programming Languages (POPL) (2010)

42. Goldberg, D.: What Every Computer Scientist Should Know About Floating-point Arithmetic. ACM Comput. Surv. **23**(1) (1991)
43. Goubault, E., Putot, S.: Static Analysis of Finite Precision Computations. In: Verification, Model Checking, and Abstract Interpretation (VMCAI) (2011)
44. Guo, H., Rubio-González, C.: Efficient Generation of Error-Inducing Floating-Point Inputs via Symbolic Execution. In: International Conference on Software Engineering (ICSE) (2020)
45. Haller, I., Slowinska, A., Neugschwandtner, M., Bos, H.: Dowsing for Overflows: A Guided Fuzzer to Find Buffer Boundary Violations. In: Security (2013)
46. Harrison, J.: Floating Point Verification in HOL Light: The Exponential Function. Formal Methods in System Design **16**(3) (2000)
47. Hatton, L., Roberts, A.: How Accurate is Scientific Software? IEEE Trans. Softw. Eng. **20** (1994)
48. IEEE, C.S.: IEEE Standard for Floating-Point Arithmetic. IEEE Std 754-2008 (2008)
49. Jacobsen, C., Solovyev, A., Gopalakrishnan, G.: A Parameterized Floating-Point Formalizaton in HOL Light. Electronic Notes in Theoretical Computer Science **317** (2015)
50. Jeannet, B., Miné, A.: Apron: A Library of Numerical Abstract Domains for Static Analysis. In: Computer Aided Verification (CAV) (2009)
51. Karlin, I., Bhatele, A., Chamberlain, B.L., Cohen, J., Devito, Z., Gokhale, M., Haque, R., Hornung, R., Keasler, J., Laney, D., Luke, E., Lloyd, S., McGraw, J., Neely, R., Richards, D., Schulz, M., Still, C.H., Wang, F., Wong, D.: LULESH Programming Model and Performance Ports Overview. Tech. Rep. LLNL-TR-608824 (2012)
52. Kroening, D., Tautschnig, M.: CBMC–C bounded model checker. In: Tools and Algorithms for the Construction and Analysis of Systems (TACAS). Springer (2014)
53. Leino, K.R.M.: This is Boogie 2 (2008), https://www.microsoft.com/en-us/research/publication/this-is-boogie-2-2/
54. Lemieux, C., Sen, K.: FairFuzz: A Targeted Mutation Strategy for Increasing Greybox Fuzz Testing Coverage. In: Automated Software Engineering (ASE) (2018)
55. Li, Y., Chen, B., Chandramohan, M., Lin, S., Liu, Y., Tiu, A.: Steelix: Program-State Based Binary Fuzzing. In: Foundations of Software Engineering (ESEC/FSE) (2017)
56. Li, Y., Ji, S., Lv, C., Chen, Y., Chen, J., Gu, Q., Wu, C.: V-Fuzz: Vulnerability-Oriented Evolutionary Fuzzing. CoRR **abs/1901.01142** (2019)
57. Liew, D., Schemmel, D., Cadar, C., Donaldson, A.F., Zähl, R., Wehrle, K.: Floating-Point Symbolic Execution: A Case Study in N-Version Programming. In: Automated Software Engineering (ASE) (2017)
58. Ma, K.K., Khoo, Y.P., Foster, J.S., Hicks, M.: Directed Symbolic Execution. In: Static Analysis Symposium (SAS) (2011)
59. Ma, L., Artho, C., Zhang, C., Sato, H., Gmeiner, J., Ramler, R.: GRT: Program-Analysis-Guided Random Testing. In: Automated Software Engineering (ASE) (2015)
60. Magron, V., Constantinides, G., Donaldson, A.: Certified Roundoff Error Bounds Using Semidefinite Programming. ACM Trans. Math. Softw. **43**(4) (2017)
61. Mahmoud, A., Venkatagiri, R., Ahmed, K., Misailovic, S., Marinov, D., Fletcher, C.W., Adve, S.V.: Minotaur: Adapting Software Testing Techniques for Hardware Errors. In: Architectural Support for Programming Languages and Operating Systems (ASPLOS) (2019)

62. Marinescu, P.D., Cadar, C.: KATCH: High-Coverage Testing of Software Patches. In: Foundations of Software Engineering (ESEC/FSE) (2013)
63. Miné, A., Mauborgne, L., Rival, X., Feret, J., Cousot, P., Kästner, D., Wilhelm, S., Ferdinand, C.: Taking Static Analysis to the Next Level: Proving the Absence of Run-Time Errors and Data Races with Astrée. In: Embedded Real Time Software and Systems (ERTS) (2016)
64. Moore, R.E., Kearfott, R.B., Cloud, M.J.: Introduction to Interval Analysis. Society for Industrial and Applied Mathematics (2009)
65. Moscato, M., Titolo, L., Dutle, A., Muñoz, C.: Automatic Estimation of Verified Floating-Point Round-Off Errors via Static Analysis. In: SAFECOMP (2017)
66. Nori, A.V., Rajamani, S.K., Tetali, S., Thakur, A.V.: The YOGI Project: Software Property Checking via Static Analysis and Testing. In: Tools and Algorithms for the Construction and Analysis of Systems (TACAS) (2009)
67. Panchekha, P., Sanchez-Stern, A., Wilcox, J.R., Tatlock, Z.: Automatically Improving Accuracy for Floating Point Expressions. In: Programming Language Design and Implementation (PLDI) (2015)
68. Rubio-González, C., Nguyen, C., Nguyen, H.D., Demmel, J., Kahan, W., Sen, K., Bailey, D.H., Iancu, C., Hough, D.: Precimonious: Tuning Assistant for Floating-point Precision. In: High Performance Computing, Networking, Storage and Analysis (SC) (2013)
69. Sanchez-Stern, A., Panchekha, P., Lerner, S., Tatlock, Z.: Finding Root Causes of Floating Point Error. In: Programming Language Design and Implementation (PLDI) (2018)
70. Schkufza, E., Sharma, R., Aiken, A.: Stochastic Optimization of Floating-Point Programs with Tunable Precision. In: Programming Language Design and Implementation (PLDI) (2014)
71. Singh, G., Püschel, M., Vechev, M.T.: Fast polyhedra abstract domain. In: Principles of Programming Languages (POPL) (2017)
72. Solovyev, A., Jacobsen, C., Rakamaric, Z., Gopalakrishnan, G.: Rigorous Estimation of Floating-Point Round-off Errors with Symbolic Taylor Expansions. In: Formal Methods (FM) (2015)
73. Wang, M., Liang, J., Chen, Y., Jiang, Y., Jiao, X., Liu, H., Zhao, X., Sun, J.: SAFL: Increasing and Accelerating Testing Coverage with Symbolic Execution and Guided Fuzzing. In: International Conference on Software Engineering: Companion (ICSE Companion) (2018)
74. Wang, X., Wang, H., Su, Z., Tang, E., Chen, X., Shen, W., Chen, Z., Wang, L., Zhang, X., Li, X.: Global Optimization of Numerical Programs via Prioritized Stochastic Algebraic Transformations. In: International Conference on Software Engineering (ICSE) (2019)
75. Wüstholz, V., Christakis, M.: Targeted Greybox Fuzzing with Static Lookahead Analysis. In: International Conference on Software Engineering (ICSE) (2020), to appear.
76. Yi, X., Chen, L., Mao, X., Ji, T.: Efficient Automated Repair of High Floating-Point Errors in Numerical Libraries. Proceedings of the ACM on Programming Languages 3(POPL) (2019)
77. Zou, D., Wang, R., Xiong, Y., Zhang, L., Su, Z., Mei, H.: A Genetic Algorithm for Detecting Significant Floating-Point Inaccuracies. In: International Conference on Software Engineering (ICSE) (2015)
78. Zou, D., Zeng, M., Xiong, Y., Fu, Z., Zhang, L., Su, Z.: Detecting Floating-Point Errors via Atomic Conditions. PACMPL 4(POPL) (2020)

Symbolic Coloured SCC Decomposition⋆

Nikola Beneš[✉], Luboš Brim, Samuel Pastva, and David Šafránek

Faculty of Informatics, Masaryk University, Brno, Czech Republic
{xbenes3,brim,xpastva,safranek}@fi.muni.cz

Abstract. Problems arising in many scientific disciplines are often modelled using edge-coloured directed graphs. These can be enormous in the number of both vertices and colours. Given such a graph, the original problem frequently translates to the detection of the graph's strongly connected components, which is challenging at this scale.
We propose a new, symbolic algorithm that computes all the monochromatic strongly connected components of an edge-coloured graph. In the worst case, the algorithm performs $O(p \cdot n \cdot \log n)$ symbolic steps, where p is the number of colours and n the number of vertices. We evaluate the algorithm using an experimental implementation based on Binary Decision Diagrams (BDDs) and large (up to 2^{48}) coloured graphs produced by models appearing in systems biology.

Keywords: strongly connected components · symbolic algorithm · edge-coloured digraphs · systems biology

1 Introduction

Processing massive data sets poses a series of interesting computational challenges. A variety of these data sets can be modelled as very large multigraphs, augmented by a specific collection of application-dependent edge attributes. These attributes are often represented as colours and the resulting formalism is called an *edge-coloured graph* [4, 10]. Geographic information systems, telecommunications traffic, or internet data are prime examples of data that are best represented as such edge-coloured graphs. For instance, in social networking, it is typically used to identify groups of nodes related to each other by some specific criteria (Sports, Health, Technology, Religion, etc.) represented as colours. Our interest in processing huge edge-coloured graphs is primarily motivated by applications taken from systems biology [5, 29] and genetics [25] where we have to deal not only with giant graphs as measured by the number of vertices and edges but also with large sets of colours. The colours in such graphs represent various parameters that influence the dynamics of a biological system [5, 9, 46].

Fundamental graph algorithms such as breadth-first search, spanning tree construction, shortest paths, decomposition into strongly connected components

---

⋆ Supported by the Czech Science Foundation grant No. 18-00178S.

J. F. Groote and K. G. Larsen (Eds.): TACAS 2021, LNCS 12652, pp. 64–83, 2021.
https://doi.org/10.1007/978-3-030-72013-1_4

(SCCs), etc., are building blocks of many practical applications. For the edge-coloured graphs, the primary research focus so far has been on some of the "classical" coloured graph problems, like the determination of the chromatic index, finding sub-graphs with a specified colour property (the coloured version of the k-linked problem), properly edge-coloured cycles and paths, alternating cycles, rainbow cliques, monochromatic cliques, monochromatic cycles, etc. [1–4, 55, 33].

To the best of our knowledge, we are not aware of any work on SCC decomposition for edge-coloured graphs, even though this problem has many important applications. For example, in biological systems, connected components represent the attractors of the system. These play an essential role in determining the system's properties, since they may correspond, for example, to the specific phenotypes of a cell [21]. The parameters (e.g. reaction rates) in such systems might be represented as edge colours in the state transition graph. The knowledge of attractors and how their structure depends on parameters is vital for understanding various biological phenomena [24, 38]. Other applications where investigation of attractors is crucial include predictions of the global climate change [52], or predictions of spreading of infectious diseases such as COVID-19 [39].

There is a serious computational problem related to the processing of massive edge-coloured graphs, even the non-coloured ones, that significantly affects the tractability of SCC decomposition. The graphs often cannot be handled with standard (explicit) representations since they are too large to be kept in the main memory. Various approaches have been considered to deal with such giant graphs: distributed-memory structures, structures for representing graphs symbolically, or storing the graphs in external memory. We review these approaches in more detail in the related work section.

In [6, 13] we have initially attacked the SCC decomposition problem for massive edge-coloured graphs by developing a parallel semi-symbolic algorithm for detecting terminal SCCs. The algorithm uses symbolic structures to represent sets of parameters, while the graph itself is represented explicitly. The results have shown that the parallel semi-symbolic algorithm is not sufficient for the practical needs to tackle large graphs representing real-world problems. Those findings have motivated us to propose an entirely symbolic approach.

In this paper, we consider *edge-coloured multi-digraphs*, i.e., multi-digraphs such that each directed edge has a colour and no two parallel (i.e., joining the same pair of vertices) edges have the same colour. Here, we refer to such graphs simply as *coloured graphs*. For coloured graphs, we can define several notions of strongly connected components involving colours. We consider the simplest case, where the SCCs are *monochromatic*, that is all their edges have the same colour [35]. This choice is motivated by the application in systems biology, as mentioned above.

We propose a novel fully symbolic algorithm for detecting *all monochromatic components* in coloured graphs which is in practice significantly faster than is achievable with a naïve execution of an algorithm for symbolic SCC decomposition scanning all colours one-by-one, in particular on massive coloured graphs. This is because in many applications, the edges are largely shared among individual colours [5] and our algorithm is capable of exploiting this fact. The algorithm conceptually follows the *lock-step* reachability approach by Bloem [14] for monochromatic digraphs. The key new ingredients behind our algorithm are a careful orchestration of the forward and backward reachability for different colours and a sophisticated selection of a set of pivots.

1.1   Related Work

The detection of SCCs in (monochromatic) digraphs is a well-known problem computable in linear time. Best serial (explicit) algorithms are Kosaraju-Sharir [50] and Tarjan [53], which are both inherently based on depth-first search. However, these algorithms do not scale for large graphs, e.g., those encountered in model-checking. Therefore, alternative approaches to SCC decomposition have been proposed (I/O efficient, parallel, symbolic algorithms).

The algorithm of Jiang [32] gives an I/O-efficient alternative based on a combination of depth-first and breadth-first search.

Efficient parallel distributed-memory algorithms avoid the inherently sequential DFS step [45] in several different ways. The Forward-Backward algorithm [26] employs a divide-and-conquer approach relying on picking a pivot state and splitting the graph in three independent (no crossing SCCs) parts. The approach of Orzan [44] uses a different distribution scheme called a colouring transformation employing a set of prioritised colours to split the graph into many parts at once. The recursive OWCTY-Backward-Forward (OBF) approach is proposed in [8]. It recursively splits the graph in a number of independent sub-graphs called OBF slices and applies to each slice the One-Way-Catch-Them-Young (OWCTY) technique. In [51] the authors utilise variants of Forward-Backward and Orzan's algorithms for optimal execution on shared-memory multi-core platforms. Finally, Bloemen et al. [15] utilise the important ability of Tarjan's algorithm to return detected SCCs on-the-fly. In particular, they present an on-the-fly parallel algorithm showing promising speedups for large graphs containing large SCCs. On another end, GPU-accelerated approaches to computing SCCs have been addressed, e.g., in [7, 30, 37, 56].

Computing SCCs of (monochromatic) digraphs symbolically is another way to handle giant graphs and has been thoroughly explored in literature. As in the case of efficient parallelisation, depth-first search is not feasible in the symbolic framework [28]. In consequence, many DFS-based algorithms cannot be easily revised to work with symbolically represented graphs. An algorithm based on forward and backward reachability performing $\mathcal{O}(n^2)$ symbolic steps was presented by Xie and Beerel in [57]. Bloem et al. present an improved $\mathcal{O}(n \cdot \log n)$ algorithm in [14]. Finally, an $\mathcal{O}(n)$ algorithm was presented by Gentilini et al. in [27, 28]. This bound has been proved to be tight in [20]. In [20], the authors argue that the algorithm from [27] is optimal even when considering more fine-grained complexity criteria, like the diameter of the graph and the diameter of the individual components. Ciardo et al. [59] use the idea of saturation [22] to speed up state exploration when computing each SCC in the Xie-Beerel algorithm, and compute the transitive closure of the transition relation using a novel algorithm based on saturation. Besides these generic algorithms, there have been recently also proposed symbolic SCC decomposition methods to deal with specific large graphs, e.g., graphs generated by Boolean networks [42, 58].

2   Problem Definition

As we have already stated in the introductory section, the SCC decomposition problem for edge-coloured graphs has remained mostly unexplored until now. We thus start this paper by introducing and formalising the notion of *coloured SCC decomposition* itself and state some of its basic properties.

Before giving exact definitions, it might be instructive to discuss the substance of the coloured SCC decomposition intuitively. There are several ways of capturing the notion of a "coloured connected component". For example, one of them is that of a colour-connectivity first introduced by Saad [47]. It is based on alternating paths in which successive edges differ in colour. However, there is no unique, universally acceptable notion of a coloured component.

In the biological application we have in mind, we want to identify a coloured component as a coloured collection of SCCs—a collection where for every colour there is a set of all relevant monochromatic SCCs. Such setting leads us to represent SCCs in the form of a relation. To that end, we first introduce such a relation for monochromatic graphs (Section 2.1) and consequently extend it to edge-coloured graphs (Section 2.2). The relation-based approach gives us also the advantage of allowing a feasible symbolic encoding of the problem.

2.1   Graphs and Strongly Connected Components

Let us first recall the standard definitions of a directed graph and its strongly connected components:

Definition 1. *A directed graph is a tuple $G = (V, E)$ where V is a set of graph vertices and $E \subseteq V \times V$ is a set of graph edges.*

We are going to use the word *graph* to mean *directed graph* in the following. We write $u \to v$ when $(u, v) \in E$ and $u \to^* v$ when $(u, v) \in E^*$, the reflexive and transitive closure of E. We say that v is *reachable* from u if $u \to^* v$. The reachability relation allows us to decompose a graph into strongly connected components, defined as follows:

Definition 2. *In a graph $G = (V, E)$, a strongly connected component (SCC) is a maximal set $W \subseteq V$ such that for all $u, v \in W$, $u \to^* v$ and $v \to^* u$. For a fixed $v \in V$, we write $SCC(G, v)$ to denote the SCC of G that contains v.*

If the graph G is clear from the context, we can simply write $SCC(v)$. A set of vertices $S \subseteq V$ is said to be *SCC-closed* if every SCC W is either fully contained inside S ($W \subseteq S$), or in its complement ($W \subseteq V \setminus S$). Notice that given a vertex v, the set of all vertices reachable from v, as well as the set of all vertices that can reach v, are both SCC-closed.

A pivotal problem in computer science is to find the SCC decomposition of G. As mentioned above, we represent the decomposition in the form of an *equivalence relation* R_{scc} such that the individual SCCs are exactly the equivalence classes of R_{scc}. The relation-based formulation of the SCC decomposition problem is the following:

Problem 1 (SCC decomposition) *Given a graph* $G = (V, E)$, *find the* SCC *decomposition relation* $R_{scc} \subseteq V \times V$ *such that* $(u, v) \in R_{scc}$ *if and only if* $SCC(u) = SCC(v)$.

Note that $SCC(u)$ is the section of the first attribute of R_{scc}, i.e. $SCC(u) = \{u \mid (u, v) \in R_{scc}\}$. We denote such a section in the following way: $SCC(u) = R_{scc}(u, \_)$. Here, u is the specific value of an attribute at which the section is taken, and $\_$ is used in place of the attributes that remain unchanged. Such notation naturally extends to relations of arbitrary arity.

2.2   Coloured SCC Decomposition Problem

We now lift the formal framework to the coloured setting. An edge-coloured graph can be seen as a succinct representation of several different graphs, all sharing the same set of vertices. Note that to emphasise the difference from the standard graphs as given in Definition 1, we sometimes call the standard graphs *monochromatic*.

Definition 3. *An* edge-coloured directed multi-graph *(coloured graph for short) is a tuple* $\mathfrak{G} = (V, C, E)$ *where* V *is a set of vertices,* C *is a set of colours and* $E \subseteq V \times C \times V$ *is a coloured edge relation.*

We also write $u \xrightarrow{c} v$ whenever $(u, c, v) \in E$. By fixing a colour $c \in C$ and keeping only the c-coloured edges (with the colour attribute removed), we obtain a monochromatic graph $\mathfrak{G}(c) = (V, \{(u, v) \mid (u, c, v) \in E\})$. We call this graph the *monochromatisation of* $\mathfrak{G}$ *with respect to* c. Intuitively, one can view the elements of C as a type of graph parametrisation where the edge structure of the graph changes based on the specific $c \in C$.

The SCC decomposition relation R_{scc} is extended to the coloured SCC decomposition relation $\mathfrak{R}_{scc}$ by relating every colour $c \in C$ with all SCCs of the monochromatisation $\mathfrak{G}(c)$. In consequence, the SCC decomposition problem is then lifted to the coloured SCC decomposition problem as follows:

Problem 2 (Coloured SCC decomposition) *Given a coloured graph* $\mathfrak{G} = (V, C, E)$, *find the* coloured SCC decomposition relation $\mathfrak{R}_{scc} \subseteq V \times C \times V$ *satisfying* $(u, c, v) \in \mathfrak{R}_{scc}$ *if and only if* $(u, v) \in R_{scc}$ *of* $\mathfrak{G}(c)$.

From this definition, we can immediately observe the following properties about the relationship of $\mathfrak{R}_{scc}$ with the terms which we have defined before:

- R_{scc} of a monochromatisation $\mathfrak{G}(c)$ is exactly the section $\mathfrak{R}_{scc}(\_, c, \_)$;
- $SCC(\mathfrak{G}(c), v)$ is exactly the section $\mathfrak{R}_{scc}(v, c, \_)$.

From this, it should be immediately clear that $\mathfrak{R}_{scc}$ contains all components of the underlying monochromatisations.

3 Algorithm

Conceptually, our algorithm follows the *lock-step* reachability approach by Bloem [14] for monochromatic graphs. The lock-step algorithm itself is based on the basic forward-backward decomposition algorithm [57]. In this section, we first briefly introduce these two algorithms in order to explain better the key ideas behind our approach and, in particular, to explain what were the main difficulties encountered in employing the concepts of these algorithms to edge-coloured graphs. Although the algorithms were originally presented as producing a set of SCCs, we reformulate them slightly using the equivalent relation-based approach as explained in the previous section. After that, we present the coloured SCC decomposition algorithm. However, before we dive into the algorithmics, let us first briefly discuss the computation model we are using.

3.1 Symbolic Computation Model

As a complexity measure of our algorithm, we consider the number of symbolic steps, or more specifically, symbolic set and relation operations that the algorithm performs. As is customary, we assume that sets of vertices (V) and colours (C) can be represented symbolically (for example, using reduced ordered binary decision diagrams [17]) as well as any relations over these sets. In particular, we often talk about *coloured vertex sets*, by which we mean the subsets of $V \times C$.

Aside from normal set operations (union, intersection, difference, product and element selection), we also require some basic relational operations, all of which we outline in Fig. 1. These extra operations tend to appear in other applications as well (such as symbolic model checking [18]), and are thus typically already available in mature symbolic computation packages.

Finally, there are several derived operators that are partially specific to our application to coloured graphs. However, these can be constructed using standard set and relation operations. The intuitive meaning of the derived operators is as follows: COLOURS returns all the colours that appear in the given coloured vertex set. PRE and POST compute the pre and post-image of a (monochromatic or coloured) set of vertices, i.e. the set of successors or predecessors of all the vertices in the given set, respectively. Finally, JOIN takes a coloured vertex set A and computes the set $\{(u, c, v) \mid (u, c) \in A, (v, c) \in A\}$.

3.2 Forward-backward Algorithm

To symbolically compute the SCCs of a graph $G = (V, E)$, Xie and Beerel [57] observed that for any vertex $v \in V$, the intersection $W = F \cap B$ of the forward reachable vertices $F = \{v' \in V \mid v \to^* v'\}$ and the backward reachable vertices $B = \{v' \in V \mid v' \to^* v\}$ is exactly the strongly connected component of G which contains v.

The algorithm thus picks an arbitrary *pivot* $v \in V$, and divides the vertices of the graph into four disjoint sets: $W, F\backslash W, B\backslash W$ and $V\backslash(F \cup B)$. This is illustrated graphically in Fig. 2 (left). The set W is then immediately reported as an SCC

Standard set operations		
pick element	$\text{PICK}(A)$	arbitrary $x \in A$
union	$A \cup B$	$\{x \mid x \in A \vee x \in B\}$
intersection	$A \cap B$	$\{x \mid x \in A \wedge x \in B\}$
difference	$A \setminus B$	$\{x \mid x \in A \wedge x \notin B\}$
product	$A \times B$	$\{(x,y) \mid x \in A \wedge y \in B\}$
Relation manipulation ($R \subseteq S_1 \times \ldots \times S_n$)		
i-th section at x	$\sigma_i(x, R)$	$\{(y_1, \ldots, y_{i-1}, y_{i+1}, \ldots, y_n) \mid$ $(y_1, \ldots, y_{i-1}, x, y_{i+1}, \ldots, y_n) \in R\}$
existential quantification of the i-th element	$\exists_i(R)$	$\bigcup_{x \in S_i} \sigma_i(x, R)$
swap	$\text{SWAP}(R \subseteq A \times B)$	$\{(y, x) \in B \times A \mid (x, y) \in R\}$
Derived operations ($G = (V, E), \mathfrak{G} = (V, C, E)$)		
colours	$\text{COLOURS}(A \subseteq V \times C)$	$\exists_1(A)$
pre-image	$\text{PRE}(G, A \subseteq V)$	$\exists_2((V \times A) \cap E)$
post-image	$\text{POST}(G, A \subseteq V)$	$\exists_1((A \times V) \cap E)$
coloured pre-image	$\text{PRE}(\mathfrak{G}, A \subseteq V \times C)$	$\exists_3((V \times \text{SWAP}(A)) \cap E)$
coloured post-image	$\text{POST}(\mathfrak{G}, A \subseteq V \times C)$	$\text{SWAP}(\exists_1((A \times V) \cap E))$
coloured join	$\text{JOIN}(A \subseteq V \times C)$	$(V \times \text{SWAP}(A)) \cap (A \times V)$

Fig. 1. Summary of symbolic operations that appear in the presented algorithms. The derived operations can be implemented using the standard and relational operations. However, typically they also have a slightly more efficient direct implementations.

of the graph, and added into the component relation: $R_{scc} \leftarrow R_{scc} \cup (W \times W)$. It is easy to see that every other SCC is fully contained within one of the three remaining sets (they are SCC-closed), and the algorithm thus recursively repeats this process independently in each set.

The correctness of the algorithm follows from the initial observation and the fact that every vertex eventually appears in W (either as a pivot or as a result of $F \cap B$). In the worst case, the algorithm performs $O(|V|^2)$ symbolic steps, since every vertex is picked as a pivot at most once and the computation of F and B requires at most $O(|V|)$ PRE/POST operations.

3.3 Lock-step Algorithm

To improve the efficiency of the forward-backward algorithm, the lock-step approach [14] uses another important observation: To compute W, it is not necessary to fully compute both F and B; only the smaller (in terms of diameter) of the two sets needs to be entirely known. With this observation, the computation of F and B can be modified in the following way: Instead of computing F and B one after the other, the computation is *interleaved* in a step-by-step manner (dovetailing). When one of the sets is fully computed, the computation of the second set is stopped. Let us call the computed set *converged* and denote it by

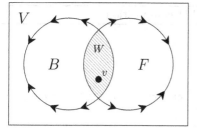
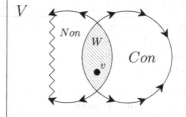

Fig. 2. Illustration of the difference between the forward-backward algorithm (left) and the lock-step algorithm (right). On the left, we fully compute both backward (B) and forward (F) reachable sets from the pivot v, identifying W as $F \cap B$. On the right, without loss of generality, assume F is fully computed first. It thus becomes converged (Con) and the computation of B (Non) is stopped before it is fully explored.

Con, and the unfinished set *non-converged* and denote it by Non. This situation is illustrated in Fig. 2 (right).

However, even when Con is fully known, we still need to finish the computation of states in Non that are inside Con to discover the whole component W. This is necessary if there are vertices w in W whose forward distance from v (i.e. the length of the path $v \rightarrow^* w$) is short while their backward distance (the length of the path $w \rightarrow^* v$) is long, or vice versa. Such vertices are thus only discovered in one of the two reachability procedures and still need to be discovered by the other one to identify the whole component. However, an important observation is that only the vertices already inside Con need to be considered in this step.

After this, the SCC can be identified and reported just as in the forward-backward algorithm. Finally, the recursion now continues in sets $Con \setminus W$ and $V \setminus Con$. This is due to Non being not fully computed; we cannot guarantee that no SCC overlaps outside of Non (Non is not necessarily SCC-closed).

The algorithm is still correct because every vertex is eventually either picked as a pivot or discovered in some W. Furthermore, due to the way Con and Non are computed guarantees that W is still a whole SCC. In terms of complexity, the algorithm performs $O(|V| \cdot \log |V|)$ symbolic steps in the worst case. To see why this is true, we may observe that every vertex appears in W exactly once, and that the smaller of the two sets $Con \setminus W$ and $V \setminus Con$, let us call it S, is always smaller than $\frac{|V|}{2}$. The authors then argue that the price of every iteration can be attributed (up to a multiplicative constant) to the vertices in $S \cup W$ and that every vertex appears in S at most $O(\log |V|)$-times.

3.4 Coloured Lock-step Algorithm

When developing an algorithm for coloured graphs, we had to deal with multiple challenges which do not appear for monochromatic graphs and require careful consideration. In the following, we refer to the pseudocode in Algorithm 1.

An important observation is that the structure of components in the graph can change arbitrarily with respect to the graph colours. In consequence, our algorithm

---

Algorithm 1: Symbolic Coloured SCC Decomposition

---

1 **Function** COLOUREDSCC($\mathfrak{G} = (V, C, E)$)
2      $\mathfrak{R}_{scc} \subseteq (V \times C \times V) \leftarrow \emptyset$;
3   DECOMPOSITION($\mathfrak{G}, \mathfrak{R}_{scc}, V \times C$);
4   **return** $\mathfrak{R}_{scc}$;

5 **Function** DECOMPOSITION($\mathfrak{G} = (V, C, E), \mathfrak{R}_{scc} \subseteq (V \times C \times V), \mathcal{V} \subseteq (V \times C)$)
6   **if** $\mathcal{V} = \emptyset$ **then return**;
7      $\mathcal{F}, \mathcal{B}, \overrightarrow{\mathcal{F}}, \overrightarrow{\mathcal{B}} \subseteq (V \times C) \leftarrow$ PIVOTS($\mathcal{V}$);
8      $\overrightarrow{\mathcal{F}_u}, \overrightarrow{\mathcal{B}_u} \subseteq (V \times C) \leftarrow \emptyset$;
9      $F_{lock}, B_{lock} \subseteq C \leftarrow \emptyset$;
10   **while** $F_{lock} \cup B_{lock} \subset$ COLOURS($\mathcal{V}$) **do**
11          $\overrightarrow{\mathcal{F}} \subseteq V \times C \leftarrow (\text{POST}(\mathfrak{G}, \overrightarrow{\mathcal{F}}) \cap \mathcal{V}) \setminus \mathcal{F}$;
12          $\overrightarrow{\mathcal{B}} \subseteq V \times C \leftarrow (\text{PRE}(\mathfrak{G}, \overrightarrow{\mathcal{B}}) \cap \mathcal{V}) \setminus \mathcal{B}$;
13          $F_{lock} \leftarrow F_{lock} \cup (\text{COLOURS}(\mathcal{V}) \setminus \text{COLOURS}(\overrightarrow{\mathcal{F}}))$;
14          $B_{lock} \leftarrow B_{lock} \cup (\text{COLOURS}(\mathcal{V}) \setminus \text{COLOURS}(\overrightarrow{\mathcal{B}}) \setminus F_{lock})$;
15          $\overrightarrow{\mathcal{F}_u} \leftarrow \overrightarrow{\mathcal{F}_u} \cup (\mathcal{F} \cap (V \times B_{lock}))$;
16          $\overrightarrow{\mathcal{B}_u} \leftarrow \overrightarrow{\mathcal{B}_u} \cup (\mathcal{B} \cap (V \times F_{lock}))$;
17          $\overrightarrow{\mathcal{F}} \leftarrow \overrightarrow{\mathcal{F}} \setminus (V \times B_{lock})$;
18          $\overrightarrow{\mathcal{B}} \leftarrow \overrightarrow{\mathcal{B}} \setminus (V \times F_{lock})$;
19          $\mathcal{F} \leftarrow \mathcal{F} \cup \overrightarrow{\mathcal{F}}$;
20          $\mathcal{B} \leftarrow \mathcal{B} \cup \overrightarrow{\mathcal{B}}$;
21   **end**
22      $Con \subseteq V \times C \leftarrow (\mathcal{F} \cap (V \times F_{lock})) \cup (\mathcal{B} \cap (V \times B_{lock}))$;
23      $\overrightarrow{\mathcal{F}} \leftarrow \overrightarrow{\mathcal{F}_u} \cap Con$;
24      $\overrightarrow{\mathcal{B}} \leftarrow \overrightarrow{\mathcal{B}_u} \cap Con$;
25   **while** $\overrightarrow{\mathcal{F}} \neq \emptyset \wedge \overrightarrow{\mathcal{B}} \neq \emptyset$ **do**
26          $\overrightarrow{\mathcal{F}} \leftarrow (\text{POST}(\mathfrak{G}, \overrightarrow{\mathcal{F}}) \cap Con) \setminus \mathcal{F}$;
27          $\overrightarrow{\mathcal{B}} \leftarrow (\text{PRE}(\mathfrak{G}, \overrightarrow{\mathcal{B}}) \cap Con) \setminus \mathcal{B}$;
28          $\mathcal{F} \leftarrow \mathcal{F} \cup \overrightarrow{\mathcal{F}}$;
29          $\mathcal{B} \leftarrow \mathcal{B} \cup \overrightarrow{\mathcal{B}}$;
30   **end**
31      $\mathcal{W} \subseteq V \times C \leftarrow \mathcal{F} \cap \mathcal{B}$;
32      $\mathfrak{R}_{scc} \leftarrow \mathfrak{R}_{scc} \cup \text{JOIN}(\mathcal{W})$;
33   DECOMPOSITION($\mathfrak{G}, \mathfrak{R}_{scc}, \mathcal{V} \setminus Con$);
34   DECOMPOSITION($\mathfrak{G}, \mathfrak{R}_{scc}, Con \setminus \mathcal{W}$);

35 **Function** PIVOTS($\mathcal{V}$)
36      $\mathcal{P} \subseteq (V \times C) \leftarrow \emptyset; \mathcal{V}' \subseteq (V \times C) \leftarrow \mathcal{V}$;
37   **while** $\mathcal{V}' \neq \emptyset$ **do**
38          $(v, c) \leftarrow$ PICK($\mathcal{V}'$);
39          $\mathcal{P} \leftarrow \mathcal{P} \cup (\{v\} \times \sigma_1(v, \mathcal{V}'))$;
40          $\mathcal{V}' \leftarrow \mathcal{V}' \setminus (V \times \text{COLOURS}(\mathcal{P}))$;
41   **end**
42   **return** $\mathcal{P}$;

---

cannot simply operate with sets of graph vertices as the normal algorithm would. To that end, we use the notion of coloured vertex sets as introduced in Section 3.1 where the symbolic operations we perform on these sets have been described.

Initially, the algorithm starts with all vertices and colours, i.e. the full set $V \times C$. However, as the components are discovered, the intermediate results may contain different vertices appearing only for certain subsets of C. As a result, we often cannot pick a single pivot vertex that would be valid for all considered colours. Instead, we aim to pick a *pivot set* $P \subseteq V \times C$ such that for every colour that still appears in $\mathcal{V}$, the set contains *exactly* one vertex. Alternatively, one can also view the pivot set as a (partial) function from C to V. This is done in the PIVOTS function.

The lock-step reachability procedure also cannot operate as in a standard graph. First of all, there can be colours where the forward reachability converges first, as well as colours where this happens for backward reachability. The algorithm thus has to account for both options simultaneously. Second, for each colour, the reachability can converge in a different number of steps. To deal with this problem, we introduce the F_{lock} and B_{lock} variables. These store the mutually disjoint sets of colours for which forward and backward reachability already converged. The lock-step procedure terminates when F_{lock} and B_{lock} contain all the colours that appear in $\mathcal{V}$.

Throughout the algorithm, we keep track of several coloured-set variables. The first two, $\mathcal{F}$ and $\mathcal{B}$, represent the forward and backward reachable sets, respectively. We then have four variables $\overrightarrow{\mathcal{F}}, \overrightarrow{\mathcal{F}_u}, \overrightarrow{\mathcal{B}}, \overrightarrow{\mathcal{B}_u}$ to represent the *frontiers* of these sets, i.e., the set of pairs (v, c) such that the vertex v has not yet been expanded in the corresponding reachability procedure for the colour c. The frontier of $\mathcal{F}$ is the set $\overrightarrow{\mathcal{F}} \cup \overrightarrow{\mathcal{F}_u}$. The sets $\overrightarrow{\mathcal{F}}$ and $\overrightarrow{\mathcal{F}_u}$ contain disjoint colours – $\overrightarrow{\mathcal{F}}$ involves those colours for which the lock-step reachability procedure has not finished yet, while $\overrightarrow{\mathcal{F}_u}$ represents the *unfinished* part of the frontier that shall be explored in the second while cycle; similarly for $\overrightarrow{\mathcal{B}}$ and $\overrightarrow{\mathcal{B}_u}$.

In the first while cycle (lines 10–21), we compute the reachability sets in the lock-step manner. Once a reachability set is completed for some colours (i.e., there are no vertices to expand with those colours), we add the colours to the corresponding F_{lock} or B_{lock} variable. Note that we ensure that F_{lock} and B_{lock} remain disjoint even if the two reachability procedures converged at the same time for certain colours—see line 14. We use F_{lock} and B_{lock} to split the newly computed frontier sets into the parts that are to be explored in the next iteration $(\overrightarrow{\mathcal{F}}, \overrightarrow{\mathcal{B}})$ and the parts that are currently left unfinished $(\overrightarrow{\mathcal{F}_u}, \overrightarrow{\mathcal{B}_u})$.

After the first while cycle, we compute the set Con that is an analogue for the converged set of the original lock-step algorithm (line 22). As already suggested above and unlike the original algorithm, this set cannot be just $\mathcal{F}$ or $\mathcal{B}$, but is instead a mixture of both, depending on the convergent colours. To compute this set, we use the F_{lock} and B_{lock} variables.

The second while cycle (lines 25–30) then completes the unfinished forward and backward reachability set, restricted to the inside of the converged set. The intersection of $\mathcal{F}$ and $\mathcal{B}$ then forms a coloured set $\mathcal{W}$ with the property that for all $c \in$ COLOURS$(\mathcal{V})$, $\mathcal{W}(\_, c)$ is a strongly connected component of $\mathfrak{G}(c)$. We create the corresponding relation using the JOIN operation, add this relation to the resulting $\mathfrak{R}_{scc}$, and recursively call the whole procedure with $\mathcal{V} \setminus Con$ and $Con \setminus \mathcal{W}$ as the base coloured sets of vertices.

Let us note that there is possibly another approach. Instead of trying to work with all colours still appearing in the coloured vertex set at once, we cold fork a new recursive procedure whenever the colour set splits due to the differences in the graph structure. For example, instead of picking multiple coloured vertices as pivots, one could pick a single vertex with a valid subset of colours and then address the remaining colours in a separate recursive call. While such approach could be to some extent beneficial in a massively parallel environment where each recursive call can be executed independently on a new CPU, the amount of forking in large systems will soon become unreasonable. More importantly, it defeats the purpose of symbolic representation which aims to minimise the number of symbolic operations.

3.5   Correctness and Complexity of the Coloured Lock-step Algorithm

Theorem 1. *Let $\mathfrak{G} = (V, C, E)$ be a coloured graph. The coloured lock-step algorithm terminates and computes the coloured SCC decomposition relation $\mathfrak{R}_{scc}$.*

Proof. We first show that the set $\mathcal{W}$ computed on line 31 indeed contains one SCC for every colour $c \in$ COLOURS$(\mathcal{V})$ and that the recursive calls of DECOMPOSITION preserve the property that $\mathcal{V}$ is SCC-closed with respect to all colours.

Let us assume that $\mathcal{V}$ is SCC-closed and let us take an arbitrary $c \in$ COLOURS$(\mathcal{V})$. The function PIVOTS chooses a set that contains exactly one pair whose colour is c, let us call this pair (v, c). Let us further assume that c is assigned into F_{lock} first (the case with B_{lock} is completely symmetric).

Let us now choose an arbitrary vertex w such that v and w are in the same SCC of $\mathfrak{G}(c)$, i.e. $v \to^* w$ and $w \to^* v$. As the first while cycle finishes, $\mathcal{F}$ contains all the pairs of the form $(u, c) \in \mathcal{V}$ where u is reachable from v in $\mathfrak{G}(c)$. Thus, it also contains (w, c) due to the fact that $\mathcal{V}$ is SCC-closed. Now, either $(w, c) \in \mathcal{B}$, or there exists a vertex x such that $w \to^* x$, $x \to^* v$ in $\mathfrak{G}(c)$ and $x \in \overrightarrow{\mathcal{B}_u}$. This means that (w, c) is added to $\mathcal{B}$ in the second while cycle. In both cases, both (v, c) and (w, c) are then added to $\mathcal{W}$. As the vertex choices were arbitrary, this proves that the SCC of v in $\mathfrak{G}(c)$ is contained in $\mathcal{W}$. Furthermore, if $(y, c) \in \mathcal{W}$ for an arbitrary y, then $v \to^* y$ and $y \to^* v$ in $\mathfrak{G}(c)$, which means that y is in $SCC(\mathfrak{G}(c), v)$. This proves that $\mathcal{W}$ contains exactly one SCC for every colour $c \in$ COLOURS$(\mathcal{V})$.

We now argue that Con is SCC-closed with respect to all colours. This immediately implies that both $\mathcal{V} \setminus Con$ and $Con \setminus \mathcal{W}$ are SCC-closed. Let us assume that there is a colour $c \in$ COLOURS$(\mathcal{V})$ and two vertices v, w in the same SCC of $\mathfrak{G}(c)$ such that $(v, c) \in Con$, but $(w, c) \notin Con$. Let us assume that $c \in F_{lock}$ (as above, the case of B_{lock} is completely symmetrical). Then $(v, c) \in \mathcal{F}$

after the first while cycle finishes. This also means that $(w, c) \in \mathcal{F}$ as the forward reachability procedure is completed for c and thus $(w, c) \in Con$, a contradiction.

What remains is to show that the algorithm terminates and that every SCC is eventually found. Termination is trivially proved by the fact that size of the set $\mathcal{V}$ always decreases in recursive calls: both $\mathcal{W}$ and Con are nonempty, because they contain the initial pivot set as a subset. Clearly, a representant of every SCC of every monochromatisation $\mathfrak{G}(c)$ is eventually chosen as a pivot. Together with the above reasoning, this implies that the algorithm is correct.   □

Theorem 2. *Let $|V|$ be the number of vertices in the coloured graph and let $|C|$ be the number of colours. The coloured lock-step algorithm performs at most $\mathcal{O}(|C| \cdot |V| \cdot \log |V|)$ symbolic steps.*

Proof. Let us first note that all the derived operations defined in Fig. 1 use only a constant number of the basic symbolic operations. As we are considering asymptotic complexity here, we can view all the operations in Fig. 1 as elementary symbolic steps.

We first make the observation that each vertex may be chosen as a part of the pivot set at most $|C|$ times. Clearly, once a vertex is included in the pivot set with a set of colours C', then, $\{v\} \times C' \subseteq Con$ (due to the monotonicity of the construction of $\mathcal{F}$ and $\mathcal{B}$) and the elements of $\{v\} \times C'$ do not appear in subsequent recursive calls. This means that the total complexity of the calls to PIVOTS is bounded by $O(|C| \cdot |V|)$ and we can exclude the calls from the rest of the complexity analysis.

We now consider the complexity of a single call to DECOMPOSITION without the subsequent recursive calls. Let us now select one of the colours for which the lock-step reachability procedure (lines 10–21) finished last, i.e., one of the colours that have been added to F_{lock} or B_{lock} in the final iteration of the cycle. Let us call this colour c. Recall that $\sigma_2(c, \mathcal{X})$ is the set of vertices with colour c in a coloured set $\mathcal{X}$.

Let us denote by $W := \sigma_2(c, \mathcal{W})$ and let S be the smaller of $\sigma_2(c, \mathcal{V} \setminus Con)$ and $\sigma_2(c, Con \setminus \mathcal{W})$. Clearly S contains at most $|V|/2$ vertices. Let $k = |S \cup W|$. We now argue that the number of symbolic steps in a given call (without the recursive calls) is bounded by $\mathcal{O}(k)$.

Assume w.l.o.g. that $c \in F_{lock}$ (a completely symmetric argument solves the case $c \in B_{lock}$). Then $\sigma_2(c, Con) = \sigma_2(c, \mathcal{F})$. If S is $\sigma_2(c, Con \setminus W)$ then k is the size of $\sigma_2(c, \mathcal{F})$. Each iteration of the first while cycle puts at least one vertex with colour c into $\mathcal{F}$; otherwise c would not be one of the last colours to finish. This means that the cycle runs for at most k iterations. This also means that the size of $\sigma_2(x, \mathcal{X})$ for all colours x and $\mathcal{X} \in \{\mathcal{F}, \mathcal{B}\}$ is also bound by k, which in turn means that the second while cycle cannot make more than $O(k)$ steps.

If S is $\sigma_2(c, \mathcal{V} \setminus Con)$ instead, let us define $B := \sigma_2(c, \mathcal{B})$ right after the first while cycle has finished. We know that $B \subseteq S \cup W$: if a vertex v were in $B \setminus S$ then $(v, c) \in Con = \mathcal{F}$ and thus $v \in W$. Again, each iteration of the first while cycle puts at least one vertex with colour c into $\mathcal{B}$; otherwise c would have been in B_{lock} before it appeared in F_{lock}. Similarly to the previous case, this means that both while cycles run for at most $O(k)$ steps.

The rest of the argument uses amortised reasoning, in a way similar to the proof in [14]. Note that each vertex is going to be an element of the set W as described above at most $|C|$ times (once for each colour). Furthermore, each vertex is going to be an element of the set S as described above at most $|C| \cdot \log |V|$ times: for each colour, the vertex can be an element of the smaller of the two sets at most $\log |V|$ times. As the cost of each single call can be charged to the vertices in $S \cup W$ as explained above, it is sufficient to charge each vertex the total cost of $|C| + |C| \cdot \log |V|$. Together, this means that the total number of symbolic steps is bounded by $O(|C| \cdot |V| \cdot \log |V|)$.   □

Note that the upper bound established by Theorem 2 is no better than the one we would get if we split the coloured graph into its monochromatic constituents and processed each monochromatic graph separately using the original lock-step algorithm [14]. We remark, however, that the coloured approach is a heuristic whose real complexity might be much smaller. Indeed, the complexity analysis in the previous proof focused on a single colour, omitting the fact than SCCs for many other colours are found at the same time. In case where the edges are largely shared among the colours, which is true in many applications, the heuristic has the potential to significantly outperform the parameter-scan approach. The situation is similar to that of the coloured model checking; see the observations made in [5].

4   Experimental Evaluation

In this section, we examine the applicability of our algorithm in real-world situations. First, we discuss how we implemented the algorithm and share some useful recommendations in this regard. We then look at how the implementation performs on real-life coloured graphs which are derived from large models considered in computational biology.

4.1   Implementation

As our symbolic set representation, we consider standard reduced ordered binary decision diagrams (ROBDDs, or just BDDs for short) [17]. The source of our edge-coloured graphs are the transition systems of *parametrised Boolean networks* (PBN) as understood in [11, 60].

Boolean networks. Normal (non-parametrised) Boolean networks [34, 46, 49, 54] appear in computational systems biology as logical models of complex biochemical processes [16]. Here, we use the asynchronous variant of BNs introduced by Thomas [54]. A Boolean network consists of Boolean variables, each having a Boolean update function. Update functions are executed non-deterministically and change the state of the Boolean variables. The semantics of such a network is a directed graph where the vertices are the possible valuations of the Boolean variables and the edges are induced by the non-deterministic execution of the update functions.

This type of models is especially challenging for symbolic analysis. It is a well-known fact, that using symbolic structures, like BDDs, to represent very large state spaces gives good results for synchronous systems, but shows its limits when trying to tackle asynchronicity (see e.g. [23]).

In the parametrised variant, the update functions can be partially unknown. This introduces a set of colours (parametrisations), each colour fully instantiating all update functions of the network. As a result, the semantics of such a model is an edge-coloured directed graph as we consider in this paper. For a full technical description of PBNs and their coloured graph semantics, please refer to [11].

Our implementation heavily relies on the existing internal libraries of our tool AEON [12], which at the moment partially supports symbolic analysis of PBNs. Specifically, AEON uses symbolic BDD-based representation of colour sets, but relies on explicit state space exploration. In this work, we extend these capabilities to fully symbolic analysis of the whole graph.

Custom operations. Aside from implementing the POST and PRE operations for a given PBN, we also choose to provide specialised implementations for the COLOURS and PIVOTS procedures. Especially for the PIVOTS procedure, this can greatly reduce the number of necessary symbolic steps, as we avoid picking pivots vertex-by-vertex.

To implement these two operations as efficiently as possible, we always order the Boolean variables in our BDDs starting from the colour and ending with vertex variables. This ensures that both PIVOTS and COLOURS can be implemented by pruning the vertex variable nodes and minimising the BDD.

Specifically, in this ordering, for COLOURS, all vertex nodes are effectively substituted with the **true** terminal node and the BDD is minimised. For PIVOTS, one (arbitrary) path of vertex variable nodes (corresponding to one pivot vertex) is preserved for every colour, and the rest of the vertex nodes are pruned.

Trimming. Finally, most graphs typically contain a large number of trivial SCCs that introduce unnecessary overhead to the main algorithm. To avoid this overhead, we additionally perform a trimming step before each invocation of DECOMPOSITION. Trimming consists of repeatedly removing all vertices which have no outgoing or no incoming edges and is employed by most symbolic SCC algorithms on standard directed graphs as well. The coloured analogue of trimming is straightforward, as it can be achieved using PRE and POST operations just as in the non-coloured case. For a coloured set of vertices $\mathcal{V}$, POST(PRE($\mathfrak{G}, \mathcal{V}) \cap \mathcal{V}) \cap \mathcal{V}$ returns only vertices which have at least one predecessor in $\mathcal{V}$. The successor variant simply exchanges the POST and PRE operations.

4.2 Experiments

We evaluated our algorithm on 7 real-world networks based on the models from the Ginsim Boolean network database [19]. The experiments were performed on a 32-core AMD Ryzen workstation with 64GB of RAM memory. All tested models are available in our source code repository.[3] Note that the smaller models

---

[3] https://github.com/sybila/biodivine-lib-param-bn/tree/tacas

Table 1. Overview of the test models for the algorithm evaluation. The times (`minutes:seconds`) refer to the total runtime of the SCC decomposition procedure. The model *variables* and *parameters* give the number of Boolean variables necessary to represent the PBN symbolically. Finally, the *graph size* and *colour set size* specifies the magnitude of $|V| \cdot |C|$ and $|C|$ for the coloured graph corresponding to the network.

Model Name	Model Variables	Model Parameters	Graph Size	Colour Set Size	Time
Asymmetric Cell Division [48]	5	48	$\sim 2^{24}$	$\sim 2^{19}$	00:09.47
Reduced TCR Signalisation [36]	10	46	$\sim 2^{24}$	$\sim 2^{14}$	00:58.35
Budding Yeast (Orlando) [43]	9	54	$\sim 2^{27}$	$\sim 2^{18}$	01:13.39
Budding Yeast (Irons) [31]	18	44	$\sim 2^{35}$	$\sim 2^{17}$	50:44.80
T-Cell Differentiation [41]	23	48	$\sim 2^{40}$	$\sim 2^{17}$	71:80.12
WG Signalling Pathway [40]	26	38	$\sim 2^{48}$	$\sim 2^{22}$	78:38.34
Full TCR Signalisation [36]	30	48	$\sim 2^{47}$	$\sim 2^{17}$	118:34.88

($< 2^{30}$) should be easy to process even on a less powerful machine, however the larger models can require substantial amounts of RAM.

The PBNs and their analysis runtime is summarised in Table 1. For each network, we specify the number of Boolean variables used by symbolic encoding, separated into model variables (vertices) and model parameters (colours), and the actual approximate size of the coloured graph. Note that not all combinations of parameters (possible graph colours) are usually biologically admissible, and these are filtered out before the coloured SCC decomposition. Hence the size of the graph is smaller than the space of all the considered BDD variables.

From the presented results, we can draw the following observations: First, fully symbolic approach allows us to scale to much larger graphs than before, especially in terms of state space. Until now, AEON was typically limited (even for an easier problem of bottom SCC detection) to vertex counts of $2^{15} - 2^{20}$, exhausting memory even for much smaller state spaces when dealing with complex parameter space. Here, we can easily handle up to 2^{30} vertices with non-trivial parameter space and we hope to push this number even higher with further optimisations to our experimental implementation.

Second, the coloured heuristic is beneficial for symbolic computation. To support this claim, we considered a monochromatic variant of the decomposition problem for the WG Signaling Pathway and tested the basic lock-step algorithm on a collection of pseudo-random monochromatisations of this graph. Processing one such monochromatisation typically required $0.5 - 1$ second. Considering the graph in question has 2359296 colours, processing the colours one-by-one would, even in ideal conditions, take well above 300 hours (more than 12 days).

5 Conclusions

In this paper we have presented a fully symbolic algorithm for detecting all monochromatic strongly connected components in edge-coloured graphs. The work has been motivated by systems sciences, namely systems biology, where the need for efficient automated analysis of components in large graphs with large sets of coloured edges is emergent. The algorithm combines several ideas inspired by existing state-of-the-art algorithms for SCC decomposition in a non-trivial way. We believe this is the first fully symbolic algorithm aiming to solve the problem efficiently.

The experimental evaluation has shown that in expected practical scenarios, the presented algorithm has a strong potential to be significantly faster than iterating a standard algorithm for SCC decomposition executed on all monochromatic sub-graphs one-by-one.

References

1. Abouelaoualim, A., Das, K.C., Faria, L., Manoussakis, Y., Martinhon, C., Saad, R.: Paths and trails in edge-colored graphs. In: LATIN 2008: Theoretical Informatics. pp. 723–735. Springer (2008)
2. Akbari, S., Alipour, A.: Multicolored trees in complete graphs. Journal of Graph Theory **54**(3), 221–232 (2007)
3. Alon, N., Gutin, G.: Properly colored hamilton cycles in edge-colored complete graphs. Random Structures & Algorithms **11**(2), 179–186 (1997)
4. Bang-Jensen, J., Gutin, G.: Alternating cycles and paths in edge-coloured multi-graphs: A survey. Discrete Mathematics **165-166**, 39 – 60 (1997)
5. Barnat, J., Brim, L., Krejci, A., Streck, A., Safranek, D., Vejnar, M., Vejpustek, T.: On parameter synthesis by parallel model checking. IEEE/ACM Transactions on Computational Biology and Bioinformatics **9**(3), 693–705 (2012)
6. Barnat, J., Beneš, N., Brim, L., Demko, M., Hajnal, M., Pastva, S., Šafránek, D.: Detecting attractors in biological models with uncertain parameters. In: Computational Methods in Systems Biology (CMSB 2017). Lecture Notes in Computer Science, vol. 10545, pp. 40–56. Springer (2017)
7. Barnat, J., Bauch, P., Brim, L., Češka, M.: Computing strongly connected components in parallel on CUDA. In: 25th IEEE International Symposium on Parallel and Distributed Processing, IPDPS 2011 - Conference Proceedings. pp. 544–555. IEEE (2011)
8. Barnat, J., Chaloupka, J., Van De Pol, J.: Distributed algorithms for SCC decomposition. J. Log. and Comput. **21**(1), 23–44 (2011)
9. Batt, G., Page, M., Cantone, I., Goessler, G., Monteiro, P.T., de Jong, H.: Efficient parameter search for qualitative models of regulatory networks using symbolic model checking. Bioinformatics **26**(18) (2010)
10. Behzad, M., Chartrand, G., Lesniak-Foster, L.: Graphs and Digraphs. Wadsworth Publishing (1979)

11. Beneš, N., Brim, L., Pastva, S., Poláček, J., Šafránek, D.: Formal analysis of qualitative long-term behaviour in parametrised boolean networks. In: Ait-Ameur, Y., Qin, S. (eds.) Formal Methods and Software Engineering. pp. 353–369. Springer International Publishing, Cham (2019)
12. Beneš, N., Brim, L., Pastva, S., Šafránek, D.: AEON: attractor bifurcation analysis of parametrised boolean networks. In: Computer Aided Verification - 32nd International Conference, CAV 2020. Lecture Notes in Computer Science, vol. 12224. Springer International Publishing, Cham (2020)
13. Beneš, N., Brim, L., Pastva, S., Poláček, J., Šafránek, D.: Formal analysis of qualitative long-term behaviour in parametrised boolean networks. In: Formal Methods and Software Engineering (ICFEM 2019). Lecture Notes in Computer Science, vol. 11852, pp. 353–369. Springer (2019)
14. Bloem, R., Gabow, H.N., Somenzi, F.: An algorithm for strongly connected component analysis in n log n symbolic steps. In: Formal Methods in Computer-Aided Design (FMCAD 2000). pp. 37–54. Lecture Notes in Computer Science, Springer-Verlag (2000)
15. Bloemen, V., Laarman, A., van de Pol, J.: Multi-core on-the-fly SCC decomposition. In: Proceedings of the 21st ACM SIGPLAN Symposium on Principles and Practice of Parallel Programming. PPoPP '16, ACM, New York, NY, USA (2016)
16. Brim, L., Češka, M., Šafránek, D.: Model checking of biological systems. In: Formal Methods for Dynamical Systems. pp. 63–112. Springer Berlin Heidelberg (2013)
17. Bryant, R.E.: Graph-based algorithms for boolean function manipulation. IEEE Trans. Comput. **35**(8), 677–691 (1986)
18. Burch, J.R., Clarke, E.M., McMillan, K.L., Dill, D.L., Hwang, L.J.: Symbolic model checking: 10^20 states and beyond. Inf. Comput. **98**(2), 142–170 (1992)
19. Chaouiya, C., Naldi, A., Thieffry, D.: Logical modelling of gene regulatory networks with ginsim. In: Bacterial Molecular Networks, pp. 463–479. Springer (2012)
20. Chatterjee, K., Dvořák, W., Henzinger, M., Loitzenbauer, V.: Lower bounds for symbolic computation on graphs: Strongly connected components, liveness, safety, and diameter. In: Proceedings of the Twenty-Ninth Annual ACM-SIAM Symposium on Discrete Algorithms (SODA 2018). pp. 2341–2356. SIAM (2018)
21. Choo, S.M., Cho, K.H.: An efficient algorithm for identifying primary phenotype attractors of a large-scale boolean network. BMC Systems Biology **10**(1), 95 (2016)
22. Ciardo, G., Marmorstein, R.M., Siminiceanu, R.: The saturation algorithm for symbolic state-space exploration. Int. J. Softw. Tools Technol. Transf. **8**(1), 4–25 (2006)
23. Couvreur, J., Thierry-Mieg, Y.: Hierarchical decision diagrams to exploit model structure. In: FORTE 2005. Lecture Notes in Computer Science, vol. 3731, pp. 443–457. Springer (2005). https://doi.org/10.1007/11562436_32
24. Deritei, D., Aird, W.C., Ercsey-Ravasz, M., Regan, E.R.: Principles of dynamical modularity in biological regulatory networks. Nature Scientific Reports **6**, 21957 (2016)
25. Dorninger, D.: Hamiltonian circuits determining the order of chromosomes. Discrete Applied Mathematics **50**(2), 159 – 168 (1994)
26. Fleischer, L.K., Hendrickson, B., Pınar, A.: On identifying strongly connected components in parallel. In: Parallel and Distributed Processing. Lecture Notes in Computer Science, vol. 1800, pp. 505–511. Springer (2000)
27. Gentilini, R., Piazza, C., Policriti, A.: Computing strongly connected components in a linear number of symbolic steps. In: Proceedings of the Twenty-Ninth Annual ACM-SIAM Symposium on Discrete Algorithms (SODA 2003). vol. 3, pp. 573–582. SIAM (2003)

28. Gentilini, R., Piazza, C., Policriti, A.: Symbolic graphs: Linear solutions to connectivity related problems. Algorithmica **50**(1), 120–158 (2008)
29. Giacobbe, M., Guet, C.C., Gupta, A., Henzinger, T.A., Paixão, T., Petrov, T.: Model checking the evolution of gene regulatory networks. Acta Informatica **54**(8), 765–787 (2017)
30. Hong, S., Rodia, N.C., Olukotun, K.: On fast parallel detection of strongly connected components (SCC) in small-world graphs. In: Proceedings of the International Conference on High Performance Computing, Networking, Storage and Analysis. SC 2013, ACM, New York, NY, USA (2013)
31. Irons, D.: Logical analysis of the budding yeast cell cycle. Journal of theoretical biology **257**(4), 543–559 (2009)
32. Jiang, B.: I/O- and CPU-optimal recognition of strongly connected components. Information Processing Letters **45**(3), 111 – 115 (1993)
33. Kano, M., Li, X.: Monochromatic and heterochromatic subgraphs in edge-colored graphs - a survey. Graphs and Combinatorics **24**(4), 237–263 (2008)
34. Kauffman, S.: Metabolic stability and epigenesis in randomly constructed genetic nets. Journal of Theoretical Biology **22**(3), 437–467 (1969)
35. Király, Z.: Monochromatic components in edge-colored complete uniform hypergraphs. European Journal of Combinatorics **35**, 374 – 376 (2014)
36. Klamt, S., Saez-Rodriguez, J., Lindquist, J.A., Simeoni, L., Gilles, E.D.: A methodology for the structural and functional analysis of signaling and regulatory networks. BMC bioinformatics **7**(1), 56 (2006)
37. Li, G., Zhu, Z., Cong, Z., Yang, F.: Efficient decomposition of strongly connected components on GPUs. Journal of Systems Architecture **60**(1), 1 – 10 (2014)
38. Li, Q., Wennborg, A., Aurell, E., Dekel, E., Zou, J.Z., Xu, Y., Huang, S., Ernberg, I.: Dynamics inside the cancer cell attractor reveal cell heterogeneity, limits of stability, and escape. Proceedings of the National Academy of Sciences **113**(10), 2672–2677 (2016)
39. Matouk, A.: Complex dynamics in susceptible-infected models for covid-19 with multi-drug resistance. Chaos, Solitons & Fractals **140**, 110257 (2020)
40. Mbodj, A., Junion, G., Brun, C., Furlong, E.E., Thieffry, D.: Logical modelling of drosophila signalling pathways. Molecular BioSystems **9**(9), 2248–2258 (2013)
41. Mendoza, L., Xenarios, I.: A method for the generation of standardized qualitative dynamical systems of regulatory networks. Theoretical Biology and Medical Modelling **3**(1), 13 (2006)
42. Mizera, A., Pang, J., Qu, H., Yuan, Q.: Taming asynchrony for attractor detection in large boolean networks. IEEE/ACM Transactions on Computational Biology and Bioinformatics **16**(1), 31–42 (2019)
43. Orlando, D.A., Lin, C.Y., Bernard, A., Wang, J.Y., Socolar, J.E., Iversen, E.S., Hartemink, A.J., Haase, S.B.: Global control of cell-cycle transcription by coupled CDK and network oscillators. Nature **453**(7197), 944–947 (2008)
44. Orzan, S.: On Distributed Verification and Verified Distribution. Ph.D. thesis, Free University Amsterdam (2005)
45. Reif, J.H.: Depth-first search is inherently sequential. Information Processing Letters **20**(5), 229 – 234 (1985)
46. Richard, A., Comet, J.P., Bernot, G.: Graph-based modeling of biological regulatory networks: Introduction of singular states. In: Computational Methods in Systems Biology (CMSB 2005). Lecture Notes in Computer Science, vol. 3082, pp. 58–72. Springer (2005)
47. Saad, R.: Sur quelques problèmes de complexité dans les graphes. Ph.D. thesis, U. de Paris-Sud, Orsay (1992)

48. Sánchez-Osorio, I., Hernández-Martínez, C.A., Martínez-Antonio, A.: Modeling asymmetric cell division in caulobacter crescentus using a boolean logic approach. In: Asymmetric Cell Division in Development, Differentiation and Cancer, pp. 1–21. Springer (2017)
49. Schwab, J.D., Kühlwein, S.D., Ikonomi, N., Kühl, M., Kestler, H.A.: Concepts in boolean network modeling: What do they all mean? Computational and Structural Biotechnology Journal **18**, 571–582 (2020)
50. Sharir, M.: A strong-connectivity algorithm and its applications in data flow analysis. Computers & Mathematics with Applications **7**(1), 67–72 (1981)
51. Slota, G.M., Rajamanickam, S., Madduri, K.: BFS and coloring-based parallel algorithms for strongly connected components and related problems. In: 2014 IEEE 28th International Parallel and Distributed Processing Symposium. pp. 550–559 (2014)
52. Steffen, W., Rockström, J., Richardson, K., Lenton, T.M., Folke, C., Liverman, D., Summerhayes, C.P., Barnosky, A.D., Cornell, S.E., Crucifix, M., Donges, J.F., Fetzer, I., Lade, S.J., Scheffer, M., Winkelmann, R., Schellnhuber, H.J.: Trajectories of the earth system in the anthropocene. Proceedings of the National Academy of Sciences **115**(33), 8252–8259 (2018)
53. Tarjan, R.E.: Depth-first search and linear graph algorithms. SIAM J. Comput. **1**(2), 146–160 (1972)
54. Thomas, R.: Boolean formalization of genetic control circuits. Journal of Theoretical Biology **42**(3), 563–585 (1973)
55. Thomason, A., Wagner, P.: Complete graphs with no rainbow path. Journal of Graph Theory **54**(3), 261–266 (2007)
56. Wijs, A., Katoen, J.P., Bošnački, D.: GPU-based graph decomposition into strongly connected and maximal end components. In: Computer Aided Verification (CAV 2014). Lecture Notes in Computer Science, vol. 8559, pp. 310–326. Springer (2014)
57. Xie, A., Beerel, P.A.: Implicit enumeration of strongly connected components and an application to formal verification. IEEE Transactions on Computer-Aided Design of Integrated Circuits and Systems **19**(10), 1225–1230 (2000)
58. Yuan, Q., Mizera, A., Pang, J., Qu, H.: A new decomposition-based method for detecting attractors in synchronous boolean networks. Science of Computer Programming **180**, 18–35 (2019)
59. Zhao, Y., Ciardo, G.: Symbolic computation of strongly connected components and fair cycles using saturation. Innov. Syst. Softw. Eng. **7**(2), 141–150 (2011)
60. Zou, Y.M.: Boolean networks with multiexpressions and parameters. IEEE/ACM Transactions on Computational Biology and Bioinformatics **10**, 584–592 (2013)

Case Studies

Local Search with a SAT Oracle for Combinatorial Optimization

Aviad Cohen, Alexander Nadel⬡✉ and Vadim Ryvchin

Intel Corporation, P.O. Box 1659, Haifa 31015, Israel
{aviad.cohen,alexander.nadel}@intel.com,vadimryv@gmail.com

Abstract. NP-hard combinatorial optimization problems are pivotal in science and business. There exists a variety of approaches for solving such problems, but for problems with complex constraints and objective functions, local search algorithms scale the best. Such algorithms usually assume that finding a non-optimal solution with no other requirements is easy. However, what if it is NP-hard? In such case, a SAT solver can be used for finding the initial solution, but how can one continue solving the optimization problem? We offer a generic methodology, called *Local Search with SAT Oracle (LSSO)*, to solve such problems. LSSO facilitates implementation of advanced local search methods, such as variable neighbourhood search, hill climbing and iterated local search, while using a SAT solver as an oracle. We have successfully applied our approach to solve a critical industrial problem of cell placement and productized our solution at Intel.

1 Introduction

Real-life *combinatorial optimization problems* are pivotal in science, operations research, engineering, economics, and business [11,13,20,21,23].

Loosely speaking, an instance of a combinatorial optimization problem deals with the minimization of an objective function over a finite set, subject to *feasibility constraints* (or, simply, *constraints*). The set of all elements satisfying the constraints is referred to as the set of *feasible solutions* (or, simply, *solutions*). In this paper, we focus on solving any problem, which can be expressed as a constraint optimization program (COP) [2]. Arguably, the vast majority of combinatorial problems, encountered in practice, fall under this category.

Many important combinatorial problems are NP-hard. For such problems, various algorithmic strategies have been devised, including complete methods, such as branch-and-bound and dynamic programming, and incomplete methods, such as greedy algorithms and local search. Each such method imposes requirements on the mathematical properties of the problem with a consequent limit on the scope of applicability.

Local search algorithms stand out from the rest in that they impose relatively mild constraints on the type of the problem to be addressed, thus providing a wide scope of applicability. Furthermore, they seem to scale better with input size relative to complete algorithms [24]. This makes local search algorithms an attractive choice. However, local search algorithms may return a low-quality solution or no solution at all, given a problem for which the mere task of finding a feasible solution is NP-hard. Henceforth, we shall refer to such problems as *NP-Hard-Feasible* problems.

© The Author(s) 2021
J. F. Groote and K. G. Larsen (Eds.): TACAS 2021, LNCS 12652, pp. 87–104, 2021.
https://doi.org/10.1007/978-3-030-72013-1_5

This paper introduces the *Local Search with SAT Oracle* (LSSO) methodology, that is, local search algorithms which use a SAT solver (or a SAT-based optimization algorithm; details appear later) as an oracle. A key advantage of our approach is that it can handle problems with complex constraints and objective functions. In particular, it can handle NP-Hard-Feasible problems.

To see how SAT solvers might be useful, consider the basic version of a local search for an optimal solution. At the beginning, the local search generates an initial solution and sets it as the current solution. Then, it enters a loop. In each iteration, it looks for a solution with a lower value of the objective function *within a neighbourhood* of the current one. If such a solution is found, it is set to be the current solution, and the execution resumes. Otherwise, the algorithm terminates and returns the current solution.

A key component of local search algorithms is the *neighbourhood function*, which assigns to each feasible solution a subset of feasible solutions, called its *neighbourhood*. Ordinarily, a neighbourhood of the current feasible solution comprises a set of solutions which can be obtained from the current solution by applying a small collection of *feasibility-preserving* perturbations to its combinatorial structure. A key concern is ensuring that neighbourhoods: (i) are polynomially searchable, and (ii) contain high-quality solutions. However, meeting *both* requirements might be challenging, since polynomial searchability implies that neighbourhoods should be small, and hence less likely to contain high-quality solutions. In addition, in the case of NP-Hard-Feasible problems, it is not clear how to achieve polynomial searchability, since a search should, in particular, be able to find a feasible solution, which is NP-hard.

Our main idea is to let the SAT solver both find an initial solution and conduct the neighbourhood search. The designer can now define feasibility constraints and neighbourhoods declaratively, that is, by a set of SAT constraints. The designer has more freedom to choose neighbourhoods, which need neither be small, nor contain only solutions close to the current solution. This is because the search of the now complex and possibly large neighbourhoods is entrusted to SAT solvers, constructed precisely to efficiently search large complex subspaces. Our approach lends itself to implementations of advanced local search variants, such as variable neighbourhood search, hill climbing and iterated local search [29].

An important feature of our algorithms is that they are *anytime*. Recall that an anytime algorithm is expected to return a valid solution even if interrupted. An anytime algorithm for an optimization problem is expected to find an *improving* set of solutions. The anytime property is essential for industrial application, since it allows the user to get an approximate solution even for very difficult instances [14, 15].

We demonstrate the usefulness of our approach by solving hard industrial instances of the NP-Hard-Feasible cell placement problem. Cell placement is one of the most important problems in VLSI automation [28]. Its most basic version concerns placing without overlap a set of rectangles on a grid, while minimizing the occupied area. In reality, the problem is more complex. Our approach has been successfully productized at Intel.

The rest of this paper is organized as follows: Sect. 2 provides the necessary background. Sect. 3 introduces our LSSO methodology. Sect. 4 shows how to solve placement with LSSO. Sect. 5 presents the experimental results. Sect. 6 concludes our paper.

2 Background

This section provides some background. Sect. 2.1 is an overview of COP. Sect. 2.2 describes the cell placement problem and shows how to reduce it to COP. Sect. 2.3 discusses how one can solve a COP using a SAT-based bit-vector solver. Sect. 2.4 reviews local search.

2.1 Constraint Optimization Program (COP)

This work presents a new methodology for solving a wide class of combinatorial optimization problems, which can be expressed as a Constraint Optimization Program, shown in Def. 1.

Definition 1 (Constraint Optimization Program (COP) [2]). *A constraint optimization program is a tuple* $(\mathcal{X}, \mathcal{D}, \mathcal{C}, \Psi)$ *where:*

1. $\mathcal{X} = \{x_1 \dots x_n\}$ *is a finite set of variables often referred to as* decision variables.
2. $\mathcal{D} = \{\mathcal{D}_1 \dots \mathcal{D}_n\}$ *is a corresponding set of* finite *domains. Without loss of generality, each* $\mathcal{D}_i$ *is assumed to be a closed bounded interval of non-negative integers.*
3. $\mathcal{C} = \{\mathcal{C}_1 \dots \mathcal{C}_m\}$ *is a finite set of constraints* $\mathcal{C}_k : \mathcal{D}_1 \times \dots \times \mathcal{D}_n \mapsto \{0, 1\}$.
4. $\Psi : \mathcal{D}_1 \times \dots \times \mathcal{D}_n \mapsto \mathbb{Z}$ *is an objective function to be minimized.*

2.2 The Cell Placement Problem

Cell Placement (Placement) is a major stage in the VLSI design cycle [8,16]. The input of the cell placement problem comprises the following components:

1. A *rectangular grid region* of M rows and N columns, on which the cells are to be placed. Row/column line numbering starts at 0 and ends at M/N, respectively.
2. A finite set $\mathcal{C}$ of *rectangular cells*. The width and the height of each cell $c \in \mathcal{C}$ are assumed to be positive integers, denoted by $c^{width} : 0 < c^{width} \leq N$ and $c^{height} : 0 < c^{height} \leq M$, respectively.
3. A set $\mathcal{R}$ of *forbidden rectangular regions*. A forbidden region $r \in \mathcal{R}$ is specified by 4 numbers $r^{west}, r^{south}, r^{east}$ and r^{north} (where, $0 \leq r^{west}, r^{east} < N; 0 \leq r^{south}, r^{north} < M; r^{east} > r^{west}; r^{north} > r^{south}$), denoting the leftmost column line, bottom row line, rightmost column line, and top row line, respectively.
4. A finite set $\mathcal{I}$ of *nets*, each consisting of a non-empty subset of cells. The nets may (and usually do) intersect.

We are interested in *feasible* placements, that is, placements in which no cell overlaps other cells or forbidden regions. Given a feasible placement, we define the *size of a net* $n \in \mathcal{I}$ as the perimeter of the box bounding its placed cells. We define the *size of the placement* as the sum of the sizes of the nets. We are required to find a feasible placement of a minimal size. An example is shown in Fig. 1.

In industrial practice, there may be additional *industrial requirements*, such as aligning some of the cells, enforcing parity constraints (i.e., the user might require the y coordinates of some of the cells to be either even or odd) [19], ensuring a minimal distance between some of the cells and others. We omit further details due to IP considerations.

Placement is NP-Hard-Feasible, since the NP-complete bin packing problem can be reduced to the decision version of the placement problem [10].

2.2.1   Constraint Optimization Program for Cell Placement. We show how to construct a COP for the cell placement problem. For each cell $c \in \mathcal{C}$, let c^{west} and c^{east} denote its leftmost and rightmost column respectively, and c^{south} and c^{north} denote its bottom and top row. Strictly speaking, it suffices to use c^{west} and c^{south} as the COP's independent variables, but it is convenient to use c^{east} and c^{north} as syntactic sugar for $c^{west} + c^{width}$ and $c^{south} + c^{height}$, respectively. The COP looks as follows:

1. *Variables:* $\{c^{west}, c^{south} \mid c \in \mathcal{C}\}$
2. *Domains:* $c^{west} \in [0 \ldots N - 1]$ and $c^{south} \in [0 \ldots M - 1]$
3. *Feasibility constraints:*
   (a) Each cell c is placed wholly within the grid region:

$$(c^{west} \geq 0) \wedge (c^{east} \leq N) \wedge (c^{south} \geq 0) \wedge (c^{north} \leq M)$$

   (b) For every pair of cells $\langle c_i, c_j \rangle$, such that $i < j$, there is no overlap:

$$(c_i^{west} \geq c_j^{east}) \vee (c_j^{west} \geq c_i^{east}) \vee (c_i^{south} \geq c_j^{north}) \vee (c_j^{south} \geq c_i^{north})$$

   (c) For every pair $\langle r, c \rangle$ of a forbidden region r and a cell c, there is no overlap:

$$(r^{west} \geq c^{east}) \vee (c^{west} \geq r^{east}) \vee (r^{south} \geq c^{north}) \vee (c^{south} \geq r^{north})$$

   (d) Constraints representing any additional industrial requirements.
4. *Objective function Ψ:* for every net $n \in \mathbb{I}$, let $\|n\|$ denote its size. We have:

$$\|n\| = \left(\max_{c \in n}(c^{east}) - \min_{c \in n}(c^{west}) \right) + \left(\max_{c \in n}(c^{north}) - \min_{c \in n}(c^{south}) \right)$$

$$\Psi = \sum_{n \in \mathbb{I}} \|n\|$$

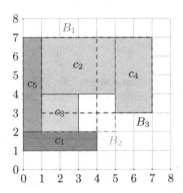

Fig. 1: Placement example [16]. A solution is shown for the problem of placing five cells c_1, c_2, c_3, c_4 and c_5 of sizes 4×1, 4×3, 2×2, 2×4 and 1×5 respectively, on a grid with $M = N = 8$. There are three nets: $n_1 = \{c_1, c_3, c_5\}$, $n_2 = \{c_2, c_3\}$ and $n_3 = \{c_2, c_4\}$ (without any forbidden regions). The bounding boxes of the nets are B_1, B_2 and B_3, respectively. The sizes of the nets, comprising the perimeters of the bounding boxes, are 20, 18 and 20, respectively. The overall placement size is $20 + 18 + 20 = 58$. The solution is an optimal one.

2.3 Solving COP with SAT

A COP can be solved with various types of solvers [2]. In particular, it is possible to solve a COP by reduction to a series of SAT solver invocations through bit-vector reasoning as explained below.

2.3.1 Bit-vector Solving and SAT.

We start with reviewing the basic terminology, related to SAT solving. A *literal* l is a Boolean variable v or its negation $\neg v$. A clause is a disjunction of literals. A formula F is in *Conjunctive Normal Form (CNF)* if it is a conjunction (set) of clauses.

A SAT solver [4] receives a CNF formula F and returns a satisfying assignment (aka, model or solution), if one exists. In *incremental SAT solving under assumptions* [5, 18], the user may invoke the SAT solver multiple times, each time with a different set of *assumption literals* (called, simply, the *assumptions*) and, possibly, additional clauses. The solver then checks the satisfiability of all the clauses provided so far, while enforcing the values of the current assumptions.

A *bit-vector variable (bit-vector)* of *width* $n = |B|$, $B = \{v_n, v_{n-1}, \ldots, v_1\}$, is a sequence of n Boolean variables, called *bits*. Bit v_1 is the Least Significant Bit (LSB) and v_n is the Most Significant Bit (MSB). A *Boolean constant* is either $\bot$ (0) or $\top$ (1). A *bit-vector constant* is a bit-vector (BV), each one of whose bits is substituted by a Boolean constant. A *bit-vector term* is either a bit-vector, a BV constant, or a result of applying an operator which returns a bit-vector (for example, BV addition, if-then-else, concatenation) over other terms and atoms. An *atom* is either a Boolean variable, a Boolean constant or a result of applying an operator, which returns a Boolean (for example, $=$ or unsigned-less-than), over BV terms and atoms. A *bit-vector formula* (also known as a *bit-vector constraint*) is recursively defined to be either an atom, a negation of a bit-vector formula, or the result of applying the Boolean operator $\wedge$ or the Boolean operator $\vee$ over two or more bit-vector formulas. See [3, 12] for a rigorous description of the BV language. A BV solver decides the satisfiability of BV formulas.

A BV formula F is *satisfiable* iff it has a *model*, that is, an assignment of BV and Boolean constants to their corresponding BV and Boolean variables, which satisfies F. In this paper, BV constants are interpreted as unsigned numbers, and BV comparison operators are interpreted as unsigned. For example, given a bit-vector $B = \{v_3, v_2, v_1\}$, the formula $F = B < 2$ has two models $\mu_1 : \mu_1(B) = 0$ and $\mu_2 : \mu_2(B) = 1$.

All the algorithms presented in this work are assumed to use the so-called *eager* BV solver [6] which, following some preprocessing, translates the input BV formula to an equisatisfiable formula in CNF and solves it with a SAT solver. Thus, we will use the notions of BV solving and SAT solving interchangeably. We also assume the BV solver to have the same incremental API as a SAT solver.

Since the variables in a COP have finite domains, both the variables and the constraints of a COP can be easily expressed as BV variables and BV constraints.

In particular, in the COP constructed for the cell placement problem in Sect. 2.2.1, the variables and the constraints can be expressed as BV variables and constraints as follows: For each cell c, we define four bit-vectors: c^{west} and c^{east} of width $\lceil \log N \rceil$ as well as c^{south} and c^{north} of width $\lceil \log M \rceil$. All the constraints in our COP involve these bit-vectors and can be expressed in terms of operators and relations available in the BV language [3]. Specifically, we implement min and max operators using a series of if-then-else operators. In addition, for every operator, we zero-extend the widths of the operands and the resulting bit-vector to prevent an overflow, whenever required.

Reducing the constraints of a COP to a BV formula and invoking BV solver suffices to find one non-optimal solution. However, for solving the optimization problem by reduction to BV, one needs an extension of BV solving to optimization.[1]

2.3.2 Extending Bit-vector Solving to Optimization.
One can extend bit-vector solving to the so-called Bit-Vector Optimization (OBV) [19] as follows:

A model μ of a BV formula F is T-minimal, for a given bit-vector T, iff $\mu(T) \leq \nu(T)$ (where the comparison is unsigned) for every model ν of F. Given a BV formula F and a term $T = \{t_n, t_{n-1}, \ldots, t_1\}$ in F, where T is called the *optimization target* (or, simply, the *target*), *Bit-Vector Optimization (OBV)* is the problem of finding a T-minimal model of F. The bits of the target T are referred to as the *target bits*.

Translating our placement COP to OBV is straightforward. We have already shown how to translate the constraints. The optimization target is constructed in the same way as the objective function Ψ is constructed in the COP.

How can one solve OBV in practice? First, one can use the following simple anytime Linear Search algorithm, implemented on top of an incremental BV solver [16,27]:

1: $solver.Assert(F)$; $\mu := solver.Sat()$ ▷ assert F and find the first solution
2: **while** μ is a solution **do**   ▷ while there is still a solution
3:     $solver.Assert(T < \mu(T))$ ▷ block all the solutions with cost $\geq \mu(T)$
4:     $\mu := solver.Sat()$ ▷ can we improve our solution?
5: **return** μ ▷ μ is guaranteed to be T-minimal

Another anytime algorithm to solve OBV is the following binary search-based algorithm, called OBV-BS [9, 19]:

1: $solver.Assert(F)$; $\mu := solver.Sat()$ ▷ assert F and find the first solution
2: $i := n$ ▷ i is the current bit number, initialized to the MSB
3: **while** $i \geq 1$ and $\mu(t_i) = \bot$ **do**   ▷ fix to $\bot$ the MSBs, assigned to $\bot$ in μ
4:     $solver.Assert(\neg t_i)$
5:     $i := i - 1$ ▷ after the loop, i will point to the first target bit, assigned $\top$
6: **while** $i \geq 1$ **do**   ▷ Check one-by-one, if we can flip the remaining target bits to $\bot$
7:     $\mu := solver.Sat(\{\neg t_i\})$ ▷ run the solver under the assumption $\neg t_i$
8:     **if** satisfiable **then**
9:        **while** ($i \geq 1$ and $\mu(t_i) = \bot$) **do** $solver.Assert(\neg t_i)$; $i := i - 1$ **endwhile**
10:     **else**
11:        $solver.Assert(t_i)$; $i := i - 1$ ▷ t_i cannot be flipped to $\bot$, so we fix it to $\top$
12: **return** μ

We have successfully applied OBV-BS for solving the problem of *fixing* an existing placement [19], closely related to the generic placement problem, we are exploring

---

[1] One cannot use MaxSAT [26]–the widely used extension of SAT to optimizing a linear Pseudo-Boolean (PB) function–to solve COP in the generic case, since the objective function is not guaranteed to be linear PB. In particular, it is *not* linear PB for placement, if only because the variables are bit-vectors, rather than Booleans.

in this work. However, both Linear Search and OBV-BS failed to scale to industrial instances of our current problem of finding an optimal placement from scratch (with Linear Search scaling somewhat better than OBV-BS).

Recently, we have introduced the so-called Polosat anytime algorithm [16], which can be used *instead* of the standard SAT solver inside Linear Search (and other SAT-based anytime optimization algorithms) to make it substantially more scalable. The idea behind Polosat, shown below, is to simulate local search using a SAT solver. We use the strictly-monotone version of Polosat [16], which assumes the availability of the so-called Boolean *observable variables (observables) Obs*, that is, a set of Boolean variables on which the objective function depends (for placement, the observables might comprise the bits of the bit-vectors, representing the sizes of the nets, for every net). Polosat is carried out by getting a model μ and then trying to improve it by repeatedly flipping observables, which have not been assigned $\bot$ in previous models:

1: **function** SOLVER.POLOSAT(assumptions)
Require: Target bit-vector T is available; Observables *Obs* are available.
2:      $\mu := solver.Sat(assumptions)$ ▷ get the first model μ
3:      $is\_good\_epoch := 1$ ▷ good epoch: an iteration, which improves μ
4:      **while** is_good_epoch **do**   ▷ one loop is an epoch
5:          $B := \{v : v \in Obs, \mu(v) = \top\}$ ▷ remove any observables, assigned $\bot$
6:          $is\_good\_epoch := 0$
7:          **while** B is not empty **do**
8:              $b_i := B.front(); B.dequeue()$
9:              $\sigma := solver.Sat(assumptions \cup \{\neg b_i\})$ ▷ trying to flip b_i
10:             **if** satisfiable **then**
11:                 **if** $\sigma(T) < \mu(T)$ **then** $\mu := \sigma$ and $is\_good\_epoch := 1$
12:                 $B := \{b : b \in B, \sigma(t) = 1\}$ ▷ remove any observables, assigned $\bot$
13:     **return** μ

To combine Polosat into Linear Search, it is sufficient to replace solver.Sat invocations by solver.Polosat invocations in the code. [2] We have shown in [16] that replacing plain SAT invocations by Polosat invocations in Linear Search makes our placement tool substantially more scalable. We reaffirm this result in Sect. 5.

Yet, despite the significant progress we had witnessed when applying Polosat, we found that combining Polosat into Linear Search is still insufficient for solving a variety of complex real-world instances of our industrial placement problem. This empirical challenge lead us to develop our LSSO methodology, presented in this paper. As we shall see, combining LSSO and Polosat makes our tool considerably more scalable, while the methodology itself is generic and can be applied to solving a wide range of optimization problems.

2.4 Local Search Algorithms

Local search strategies [1] are a collection of *algorithmic templates*. An algorithmic template specifies the main flow of an algorithm, but leaves some details unimple-

---

[2] Polosat also uses polarity fixing strategies, such as TORC [14,17], omitted here; please refer to [16] for details. Additional non-anytime OBV algorithms are introduced in [19,22].

mented. By implementing these details for a specific problem, one obtains an algorithmic solution for that problem.

2.4.1   Basic Local Search Strategy. The basic strategy generates an initial feasible solution and sets it as the *current solution*. Then, it enters a loop. In each iteration, it looks within a *neighbourhood* of the current solution for a feasible solution with a lower value of the objective function. If one is found, it is set to be the current solution. Otherwise, the algorithm is terminated returning the current solution. Note that this version is guaranteed to stop; it does so, when it reaches a *local minimum* of the objective function with respect to the neighbourhood used.

To turn this algorithmic template into a complete algorithm, one has to implement the following *problem-dependent* items: (i) A procedure for generating an initial feasible element. (ii) A *neighbourhood function* assigning to each solution a subset of solutions. (iii) An algorithm for searching the neighbourhood for a better solution.

2.4.2   Neighbourhood Functions. A key factor, which affects both the complexity of the search and the quality of the resulting solution, is the selection of a *neighbourhood function*. In theory, the selection ought to depend on a mathematical analysis of the structure of the feasible set and the profile of the objective function. For complex problems, such an analysis is usually beyond reach. The classical approach to neighbourhood definition is based on the following problem-independent general principles:

1. Drawing on an analogy to optimization algorithms in the continuous case (such as gradient descent or line search), a neighbourhood should be so defined as to make its elements "close" to the current solution. So, typically, the neighbourhood of a feasible solution is specified by a small class of *feasibility-preserving* modifications/perturbations to its combinatorial structure.
2. A neighbourhood should be so defined as to ensure that it is *polynomially searchable*. Hence, unless we have a sophisticated non-exhaustive neighbourhood search algorithm, neighbourhoods should be small.

However, as we have argued in Sect. 1, this approach is not without issues. In particular, feasibility-preserving perturbations may not be easy to find, especially for NP-Hard-Feasible problems, while having small neighbourhoods implies a low likelihood of high-quality solutions.

2.4.3   Advanced Versions of Local Search. A disadvantage of the basic version of local search is that it may stop at a local minimum of a poor quality, if too small a region of the feasible space is explored. To circumvent this outcome, advanced variants enabling an exploration of larger portions of the feasible space have been devised [7, 29]. Those described here provide some mechanism to escape from the local minimum to "nearby" solutions and resume the search from there. They have been designed to accommodate situations, where local minima are not distributed uniformly in the feasibility space, but are rather clustered in close proximity [25].

The *variable neighbourhood search* approach uses multiple neighbourhoods to escape from local minima. It relies on the fact that a local minimum with respect to one neighbourhood need not be a local minimum with respect to another (if the latter is not contained in the former). The algorithm maintains a set of neighbourhood functions. Once a local minimum with respect to the current neighbourhood is reached, the neighbourhood is switched, and the search is resumed.

The *hill climbing* method allows the selection of a non-improving solution, once a local minimum is reached. Since the objective function no longer monotonically decreases, there is now a possibility of a cycle: a solution may be visited more than once forcing the search into an infinite loop. One can deal with this problem in various ways: ignore it and let the algorithm run until the timeout expires, use randomization, or introduce data structures that keep track of the search history and prohibit solutions that have already been encountered. The latter approach is referred to as *tabu search*.

Another idea is to use *large neighbourhoods*. This approach increases the size of the explored region and the likelihood of better solutions. However, large neighbourhood search may become intractable.

The *iterated local search* approach can be viewed as "a local search within a local search". In each iteration of the search, it uses a *subsidiary search algorithm* to explore iteratively a feasible sub-space. Once a local minimum is returned, a new search is initiated in a region, whose elements are obtained by "perturbing" the recent solution.

All the above approaches can be implemented within our LSSO framework. The key difference between LSSO and previous approaches is using SAT or Polosat as an oracle for both finding the initial solution and carrying out the neighbourhood search.

3   Local Search with SAT Oracle (LSSO)

This section introduces the main contribution of our paper. We propose using SAT as an oracle in local search algorithms to address the scalability and quality issues that arise in the classical local search algorithms, especially, given an NP-Hard-Feasible problem.

Given a combinatorial optimization problem, the first stage in designing an LSSO solution is expressing the problem as a COP.

In the second stage, the COP decision variables are translated to bit-vectors, and the feasibility constraints are translated to a BV formula (including any additional industrial requirements). One might experiment with several alternative formulations and select the one deemed best.

The third step is defining the so-called neighbourhood generators. A *neighbourhood generator* $\mathcal{N}(\mu)$ accepts as an input a solution μ (that is, a model to the bit-vector formula, representing the COP), and generates *neighbourhood constraints*. The set of all the assignments which satisfy the feasibility and neighbourhood constraints constitutes the neighbourhood of the solution. Thus, finding such an assignment amounts to finding an element of the neighbourhood of μ.

A key ingredient of our methodology is the adoption of a neighbourhood concept, which differs significantly from the classical one, described in Sect. 2.4.2:

1. The neighbourhood need not be small and need not contain (only) elements "close" to the current solution.

2. Normally, $\mathcal{N}(\mu)$ should generate constraints which ensure a cost lower than that of μ. If such a formulation is possible, then an iteration of the local search algorithm merely needs to find a model to these constraints in order to progress.
3. If the objective function is too complex to model in its entirety, a neighbourbood generator might attempt to ensure a better value for the objective function by imposing constraints on the objective function's sub-components. For example, when the objective function is a very large sum of bit-vector terms, one might impose constraints on the sum's terms or small partial sums thereof.
4. Notwithstanding the above, neighbourhood generators may support *hill climbing*, in which case, the constraints are so formulated as to admit non-improving solutions.

Note that, in our approach, neighbourhoods direct the search to "higher-quality" regions with respect to the current solution, regardless of the algorithmic difficulties of searching such regions. This is another key aspect of our approach: we trust SAT solvers to search complex sub-spaces efficiently.

Having discussed neighbourhoods, we are now ready to describe the simplest LSSO implementation:

1. A BV solver instance is created and the COP is provided to the solver. Specifically, we represent the COP's decision variables as bit-vectors, where the widths are chosen to accommodate the largest values. We provide the feasibility constraints to the solver as BV constraints. Then, we implement neighbourhood generators, which, given a feasible solution, return a set of BV constraints defining its neighbourhood.
2. The local search is carried out as follows:
   (a) The algorithm obtains an initial solution by asserting the feasibility constraints and asking the solver for a model. This model is set as the *current solution* μ.
   (b) The algorithm enters a loop, in which the solver operates in incremental mode. In each iteration, the algorithm calls the neighbourhood generator with the current solution as input, to generate a list of BV constraints. These are provided to the solver, which is asked for a model. If a model α is found, μ is set to α. Otherwise, the algorithm terminates returning μ.

The neighbourhood constraints can be given to the solver as either *assumptions* or *assertions*. This leads to two types of search, providing a tradeoff between execution time and quality:

1. *Non-speculative search*: the neighbourhood constraints are passed to the solver as *assertions*. Once assertions are passed to the solver, they are enforced in all ensuing iterations. The search proceeds through a monotone sequence of decreasing neighbourhoods until a local minimum is reached. Thus, the search is localized and is relatively fast at the possible expense of quality.
2. *Speculative search*: the neighbourhood constraints are passed to the solver as *assumptions*. The neighbourhood constraints are valid only for one iteration. Thus, the current neighbourhood is not intersected with previous neighbourhoods and a larger portion of the feasibility space will be explored. The search is expected to be slower, since the SAT solver handles assumptions less efficiently than assertions [18], but the quality of resulting solution is expected to be better, since the search can explore a greater part of the feasibility space, especially so by variable neighbourhood search and hill climbing.

Alg. 1 depicts our implementation of LSSO. The algorithm receives four inputs. The Boolean inputs $\mathcal{VNS}$, $\mathcal{HC}$, and $\mathcal{SPEC}$ specify whether variable neighbourhood search, hill climbing, and speculative search are to be used. All combinations are possible, except that *hill climbing requires speculative search*. The input $\mathcal{N}_{max}$ applies to variable neighbourhood search. It specifies an upper bound on the number of consecutive neighbourhood switches without finding a solution. If that bound is exceeded, the algorithm terminates with the current solution. To effect variable neighbourhood search, the algorithm uses a predefined list of neighbourhood generators $\mathcal{N} = [\mathcal{N}_0(\mu), \mathcal{N}_1(\mu) \ldots]$. The first generator $\mathcal{N}_0(\mu)$ is considered the default and is used most of the time. The others are used to escape local minima.

Alg. 1 carries out iterated local search with Polosat as an oracle, where the observables are recommended to be set to the bits of the inputs of the objective function. One can also replace the Polosat invocation by an ordinary SAT invocation.

4 LSSO Algorithms for the Cell Placement Problem

This section presents our LSSO-based placement algorithms. All the algorithms are instantiations of Alg. 1 with different sets of parameters. The BV constraints are generated by translating the COP constraints, as discussed in Sect. 2.3. Each algorithm uses some of the neighbourhood generators defined in Sect. 4.1.

The algorithms are presented in Sect. 4.2. None of the algorithms define the target bit-vector explicitly, since they rely on local search instead of OBV solving. By default, the algorithms use Polosat as the oracle, where the observables comprise all the bits of the bit-vectors, representing the sizes of the nets, where the size of net n is given by the following bit-vector term (for every intermediate term and the resulting term $\|n\|$, its width is set to the minimal possible width which prevents an overflow, where the operators are zero-extended, whenever required):

$$\|n\| = \left(\max_{c \in n}(c^{east}) - \min_{c \in n}(c^{west}) \right) + \left(\max_{c \in n}(c^{north}) - \min_{c \in n}(c^{south}) \right)$$

4.1 Neighbourhood Generators

4.1.1 Neighbourhood Generator N_1.

Let μ be a placement, that is, a model to the bit-vector formula representing the feasibility constraints. The neighbourhood $N_1(\mu)$ is designed for a highly localized fast search at the possible expense of quality. To this end, the constraints corresponding to $N_1(\mu)$ force a decrease of the objective function in a very constrained manner, so as to help the solver to come back quickly. $N_1(\mu)$ consists of all of legal placements, for which all the nets are no bigger and at least one net is smaller than under μ, thus ensuring a lower cost. The constraints are:

$$\overbrace{\left(\bigwedge_{n \in \mathbb{I}} (\|n\| \leq \mu(\|n\|)) \right)}^{each\ net\ is\ no\ bigger} \bigwedge \overbrace{\left(\bigvee_{n \in \mathbb{I}} (\|n\| < \mu(\|n\|)) \right)}^{at\ least\ one\ net\ is\ smaller}$$

Algorithm 1 Local Search with SAT Oracle (LSSO)

1: **procedure** LOCALSEARCH($\mathcal{VNS} = \top, \mathcal{HC} = \top, \mathcal{SPEC} = \top, \mathcal{N}_{max} = 10$)
Require: $\mathcal{L}$ ▷ feasibility constraints
Require: $\mathcal{N} := [\mathcal{N}_0(\mu), \mathcal{N}_1(\mu) \dots]$ ▷ neighbourhood constraints generators
Require: $\mathcal{J}(x)$ ▷ hill climbing constraints generator
      ▷ From now on, confine the search to the feasible space
2:     $solver.Assert(\mathcal{L})$
3:     $current \leftarrow solver.Sat()$ ▷ find the initial solution
4:     **if** $\neg current$ **then return** None   ▷ the problem is unsatisfiable
      ▷ Loop initialization
5:     $best \leftarrow current$
6:     $stop \leftarrow \bot$ ▷ stopping condition
7:     $jump \leftarrow \bot$ ▷ indicates whether hill climbing should be attempted
8:     $i \leftarrow 0$ ▷ current neighbourhood index
9:     **while** $\neg stop$ **do**
      ▷ Compute neighbourhood constraints
10:        **if** $\mathcal{HC} \wedge jump$ **then**   ▷ hill climbing is required
11:            $neighbourhood\_constraints := \mathcal{J}(current)$
12:        **else**   ▷ hill climbing is not required
13:            $neighbourhood\_constraints := \mathcal{N}[i](current)$
      ▷ If the mode is speculative, constraints are assumptions; otherwise they are assertions
14:        **if** $\mathcal{SPEC}$ **then**
15:            $assertions := []; assumptions := neighbourhood\_constraints$
16:        **else**
17:            $assertions := neighbourhood\_constraints; assumptions := []$
      ▷ Search for the next solution
18:        $solver.Assert(assertions)$
19:        $next \leftarrow solver.Polosat(assumptions)$
20:        **if** $next$ **then**   ▷ found a solution
21:            $current \leftarrow next; i \leftarrow 0; jump \leftarrow \bot$
22:            **if** $current.cost < best.cost$ **then** $best \leftarrow current$
23:            **continue**
      ▷ ▷ ▷ Solution not found
      ▷ If we are in variable neighbourhood mode and the number of consecutive neighbourhood switches without a model has not exceeded the bound, move to next neighbourhood
24:        **if** $\mathcal{VNS} \wedge (i < (\mathcal{N}_{max} - 1))$ **then**
25:            $i \leftarrow i + 1$
26:            **continue**
      ▷ If we are in hill climbing mode, and have exhausted the bound on neighbourhood switches without getting a model, and hill climbing has not already been attempted in this iteration, attempt it in the next iteration
27:        **if** $\mathcal{HC} \wedge \neg jump$ **then**
28:            $jump \leftarrow \top$
29:            **continue**
      ▷ If we got here, we are stuck and need to terminate
30:        $stop \leftarrow \top$
31:   **return** $best$

4.1.2 N_2: a Family of Neighbourhood Generators.

The N_2 family is designed for *variable neighbourhood search*. Each of its neighbourhoods strictly contains N_1 and allows the objective function to decrease in more ways. This implies higher quality solutions at the expense of slower convergence. To define the N_2 family, let $\alpha = \|\mathbb{I}\|$ be the number of the nets and assume $\alpha \geq 3$. For each permutation σ of $[1 \dots \alpha]$ and positive number $2 \leq d < \alpha$ we define a neighbourhood function $N_2[\sigma, d](\mu)$ as follows: Let $n_{\sigma(1)}, \dots n_{\sigma(\alpha)}$ be the permuted sequence of the nets. Partition this sequence into $\lceil \alpha/d \rceil$ segments of size d (last segment could be shorter). The neighbourhood $N_2[\sigma, d](\mu)$ consists of all of legal placements, for which the sum of the net sizes of each segment is no bigger than under μ, and the sum of at least one segment is smaller. Note that this ensures a cost lower than the placement under μ. By choosing different pairs $\langle \sigma, d \rangle$, one may obtain different neighbourhoods. The constraints are:

$$\left(\overbrace{\bigwedge_{k=1}^{\lceil \alpha/d \rceil} \left(\sum_{i=(k-1)d+1}^{\min(kd,\alpha)} \|n_{\sigma(i)}\| \leq \sum_{i=(k-1)d+1}^{\min(kd,\alpha)} \mu(\|n_{\sigma(i)}\|) \right)}^{each\ sum\ is\ no\ bigger} \right)$$

$$\bigwedge$$

$$\left(\overbrace{\bigvee_{k=1}^{\lceil \alpha/d \rceil} \left(\sum_{i=(k-1)d+1}^{\min(kd,\alpha)} \|n_{\sigma(i)}\| < \sum_{i=(k-1)d+1}^{\min(kd,\alpha)} \mu(\|n_{\sigma(i)}\|) \right)}^{at\ least\ one\ sum\ is\ smaller} \right)$$

4.1.3   Hill-climbing Neighbourhood Generator N_3.

N_3 is designed to implement *hill climbing*. We reason as follows: If the current placement is not a global minimum, there exists a placement with at least one smaller net. Hence, to *tunnel away* from the local minimum, we generate the following neighbourhood constraints:

$$\overbrace{\bigvee_{n \in \mathbb{I}} \|n\| < \mu(\|n\|)}^{at\ least\ one\ net\ is\ smaller}$$

4.2   LSSO-based Algorithms for Placement

All the algorithms below are instantiations of Alg. 1; they use lists of neighbourhood generators, composed of the ones defined in Sect. 4.1, where hill climbing is carried out by using the neighbourhood generator N_3. Due to project deadline constraints, we did not explore other combinations.

1. `single_nbr_nonspec`
   (a) parameters: $\mathcal{VNS} = \bot$, $\mathcal{HC} = \bot$, $\mathcal{SPEC} = \bot$, $\mathcal{N}_{max} = 1$.
   (b) list of neighbourhood generators: $[N_1]$

2. `many_nbr_nonspec`
   (a) parameters: $\mathcal{VNS} = \top, \mathcal{HC} = \bot, \mathcal{SPEC} = \bot, \mathcal{N}_{max} = 10$.
   (b) list of neighbourhood generators: $N_2[\sigma, d](\mu)$, enumerated by drawing σ and d by a pseudo-random generator.
3. `many_env_spec`
   (a) parameters: $\mathcal{VNS} = \top, \mathcal{HC} = \bot, \mathcal{SPEC} = \top, \mathcal{N}_{max} = 10$.
   (b) list of neighbourhood generators: the first generator is N_1 and the rest are $N_2[\sigma, d](\mu)$, enumerated by drawing σ and d by a pseudo-random generator.
4. `many_env_spec_hill_clmb`
   (a) parameters: $\mathcal{VNS} = \bot, \mathcal{HC} = \top, \mathcal{SPEC} = \top, \mathcal{N}_{max} = 1$.
   (b) list of neighbourhood generators: $[N_1]$
   (c) neighbourhood generator N_3 is used for hill climbing.

5 Experimental Results

We study the performance of the following algorithms within our placement tool:

1. Algorithms which use `Polosat` as the satisfiability oracle:
   (a) `ls` (Linear Search, described in Sect. 2.3.2, with `Polosat` as the oracle)
   (b) `single_nbr_nonspec` (see Sect. 4.2)
   (c) `many_nbr_nonspec` (see Sect. 4.2)
   (d) `many_env_spec` (see Sect. 4.2)
   (e) `many_env_spec_hill_clmb` (see Sect. 4.2)
2. Algorithms which use standard SAT solving as the satisfiability oracle:
   (a) `bs_no_polosat` [19]: `OBV-BS` (see Sect. 2.3.2).
   (b) `ls_no_polosat`: Linear Search with SAT as the oracle
   (c) `many_env_spec_hill_clmb_no_polosat`: `many_env_spec_hill_clmb` with SAT instead of `Polosat` (to study the impact of disabling `Polosat` on LSSO, we chose `many_env_spec_hill_clmb`, since, as we shall soon see, it outperforms the other LSSO algorithms in a pairwise comparison).
3. `virtual-best`: represents the best result of the above algorithms per timeout.

We used an extensive set of 1200 proprietary industrial designs of various sizes and complexities. The sizes of the grids (where a *grid size* is the width N multiplied by the height M) can be characterized as follows: a) Minimum size = 70; b) Maximum = 364000; c) Average $\approx$ 4643; d) Standard deviation $\approx$ 18829. We used machines with 32Gb of memory running Intel® Xeon® processors with 3Ghz CPU frequency.

We ran the algorithms for 600 seconds and measured the quality of the placement at different time intervals. Fig. 2 shows our main results. For each algorithm and time interval, Fig. 2 displays a score which represents the quality. The score is a real number between 0 and 1 inclusive, where the closer the score is to 1 the better. For each algorithm and time interval, the score is computed as follows: we compute the average value of the following score-per-instance: (the result of virtual-best in 600 sec.) / (the result of the current algorithm within the current time interval). Our conclusions:

First, when using SAT as the oracle, Linear Search (ls_no_polosat) outperforms OBV-BS (bs_no_polosat), demonstrating that OBV-BS is not useful when the optimization target is a complex arithmetic expression (rather than a vector of lexicographically ordered bits, where each bit is a result of a separate calculation as in [19]). Based on this result, we preferred Linear Search over OBV-BS as the baseline algorithm.

Second, confirming the conclusion of [16], Polosat makes Linear Search substantially more efficient (compare ls to ls_no_polosat).

Third, and more importantly in the context of this work, our best novel LSSO algorithm even without Polosat (many_env_spec_hill_clmb_no_polosat) is almost as efficient as Linear Search with Polosat (ls), the latter being the state-of-the-art in solving placement [16]. Moreover, the best Polosat-based LSSO algorithm (many_env_spec_hill_clmb) is significantly more efficient than both aforementioned algorithms. This result justifies the usage of both major components of our solution: LSSO–the high-level local search on top a satisfiability oracle, presented in this paper, and Polosat [16]–the low-level local search simulation with SAT.

Finally, the virtual best algorithm yields the absolutely best result, providing evidence that development of different LSSO algorithms pays off.

Additionally, Table 1 shows a pairwise comparison between our four Polosat-based LSSO algorithms. many_env_spec_hill_clmb outperforms the others.

Table 2 offers a fine-grained comparison between our best novel LSSO algorithm many_env_spec_hill_clmb and the Polosat-based Local Search ls, the latter being the state-of-the-art in solving placement [16]. The comparison is provided per grid size category and for two different timeouts. LSSO improves the performance significantly for every input size category for both timeouts. Comparing the results for the two timeouts on the biggest instances shows that increasing the timeout makes the gap between LSSO and ls more significant, given large grids.

Finally, Table 3 shows the unique contribution of each algorithm to the virtual best in 600 sec. (we dismissed all the instances on which there was more than one best-performing solver). Notably, each of the LSSO algorithms is a contributor. Surprisingly, many_nbr_nonspec contributes more than many_env_spec_hill_clmb, despite the latter algorithm outperforming the former in a pairwise comparison. A possible explanation is that we ran many_nbr_nonspec with Polosat only, while many_env_spec_hill_clmb was run twice with Polosat and SAT. Another surprising result is the significant contribution of many_env_spec_hill_clmb_no_polosat, second only to many_nbr_nonspec, implying that a SAT-based LSSO algorithm should be part of any parallel portfolio.

	many_nbr_nonspec	single_nbr_nonspec	many_env_spec
many_env_spec_hill_clmb	(730 141 329)	(813 253 134)	(227 893 80)
many_nbr_nonspec		(815 147 238)	(344 170 686)
single_nbr_nonspec			(130 280 790)

Table 1: Pairwise comparison between LSSO algorithms for the timeout of 600 sec. Each non-empty cell (r, c) contains a comparison between Algorithm R in row r and Algorithm C in column c. The value (w d l) in each non-empty cell is interpreted as follows: R outscored C on w instances; there was a draw on d instances; C outscored R on l instances.

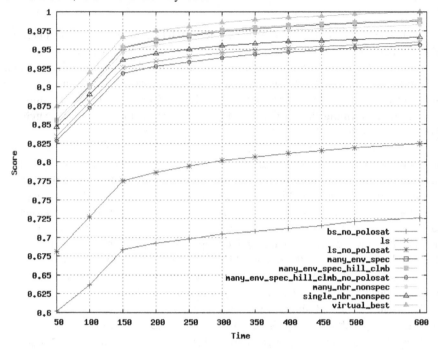

Fig. 2: Comparing Algorithms Over Time

Grid size	Timeout of 600 seconds			Timeout of 300 seconds		
	ls is better	Draw	LSSO is better	ls is better	Draw	LSSO is better
≤ 500	27	62	337	21	56	349
> 500 & ≤ 10000	57	74	551	57	91	534
> 10000	17	28	47	18	40	34

Table 2: Comparing the best Polosat-based LSSO algorithm (many_env_spec_hill_clmb) to the Polosat-based Linear Search (ls), the latter comprising the previous state-of-the-art.

6   Conclusion

We have presented a new methodology for solving NP-hard combinatorial optimization problems, called Local Search with SAT Oracle (LSSO). Our approach can handle problems for which finding even one feasible solution is already NP-hard. LSSO applies local search which uses a SAT solver or the SAT-based optimization algorithm Polosat as an oracle. We have introduced a generic algorithm which integrates different local search schemes within the LSSO framework. Furthermore, we have implemented our approach in an industrial tool for solving the cell placement problem in VLSI and have shown that our new LSSO approach makes the tool substantially more efficient. Our tool has been successfully productized at Intel.

Algorithm	Contribution	Algorithm	Contribution
many_nbr_nonspec	240	ls	33
many_env_spec_hill_clmb_no_polosat	181	many_env_spec	21
many_env_spec_hill_clmb	79	ls_no_polosat	12
single_nbr_nonspec	54	bs_no_polosat	8

Table 3: Unique contribution to the virtual best per algorithm (sorted by the contribution).

References

1. E. Aarts and J. K. Lenstra. *Local Search in Combinatorial Optimization*. John Wiley, USA, 1st edition, 1997.
2. T. Achterberg. *Constraint Integer Programming*. PhD thesis, 2007. Chapter 1.
3. C. Barrett, P. Fontaine, and C. Tinelli. The SMT-LIB Standard: Version 2.6. Technical report, Department of Computer Science, The University of Iowa, 2017. Available at www.SMT-LIB.org.
4. A. Biere, M. Heule, H. van Maaren, and T. Walsh, editors. *Handbook of Satisfiability*, volume 185 of *Frontiers in Artificial Intelligence and Applications*. IOS Press, 2009.
5. N. Eén and N. Sörensson. An extensible SAT-solver. In *SAT*, pages 502–518, 2003.
6. V. Ganesh and D. L. Dill. A decision procedure for bit-vectors and arrays. In W. Damm and H. Hermanns, editors, *Computer Aided Verification, 19th International Conference, CAV 2007, Berlin, Germany, July 3-7, 2007, Proceedings*, volume 4590 of *Lecture Notes in Computer Science*, pages 519–531. Springer, 2007.
7. M. Gendreau and J.-Y. Potvin. *Handbook of Metaheuristics*. Springer Publishing Company, Incorporated, 2nd edition, 2010.
8. S. Held, B. Korte, D. Rautenbach, and J. Vygen. Combinatorial optimization in VLSI design. In V. Chvátal, editor, *Combinatorial Optimization - Methods and Applications*, volume 31 of *NATO Science for Peace and Security Series - D: Information and Communication Security*, pages 33–96. IOS Press, 2011.
9. D. E. Knuth. *The Art of Computer Programming, Volume 4, Fascicle 6: Satisfiability*. Addison Wesley, December 2015.
10. R. Korf, M. Moffitt, and M. Pollack. Optimal rectangle packing. *Annals OR*, 179:261–295, September 2010.
11. B. Korte and J. Vygen. *Combinatorial Optimization Theory and Algorithms*. Springer, 2018.
12. D. Kroening and O. Strichman. Bit vectors. In *Decision Procedures: An Algorithmic Point of View*, pages 135–156. Springer Berlin Heidelberg, Berlin, Heidelberg, 2016.
13. J. Lee. *A First Course in Combinatorial Optimization*. Cambridge University Press, 2005.
14. A. Nadel. Anytime weighted MaxSAT with improved polarity selection and bit-vector optimization. In C. W. Barrett and J. Yang, editors, *2019 Formal Methods in Computer Aided Design, FMCAD 2019, San Jose, CA, USA, October 22-25, 2019*, pages 193–202. IEEE, 2019.
15. A. Nadel. Anytime algorithms for MaxSAT and beyond. In *2020 Formal Methods in Computer Aided Design, FMCAD 2020, Haifa, Israel, September 21-24, 2020*, page 1. IEEE, 2020.
16. A. Nadel. On optimizing a generic function in SAT. In *2020 Formal Methods in Computer Aided Design, FMCAD 2020, Haifa, Israel, September 21-24, 2020*, pages 205–213. IEEE, 2020.
17. A. Nadel. Polarity and variable selection heuristics for SAT-based anytime MaxSAT. *J. Satisf. Boolean Model. Comput.*, 12(1):17–22, 2020.
18. A. Nadel and V. Ryvchin. Efficient SAT solving under assumptions. In *Theory and Applications of Satisfiability Testing - SAT 2012 - 15th International Conference, Trento, Italy, June 17-20, 2012. Proceedings*, pages 242–255, 2012.
19. A. Nadel and V. Ryvchin. Bit-vector optimization. In *TACAS 2016*, pages 851–867, 2016.
20. G. L. Nemhauser and L. A. Wolsey. *Integer and Combinatorial Optimization*. Wiley interscience series in discrete mathematics and optimization. Wiley, 1988.
21. C. H. Papadimitriou and K. Steiglitz. *Combinatorial Optimization: Algorithms and Complexity*. Prentice-Hall, 1982.

22. A. Petkovska, A. Mishchenko, M. Soeken, G. D. Micheli, R. K. Brayton, and P. Ienne. Fast generation of lexicographic satisfiable assignments: enabling canonicity in SAT-based applications. In F. Liu, editor, *Proceedings of the 35th International Conference on Computer-Aided Design, ICCAD 2016, Austin, TX, USA, November 7-10, 2016*, page 4. ACM, 2016.

23. R. Poler, J. Mula, and M. Dìaz-Madroñero. *Operations Research Problems: Statements and Solutions*. Springer, London, 2014.

24. S. Prestwich. Combining the scalability of local search with the pruning techniques of systematic search. *Annals of Operations Research*, 115:51–72, September 2002.

25. F. Rothlauf. *Design of Modern Heuristics*. Natural Computing Series. Springer, 2011.

26. O. Roussel and V. M. Manquinho. Pseudo-boolean and cardinality constraints. In A. Biere, M. Heule, H. van Maaren, and T. Walsh, editors, *Handbook of Satisfiability*, volume 185 of *Frontiers in Artificial Intelligence and Applications*, pages 695–733. IOS Press, 2009.

27. R. Sebastiani and S. Tomasi. Optimization in SMT with LA(Q) cost functions. In B. Gramlich, D. Miller, and U. Sattler, editors, *Automated Reasoning - 6th International Joint Conference, IJCAR 2012, Manchester, UK, June 26-29, 2012. Proceedings*, volume 7364 of *Lecture Notes in Computer Science*, pages 484–498. Springer, 2012.

28. N. A. Sherwani. *Algorithms for VLSI physical design automation*. Kluwer, 3 edition, November 1998.

29. E.-G. Talbi. *Metaheuristics: From Design to Implementation*. Wiley Publishing, 2009.

Analyzing Infrastructure as Code to Prevent Intra-update Sniping Vulnerabilities

Julien Lepiller[1], Ruzica Piskac (✉)[1], Martin Schäf[2], and Mark Santolucito[3]

[1] Yale University, New Haven, USA {julien.lepiller,ruzica.piskac}@yale.edu
[2] Amazon Web Services, NYC, USA schaef@amazon.com
[3] Barnard College, Columbia University, NYC, USA msantolu@barnard.edu

Abstract. Infrastructure as Code is a new approach to computing infrastructure management that allows users to leverage tools such as version control, automatic deployments, and program analysis for infrastructure configurations. This approach allows for faster and more homogeneous configuration of a complete infrastructure. Infrastructure as Code languages, such as CloudFormation or TerraForm, use a declarative model so that users only need to describe the desired state of the infrastructure. However, in practice, these languages are not processed atomically. During an upgrade, the infrastructure goes through a series of intermediate states. We identify a security vulnerability that occurs during an upgrade even when the initial and final states of the infrastructure are secure, and we show that those vulnerability are possible in Amazon's AWS and Google Cloud. We call such attacks intra-update sniping vulnerabilities. In order to mitigate this shortcoming, we present a technique that detects such vulnerabilities and pinpoints the root causes of insecure deployment migrations. We implement this technique in a tool, Häyhä, that uses dataflow graph analysis. We evaluate our tool on a set of open-source CloudFormation templates and find that it is scalable and could be used as part of a deployment workflow.

1 Introduction

Managing an infrastructure of thousands of hosts, with different software and servers is nearly impossible to do manually. A relatively new approach to infrastructure management is called *Infrastructure as Code* (IaC). This has given rise to many different tools with a shared goal: helping system administrators manage their infrastructure in the same way as they manage code. Some tools, like Ansible [20], Puppet [23] or Chef [6] are Configuration Management tools: they allow the administrator to specify the entire configuration of one or more running machines and automatically deploy it by connecting to that machine and performing administrative tasks on behalf of the administrator. These tools automatically detect and apply the steps necessary to switch from the current state of a machine to the desired state, specified by the administrator. Similarly, tools like Amazon's CloudFormation [3] or Hashicorp's Terraform [11] read a description of the desired infrastructure and automatically take the necessary

© The Author(s) 2021
J. F. Groote and K. G. Larsen (Eds.): TACAS 2021, LNCS 12652, pp. 105–123, 2021.
https://doi.org/10.1007/978-3-030-72013-1_6

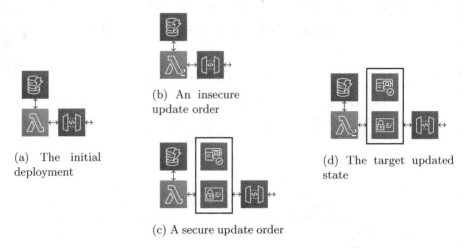

(a) The initial
deployment

(b) An insecure
update order

(c) A secure update order

(d) The target updated
state

Fig. 1: A deployment of a computation (the orange lambda), accessing a database (the blue disk stack), which is accessible to the outside world through an API (the purple gateway). The upgrade should change the computation to access more sensitive data (the lambda with the subscript 2), but be authenticated through a user check (the red identification checks).

steps to deploy that infrastructure. In CloudFormation, an infrastructure configuration is declared as a set of *resources*.

Benefits of IaC are well-known among practitioners: the entire infrastructure is described accurately by a configuration file, making it easy to debug or visualize the infrastructure. This way the infrastructure can be version controlled and documented as any other programming language. The tools help guarantee identical configuration of hosts, making it an essential practice for security and maintainability.

However, for all the benefits IaC brings, it also opens new security vulnerabilities. We have identified a new class of vulnerability issues that appear while the tool is operating on the infrastructure. In order to decrease infrastructure upgrade times, deployment tools typically will run many operations in parallel. We argue that this parallelism, as well as the global naming used in these infrastructures, can lead to discrepancies during the upgrade that lead to a violation of the intended security policy, *even if* the initial infrastructure *and* the target infrastructure are both perfectly secure. We empirically validate our claims by reenacting this vulnerability in both, Amazon's AWS and in Google Cloud.

1.1   Proof of Concept

When upgrading the infrastructure, if operators do not provide enough dependencies, ie. they do not impose an ordering on upgrade operations, a security policy and a protected service might be upgraded in an order that exposes private data. Consider an example given in Figure 1: an API service that replies to any request with some benign information, as depicted in Fig. 1a. The service is upgraded so that the API returns private information about users, and the security policy is modified to allow only authenticated users to access the service, as shown in Figure 1d. This architecture is a core architectural building block for serverless computing. This same configuration is recommended in AWS's "Well Architected" developer guideline series [1]. The upgrade code is functionally correct and implements the desired change, but the user did not specify ordering constraints. However, without such constraints, there are two possible upgrade plans. First, as shown in Figure 1b, the backend computation may be updated first. In this case, since the authentication has not yet been added to the API, there is a short period of time where private data is publicly accessible. The amount of time this information is exposed depends on the cloud service provider and the particulars of the infrastructure, but typically ranges on the order of seconds to minutes. We call this kind of attack intra-update sniping vulnerability. The second possible upgrade order, shown in Figure 1c, implements the desired secure update order. Enforcing the second ordering requires the user to explicitly specify an ordering constraint that the authentication must be added before the backend computation is updated.

Another instance of intra-update sniping vulnerability happens when components are added or removed from an infrastructure, but no ordering constraints are given between them and components that use them. As an example, suppose a user is adding a lamda that reads data from a new S3 bucket. If no dependency is specified, the lambda could be created and connected to the bucket before CloudFormation recognizes that the bucket is already owned. The attacker who owns this bucket may then inject their data into the user's system during the time it takes CloudFormation to notice the naming conflict and roll back the migration. This is related to the issue of S3 bucket namesquatting [15].

Although this paper is mostly focused on Amazon's infrastructure, we have successfully reproduced a similar scenario in Google Cloud, demonstrating that intra-update sniping vulnerabilities are not limited to one cloud provider. We reported this issue to Google, and although they acknowledged the problem, they explicitly stated that it is the responsibility of the user to ensure the security of their deployment.

1.2   Detecting Intra-update Sniping Vulnerabilities

We propose a tool, Häyhä, that detects possible intra-update sniping vulnerabilities and proposes solutions to users. Häyhä allows CloudFormation users to check the security of planned updates to their infrastructure, before they actually deploy the update. Although our tool is specifically engineered to work with CloudFormation, this class of vulnerabilities is not limited to it, and the proposed solution is generic enough to be adopted in any other Infrastructure as Code language.

The main challenge in detecting intra-update sniping vulnerabilities is in determining the underlying issue with common deployment models that lead to the security vulnerability. We identify parallelism and in-place upgrades as the root causes, arguing there is a trade-off in Infrastructure as Code between security and scalability. On the opposite side of this trade-off, some practitioners advocate for Immutable Infrastructure [12] management, which re-builds the entire infrastructures from scratch on each update and only switches atomically to the new infrastructure when it is ready. This practice would guarantee atomicity of updates to the infrastructure and the absence of intra-update sniping vulnerabilities. However, this comes with a huge cost in terms of scalability and does not apply well when statefulness is required (for example, migrating an existing database), making it a less attractive practice.

Naturally, there is a connection between intra-update sniping vulnerability and the problem of data races and concurrent access. Our proposed solution, of adding ordering constraints, is somewhat similar to generic tools in the concurrency domain, such as memory barriers or locks [19,16,24], that add constraints to the order of execution of a program. However, the focus of our work are configuration files that describe infrastructure, not programs. We cannot simply apply existing work, because these configuration files do not have a formal semantics, creating this way an additional challenge for our problem domain.

In summary, we identify the following key contributions of this paper:

- The description of intra-update sniping vulnerabilities and how they arise in IaC services, with examples in AWS and Google Cloud.
- An intermediate representation of IaC configurations that allows us to reason about security and network properties of a deployment, as well as about changes in deployments.
- A tool, Häyhä [17] that statically checks for potential intra-update sniping vulnerabilities in a proposed infrastructure update.
- An evaluation on CloudFormation files scraped from GitHub, showing Häyhä scales and runs fast enough to be adopted into developer workflows.

2   A Model for Infrastructure as Code

Our tool, Häyhä, detects the possibility of a sniping attack in future deployments. It analyzes the given deployment and raises alarms when it detects potential security issues. The tool follows steps that we further detail in this section.

Step 1: Internal representation. First, Häyhä reads the configuration of the current and target infrastructure and translates them to the internal representation. This representation is a dataflow graph identifying which component of the infrastructure has access to which other components, and under which security assumptions. Figure 2 shows two such simplified dataflow graphs that our tool built from arch in Fig. 1. From this graph, Häyhä learns the desired security level of each component. In this section we describe how to compute security levels of resources in a given CloudFormation file: in Section 2.1 we describe the concrete syntax of a general CloudFormation file and how it applies

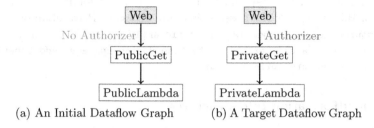

(a) An Initial Dataflow Graph   (b) A Target Dataflow Graph

Fig. 2: Dataflow graphs derived from an infrastructure

to other IaC tools; in Section 2.2 we describe how we model an infrastructure in terms of network communication and security; finally, in Section 2.3 we show the execution semantics and computation of the security level of resources in an infrastructure.

Step 2: Capturing all potential upgrade states. After the initial and target configurations are converted to our model, Häyhä builds an *upgrade state*, designed to represent every possible intermediate infrastructure that could exist during the upgrade. In Section 2.4 we formally define the upgrade semantics from an initial state to a target state in terms of our model, while in Section 3.1 we show how the upgrade state is built in practice. Figure 3 shows such a state, in form of a graph, which contains a path (*Web* to *PublicGet* to *PrivateLambda*) allowing any user on the web to access a sensitive resource in a non-secure manner. Finally, in Section 3.2 we discuss how dependency relations refine the upgrade state.

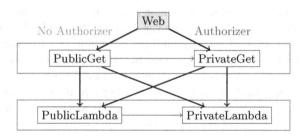

Fig. 3: Upgrade State with a Path Exposing a Security Vulnerability

Step 3: Analysis. (Section 3.3) Häyhä computes an over-approximation of the intermediate states and the security level of their nodes in order to answer two questions: 1) is every node in every possible intermediate state at least as secure as the corresponding node in the initial or target configuration? and 2) does every node in every possible intermediate state communicate only with existing nodes? Any possible violation is reported to the user so they can take action and modify their target configuration accordingly. For example, using the

`DependsOn` keyword, one can enforce build orders in a CloudFormation file. For Figure 3, Häyhä reports the possible insecure access to PrivateLambda:

> `Resource PrivateLambda is not sufficiently protected, it needs at`
> `least Authorizer and is protected by None during upgrade. Add DependsOn`
> `properties to ensure correct security.`

2.1   CloudFormation Infrastructures

CloudFormation uses a declarative language in which users can specify the desired state of their system. An example of a CloudFormation file is given on the left side of Figure 4. It shows a simplified example of an infrastructure in which an API can be called to access the result of running a Lambda (a simple function). There are no formal semantics for CloudFormation files [4,9] – they are simply YAML or JSON files created from the given AWS CloudFormation templates. Other tools, such as Terraform by HashiCorp, follow a similar template-based design.

To formalize the behavior of IaC languages, we would also need to formalize the precise behavior of components. However, these components are very diverse, ranging from firewalls and HTTP servers to general purpose machines or even entire network configurations. Fortunately, the intra-update sniping vulnerability is independent from the precise behavior of individual components, and we only need to analyze the network and security behavior of the infrastructure. We only track the security level of requests, and abstract away from their content. To describe our model, we need to introduce three concepts used in IaC:

A component of the infrastructure is called a *resource*. Every configuration file declares a set of resources and their configurations (e.g. Figure 4). Some resources, like the *LambdaExecutionRole* and the *LambdaPermission* are security resources, and they prevent an unauthorized use of other resources. Other resources, like the *GreetingLambda* and the *GreetingRequestGET* are actual running processes, the later also being publicly accessible. Finally, some resources do not correspond to a running process, but to a group of resources such as *GreetingApi* that gives some configuration value to every resource in the group.

A resource's configuration may reference other resources, and we record that information in our model. Based on the CloudFormation documentation, we distinguish different types of references that we list below:

- **network references(r, r')** are directed network connections between two components r and r', that allow r to send requests to r', and receive answers.
- **incoming protection references(r, s)** protect all incoming requests to a resource r, using a security resource s.
- **outgoing protection references(r, s)** protect all outgoing requests from a resource r, using a security resource s.
- **connection protection references(r, r', s)** protect a specific connection between two resources r and r' using a security resource s.
- **collection references(c, r)** specify a resource r is in a specific collection resource c.

CloudFormation File	Corresponding Model

{ "Resources": {
"LambdaPermission": {
  "Type": "AWS::Lambda::Permission",
  "Properties": {
    "FunctionName": "GreetingLambda",
    "SourceArn": "GreetingApi"
  }
},
"GreetingLambda": {
  "Type": "AWS::Lambda::Function",
  "Properties": {
    "Role": "LambdaExecutionRole"
  }
},
"GreetingRequestGET": {
  "Type": "AWS::ApiGateway::Method",
  "Properties": {
    "Integration": "GreetingLambda",
    "RestApiId": "GreetingApi"
  }
},
"GreetingApi": {
  "Type": "AWS::ApiGateway::Api"
},
"LambdaExecutionRole": {
  "Type": "AWS::IAM::Role"
  "Properties": {
    ...
}}}}
	LambdaPermission [*security*]
	intrinsic security: LambdaPermission,
	
	connection security(GreetingApi, GreetingLambda, *this*)
	
	GreetingLambda
	intrinsic security: ⊤
	
	GreetingRequestGET [*public*]
	intrinsic security: ⊤,
	
	network(*this*, GreetingLambda),
	collects(GreetingApi, *this*)
	
	GreetingApi [*collection*]
	intrinsic security: ⊤

Fig. 4: Mapping Between a CloudFormation File and our Model

Each of these reference types can be present in any resource, any number of time. The resource it is declared in can take any role in the relation that it defines, and we represent the resource as *this* in the model, as shown on the right side of Figure 4.

In CloudFormation, a dependency is declared by using e.g. the *DependsOn* keyword. A dependency restricts the order in which updates can occur: before a resource can be updated, all the resources it depends on must have been updated.

2.2   Model of a CloudFormation Infrastructure

We now describe a model for a CloudFormation infrastructure. We define a *state* $S = (R, D)$ as a set of resources and a partial order that represents the dependency relation between resources. A resource is a tuple composed of a name (string), a type, an intrinsic security context, an origin flag, the different types of references discussed above, and the original configuration of the resource.

With $(id, id') \in D$ we denote that id depends on id', and that id cannot be upgraded until id' is upgraded.

The origin flag denotes whether the resource comes from the initial state or the target state during an upgrade, but it is not used at all when dealing with a single state. Similarly, the original configuration's type is not further defined, and depends on the vendor. It is not used for a single deployment, and we only use it to check for equality of resources when updating an existing deployment.

Inspired by Abstract Interpretation [10], we define a security context as an abstract domain with a partial order and some abstract operations: a top, a bottom, a meet, and a join. When two security contexts are comparable ($x \sqsubseteq y$), we say that x is less permissive than y, or that x is more secure than y.

We define predicates that can help us to express some properties of resources in a specific state S: $collection(r)$, resp. $security(r)$, means that r is a resource whose type is that of a collection resource, resp. a security resource. We use $public(r)$ to denote when r is a resource whose type is that of a resource that can be accessed from anywhere on the internet (although this might be restricted with security references), or if it is contained in a collection that is itself publicly accessible.

Definition 1 (connection). *A connection is possible between two resources when there is a network reference between them or resources that collects them.*

$$ref(r, r') \iff \exists c, c'. \wedge \begin{cases} network\ reference(c, c') \\ r = c \vee collects(c, r) \\ r' = c' \vee collects(c', r') \end{cases}$$

The security of a connection is the minimum security level a request from r must have to be able to reach r' directly. This definition reflects the fact that, when a connection is secured by multiple security resources, it must have sufficient authority to be accepted by *all* of them.

Definition 2 (connection security).

$$security(r, r') \iff \sqcap \left\{ sec(s) \middle| \exists c, c'. \vee \begin{cases} incoming\ protection(c, s) \\ outgoing\ protection(c', s) \\ connection\ protection(c, c', s) \\ with\ \wedge \begin{cases} (r = c \vee collects(c, r)) \\ (r' = c' \vee collects(c', r')) \end{cases} \end{cases} \right\}$$

2.3 Execution Semantics

The execution semantics for our intermediate representation is given below. The semantics explains which resources are allowed to talk to which resources, and under which security level. When we write $L \vdash r \to r'$, it means that r is allowed to send a request to r', under the security level L.

A request can come from the internet (represented with the constant W) and reach a public resource r' if it has a sufficient security level L. Similarly, a request can come from a resource r and reach r' if it has a sufficient security level, r' is not a collection, and both resources have an adequate configuration that allows them to communicate.

$$\text{OutsideRequest} \frac{r' \in R \quad \neg collection(r') \quad L \sqsubseteq security(W, r') \quad public(r')}{L \vdash W \to r'}$$

$$\text{InternalRequest} \frac{(r,r') \in R^2 \quad \neg collection(r') \quad L \sqsubseteq security(r,r') \quad ref(r,r')}{L \vdash r \to r'}$$

A path P is a finite sequence of resources whose first resource is public, and subsequent resources can be reached from the previous, using the above semantics under some security level. The security of a path is then defined as the minimal security level under which every node can be reached in the above semantics:

$$security((r_1,\ldots,r_n)) = \wedge_{i=1}^{n} security(r_{i-1}, r_i)$$

with $r_0 = W$. We note $W \to^* r$ the set of paths whose last element is r. Similarly, the security of a node is defined as the minimal security level under which the node can be reached by at least one path:

$$Sec(r) = \vee \{security(P) | P \in W \to^* r\}$$

When the infrastructure, under which we consider the security of resources, is not clear from the context, we clarify that with a subscript $Sec_S(r)$.

Definition 3 (Substate). *When comparing two states, S_1 and S_2, we say that $S_1 \subseteq S_2$ when*

- *Every resource of S_1 is a resource of S_2 and*
- *For every pair of resources r, r' in S_1, if $L \vdash r \to r'$ holds in S_1, then it also holds in S_2.*

Our first lemma states that, when a state is a substate of another, its nodes are at least as secure as the other.

Lemma 1 (Substate Security).
$\forall S_1, S_2. \; \forall id \in S_1. \; S_1 \subseteq S_2 \implies Sec_{S_1}(id) \sqsubseteq Sec_{S_2}(id)$

Proof. We note that by definition, id is in both states. Additionally, any path in S_1 is also a path in S_2, and since the security of connections in S_1 is more secure than the same connections in S_2, the security of paths in S_1 is greater than the security of the same paths in S_2.

The security of a node is the meet of the security of paths that lead to it in the state. Paths that lead to id is S_2 are the paths that lead to it in S_1, and potentially additional paths. Therefore, the security of id in S_1 is greater than in S_2.

2.4 Upgrade Semantics and Security Policy

In IaC tools, an upgrade changes a given infrastructure state to a new state. This is done by upgrading each node that needs to be changed as specified by the new configuration. Generally, nodes are upgraded in an unspecified order, even in parallel, to improve deployment speed. Node updates are sent asynchronously to every service that needs to be updated, and there are dozens if not hundreds of steps each service must take to complete its update. When these upgrades are sent in parallel, it is difficult to reason about the state of the system as the running time for a node upgrade depends on the latency of the service. To model this behavior, we define an interleaving semantics for upgrades.

An upgrade starts in an initial state S_i and ends in a target state S_t. Additional dependency ordering information is provided by the relation D of the target state.

The configuration of an identifier can be updated if all its dependencies are already updated ($\forall id', (id, id') \in R \implies S(id') = S_t(id')$), and it has not been updated yet:

$$\text{UpgradeConf} \frac{S(id) \neq S_t(id) \quad \forall id', (id, id') \in R \implies S(id') = S_t(id')}{S \to S[id \leftarrow S_t(id)]}$$

A new resource can be created under the same conditions, if it was not present in the initial state:

$$\text{UpgradeAdd} \frac{id \notin S \quad \forall id', R(id, id') \implies S(id') = S_t(id')}{S \to S[id \leftarrow S_t(id)]}$$

An identifier can be removed, if it is not in the target state:

$$\text{UpgradeDel} \frac{id \notin S_t \quad id \in S}{S \to S \setminus id}$$

We collect every accessible intermediate state in a set denoted by Acc:

$$\text{AccInit} \frac{}{S_i \in Acc} \qquad \text{AccNext} \frac{S \in Acc \quad S \to S'}{S' \in Acc}$$

Note that, in the absence of any dependency, Acc contains every combination where each resource is either at its initial or target configuration, leading to 2^n possible intermediate states when n is the number of changed resources.

We next show that, when two identifiers are in a dependency relation, some intermediate states are not possible. For ease of expressing this lemma, we extend equality to also check whether id is in the domain of S. If id is neither in S nor S', we have $S(id) = S'(id)$. Otherwise, id must be in both and associated to the same configuration for the equality to hold.

Lemma 2 (Dependency Restriction).
$\forall (id, id') \in R, S \in Acc \implies S(id) \neq S_t(id) \vee S(id') \neq S_i(id') \vee S_t(id) = S_i(id) \vee S_t(id') = S_i(id')$

Proof. By induction of $S \in Acc$ and by case analysis on the inequality that holds in the inductive case.

We now define the security policy as:

Definition 4 (Security Policy). *A deployment from S_i to S_t is secure iff:*

$$\forall S \in Acc, \forall id, \begin{cases} Sec(S, id) \sqsubseteq Sec(S_i, id) & \text{if } S_i(id) = S(id) \\ Sec(S, id) \sqsubseteq Sec(S_t, id) & \text{if } S_t(id) = S(id) \\ Sec(S, id) = \bot & \text{otherwise (id is not in S)} \end{cases}$$

Our work focuses on security issues that happen during upgrades, assuming that the initial and target states are both secure. We require that in any intermediate state any resource is at least as secure as their counterpart in the initial or target state, depending on where their configuration comes from.

3 Architectural Design of the Häyhä Tool

3.1 Upgrade States

To verify the security of intermediate states, we could compute all the possible intermediate states and pass them to existing tools that could check the security of such states. However, this approach has two main drawbacks. First, we would need to construct 2^n intermediate states, which does not scale for large infrastructure changes. Second, the result of such tools would not be easy to understand for end users, as they would report issues with states that are not defined or even considered by the user. Our goal is a tool that is both scalable and able to provide suggestions on how to change the target configuration, not some hidden intermediate configuration.

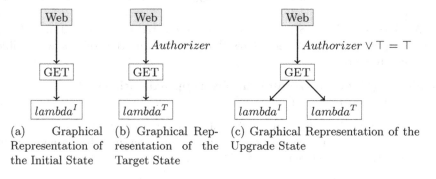

(a)   Graphical Representation of the Initial State (b) Graphical Representation of the Target State (c) Graphical Representation of the Upgrade State

Fig. 5: Example Upgrade State

To address scalability we introduce *upgrade states* which represent multiple states on which we can apply the same execution semantics. Recall that a state is composed of a list of resources with their origin, type and references, and of a dependency relation. An upgrade state is composed in the same way. The set of resources is the union of the resources from the initial and target states, excluding initial resources that only differ from their target counterpart by their provenance flag. When resources are added or removed from an infrastructure, we introduce an empty resource for each of them. They represent the absence of these resources. The dependency relation of the upgrade state is the dependency relation of the target state.

The execution semantics of an upgrade state is the same as the execution semantics of a normal state. Since the upgrade state represents multiple versions of the same resources at the same time, we need to change the definition of the security level of a connection between resources. An example of an upgrade state is given in Figure 5. The initial state has an API, a GET method and a lambda, and everything is public. The target state modifies the lambda and adds an authorizer. The upgrade state is comprised of the unchanged API, the target authorizer (with an empty resource as its initial counterpart), the GET method (which did not change), and the two variants of the lambda. The connection to the GET method is protected either by the empty node ($\top$) or the target authorizer. The minimal security level for this connection is therefore $\top$.

In summary, when a security resource is relevant for a connection, we need to consider its counterpart that has a different provenance flag. If it is also relevant, the connection is protected by the disjunction of the security level of these resources (they cannot both exist at the same time, but one of them exists at any given time). If it is not relevant, the upgrade state represents at least one case where the security resource is not relevant, meaning that the connection is protected by the disjunction of the first security level and $\top$, which is $\top$ (no security at all). If the counterpart is an empty resource, the upgrade state represents at least one case where the security resource was deleted (or not yet added), so the connection is also unprotected. If there is no counterpart, the connection is simply protected by the resource, because it does not change in any way during the upgrade.

We denote by $U(S_i, S_t)$ the upgrade state created from the initial state S_i and the target state S_t. We now show that this state indeed collects all possible intermediate states.

Lemma 3 (Upgrade Graph is an Overapproximation).
$\forall S \in Acc.S \subseteq U(S_i, S_t)$

Proof. To apply the definition, we first show resources of S are resources of U. Then, we show that any connection in S is a connection in U, because resources come with the same references in both states.

3.2 Splitting Dependencies

We have seen that the upgrade state created from the initial and target configurations is an over-approximation of all the intermediate states, when we do not consider dependencies. Because dependencies reduce the number of intermediate states, the upgrade state might not be precise enough and might produce a warning when no actual intermediate states violate the security policy.

Variants. When the state has two nodes A and A' with the same identifier, but a different label, we call them a variant of one another. When A belongs to the initial configuration and A' to the target configuration, (A, A') is called an upgrade pair.

We refine the upgrade state by splitting it along a dependency. Considering a state S, its dependency relation D, and two target resources $(A', B') \in D$, the split of S, $split(S, A', B')$ is a set of upgrade states. Suppose A' and B' are, respectively, part of an upgrade pair (A, A') and (B, B'). Then, $split(S, A', B')$ is the set of three upgrade states, where only one of A or A' remains, and only one of B or B'. We exclude the case where A' and B remain. When any of these nodes does not exist, the number of possible combination is reduced. When only A' and B exist in S, we have found an impossible situation, and the result of splitting is the empty set.

Although this process creates an exponential number of states, the number of dependencies tends to be limited in practice, because they slow upgrades down. At the same time, a big number of dependencies actually reduces the number of possible intermediate states, until every node is in a dependency, in which case there are exactly n intermediate states.

We now prove that splitting the upgrade state is correct, in the sense that the set of states $split(S)$ still contains all the possible intermediate states (Acc):

Theorem 1 (Correct Split).
  $\forall S \in Acc.\ \exists u \in split(U(S_i, S_t)).\ S \subseteq u$

Proof. Let us take a state $S \in Acc$ from the set of all possible intermediate states. Since splitting a state according to a dependency preserves the states from Acc (Lemma 4 below), we can consider every dependency and split them in any order. Initially, it holds that $S \subseteq U(S_i, S_t)$, using Lemma 3.

Consider an upgrade state u such that $S \subseteq u$ and $D(id, id')$. By Lemma 4, we can find a state $u' \in split(u, id, id')$ such that $S \subseteq u'$.

After applying this for each dependency, u' is one of the states resulting from $split(U(S_i, S_t))$, and the claim of the theorem holds.

The following intermediate lemma is needed to prove the correction of the split. It states that if a state contains one of the accessible states, splitting a dependency in it results in a set of states, where one of them still contains this intermediate state.

Lemma 4 (Split Graphs). $\forall S \in Acc.\ \forall (id, id') \in D.\ S \subseteq u \implies \exists u' \in split(u, id, id'), S \subseteq u'$

Proof. Take (A, A') the upgrade pair whose identifier is id. Similarly, take (B, B') the upgrade pair whose identifier is id'. Since $S \in Acc$, A' and B cannot both exist at the same time in S (Lemma 2). Since $S \subseteq u$, we also know that u has at least one variant of id and one variant of id', the ones that are present in S.

The states from $split(u, id, id')$ are composed of the same nodes as u, except for id and id', where they all have one of the four possible combinations of initial and target states, except for the pair A', B. Since S doesn't have them both either, one states has the same variants of id and id' as S, and we call it u'. We now show that $S \subseteq u'$.

First, we note that u' has the same nodes as u, except for those with identifier id and id'. For any resource in S, the resource was present in u, so it is also in u', unless it has identifier id or id'. For this last cases, we note that u' is defined to contain the same variants as S, so the resources of S are also resources of u'.

Second, if we take $L \vdash r \rightarrow r'$ in S, we can use the same reasoning as in Lemma 3 to conclude that is also holds in u'. Thus we conclude that $S \subseteq u'$.

3.3   Finding Vulnerabilities

After Häyhä constructs the upgrade state, the next step is to check for security issues. Although we could split the upgrade state recursively until no dependency remains, a more interesting strategy is to immediately check the upgrade state for issues. If none is found, it is not necessary to refine the upgrade state. Otherwise, we try to find a relevant dependency and split the upgrade state on it, running the analysis on the resulting states, splitting on other dependencies as needed.

Our analysis detects two types of issues: first, if an empty node is accessible, it might be used by the infrastructure at a point it is not registered by the owner of the infrastructure. This is the case for a new node that is accessible before it is created. When that node is a resource that can be claimed by a third party (such as an S3 bucket), the attacker might be able to register it before the user. Similarly, for a deleted resource, an attacker could register it for themselves before the user stops using it.

Second, the security context of every node in the upgrade state is compared to the security of the same node in the initial or target state (depending on its provenance flag). When its security is strictly lower than the security of the node in the state it comes from, or incomparable, we raise an alarm because there is an intermediate step where the resource might not be sufficiently protected.

Using Lemma 1 and Theorem 1, when the security of a node in a possible intermediate state (collected in Acc) is insufficient, the security of that node in at least one split upgrade state is even lower. Therefore, if there is a violation of the security property, our tool will detect it.

4   Experiments

Häyhä is designed to be used before the deployment of a CloudFormation update, and it is crucial that Häyhä does not interrupt developer workflow. Our goal was, therefore, to evaluate the scalability of Häyhä on a variety of real-world CloudFormation updates. To do this, we collected 36 CloudFormation files from GitHub, where each file had a history of updates (commits). We ran Häyhä against every update recorded in GitHub to that file, and measured the running time. We found that our analysis completed within one seconds for all files – we believe that these results indicate that Häyhä could be integrated in developer workflow with minimal disruption to the user. The details of the evaluation dataset are given in Fig. 6.

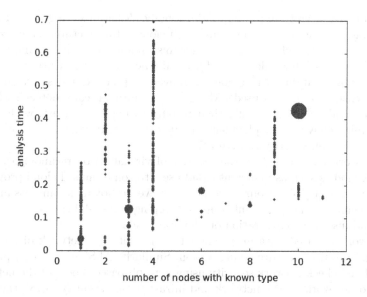

Fig. 6: Analysis time of various CloudFormation files from GitHub. Point size is proportional to the number of updated resources, which are between 0 and 31.

To collect the set of GitHub CloudFormation files used in our scalability benchmark, we searched GitHub using the web search tool for code with the keyword `AWSTemplateFormatVersion` - which is a required keyword for any Cloud-Formation file. We then filtered by the `.yaml` extension, and further manually filtered for valid CloudFormation files (as opposed to other languages with overlap). Since we wanted to track updates to these files, we also filtered manually to find only files that had a revision history (≥ 2 commits for the file).

While we showed that Häyhä scales well on real world data, we did not identify any instances of intra-update sniping vulnerability in these files. This is an expected result, as the CloudFormation files we found on GitHub were generally designed as templates that developers would customize to their own needs. We believe application-focused CloudFormation files are not often uploaded, since CloudFormation files can contain sensitive and proprietary information (e.g. infrastrucuture design). In order to run a large-scale analysis to check for past instances of intra-update sniping vulnerability, we would need access to a repository of the private user data for many CloudFormation users.

5 Related Work

Following the development and use of Infrastructure as Code (IaC) practices, many threats and security challenges were recognized [26,27]. The security risks that have been identified in IaC have thus far remained similar to existing vulnerabilities arising from poor security practices, such as infrequent key rotation and hard-coded secret values [25]. Additionally, despite existing recommendations and good practices when dealing with cloud infrastructure, many existing deployments are still left insecure by user misconfigurations. For example, storage "buckets" which host files, should generally be configured by user to disallow world readable/writable permissions. However, in practice, users struggle with this [8]. Existing work has used SMT solver to automatically detect such vulnerabilities and help users secure their resources [4,9]. In contrast, we focus on the dynamic behavior of deployment updates that occur when using IaC tools, and their effect on security configuration.

Much work has focused on the security of virtualization technologies based on attack models such as malicious cloud users to compromised cloud providers, as summarized in [13]. In our work however, we do not make any assumption on the specific technology, as intra-update sniping vulnerabilities rely mostly on timing and insecure configuration on the user's side.

Our work is based on a graph model of the dataflow network of resources created in an infrastructure configuration. Similarly, Al-Shaer et al [2] propose to model and check network security using a graph-based model of the network. As with other work on the network and infrastructure security [5,18], the focus of the analysis is on the security of static network topologies, instead of the security of a moving topology, as we have in this paper. The analysis of security in static networks and static information flow models [21] is complementary to our work, as we assume the initial and target infrastructure are secure.

Beyond network configurations, there has been work in the analysis of configuration files. In particular, static analysis has been used to check that IaC configurations are idempotent [14,30], an important property for maintaining reproducibility of infrastructure. The reproducibility of infrastructure is known to be a challenge [7], despite IaC being declarative and version controlled. Further efforts have used probabilistic modelling to learn constraints on configurations [22,28,29].

6   Conclusion

We have identified a new class of vulnerability that applies to Infrastructure as Code services, intra-update sniping vulnerabilities, that arise from a lack of ordering in upgrading resources. We presented a tool, Häyhä, that detects such vulnerabilities in CloudFormation, and gives feedback to users on how securely update their infrastructure deployment. Our evaluation shows the scalability of Häyhä by running it on existing configurations from GitHub and found that it runs quickly enough to be usable in practice.

Acknowledgement

This work was completed while working on the grant supported by the National Science Foundation under Grant No. CCF-1715387, and partially supported by the Office of Naval Research under Grant N00014-17-1-2787.

References

1. Julian Wood: Building well-architected serverless applications: Controlling serverless API access. AWS Compute Blog, https://aws.amazon.com/blogs/compute/building-well-architected-serverless-applications-controlling-serverless-api-access-part-1/
2. Al-Shaer, E., Marrero, W., El-Atawy, A., ElBadawi, K.: Network configuration in a box: towards end-to-end verification of network reachability and security. In: 2009 17th IEEE International Conference on Network Protocols (2009)
3. Amazon.com, Inc: CloudFormation, aws.amazon.com
4. Backes, J., Bolignano, P., Cook, B., Dodge, C., Gacek, A., Luckow, K., Rungta, N., Tkachuk, O., Varming, C.: Semantic-based automated reasoning for AWS access policies using smt. In: 2018 Formal Methods in Computer Aided Design (FMCAD). IEEE (2018)
5. Ball, T., Bjørner, N., Gember, A., Itzhaky, S., Karbyshev, A., Sagiv, M., Schapira, M., Valadarsky, A.: Vericon: towards verifying controller programs in software-defined networks. In: Proceedings of the 35th ACM SIGPLAN Conference on Programming Language Design and Implementation (2014)
6. Chef misc, Inc: Chef, https://www.chef.io
7. Cito, J., Schermann, G., Wittern, J.E., Leitner, P., Zumberi, S., Gall, H.C.: An empirical analysis of the docker container ecosystem on github. In: 2017 IEEE/ACM 14th International Conference on Mining Software Repositories (MSR). IEEE (2017)
8. Continella, A., Polino, M., Pogliani, M., Zanero, S.: There's a hole in that bucket! a large-scale analysis of misconfigured S3 buckets. In: Proceedings of the 34th Annual Computer Security Applications Conference. ACSAC '18, Association for Computing Machinery, New York, NY, USA (2018)
9. Cook, B.: Formal reasoning about the security of amazon web services. In: Chockler, H., Weissenbacher, G. (eds.) Computer Aided Verification (CAV). Springer International Publishing (2018)
10. Cousot, P., Cousot, R.: Abstract interpretation: A unified lattice model for static analysis of programs by construction or approximation of fixpoints. In: Proc. of the 4th Symp. on Principles of Programming Languages. ACM (1977)
11. Hashicorp: Terraform, https://www.terraform.io
12. Hashicorp: What is mutable vs. immutable infrastructure?, https://www.hashicorp.com/resources/what-is-mutable-vs-immutable-infrastructure/
13. Huang, W., Ganjali, A., Kim, B.H., Oh, S., Lie, D.: The state of public infrastructure-as-a-service cloud security. ACM Comput. Surv. **47**(4) (Jun 2015)
14. Hummer, W., Rosenberg, F., Oliveira, F., Eilam, T.: Testing idempotence for infrastructure as code. In: ACM/IFIP/USENIX International Conference on Distributed Systems Platforms and Open Distributed Processing. Springer (2013)
15. Ian Mckay: S3 Bucket Namesquatting - Abusing predictable S3 bucket names, https://onecloudplease.com/blog/s3-bucket-namesquatting
16. Ponce-de León, H., Furbach, F., Heljanko, K., Meyer, R.: Portability analysis for weak memory models porthos: One tool for all models. In: Ranzato, F. (ed.) Static Analysis Symposium. pp. 299–320. Springer International Publishing, Cham (2017)
17. Lepiller, J., Piskac, R., Schäf, M., Santolucito, M.: Häyhä (2021), https://gitlab.com/rose-yale/hayha
18. Liu, J., Hallahan, W., Schlesinger, C., Sharif, M., Lee, J., Soulé, R., Wang, H., Cascaval, C., McKeown, N., Foster, N.: P4v: Practical verification for programmable data planes. In: Proceedings of the 2018 Conference of the ACM Special

Interest Group on Data Communication. SIGCOMM '18, Association for Computing Machinery, New York, NY, USA (2018)

19. Meshman, Y., Dan, A.M., Vechev, M.T., Yahav, E.: Synthesis of memory fences via refinement propagation. In: Müller-Olm, M., Seidl, H. (eds.) Static Analysis - 21st International Symposium, SAS 2014, Munich, Germany, September 11-13, 2014. Proceedings. Lecture Notes in Computer Science, vol. 8723, pp. 237–252. Springer (2014)

20. Michael DeHaan and Contributors: Ansible, https://www.ansible.com

21. Parker, J., Vazou, N., Hicks, M.: Lweb: Information flow security for multi-tier web applications. Proc. ACM Program. Lang. 3(POPL) (Jan 2019)

22. Piskac, R.: New applications of software synthesis: Verification of configuration files and firewall repair. In: Podelski, A. (ed.) Static Analysis Symposium (SAS). Springer International Publishing (2018)

23. Puppet, Inc: Puppet, https://www.puppet.com

24. Raad, A., Doko, M., Rožić, L., Lahav, O., Vafeiadis, V.: On library correctness under weak memory consistency: Specifying and verifying concurrent libraries under declarative consistency models. Proc. ACM Program. Lang. 3(POPL) (Jan 2019). https://doi.org/10.1145/3290381, https://doi.org/10.1145/3290381

25. Rahman, A., Parnin, C., Williams, L.: The seven sins: Security smells in infrastructure as code scripts. In: 2019 IEEE/ACM 41st International Conference on misc Engineering (ICSE) (2019)

26. Rahman, A.A.U., Williams, L.: misc security in devops: Synthesizing practitioners' perceptions and practices. In: 2016 IEEE/ACM International Workshop on Continuous misc Evolution and Delivery (CSED) (2016)

27. Rahman, A., Parnin, C., Williams, L.: The seven sins: security smells in infrastructure as code scripts. In: 2019 IEEE/ACM 41st International Conference on Software Engineering (ICSE). pp. 164–175. IEEE (2019)

28. Santolucito, M., Zhai, E., Dhodapkar, R., Shim, A., Piskac, R.: Synthesizing configuration file specifications with association rule learning. Proceedings of the ACM on Programming Languages 1(OOPSLA) (2017)

29. Santolucito, M., Zhai, E., Piskac, R.: Probabilistic automated language learning for configuration files. In: International Conference on Computer Aided Verification. Springer (2016)

30. Shambaugh, R., Weiss, A., Guha, A.: Rehearsal: A configuration verification tool for puppet. In: ACM SIGPLAN Conference on Programming Language Design and Implementation (PLDI) (2016)

Proof Generation/Validation

Certifying Proofs in the First-Order Theory of Rewriting*

Fabian Mitterwallner[1] (✉), Alexander Lochmann[1],
Aart Middeldorp[1], and Bertram Felgenhauer[2]

[1] Department of Computer Science, University of Innsbruck, Innsbruck, Austria
fabian.mitterwallner@uibk.ac.at, alexander.lochmann@uibk.ac.at,
aart.middeldorp@uibk.ac.at
[2] Innsbruck, Austria
int-e@gmx.de

Abstract. The first-order theory of rewriting is a decidable theory for linear variable-separated rewrite systems. The decision procedure is based on tree automata techniques and recently we completed a formalization in the Isabelle proof assistant. In this paper we present a certificate language that enables the output of software tools implementing the decision procedure to be formally verified. To show the feasibility of this approach, we present FORT-h, a reincarnation of the decision tool FORT with certifiable output, and the formally verified certifier FORTify.

1 Introduction

Many properties of rewrite systems can be expressed as logical formulas in the first-order theory of rewriting. This theory is decidable for the class of linear variable-separated rewrite systems, which includes all ground rewrite systems. The decision procedure is based on tree automata techniques and goes back to Dauchet and Tison [7]. It is implemented in FORT [17,18]. FORT takes as input one or more rewrite systems $\mathcal{R}_0, \mathcal{R}_1, \ldots$ and a formula φ, and determines whether or not the rewrite systems satisfy the property expressed by φ, in which case it reports yes or no. FORT may not reach a conclusion due to limited resources.

For properties related to confluence and termination, designated competitions (CoCo [15], termCOMP [9]) of software tools take place regularly. Occasionally, yes/no conflicts appear. Since the participating tools typically couple a plethora of techniques with sophisticated search strategies, human inspection of the output of tools to determine the correct answer is often not feasible. Hence certified categories were created in which tools must output a formal certificate. This certificate is verified by CeTA [21], an automatically generated Haskell program using the code generation feature of Isabelle. This requires not only that the underlying techniques are formalized in Isabelle, but the formalization must be executable for code generation to apply. During the time-consuming formalization process, mistakes in papers are sometimes brought to light.

---

* This research is supported by FWF (Austrian Science Fund) project P30301.

J. F. Groote and K. G. Larsen (Eds.): TACAS 2021, LNCS 12652, pp. 127–144, 2021.
https://doi.org/10.1007/978-3-030-72013-1_7

Since 2017 we are concerned with the question of how to ensure the correctness of the answers produced by FORT. The certifier CeTA supports a great many techniques for establishing concrete properties like termination and confluence, but the formalizations in the underlying Isabelle Formalization of Rewriting (IsaFoR)[3] are orthogonal to the ones required for supporting the decision procedure underlying FORT. We recently completed the formalization of the automata constructions involved in the decision procedure [14]. Earlier fragments were described in [8,13]. In this paper we put these efforts to the test. More precisely, we

1. present a certificate language which is rich enough to express the various automata operations in decision procedures for the first-order theory of rewriting as well as numerous predicate symbols that may appear in formulas in this theory,
2. describe the tasks required to turn the formalization described in [14] into verified code to check certificates within reasonable time,
3. present a new reincarnation of FORT in Haskell, named FORT-h, which is capable of producing certificates.

The remainder of the paper is organized as follows. The next section briefly recapitulates the first-order theory of rewriting and the variant of the decision procedure described in [14]. Sections 3 and 4 describe the representation of formulas in certificates and the certificate language. In Section 5 we describe how certificates are validated by FORTify, the verified Haskell program obtained from the Isabelle formalization. Section 6 describes FORT-h. Experimental results are presented in Section 7, before we conclude in Section 8.

2   Preliminaries

Familiarity with term rewriting [2] and tree automata [6] is useful, but we briefly recall important definitions and notation that we use in the remainder.

Terms $\mathcal{T}(\mathcal{F}, \mathcal{V})$ are constructed from a signature $\mathcal{F}$, consisting of function symbols with fixed arities, and a set of variables $\mathcal{V}$. A term rewrite system (TRS for short) $\mathcal{R}$ consists of rewrite rules $\ell \to r$ between terms ℓ and r. Instead of the usual restrictions $\ell \notin \mathcal{V}$ and $\mathcal{V}ar(r) \subseteq \mathcal{V}ar(\ell)$, we require $\mathcal{V}ar(\ell) \cap \mathcal{V}ar(r) = \varnothing$. Here $\mathcal{V}ar(t)$ denotes the set of variables in a term t. Moreover, ℓ and r are assumed to be linear terms (i.e., variables occur at most once). The conditions on the rewrite rules are necessary to ensure decidability of the first-order theory of rewriting for these *linear variable-separated* TRSs. The (one-step) rewrite relation of a TRS $\mathcal{R}$ is denoted by $\to_\mathcal{R}$. A term t is ground if $\mathcal{V}ar(t) = \varnothing$. The set of ground terms is denoted by $\mathcal{T}(\mathcal{F})$.

The first-order theory of rewriting is defined over a language $\mathcal{L}$ containing the predicate symbols $\to$, $\to^*$, $=$, and many more. As models, we consider finite linear variable-separated TRSs $\mathcal{R}$ over signatures $\mathcal{F}$ such that $\mathcal{T}(\mathcal{F})$ is nonempty. The set $\mathcal{T}(\mathcal{F})$ serves as domain for the variables in formulas over $\mathcal{L}$. The

---

[3] http://cl-informatik.uibk.ac.at/software/ceta/

interpretation of the predicate symbol $\rightarrow$ in $\mathcal{R}$ is the one-step rewrite relation $\rightarrow_{\mathcal{R}}$ over $\mathcal{T}(\mathcal{F})$, $\rightarrow^*$ denotes the restriction of $\rightarrow^*_{\mathcal{R}}$ to terms in $\mathcal{T}(\mathcal{F})$, and $=$ is interpreted as the identity relation on $\mathcal{T}(\mathcal{F})$. Since we use ground terms as carrier, formulas in the first-order theory of rewriting express properties on ground terms. For instance, the following formula φ expresses the property of having unique normal forms (UNR):

$$\forall s \, \forall t \, \forall u \, (s \rightarrow^* t \wedge \neg \exists v \, (t \rightarrow v) \wedge s \rightarrow^* u \wedge \neg \exists v \, (u \rightarrow v) \implies t = u)$$

To use φ for establishing UNR for arbitrary terms (i.e., terms in $\mathcal{T}(\mathcal{F}, \mathcal{V})$) two additional constant symbols need to be added to the signature [18]. (More on this in Section 8.) Additional predicates in $\mathcal{L}$ increase the expressive power and also allow expressing properties more compactly. For instance, we can write $\mathsf{NF}(t)$ for $\neg \exists v \, (t \rightarrow v)$ and $s \rightarrow^! t$ for $s \rightarrow^* t \wedge \neg \exists v \, (t \rightarrow v)$. In Section 3 we present a grammar that describes the available constructions for predicates. All predicates that can be represented using these constructions are supported in our decision procedure.

The decision procedure is based on tree automata that recognize relations on ground terms. Here we give a brief summary. More information can be found in [6] and [14]. A tree automaton $\mathcal{A} = (\mathcal{F}, Q, Q_f, \Delta)$ consists of a finite signature $\mathcal{F}$, a finite set Q of states, disjoint from $\mathcal{F}$, a subset $Q_f \subseteq Q$ of final states, and a set of transition rules Δ. Transition rules have one of the following two shapes: $f(p_1, \ldots, p_n) \rightarrow q$ with $f \in \mathcal{F}$ and $p_1, \ldots, p_n, q \in Q$, or $p \rightarrow q$ with $p, q \in Q$. The latter are called epsilon transitions. Transition rules can be viewed as rewrite rules between ground terms in $\mathcal{T}(\mathcal{F} \cup Q)$. The induced rewrite relation is denoted by $\rightarrow_\Delta$ or $\rightarrow_{\mathcal{A}}$. A ground term $t \in \mathcal{T}(\mathcal{F})$ is accepted by $\mathcal{A}$ if $t \rightarrow^*_{\mathcal{A}} q$ for some $q \in Q_f$. The set of all accepted terms is denoted by $L(\mathcal{A})$ and a set L of ground terms is regular if $L = L(\mathcal{A})$ for some tree automaton $\mathcal{A}$.

We encode n-tuples with $n \geqslant 1$ of ground terms as terms over an enriched signature, as follows. We write $\mathcal{F}^{(n)}$ for the signature $(\mathcal{F} \cup \{\perp\})^n$ where $\perp \notin \mathcal{F}$ is a fresh constant. The arity of a symbol $f_1 \cdots f_n \in \mathcal{F}^{(n)}$ is the maximum of the arities of $f_1, \ldots, f_n$. The encoding of terms $t_1, \ldots, t_n \in \mathcal{T}(\mathcal{F})$ is the unique term $\langle t_1, \ldots, t_n \rangle \in \mathcal{T}(\mathcal{F}^{(n)})$ such that $\mathcal{P}os(\langle t_1, \ldots, t_n \rangle) = \mathcal{P}os(t_1) \cup \cdots \cup \mathcal{P}os(t_n)$ and $\langle t_1, \ldots, t_n \rangle(p) = f_1 \cdots f_n$ where $f_i = t_i(p)$ if $p \in \mathcal{P}os(t_i)$ and $f_i = \perp$ otherwise, for all $p \in \mathcal{P}os(\langle t_1, \ldots, t_n \rangle)$ and $1 \leqslant i \leqslant n$. As an example, for the terms $s = \mathsf{f}(\mathsf{g}(\mathsf{a}), \mathsf{f}(\mathsf{b}, \mathsf{b}))$, $t = \mathsf{g}(\mathsf{g}(\mathsf{a}))$, and $u = \mathsf{f}(\mathsf{b}, \mathsf{g}(\mathsf{a}))$ we obtain $\langle s, t, u \rangle = \mathsf{fgf}(\mathsf{ggb}(\mathsf{aa}\perp), \mathsf{f}\perp\mathsf{g}(\mathsf{b}\perp\mathsf{a}, \mathsf{b}\perp\perp))$. An n-ary relation on ground terms is regular if its encoding is accepted by a tree automaton operating on terms in $\mathcal{T}(\mathcal{F}^{(n)})$. Such an automaton is called an RR_n automaton and regular n-ary relations are called RR_n relations. The i-th cylindrification of an RR_n relation R over $\mathcal{T}(\mathcal{F})$ is the RR_{n+1} relation $\{(t_1, \ldots, t_{i-1}, u, t_i, \ldots, t_n) \mid (t_1, \ldots, t_n) \in R$ and $u \in \mathcal{T}(\mathcal{F})\}$.

Besides RR_n automata, the decision procedure makes use of ground tree transducers (GTTs for short). A GTT is a pair $\mathcal{G} = (\mathcal{A}, \mathcal{B})$ of tree automata over the same signature $\mathcal{F}$. A pair (s, t) of ground terms in $\mathcal{T}(\mathcal{F})$ is accepted by $\mathcal{G}$ if $s \rightarrow^*_{\mathcal{A}} u \, {}_{\mathcal{B}}{\leftarrow}^* t$ for some term $u \in \mathcal{T}(\mathcal{F} \cup Q)$. Here Q is the combined set of states of $\mathcal{A}$ and $\mathcal{B}$. The set of all such pairs is denoted by $L(\mathcal{G})$. We denote by

$L_a(\mathcal{G})$ the set of all pairs (s,t) such that $s \to_{\mathcal{A}}^* q \;_{\mathcal{B}}^*{\leftarrow} t$ for some state $q \in Q$. A binary relation R on ground terms is a(n anchored) GTT relation if there exists a GTT $\mathcal{G}$ such that $R = L(\mathcal{G})$ ($R = L_a(\mathcal{G})$). The decision procedure for the first-order theory of rewriting described in [7] and implemented in FORT uses GTTs, the formalized variant described in [14] uses anchored GTTs (aGTTs), which have better closure properties. Both are supported in our certificate language, but FORT-h and FORTify use anchored GTTs since they permit us to model more predicates while reducing the need for ad-hoc constructions that need to be turned into executable (verified) code.

The decision procedure for the first-order theory of rewriting constructs RR_n automata for the subformulas in a bottom-up fashion. GTTs (aGTTs) come into play for some of the atomic subformulas consisting of predicate symbols and variables. Closure properties take care of the logical structure of formulas. A final emptiness check determines whether the formula is satisfied for the TRS given as input to the decision procedure. Rather than formally stating the properties involved, we illustrate the decision procedure on an example.

Example 1. Consider the formula $\varphi = \forall s\, \exists t\, (s \to^* t \wedge \mathsf{NF}(t))$, which expresses the normalization property of TRSs. To determine whether a TRS $\mathcal{R}$ over a signature $\mathcal{F}$ satisfies φ, we first construct an RR_1 automaton $\mathcal{A}_1$ that accepts the ground normal forms in $\mathcal{T}(\mathcal{F})$, using an algorithm first described in [5] and recently formalized in [13]. For the subformula $s \to^* t$ we construct a GTT $\mathcal{G}_1$ for the parallel rewrite relation $\twoheadrightarrow_{\mathcal{R}}$. Since GTT relations are effectively closed under transitive closure (while RR_2 relations are not), we obtain a GTT $\mathcal{G}_2$ for $\to_{\mathcal{R}}^*$. This GTT is transformed into an RR_2 automaton $\mathcal{A}_2$. (In the formalized decision procedure described in [14], an RR_2 automaton for $\to^*$ is constructed from an anchored GTT for the root step relation $\to_{\mathcal{R}}^\epsilon$, using suitable closure properties of anchored GTT and RR_2 relations.) We cylindrify the RR_1 automaton $\mathcal{A}_1$ into an RR_2 automaton $\mathcal{A}_3$ that accepts $\mathcal{T}(\mathcal{F}) \times \mathsf{NF}_{\mathcal{R}}$. A product construction involving $\mathcal{A}_2$ and $\mathcal{A}_3$ produces an RR_2 automaton $\mathcal{A}_4$ for the subformula $s \to^* t \wedge \mathsf{NF}(t)$. Projection yields an RR_1 automaton $\mathcal{A}_5$ corresponding to $\exists t\, (s \to^* t \wedge \mathsf{NF}(t))$. So φ holds if and only if $L(\mathcal{A}_5) = \mathcal{T}(\mathcal{F})$. In FORT the $\forall$ quantifier is transformed into the equivalent $\neg\exists\neg$. Hence complementation is used to obtain an RR_1 automaton $\mathcal{A}_6$ and the existential quantifier is implemented using projection. This gives an RR_0 automaton $\mathcal{A}_7$ which either accepts the empty relation $\varnothing$ or the singleton set $\{()\}$ consisting of the nullary tuple $()$. The outermost negation gives rise to another complementation step. The final RR_0 automaton $\mathcal{A}_8$ is tested for emptiness: $L(\mathcal{A}_8) = \varnothing$ if and only the TRS $\mathcal{R}$ does not satisfy φ.

3 Formulas

The first step in the certification process is to translate formulas in the first-order theory of rewriting into a format suitable for further processing. We adopt de Bruijn indices [4] to avoid alpha renaming.

Example 2. Consider the formula

```
forall s, t, u ([0] s ->* t & [1] s ->* u =>
        exists v ([1] t ->* v & [0] u ->* v))
```

in FORT syntax. It expresses the *commutation* of two TRSs, indicated by the indices 0 and 1. Using de Bruijn indices for the term variables s, t, u, v produces

$$\forall\forall\forall (2 \to_0^* 1 \wedge 2 \to_1^* 0) \implies \exists (2 \to_1^* 0 \wedge 1 \to_0^* 0)$$

We refer to Example 4 for further explanation.

The formal syntax of formulas in certificates is given below. Angle brackets $\langle\ \rangle$ are used for non-terminal symbols. Here $\langle rr_2 \rangle$ denotes the supported binary regular relations, which are formally defined after Example 3. Likewise, $\langle rr_1 \rangle$ stands for regular sets (which are identified with unary regular relations).

$$
\begin{aligned}
\langle formula \rangle ::=\ & (\texttt{rr1}\,\langle rr_1 \rangle\,\langle term \rangle) \mid (\texttt{rr2}\,\langle rr_2 \rangle\,\langle term \rangle\,\langle term \rangle) \\
& \mid (\texttt{and}\,\langle formula \rangle\,*) \mid (\texttt{or}\,\langle formula \rangle\,*) \mid (\texttt{not}\,\langle formula \rangle) \\
& \mid (\texttt{forall}\,\langle formula \rangle) \mid (\texttt{exists}\,\langle formula \rangle) \mid (\texttt{true}) \mid (\texttt{false}) \\
& \mid (\texttt{restrict}\,\langle formula \rangle\,(\,\langle trs \rangle\,+\,))
\end{aligned}
$$

$$\langle term \rangle ::= \langle nat \rangle \qquad \langle trs \rangle ::= \langle nat \rangle \mid \langle nat \rangle\,- \qquad \langle nat \rangle ::= 0 \mid 1 \mid 2 \mid \cdots$$

De Bruijn indices are used for $\langle term \rangle$ variables and $\langle nat \rangle$- denotes a TRS with index $\langle nat \rangle$ in which the left- and right-hand sides of the rules have been swapped. The class of linear variable-separated TRSs is closed under this operation. We use it to represent the conversion relation $\leftrightarrow^*$ of a TRS $\mathcal{R}$ as the reachability relation $\to^*$ induced by the TRS $\mathcal{R} \cup \mathcal{R}^-$.

Example 3. The commutation property in Example 2 is rendered as follows:

```
(forall (forall (forall (or (not (and (rr2 (step* (0)) 2 1)
    (rr2 (step* (1)) 2 0))) (exists (and (rr2 (step* (1)) 2 0)
    (rr2 (step* (0)) 1 0)))))))
```

Here $(\texttt{step*}\ (0))$ denotes the RR_2 relation $\to^*$ induced by the first TRS (which is indexed by 0) and $(\texttt{rr2}\ (\texttt{step*}\ (1))\ 2\ 0)$ represents the subformula `[1] t ->* v` of the FORT formula in Example 2.

We continue with the certificate syntax of RR_1 and RR_2 relations:

$$
\begin{aligned}
\langle rr_1 \rangle ::=\ & (\texttt{terms}) \mid (\texttt{nf}\,(\langle trs \rangle\,+\,)) \mid (\texttt{inf}\,\langle rr_2 \rangle) \mid (\texttt{proj}\,(1\,|\,2)\,\langle rr_2 \rangle) \\
& \mid (\texttt{union}\,\langle rr_1 \rangle\,\langle rr_1 \rangle) \mid (\texttt{inter}\,\langle rr_1 \rangle\,\langle rr_1 \rangle) \mid (\texttt{diff}\,\langle rr_1 \rangle\,\langle rr_1 \rangle)
\end{aligned}
$$

$$
\begin{aligned}
\langle rr_2 \rangle ::=\ & (\texttt{gtt}\,\langle gtt \rangle\,\langle pos \rangle\,\langle num \rangle) \mid (\texttt{product}\,\langle rr_1 \rangle\,\langle rr_1 \rangle) \mid (\texttt{id}\,\langle rr_1 \rangle) \\
& \mid (\texttt{union}\,\langle rr_2 \rangle\,\langle rr_2 \rangle) \mid (\texttt{inter}\,\langle rr_2 \rangle\,\langle rr_2 \rangle) \mid (\texttt{diff}\,\langle rr_2 \rangle\,\langle rr_2 \rangle) \\
& \mid (\texttt{comp}\,\langle rr_2 \rangle\,\langle rr_2 \rangle) \mid (\texttt{inverse}\,\langle rr_2 \rangle)
\end{aligned}
$$

$\langle pos \rangle$ ::= >= | e | > $\langle num \rangle$ ::= >= | 1 | >

$\langle gtt \rangle$ ::= (root-step ($\langle trs \rangle$ +)) | (inverse $\langle gtt \rangle$) | (union $\langle gtt \rangle$ $\langle gtt \rangle$)
     | (acomp $\langle gtt \rangle$ $\langle gtt \rangle$) | (gcomp $\langle gtt \rangle$ $\langle gtt \rangle$) | (inter $\langle gtt \rangle$ $\langle gtt \rangle$)
     | (acomplement $\langle gtt \rangle$) | (atc $\langle gtt \rangle$) | (gtc $\langle gtt \rangle$)

Here (terms) refers to $\mathcal{T}(\mathcal{F})$, (nf ($\langle trs \rangle$ +)) to the normal forms (NF) induced by the union of the underlying TRSs, and (inf $\langle rr_2 \rangle$) to the infinity predicate (INF_R) which is satisfied by all terms having infinitely many successors with respect to the relation R. Furthermore, (proj (1 | 2) $\langle rr_2 \rangle$) denotes projection (π) to the first (second) argument, (gtt $\langle gtt \rangle$ $\langle pos \rangle$ $\langle num \rangle$) the transformation of a GTT relation into an RR_2 relation with corresponding context closure (cf. [14, Section 3]), (id $\langle rr_1 \rangle$) the identity relation on the underlying set, and (gtc $\langle gtt \rangle$) ((atc $\langle gtt \rangle$)) the (anchored) transitive closure of the underlying (anchored) GTT relation.

The constructs defined above closely correspond to the formalized closure operations for the predicates in the first-order theory of rewriting, reported in [14] and summarized below:

$$
\begin{aligned}
A &::= \rightarrow_\epsilon | A^- | A \cup A | A^+ | A^{\widehat{+}} | A \circ A | A \widehat{\circ} A | A^c | A \cap A \\
R &::= A | R_p^n | R \cup R | R \cap R | R^- | T \times T | =_T \\
T &::= \mathcal{T}(\mathcal{F}) | \mathsf{NF} | \mathsf{INF}_R | T \cup T | T \cap T | T^c | \pi_1(R) | \pi_2(R) \\
n &::= \geqslant | 1 | > \qquad p ::= \geqslant | \epsilon | >
\end{aligned}
$$

Here A are anchored GTT relations ($\langle gtt \rangle$), R are RR_2 relations ($\langle rr_2 \rangle$), and T are regular sets of ground terms ($\langle rr_1 \rangle$).

For convenience of tool authors, we add a few other constructs to $\langle rr_2 \rangle$. The certifier expands these to a sequence of basic constructs given above.

$\langle rr_2 \rangle$ ::= $\cdots$ | (step ($\langle trs \rangle$ +)) | (step= ($\langle trs \rangle$ +))
     | (step+ ($\langle trs \rangle$ +)) | (step* ($\langle trs \rangle$ +)) | (equality)
     | (parallel-step ($\langle trs \rangle$ +)) | (root-step+ ($\langle trs \rangle$ +))
     | (non-root-step ($\langle trs \rangle$ +)) | (join ($\langle trs \rangle$ +))

The complete list can be obtained from the accompanying website.

4 Certificates

A certificate for a first-order formula φ explains how the corresponding RR_n automaton is constructed. We adopt a line-oriented natural deduction style. The automata are implicit. This is a deliberate design decision to keep certificates small. More importantly, it avoids having to check equivalence of finite tree automata, which is EXPTIME-complete [6, Section 1.7].

$\langle certificate \rangle$ ::= ($\langle item \rangle$ $\langle inference \rangle$ $\langle formula \rangle$ $\langle info \rangle$ *) $\langle certificate \rangle$

$$| \; (\text{empty} \, \langle \textit{item} \rangle) \; | \; (\text{nonempty} \, \langle \textit{item} \rangle)$$

$$\langle \textit{item} \rangle \; ::= \; \langle \textit{nat} \rangle \qquad \langle \textit{info} \rangle \; ::= \; (\text{size} \, \langle \textit{nat} \rangle \, \langle \textit{nat} \rangle \, \langle \textit{nat} \rangle) \; | \; \cdots$$

$$\langle \textit{inference} \rangle \; ::= \; (\text{rr1} \, \langle \textit{rr}_1 \rangle \, \langle \textit{term} \rangle) \; | \; (\text{rr2} \, \langle \textit{rr}_2 \rangle \, \langle \textit{term} \rangle \, \langle \textit{term} \rangle)$$

$$| \; (\text{and} \, \langle \textit{item} \rangle \, * \,) \; | \; (\text{or} \, \langle \textit{item} \rangle \, * \,) \; | \; (\text{not} \, \langle \textit{item} \rangle)$$

$$| \; (\text{exists} \, \langle \textit{item} \rangle) \; | \; (\text{nnf} \, \langle \textit{item} \rangle) \; | \; \cdots$$

Currently the $\langle \textit{info} \rangle$ field only serves as an interface between the tool (which provides the certificate) and the certifier to compare the sizes of the constructed automata. In the future we plan to extend this field with concrete automata. This allows to test language equivalence of a tree automaton computed by a tool that supports our certificate language and the one reconstructed by FORTify, thereby providing tool authors with a mechanism to trace buggy constructions in case a certificate is rejected.

We revisit Example 1 to illustrate the construction of certificates.

Example 4. The formula $\varphi = \forall s \exists t \, (s \to^* t \land \mathsf{NF}(t))$ expressing normalization is rendered as $\varphi' = \forall \exists (1 \to_0^* 0 \land 0 \in \mathsf{NF}[0])$ in de Bruijn notation. Here 1 refers to the variable s, the second and third occurrences of 0 refer to t, and the last occurrence of 0 refer to the first (and only) TRS, which has index 0. We construct the certificate bottom-up, to mimic the decision procedure. The first line is for $\mathsf{NF}[0]$:

```
(0 (rr1 (nf (0)) 0) (rr1 (nf (0)) 0))
```

The components can be read as follows:

- $\langle \textit{item} \rangle = 0$ denotes the first step in our proof,
- $\langle \textit{inference} \rangle = $ rr1 (nf (0)) 0 construct the automaton that accepts the normal forms and keeps track of the variable 0,
- $\langle \textit{formula} \rangle = $ rr1 (nf (0)) 0 denotes the subformula $0 \in \mathsf{NF}[0]$; it is satisfiable if and only if the automaton constructed using the description in $\langle \textit{inference} \rangle$ is not empty.

The apparent redundancy will disappear when we continue. We proceed by expressing the relation $\to_0^*$ and subsequently make sure that the second component of $\to_0^*$ is in normal form:

```
(1 (rr2 (step* (0)) 1 0) (rr2 (step* (0)) 1 0))
(2 (and (1 0)) (and ((rr2 (step* (0)) 1 0) (rr1 (nf (0)) 0))))
```

Line 1 is similar to line 0. The inference step and 1 0 in line 2 constructs an RR_2 automaton that accepts the intersection of the relations modeled in lines 1 and 0. This automaton corresponds to $\mathcal{A}_4$ in Example 1. The cylindrification step from $\mathcal{A}_1$ to $\mathcal{A}_3$ in Example 1 is left implicit. We continue with the projection of variable 0 and afterwards complement the resulting automaton. This is done by an exists followed by a not inference step:

```
(3 (exists 2) (exists (and ((rr2 (step* (0)) 1 0)
   (rr1 (nf (0)) 0)))))
(4 (not 3) (not (exists (and ((rr2 (step* (0)) 1 0)
   (rr1 (nf (0)) 0))))))
```

The inference steps until this point describe the construction of $\mathcal{A}_6$ in Example 1. We complete the certificate by introducing the remaining operators:

```
(5 (exists 4) (exists (not (exists (and ((rr2 (step* (0)) 1 0)
   (rr1 (nf (0)) 0)))))))
(6 (not 5) (not (exists (not (exists (and ((rr2 (step* (0)) 1 0)
   (rr1 (nf (0)) 0))))))))
(7 (nnf 6) (forall (exists (and ((rr2 (step* (0)) 1 0)
   (rr1 (nf (0)) 0))))))
(nonempty 7)
```

The nnf inference step does not modify the tree automaton computed in step 6 (which corresponds to $\mathcal{A}_8$ in Example 1) but checks the equivalence of the formula in line 6 with the one of line 7, which corresponds to the input formula φ'. The equivalence check incorporates $\forall$ elimination, negation normal form, and associativity, commutativity and idempotency of $\wedge$ and $\vee$. In the future we might add support for additional equivalences in first-order logic. The final step (nonempty 7) checks that $L(\mathcal{A}_8) \neq \varnothing$. So this certificate claims that the input TRS is normalizing. For TRSs that do not satisfy φ, the final line in the certificate would be (empty 7).

In the previous example we intentionally skipped over some details to convey the underlying intuition. First of all, the $\langle rr_2 \rangle$ construct (step* (0)) is derived and internally unfolded via (anchored) GTTs into

```
(gtt (gtc (root-step 0)) >= >)
```

Starting from an anchored GTT that accepts the root step relation induced by the first (and only) TRS in the list, an application of the GTT transitive closure operation followed by a multi-hole context closure operation with at least one hole that may appear in any position, an RR_2 automaton that accepts the relation $\to_0^*$ is constructed. We also mentioned that cylindrification is implicit. The same holds for the projection operation that is used in the exists inference steps. A projection takes place in the first component if the variable 0 is present in the list of variables, otherwise the inference step preserves the automaton. This approach is sound as variables indicate the relevant components of the RR_n automaton. Thanks to the de Bruijn representation, the innermost quantifier refers to variable 0, the first component in the given RR_n automaton. However we must keep track of all variables occurring in the surrounding formula and update that list accordingly.

5   FORTify

The example in the preceding section makes clear that a certificate can be viewed as a recipe for the certifier to perform certain operations on automata and for-

nulas to confirm the final (non-)emptiness claim. In particular, checking a certificate is expensive because the decision procedure for the first-order theory is
replayed using code-generated operations from a verified version of the decision
procedure. In this section we describe the steps we performed to turn the Isabelle formalization of the decision procedure described in [14] into our certifier
FORTify.

We use the FOL-Fitting library [3], which is part of the Archive of Formal
Proofs,[4] to connect the first-order theory of rewriting and first-order logic. The
translation is more or less straightforward. We interpret RR_1 constructions as
predicates and RR_2 construction as relations in first-order logic and prove both
interpretations to be semantically equivalent:

lemma *eval_formula $\mathcal{F}$ Rs α f =*
  eval α undefined (for_eval_rel $\mathcal{F}$ Rs) (form_of_formula f)

With this equivalence we are able to define the semantics of formulas:

definition *formula_satisfiable* **where**
  formula_satisfiable $\mathcal{F}$ Rs f $\longleftrightarrow$ ($\exists \alpha$. range $\alpha \subseteq \mathcal{T}_G \mathcal{F} \wedge$
  eval_formula $\mathcal{F}$ Rs α f)

definition *formula_unsatisfiable* **where**
  formula_unsatisfiable $\mathcal{F}$ Rs fm $\longleftrightarrow$ (formula_satisfiable $\mathcal{F}$ Rs fm = False)

definition *correct_certificate* **where**
  correct_certificate $\mathcal{F}$ Rs claim infs n $\equiv$
    (claim = Empty $\longleftrightarrow$ (formula_unsatisfiable (fset $\mathcal{F}$) (map fset Rs)
    (fst (snd (snd (infs ! n)))))) $\wedge$
    claim = Nonempty $\longleftrightarrow$ formula_satisfiable (fset $\mathcal{F}$) (map fset Rs)
    (fst (snd (snd (infs ! n)))))))

Last but not least we define the important function `check_certificate` which
takes as input a signature, a list of TRSs, a boolean, a formula, and a certificate.
This function first verifies that the given formula and the claim corresponds to
the ones referenced in the certificate and afterwards checks the integrity of the
certificate. The following lemmata, which are formally proved in Isabelle, state
the correctness of the `check_certificate` function:

lemma *check_certificate $\mathcal{F}$ Rs A fm (Certificate infs claim n) = Some B*
  $\Longrightarrow$ fm = fst (snd (snd (infs ! n))) $\wedge$ A = (claim = Nonempty)

lemma *check_certificate $\mathcal{F}$ Rs A fm (Certificate infs claim n) = Some B*
  $\Longrightarrow$ (B = True $\longrightarrow$ correct_certificate $\mathcal{F}$ Rs claim infs n) $\wedge$
  (B = False $\longrightarrow$ correct_certificate $\mathcal{F}$ Rs (case claim of
  Empty $\Rightarrow$ Nonempty | Nonempty $\Rightarrow$ Empty) infs n)

---

[4] https://www.isa-afp.org

The first lemma ensures that our check function verifies that the provided parameters *fm* (formula) and *A* (answer satisfiable/unsatisfiable) match the formula and the claim stated in the certificate. The second lemma is the key result. It states that the check function returns Some True if and only if the certificate is correct. The only-if case is hidden in the last two lines. More precisely, if the claim of the certificate is wrong then negating the claim (the first-order theory of rewriting is complete) leads to a correct certificate. Therefore, if our check function returns Some None then the certificate is correct after negating the claim.

Our check function returns None if the global assumptions (the input TRS is not linear variable-separated, the signature is not empty, etc.) are not fulfilled. We plan to extend the check_certificate function in the near future such that it reports these kind of errors.

A central part of the formalization is to obtain a trustworthy decision procedure to verify certificates. Hence we use the code generation facility of Isabelle/HOL to produce an executable version of our check_certificate function. Isabelle's code generation facility is able to derive executable code for our constructions with the exception of inductively defined sets. In [8, Section 7] an abstract *Horn inference system* for finite sets is introduced to overcome this limitation. We use this framework to obtain executable code for the following constructions defined as inductive sets:

- reachable and productive states of a tree automaton,
- states of tree automata obtained by the subset construction,
- epsilon transitions for the composition and transitive closure constructions of (anchored) GTTs,
- an inductive set needed for the tree automaton for the infinity predicate.

At this point we can use Isabelle's code generation to obtain an executable check function. However, more effort is needed to obtain an efficient check function. Checking the certificate in Example 6 below did not terminate after more than 24 hours computation time. We used the profiling capabilities of the Glasgow Haskell Compiler (GHC) to analyze the generated code. This revealed that most of the time was spent on checking membership. Since the computed tree automata can grow very large, the use of lists as underlying data structure for sets in the generated code is a bottleneck.

To overcome this problem we decided to use the container framework of Lochbihler [12]. In our case, the setup involved a non-trivial overhead as the container framework requires multiple class instances for data types used inside sets. Some of these instances could be derived automatically by the deriving framework of Sternagel and Thiemann [20]. Afterwards Isabelle's code generation was able to generate a check_certificate function that uses red-black trees as underlying data structure for sets.

Sadly, the function was still infeasible for the certificate in Example 6. This time the power set construction, which is exponential in worst case, turned out to be the culprit. In this construction we compute the transitive closure of the present epsilon transitions multiple times. Adding an explicit construction to

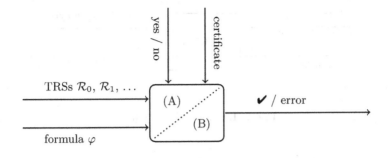

Fig. 1. Certificate validation with FORTify.

remove epsilon transitions from tree automata solved this issue. To make a long story short, after further modifications we were able to verify the certificate for Example 6 in a little less than 3 minutes, which we consider fast enough for a first prototype. The resulting code-generated certifier is called FORTify.

The overall design of FORTify is shown in Figure 1. It can be viewed as two separate modules A and B. Module B is the verified Haskell code base that is generated by Isabelle's code generation facility, containing the check_certificate function and the data type declarations for formulas and certificates. To use this functionality, we wrote a parser which translates strings representing formulas (signatures, TRSs, certificates) to semantically equivalent formulas (signatures, TRSs, certificates) represented in the data types obtained from the generated code. This was done in Haskell and refers to module A in Figure 1. Module A accepts formulas in FORT syntax. Hence it also applies the conversion to the de Bruijn representation. After the translation in module A, the check_certificate function in module B is executed and its output is reported.

Importantly, the code in module A is not verified in Isabelle. Correctness of FORTify must therefore assume correctness of module A as well as the correctness of the Glasgow Haskell Compiler, which we use to generate a standalone executable from the generated code.

6   FORT-h

FORT-h is a new decision tool for the first order theory of rewriting. It is a reimplementation of the decision mode of the previous FORT tool [18] based on a modified decision procedure. The decision procedure, like the formalization, is based on anchored GTTs. The new tool is implemented in Haskell whereas FORT is written in Java.

FORT-h supports all features of FORT while extending the domain of supported TRSs from left-linear right-ground TRSs to *linear variable-separated* ones. While FORT could technically take such TRSs as input, it is unsound when checking non-ground properties on them.

Fig. 2. Interface of FORT-h.

Example 5. To check confluence of the linear variable-separated TRS

$$g(g(x)) \to g(y) \qquad\qquad a \to g(a)$$

FORT-h can be called with

```
> ./fort-h "CR" input.trs
NO
```

where `input.trs` is a text file containing the rewrite system. The tool correctly states that NO the system is not confluent. However, FORT incorrectly identifies this as confluent due to the lack of support for variables appearing in right-hand sides of rules.

FORT-h took part in the 2020 edition of the Confluence Competition, competing in five categories: COM, GCR, NFP, UNC and UNR. Even though it does not support many problems tested in the competition, due to the restriction to linear variable-separated TRSs, it was able to win the category for most YES results in UNR. The tool expects as input a formula φ and one or more TRSs, as seen in Figure 2. It then outputs the answer YES or NO depending on whether φ is satisfied or not by the given TRSs. FORT-h may be passed some additional options:

`-c FILE:` causes FORT-h to write a certificate to the given `FILE`,
`-i:` enables the additional ⟨*info*⟩ in the inference steps in the certificate,
`-v:` enables verbose output (e.g. showing the internal formula representation).
`-w:` enables witness generation.

As an example of the latter, consider Example 5 and the call

```
> fort-h -w "CR" input.trs
NO
formula body / witness:
    (0 (<- o ->*) 1 & ~ 0 (->* o *<-) 1)
    0 = g(_00())
    1 = g(_01())
```

So in addition to the answer NO, it also outputs a counter example for the given formula consisting of the two terms `g(_00())` and `g(_01())`. Here _00 and _01 are additional constants required to reduce confluence to ground-confluence, and represent variables. The terms should therefore be read as $g(x)$ and $g(y)$.

Internally FORT-h represents formulas using de Bruijn indices as described in Section 4. Additionally, universal quantifiers and implications are eliminated, and negations are pushed as far as possible to the atomic subformulas. The tool then traverses the formula in a bottom-up fashion, constructing the corresponding anchored GTTs and RR_n automata. During this traversal we also keep track of the steps taken, to construct the certificate if necessary. To improve performance the automata are cached and reused for equal subformulas. The tree automaton representing the whole formula is then checked for emptiness. If the accepted language is empty, FORT-h reports NO, otherwise it outputs YES.

7   Experiments

The experiments described in this section were run on a computer with a Intel(R) Core(TM) i7-5930K CPU with 6 cores at 3.50GHz.

In the 2019 edition of the Confluence Competition [15] three tools contested the commutation (COM) category:[5] ACP [1], CoLL [19], and FORT. On input problem COPS #1118 the tools gave conflicting answers.

Example 6. COPS #1118 is about the commutation of the TRSs COPS #669

$$a \to c \qquad f(a) \to b \qquad b \to b \qquad b \to h(b, h(c, a))$$

and COPS #695

$$h(a, a) \to c \qquad b \to h(b, a) \qquad b \to a \qquad f(c) \to c \qquad c \to a$$

To determine the correct answer we use FORT-h to produce a certificate for ground-confluence by calling

```
> fort-h -c cert -i "GCom([0],[1])" 1118.trs
YES
```

This produces the following certificate:

```
0 (rr2 (comp (inverse (step* (1))) (step* (0))) 0 1)
  (rr2 (comp (inverse (step* (1))) (step* (0))) 0 1)
  (size 13 53 0))
1 (rr2 (comp (step* (0)) (inverse (step* (1)))) 0 1)
  (rr2 (comp (step* (0)) (inverse (step* (1)))) 0 1)
  (size 11 47 0))
2 (not 1) (not (rr2 (comp (step* (0)) (inverse (step* (1)))) 0 1))
3 (and (0 2))
  (and ((rr2 (comp (inverse (step* (1))) (step* (0))) 0 1)
    (not (rr2 (comp (step* (0)) (inverse (step* (1)))) 0 1))))
4 (exists 3)
```

---

[5] https://cops.uibk.ac.at/results/?y=2019&c=COM

Table 1. FORT(-h) run on GCR formulas with a 60 s timeout (FORTify with 600 s).

	YES	∅-time	✔	NO	∅-time	✔	∞	total (✔) time
(1) FORT-h	36	0.26 s	10	84	0.56 s	16	2	176.23 s (17.6 h)
FORT	37	0.31 s	—	82	0.52 s	—	3	234.08 s
(2) FORT-h	37	1.48 s	10	84	0.09 s	16	1	122.55 s (17.8 h)
FORT	37	0.32 s	—	82	0.50 s	—	3	233.20 s
(3) FORT-h	36	0.45 s	6	83	0.08 s	9	3	202.64 s (18.2 h)
FORT	37	0.32 s	—	82	0.55 s	—	3	236.69 s

```
    (exists (and ((rr2 (comp (inverse (step* (1))) (step* (0))) 0 1)
       (not (rr2 (comp (step* (0)) (inverse (step* (1)))) 0 1))))))
(5 (exists 4)
    (exists (exists (and ((rr2 (comp (inverse (step* (1)))
       (step* (0))) 0 1) (not (rr2 (comp (step* (0))
       (inverse (step* (1)))) 0 1)))))))
(6 (not 5)
    (not (exists (exists (and (
       (rr2 (comp (inverse (step* (1))) (step* (0))) 0 1)
       (not (rr2 (comp (step* (0)) (inverse (step* (1)))) 0 1)))))))
(7 (nnf 6)
    (forall (forall (or (
       (not (rr2 (comp (inverse (step* (1))) (step* (0))) 0 1))
       (rr2 (comp (step* (0)) (inverse (step* (1)))) 0 1))))))
(nonempty 7)
```

When passing this certificate to FORTify, after 2 minutes and 57 seconds the output `Certified` is produced, so we can be assured that the TRSs do commute. Note that the inference steps 0 and 1 contain the optional size information. Here (`size k m n`) means the underlying RR_n automaton constructed by FORT-h contains k final states, m transitions, and n epsilon transitions.

We also ran some experiments comparing FORT-h to FORT. The problems for these experiments are taken from the Confluence Problems database (COPS), and consists of 122 left-linear right-ground TRSs. Note that FORT-h implements no parallelism, while FORT does. For the first two experiments we chose a timeout of 60 seconds for the decision tools and 600 seconds for FORTify. The formulas were taken from the experiments reported in [17]. The first three

$$\forall s \forall t \forall u \, (s \to^* t \land s \to^* u \implies t \downarrow u) \tag{1}$$

$$\forall s \forall t \forall u \, (s \to^* t \land s \to u \implies t \downarrow u) \tag{2}$$

$$\forall t \forall u \, (t \leftrightarrow^* u \implies t \downarrow u) \tag{3}$$

denote different but equivalent formulations of ground-confluence (GCR).

The results are shown in Table 1, where the YES (NO) column shows the number of systems determined to be (non-)ground-confluent together with average time (∅-time) the tool took. The ∞ column is the number of timeouts.

To compare overall performance the *total time* column contains the sum of all runtimes, including timeouts but excluding the time taken by FORTify. The ✔ columns show the numbers of certifiable results as well as the overall time taken by FORTify (✔-time). These results show that, even though they have the same meaning, the choice of formula has an impact on performance. Interestingly FORT-h is generally faster and can solve more problems than FORT even though it can not take advantage of any parallelism. This performance advantage is more prominent in systems which are non-confluent. For problems with the answer YES, FORT can still prove more. The table also shows that FORTify can only certify a small portion the results. This is due to the performance of the certifier, since all other problems time out. It is also apparent that formulas containing conversion ($\leftrightarrow^*$) are especially slow. No wrong results by the decision tools where identified.

The second set of formulas represents the normal form property, restricted to ground terms (GNFP):

$$\forall t \forall u \, (t \leftrightarrow^* u \wedge \mathsf{NF}(u) \implies t \rightarrow^* u) \tag{4}$$

$$\forall s \forall t \forall u \, (s \rightarrow t \wedge s \rightarrow^! u \implies t \rightarrow^* u) \tag{5}$$

$$\forall t \, (\mathsf{WN}(t) \implies \mathsf{CR}(t)) \tag{6}$$

The results for these are shown in Table 2. The same pattern is observed, where even though both can (dis)prove satisfaction for the same formulas, FORT-h is faster overall.

For the last experiment we test performance on properties over two TRSs. This is done by checking ground-commutation (GCOM) for all pairs of systems form the dataset, resulting in 7503 problems. A timeout of 60 seconds was used. The results, presented in Table 3, show that FORT-h is ahead here as well, (dis)proving more problems and doing so in significantly less time.

Full details of the experiments are available from the website[6] accompanying this paper. Precompiled binaries of FORT-h and FORTify are available from the same site. We also present a few additional experiments with FORTify.

---

[6] https://fortissimo.uibk.ac.at/tacas2021

Table 2. FORT(-h) run on GNFP formulas with a 60 s timeout (FORTify with 600 s).

	YES	∅-time	✔	NO	∅-time	✔	∞	total	(✔) time
(4) FORT-h	59	0.70 s	31	63	0.07 s	20	0	45.62 s	(14.6 h)
FORT	59	0.23 s	—	63	0.39 s	—	0	38.16 s	
(5) FORT-h	59	0.03 s	46	63	0.01 s	50	0	2.55 s	(6.3 h)
FORT	59	0.22 s	—	63	0.30 s	—	0	31.83 s	
(6) FORT-h	59	0.05 s	42	62	0.12 s	45	1	70.51 s	(8.6 h)
FORT	59	0.31 s	—	62	0.64 s	—	1	117.86 s	

Table 3. FORT(-h) run on GCOM with a 60 s timeout (FORTify with 600 s).

	YES	∅-time	✔	NO	∅-time	✔	∞	total (✔) time
FORT-h	1381	0.16 s	878	6120	0.03 s	3666	2	517.32 s (681.5 h)
FORT	1354	1.46 s	—	6100	0.94 s	—	49	10670.89 s

8 Conclusion

In this paper we presented FORTify, a certifier for the first-order theory of rewriting for linear variable-separated TRSs, together with an expressive certificate language for formulas and proofs. Moreover, a new implementation of the decision procedure for the theory of rewriting, FORT-h, is capable of producing certificates in this language.

We mention three topics which require further research. First of all, many certificates produced by FORT-h cannot be validated by the current version of FORTify within reasonable time. We will further improve the algorithms and data structures used in the `check-certificate` function. A natural candidate for optimization is the transitive closure algorithm generated by Isabelle, which always takes cubic time. Currently, sharing only takes place in the inference rules. Expanding this to the individual constructions will be the next step. Also trimming of anchored GTTs could improve the run time. In the current state of the formalization only trimming of GTTs is proved to be sound. Profiling will be used to determine other candidates that are likely to have a large impact on the validation time.

A second topic for future research is the certification of properties on open (i.e., non-ground) terms. In [8,16,18] conditions are presented to reduce properties related to confluence to the corresponding properties on ground terms, by adding additional constants to the signature. These results need to be formalized in Isabelle and the certificate language needs to be extended, before FORTify can be used to certify the corresponding categories in the Confluence Competition. We plan to define signature extensions directly in formulas, to offer the most flexibility. A related issue is the support for many-sorted signatures in the Isabelle formalization. FORT-h already supports many-sorted TRSs, which is the format in the GCR category of CoCo.

A third topic is improving the efficiency of FORT-h. We anticipate that supporting parallelism will further speed up FORT-h, especially for large formulas. Preprocessing techniques that go beyond the mere transformation to negation normal form will be helpful to obtain equivalent formulas that reduce the size of the ensuing tree automata in the decision procedure. In [10] similar ideas are applied to WSkS, in connection with MONA [11].

Acknowledgments. We thank René Thiemann for giving valuable advice on how to improve the efficiency of the generated code. The comments by the anonymous reviewers improved the presentation.

References

1. Aoto, T., Yoshida, J., Toyama, Y.: Proving confluence of term rewriting systems automatically. In: Treinen, R. (ed.) Proc. 20th International Conference on Rewriting Techniques and Applications. Lecture Notes in Computer Science, vol. 5595, pp. 93–102 (2009). https://doi.org/10.1007/978-3-642-02348-4_7
2. Baader, F., Nipkow, T.: Term Rewriting and All That. Cambridge University Press (1998). https://doi.org/10.1017/CBO9781139172752
3. Berghofer, S.: First-order logic according to Fitting. Archive of Formal Proofs (2007), https://isa-afp.org/entries/FOL-Fitting.html, Formal proof development
4. de Bruijn, N.G.: Lambda calculus notation with nameless dummies: A tool for automatic formula manipulation, with application to the Church–Rosser theorem. Indagationes Mathematicae 34(5), 381–392 (1972). https://doi.org/10.1016/1385-7258(72)90034-0
5. Comon, H.: Sequentiality, monadic second-order logic and tree automata. Information and Computation 157(1-2), 25–51 (2000). https://doi.org/10.1006/inco.1999.2838
6. Comon, H., Dauchet, M., Gilleron, R., Löding, C., Jacquemard, F., Lugiez, D., Tison, S., Tommasi, M.: Tree automata techniques and applications (2008), http://tata.gforge.inria.fr/
7. Dauchet, M., Tison, S.: The theory of ground rewrite systems is decidable. In: Proc. 5th IEEE Symposium on Logic in Computer Science. pp. 242–248 (1990). https://doi.org/10.1109/LICS.1990.113750
8. Felgenhauer, B., Middeldorp, A., Prathamesh, T.V.H., Rapp, F.: A verified ground confluence tool for linear variable-separated rewrite systems in Isabelle/HOL. In: Mahboubi, A., Myreen, M.O. (eds.) Proc. 8th ACM SIGPLAN International Conference on Certified Programs and Proofs. pp. 132–143 (2019). https://doi.org/10.1145/3293880.3294098
9. Giesl, J., Rubio, A., Sternagel, C., Waldmann, J., Yamada, A.: The termination and complexity competition. In: Beyer, D., Huisman, M., Kordon, F., Steffen, B. (eds.) Proc. 25th International Conference on Tools and Algorithms for the Construction and Analysis of Systems. Lecture Notes in Computer Science, vol. 11429, pp. 156–166 (2019). https://doi.org/10.1007/978-3-030-17502-3_10
10. Havlena, V., Holík, L., Lengal, O., Vales, O., Vojnar, T.: Antiprenexing for WSkS: A little goes a long way. In: Albert, E., Kovacs, L. (eds.) Proc. 23rd International Conference on Logic for Programming, Artificial Intelligence, and Reasoning. EPiC Series in Computing, vol. 73, pp. 298–316 (2020). https://doi.org/10.29007/6bfc
11. Klarlund, N., Møller, A., Schwartzbach, M.I.: MONA implementation secrets. International Journal of Foundations of Computer Science 13(4), 571–586 (2002). https://doi.org/10.1142/S012905410200128X
12. Lochbihler, A.: Light-weight containers for Isabelle: Efficient, extensible, nestable. In: Blazy, S., Paulin-Mohring, C., Pichardie, D. (eds.) Proc. 4th International Conference on Interactive Theorem Proving. Lecture Notes in Computer Science, vol. 7998, pp. 116–132 (2013). https://doi.org/10.1007/978-3-642-39634-2_11
13. Lochmann, A., Middeldorp, A.: Formalized proofs of the infinity and normal form predicates in the first-order theory of rewriting. In: Biere, A., Parker, D. (eds.) Proc. 26th International Conference on Tools and Algorithms for the Construction and Analysis of Systems. Lecture Notes in Computer Science, vol. 12079, pp. 178–194 (2020). https://doi.org/10.1007/978-3-030-45237-7_11

14. Lochmann, A., Middeldorp, A., Mitterwallner, F., Felgenhauer, B.: A verified decision procedure for the first-order theory of rewriting for linear variable-separated rewrite systems variable-separated rewrite systems in Isabelle/HOL. In: Hrițcu, C., Popescu, A. (eds.) Proc. 10th ACM SIGPLAN International Conference on Certified Programs and Proofs. pp. 250–263 (2021). https://doi.org/10.1145/3437992.3439918
15. Middeldorp, A., Nagele, J., Shintani, K.: Confluence competition 2019. In: Beyer, D., Huisman, M., Kordon, F., Steffen, B. (eds.) Proc. 25th International Conference on Tools and Algorithms for the Construction and Analysis of Systems. Lecture Notes in Computer Science, vol. 11429, pp. 25–40 (2019). https://doi.org/10.1007/978-3-030-17502-3_2
16. Mitterwallner, F.: Extending Tools for Confluence and Related Properties of Rewrite Systems. Master's thesis, University of Innsbruck (2020)
17. Rapp, F., Middeldorp, A.: Automating the first-order theory of left-linear right-ground term rewrite systems. In: Kesner, D., Pientka, B. (eds.) Proc. 1st International Conference on Formal Structures for Computation and Deduction. Leibniz International Proceedings in Informatics, vol. 52, pp. 36:1–36:12 (2016). https://doi.org/10.4230/LIPIcs.FSCD.2016.36
18. Rapp, F., Middeldorp, A.: FORT 2.0. In: Galmiche, D., Schulz, S., Sebastiani, R. (eds.) Proc. 9th International Joint Conference on Automated Reasoning. LNAI, vol. 10900, pp. 81–88 (2018). https://doi.org/10.1007/978-3-319-94205-6_6
19. Shintani, K., Hirokawa, N.: CoLL: A confluence tool for left-linear term rewrite systems. In: Felty, A.P., Middeldorp, A. (eds.) Proc. 25th International Conference on Automated Deduction. Lecture Notes in Computer Science, vol. 9195, pp. 127–136 (2015). https://doi.org/10.1007/978-3-319-21401-6_8
20. Sternagel, C., Thiemann, R.: Deriving class instances for datatypes. Archive of Formal Proofs (2015), https://isa-afp.org/entries/Deriving.html, Formal proof development
21. Thiemann, R., Sternagel, C.: Certification of termination proofs using CeTA. In: Berghofer, S., Nipkow, T., Urban, C., Wenzel, M. (eds.) Proc. 22nd International Conference on Theorem Proving in Higher Order Logics. Lecture Notes in Computer Science, vol. 5674, pp. 452–468 (2009). https://doi.org/10.1007/978-3-642-03359-9_31

Syntax-Guided Quantifier Instantiation*

Aina Niemetz[1], Mathias Preiner[1(✉)], Andrew Reynolds[2],
Clark Barrett[1], and Cesare Tinelli[2]

[1] Stanford University, Stanford, USA
preiner@cs.stanford.edu
[2] The University of Iowa, Iowa City, USA

Abstract. This paper presents a novel approach for quantifier instantiation in Satisfiability Modulo Theories (SMT) that leverages syntax-guided synthesis (SyGuS) to choose instantiation terms. It targets quantified constraints over background theories such as (non)linear integer, reals and floating-point arithmetic, bit-vectors, and their combinations. Unlike previous approaches for quantifier instantiation in these domains which rely on theory-specific strategies, the new approach can be applied to any (combined) theory, when provided with a grammar for instantiation terms for all sorts in the theory. We implement syntax-guided instantiation in the SMT solver CVC4, leveraging its support for enumerative SyGuS. Our experiments demonstrate the versatility of the approach, showing that it is competitive with or exceeds the performance of state-of-the-art solvers on a range of background theories.

1 Introduction

Modern Satisfiability Modulo Theories (SMT) solvers are highly efficient tools, capable of reasoning about constraints over a wide range of logical theories, including (non-linear) real and integer arithmetic, fixed-size bit-vectors, and floating-point arithmetic. Their core algorithms are designed primarily for quantifier-free constraints, but various extensions have been shown to work well also for quantified constraints in many cases. Quantified reasoning in SMT has many practical applications, including software verification, automated theorem proving, and synthesis.

Current SMT solvers handle quantified constraints in a variety of ways, with a degree of effectiveness that usually depends on the background theory. For instance heuristic instantiation techniques such as E-matching [15] are used for quantified formulas with heavy use of uninterpreted functions. These heuristic instantiation techniques are refutationally incomplete but they can be highly effective, in particular in the context of verification applications. For quantified constraints over a particular background theory, such as linear arithmetic or fixed-size bit-vectors, on the other hand, SMT solvers resort to an entirely different set of techniques. While also based on quantifier instantiation, these other

---

* This work was supported in part by DARPA (award no. FA8650-18-2-7861), NSF (award no. 1656926) and ONR (award no. N68335-17-C-0558).

© The Author(s) 2021
J. F. Groote and K. G. Larsen (Eds.): TACAS 2021, LNCS 12652, pp. 145–163, 2021.
https://doi.org/10.1007/978-3-030-72013-1_8

techniques tend to be counterexample-guided and can be complete for theories and fragments of first-order logic that admit quantifier elimination.

Specific previous work in the latter direction includes counterexample-guided quantifier instantiation techniques for linear arithmetic [25] and fixed-size bit-vectors [18,20]. The key to developing each of them is to devise an appropriate, theory-specific *selection function*, which determines a term selection strategy for instantiating universal quantifiers. For some logics, e.g., linear arithmetic, selection functions can be based on the notion of elimination set found in classic algorithms for quantifier elimination [9,14]. However, since many theories used in practice do not admit quantifier elimination, the design of a good selection function is usually non-trivial. These challenges are further magnified when reasoning in combinations of multiple theories.

We propose a novel, *syntax-guided quantifier instantiation (SyQI)* approach, which is both general-purpose and highly effective for quantified formulas in background theories such as (non)linear integer, reals and floating-point arithmetic, and their combinations. The new approach leverages an embedding of a solver for the syntax-guided synthesis (SyGuS) problem [1] within an SMT solver in order to choose terms for quantifier instantiation in a counterexample-guided manner. It is theory-agnostic and only requires the specification, via a grammar, of the set of terms to consider for each sort in the theory when instantiating quantifiers.[3] Since it can be applied to quantified formulas in any background theory, it is more general in scope than previous work [20]. Our approach is intended for logics such as quantified floating-point arithmetic, which would benefit from counterexample-guided quantifier instantiation, but for which appropriate selection function are not obvious. We show that the use of syntax-guided synthesis gives us the flexibility to develop variants of our approach that are highly competitive with the state of the art in SMT solving. More specifically, this paper makes the following *contributions*:

- We present and prove correct a simple yet novel quantifier instantiation approach that leverages syntax-guided synthesis for selecting instantiations.
- We explore variants of the approach along several dimensions, including the choice of symbols to include in grammars for various background theories.
- We implement this technique in the SMT solver CVC4 [5] and show that it performs remarkably well in a wide variety of SMT logics. In particular, it improves upon the state of the art for solving quantified formulas over floating-point arithmetic, and is highly competitive for non-linear integer arithmetic and certain combined logics that involve fixed-size bit-vectors.

Related Work. Handling quantified formulas in SMT solvers is a long-standing challenge. Early approaches for quantified formulas were largely based on E-matching [8,10,15]. They have been later supplemented with techniques that rely on models for establishing satisfiability [11,26], and on conflict finding to accelerate the search for unsatisfiability [27]. Pragmatic enumerative approaches

---

[3] Our implementation provides a default grammar for all supported sorts. In general, grammars can also be provided by the user. We do not explore this option here.

for quantifier instantiation have also been explored and shown to increase the precision of SMT solvers on inputs involving uninterpreted functions where E-matching is incomplete [21]. The approach we describe here is also enumerative in nature; however, it leverages syntax-guided synthesis for choosing instantiations and does not target inputs with uninterpreted functions.

For quantified formulas over a single background theory, counterexample-guided approaches have been considered by Bjørner and Janota [6] and by Reynolds et al. [25], targeting primarily quantified linear integer/real arithmetic. For theories of other data types (e.g., bit-vectors), most approaches use *value-based* instantiation, where concrete variable assignments for a set of quantifier-free formulas derived from the negation of the input formula (the counterexamples) provide instantiations for the universal variables. In the SMT solver Z3 [16], model-based quantifier instantiation (MBQI) [11] is combined with a template-based model finding procedure [29]. A recent line of work by Niemetz et al. [18] leverages invertibility conditions in a counterexample-guided loop for quantifier instantiation of formulas in the theory of fixed-size bit-vectors. Brain et al. [7] lift the concept of invertibility conditions to the theory of floating-point arithmetic and presented a preliminary quantifier elimination procedure for a fragment of the theory based on these conditions. Another approach for lazy quantifier elimination for bit-vector formulas is explored by Vediramana Krishnan et al. [12], based on iterative approximate quantifier elimination.

Reynolds et al. [24] leverage counterexample-guided quantifier instantiation (CEGQI) to efficiently solve a restricted but practically useful form of syntax-guided synthesis problems. In contrast, the work in this paper has the dual goal of leveraging enumerative syntax-guided synthesis to establish a strategy for quantifier instantiation of (first-order) quantified formulas.

SyGuS techniques to solve quantified problems were previously explored by Preiner et al. in [20]. However, instead of focusing on quantifier instantiation they combined enumerative syntax-guided synthesis with value-based quantifier instantiation to synthesize Skolem functions for existential variables.

2   Background

We assume the usual notions and terminology of many-sorted first-order logic with equality (denoted by $\approx$). Let S be a set of *sort symbols*. For every $\sigma \in S$, let X_σ be an infinite set of *variables of sort* σ. Let $X = \bigcup_{\sigma \in S} X_\sigma$. Let Σ be a *signature* consisting of a set $\Sigma^s \subseteq S$ of sort symbols and a set Σ^f of interpreted (and sorted) function symbols $f^{\sigma_1 \cdots \sigma_n \sigma}$ with arity $n \geq 0$ and $\sigma_1, ..., \sigma_n, \sigma \in \Sigma^s$. We assume that Σ includes a Boolean sort Bool and the Boolean values $\top$ (true) and $\bot$ (false). Let $\mathcal{I}$ be a Σ-*interpretation* that maps: each sort $\sigma \in \Sigma^s$ to a non-empty set $\sigma^{\mathcal{I}}$ (the *domain* of $\mathcal{I}$), with $\mathsf{Bool}^{\mathcal{I}} = \{\top, \bot\}$; each variable $x \in X_\sigma$ to an element $x^{\mathcal{I}} \in \sigma^{\mathcal{I}}$; and each function $f^{\sigma_1 \cdots \sigma_n \sigma} \in \Sigma^f$ to a total function $f^{\mathcal{I}}: \sigma_1^{\mathcal{I}} \times ... \times \sigma_n^{\mathcal{I}} \to \sigma^{\mathcal{I}}$ if $n > 0$, and to an element in $\sigma^{\mathcal{I}}$ if $n = 0$.

We assume the usual definition of well-sorted terms, literals, and formulas as Bool terms with variables in X and symbols in Σ, and refer to them as Σ-

terms, Σ-atoms, and so on. A *ground* term/formula is a Σ-term/formula without variables. We define $\boldsymbol{x} = (x_1, ..., x_n)$ as a tuple of variables and write $Q\boldsymbol{x}.\varphi$ with $Q \in \{\forall, \exists\}$ for a *quantified* formula $Qx_1.\cdots Qx_n.\varphi$. A formula is *universal* if it has the form $\forall \boldsymbol{x}.\,P$ where P is a quantifier-free formula. For simplicity, *we consider only universal quantifiers* since existential quantifiers can be rewritten in terms of universal ones. We use $\mathrm{Lit}(\varphi)$ to denote the set of Σ-literals of Σ-formula φ. For a Σ-term or Σ-formula e, we use $e[\boldsymbol{x}]$ to indicate that the free variables of e are in $\boldsymbol{x}$. For a tuple of Σ-terms $\boldsymbol{t} = (t_1, ..., t_n)$, we write $e[\boldsymbol{t}]$ for the term or formula obtained from e by simultaneously replacing each occurrence of x_i in e by t_i. If t is a Σ-term/formula and $\mathcal{I}$ a Σ-interpretation, we write $t^{\mathcal{I}}$ to denote the meaning of t in $\mathcal{I}$. We use the usual inductive definition of a satisfiability relation $\models$ between Σ-interpretations and Σ-formulas.

A *theory* T is a pair (Σ, I), where Σ is a signature and I is a non-empty class of Σ-interpretations (the *models* of T) that is closed under variable reassignment, i.e., every Σ-interpretation that only differs from an $\mathcal{I} \in I$ in how it interprets variables is also in I. A Σ-formula φ is *T-satisfiable* (resp. *T-unsatisfiable*) if it is satisfied by some (resp. no) interpretation in I; it is *T-valid* if it is satisfied by all interpretations in I.

Enumerative SyGuS using an Embedding into Datatypes. A syntax-guided synthesis problem for an n-ary function f in a background theory T consists of a set of semantic restrictions (a *specification*) for f, given as a (second-order) T-formula of the form $\exists f.\,\varphi[f]$, and a set of syntactic restrictions on the solutions for f, typically expressed as a *context-free grammar*. A solution to such a problem is a term $t[x_1, \ldots, x_n]$ that satisfies the syntactic restrictions and is such that the formula $\varphi[\lambda x_1, \ldots, x_n.t]$ is T-valid.

As shown in previous work [24], syntactic restrictions for the bodies of functions to synthesize can be conveniently represented as a set of *(algebraic) datatypes*. The setting in this paper is simpler. Instead of synthesizing terms corresponding to function bodies, we use context-free-grammars for defining a set of (first-order) terms in a given theory, possibly containing free function symbols. For instance, let a and b be free constants of sort Int. The context-free grammar R below specifies a set of integer (Z) and Boolean (B) terms:

$$Z ::= 0 \mid 1 \mid a \mid b \mid Z + Z \mid Z - Z \mid \mathsf{ite}(B, Z, Z) \tag{1}$$

$$B ::= B \geq B \mid Z \approx Z \mid \neg B \mid B \wedge B \tag{2}$$

Given such a grammar, our SyGuS solver generates the following mutually recursive datatypes:

$$\mathcal{Z} = \mathsf{zero} \mid \mathsf{one} \mid \mathsf{a} \mid \mathsf{b} \mid \mathsf{plus}(\mathcal{Z}, \mathcal{Z}) \mid \mathsf{minus}(\mathcal{Z}, \mathcal{Z}) \mid \mathsf{ite}(\mathcal{B}, \mathcal{Z}, \mathcal{Z}) \tag{3}$$

$$\mathcal{B} = \mathsf{geq}(\mathcal{Z}, \mathcal{Z}) \mid \mathsf{eq}(\mathcal{Z}, \mathcal{Z}) \mid \mathsf{not}(\mathcal{B}) \mid \mathsf{and}(\mathcal{B}, \mathcal{B}) \tag{4}$$

Each datatype constructor, listed on the right-hand side of each equation, corresponds to a production rule of R, e.g., plus corresponds to the rule $Z ::= Z + Z$. Given a datatype value v, we write $\mathbf{to\_term}(v)$ to denote the term that v represents, e.g., $\mathbf{to\_term}(\mathsf{plus}(\mathsf{a}, \mathsf{b}))$ is the term $a + b$.

In previous work [22, 24], a *smart* enumerative approach for syntax-guided synthesis was presented and implemented in CVC4. In that work, the generation of terms is based on finding solutions for an evolving set of constraints in an extension of the quantifier-free fragment of algebraic datatypes, for which some SMT solvers have dedicated decision procedures [3, 23]. In the remainder of this paper, we write T_D to denote the theory of datatypes over a signature Σ_D of *constructor* and *selector* symbols. The signature Σ_D includes (parametric) datatype sorts that are interpreted as the universe of a term algebra over the constructors. Selectors are interpreted as functions that extract the immediate subterms of a constructor term.

In our setting, datatype constraints are used to express syntactic restrictions on the terms in the original theory. For instance, in case of the example theory and corresponding datatypes $\mathcal{Z}$ and $\mathcal{B}$ defined above, we can write a datatype constraint that is falsified by all terms of the form $\mathsf{plus}(\mathsf{zero}, t)$ where t is a constructor term of sort $\mathcal{Z}$. This corresponds to ruling out terms of the form $(0 + \ldots)$ in the original theory where s is a term of sort Int. In more detail, for a datatype term d, we write $\mathsf{is}_C(d)$ to denote the *discriminator* predicate, which is satisfied exactly when d is interpreted as a datatype value whose top constructor is C. We write $\mathsf{sel}_{\sigma,n}(d)$ to denote a *shared selector* [28] applied to d, interpreted as the nth child of d with sort σ if one exists, and as an arbitrary element of σ otherwise. These symbols are used for constructing *blocking constraints*. For example, we can write $\neg\mathsf{is}_{\mathsf{plus}}(d) \vee \neg\mathsf{is}_{\mathsf{zero}}(\mathsf{sel}_{\mathcal{Z},1}(d))$ to state the constraint above that d cannot be interpreted as any datatype value corresponding to an Int term of the form $(0 + \ldots)$. In the context of syntax-guided synthesis, a constraint like this is added, for instance, to filter out redundant terms (like $0 + \ldots$) or terms already known to falsify the synthesis conjecture.

Our approach for syntax-guided instantiation relies on a notion of *evaluation variables*. A related, more general, notion of evaluation functions was used in the context of syntax-guided synthesis (see Section 2 of [22] for details). Let d be a term of a datatype sort encoding a grammar over terms of sort σ. We write e_d to denote a free constant of sort σ, which we call the evaluation variable for d. We use evaluation variables to determine which terms to use in instantiations of quantified formulas. The algorithm given in the following section will add constraints that force the interpretation of e_d to be equal to $\mathsf{to\_term}(d^{\mathcal{I}})$ in interpretations $\mathcal{I}$. A simple example of such a constraint is $\mathsf{is}_{\mathsf{a}}(d) \Rightarrow \mathsf{e}_d \approx a$, stating that the evaluation variable e_d for d is equal to the free constant a of integer type when d is interpreted as the datatype value a.

3   SyGuS Quantifier Instantiation (SyQI)

Our new SyGuS-based instantiation approach combines counterexample-guided quantifier instantiation (CEGQI) with smart enumerative SyGuS techniques to synthesize terms for quantifier instantiation. In essence, it is an algorithm that tries to synthesize a term t for a variable x in a given formula $\forall x.\, P[x]$ such that $\neg P[t]$ holds. For synthesis purposes, each quantified variable is associated with

---

Algorithm 1 Main algorithms of the SyQI approach.

1: **procedure syqi**($\{Q_1, \ldots, Q_n\}, G$)
2:    **for** $Q_j \in \{Q_1, \ldots, Q_n\}$ with $Q_j = \forall \boldsymbol{x}. P[\boldsymbol{x}]$ **do**
3:       **for** $x \in \boldsymbol{x}$ **do**
4:          Let d_x be a fresh global constant of datatype sort **grammar**$_{\mathcal{S}}(x)$
5:          $G := G \cup \{l_j \Rightarrow \neg P[\mathbf{e}_{\boldsymbol{d_x}}]\}$ with fresh Boolean constant l_j and fresh $\mathbf{e}_{d_x}$
6:    **repeat**
7:       **if check**$(G) = unsat$ **then return** $unsat$
8:       $r, \mathcal{I} := \mathbf{check}(G \wedge (l_1 \vee \ldots \vee l_n))$
9:       **if** $r = unsat$ **then return** sat
10:      **for** $l_j \in \{l_1, \ldots, l_n\}$ such that $l_j^{\mathcal{I}} = \top$ **do**
11:         $G := G \cup \mathbf{select\_lemmas}_{\mathcal{L}}(Q_j, \mathcal{I})$

12: **procedure select_lemmas**$_{\mathcal{L}}(\forall x_1, \ldots, x_p. P[x_1, \ldots, x_p], \mathcal{I})$
13:   $L := \emptyset$
14:   **for** $x_i \in \{x_1, \ldots, x_p\}$ **do**
15:      $t_i := \mathbf{to\_term}(d_{x_i}^{\mathcal{I}})$
16:      $L := L \cup \{\mathbf{explain}(d_{x_i} \approx d_{x_i}^{\mathcal{I}}) \Rightarrow \mathbf{e}_{d_{x_i}} \approx \mathbf{to\_term}(d_{x_i}^{\mathcal{I}})\}$
17:      **return** non-empty subset of $\{P[t_1, \ldots, t_p]\} \cup L$ based on selection strategy $\mathcal{L}$

---

a SyGuS grammar based on the sort of the variable. For example, our algorithm uses a bit-vector-specific grammar to synthesize bit-vector terms as possible instantiations of quantified variables of bit-vector sort. Our SyGuS solver suggests instantiations based on such grammars and an evolving set of constraints on the instance term. The main advantage of this instantiation approach is that it does not require theory-specific quantifier instantiation algorithms. Its only theory-specific aspects are the construction of the grammar for each theory sort and the satisfiability checks performed on the generated instances.

Algorithm 1 shows the two main procedures **syqi** and **select_lemmas**$_{\mathcal{L}}$ of our SyGuS instantiation approach. To simplify the exposition, we describe the restricted case where the quantified input formula are all universal. Our implementation in CVC4, however, applies to the general case through a lazy conversion to DNF and resolution of quantifier alternations.

Procedure **syqi** takes as argument a set $\{Q_1, \ldots, Q_n\}$ of *universal* (quantified) T-formulas and a set G of *ground* T-formulas. As an initial step, and prior to solving the problem, we generate a lemma for each quantified formula Q_i as part of our counterexample-guided quantifier instantiation approach (lines 2-5). We first create a fresh datatype constant d_x of sort **grammar**$_{\mathcal{S}}(x)$ for each variable $x \in \boldsymbol{x}$ in each input formula $\forall \boldsymbol{x}. P[\boldsymbol{x}]$. The datatype sort **grammar**$_{\mathcal{S}}(x)$ is constructed from a SyGuS grammar determined by the sort of variable x. The language generated by the grammar includes ground terms from Q_i and G of the same sort. These terms are chosen following a selection strategy $\mathcal{S}$, which we describe in Section 3.1. Apart from running **check**, used as a black box, **grammar**$_{\mathcal{S}}$ implements the only theory-specific handling of our procedure. Finally, we add to G a lemma of the form $l_i \Rightarrow \neg P[\mathbf{e}_{d_x}]$ for each quantified formula, where l_i is a fresh Boolean constant (the counterexample literal for Q_i). Thanks to l_i being fresh, this preserves the satisfiability of G. The notation $\mathbf{e}_{d_x}$ is a shorthand for $(\mathbf{e}_{d_{x_1}}, \ldots, \mathbf{e}_{d_{x_m}})$, the tuple of evaluation variables for each d_x of $x \in \boldsymbol{x}$. The purpose of a counterexample lemma is twofold. First, it indicates whether a quantified formula Q_i is *active* (l_i assigned to true) or *inactive* (l_i assigned to false). Second, it focuses on finding counterexamples that falsify the body of Q_i.

The main loop of procedure **syqi** is provided in lines 6-11. Each iteration starts with a quantifier-free satisfiability check (performed by procedure **check** on line 7) on the current set of ground formulas G in the combined theory $T \cup T_D$. If G is unsatisfiable, procedure **syqi** returns *unsat*. If G is satisfiable, the procedure further checks whether it can find a counterexample for any of the quantified formulas $Q_1, \ldots, Q_n$, which is done by checking the satisfiability of $G \wedge (l_1 \vee \ldots \vee l_n)$. If the check returns *unsat* then no more counterexamples can be found; the algorithm concludes that input set is satisfiable and returns *sat*. The reason is that, in this case, the set G is satisfiable and entails each input formula, as proven later in this section. If the second call to **check** (line 8) returns *sat*, it additionally returns (a finite representation of) a model $\mathcal{I}$ for the current set of ground formulas G. Since $\mathcal{I}$ satisfies $l_1 \vee \ldots \vee l_n$, it does not satisfy at least one quantified formula in $Q_1, \ldots, Q_n$.[4] For each active quantified formula in $\mathcal{I}$, we generate new lemmas via procedure **select_lemmas**$_{\mathcal{L}}$ (lines 10-11), and repeat the main loop of the algorithm. Note that the second satisfiability check can be avoided by employing a special decision heuristic for counterexample literals l_i in the SAT solver. The decision heuristic will always assign a counterexample literal l_i to true on a decision. Consequently, l_i can only be assigned to false in a candidate interpretation $\mathcal{I}$ if $\neg l_i$ is entailed by the set of ground formulas G.

Procedure **select_lemmas**$_{\mathcal{L}}$ takes a formula $\forall \boldsymbol{x}. P[\boldsymbol{x}]$ and a model $\mathcal{I}$ as arguments and generates a set of lemmas based on $\mathcal{I}$ and selection strategy $\mathcal{L}$. The procedure maintains the invariant of always returning a set of lemmas L where $L \setminus G$ is non-empty. This set L includes a single *instantiation lemma* (of the form $P[t]$) and an *evaluation unfolding lemmas* (see below) for each variable $x \in \boldsymbol{x}$. The returned lemmas are generated based on one of three *lemma selection strategies*: priority-inst, priority-eval, and interleave. Strategy interleave selects both the instantiation lemma and a set of evaluation unfolding lemmas at the same time. Strategies priority-inst and priority-eval give priority to instantiation lemmas and evaluation unfolding lemmas, respectively; i.e., strategy priority-inst selects the instantiation lemma and only selects evaluation unfolding lemmas if the instantiation lemma was already in G. Analogously, priority-eval gives priority to evaluation unfolding lemmas.

The various lemmas are constructed as follows. For each variable $x \in \boldsymbol{x}$ we use the model value $d_x^{\mathcal{I}}$ of datatype constant d_x to construct the corresponding term **to_term**$(d_x^{\mathcal{I}})$ in the theory of variable x (line 15). The constructed term corresponds to a term synthesized by the SyGuS extension of our datatypes

---

[4] Note that this does not mean the quantified formula is unsatisfiable, only that it is not satisfied in $\mathcal{I}$.

solver based on the grammar specified for x. To ensure that d_x evaluates to the same values as term $\textbf{to\_term}(d_x^{\mathcal{I}})$ under model value $d_x^{\mathcal{I}}$, we generate the evaluation unfolding lemma $\textbf{explain}(d_x \approx d_x^{\mathcal{I}}) \Rightarrow \textsf{e}_{d_x} \approx \textbf{to\_term}(d_x^{\mathcal{I}})$. The explanation for the model value $d_x^{\mathcal{I}}$ is expressed in terms of discriminator predicates. For example, if value $d_x^{\mathcal{I}}$ represents term $a + b$, the procedure generates lemma $\textsf{is}_{\textsf{plus}}(d_x) \wedge \textsf{is}_{\textsf{a}}(\textsf{sel}_{\mathcal{Z},1}(d_x)) \wedge \textsf{is}_{\textsf{b}}(\textsf{sel}_{\mathcal{Z},2}(d_x)) \Rightarrow \textsf{e}_{d_x} = a + b$. As a last step, $\textbf{select\_lemmas}_{\mathcal{L}}$ selects a non-empty subset of the generated instantiation lemma $P[t_1, \ldots, t_p]$ (where each t_i is $\textbf{to\_term}(d_{x_i}^{\mathcal{I}})$) and the evaluation unfolding lemmas L according to the lemma selection strategy $\mathcal{L}$.

We now discuss the correctness properties of our approach. In the following, we say a grammar R for sort σ is *complete*, if for all interpretations $\mathcal{I}$ and values v of sort σ, it generates at least one term t such that $t^{\mathcal{I}} = v$. Note that we only consider complete grammars in this paper. We say a lemma selection strategy $\mathcal{L}$ is *fair* wrt a set of formulas G if it returns a set of lemmas that contain at least one lemma inequivalent to each formula in G whenever such lemma exists.

Theorem 1. *Let T be a theory with signature Σ, let F be a set of universal formulas $\{Q_1, \ldots, Q_n\}$ and G_0 is a set of quantifier-free formulas. If all grammars constructed by the calls to $\textbf{grammar}_S$ in $\textbf{syqi}$ are complete and the selection strategy $\mathcal{L}$ used for $\textbf{select\_lemmas}_{\mathcal{L}}$ is fair, then the following statements hold:*

1. *(Refutation Soundness) If $\textbf{syqi}(F, G_0)$ returns unsat, $F \cup G_0$ is T-unsatisfiable.*
2. *(Model soundness) If $\textbf{syqi}(F, G_0)$ returns sat, $F \cup G_0$ is T-satisfiable.*
3. *(Progress) Let G_i be the current state of the set of ground formulas G after i iterations of $\textbf{syqi}$ (lines 6-11). Each iteration $i + 1$ adds at least one new formula to G_i, so that $G_{i+1} \setminus G_i \neq \emptyset$.*

Conceptually, the proof of refutational soundness relies on the fact that all lemmas added to G are entailed by the input or maintain equisatisfiability with respect to the input. The proof of model soundness relies on the fact that when G collectively entails the negation of (all) quantified formulas, then the current model $\mathcal{I}$ for G must be a model for all quantified formulas. Procedure $\textbf{syqi}$ is not terminating in general. However, the progress property guarantees that the algorithm does not get stuck in a single state and keeps making progress towards refining the set of possible models by ruling out at least one candidate model at each iteration of the procedure's main loop.

Proof. For brevity, we show these statements for the case of $n = 1$ and where Q_1 is $\forall \boldsymbol{x}. P[\boldsymbol{x}]$; the proof can be easily lifted to $n > 1$. When $\textbf{syqi}(F, G_0)$ terminates, the internal set G is the union of:

- The initial quantifier-free formula G_0,
- The counterexample lemma G_{cex} of the form $l \Rightarrow \neg P[\boldsymbol{e}_{d_x}]$ added on line 5,
- A set of instantiations G_{inst} of the form $P[\boldsymbol{t}]$, and
- A set of evaluation lemmas G_{ev} of the form $C[d] \Rightarrow \textsf{e}_d \approx t$.

To show (1), assume that φ is satisfied by some Σ-interpretation $\mathcal{J}$, where without loss of generality assume that $l^{\mathcal{J}}$ is false. Let $\mathcal{I}$ be a $\Sigma \cup \Sigma_{\mathsf{D}}$-interpretation that extends $\mathcal{J}$ such that for each evaluation variable e_d, the interpretation of d in $\mathcal{I}$ is such that $\mathbf{to\_term}(d^{\mathcal{I}})^{\mathcal{I}} = \mathsf{e}_d^{\mathcal{I}}$. Such a value exists since our grammars are complete by assumption. We show that $\mathcal{I}$ satisfies each formula ψ in G. If $\psi \in G_0$, then this holds since $\mathcal{J}$ satisfies φ, and hence, by extension $\mathcal{I}$ does as well. If $\psi \in G_{cex}$, then ψ is satisfied by $\mathcal{I}$ since it interprets l_i as false. If $\psi \in G_{inst}$ is an instantiation lemma of some Q_i, then it is satisfied by $\mathcal{I}$ since $\mathcal{J}$ also satisfies Q_i. If $\psi \in G_{ev}$ is an evaluation lemma, this is satisfied by our construction of $d^{\mathcal{I}}$. Thus φ is T-satisfiable, then G must be $(T \cup T_{\mathsf{D}})$-satisfiable. Thus, since $\mathbf{syqi}(F, G_0)$ returns $unsat$ when G is $(T \cup T_{\mathsf{D}})$-unsatisfiable, this means that $F \cup G_0$ must be T-unsatisfiable as well.

To show (2), if $\mathbf{syqi}(F, G_0)$ returns sat, then the set G is satisfied by some $\Sigma \cup \Sigma_{\mathsf{D}}$-interpretation and $G \cup \{l_1\}$ is unsatisfiable. Let $\mathcal{J}$ be the Σ-interpretation that interprets all symbols in Σ the same as in $\mathcal{I}$. Since $G \cup \{l_1\}$ is unsatisfiable, we have that $G_0 \cup G_{inst} \cup G_{ev} \cup \{\neg P[\mathsf{e}_{d_x}]\}$ is $T \cup T_{\mathsf{D}}$-unsatisfiable. Since all Σ-interpretations can be lifted to a $\Sigma \cup \Sigma_{\mathsf{D}}$-interpretation satisfying G_{ev}, it must also be the case that $G_0 \cup G_{inst} \cup \{\neg P[\mathsf{e}_{d_x}]\}$ is T-unsatisfiable. Hence, all models of $G_0 \cup G_{inst}$ must make $P[\mathsf{e}_{d_x}]$ true. Since e_{d_x} does not occur in $G_0 \cup G_{inst}$, this implies that all models of $G_0 \cup G_{inst}$ satisfy $\forall x.\, P[x]$. Since $G_0 \cup G_{inst} \subseteq G$ and $\mathcal{I}$ satisfies G, we have that $\mathcal{J}$ satisfies $\{\forall x.P[x]\} \cup G$.

To show (3), assume $ad\ absurdum$ that G is satisfied by a $T \cup T_{\mathsf{D}}$-interpretation $\mathcal{I}$ where $\mathbf{to\_term}(d_x{}^{\mathcal{I}}) = t$ and Q_1 is active in $\mathcal{I}$. Also assume that G contains the evaluation unfolding lemmas for $d_x{}^{\mathcal{I}}$ and the instantiation lemma $P[t]$. Due to the former, we have that $\mathsf{e}_{d_x}{}^{\mathcal{I}} = t^{\mathcal{I}}$. Since Q_1 is active in $\mathcal{I}$, $\mathcal{I}$ satisfies $\neg P[\mathsf{e}_{d_x}]$. However, $P[t]$ is also satisfied by $\mathcal{I}$, a contradiction. Thus, at least one of the lemmas returned by $\mathbf{select\_lemmas}_{\mathcal{L}}$ for Q_1 must be inequivalent to the lemmas in G, due to our assumption that $\mathcal{L}$ is a fair selection strategy. $\square$

3.1   Grammar Construction

For quantifier instantiation, we focus on the theories of fixed-size bit-vectors, floating-point numbers, integers, and reals as defined by the SMT-LIB 2 standard [4]. The signature of the theory of fixed-size bit-vectors includes a unique sort for each positive bit-vector width n, denoted here as $\mathsf{BV}_{[n]}$. The signature of the theory of floating-point numbers includes a rounding-mode sort RM and a unique floating-point sort for each combination of positive exponent width e and significand width s, denoted here as $\mathsf{FP}_{[e,s]}$. The theories of Integers and Reals include the integer sort Int and the real sort Real, respectively. For each of these sorts we define a SyGuS grammar that includes the following operators and constants.

$$R_{\mathrm{BV}} : \{\sim, -, \&, |, \oplus, +, \cdot, \div, \div_s, \mathrm{mod}, \mathrm{mod}_s \ll, \gg, \gg_a, 0, 1, \mathrm{ones}, \mathrm{smin}, \mathrm{smax}\}$$

$$R_{\mathrm{FP}} : \{-, \mathrm{abs}, \mathrm{rem}, \sqrt{}, \mathrm{rti}, +, \cdot, \div, \mathrm{fma}, \mathrm{NaN}, \pm\infty, \pm 0, \pm\mathrm{min}^s, \pm\mathrm{max}^s, \pm\mathrm{min}^n, \pm\mathrm{max}^n\}$$

$$R_{\mathrm{RM}} : \{\mathrm{RNA}, \mathrm{RNE}, \mathrm{RTE}, \mathrm{RTP}, \mathrm{RTZ}\} \qquad R_{\mathrm{Int}} : \{+, -, 0, 1\} \qquad R_{\mathrm{Real}} : \{+, -, \div, 0, 1\}$$

Theory	Symbol	SMT-LIB Syntax	Sort
	$\sim, -$	bvnot, bvneg	$BV_{[n]} \to BV_{[n]}$
	$\&, |, \oplus$	bvand, bvor, bvxor	$BV_{[n]} \times BV_{[n]} \to BV_{[n]}$
BV	$\ll, \gg, \gg_a$	bvshl, bvlshr, bvashr	$BV_{[n]} \times BV_{[n]} \to BV_{[n]}$
	$+, -, \cdot$	bvadd, bvsub, bvmul	$BV_{[n]} \times BV_{[n]} \to BV_{[n]}$
	$\div, \div_s, \mathrm{mod}, \mathrm{mod}_s$	bvudiv, bvsdiv, bvurem, bvsrem	$BV_{[n]} \times BV_{[n]} \to BV_{[n]}$
	$-, \mathrm{abs}$	fp.neg, fp.abs	$FP_{[e,s]} \to FP_{[e,s]}$
	rem	fp.rem	$FP_{[e,s]} \times FP_{[e,s]} \to FP_{[e,s]}$
FP	$\sqrt{}$, rti	fp.sqrt, fp.roundToIntegral	$RM \times FP_{[e,s]} \to FP_{[e,s]}$
	$+, \cdot, \div$	fp.add, fp.mul, fp.div	$RM \times FP_{[e,s]} \times FP_{[e,s]} \to FP_{[e,s]}$
	fma	fp.fma	$RM \times FP_{[e,s]} \times FP_{[e,s]} \times FP_{[e,s]} \to FP_{[e,s]}$
Ints	$+, -$	$+, -$	$Int \times Int \to Int$
Reals	$+, -, \div$	$+, -, /$	$Real \times Real \to Real$

Table 1. Set of operators considered in SyGuS grammars.

The (non-constant) operators and their SMT-LIB names and types are listed in Table 1. Note that we further restrict the division operator $\div$ of sort Real to division by value, i.e., we do not allow division by an arbitrary term of sort Real. We also add a set of special values of the corresponding sort to each default grammar. We represent *bit-vector* values of sort $BV_{[n]}$ as bit-strings of length n, where the left-most bit is the most significant bit. For *floating-point* values of sort $FP_{[e,s]}$, we use bit strings where the left-most bit indicates the sign, the following e bits represent the exponent, and the remaining bits the significand. For the theory of fixed-size bit-vectors, we use $smax_{[n]}$ or $smin_{[n]}$ for the *maximum* or *minimum signed value* of width n, e.g., $smax_{[4]} = 0111$ and $smin_{[4]} = 1000$, and $ones_{[n]}$ for the maximum unsigned value, e.g., $ones_{[4]} = 1111$. For the theory of floating-point numbers, we use ± 0 for *positive* and *negative zero*, $\pm\infty$ for *positive* and *negative infinity*, and NaN for *not a number*, e.g., $-0_{[3,5]} = 10000000$ and $+\infty_{[3,5]} = 01110000$. We further use $\pm\mathrm{min}^s$ for the *positive* and *negative smallest subnormal*, $\pm\mathrm{max}^s$ for the *positive* and *negative largest subnormal*, $\pm\mathrm{min}^n$ for the *positive* and *negative smallest normal*, and $\pm\mathrm{max}^n$ for the *positive* and *negative largest normal*, e.g., $-\mathrm{max}^s_{[3,5]} = 10001111$ and $+\mathrm{min}^n_{[3,5]} = 00010000$. In the definition of grammar R_{FP} above, we use symbol $\pm$ to indicate that both the positive and negative variant of a special value is included in the grammar.

We extend the above set of default grammars (**grammar**$_S$ in Algorithm 1) with ground terms that occur in an input set $\{Q_1, \ldots, Q_n\} \cup G_0$ based on the sort of variable $x \in \boldsymbol{x}$ in $Q_i = \forall \boldsymbol{x}. P[\boldsymbol{x}]$ and a *term selection strategy*. This strategy is based on the following two factors. We consider three modes for the *scope* of ground terms: (1) ground terms that occur in quantified formula Q_i (strategy in) (2) ground terms that occur in the set of ground formulas G (strategy out), and (3) the union of (1) and (2) (strategy both). We consider three modes for the *size* of ground terms, defined as the number of subterms a term consists of: (a) terms of *minimal* size, i.e., constants that occur in a term (strategy min) (b) terms of *maximal* size (strategy max), and (c) the union of (a) and (b) (strategy both). For example, for a ground term $a + b \cdot c$, strategy min will select a, b, c, max will select $a + b \cdot c$, and both will select $a, b, c, a + b \cdot c$. Each of the scope and size modes may be combined, giving $3 * 3 = 9$ possible term selection strategies.

Example 1. Let $Q = \forall x.\, x \cdot x \not\approx a \cdot a + b \cdot b + 2 \cdot a \cdot b$ where x, a, b have integer type and suppose we run $\mathbf{syqi}(\{Q\}, \emptyset)$. The algorithm first constructs the grammar $\mathbf{grammar}_S(x)$ for x, where we assume term selection strategy S with scope in and size min, which considers ground terms that occur in Q and are of minimal size (2, a, and b). This grammar is encoded as the following datatype $\mathcal{Z}$:

$$\mathcal{Z} = \mathsf{zero} \mid \mathsf{one} \mid \mathsf{plus}(\mathcal{Z}, \mathcal{Z}) \mid \mathsf{minus}(\mathcal{Z}, \mathcal{Z}) \mid \mathsf{two} \mid \mathsf{a} \mid \mathsf{b}$$

The algorithm introduces a fresh datatype variable d_x of type $\mathcal{Z}$, a fresh integer variable e_{d_x} of integer type, and adds $l \Rightarrow \mathsf{e}_{d_x} \cdot \mathsf{e}_{d_x} \approx a \cdot a + b \cdot b + 2 \cdot a \cdot b$ to the internal set G of ground formulas, where l is a fresh Boolean variable. In the first iteration of the loop, we have that G (and $G \cup \{l\}$) are satisfiable. Hence, the algorithm calls $\mathbf{select\_lemmas}_{\mathcal{L}}$ on Q and a model $\mathcal{I}$ for G; assume that $d_x^{\mathcal{I}} = \mathsf{zero}$ and $\mathsf{e}_{d_x}^{\mathcal{I}} = a^{\mathcal{I}} = b^{\mathcal{I}} = 0$. Based on the lemma selection strategy, we may choose to add the instantiation lemma $0 \cdot 0 \not\approx a \cdot a + b \cdot b + 2 \cdot a \cdot b$, or the evaluation lemma $\mathsf{is}_{\mathsf{zero}}(d_x) \Rightarrow \mathsf{e}_{d_x} \approx 0$, or both lemmas to G. Assuming both lemmas are added to G, the next iteration of the loop will consider a new model $\mathcal{I}'$ where $d_x^{\mathcal{I}'} \neq \mathsf{zero}$ and $\mathsf{e}_{d_x}^{\mathcal{I}'} \neq 0$. The algorithm will continue finding models with new values for d_x, until it finds a model $\mathcal{I}''$ where $d_x^{\mathcal{I}''} = \mathsf{plus}(\mathsf{a}, \mathsf{b})$. At this point the instantiation lemma $(a + b) \cdot (a + b) \not\approx a \cdot a + b \cdot b + 2 \cdot a \cdot b$ will be added to G, which is equivalent to false, and $\mathbf{syqi}$ will terminate with *unsat*.   □

3.2   Implementation Details

We implemented syntax-guided quantifier instantiation in the CVC4 [5] solver, which has support for a wide range of background theories, covering all those in the SMT-LIB standard library [2]. CVC4 is based on the CDCL(T) (formerly DPLL(T)) framework [19]. This framework integrates a propositional SAT solver, which attempts to find a Boolean assignment that propositionally satisfies the input formula, with one or more specialize theory solvers, which monitor the assignments made by the SAT solver to theory literal and flag a conflict if the assignments are ever inconsistent in their theory.

Our SyQI technique is implemented as a module of the subsolver of CVC4 that handles quantified formulas. We leverage CVC4's support for smart enumerative SyGuS as described in Reynolds et al. [22]. Specifically, the **check** method in line 7 in Algorithm 1 involves calling the (combination) of quantifier-free theory solvers, which includes an extension of the theory of datatypes described in the following.

Symmetry Breaking for Smart Enumerative Synthesis. As described in previous work [22, 24], CVC4 uses advanced techniques for *symmetry breaking* for the datatypes over which context-free grammars are embedded. The quantifier-free datatype theory solver in CVC4 is extended to issue symmetry blocking clauses based on reasoning about such datatypes, so that the models we generate for a datatype variable d are such that $\textbf{to\_term}(d)$ is unique with respect to rewriting. For example, the terms $a + b$ and $b + a$ are equivalent, and in CVC4, one will be rewritten to the other. Thus, we know that we only have to consider one variant, e.g., $a + b$. Hence, the extended datatypes solver may issue the blocking clause $\neg \textsf{is}_{\textsf{plus}}(d) \vee \neg \textsf{is}_b(\textsf{sel}_{\mathcal{Z},1}(d)) \vee \neg \textsf{is}_a(\textsf{sel}_{\mathcal{Z},2}(d))$, effectively stating that the term associated with d should not be $b + a$. This technique is highly valuable for syntax-guided synthesis, since it reduces the set of terms considered in the search for candidate solutions. In the context of this work, these techniques are of great importance, since they guarantee that our algorithm does not consider multiple instantiations over tuples of pairwise equivalent terms.

Quantified Formulas within Boolean Structure and Nested Quantification. As mentioned earlier, while not shown in Algorithm 1, our approach uses standard techniques for handling qeneral quantified formulas, in particular with quantifiers that occur below Boolean connectives. In the context of CDCL(T), for each quantified formula Q_i of the form $\forall \boldsymbol{x}.\, P[\boldsymbol{x}]$, the propositional model of our Boolean structure may either assign Q_i to true or false, or leave it unassigned. Quantified formulas that are assigned to false are *Skolemized*, i.e., a lemma of the form $\neg Q_i \Rightarrow \neg P[\boldsymbol{k}]$, where $\boldsymbol{k}$ are fresh constants, is returned to the SAT solver. Quantified formulas that are unassigned are ignored. Quantified formulas that are assigned to true are either active or inactive based on the value assigned to their counterexample literals. Those that are active are processed via $\textbf{select\_lemmas}_{\mathcal{L}}$. In practice, instantiation lemmas are guarded so that $Q_i \Rightarrow P[t]$ is returned to the SAT solver, meaning that the conclusion only holds when Q_i is assigned to true. Furthermore, each Q_i may have nested quantification, that is, the formula P the counterexample lemma $l_i \Rightarrow \neg P[\mathbf{e}_{d_x}]$ may contain quantified subformulas. Those quantified formulas are then processed by our full algorithm in the same way as quantified formulas from the input.

4   Experiments

We implemented our approach in the SMT solver CVC4 [5]. We provide here an extensive evaluation of the techniques and strategies described in Section 3. We first evaluate term and lemma selection strategies for grammar construction, and then compare the performance of our best configuration against Z3 [16], the only state-of-the-art SMT solver besides CVC4 that supports all the logics supported by our implementation.

We performed all experiments on a cluster with Intel Xeon CPU E5-2620 CPUs with 2.1GHz and 128GB memory. We used a time limit of 300 seconds, and an 8GB memory limit for each solver/benchmark pair and count memory out as time out. We evaluate here all configurations on all quantified logics in SMT-LIB [2] that do not contain uninterpreted functions (UF). As an exception, we include the logic UFBV, since the benchmarks in this logic rely

Strategy	Solved	Sat	Unsat	TO	MO	Uniq	Time[s]
Term Selection Strategies							
both-max	12865	825	12040	2871	10	8	886137.3
both-both	12848	823	12025	2887	11	12	892219.8
both-min	12843	819	12024	2893	10	10	893808.7
in-both	12688	831	11857	3052	6	6	939886.7
in-min	12673	828	11845	3065	8	4	944167.2
in-max	12667	832	11835	3067	12	7	944952.3
out-both	12660	785	11875	3081	5	3	948301.4
out-min	12643	788	11855	3098	5	2	954925.1
out-max	12616	774	11842	3127	3	6	961683.9
Lemma Selection Strategies							
interleave	12848	823	12025	2887	11	60	892272.2
priority-inst	12838	821	12017	2893	15	49	897454.3
priority-eval	12721	821	11900	3019	6	52	938443.4

Table 2. Selection strategies on considered logics (15,746 benchmarks).

almost entirely on BV reasoning only. We generally exclude logics with UF since for such logics counterexample-guided techniques, as in our approach, are not expected to be more effective than heuristic instantiation techniques such as E-matching, which we confirmed in a preliminary evaluation. Overall, we include logics BV (bit-vectors), FP (floating-point arithmetic), LIA (linear integer arithmetic), LRA (linear real arithmetic), NIA (non-linear integer arithmetic), NRA (non-linear real arithmetic), and their combinations BVFP, BVFPLRA, FPLRA, and UFBV. In total, our benchmark set consists of 15,746 benchmarks.

Term Selection for Grammar Construction. As a first experiment, we determine the best combination of scope-based and size-based ground term selection strategies for grammar construction as introduced in Section 3.1. We combine strategies based on scope with strategies based on term size into *nine* selection strategies: in-min, in-max, in-both, out-min, out-max, out-both, both-min, both-max, both-both. The results for our SyGuS instantiation approach with these strategies enabled is shown in Table 2. Note that preliminary experiments identified lemma selection strategy interleave as the best. Hence, we use strategy interleave as the lemma selection strategy for this experiment.

Overall, using strategy both for the scope performs best. Furthermore, for this strategy all three size-based strategies perform equally well. For the remaining experiments, we use strategy both-both as the term selection strategy for grammar construction, where both minimal and maximal ground terms are selected from both the quantified formula Q_i (containing the variable we construct a grammar for) and the set of ground formulas G. Note that we choose the more general strategy both-both over strategy both-max even though both-max performs slightly better.

Lemma Selection. In our second experiment, we determine the best lemma selection strategy out of the three strategies priority-inst, priority-eval and interleave described in Section 3. The results are shown in Table 2. Note that we use the previously determined best term selection strategy both-both in this experiment.

The best overall strategy is interleave, indicating that it is beneficial to consider instantiation lemmas and evaluation unfolding lemmas in parallel. On the other hand, prioritizing evaluation lemmas over instantiation lemmas (priority-eval) performed significantly worse than the other two configurations. Since this strategy prioritizes evaluation lemmas, it has the advantage over other configurations of delaying instantiations until we obtain an interpretation $\mathcal{I}$ where the interpretation of e_{d_x} is consistent with respect to d_x, i.e., $e_{d_x}^{\mathcal{I}} = \text{to\_term}(d_x)^{\mathcal{I}}$. As a consequence, prioritizing evaluation lemmas puts more effort into finding terms in instantiation that are guaranteed to refine the current candidate model $\mathcal{I}$. However, we conclude from these results that it is often effective to consider instantiations in an eager fashion, either in parallel or even before considering evaluation lemmas. This is likely because instantiation lemmas may often refine the set of possible models even when G does not yet force our evaluation variables to have an interpretation that is consistent with their corresponding datatype values. Nevertheless, we found that evaluation lemmas are often necessary in practice for ensuring our procedure does not get stuck on a single model. When only instantiation lemmas are used, our procedure often terminates the loop with no new lemmas. This is to be expected, as such a strategy violates the requirements for the progress property of Theorem 1.

In the remaining experiment, we use strategy interleave as the lemma selection strategy since it performs slightly better than priority-inst.

Comparison Against Other Techniques. Finally, we compare our SyGuS instantiation approach against other techniques implemented in CVC4, the state-of-the-art SMT solvers Z3 [16] (version 4.8.9) and Boolector [17] (version 3.2.1), and the superposition-based theorem prover Vampire [13] (version 4.5.1). Note that Boolector implements counterexample-guided model synthesis [20] but only supports the SMT-LIB logic BV, whereas Vampire supports LIA, LRA, NIA, and NRA. We consider the following four configurations of CVC4: **ematch**: with E-matching [15] enabled; **cegqi**: with CEGQI for linear arithmetic [25] and bit-vectors [18] enabled, falls back to value-based instantiation techniques for other theories; **enum**: with enumerative instantiation [21] enabled; **syqi**: with our SyGuS instantiation approach enabled. We use strategy both-both for term selection, and interleave for lemma selection.

The results are summarized in Table 3. First, note that Z3 disagrees on 10 benchmarks in logic FP with the other four CVC4 configurations. This is due to a known problem in Z3 related to operator rem, where it answers *sat* instead of *unsat*. We do not count these 10 benchmarks as solved and give the number of disagreements in parenthesis marked with a * in Table 3.

Overall, note that E-matching (**ematch**) performs very poorly on these benchmark sets. This is not surprising since it is designed with a focus on problems with uninterpreted functions. To a lesser extent, enumerative instantiation (**enum**) also performs poorly, probably also due to the fact that it is not designed for inputs without uninterpreted functions. In detail, both this configuration and

Logic		syqi	cegqi	ematch	enum	Z3	Boolector	Vampire
BV	sat	269	411	203	204	566	620	-
(5846)	unsat	4752	5039	3846	4699	4934	4889	-
	unsolved	825	396	1797	943	346	337	-
BVFP	sat	113	110	26	29	174	-	-
(224)	unsat	14	4	4	14	11	-	-
	unsolved	97	110	194	181	39	-	-
BVFPLRA	sat	103	95	67	67	164	-	-
(185)	unsat	5	5	5	6	5	-	-
	unsolved	77	85	113	112	16	-	-
FP	sat	34	28	23	23	47	-	-
(2484)	unsat	2117	1899	83	1615	1923	-	-
	unsolved	333	557	2378	846	504 (10)*	-	-
FPLRA	sat	17	17	13	13	18	-	-
(27)	unsat	0	0	0	0	0	-	-
	unsolved	10	10	14	14	9	-	-
LIA	sat	188	199	19	19	189	-	5
(607)	unsat	319	357	46	171	295	-	310
	unsolved	100	51	542	417	123	-	292
LRA	sat	79	593	461	461	740	-	0
(2419)	unsat	955	1306	1018	1117	1454	-	871
	unsolved	1385	520	940	841	225	-	1548
NIA	sat	12	11	6	6	12	-	0
(20)	unsat	7	8	1	5	5	-	6
	unsolved	1	1	13	9	3	-	14
NRA	sat	0	0	0	0	2	-	0
(3813)	unsat	3781	3781	3703	3768	3806	-	3803
	unsolved	32	32	110	45	5	-	10
UFBV	sat	8	8	8	8	26	-	-
(121)	unsat	74	53	47	66	72	-	-
	unsolved	39	60	66	47	23	-	-
Total	sat	**823**	**1472**	**826**	**830**	**1938**	-	-
(15746)	unsat	**12024**	**12452**	**8753**	**11461**	**12505**	-	-
	unsolved	**2899**	**1822**	**6167**	**3455**	**1293 (10)***	-	-

Table 3. SyQI vs. other techniques, Z3, Boolector, and Vampire (15,746 benchmarks).

syqi are enumerative in nature. The former uses a selection strategy based on the evolving ground terms in the current context, whereas the latter uses a fixed grammar built from the initial set of terms. In a sense, syqi leverages the power of a grammar for discovering new terms, whereas enum adapts to what terms are generated by instantiations. Overall, syqi solves 556 more benchmarks than enumerative instantiation, justifying the need for a syntax-guided approach for instantiation for inputs that are rich in background theories.

Our results show that syqi is remarkably competitive when compared to cegqi, which uses the best known theory-specific instantiation strategies. The performance of syntax-guided instantiation matches or exceeds counterexample-guided instantiation on logics BVFP, BVFPLRA, FP, FPLRA, NIA, NRA, and UFBV. In particular, for quantified floating-point arithmetic (FP), the performance of syqi significantly outperforms cegqi, where it solves 224 more benchmarks. We attribute this to the fact that **cegqi** only performs value-based instantiation, whereas the use of grammars is effective in determining useful symbolic terms to use in instantiations for this theory. Interestingly, **syqi** solves the only satisfiable benchmark in the NIA category that is unsolved by **cegqi**, meaning that in a portfolio setting with all available configurations, CVC4 solves all benchmarks in this category. On the other hand, counterexample-guided instantiation outperforms **syqi** on logics such as LIA, LRA, and BV, where well-established instantiation strategies exist. Syntax-guided techniques are especially ineffective for linear real arithmetic, since it is often important to construct specific real constants based on solving sets of linear (in)equalities [25].

Comparing all configurations of CVC4 with Z3, Boolector, and Vampire, we see that in some logics like LIA and NIA, counterexample-guided instantiation in CVC4 outperforms Z3 and Vampire, whereas in other logics like NRA, UFBV, and many logics that combine BV, FP and LRA, Z3 performs best. For the logic BV, Boolector outperforms CVC4 and Z3; however, CVC4 solves the most unsatisfiable instances. The **syqi** configuration performs best on the floating-point benchmarks, where it solves 181 more than the closest competitor. When comparing the four CVC4 configurations in terms of uniquely solved instances, **cegqi** uniquely solves 660 instances, **syqi** 119 instances, **enum** 117 instances, and **ematch** not a single one. Between configurations **cegqi** and **syqi**, the former uniquely solves 1479 instances, and the latter 402 instances.

In summary, theory-specific approaches as implemented in CVC4, Z3, and Boolector outperform **syqi** in categories where instantiation strategies are highly mature, such as linear integer and real arithmetic, and fixed-width bit-vectors. Nevertheless, our evaluation demonstrates the versatility of the approach, especially for benchmarks using quantified floating-point arithmetic or combined theories where no good approach to quantifier instantiation was known.

5   Conclusion

We have presented a syntax-guided approach for quantifier instantiation and implemented it in the SMT solver CVC4. Our experiments show that our approach is a viable alternative to theory-specific quantifier instantiation techniques and can be applied to a wide range of logics. In particular, for the theory of floating-point arithmetic, syntax-guided instantiation in CVC4 significantly outperforms the state of the art. In future work, we plan to tune our grammar construction based on an analysis of which terms are more likely to appear in conflicts, which can potentially be done automatically. Another direction of future work is to provide an interface that would allow users to supply their own grammars for use in SyQI, similarly to the user-provided triggers for E-matching. We also plan to use our approach as a baseline for quantified logics in recent (and future) new theories. Currently, support in SMT solvers is highly limited, for instance, for quantified formulas involving the theory of strings and regular expressions. Syntax-guided instantiation can serve as a baseline for potential user applications that rely on quantified formulas in these theories.

References

1. Alur, R., Bodík, R., Juniwal, G., Martin, M.M.K., Raghothaman, M., Seshia, S.A., Singh, R., Solar-Lezama, A., Torlak, E., Udupa, A.: Syntax-guided synthesis. In: Formal Methods in Computer-Aided Design, FMCAD 2013, Portland, OR, USA, October 20-23, 2013. pp. 1–8. IEEE (2013), http://ieeexplore.ieee.org/document/6679385/
2. Barrett, C., Fontaine, P., Tinelli, C.: The Satisfiability Modulo Theories Library (SMT-LIB) (2020), http://www.SMT-LIB.org
3. Barrett, C., Shikanian, I., Tinelli, C.: An abstract decision procedure for satisfiability in the theory of recursive data types. Electr. Notes Theor. Comput. Sci. **174**(8), 23–37 (2007). https://doi.org/10.1016/j.entcs.2006.11.037
4. Barrett, C., Stump, A., Tinelli, C.: The SMT-LIB Standard: Version 2.0. In: Gupta, A., Kroening, D. (eds.) Proceedings of the 8th International Workshop on Satisfiability Modulo Theories (Edinburgh, UK) (2010)
5. Barrett, C.W., Conway, C.L., Deters, M., Hadarean, L., Jovanovic, D., King, T., Reynolds, A., Tinelli, C.: CVC4. In: Gopalakrishnan, G., Qadeer, S. (eds.) Computer Aided Verification - 23rd International Conference, CAV 2011, Snowbird, UT, USA, July 14-20, 2011. Proceedings. Lecture Notes in Computer Science, vol. 6806, pp. 171–177. Springer (2011). https://doi.org/10.1007/978-3-642-22110-1_14
6. Bjørner, N., Janota, M.: Playing with quantified satisfaction. In: Fehnker, A., McIver, A., Sutcliffe, G., Voronkov, A. (eds.) 20th International Conferences on Logic for Programming, Artificial Intelligence and Reasoning - Short Presentations, LPAR 2015, Suva, Fiji, November 24-28, 2015. EPiC Series in Computing, vol. 35, pp. 15–27. EasyChair (2015), https://easychair.org/publications/paper/jmM
7. Brain, M., Niemetz, A., Preiner, M., Reynolds, A., Barrett, C.W., Tinelli, C.: Invertibility conditions for floating-point formulas. In: Dillig, I., Tasiran, S. (eds.) Computer Aided Verification - 31st International Conference, CAV 2019, New York City, NY, USA, July 15-18, 2019, Proceedings, Part II. Lecture Notes in Computer Science, vol. 11562, pp. 116–136. Springer (2019). https://doi.org/10.1007/978-3-030-25543-5_8
8. Detlefs, D., Nelson, G., Saxe, J.B.: Simplify: a theorem prover for program checking. J. ACM **52**(3), 365–473 (2005). https://doi.org/10.1145/1066100.1066102
9. Ferrante, J., Rackoff, C.: A decision procedure for the first order theory of real addition with order. SIAM J. Comput. **4**(1), 69–76 (1975). https://doi.org/10.1137/0204006
10. Ge, Y., Barrett, C.W., Tinelli, C.: Solving quantified verification conditions using satisfiability modulo theories. In: Pfenning, F. (ed.) Automated Deduction - CADE-21, 21st International Conference on Automated Deduction, Bremen, Germany, July 17-20, 2007, Proceedings. Lecture Notes in Computer Science, vol. 4603, pp. 167–182. Springer (2007). https://doi.org/10.1007/978-3-540-73595-3_12
11. Ge, Y., de Moura, L.M.: Complete instantiation for quantified formulas in satisfiabiliby modulo theories. In: Bouajjani, A., Maler, O. (eds.) Computer Aided Verification, 21st International Conference, CAV 2009, Grenoble, France, June 26 - July 2, 2009. Proceedings. Lecture Notes in Computer Science, vol. 5643, pp. 306–320. Springer (2009). https://doi.org/10.1007/978-3-642-02658-4_25
12. K., H.G.V., Fedyukovich, G., Gurfinkel, A.: Word level property directed reachability. In: IEEE/ACM International Conference On Computer Aided Design, ICCAD 2020, San Diego, CA, USA, November 2-5, 2020. pp. 107:1–107:9. IEEE (2020). https://doi.org/10.1145/3400302.3415708

13. Kovács, L., Voronkov, A.: First-order theorem proving and vampire. In: Sharygina, N., Veith, H. (eds.) Computer Aided Verification - 25th International Conference, CAV 2013, Saint Petersburg, Russia, July 13-19, 2013. Proceedings. Lecture Notes in Computer Science, vol. 8044, pp. 1–35. Springer (2013). https://doi.org/10.1007/978-3-642-39799-8_1

14. Loos, R., Weispfenning, V.: Applying linear quantifier elimination. Comput. J. **36**(5), 450–462 (1993). https://doi.org/10.1093/comjnl/36.5.450

15. de Moura, L.M., Bjørner, N.: Efficient e-matching for SMT solvers. In: Pfenning, F. (ed.) Automated Deduction - CADE-21, 21st International Conference on Automated Deduction, Bremen, Germany, July 17-20, 2007, Proceedings. Lecture Notes in Computer Science, vol. 4603, pp. 183–198. Springer (2007). https://doi.org/10.1007/978-3-540-73595-3_13

16. de Moura, L.M., Bjørner, N.: Z3: an efficient SMT solver. In: Ramakrishnan, C.R., Rehof, J. (eds.) Tools and Algorithms for the Construction and Analysis of Systems, 14th International Conference, TACAS 2008, Held as Part of the Joint European Conferences on Theory and Practice of Software, ETAPS 2008, Budapest, Hungary, March 29-April 6, 2008. Proceedings. Lecture Notes in Computer Science, vol. 4963, pp. 337–340. Springer (2008). https://doi.org/10.1007/978-3-540-78800-3_24

17. Niemetz, A., Preiner, M., Biere, A.: Boolector 2.0. J. Satisf. Boolean Model. Comput. **9**(1), 53–58 (2014). https://doi.org/10.3233/sat190101

18. Niemetz, A., Preiner, M., Reynolds, A., Barrett, C.W., Tinelli, C.: On solving quantified bit-vector constraints using invertibility conditions. Formal Methods in System Design pp. 1572–8102 (2021). https://doi.org/10.1007/s10703-020-00359-9

19. Nieuwenhuis, R., Oliveras, A., Tinelli, C.: Solving SAT and SAT Modulo Theories: from an abstract Davis-Putnam-Logemann-Loveland Procedure to DPLL(T). Journal of the ACM **53**(6), 937–977 (Nov 2006)

20. Preiner, M., Niemetz, A., Biere, A.: Counterexample-guided model synthesis. In: Legay, A., Margaria, T. (eds.) Tools and Algorithms for the Construction and Analysis of Systems - 23rd International Conference, TACAS 2017, Held as Part of the European Joint Conferences on Theory and Practice of Software, ETAPS 2017, Uppsala, Sweden, April 22-29, 2017, Proceedings, Part I. Lecture Notes in Computer Science, vol. 10205, pp. 264–280 (2017). https://doi.org/10.1007/978-3-662-54577-5_15

21. Reynolds, A., Barbosa, H., Fontaine, P.: Revisiting enumerative instantiation. In: Beyer, D., Huisman, M. (eds.) Tools and Algorithms for the Construction and Analysis of Systems - 24th International Conference, TACAS 2018, Held as Part of the European Joint Conferences on Theory and Practice of Software, ETAPS 2018, Thessaloniki, Greece, April 14-20, 2018, Proceedings, Part II. Lecture Notes in Computer Science, vol. 10806, pp. 112–131. Springer (2018). https://doi.org/10.1007/978-3-319-89963-3_7

22. Reynolds, A., Barbosa, H., Nötzli, A., Barrett, C.W., Tinelli, C.: cvc4sy: Smart and fast term enumeration for syntax-guided synthesis. In: Dillig, I., Tasiran, S. (eds.) Computer Aided Verification - 31st International Conference, CAV 2019, New York City, NY, USA, July 15-18, 2019, Proceedings, Part II. Lecture Notes in Computer Science, vol. 11562, pp. 74–83. Springer (2019). https://doi.org/10.1007/978-3-030-25543-5_5

23. Reynolds, A., Blanchette, J.C.: A decision procedure for (co)datatypes in SMT solvers. In: Felty, A.P., Middeldorp, A. (eds.) Automated Deduction - CADE-25 - 25th International Conference on Automated Deduction, Berlin, Germany, August

1-7, 2015, Proceedings. Lecture Notes in Computer Science, vol. 9195, pp. 197–213. Springer (2015). https://doi.org/10.1007/978-3-319-21401-6_13, https://doi.org/10.1007/978-3-319-21401-6_13

24. Reynolds, A., Deters, M., Kuncak, V., Tinelli, C., Barrett, C.W.: Counterexample-guided quantifier instantiation for synthesis in SMT. In: Kroening, D., Pasareanu, C.S. (eds.) Computer Aided Verification - 27th International Conference, CAV 2015, San Francisco, CA, USA, July 18-24, 2015, Proceedings, Part II. Lecture Notes in Computer Science, vol. 9207, pp. 198–216. Springer (2015). https://doi.org/10.1007/978-3-319-21668-3_12

25. Reynolds, A., King, T., Kuncak, V.: Solving quantified linear arithmetic by counterexample-guided instantiation. Formal Methods Syst. Des. **51**(3), 500–532 (2017). https://doi.org/10.1007/s10703-017-0290-y

26. Reynolds, A., Tinelli, C., Goel, A., Krstic, S., Deters, M., Barrett, C.W.: Quantifier instantiation techniques for finite model finding in SMT. In: Bonacina, M.P. (ed.) Automated Deduction - CADE-24 - 24th International Conference on Automated Deduction, Lake Placid, NY, USA, June 9-14, 2013. Proceedings. Lecture Notes in Computer Science, vol. 7898, pp. 377–391. Springer (2013). https://doi.org/10.1007/978-3-642-38574-2_26

27. Reynolds, A., Tinelli, C., de Moura, L.M.: Finding conflicting instances of quantified formulas in SMT. In: Formal Methods in Computer-Aided Design, FMCAD 2014, Lausanne, Switzerland, October 21-24, 2014. pp. 195–202. IEEE (2014). https://doi.org/10.1109/FMCAD.2014.6987613

28. Reynolds, A., Viswanathan, A., Barbosa, H., Tinelli, C., Barrett, C.: Datatypes with shared selectors. In: Automated Reasoning - 9th International Joint Conference, IJCAR 2018, Held as Part of the Federated Logic Conference, FloC 2018, Oxford, UK, July 14-17, 2018, Proceedings. pp. 591–608 (2018). https://doi.org/10.1007/978-3-319-94205-6_39

29. Wintersteiger, C.M., Hamadi, Y., de Moura, L.M.: Efficiently solving quantified bit-vector formulas. In: Bloem, R., Sharygina, N. (eds.) Proceedings of 10th International Conference on Formal Methods in Computer-Aided Design, FMCAD 2010, Lugano, Switzerland, October 20-23. pp. 239–246. IEEE (2010), http://ieeexplore.ieee.org/document/5770955/

Making Theory Reasoning Simpler

Giles Reger[1], Johannes Schoisswohl[1(✉)], and Andrei Voronkov[1,2]

[1] University of Manchester, Manchester, UK
[2] EasyChair, Manchester, UK
johannes.schoisswohl@manchester.ac.uk

Abstract Reasoning with quantifiers and theories is at the core of many
applications in program analysis and verification. Whilst the problem is
undecidable in general and hard in practice, we have been making large
pragmatic steps forward. Our previous work proposed an instantiation
rule for theory reasoning that produced pragmatically useful instances.
Whilst this led to an increase in performance, it had its limitations as
the rule produces ground instances which (i) can be overly specific, thus
not useful in proof search, and (ii) contribute to the already problematic
search space explosion as many new instances are introduced. This paper
begins by introducing that specifically addresses these two concerns as it
produces general solutions and it is a simplification rule, i.e. it replaces an
existing clause by a 'simpler' one. Encouraged by initial success with this
new rule, we performed an experiment to identify further common cases
where the complex structure of theory terms blocked existing methods.
This resulted in four further simplification rules for theory reasoning. The
resulting extensions are implemented in the VAMPIRE theorem prover
and evaluated on SMT-LIB, showing that the new extensions result in
a considerable increase in the number of problems solved, including 90
problems unsolved by state-of-the-art SMT solvers.

1 Introduction

Many applications of reasoning in program analysis and verification depend on
reasoning with the first-order theory of arithmetic, often in combination with
other theories and quantifiers. A common approach to this problem is via Satisfiability Modulo Theory (SMT) solving, which has strong support for decidable
theories but may struggle to scale in the presence of quantifiers. Conversely,
superposition-based first-order solvers handle quantifiers naturally and have, recently, been extended to reason with theories [2,3,5,6,9,13,16,21]. Such solvers
are based on a *saturation loop* and tend to suffer from *search space explosion*.
This is compounded by the effective but explosive use of *theory axioms*, leading
to the derivation of numerous inconsequential consequences of the theory. So far
we have attempted to control this explosive behaviour [10,17] but now we aim
to eliminate some of it. This paper introduces a set of *simplification rules* for
reasoning in the theory of (any combination of linear or non-linear real, rational,
or integer) arithmetic, i.e. rules that make reasoning in arithmetic simpler.

© The Author(s) 2021
J. F. Groote and K. G. Larsen (Eds.): TACAS 2021, LNCS 12652, pp. 164–180, 2021.
https://doi.org/10.1007/978-3-030-72013-1_9

This work was motivated by our previous attempt [20] to find useful instances of first-order clauses that would be otherwise difficult to find via reasoning with theory axioms. For example, when considering the two clauses

$$r(7x) \qquad \neg r(6 + y) \vee p(y)$$

our previous work would apply resolution on $r(7x)$ and $\neg r(6+y)$ using *unification with abstraction* to produce the clause $7x \neq 6 + y \vee p(y)$ and then applied *theory instantiation*, utilising an SMT solver to find the substitution $\{x \mapsto 1, y \mapsto 1\}$, producing the instance $p(1)$. This may or may not be useful to proof search and, crucially, we need to keep performing inferences with the original clauses in case it is not. In this case, we would prefer to instantiate with $\{y \mapsto 7x - 6\}$ to produce $7x \neq 6 + (7x - 6) \vee p(7x - 6)$, which can be reduced to $p(7x - 6)$. This is a *general* solution (being logically equivalent) that is also *simpler* – in this case it has fewer variables than the original clause. Hence, we replace the clause by the more general result, aiding proof search and preventing the addition of unnecessary instances.

The above was motivated by the observation that we would often see clauses of the form $\widehat{k}x \neq t \vee C[x]$ (for numeral $\widehat{k}$, variable x, and term t) and expend much effort using theory axioms to rewrite $\widehat{k}x \neq t$ into $x \neq \frac{t}{k}$. This led us to conduct an experiment to identify other common cases where arithmetic clauses could be simplified. An immediate observation is that, if x ranges over the reals, $p(7x - 6)$ can be instantiated with $\{x \mapsto \frac{(y+6)}{7}\}$ to produce $p(y)$. Furthermore, in the above example we no longer need to employ the expensive unification with abstraction as we can instantiate $r(7x)$ with $\{x \mapsto \frac{z}{7}\}$ to produce $r(z)$ and then resolve with $r(6 + y) \vee p(y)$ to produce $p(y)$ directly.

Another observation was that a large amount of effort was expended by the theorem prover reordering sums and products to expose seemingly obvious structure. For example, taking $(3t + x) + 2t$ and producing $5t + x$ requires three theory axioms and 12 rewriting steps. To combat this, we introduce an evaluation method that flattens sums and products, reorders and simplifies them, before reintroducing the necessary bracketed structure. A related common issue was the occurrence of terms that could easily be *cancelled*, such as in $4x + 3 < 4x + 10$, again requiring significant rewriting effort that can be replaced by a special rule.

This paper does not present the exploratory experimentation described above but focusses instead on the fruits of this work. After introducing the necessary preliminaries (Sec. 2), we make the following contributions:

- A new *Gaussian Variable Elimination* rule (Sec. 3) that eliminates variables if they can be described completely in terms of other variables.
- A set of *Arithmetic Subterm Generalisation* rules (Sec. 4) that replace clauses with obvious generalisations, as in the above cases of replacing $p(7x - 6)$ with $p(y)$ and $r(7x)$ with $r(x)$.
- A general approach to the *evaluation* of terms involving arithmetic (Sec. 5), including a special rule to handle a surprisingly common corner case involving unary minus.

– A rule for *cancelling* subterms, e.g. in $4x + 3 < 4x + 10$ (Sec. 6)

These rules are all implemented in the VAMPIRE [1,14] theorem prover. Our experimental evaluation (Sec. 7) shows that the new rules significantly improve the number of problems (from SMT-LIB) that VAMPIRE can solve. Our final experiment shows that the new VAMPIRE can solve 1,052 problems unsolved by VAMPIRE 4.5, 1,056 problems unsolved by CVC4, and 1,350 problems unsolved by Z3 — given their complementary nature, this equates to 90 problems unsolved by any of these state-of-the-art solvers.

2   Preliminaries and Related Work

First-Order Logic and Theories. We consider a many-sorted first-order logic with equality. A *signature* is a pair $\Sigma = (\Xi, \Omega)$ where Ξ is a set of *sorts* and Ω a set of *predicate* and *function* symbols with associated argument and return sorts from Ξ. *Terms* are of the form c, x, or $f(t_1, \ldots, t_n)$ where f is a *function symbol* of arity $n \geq 1$, $t_1, \ldots, t_n$ are terms, c is a zero arity function symbol (i.e. a constant) and x is a variable. We assume that all terms are well-sorted and write $t : \sigma$ if term t has sort σ. Atoms are of the form $p(t_1, \ldots, t_n)$, q or $t_1 \simeq_s t_2$ where p is a predicate symbol of arity n, $t_1, \ldots, t_n$ are terms, q is a zero arity predicate symbol and for each sort $s \in \Xi$, $\simeq_s$ is the *equality symbol for the sort* s. We write simply $\simeq$ when s is known from the context or irrelevant. A *literal* is either an atom A, in which case we call it *positive*, or a negation of an atom $\neg A$, in which case we call it *negative*. When L is a negative literal $\neg A$ and we write $\neg L$, we mean the positive literal A. For negative literals with binary predicates $\neg(t_1 \Diamond t_2)$ (like, e.g. equality), we sometimes write $t_1 \not\Diamond t_2$.

A *clause* is a disjunction of literals $L_1 \vee \ldots \vee L_n$ for $n \geq 0$. We disregard the order of literals and treat a clause as a multiset. When $n = 0$ we speak of the *empty clause*, which is always false. When $n = 1$ a clause is called a *unit clause*. Variables in clauses are considered to be universally quantified. Standard methods exist to transform an arbitrary first-order formula into clausal form (e.g. [15] and our recent work in [19]).

In the following we use *expression* to mean a term, an atom, a literal, or a clause. We write $E[t]_p$ to denote an expression E containing a term t at position p (a position is a unique point in an expression's syntax tree) and may then write $E[s]_p$ to denote the same expression with t replaced by term s at p. We will normally leave the position p as implicit. A *substitution* is any θ of the form $\{x_1 \mapsto t_1, \ldots, x_n \mapsto t_n\}$, where $n \geq 0$. $E\theta$ is the expression obtained from E by the simultaneous replacement of each x_i by t_i. An expression is *ground* if it contains no variables. An *instance* of E is any expression $E\theta$ and a *ground instance* of E is any instance of E that is ground. A *unifier* of two terms, atoms or literals E_1 and E_2 is a substitution θ such that $E_1\theta = E_2\theta$. It is known that if two expressions have a unifier, then they have a so-called most general unifier.

We assume a standard notion of a (first-order, many-sorted) *interpretation* $\mathcal{I}$, which assigns a non-empty domain $\mathcal{I}_s$ to every sort $s \in \Xi$, and maps every function symbol f to a function $\mathcal{I}_f$ and every predicate symbol p to a relation $\mathcal{I}_p$ on these domains so that the mapping respects sorts. We call $\mathcal{I}_f$ the *interpretation of f in $\mathcal{I}$*, and similarly for $\mathcal{I}_p$ and $\mathcal{I}_s$. Interpretations are also sometimes called *first-order structures*. A *sentence* is a closed formula, i.e. with no free variables. We use the standard notions of validity and satisfiability of sentences in such interpretations. An interpretation is a *model* for a set of clauses if (the universal closure of) each of these clauses is true in the interpretation.

A *theory $\mathcal{T}$* is identified by a class of interpretations. A sentence is *satisfiable* in $\mathcal{T}$ if it is true in at least one of these interpretations and *valid* if it is true in all of them. A function (or predicate) symbol f is called *uninterpreted* in $\mathcal{T}$, if for every interpretation $\mathcal{I}$ of $\mathcal{T}$ and every interpretation $\mathcal{I}'$ which agrees with $\mathcal{I}$ on all symbols apart from f, $\mathcal{I}'$ is also an interpretation of $\mathcal{T}$. A theory is called *complete* if, for every sentence F of this theory, either F or $\neg F$ is valid in this theory. Evidently, every theory of a single interpretation is complete. We can define satisfiability and validity of arbitrary formulas in an interpretation in a standard way by treating free variables as new uninterpreted constants.

The theories we will deal with are the theories of integer, rational, and real arithmetic with uninterpreted functions, denoted by $\mathcal{T}_\mathbb{Z}$, $\mathcal{T}_\mathbb{Q}$, and $\mathcal{T}_\mathbb{R}$, which fix the interpretation of a distinguished sort $\sigma_\mathbb{Z}$, $\sigma_\mathbb{Q}$, and $\sigma_\mathbb{R}$ to the set of mathematical integers $\mathbb{Z}$, rationals $\mathbb{Q}$, and reals $\mathbb{R}$ respectively, and assign the usual meanings to the function and predicate symbols $\{+, -, <, \leq, \cdot\}$. By $\overline{k}$, we denote the numeral interpreted as k in any of these theories. We consider signatures over these theories to additionally contain uninterpreted functions, and predicates, hence, in contrast to the case without unintpreted functions, for none of these theories there is a sound and complete proof system (see e.g. [13]).

Unless stated differently, we use the symbols x, y, z for variables, s, t, u for terms, C, D for clauses, p, q, r for predicate symbols, f, g, h for function symbols, and σ for substitutions, and sorts, with sometimes suffixes being added.

Term Orderings. A *simplification ordering* (see, e.g. [8]) on terms is an ordering that is *well-founded, monotonic, stable under substitutions* and has the *subterm property*. Such an ordering captures a notion of *simplicity*, i.e. $t_1 \prec t_2$ implies that t_1 is in some way simpler than t_2. VAMPIRE uses the Knuth-Bendix ordering [12], which is parametrized by total precedence ordering on function and predicate symbols $\ll$. This is total on ground terms and partial on non-ground ones, leading to the possibility of *incomparable* terms, e.g. $f(x, a)$ and $f(b, y)$. A simplification ordering $\prec$ on terms can be extended to a simplification ordering on literals and clauses, using a multiset extension of orderings. For simplicity, we will use $\prec$ to refer to the term ordering and its lifting. Whenever $E_1 \prec E_2$ $(E_2 \prec E_1)$ we say that E_1 is smaller (bigger) than E_2. An equality literal $t \simeq s$ is *oriented* if $t \prec s$ or $s \prec t$.

Saturation-Based Proof Search. We introduce our new rules within the context of saturation-based proof search. The general idea in saturation is to maintain two sets of *Active* and *Passive* clauses. A saturation-loop then selects a clause C from *Passive*, places C in *Active*, applies *generating inferences* between C and clauses in *Active*, and finally places newly derived clauses in *Passive* after applying some retention tests. The retention tests involve checking whether the new clause is itself redundant (i.e. a tautology) or redundant with respect to existing clauses (implied by a set of smaller clauses in *Active* ∪ *Passive*). Rules that remove the parent clause immediately from the search space without performing a retention test are called immediate simplification rules. Whenever there are applicable immediate simplification rules, the first one wrt. some fixed ordering is chosen to be applied to the selected clause instead of applying any other rule. The rules introduced in this paper are all introduced as immediate simplification rules. However, as mentioned later, not all of them strictly obey the requirement that the result is *smaller*. Normally this would have implications on the *completeness* of the approach but we lose completeness when we start reasoning with theories. This leads us to a trade-off between the potential loss of some proofs by missing some inferences, and the potential gain via simplifying proof search. Our later experimental results show that forgoing completeness is of pragmatic interest.

Superposition Calculus. VAMPIRE works with the superposition and resolution calculus (see our previous work [11,14] for a description). The calculus itself is not of direct interest to this work. We do, however, draw attention to two rules. Firstly, the *Equality Resolution* rule

$$\frac{s \not\simeq t \vee C}{C\theta} \qquad \theta \text{ is a most general unifier of } s \text{ and } t$$

is a starting point for both our previous theory instantiation work and the Gaussian Variable Elimination rule introduced later (Sec. 3). Secondly, we draw attention to the *Demodulation* (or rewriting by unit equalities) rule

$$\frac{l \simeq r \quad L[t] \vee C}{L[r\theta] \vee C}$$

where $l\theta = t, r\theta \prec l\theta$, and $(l \simeq r)\theta \prec L[t] \vee C$. This is of interest as later we will need to take special care of the last side-condition when evaluating terms.

Theory Reasoning. To perform theory reasoning within this context it is common to do two things. Firstly, to *evaluate* new clauses to put them in a common form (e.g. rewrite all inequalities in terms of <) and evaluate ground theory terms and literals (e.g. $1+2$ becomes 3 and $1 < 2$ becomes *false*). More complex evaluation is possible and is the subject of this work (see Section 5). Secondly, relevant theory axioms can be added to the initial search space. For example, if the input clauses use the + symbol one can add the axioms $x + y \simeq y + x$ and $x + 0 \simeq x$, among others.

In addition to these basic methods, VAMPIRE also employs a number of other techniques. *AVATAR modulo theories* [16] uses an SMT solver within the context of clause splitting to ensure that the ground part of any chosen clause splits are theory-consistent. The previously mentioned *unification with abstraction* and *theory instantiation* [20] rules support lazy unification modulo theories and pragmatic instantiation. Theory axiom usage can be controlled by the *set of support* strategy [17] or layered clause selection [10]. Both approaches de-prioritise reasoning with theory axioms.

3   Gaussian variable elimination

Recall the example $7x \neq 6 + y \lor p(y)$ from the Introduction (Sec. 1) where we want to identify the substitution $\{y \mapsto 7x - 6\}$ to produce the simpler instance $p(7x - 6)$. Our general approach is to *rewrite* $7x \neq 6 + y$ in terms of y and then apply the standard *Equality Resolution* rule introduced in Sec. 2. This gives us the straightforward rule:

$$\frac{s \not\approx t \lor C[x]}{C[u]} \text{ gve}$$

where $x : \sigma_{\mathbb{Z}}$, $x : \sigma_{\mathbb{Q}}$, or $x : \sigma_{\mathbb{R}}$, $\langle s, t \rangle \Longrightarrow^{*}_{\text{gve}} \langle x, u \rangle$, or $\langle t, s \rangle \Longrightarrow^{*}_{\text{gve}} \langle x, u \rangle$ and x is not a subterm of u. The relation $\Longrightarrow^{*}_{\text{gve}}$ is the reflexive, and transitive closure of the relation $\Longrightarrow_{\text{gve}}$ which can be defined as follows.

$$\langle s + t, u \rangle \Longrightarrow_{\text{gve}} \langle s, u + (-t) \rangle$$
$$\langle s + t, u \rangle \Longrightarrow_{\text{gve}} \langle t, u + (-s) \rangle \qquad \langle -s, t \rangle \Longrightarrow_{\text{gve}} \langle s, -t \rangle$$

$$\langle s \cdot \widehat{t}, u \rangle \Longrightarrow_{\text{gve}} \langle s, u / t \rangle \qquad \text{if } t \neq 0, \text{ and } \widehat{t} : \sigma_{\mathbb{Q}}, \text{ or } \widehat{t} : \sigma_{\mathbb{R}}$$
$$\langle \widehat{s} \cdot t, u \rangle \Longrightarrow_{\text{gve}} \langle t, u / s \rangle \qquad \text{if } s \neq 0, \text{ and } \widehat{s} : \sigma_{\mathbb{Q}}, \text{ or } \widehat{t} : \sigma_{\mathbb{R}}$$

$$\langle s / \widehat{t}, u \rangle \Longrightarrow_{\text{gve}} \langle s, u \cdot t \rangle \qquad \text{if } t \neq 0, \text{ and } \widehat{t} : \sigma_{\mathbb{Q}}, \text{ or } \widehat{t} : \sigma_{\mathbb{R}}$$

It should be noted that $\Longrightarrow_{\text{gve}}$ is not normalising. The pair $\langle s_1 + s_2, t \rangle$ can, for example, be rewritten to $\langle s_1, t - s_2 \rangle$, as well as to $\langle s_2, t - s_1 \rangle$. But due to the fact that there is at most a linear number of such rewritings, we can enumerate all of them and choose the first $\langle x, t \rangle$, such that x is not a subterm of t. Further choice comes from the fact that we can either rewrite based on $\langle l, r \rangle$, or based on $\langle r, l \rangle$. Looking at our example, we could rewrite

$$\langle 6 + y, 7x \rangle \Longrightarrow_{\text{gve}} \langle y, 7x - 6 \rangle$$

but also

$$\langle 7x, 6 + y \rangle \Longrightarrow_{\text{gve}} \langle x, (6 + y) / 7 \rangle$$

if x is not of integer sort, leaving us with a choice. Another source of choice comes from the fact that our premise can contain multiple negative equalities. Any of those could potentially be used to rewrite the rest of the clause.

Since application of the rule, will yield a logically equivalent conclusion, with fewer literals and fewer distinct variables, we make an arbitrary choice. For the same reason, we implement this as a simplification rule (thus removing the premise from the search space) even though the conclusion will often be incomparable to (not smaller than) the premise.

To further demonstrate this rule we consider the additional example

$$\frac{\dfrac{\dfrac{\dfrac{\dfrac{p(7xxxy - 6)}{p(7xxx - 6)}\ \mathsf{asg}^{\cdot}_{\mathsf{var}}}{p(7x - 6)}\ \mathsf{asg}^{\mathsf{pow}}_{\mathsf{var}}}{p(x - 6)}\ \mathsf{asg}^{\cdot}_{\mathsf{num}}}{p(x)}\ \mathsf{asg}^{+}$$

Figure 1. Illustration of the 4 generalization rules, in the theory of Reals.

$$\frac{\dfrac{\dfrac{\dfrac{\dfrac{x + y \neq 36 \vee x + 3y \neq 90 \vee p(x, y)}{(36 - y) + 3y \neq 90 \vee p(36 - y, y)}\ \mathsf{gve}}{36 + 2y \neq 90 \vee p(36 - y, y)}\ \mathsf{eval}}{\vee\ p(36 - (90 - 36)/2, (90 - 36)/2)}\ \mathsf{gve}}{p(9, 27)}\ \mathsf{eval}$$

which highlights the need to interleave *evaluation* between successive Gaussian elimination steps — we discuss our evaluation strategy below.

4 Arithmetic subterm generalization

Taking a closer look at the choice for our example from the previous section, we see that we could have instantiated the premise $y + 6 \not\simeq 7x \vee p(y)$ either with $\{y \mapsto 7x - 6\}$ to get $p(7x - 6)$, or with $\{x \mapsto (6 + y) \,/\, 7\}$ to obtain $p(y)$ (again, assuming that x is not of integer sort). Both of the clauses are logically equivalent in $\mathcal{T}_{\mathbb{Q}}$, and $\mathcal{T}_{\mathbb{R}}$, since the earlier is an instance of the latter, and the latter implies the earlier as we can apply the substitution $\{x \mapsto (y + 6) \,/\, 7\}$ and simplify the result to the earlier clause. Obviously this kind of reasoning can be applied for any linear subterm $\widehat{k} \cdot x + d$ where $k \neq 0$.

Splitting this idea into multiple rules lets us take these generalizations further. Therefore we propose 4 rules for arithmetic subterm generalization, that are illustrated in a single example in Figure 1.

Since we do not want the applicability of our generalization rules to depend on associativity and commutativity (AC) we will formulate them modulo AC. For this purpose we introduce the following notation. We use $C[t]_{AC}$ to denote a clause that contains the subterm t modulo AC. Further we use $C[t']_{AC}$ to denote the same clause, but all occurrences of t modulo AC, being replaced by t'.

Addition Generalization

$$\frac{C[x + t_1 + \ldots + t_n]_{AC}}{C[x]_{AC}}\ \mathsf{asg}^{+}$$

where

  – $x : \sigma$ for some $\sigma \in \{\sigma_{\mathbb{Z}}, \sigma_{\mathbb{Q}}, \sigma_{\mathbb{R}}\}$

- all occurrences of x are in the subterm $x + t_1 + \ldots + t_n$ (modulo AC)
- x is not a subterm of t_i

The first rule deals with the case where a clause contains a sum with a variable as summand. Such a sum can be generalized by applying the substitution $\{x \mapsto x - t_1 - \ldots - t_n\}$, and simplifying the result.

Numeral Multiplication Generalization

$$\frac{C[\widehat{k} \cdot x \cdot t_1 \cdot \ldots \cdot t_n]_{AC}}{C[x \cdot t_1 \cdot \ldots \cdot t_n]_{AC}} \ \mathsf{asg}'_{\mathsf{num}}$$

where

- $x : \sigma$ for some $\sigma \in \{\sigma_{\mathbb{Q}}, \sigma_{\mathbb{R}}\}$
- all occurrences of x are in the term $\widehat{k} \cdot x \cdot t_1 \cdot \ldots \cdot t_n$ (modulo AC)
- x is not a subterm of t_i

In the second rule we generalize a product that contains one variable that occurs only once in this product. Its soundness is justified by the substitution $\{x \mapsto \frac{\widehat{x}}{k}\}$.

Variable Multiplication Generalization

$$\frac{C[x \cdot x_1 \cdot \ldots \cdot x_n]_{AC}}{C[x]_{AC}} \ \mathsf{asg}'_{\mathsf{var}}$$

where

- $x : \sigma$ for some $\sigma \in \{\sigma_{\mathbb{Z}}, \sigma_{\mathbb{Q}}, \sigma_{\mathbb{R}}\}$
- all occurrences of x, x_i are in the term $x \cdot x_1 \cdot \ldots \cdot x_n$ (modulo AC)
- $x \neq x_i$

In this rule we generalize subterms that are products of variables, containing redundant variables. The rule is sound since we can replace x_i by $\widehat{1}$.

Variable Power Generalization

$$\frac{C[x^n]_{AC}}{C[x^k]_{AC}} \ \mathsf{asg}^{\mathsf{pow}}_{\mathsf{var}}$$

where

- $x : \sigma_{\mathbb{R}}$
- x^n is an abbreviation for $x \cdot x \cdot \ldots \cdot x$
- $k = \begin{cases} 1 & \text{if } n \text{ is odd} \\ 2 & \text{if } n \text{ is even} \end{cases}$
- all occurrences of x are in the term x^n (modulo AC)

The last rule lets us generalize away redundant powers of variables. Its soundness is guaranteed by the fact, that for Real numbers the co-domains of x^n and x^k are the same.

All of the above rules produce a result that is smaller with respect to any simplification ordering due to the removal of terms, justifying their implementation as immediate simplifications.

5   Evaluation

As mentioned above, reasoning with arithmetic often requires us to be able to *evaluate* terms — evaluations such as $3 + 3 \implies 6$ and $f(x) + 0 \implies f(x)$ are straightforward but we also want to support evaluations such as $(3t + x) + 2t \implies 5t + x$ for variable x and arbitrary term t. We introduce a new method for this (replacing a previous ad-hoc method implemented in VAMPIRE). The general idea is to first rewrite terms into a special *normal form*, apply simplifying steps that preserve this form, and then *denormalise* to obtain standard terms again. We describe the three steps in detail below.

Normalization. This step removes the need to take care of reordering and bracketing of terms. Our general normal form is as follows

$$\widehat{c_1} \cdot (t_{1,1} \cdot \ldots \cdot t_{1,k_1}) + \ldots + \widehat{c_n} \cdot (t_{n,1} \cdot \ldots \cdot t_{1,k_n})$$

where $t_{i,j} \prec_1 t_{i,j+1}$ and $(t_{i,1} \cdot \ldots \cdot t_{i,k_i}) \prec_2 (t_{i+1,1} \cdot \ldots \cdot t_{i+1,k_{i+1}})$. To get to this normal form we rewrite $-t$ as $-1 \cdot t$, rewrite $t \mathbin{/} \widehat{c}$ as $t \cdot \widehat{\frac{1}{c}}$, rewrite t as $1 \cdot t$ where necessary, and sort with respect to $\prec_1$ and $\prec_2$. Both relations $\prec_1$, and $\prec_2$ need to be strict total orderings, on terms, and $\prec_1$-sorted lists of terms respectively. VAMPIRE uses so-called aggressive sharing for terms, meaning that for each distinct term there is at most one instance present in memory, and copies are being made by copying the term's id. Hence we can define $\prec_1$ as comparing the ids of two terms. We use the same approach for $\prec_2$.

Simplification. Once in normal form, terms can be simplified by joining coefficients for identical terms and removing terms multiplied by zero. This can be given as follows:

$$\widehat{c} \cdot t \cdot \ldots \widehat{d} \ldots \cdot u \implies_{\text{eval}} \widehat{cd} \cdot t \cdot \ldots \cdot u$$

$$s + \ldots \widehat{c_1} \cdot t + \widehat{c_2} \cdot t \ldots + u \implies_{\text{eval}} s + \ldots \widehat{c_1 + c_2} \cdot t \ldots + u$$

$$s + \ldots + \widehat{0} \cdot t + \ldots + u \implies_{\text{eval}} s + \ldots + u$$

If we would generate an empty sum by removing an addition we will simplify to $\widehat{0}$ instead. All of these steps can be implemented in linear time and in a bottom up manner, since we firstly can rely on the terms being sorted by the non-numeral parts of their summands, and secondly on a numeral part of a product being on a fixed position.

Denormalisation. Finally, as the normal form contains redundant information (such as $1 \cdot t + \ldots$ instead of $t + \ldots$) we need to *denormalise* as follows:

$$-1 \cdot (t_1 \cdot \ldots \cdot t_n) \implies (t_1 \cdot (\ldots \cdot (t_{n-1} \cdot (- t_n)) \ldots))$$

$$1 \cdot (t_1 \cdot \ldots \cdot t_n) \implies (t_1 \cdot (\ldots \cdot (t_{n-1} \cdot t_n) \ldots))$$

We define the rule eval to be the chain of normalising, simplifying and de-normalising a clause in a bottom-up manner, which is only applied if the step of simplification is successful for some subterm. The reason for not always applying the rules is to prevent arbitrary reordering of sums and products, which in many cases leads to conclusions being bigger than the premise. This can have significant consequences beyond perturbing proof search. Consider the following scenario involving the Demodulation rule (see Sec. 2).

$$\frac{\dfrac{x + y \simeq y + x \qquad k = a + \cancel{(b + c)}}{k = a + (c + b)} \text{ demodulation}}{k = a + (b + c)} \text{ eval}$$

This process would repeat itself ad infinitum as the initial clause is deleted, replaced by an identical clause. Evaluation would violate the side-condition that should have prevented this, if we would not insist on the step of simplification being successful for the rule to be applied.

In most cases this inference rule is a true simplification wrt. our simplification ordering, since we eliminate at least one symbol in each of the cases in the step *simplification*. Due to generating sometimes bigger terms in the *normalisation*, like in the case $x + x \Rightarrow 1 \cdot x + 1 \cdot x \Rightarrow 2 \cdot x$ we sometimes violate the simplification ordering. Due to the fact that these cases do not occur too frequently, and completeness is not possible in our base theories, we ignore these violations.

During experimentation, we discovered many cases where a unary minus blocks our evaluation rule. Consider the following desired derivation

$$\frac{\dfrac{\dfrac{y + t \neq x \vee C[y + -x]}{C[y + -(y + t)]}}{C[y + (-y + -t)]}}{C[t]}$$

This is not currently possible as the weight of $-y + -t$ is 5, which is larger than the weight of $-(y + t)$, meaning the second step is not a simplification.

We introduce a simple fix by modifying the weight function and symbol precedence of the Knuth-Bendix ordering as follows:

1. We let $-$ to be weight 0 (for every sorted version of $-$)
2. We let $-$ be the *largest* symbol among symbols of its sort

As a result we can use the following rewrite rule as an additional simplifaction rule, since the right hand side has the same weight as the left hand side, but $-$, the outer most symbol on the left hand side, has higher precedence than $+$ the one on the right hand side.

$$- (x + y) \Longrightarrow_{\text{push}-} (-x) + (-y)$$

6   Cancellation

The motivation for our last rule was two-fold. Firstly evaluation of constant predicates can be helpful in some cases, but fails in seemingly trivial cases. One example for a case like this is the redundant literal $4x + 3 < 4x + 10$. The simple approach of evaluating interpreted predicates fails since we are dealing with non-ground symbols. However it can be simplified to a ground term that can then be evaluated, by cancelling away the $4x$ on both sides of the inequality.

The second motivation were cases where unification with abstraction yields literals in which gve could almost be applied but require a step of cancellation. An example for such a case is the derivation

$$\cfrac{\cfrac{\cfrac{p(5x) \qquad \neg p(3x) \vee C[x]}{3x \neq 5x \vee C[x]}}{0 \neq 2x \vee C[x]} \text{ cancel}}{C[0]} \text{ gve}$$

In order to resolve both of these cases we propose the inference rule cancellation cancel, which consists of the following two symmetric cases depending on which side is cancelled.

$$\frac{s + \ldots \widehat{n}t \ldots + u \, \Diamond v + \ldots \widehat{n}t \ldots + w \vee C}{s + \ldots + u \, \Diamond v + \ldots + w \vee C} \text{ cancel}$$

where

- $\Diamond \in \{\simeq, \not\simeq, <, \not<, \leq, \not\leq\}$

$$\frac{s + \ldots \widehat{n}t \ldots + u \, \Diamond v + \ldots \widehat{m}t \ldots + w \vee C}{s + \ldots + u \, \Diamond v + \ldots \widehat{m - n}t \ldots + w \vee C} \text{ cancel}$$

where

- $\widehat{m - n} \ll \widehat{n - m}$
- $\Diamond \in \{\simeq, \not\simeq, <, \not<, \leq, \not\leq\}$

$$\frac{s + \ldots \widehat{n}t \ldots + u \, \Diamond v + \ldots \widehat{m}t \ldots + w \vee C}{s + \ldots \widehat{n - m}t \ldots + u \, \Diamond v + \ldots + w \vee C} \text{ cancel}$$

where

- $\widehat{n - m} \ll \widehat{m - n}$
- $\Diamond \in \{\simeq, \not\simeq, <, \not<, \leq, \not\leq\}$

In order for the rule to not be sensitive to associativity and commutativity, we perform the same steps of normalisation and denormalisation as for the rule eval. Again we will only simplify a clause, if cancellation itself, not only normalisation and denormalisation, is applicable.

The rule is a simplification rule since the number of symbols is reduced with (almost) every application of the cancellation.

Table 1. Compares the number of problems solved with any configuration where a new option is enabled to the ones where it is disabled, with a runtime of 10 seconds. The column "both" lists how many were solved in either case. The columns "on", and "off" list how many additional problems could have been solved with the option enabled, or disabled respectively.

	on	both	off
gve	**121**	3372	104
eval	323	2927	**347**
asg	**440**	2859	298
push⁻	**112**	3378	107
cancel	**576**	2749	272

7 Experimental evaluation

We describe two experiments to establish the impact of the new rules. The first experiment compares the new rules to each other, whilst the second experiment aims to determine how helpful the new rules will be in designing extensions to VAMPIRE's portfolio mode. This is a standard approach to evaluating the benefit of new features in an automated theorem prover [18].

Experimental Setup. We implemented the rules as immediate simplification rules in VAMPIRE 4.5 (the implementation is available from the GitHub repository linked from the VAMPIRE website [1], on the branch `integer-arithemtic`). We selected a suitable subset of problems as follows. We started with the set problems of 56,210 from SMT-LIB that involve quantifiers and arithmetic. In a first step we filtered out benchmarks that VAMPIRE could solve within 1 second in **both** default mode (which involves a simpler version of the rule eval), and in default mode with eval enabled. Our main experiments were carried out on the remaining set of 21,512 benchmarks, we which will refer to as **B**. Filtering out trivial benchmarks avoids the results containing noise from benchmarks that can easily be solved and is an approach recently adopted by SMT-COMP [22]. Experiments are run on a Linux cluster where each node contains two octa-core 2.1 GHz Intel Xeon processors and 160GB of RAM. The raw results of our experiments can be found on GitHub[3].

Experiment 1. In our first experiment we wanted to find out which are the best combinations of new rules, and whether the rules themselves have a positive impact on proof search. Therefore we ran VAMPIRE in each of the 32 configurations **C** resulting from enabling or disabling each of the 5 groups of rules (asg, gve, eval, push⁻, and cancel) over **B** with a timeout of 10 seconds.

The results are given in Table 1 showing the total number of problems solved and the problems gained/lost when compared to the default mode with no options set. Each row represents the combination (union) of 16 strategies where

---

[3] https://github.com/vprover/vampire_publications/tree/master/
experimental_data/TACAS-2021-THEORY-REASONING

Table 2. The top 10 strategies in the greedy ranking of configurations.

solved	id	eval	gve	asg	push⁻	cancel
2546	15	✓	✓	✓	✓	✓
548	24		✓			
136	27	✓			✓	✓
63	22			✓	✓	
51	9	✓	✓			✓
38	4	✓		✓		
27	23			✓	✓	✓
20	26		✓	✓		
19	25		✓			✓
18	5	✓		✓		✓

Table 3. The symmetric difference in number of problems solved between the three new strategies in portfolio mode against VAMPIRE 4.5. Each cell indicates the number of problems solved by the row solver unsolved by the column solver. The column unique lists how many problems each strategy could solve that no other strategy could. The strategy VAMPIRE * is what we can solve with either of the three other strategies. VAMPIRE * is not taken into account for uniqueness.

strategy	total	unique	VAMPIRE *	15	24	27	VAMPIRE 4.5
VAMPIRE *	7511	0	0	622	937	932	1052
15	6889	64	0	0	865	729	824
24	6574	12	0	550	0	261	366
27	6579	2	0	419	266	0	165
VAMPIRE 4.5	6506	10	47	441	298	92	0

that option is turned on. This shows that, with the exception of evaluation, the gains outweigh the losses, sometimes considerably. This result for evaluation tells us that the other rules can still operate effectively without our new evaluation and, further, that the two evaluation methods are in some sense complementary. Therefore, whilst we explore this further, we will keep both evaluation methods. The most significant gains are with cancellation, which may be related to the fact that it is applicable to inequalities as well as equalities.

Greedy Ranking. Another way of looking at the results of Experiment 1 is to create a greedy ranking *rank* of all configurations **C**, starting with the set of all configurations, and ranking the configuration solving the most benchmarks in **B** as the best, ranking the one that solves most of the remaining benchmarks as second, and so on. The top 10 strategies in this ranking are given in Table 2. The overall best strategy uses all 5 of the new rules. Interestingly, the second best strategy only uses the gve rule. This ranking indicates the most promising strategies to use in our next experiment.

Experiment 2 In our second experiment we wanted to see how many new problems we can solve with the new simplification rules compared to our current

Table 4. Comparing our new approach, VAMPIRE *, against VAMPIRE 4.5, CVC4, and Z3 with results separated by logic. The notation $(+a, -b)$ means that the solver solved a problems the new VAMPIRE could not solve, and the new vampire could solve b the other solver couldn't. The entries $a(b)$ in the column VAMPIRE *, list the number a of problems that could be solved by our new rules, and b the number of these problems that could not be solved by any of the other solvers.

	count	VAMPIRE *	VAMPIRE 4.5	CVC4	Z3
ALIA	24	14 (0)	12 (+0, -2)	23 (+9, -0)	**24** (+10, -0)
AUFDTLIA	134	39 (0)	39 (+0, -0)	**86** (+47, -0)	80 (+45, -4)
AUFLIA	862	312 (4)	311 (+4, -5)	295 (+84, -101)	**331** (+148, -129)
AUFLIRA	1697	1364 (0)	1354 (+0, -10)	**1455** (+101, -10)	1453 (+102, -13)
AUFNIA	3	**0** (0)	**0** (+0, -0)	**0** (+0, -0)	**0** (+0, -0)
AUFNIRA	509	**87** (2)	81 (+2, -8)	**87** (+20, -20)	63 (+16, -40)
LIA	246	79 (0)	78 (+0, -1)	**246** (+167, -0)	230 (+155, -4)
LRA	2043	1013 (41)	365 (+0, -648)	1528 (+635, -120)	**1756** (+883, -140)
NIA	11	1 (0)	1 (+0, -0)	9 (+9, -1)	5 (+4, -0)
NRA	101	92 (0)	91 (+0, -1)	72 (+0, -20)	**96** (+9, -5)
UFDTLIA	274	**120** (4)	115 (+0, -5)	40 (+3, -83)	34 (+1, -87)
UFDTLIRA	33	0 (0)	0 (+0, -0)	**33** (+33, -0)	**33** (+33, -0)
UFLIA	4833	1924 (23)	1829 (+30, -125)	**2314** (+501, -111)	1899 (+315, -340)
UFLRA	7	2 (0)	2 (+0, -0)	2 (+0, -0)	**5** (+3, -0)
UFNIA	10735	2463 (16)	2227 (+11, -247)	**4928** (+3055, -590)	3858 (+1983, -588)
Any Logic	21512	7510 (90)	6505 (+47, -1052)	**11118** (+4664, -1056)	9867 (+3707, -1350)

best effort in VAMPIRE 4.5. Therefore we ran VAMPIRE with the three top ranking configurations of experiment 3 forced added on top of VAMPIRE's portfolio mode. The portfolio mode executes a sequence of strategies heuristically chosen based on problem features. Forcing a configuration of new options on top of this forces each strategy to make use of the new options. We ran this experiment over **B** with a timeout of 200 seconds.

Results are given in Table 3 and show that the new rules allow VAMPIRE to solver considerably more problems (1052) than it could before whilst losing relatively few (47). The best configuration of options (all five new rules) solves the most with the other two configurations solving roughly the same. The interesting point here is that they remain complementary, solving a large number of problems uniquely. These are the exact conditions we require for producing a new, powerful portfolio mode. It is likely that performance will improve even further when also considering other option combinations.

Finally, Table 4 compares the number of problems solved by either of the three top strategies – referred to as VAMPIRE* – against VAMPIRE 4.5, Z3 [7] and CVC4 [4]. Results are further separated by the logic in which the benchmarks belong — A stands for <u>A</u>rrays, UF stands for <u>U</u>ninterpreted <u>F</u>unctions, DT stands for <u>D</u>ata <u>T</u>ypes, L stands for <u>L</u>inear, N for <u>N</u>on-linear, I stands for <u>I</u>ntegers, R stands for <u>R</u>eals, with the final A standing for <u>A</u>rithmetic. Here we notice that the new rules make a considerable impact in the case of pure linear real arithmetic. This is likely due to the fact that the asg allows us to fully generalise away most linear terms and gve will be broadly applicable without uninterpreted functions. It is interesting to note that, whilst the new VAMPIRE solves fewer problems than CVC4, and Z3 overall, it solves many (1056, and 1350) problems that the other provers do not solve. The most striking result is that we can solve 90 new problems, neither VAMPIRE 4.5 nor either of the state-of-the-art SMT solvers could solve.

8   Conclusion

We have motivated and introduced five new simplification rules for reasoning in the theory of arithmetic within saturation-based first-order theorem provers. These rules were implemented within the VAMPIRE theorem prover and demonstrated to improve the reasoning power on problems taken from SMT-LIB. It remains future work to explore the ideal combinations of these rules and existing proof search heuristics. It also remains an open question whether we can design an evaluation rule and modified simplification ordering that ensures that every evaluation that we want to perform is a true simplification. As demonstrated, this is not necessary pragmatically but would be satisfying theoretically.

References

1. Vampire website. https://vprover.github.io/.
2. E. Althaus, E. Kruglov, and C. Weidenbach. Superposition modulo linear arithmetic SUP(LA). In *Frontiers of Combining Systems, 7th International Symposium, FroCoS 2009, Trento, Italy, September 16-18, 2009. Proceedings*, vol. 5749 of *Lecture Notes in Computer Science*, pp. 84–99. Springer, 2009.
3. L. Bachmair, H. Ganzinger, and U. Waldmann. Refutational theorem proving for hierarchic first-order theories. *Appl. Algebra Eng. Commun. Comput.*, 5:193–212, 1994.
4. C. Barrett, C. Conway, M. Deters, L. Hadarean, D. Jovanovic, T. King, A. Reynolds, and C. Tinelli. CVC4. In *Proceedings of the 23rd International Conference on Computer Aided Verification*, number 6806 in Lecture Notes in Computer Science, pp. 171–177. Springer-Verlag, 2011.
5. P. Baumgartner and U. Waldmann. Hierarchic Superposition With Weak Abstraction. In *Proceedings of the 24th International Conference on Automated Deduction*, number 7898 in Lecture Notes in Artificial Intelligence, pp. 39–57. Springer-Verlag, 2013.
6. M. P. Bonacina, C. Lynch, and L. M. de Moura. On deciding satisfiability by theorem proving with speculative inferences. *J. Autom. Reasoning*, 47(2):161–189, 2011.
7. L. M. de Moura and N. Bjørner. Z3: an efficient SMT solver. In *Proc. of TACAS*, vol. 4963 of *LNCS*, pp. 337–340, 2008.
8. N. Dershowitz and D. A. Plaisted. Rewriting. In *Handbook of Automated Reasoning*, vol. I, chapter 9, pp. 535–610. Elsevier Science, 2001.
9. H. Ganzinger and K. Korovin. Theory instantiation. In *Logic for Programming, Artificial Intelligence, and Reasoning, 13th International Conference, LPAR 2006, Phnom Penh, Cambodia, November 13-17, 2006, Proceedings*, vol. 4246 of *Lecture Notes in Computer Science*, pp. 497–511. Springer, 2006.

10. B. Gleiss and M. Suda. Layered clause selection for theory reasoning. In *Automated Reasoning*, pp. 402–409. Springer International Publishing, 2020.
11. K. Hoder, G. Reger, M. Suda, and A. Voronkov. Selecting the selection. In *Automated Reasoning: 8th International Joint Conference, IJCAR 2016, Coimbra, Portugal, June 27 – July 2, 2016, Proceedings*, pp. 313–329. Springer International Publishing, 2016.
12. D. Knuth and P. Bendix. Simple word problems in universal algebra. In *Computational Problems in Abstract Algebra*, pp. 263–297. Pergamon Press, 1970.
13. K. Korovin and A. Voronkov. Integrating linear arithmetic into superposition calculus. In *Computer Science Logic, 21st International Workshop, CSL 2007, 16th Annual Conference of the EACSL, Lausanne, Switzerland, September 11-15, 2007, Proceedings*, vol. 4646 of *Lecture Notes in Computer Science*, pp. 223–237. Springer, 2007.
14. L. Kovács and A. Voronkov. First-order theorem proving and Vampire. In *CAV 2013*, vol. 8044 of *Lecture Notes in Computer Science*, pp. 1–35, 2013.
15. A. Nonnengart and C. Weidenbach. Computing small clause normal forms. In *Handbook of Automated Reasoning (in 2 volumes)*, pp. 335–367. Elsevier and MIT Press, 2001.
16. G. Reger, N. Bjørner, M. Suda, and A. Voronkov. AVATAR modulo theories. In *GCAI 2016. 2nd Global Conference on Artificial Intelligence*, vol. 41 of *EPiC Series in Computing*, pp. 39–52. EasyChair, 2016.
17. G. Reger and M. Suda. Set of support for theory reasoning. In *IWIL Workshop and LPAR Short Presentations*, vol. 1 of *Kalpa Publications in Computing*, pp. 124–134. EasyChair, 2017.
18. G. Reger, M. Suda, and A. Voronkov. The challenges of evaluating a new feature in Vampire. In *Proceedings of the 1st and 2nd Vampire Workshops*, vol. 38 of *EPiC Series in Computing*, pp. 70–74. EasyChair, 2016.
19. G. Reger, M. Suda, and A. Voronkov. New techniques in clausal form generation. In *GCAI 2016. 2nd Global Conference on Artificial Intelligence*, vol. 41 of *EPiC Series in Computing*, pp. 11–23. EasyChair, 2016.
20. G. Reger, M. Suda, and A. Voronkov. Unification with abstraction and theory instantiation in saturation-based reasoning. In *International Conference on Tools and Algorithms for the Construction and Analysis of Systems*, pp. 3–22. Springer, 2018.
21. P. Rümmer. A Constraint Sequent Calculus for First-Order Logic with Linear Integer Arithmetic. In *Proceedings of the 15th International Conference on Logic for Programming Artificial Intelligence and Reasoning*, number 5330 in Lecture Notes in Artificial Intelligence, pp. 274–289. Springer-Verlag, 2008.
22. T. Weber, S. Conchon, D. Déharbe, M. Heizmann, A. Niemetz, and G. Reger. The smt competition 2015–2018. *Journal on Satisfiability, Boolean Modeling and Computation*, 11(1):221–259, 2019.

Deductive Stability Proofs for Ordinary Differential Equations*

Yong Kiam Tan$^{(\boxtimes)}$ (iD) and André Platzer$^{(\boxtimes)}$ (iD)

Computer Science Department, Carnegie Mellon University, Pittsburgh, USA
{yongkiat,aplatzer}@cs.cmu.edu

Abstract. Stability is required for real world controlled systems as it ensures that those systems can tolerate small, real world perturbations around their desired operating states. This paper shows how stability for continuous systems modeled by ordinary differential equations (ODEs) can be formally verified in differential dynamic logic (dL). The key insight is to specify ODE stability by suitably nesting the dynamic modalities of dL with first-order logic quantifiers. Elucidating the logical structure of stability properties in this way has three key benefits: *i)* it provides a flexible means of formally specifying various stability properties of interest, *ii)* it yields rigorous proofs of those stability properties from dL's axioms with dL's ODE safety and liveness proof principles, and *iii)* it enables formal analysis of the relationships between various stability properties which, in turn, inform proofs of those properties. These benefits are put into practice through an implementation of stability proofs for several examples in KeYmaera X, a hybrid systems theorem prover based on dL.

Keywords: differential equations, stability, differential dynamic logic

1 Introduction

The study of stability has its roots in efforts to understand mechanical systems, particularly those arising in celestial mechanics [15,19,30]. Today, it is an important part of numerous applications in dynamical systems [34] and control theory [14,18]. This paper studies proofs of stability for continuous dynamical systems described by *ordinary differential equations* (ODEs), such as those used to model feedback control systems [14,18]. For such systems, ODE stability is a key correctness requirement [2] that deserves fully rigorous proofs *alongside* other key properties such as safety and liveness of those ODEs [28,36]. Despite this, formal stability verification has received less attention compared to proofs of safety and liveness, e.g., through reachability or deductive techniques [8].

Stability for a continuous system (or ODEs) requires that *i)* its system state always stays close to some desired operating state(s) when initially slightly perturbed from those operating state(s), and *ii)* those perturbations are eventually dissipated so the system returns to a desired operating state. These properties

---

* This research was sponsored by the AFOSR under grant number FA9550-16-1-0288. The first author was supported by A*STAR, Singapore.

J. F. Groote and K. G. Larsen (Eds.): TACAS 2021, LNCS 12652, pp. 181–199, 2021.
https://doi.org/10.1007/978-3-030-72013-1_10

are especially crucial for engineered systems because they must be robust to real world perturbations deviating from idealized system models. Simple pendulums provide canonical examples of stability phenomena: they are always observed to settle in the rest position of Fig. 1 (bottom) after some time regardless of how they are initially released. In contrast, the inverted pendulum in Fig. 1 (top) is *theoretically* also at a resting position but can only be observed transiently in practice because the slightest real world perturbation will cause the pendulum to fall due to gravity. Stability explains these observations—the resting position is (asymptotically) stable while the inverted position is unstable and requires active control to ensure its stability. Proofs of safety and liveness properties are still required for the inverted pendulum under control, e.g., its controller must never generate unsafe amounts of torque and the pendulum must eventually reach the inverted position. The *triumvirate* of safety, liveness, and stability is required for holistic correctness of the inverted pendulum controller.

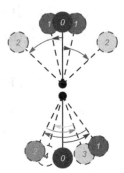

Fig. 1. A pendulum (in green) hung by a rigid rod from a pivot (in black) perturbed from its resting state (bottom) and from its inverted, upright position (top). Perturbed states (with dashed boundaries) are faded out to show the progression of time.

The classical way of distinguishing the aforementioned stability situations is by designing a *Lyapunov function* [19], i.e., an energy-like auxiliary measure satisfying certain *arithmetical conditions* [14,18,31] which implies that the auxiliary energy decreases along system trajectories towards local minima at the stable resting state(s), see Fig. 2. Prior approaches [1,12,17,21,33] have emphasized the need to formally verify those arithmetical conditions in order to guarantee that a conjectured Lyapunov function correctly implies stability for a given system.

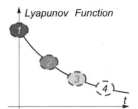

Fig. 2. A Lyapunov function that decreases along the pendulum trajectory shown in Fig. 1 (bottom).

This paper shows how deductive proofs of ODE stability can be carried out in differential dynamic logic (dL) [25,26,27], a logic for *deductive verification* of hybrid systems.[1] The key insight is that stability properties can be specified by suitably nesting the dynamic modalities of dL with quantifiers of first-order logic. The resulting specifications are amenable to rigorous proof by combining dL's ODE safety [28] and liveness [36] proof principles with real arithmetic and first-order quantifier reasoning. This makes it possible to *syntactically derive* stability for a given system from the small set of dL axioms which, in turn, enables trustworthy stability proofs in the KeYmaera X theorem prover for hybrid systems [11,26]. Notably, this approach directly verifies *stability specifications*, which

---

[1] Hybrid systems are mathematical models describing discrete and continuous dynamics, and interactions thereof. This paper's formal understanding of ODE stability is crucial for subsequent investigation of hybrid systems stability [5,13,20].

goes beyond verifying arithmetic that imply those specifications [1,12,17,21,33]. This is crucial for advanced stability notions because those variations generally require subtle twists to the required arithmetical conditions on their Lyapunov functions [14]; proofs of stability specifications alleviate the onus on system designers to correctly pick and check the appropriate conditions for their applications. Section 3 shows how various stability properties for ODE equilibria can be formally specified and proved in dL with Lyapunov function techniques. Section 4 generalizes those stability specifications, yielding unambiguous formal specifications of advanced stability properties from the literature [14,18], along with their derived proof rules. These specifications also provide rigorous insights into the logical relationship between various stability notions, which are used to inform their respective proofs. Section 5 illustrates the practicality of this paper's dL approach through several stability case studies formalized in KeYmaera X.

All omitted definitions and proofs are available in the supplement [35].

2   Background: Differential Dynamic Logic

This section briefly recalls the syntax and semantics of dL, focusing on its continuous fragment which has a complete axiomatization for ODE invariants [28]. Full presentations of dL, including its discrete fragment, are elsewhere [26,27].

Syntax and Semantics. The grammar of dL terms is as follows, where $x \in \mathcal{V}$ is a variable and $c \in \mathbb{Q}$ is a rational constant. These terms are polynomials over $\mathcal{V}$ (extensions with Noetherian functions [28] such as $\exp, \sin, \cos$ are possible):

$$p, q ::= x \mid c \mid p + q \mid p \cdot q$$

The grammar of dL formulas is as follows, where $\sim \in \{=, \neq, \geq, >, \leq, <\}$ is a comparison operator and α is a hybrid program:

$$\phi, \psi ::= p \sim q \mid \phi \wedge \psi \mid \phi \vee \psi \mid \neg \phi \mid \forall v\, \phi \mid \exists v\, \phi \mid [\alpha]\phi \mid \langle \alpha \rangle \phi$$

This grammar features atomic comparisons ($p \sim q$), propositional connectives ($\neg, \wedge, \vee$), first-order quantifiers over the reals ($\forall, \exists$), and the box ($[\alpha]\phi$) and diamond ($\langle \alpha \rangle \phi$) modality formulas which express that all or some runs of hybrid program α satisfy ϕ, respectively. The modalities $[\cdot], \langle \cdot \rangle$ can be freely nested with first-order and modal connectives, which is crucial for the specification of stability properties in Sections 3 and 4. Formulas not containing the modalities are formulas of first-order real arithmetic and are written as P, Q, R.

This paper focuses on the *continuous* fragment of hybrid programs $\alpha \equiv x' = f(x) \,\&\, Q$, where $x' = f(x)$ is an n-dimensional system of ordinary differential equations (ODEs), $x'_1 = f_1(x), \ldots, x'_n = f_n(x)$, over variables $x = (x_1, \ldots, x_n)$, the LHS x'_i is the time derivative of x_i and the RHS $f_i(x)$ is a polynomial over variables x. The evolution domain constraint Q specifies the set of states in which the ODE is allowed to evolve continuously. When Q is the formula *true*, the ODE is also written as $x' = f(x)$. For n-dimensional vectors x, y, the dot product is $x \cdot y \overset{\text{def}}{=} \sum_{i=1}^{n} x_i y_i$ and $\|x\|^2 \overset{\text{def}}{=} \sum_{i=1}^{n} x_i^2$ denotes the squared Euclidean norm. Variables $z \in \mathcal{V} \setminus \{x\}$ not occurring on the LHS of ODE $x' = f(x)$ are *parameters* that remain constant along ODE solutions. The following parametric ODE model of a simple pendulum is used as a running example.

Example 1 (Pendulum model). The ODE $\alpha_p \equiv \theta' = \omega, \ \omega' = -\frac{g}{L}\sin(\theta) - b\omega$ models a pendulum (illustrated below) suspended from a pivot by a rod of length L, where θ is the angle of displacement, ω is the angular velocity of the pendulum, and $g > 0$ is the gravitational constant. Parameter $a = \frac{g}{L}$ is a positive scaling constant and parameter $b \geq 0$ is the coefficient of friction for angular velocity. The symbolic parameters a, b make analysis of α_p apply to a range of concrete values, e.g., pendulums that are suspended by a long rod (with large L) are modeled by small positive values of a, while frictionless pendulums have $b = 0$.

A simplification of α_p is used because stability analyses often concern the behavior of the pendulum near its resting (or inverted) state where $\theta = 0$. For such nearby states with $\theta \approx 0$, the small angle approximation $\sin(\theta) \approx \theta$ yields a linear ODE:[2]

$$\alpha_l \equiv \theta' = \omega, \ \omega' = -a\theta - b\omega \tag{1}$$

An *inverted* pendulum is modeled by a similar ODE (illustrated on the right) under a change of coordinates. Such a pendulum requires an external torque input $u(\theta, \omega)$ to maintain its stability; $u(\theta, \omega)$ is determined and proved correct in Section 5.

$$\alpha_i \equiv \theta' = \omega, \ \omega' = a\theta - b\omega - u(\theta, \omega) \tag{2}$$

States $\nu : \mathcal{V} \to \mathbb{R}$ assign real values to each variable in $\mathcal{V}$; the set of all states is $\mathbb{S}$. The semantics of dL formula ϕ is the set of states $\llbracket \phi \rrbracket \subseteq \mathbb{S}$ in which ϕ is true [26,27], where the semantics of first-order logical connectives are defined as usual, e.g., $\llbracket \phi \wedge \psi \rrbracket = \llbracket \phi \rrbracket \cap \llbracket \psi \rrbracket$. For ODEs, the semantics of the modal operators is as follows.[3] Let $\nu \in \mathbb{S}$ and $\boldsymbol{\varphi} : [0, T) \to \mathbb{S}$ for some $0 < T \leq \infty$, be the unique, right-maximal solution [6] to ODE $x' = f(x)$ with initial value $\boldsymbol{\varphi}(0) = \nu$:

$\nu \in \llbracket [x' = f(x) \,\&\, Q]\phi \rrbracket$ iff for all $0 \leq \tau < T$ where $\boldsymbol{\varphi}(\zeta) \in \llbracket Q \rrbracket$ for all $0 \leq \zeta \leq \tau$:
$$\boldsymbol{\varphi}(\tau) \in \llbracket \phi \rrbracket$$
$\nu \in \llbracket \langle x' = f(x) \,\&\, Q \rangle \phi \rrbracket$ iff there exists $0 \leq \tau < T$ such that:
$$\boldsymbol{\varphi}(\tau) \in \llbracket \phi \rrbracket \text{ and } \boldsymbol{\varphi}(\zeta) \in \llbracket Q \rrbracket \text{ for all } 0 \leq \zeta \leq \tau$$

For a formula P the ε-neighborhood of P with respect to x is defined as $\mathcal{U}_\varepsilon(P) \overset{\text{def}}{=} \exists y \left(\|x - y\|^2 < \varepsilon^2 \wedge P(y) \right)$, where the existentially quantified variables y are fresh in P. The neighborhood formula $\mathcal{U}_\varepsilon(P)$ characterizes the set of states within distance ε from P, with respect to the dynamically evolving variables x.

---

[2] This linearization is justified by the Hartman-Grobman theorem [6]. A nonlinear polynomial approximation, such as $\sin(\theta) \approx \theta - \frac{\theta^3}{6}$, can also be used.

[3] The semantics of dL formulas is defined compositionally elsewhere [26,27].

This is useful for syntactically expressing small ε perturbations in the stability definitions of Sections 3 and 4. For formulas P of first-order real arithmetic, the ε-neighborhood, $\mathcal{U}_\varepsilon(P)$, can be equivalently expressed in quantifier-free form by quantifier elimination [4]. For example, $\mathcal{U}_\varepsilon(x = 0)$ is equivalent to the formula $\|x\|^2 < \varepsilon^2$. Formulas $\overline{P}$ and ∂P are the syntactically definable topological closure and boundary of the set characterized by P, respectively [4].

Proof Calculus. All derivations and proof rules are presented in a classical sequent calculus. The semantics of *sequent* $\Gamma \vdash \phi$ is equivalent to the formula $(\bigwedge_{\psi \in \Gamma} \psi) \rightarrow \phi$. A sequent is valid iff its corresponding formula is valid. Completed branches in a sequent proof are marked with $*$. Assumptions $\psi \in \Gamma$ that have only ODE parameters as free variables remain true along ODE evolutions and are soundly kept across ODE deduction steps [26,27]. First-order real arithmetic is decidable [4] so we assume such a decision procedure and label proof steps with ℝ when they follow from real arithmetic. Axioms and proof rules are *derivable* iff they can be deduced from sound dL axioms and proof rules [26,27].

Formula I is an *invariant* of the ODE $x' = f(x) \,\&\, Q$ iff the formula $I \rightarrow [x' = f(x) \,\&\, Q]I$ is valid. The dL proof calculus is *complete* for ODE invariants [28], i.e., any true ODE invariant expressible in first-order real arithmetic can be proved in the calculus. The calculus also supports refinement reasoning [36] for proving ODE liveness properties $P \rightarrow \langle x' = f(x) \,\&\, Q \rangle R$, which says that the goal R is reached along the ODE $x' = f(x) \,\&\, Q$ from precondition P.

An important syntactic tool for reasoning with ODE $x' = f(x)$ is the *Lie derivative* of term p defined as $\dot{p} \stackrel{\text{def}}{=} \sum_{x_i \in x} \frac{\partial p}{\partial x_i} f_i(x)$, whose semantic value is equal to the time derivative of the value of p along solutions φ of the ODE [26,28]. They are provably definable in dL using syntactic differentials [26].

3 Asymptotic Stability of an Equilibrium Point

This section presents Lyapunov's classical notion of asymptotic stability [19] and its formal specification in dL. This formalization enables the derivation of dL stability proof rules with *Lyapunov functions* [14,18,19,31]. Several related stability concepts are formalized in dL, along with their relationships and rules.

3.1 Mathematical Preliminaries

An *equilibrium point* of ODE $x' = f(x)$ is a point $x_0 \in \mathbb{R}^n$ where $f(x_0) = 0$, so a system that starts at x_0 stays at x_0 along its continuous evolution. Such points are often interesting in real-world systems, e.g., the equilibrium point $\theta = 0, \omega = 0$ for α_l from (1) is the resting state of a pendulum. For a controlled system, equilibrium points often correspond to desired steady system states where no further continuous control input (modeled as part of $f(x)$) is required [18].

For brevity, assume the origin $0 \in \mathbb{R}^n$ is an equilibrium point of interest. Any other equilibrium point(s) of interest $x_0 \in \mathbb{R}^n$ can be translated to the origin with the change of coordinates $x \mapsto x - x_0$ for the ODE (see supplement [35]).

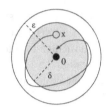 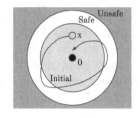

Fig. 3. Solutions from points in the δ ball around the origin, like the green initial point x, remain within the ε ball around the origin $0 \in \mathbb{R}^n$ (black dot) and asymptotically approach the origin. The latter two plots illustrate how asymptotic stability for an ODE can be broken down into a pair of (quantified) ODE safety and liveness properties.

The following definition of asymptotic stability is standard [14,18,31].[4]

Definition 2 (Asymptotic stability [14,18,31]). *The origin* $0 \in \mathbb{R}^n$ *of ODE* $x' = f(x)$ *is*

- ***stable*** *if, for all* $\varepsilon > 0$, *there exists* $\delta > 0$ *such that for all initial states* $x = x(0)$ *with* $\|x\| < \delta$, *the right-maximal ODE solution* $x(t) : [0, T) \to \mathbb{R}^n$ *satisfies* $\|x(t)\| < \varepsilon$ *for all times* $0 \le t < T$,
- ***attractive*** *if there exists* $\delta > 0$ *such that for all* $x = x(0)$ *with* $\|x\| < \delta$, *the right-maximal ODE solution* $x(t) : [0, T) \to \mathbb{R}^n$ *satisfies* $\lim_{t \to T} x(t) = 0$,
- ***asymptotically stable*** *if it is stable and attractive.*

These definitions can be understood using the resting state of the pendulum from Fig. 1 (bottom) which is asymptotically stable. When the pendulum is given a light push from its bottom resting state (formally, $\|x\| < \delta$), it gently oscillates near that resting state (formally, $\|x(t)\| < \varepsilon$). In the presence of friction, these oscillations eventually dissipate so the pendulum asymptotically returns to its resting state (formally, $\lim_{t \to T} x(t) = 0$). This behavior is *local*, i.e., for any given $\varepsilon > 0$, there *exists* a sufficiently small $\delta > 0$ perturbation of the initial state that results in gentle oscillations with $\|x(t)\| < \varepsilon$, see Fig. 3 (left). A strong push, e.g., with $\delta > \varepsilon$, could instead cause the pendulum to spin around on its pivot.

Remark 3. Stability and attractivity *do not* imply each other [31, Chapter I.2.7]. However, if the origin is stable, attractivity can be defined in a simpler way. This is proved in dL, after characterizing stability and attractivity syntactically.

3.2 Formal Specification

The formal specification of asymptotic stability in dL combines *i)* the dynamic modalities of dL, which are used to quantify over the dynamics of the ODE, and *ii)* the first-order logic quantifiers, which are used to express combinations of (topologically) local and asymptotic properties of those dynamics.

---

[4] Some definitions require, or implicitly assume, right-maximal solutions $x(t)$ to be global, i.e., with $T = \infty$, see [18, Definition 4.1] and associated discussion. The definitions presented here are better suited for subsequent generalizations.

Lemma 4 (Asymptotic stability in dL). *The origin of ODE $x' = f(x)$ is, respectively, i)* **stable,** *ii)* **attractive,** *and iii)* **asymptotically stable** *iff the* dL *formulas i)* Stab$(x' = f(x))$, *ii)* Attr$(x' = f(x))$, *and iii)* AStab$(x' = f(x))$ *respectively are valid. Variables ε, δ are fresh, i.e., not in $x, f(x)$.*

$$\text{Stab}(x' = f(x)) \equiv \forall \varepsilon{>}0 \, \exists \delta{>}0 \, \forall x \, (\mathcal{U}_\delta(x = 0) \to [x' = f(x)]\mathcal{U}_\varepsilon(x = 0))$$

$$\text{Attr}(x' = f(x)) \equiv \exists \delta{>}0 \, \forall x \, (\mathcal{U}_\delta(x = 0) \to \text{Asym}(x' = f(x), x = 0))$$

$$\text{AStab}(x' = f(x)) \equiv \text{Stab}(x' = f(x)) \wedge \text{Attr}(x' = f(x))$$

Formula Asym$(x' = f(x), P) \equiv \forall \varepsilon{>}0 \, \langle x' = f(x) \rangle [x' = f(x)]\mathcal{U}_\varepsilon(P)$ *characterizes the set of states that asymptotically approach P along ODE solutions.*

Formula Stab$(x' = f(x))$ is a syntactic dL rendering of the corresponding quantifiers from Def. 2. The safety property $\mathcal{U}_\delta(x = 0) \to [x' = f(x)]\mathcal{U}_\varepsilon(x = 0)$ expresses that solutions starting from the δ-neighborhood of the origin always (for all times) stay safely in the ε-neighborhood, as visualized in Fig. 3 (middle). Formula Attr$(x' = f(x))$ uses the subformula Asym$(x' = f(x), x = 0)$ which characterizes the limit in Def. 2. Recall $\lim_{t \to T} x(t) = 0$ iff for all $\varepsilon > 0$ there exists a time τ with $0 \leq \tau < T$ such that for all times t with $\tau \leq t < T$, the solution satisfies $\|x(t)\| < \varepsilon$, i.e., the limit requires for all distances $\varepsilon > 0$, the ODE solution will *eventually always* be within distance ε of the origin, as visualized in Fig. 3 (right). This limit is characterized using nested $\langle \cdot \rangle [\cdot]$ modalities, together with first-order quantification according to Def. 2. More generally, formula Asym$(x' = f(x), P)$ characterizes the set of initial states where the right-maximal ODE solution asymptotically approaches P; this set is known as the *region of attraction* of P [18]. Thus, attractivity requires that the region of attraction of the origin contains an open neighborhood $\mathcal{U}_\delta(x = 0)$ of the origin.

From Lemma 4, proving validity of the formula AStab$(x' = f(x))$ yields a rigorous proof of asymptotic stability for $x' = f(x)$. However, if the origin is stable, then attractivity can be provably simplified with the following corollary.

Corollary 5 (Stable attractivity). *The following axiom is derivable in* dL.
SAttr Stab$(x' = f(x)) \to \big(\text{Asym}(x' = f(x), x{=}0) \leftrightarrow \forall \varepsilon{>}0 \, \langle x' = f(x) \rangle \mathcal{U}_\varepsilon(x{=}0)\big)$

Corollary 5 simplifies the syntactic characterization of the region of attraction for stable equilibria from a nested $\langle \cdot \rangle [\cdot]$ formula to a $\langle \cdot \rangle$ formula, which is then directly amenable to ODE liveness reasoning [36]. This corollary is used to simplify proofs of asymptotic stability, as explained next.

3.3 Lyapunov Functions

Lyapunov functions are the standard tool for showing stability of general, nonlinear ODEs [14,18,31] and finding suitable Lyapunov functions is an important problem in its own right [1,9,12,17,21,23,24,33,37]. This section shows how a candidate Lyapunov function, once found, can be used to rigorously prove stability. The following proof rules derive Lyapunov stability arguments [14,18,31] syntactically in dL.

Lemma 6 (Lyapunov functions). *The following Lyapunov function proof rules are derivable in* dL.

$$\text{Lyap}_{\geq} \quad \frac{\vdash f(0) = 0 \wedge v(0) = 0 \quad \vdash \exists \gamma{>}0 \, \forall x \left(0{<}\|x\|^2{\leq}\gamma^2 \rightarrow v > 0 \wedge \dot{v} \leq 0\right)}{\vdash \text{Stab}(x' = f(x))}$$

$$\text{Lyap}_{>} \quad \frac{\vdash f(0) = 0 \wedge v(0) = 0 \quad \vdash \exists \gamma{>}0 \, \forall x \left(0{<}\|x\|^2{\leq}\gamma^2 \rightarrow v > 0 \wedge \dot{v} < 0\right)}{\vdash \text{AStab}(x' = f(x))}$$

Rules $\text{Lyap}_{\geq}$, $\text{Lyap}_{>}$ use the Lyapunov function v as an auxiliary, energy-like function near the origin which is positive and has non-positive (resp. negative $\text{Lyap}_{>}$) derivative $\dot{v}$. This guarantees that v is non-increasing (resp. decreasing) along ODE solutions near the origin, see Fig. 2. The right premise of both rules use $\exists \gamma{>}0 \, \forall x \left(0{<}\|x\|^2{\leq}\gamma^2 \rightarrow \cdots\right)$ to require that the Lyapunov function conditions are true in a γ-neighborhood of the origin. The subtle difference in sign condition for $\dot{v}$ between rules $\text{Lyap}_{\geq}$, $\text{Lyap}_{>}$ is illustrated for the pendulum.

Example 7 (Pendulum asymptotic stability). For ODE α_l from (1), a suitable Lyapunov function for proving its stability [18] is $v = a\frac{\theta^2}{2} + \frac{(b\theta+\omega)^2+\omega^2}{4}$, where the Lie derivative of v along α_l is $\dot{v} = -\frac{b}{2}(a\theta^2+\omega^2)$. Stability[5] is formally proved in dL for *any* parameter values $a > 0, b \geq 0$ using rule $\text{Lyap}_{\geq}$ because both of its resulting arithmetical premises are provable by ℝ. The full dL derivation, also used in KeYmaera X (Section 5), is shown in the proof of Lemma 6 [35].

When $b > 0$, i.e., friction is non-negligible, an identical derivation with $\text{Lyap}_{>}$ instead of $\text{Lyap}_{\geq}$ proves asymptotic stability because $-\frac{b}{2}(a\theta^2 + \omega^2)$ is negative except at the origin. Indeed, displacements to the pendulum's resting state can only be dissipated in the presence of friction, not when $b = 0$.

3.4   Asymptotic Stability Variations

Asymptotic stability is a strong guarantee about the local behavior of ODE solutions near equilibrium points of interest. In certain applications, stronger stability guarantees may be needed for those equilibria [18]. This section examines two standard stability variations, shows how they can be proved in dL, and formally analyzes their logical relationship with asymptotic stability.

Exponential stability As the name suggests, the first stability variation, exponential stability, guarantees an exponential rate of convergence towards the equilibrium point from an initial displacement. This is useful, e.g., for bounding the time spent by a perturbed system far away from its desired operating state.

Definition 8 (Exponential stability [14,18,31]). *The origin $0 \in \mathbb{R}^n$ of ODE $x' = f(x)$ is **exponentially stable** if there are positive constants $\alpha, \beta, \delta > 0$ such that for all initial states $x = x(0)$ with $\|x\| < \delta$, the right-maximal ODE solution $x(t) : [0, T) \rightarrow \mathbb{R}^n$ satisfies $\|x(t)\| \leq \alpha\|x(0)\| \exp\left(-\beta t\right)$ for all times $0 \leq t < T$.*

---

[5] For the trigonometric pendulum ODE α_p from Example 1, the Lyapunov function $v = a(1 - \cos(\theta)) + \frac{(b\theta+\omega)^2+\omega^2}{4}$ with Lie derivative $\dot{v} = -\frac{b}{2}(a\theta\sin(\theta)+\omega^2)$ proves its stability [18] but requires arithmetic reasoning over trigonometric functions.

Exponential stability bounds the norm of solutions to ODE $x' = f(x)$ near the origin by a decaying exponential. It is specified in dL as follows.

Lemma 9 (Exponential stability in dL). *The origin of ODE $x' = f(x)$ is* **exponentially stable** *iff the following dL formula is valid. Variables α, β, δ, y are fresh, i.e., not in $x, f(x)$.*

$$\mathrm{EStab}(x' = f(x)) \equiv \exists \alpha{>}0\, \exists \beta{>}0\, \exists \delta{>}0\, \forall x\, (\mathcal{U}_\delta(x = 0) \to$$
$$[y := \alpha^2 \|x\|^2; x' = f(x), y' = -2\beta y]\, \|x\|^2 \le y)$$

The discrete assignment $y := \alpha^2 \|x\|^2$ sets the value of variable y to that of $\alpha^2 \|x\|^2$ and ; denotes sequential composition of hybrid programs [26,27].

Formula $\mathrm{EStab}(x' = f(x))$ uses a fresh variable y with ODE $y' = -2\beta y$ and initialized to $\alpha^2 \|x\|^2$ so that y *differentially axiomatizes* [28] the (squared) decaying exponential function $\alpha^2 \|x(0)\|^2 \exp(-2\beta t)$ along ODE solutions. Such an implicit (polynomial) characterization of exponential decay allows syntactic proof steps to use decidable real arithmetic reasoning.

Lemma 10 (Lyapunov function for exponential stability). *The following Lyapunov function proof rule for exponential stability is derivable in dL, where $k_1, k_2, k_3 \in \mathbb{Q}$ are positive constants.*

$$\mathrm{Lyap_E} \frac{\vdash \exists \gamma{>}0\, \forall x\, (\|x\|^2 {\le} \gamma^2 \to k_1^2 \|x\|^2 \le v \le k_2^2 \|x\|^2 \land \dot{v} \le -2k_3 v)}{\vdash \mathrm{EStab}(x' = f(x))}$$

Rule $\mathrm{Lyap_E}$ enables proofs of exponential stability in dL. In fact, the proof of Lemma 10 (see supplement [35]) yields concrete, *quantitative* bounds, where $\mathrm{EStab}(x' = f(x))$ is explicitly witnessed with scaling constant $\alpha = \frac{k_2}{k_1}$ and decay rate $\beta = k_3$. These can be used to calculate time bounds when the system state will return sufficiently close to the origin. Similarly, the disturbance δ in $\mathrm{EStab}(x' = f(x))$ is quantitatively witnessed by $\frac{k_1}{k_2}\gamma$ for any γ witnessing validity of the premise of rule $\mathrm{Lyap_E}$. This yields a provable estimate of the region around the origin where exponential stability holds; this latter estimate is explored next.

Region of attraction Formulas $\mathrm{Attr}(x' = f(x))$ and $\mathrm{EStab}(x' = f(x))$ both feature a subformula of the form $\exists \delta > 0\, \forall x\, (\mathcal{U}_\delta(x = 0) \to \cdots)$ which expresses that attractivity (or exponential stability) is locally true in *some* δ neighborhood of the origin. In many applications, it is useful to find and rigorously prove that a given set is attractive or exponentially stable with respect to the origin [18, Chapter 8.2]. The second stability variation yields *provable* subsets of the region of attraction, including the special case where it is the entire state space. This is formalized using the following variants of $\mathrm{Attr}(x' = f(x))$ and $\mathrm{EStab}(x' = f(x))$ within a region given by a formula P.

$$\mathrm{Attr}^P(x' = f(x), P) \equiv \forall x\, (P \to \mathrm{Asym}(x' = f(x), x = 0))$$
$$\mathrm{EStab}^P(x' = f(x), P) \equiv \exists \alpha{>}0\, \exists \beta{>}0\, \forall x\, (P \to$$
$$[y := \alpha^2 \|x\|^2; x' = f(x), y' = -2\beta y]\, \|x\|^2 \le y)$$

The formula $\text{Attr}^P(x' = f(x), P)$ is valid iff the set characterized by P is a subset of the origin's region of attraction [18]. For example, $\text{Attr}(x' = f(x))$ is $\exists \delta > 0 \, \text{Attr}^P(x' = f(x), \mathcal{U}_\delta(x = 0))$. This generalization is useful for formalizing stronger notions of stability in dL, such as the following *global* stability notions [14,18]. For brevity, dL specifications of the stability properties (in **bold**) are given below with mathematical definitions deferred to the supplement [35].

Lemma 11 (Global stability in dL). *The origin of ODE $x' = f(x)$ is **globally asymptotically stable** iff the dL formula $\text{Stab}(x' = f(x)) \wedge \text{Attr}^P(x' = f(x), true)$ is valid. The origin is **globally exponentially stable** iff the dL formula $\text{EStab}^P(x' = f(x), true)$ is valid.*

Global stability ensures that *all* perturbations to the system state are eventually dissipated. Their proof rules are similar to $\text{Lyap}_>$ and Lyap_E respectively.

Lemma 12 (Lyapunov function for global stability). *The following Lyapunov function proof rules for global asymptotic and exponential stability are derivable in dL. In rule Lyap_E^G, $k_1, k_2, k_3 \in \mathbb{Q}$ are positive constants.*

$$\text{Lyap}_>^G \quad \frac{\vdash f(0){=}0 \wedge v(0){=}0 \quad x{\neq}0 \vdash v{>}0 \wedge \dot{v}{<}0 \quad \vdash \forall b \, \exists \gamma{>}0 \, \forall x \, (v{\leq}b{\rightarrow}\mathcal{U}_\gamma(x{=}0))}{\vdash \text{Stab}(x' = f(x)) \wedge \text{Attr}^P(x' = f(x), true)}$$

$$\text{Lyap}_E^G \quad \frac{\vdash k_1^2 \|x\|^2 \leq v \leq k_2^2 \|x\|^2 \wedge \dot{v} \leq -2k_3 v}{\vdash \text{EStab}^P(x' = f(x), true)}$$

Example 13 (Pendulum global exponential stability). For simplicity, instantiate Example 7 with parameters $a = 1, b = 1$. The Lyapunov function then simplifies to $v = \frac{\theta^2}{2} + \frac{(\theta+\omega)^2 + \omega^2}{4}$ with Lie derivative $\dot{v} = -\frac{(\theta^2+\omega^2)}{2}$, which satisfies the real arithmetic inequalities $\frac{\theta^2+\omega^2}{4} \leq v \leq \theta^2 + \omega^2$ and $\dot{v} \leq -\frac{1}{2}v$. Thus, rule Lyap_E^G proves global exponential stability of α_l with $k_1 = \frac{1}{2}$, $k_2 = 1$, and $k_3 = \frac{1}{4}$. An important caveat is that Example 7 used a local small angle approximation, so this global phenomenon does *not* hold for a real world pendulum (nor for α_p).

Logical relationships With the proliferation of stability variations just introduced, it is useful to take stock of their logical relationships. An important example of such a relationship is shown in the following corollary.

Corollary 14 (Exponential stability implies asymptotic stability). *The following axioms are derivable in dL.*
EStabStab $\text{EStab}(x' = f(x)) \rightarrow \text{Stab}(x' = f(x))$

EStabAttr $\text{EStab}^P(x' = f(x), P) \rightarrow \text{Attr}^P(x' = f(x), P)$

Derived axioms EStabStab, EStabAttr show that exponential stability implies asymptotic stability. In proofs, EStabAttr allows the region of attraction to be estimated using the region where solutions are exponentially bounded.

4 General Stability

This section provides stability definitions and proof rules that generalize stability for an equilibrium point from Section 3 to the stability of sets. These definitions are useful when the desired stable system state(s) is not modeled by a single equilibrium point, but may instead, e.g., lie on a periodic trajectory [18], a hyperplane, or a continuum of equilibrium points within the state space [14]. The generalized definition is used to formalize two stability notions from the literature [14,18], and to justify their Lyapunov function proof rules.

4.1 General Stability and General Attractivity

The following *general stability* formula defines stability in dL with respect to an ODE $x' = f(x)$ and formulas P, R. The quantified variables ε, δ are assumed to be fresh by bound renaming, i.e., do not appear in $x, f(x), P$ or R.

$$\mathrm{Stab}^{\mathrm{P}}_{\mathrm{R}}(x' = f(x), P, R) \equiv \forall \varepsilon{>}0 \,\exists \delta{>}0 \,\forall x \left(\mathcal{U}_\delta(P) \to [x' = f(x)]\mathcal{U}_\varepsilon(R)\right)$$

This formula generalizes stability of the origin $\mathrm{Stab}(x' = f(x))$ by adding two logical tuning knobs that can be intuitively understood as follows. The *precondition* P characterizes the initial states from which the system state is expected to be disturbed by some disturbance δ. The *postcondition* R characterizes the set of desired operating states that the system must remain close (within the ε neighborhood of R) after being disturbed from its initial states.

The *general attractivity* formula similarly generalizes $\mathrm{Attr}^{\mathrm{P}}(x' = f(x), P)$ with a postcondition R towards which the ODE solutions from initial states satisfying precondition P are asymptotically attracted.

$$\mathrm{Attr}^{\mathrm{P}}_{\mathrm{R}}(x' = f(x), P, R) \equiv \forall x \left(P \to \mathrm{Asym}(x' = f(x), R)\right)$$

Lemma 15 (General Lyapunov functions). *The following Lyapunov function proof rule for general stability with two stacked premises is derivable in* dL.

$$\mathrm{GLyap} \quad \cfrac{\vdash P \to R \qquad \vdash \forall \varepsilon{>}0 \,\exists 0{<}\gamma{\le}\varepsilon \,\exists k \left(\begin{array}{l} \forall x \left(\partial(\mathcal{U}_\gamma(R)) \to v \ge k\right) \wedge \\ \exists 0{<}\delta{\le}\gamma \,\forall x \left(\mathcal{U}_\delta(P) \to R \vee v{<}k\right) \wedge \\ \forall x \left(R{\vee}v{<}k \to [x' = f(x) \,\&\, \overline{\mathcal{U}_\gamma(R)}](R{\vee}v{<}k)\right) \end{array}\right)}{\vdash \mathrm{Stab}^{\mathrm{P}}_{\mathrm{R}}(x' = f(x), P, R)}$$

Rule GLyap proves general stability for precondition P and postcondition R. It generalizes the Lyapunov function reasoning underlying rule $\mathrm{Lyap}_\ge$ to support arbitrary pre- and postconditions. The conjunct $\forall x \left(\partial(\mathcal{U}_\gamma(R)) \to v \ge k\right)$ requires $v{\ge}k$ on the boundary of $\mathcal{U}_\gamma(R)$ while the middle conjunct requires $v{<}k$ for some small neighborhood of P excluding R. The conjunct $\forall x \left(R{\vee}v{<}k \to \cdots\right)$ asserts that $R \vee v < k$ is an invariant of the ODE *within* closed domain $\overline{\mathcal{U}_\gamma(R)}$. When R is a formula of first-order real arithmetic, this invariance question is provably equivalent in dL to a formula of real arithmetic [28], so the premise of rule GLyap is, *in theory*, decidable by ℝ for a given candidate Lyapunov function v. In practice, it is prudent to consider specialized stability notions, for which the premise of rule GLyap can be arithmetically simplified. Proof rules for generalized attractivity are also derivable for specialized instances.

4.2   Specialization

General stability specializes to several stability notions in the literature. For brevity, dL specifications of the stability properties (in **bold**) are given below with mathematical definitions deferred to the supplement [35].

Set Stability   An important special case is when the desired operating states are exactly the states from which disturbances are expected, i.e., $R \equiv P$. This leads to the notion of **set stability** of the set characterized by P [14,18].

Lemma 16 (Set Stability in dL). *For the ODE $x' = f(x)$, the set characterized by formula P is i) **stable**, ii) **attractive**, iii) **asymptotically stable**, and iv) **globally asymptotically stable** iff the following dL formulas are valid:*

i) $\mathrm{Stab}_{\mathrm{R}}^{\mathrm{P}}(x' = f(x), P, P)$,
ii) $\exists \delta {>} 0 \; \mathrm{Attr}_{\mathrm{R}}^{\mathrm{P}}(x' = f(x), \mathcal{U}_\delta(P), P)$,
iii) $\mathrm{Stab}_{\mathrm{R}}^{\mathrm{P}}(x' = f(x), P, P) \wedge \exists \delta {>} 0 \; \mathrm{Attr}_{\mathrm{R}}^{\mathrm{P}}(x' = f(x), \mathcal{U}_\delta(P), P)$, *and*
iv) $\mathrm{Stab}_{\mathrm{R}}^{\mathrm{P}}(x' = f(x), P, P) \wedge \mathrm{Attr}_{\mathrm{R}}^{\mathrm{P}}(x' = f(x), true, P)$

The intuition for Lemma 16 is similar to Lemmas 4 and 11, except formula P (instead of the origin) characterizes the set of desirable states. An application of set stability is shown in the following example.

Example 17 (Tennis racket theorem [3]). The following system of ODEs models the rotation of a 3D rigid body [6,14], where x_1, x_2, x_3 are angular velocities and $I_1 > I_2 > I_3 > 0$ are the principal moments of inertia along the respective axes.

$$\alpha_r \equiv x_1' = \frac{I_2 - I_3}{I_1} x_2 x_3, \quad x_2' = \frac{I_3 - I_1}{I_2} x_3 x_1, \quad x_3' = \frac{I_1 - I_2}{I_3} x_1 x_2$$

When such a rigid object is spun or rotated on each of its axes, a well-known physical curiosity [3] is that the rotation is stable in the first and third axes, whilst additional (unstable) twisting motion is observed for the intermediate axis. Mathematically, a perfect rotation, e.g., around x_1, corresponds to a (large) initial value for x_1 with no rotation in the other axes, i.e., $x_2 = 0$, $x_3 = 0$. Accordingly the real world observation of stability for rotations about the first principal axis is explained by stability with respect to small perturbations in x_2, x_3, as formally specified by formula (3) below. Note that the set characterized by formula $x_2 = 0 \wedge x_3 = 0$ is the entire x_1 axis, not just a single point. Similarly, rotations are stable around the third principal axis iff formula (4) is valid.

$$\mathrm{Stab}_{\mathrm{R}}^{\mathrm{P}}(\alpha_r, x_2 = 0 \wedge x_3 = 0, x_2 = 0 \wedge x_3 = 0) \tag{3}$$

$$\mathrm{Stab}_{\mathrm{R}}^{\mathrm{P}}(\alpha_r, x_1 = 0 \wedge x_2 = 0, x_1 = 0 \wedge x_2 = 0) \tag{4}$$

The validity of formulas (3) and (4) are proved in Example 20.

The formal specification of set stability yields three provable logical consequences which are important stepping stones for the set stability proof rules.

Corollary 18 (Set stability properties). *The following axioms are derivable in* dL. *In axiom SClosure, formula* $\overline{P}$ *characterizes the topological closure of formula P. In axiom SClosed, formula P characterizes a closed set.*

SetSAttr
$$\begin{aligned} &\text{Stab}_R^P(x' = f(x), P, P) \\ &\quad \to \big(\text{Asym}(x' = f(x), P) \leftrightarrow \forall \varepsilon{>}0 \, \langle x' = f(x) \rangle \, \mathcal{U}_\varepsilon(P) \big) \end{aligned}$$

SClosure $\text{Stab}_R^P(x' = f(x), P, P) \leftrightarrow \text{Stab}_R^P(x' = f(x), \overline{P}, \overline{P})$

SClosed $\text{Stab}_R^P(x' = f(x), P, P) \to \forall x \big(P \to [x' = f(x)]P \big)$

Axiom SetSAttr generalizes SAttr and provides a syntactic simplification of the region of attraction for formula P when P is stable. Axiom SClosure says that stability of P is equivalent to stability of its closure $\overline{P}$, because for any perturbation $\delta > 0$, the neighborhoods $\mathcal{U}_\delta(P)$ and $\mathcal{U}_\delta(\overline{P})$ are provably equivalent in real arithmetic. Axiom SClosed says that for closed formulas P, invariance of P is a necessary condition for stability of P. Without loss of generality, it suffices to develop proof rules for stability of formulas characterizing closed (using SClosure) and invariant (using SClosed) sets. Indeed, standard definitions of set stability [14,18] usually assume that the set of concern is closed and invariant.

Lemma 19 (Set stability Lyapunov functions). *The following Lyapunov function proof rules for set stability are derivable in* dL. *In derived rules SLyap$_\geq$ and SLyap$_>$, formula P characterizes a compact (i.e., closed and bounded) set. In derived rule SLyap$_\geq^*$, the two premises are stacked.*

SLyap$_\geq$
$$\frac{P \vdash [x' = f(x)]P \quad \neg P \vdash v > 0 \wedge \dot{v} \leq 0 \quad \partial P \vdash v \leq 0}{\vdash \text{Stab}_R^P(x' = f(x), P, P)}$$

SLyap$_>$
$$\frac{P \vdash [x' = f(x)]P \quad \neg P \vdash v > 0 \wedge \dot{v} < 0 \quad \partial P \vdash v \leq 0}{\vdash \text{Stab}_R^P(x' = f(x), P, P) \wedge \exists \delta{>}0 \, \text{Attr}_R^P(x' = f(x), \mathcal{U}_\delta(P), P)}$$

SLyap$_\geq^*$
$$\frac{\begin{array}{c} P \vdash [x' = f(x)]P \\[4pt] \vdash \forall \varepsilon{>}0 \, \exists 0{<}\gamma{\leq}\varepsilon \left(\begin{array}{l} \exists k \left(\begin{array}{l} \forall x \, (\partial(\mathcal{U}_\gamma(P)) \to v \geq k) \wedge \\ \exists 0{<}\delta{\leq}\gamma \, \forall x \, (\mathcal{U}_\delta(P) \wedge \neg P \to v < k) \end{array} \right) \wedge \\ \forall x \, (\mathcal{U}_\gamma(P) \wedge \neg P \to \dot{v} \leq 0) \end{array} \right) \end{array}}{\vdash \text{Stab}_R^P(x' = f(x), P, P)}$$

All three proof rules have the necessary premise $P \vdash [x' = f(x)]P$ which says that formula P is an invariant of the ODE $x' = f(x)$. Rules SLyap$_\geq$, SLyap$_>$ are slight generalizations of Lyapunov function proof rules for set stability [14] and they respectively generalize rules Lyap$_\geq$, Lyap$_>$ to prove stability for an invariant P. Importantly, both rules assume that P characterizes a compact, i.e., closed and bounded set, which simplifies the arithmetical conditions on v in their premises. The rule *without* the boundedness requirement on P suggested in the remark after [18, Definition 8.1], is unsound, see supplement [35].

For asymptotic stability (in rule SLyap$_>$), boundedness also guarantees that perturbed ODE solutions always exist for sufficient duration, which is a fundamental step in the ODE liveness proofs [36]. Rule SLyap$^*_\geq$ is derived from rule GLyap using invariance of P by the first premise; it provides a means of formally proving the set stability properties (3) and (4) from Example 17.

Example 20 (Stability of rigid body motion). The proof for (3) uses the Lyapunov function $v = \frac{1}{2}(\frac{I_1-I_2}{I_3}x_2^2 - \frac{I_3-I_1}{I_2}x_3^2)$, whose Lie derivative is $\dot{v} = 0$, and rule SLyap$^*_\geq$ with formula $P \equiv x_2 = 0 \wedge x_3 = 0$. The proof for (4) is symmetric. For the top premise of rule SLyap$^*_\geq$, formula P is a provable invariant [28] of the ODE α_r. The bottom premise, although arithmetically complicated, can be simplified by choosing $\gamma = \varepsilon$ and deciding the resulting formula by ℝ.

Recall that the x_1 axis is *not* a compact set so neither of the standard proof rules for set stability SLyap$_\geq$, SLyap$_>$ would be sound for this proof.

Epsilon-Stability Motivated by numerical robustness of proofs of stability, Gao et al. [12] define ε-stability for ODEs. The following dL characterization shows how ε-stability can be understood as an instance of general stability.

Lemma 21 (ε-Stability in dL). *The origin of ODE $x' = f(x)$ is ε-stable for constant $\varepsilon > 0$ iff the dL formula $\mathrm{Stab}_R^P(x' = f(x), x = 0, \mathcal{U}_\varepsilon(x = 0))$ is valid.*

Unlike set stability, ε-stability is an instance of general stability where the pre- and postconditions differ. In ε-stability, systems are perturbed from the precondition $x = 0$ (the origin), but the postcondition enlarges the set of desired states to a $\varepsilon > 0$ neighborhood of the origin, which is considered indistinguishable from the origin itself [12]. An immediate consequence of Lemma 21 is that rule GLyap can be used to prove ε-stability, as shown in the next section.

5   Stability in KeYmaera X

This section puts the dL stability specifications and derivations from the preceding sections into practice through proofs for several case studies in the KeYmaera X theorem prover [11].[6] Examples 7, 13, 17, 20 have also been formalized. The insights from these proofs are discussed after an overview of the case studies.

Inverted Pendulum. The stability of the resting state of the pendulum is investigated in Examples 7 and 13. For the inverted pendulum α_i from (2), the controlled torque $u(\theta, \omega)$ must be designed and rigorously proved to ensure *feedback stabilization* [18] of the inverted position. A standard PD (Proportional-Derivative) controller can be used for stabilization, where the control input has the form $u(\theta, \omega) = k_1\theta + k_2\omega$ for tuning parameters k_1, k_2. Asymptotic stability of the inverted position is achieved for any control parameter choice where $k_1 > a$ and $k_2 > -b$. The sequent $a > 0, b \geq 0, k_1 > a, k_2 > -b \vdash \mathrm{AStab}(\alpha_i)$ is proved in KeYmaera X using the Lyapunov function $\frac{(k_1-a)\theta^2}{2} + \frac{(((b+k_2)\theta+\omega)^2+\omega^2)}{4}$.

---

[6] See https://github.com/LS-Lab/KeYmaeraX-projects/blob/master/stability

Frictional Tennis Racket Theorem. The stability of a 3D rigid body is investigated for α_r in Examples 17 and 20. The following ODEs model additional frictional forces that oppose the rotational motion in each axis of the rigid body, where $\alpha_1, \alpha_2, \alpha_3 > 0$ are positive coefficients of friction:

$$\alpha_f \equiv x_1' = \frac{I_2 - I_3}{I_1} x_2 x_3 - \alpha_1 x_1, \quad x_2' = \frac{I_3 - I_1}{I_2} x_3 x_1 - \alpha_2 x_2, \quad x_3' = \frac{I_1 - I_2}{I_3} x_1 x_2 - \alpha_3 x_3$$

In the presence of friction, rotations of the rigid body are globally asymptotically stable in the first and third principal axes, as proved in KeYmaera X.

$$\Gamma \equiv I_1 > I_2, I_2 > I_3, I_3 > 0, \alpha_1 > 0, \alpha_2 > 0, \alpha_3 > 0$$

$$\Gamma \vdash \mathrm{Stab}_R^P(\alpha_f, x_2{=}0 \wedge x_3{=}0, x_2{=}0 \wedge x_3{=}0) \wedge \mathrm{Attr}_R^P(\alpha_f, \mathit{true}, x_2{=}0 \wedge x_3{=}0)$$

$$\Gamma \vdash \mathrm{Stab}_R^P(\alpha_f, x_1{=}0 \wedge x_2{=}0, x_1{=}0 \wedge x_2{=}0) \wedge \mathrm{Attr}_R^P(\alpha_f, \mathit{true}, x_1{=}0 \wedge x_2{=}0)$$

Both asymptotic stability properties are proved using $\mathrm{SLyap}_{\geq}^*$ and the liveness property [36] that the kinetic energy $I_1 x_1^2 + I_2 x_2^2 + I_3 x_3^2$ of the system tends to zero over time. The latter property implies that solutions of α_f exist globally and that the values of x_1, x_2, x_3 asymptotically tend to zero, which proves global asymptotic stability with the aid of SetSAttr. Even though a proof rule for (global) asymptotic stability of general nonlinear ODEs and unbounded sets is not available (Section 4), this example shows that formalized stability properties can still be proved on a case-by-case basis using dL's ODE reasoning principles.

Moore-Greitzer Jet Engine [12]. The origin of the ODE modeling a simplified jet engine $\alpha_m \equiv x_1' = -x_2 - \frac{3}{2} x_1^2 - \frac{1}{2} x_1^3, \ x_2' = 3 x_1 - x_2$ is ε-stable for $\varepsilon = 10^{-10}$ [12]. The sequent $\varepsilon = 10^{-10} \vdash \mathrm{Stab}_R^P(\alpha_m, x_1^2 + x_2^2 = 0, x_1^2 + x_2^2 < \varepsilon^2)$ is proved in KeYmaera X. The key proof ingredients are an ε-Lyapunov function [12] and manual arithmetic steps, e.g., instantiating existential quantifiers appearing in the specification of ε-stability with appropriate values [12].

Other Examples [1]. Stability for several ODEs with Lyapunov functions generated by an inductive synthesis technique [1, Examples 5–11] were successfully verified in KeYmaera X. The proof for the largest, 6-dim. nonlinear ODE [1, Example 5] required substantial manual arithmetic reasoning in KeYmaera X.[7]

The arithmetical conditions in [1, Equation 1] are identical to the premises of rule Lyap$_{\geq}$ except it unsoundly omits the condition $v(0) = 0$, see supplement [35]. The generated Lyapunov functions remain correct because the inductive synthesis technique [1] implicitly guarantees this omitted condition.

Summary. These case studies demonstrate the feasibility of carrying out proofs of various (advanced) stability properties within KeYmaera X using this paper's stability specifications. The proofs share similar high-level proof structure, which suggests that proof automation could significantly reduce proof effort [10]. Such automation should also support user input of key insights for difficult reasoning steps, e.g., real arithmetic reasoning with nested, alternating quantifiers.

---

[7] The Lyapunov function in [1, Example 5] does *not* work for its associated ODE. It works if the ODE is corrected with $\dot{x}_1 = -x_1^3 + 4x_2^3 - 6x_3 x_4$, as in the literature [23].

6 Related Work

Stability is a fundamental property of interest across many different fields of mathematics [6,15,19,30,31,34] and engineering [14,18,20]. This related work discussion focuses on formal approaches to stability of ODEs.

Logical specification of stability. Rouche, Habets, and Laloy [31] provide a pioneering example of using logical notation to specify and classify stability properties of ODEs. Alternative logical frameworks have also been used to specify stability and related properties: stability is expressed in HyperSTL [22] as a hyperproperty relating the trace of an ODE against two constant traces; ϵ-stability is studied in the context of δ-complete reasoning over the reals [12]; region stability for hybrid systems [29] is discussed using CTL*; the syntactic specification of $\text{Asym}(x' = f(x), P)$ resembles the limit definition using filters [16]. This paper uses dL as a *sweet spot* logical framework, general enough to specify various stability properties of interest, e.g., asymptotic or exponential stability, and the stability of sets, while also enabling syntactic proofs of those properties.

Formal verification of stability. There is a vast literature on finding Lyapunov functions for stability, e.g., through numerical [24,23,37] and algebraic methods [9,21]. Formal approaches are often based on finding Lyapunov function candidates and *certifying* the correctness of those generated candidates [1,12,17,33]. This paper's approach enables highly trustworthy certification of those candidates in dL and KeYmaera X, with stability proof rules that are soundly *derived* from dL's parsimonious axiomatization [25,26,27], as implemented in KeYmaera X [11,26]. Sections 4 and 5 further show that this paper's approach supports verification of advanced stability properties [12,14,18] within the same dL framework. New stability proof rules like GLyap can also be soundly and *syntactically* justified in dL without the need for (low-level) semantic reasoning about the underlying ODE mathematics. As an example of the latter, semantic approach, LaSalle's invariance principle is formalized in Coq [7] and used to verify the correctness of an inverted pendulum controller [32].

7 Conclusion

This paper shows how ODE stability can be formalized in dL using the key idea that stability properties are $\forall/\exists$-quantified dynamical formulas. These specifications, their proof rules, and their logical relationships are all syntactically derived from dL's sound proof calculus. This further enables trustworthy KeYmaera X proofs that rigorously verify *every step* in an ODE stability argument, from arithmetical premises down to dynamical reasoning for ODEs. Directions for future work include *i)* formalization of stability with respect to perturbations of the system dynamics, and *ii)* generalizations of stability to hybrid systems.

Acknowledgments. We thank Brandon Bohrer, Stefan Mitsch, and the anonymous reviewers for their helpful feedback on KeYmaera X and this paper.

References

1. Ahmed, D., Peruffo, A., Abate, A.: Automated and sound synthesis of Lyapunov functions with SMT solvers. In: Biere, A., Parker, D. (eds.) TACAS. LNCS, vol. 12078, pp. 97–114. Springer (2020). https://doi.org/10.1007/978-3-030-45190-5_6
2. Alur, R.: Principles of Cyber-Physical Systems. MIT Press (2015)
3. Ashbaugh, M.S., Chicone, C.C., Cushman, R.H.: The twisting tennis racket. Journal of Dynamics and Differential Equations **3**, 67–85 (1991). https://doi.org/10.1007/BF01049489
4. Bochnak, J., Coste, M., Roy, M.F.: Real Algebraic Geometry. Springer, Heidelberg (1998). https://doi.org/10.1007/978-3-662-03718-8
5. Branicky, M.S.: Introduction to hybrid systems. In: Hristu-Varsakelis, D., Levine, W.S. (eds.) Handbook of Networked and Embedded Control Systems, pp. 91–116. Birkhäuser (2005). https://doi.org/10.1007/0-8176-4404-0_5
6. Chicone, C.: Ordinary Differential Equations with Applications. Springer, New York, second edn. (2006). https://doi.org/10.1007/0-387-35794-7
7. Cohen, C., Rouhling, D.: A formal proof in Coq of LaSalle's invariance principle. In: Ayala-Rincón, M., Muñoz, C.A. (eds.) ITP. LNCS, vol. 10499, pp. 148–163. Springer (2017). https://doi.org/10.1007/978-3-319-66107-0_10
8. Doyen, L., Frehse, G., Pappas, G.J., Platzer, A.: Verification of hybrid systems. In: Clarke, E.M., Henzinger, T.A., Veith, H., Bloem, R. (eds.) Handbook of Model Checking, pp. 1047–1110. Springer, Cham (2018). https://doi.org/10.1007/978-3-319-10575-8_30
9. Forsman, K.: Construction of Lyapunov functions using Gröbner bases. In: CDC. vol. 1, pp. 798–799. IEEE (1991). https://doi.org/10.1109/CDC.1991.261424
10. Fulton, N., Mitsch, S., Bohrer, B., Platzer, A.: Bellerophon: Tactical theorem proving for hybrid systems. In: Ayala-Rincón, M., Muñoz, C.A. (eds.) ITP. LNCS, vol. 10499, pp. 207–224. Springer (2017). https://doi.org/10.1007/978-3-319-66107-0_14
11. Fulton, N., Mitsch, S., Quesel, J., Völp, M., Platzer, A.: KeYmaera X: an axiomatic tactical theorem prover for hybrid systems. In: Felty, A.P., Middeldorp, A. (eds.) CADE. LNCS, vol. 9195, pp. 527–538. Springer, Cham (2015). https://doi.org/10.1007/978-3-319-21401-6_36
12. Gao, S., Kapinski, J., Deshmukh, J.V., Roohi, N., Solar-Lezama, A., Aréchiga, N., Kong, S.: Numerically-robust inductive proof rules for continuous dynamical systems. In: Dillig, I., Tasiran, S. (eds.) CAV. LNCS, vol. 11562, pp. 137–154. Springer (2019). https://doi.org/10.1007/978-3-030-25543-5_9
13. Goebel, R., Sanfelice, R.G., Teel, A.R.: Hybrid Dynamical Systems: Modeling, Stability, and Robustness. Princeton University Press (2012)
14. Haddad, W.M., Chellaboina, V.: Nonlinear Dynamical Systems and Control: A Lyapunov-Based Approach. Princeton University Press (2008)
15. Hirsch, M.W.: The dynamical systems approach to differential equations. Bull. Amer. Math. Soc. (N.S.) **11**(1), 1–64 (07 1984)
16. Hölzl, J., Immler, F., Huffman, B.: Type classes and filters for mathematical analysis in Isabelle/HOL. In: Blazy, S., Paulin-Mohring, C., Pichardie, D. (eds.) ITP. LNCS, vol. 7998, pp. 279–294. Springer (2013). https://doi.org/10.1007/978-3-642-39634-2_21
17. Kapinski, J., Deshmukh, J.V., Sankaranarayanan, S., Aréchiga, N.: Simulation-guided Lyapunov analysis for hybrid dynamical systems. In: Fränzle, M., Lygeros, J. (eds.) HSCC. pp. 133–142. ACM (2014). https://doi.org/10.1145/2562059.2562139

18. Khalil, H.K.: Nonlinear systems. Macmillan Publishing Company, New York (1992)
19. Liapounoff, A.: Probléme général de la stabilité du mouvement. Annales de la Faculté des sciences de Toulouse : Mathématiques **9**, 203–474 (1907)
20. Liberzon, D.: Switching in Systems and Control. Systems & Control: Foundations & Applications, Birkhäuser (2003). https://doi.org/10.1007/978-1-4612-0017-8
21. Liu, J., Zhan, N., Zhao, H.: Automatically discovering relaxed Lyapunov functions for polynomial dynamical systems. Math. Comput. Sci. **6**(4), 395–408 (2012). https://doi.org/10.1007/s11786-012-0133-6
22. Nguyen, L.V., Kapinski, J., Jin, X., Deshmukh, J.V., Johnson, T.T.: Hyperproperties of real-valued signals. In: Talpin, J., Derler, P., Schneider, K. (eds.) MEMOCODE. pp. 104–113. ACM (2017). https://doi.org/10.1145/3127041.3127058
23. Papachristodoulou, A., Prajna, S.: On the construction of Lyapunov functions using the sum of squares decomposition. In: CDC. vol. 3, pp. 3482–3487. IEEE (2002). https://doi.org/10.1109/CDC.2002.1184414
24. Parrilo, P.A.: Structured semidefinite programs and semialgebraic geometry methods in robustness and optimization. Ph.D. thesis, California Institute of Technology (2000)
25. Platzer, A.: The complete proof theory of hybrid systems. In: LICS. pp. 541–550. IEEE Computer Society (2012). https://doi.org/10.1109/LICS.2012.64
26. Platzer, A.: A complete uniform substitution calculus for differential dynamic logic. J. Autom. Reasoning **59**(2), 219–265 (2017). https://doi.org/10.1007/s10817-016-9385-1
27. Platzer, A.: Logical Foundations of Cyber-Physical Systems. Springer, Cham (2018). https://doi.org/10.1007/978-3-319-63588-0
28. Platzer, A., Tan, Y.K.: Differential equation invariance axiomatization. J. ACM **67**(1) (2020). https://doi.org/10.1145/3380825
29. Podelski, A., Wagner, S.: Model checking of hybrid systems: From reachability towards stability. In: Hespanha, J.P., Tiwari, A. (eds.) HSCC. LNCS, vol. 3927, pp. 507–521. Springer (2006). https://doi.org/10.1007/11730637_38
30. Poincaré, H.: Les méthodes nouvelles de la mécanique céleste. Gauthier-Villars, Paris (1892–1899)
31. Rouche, N., Habets, P., Laloy, M.: Stability Theory by Liapunov's Direct Method. Springer, New York (1977). https://doi.org/10.1007/978-1-4684-9362-7
32. Rouhling, D.: A formal proof in Coq of a control function for the inverted pendulum. In: Andronick, J., Felty, A.P. (eds.) CPP. pp. 28–41. ACM (2018). https://doi.org/10.1145/3167101
33. Sankaranarayanan, S., Chen, X., Ábrahám, E.: Lyapunov function synthesis using Handelman representations. In: Tarbouriech, S., Krstic, M. (eds.) NOLCOS. pp. 576–581. IFAC (2013). https://doi.org/10.3182/20130904-3-FR-2041.00198
34. Strogatz, S.H.: Nonlinear Dynamics and Chaos: With Applications to Physics, Biology, Chemistry, and Engineering. Westview Press, Boulder, CO, second edn. (2015)
35. Tan, Y.K., Platzer, A.: Deductive stability proofs for ordinary differential equations. CoRR **abs/2010.13096** (2020), https://arxiv.org/abs/2010.13096
36. Tan, Y.K., Platzer, A.: An axiomatic approach to existence and liveness for differential equations. Formal Aspects Comput. (to appear). https://doi.org/10.1007/s00165-020-00525-0
37. Topcu, U., Packard, A.K., Seiler, P.J.: Local stability analysis using simulations and sum-of-squares programming. Autom. **44**(10), 2669–2675 (2008). https://doi.org/10.1016/j.automatica.2008.03.010

Tool Papers

An SMT-Based Approach for Verifying Binarized Neural Networks

Guy Amir[1], Haoze Wu[2], Clark Barrett[2], and Guy Katz[1][✉]

[1] The Hebrew University of Jerusalem, Jerusalem, Israel
{guy.amir2, g.katz}@mail.huji.ac.il
[2] Stanford University, Stanford, USA
{haozewu, barrett}@cs.stanford.edu

Abstract. Deep learning has emerged as an effective approach for creating modern software systems, with neural networks often surpassing hand-crafted systems. Unfortunately, neural networks are known to suffer from various safety and security issues. Formal verification is a promising avenue for tackling this difficulty, by formally certifying that networks are correct. We propose an SMT-based technique for verifying *binarized neural networks* — a popular kind of neural network, where some weights have been binarized in order to render the neural network more memory and energy efficient, and quicker to evaluate. One novelty of our technique is that it allows the verification of neural networks that include both binarized and non-binarized components. Neural network verification is computationally very difficult, and so we propose here various optimizations, integrated into our SMT procedure as deduction steps, as well as an approach for parallelizing verification queries. We implement our technique as an extension to the Marabou framework, and use it to evaluate the approach on popular binarized neural network architectures.

1 Introduction

In recent years, *deep neural networks* (*DNNs*) [21] have revolutionized the state of the art in a variety of tasks, such as image recognition [12,37], text classification [39], and many others. These DNNs, which are artifacts that are generated automatically from a set of training data, generalize very well — i.e., are very successful at handling inputs they had not encountered previously. The success of DNNs is so significant that they are increasingly being incorporated into highly-critical systems, such as autonomous vehicles and aircraft [7,30].

In order to tackle increasingly complex tasks, the size of modern DNNs has also been increasing, sometimes reaching many millions of neurons [46]. Consequently, in some domains, DNN size has become a restricting factor: huge networks have a large memory footprint, and evaluating them consumes both time and energy. Thus, resource-efficient networks are required in order to allow DNNs to be deployed on resource-limited, embedded devices [23,42].

One promising approach for mitigating this problem is via DNN *quantization* [4,27]. Ordinarily, each edge in a DNN has an associated weight, typically

© The Author(s) 2021
J. F. Groote and K. G. Larsen (Eds.): TACAS 2021, LNCS 12652, pp. 203–222, 2021.
https://doi.org/10.1007/978-3-030-72013-1_11

stored as a 32-bit floating point number. In a quantized network, these weights are stored using fewer bits. Additionally, the *activation functions* used by the network are also quantized, so that their outputs consist of fewer bits. The network's memory footprint thus becomes significantly smaller, and its evaluation much quicker and cheaper. When the weights and activation function outputs are represented using just a single bit, the resulting network is called a *binarized neural network* (*BNN*) [26]. BNNs are a highly popular variant of a quantized DNN [10, 40, 56, 57], as their computing time can be up to 58 times faster, and their memory footprint 32 times smaller, than that of traditional DNNs [45]. There are also network architectures in which some parts of the network are quantized, and others are not [45]. While quantization leads to some loss of network precision, quantized networks are sufficiently precise in many cases [45].

In recent years, various security and safety issues have been observed in DNNs [33, 48]. This has led to the development of a large variety of verification tools and approaches (e.g., [16, 25, 33, 52], and many others). However, most of these approaches have not focused on binarized neural networks, although they are just as vulnerable to safety and security concerns as other DNNs. Recent work has shown that verifying quantized neural networks is PSPACE-hard [24], and that it requires different methods than the ones used for verifying non-quantized DNNs [18]. The few existing approaches that do handle binarized networks focus on the *strictly binarized* case, i.e., on networks where *all* components are binary, and verify them using a SAT solver encoding [29, 43]. Neural networks that are only partially binarized [45] cannot be readily encoded as SAT formulas, and thus verifying these networks remains an open problem.

Here, we propose an SMT-based [5] approach and tool for the formal verification of binarized neural networks. We build on top of the Reluplex algorithm [33],[3] and extend it so that it can support the *sign* function,

$$\text{sign}(x) = \begin{cases} x < 0 & -1 \\ x \geq 0 & 1. \end{cases}$$

We show how this extension, when integrated into Reluplex, is sufficient for verifying BNNs. To the best of our knowledge, the approach presented here is the first capable of verifying BNNs that are not strictly binarized. Our technique is implemented as an extension to the open-source Marabou framework [2, 34]. We discuss the principles of our approach and the key components of our implementation. We evaluate it both on the XNOR-Net BNN architecture [45], which combines binarized and non-binarized parts, and on a strictly binarized network.

The rest of this paper is organized as follows. In Section 2, we provide the necessary background on DNNs, BNNs, and the SMT-based formal verification of DNNs. Next, we present our SMT-based approach for supporting the sign activation function in Section 3, followed by details on enhancements and optimizations for the approach in Section 4. We discuss the implementation of our tool in Section 5, and its evaluation in Section 6. Related work is discussed in Section 7, and we conclude in Section 8.

---

[3] [33] is a recent extended version of the original Reluplex paper [31].

2 Background

Deep Neural Networks. A deep neural network (DNN) is a directed graph, where the nodes (also called neurons) are organized in layers. The first layer is the *input layer*, the last layer is the *output layer*, and the intermediate layers are the *hidden layers*. When the network is evaluated, the input neurons are assigned initial values (e.g., the pixels of an image), and these values are then propagated through the network, layer by layer, all the way to the output layer. The values of the output neurons determine the result returned to the user: often, the neuron with the greatest value corresponds to the output class that is returned. A network is called *feed-forward* if outgoing edges from neurons in layer i can only lead to neurons in layer j if $j > i$. For simplicity, we will assume here that outgoing edges from layer i only lead to the consecutive layer, $i + 1$.

Each layer in the neural network has a *layer type*, which determines how the values of its neurons are computed (using the values of the preceding layer's neurons). One common type is the *weighted sum* layer: neurons in this layer are computed as a linear combination of the values of neurons from the preceding layer, according to predetermined edge weights and biases. Another common type of layer is the *rectified linear unit* (*ReLU*) layer, where each node y is connected to precisely one node x from the preceding layer, and its value is computed by $y = \mathrm{ReLU}(x) = \max(0, x)$. The *max-pooling* layer is also common: each neuron y in this layer is connected to multiple neurons $x_1, \ldots, x_k$ from the preceding layer, and its value is given by $y = \max(x_1, \ldots, x_k)$.

More formally, a DNN N with k inputs and m outputs is a mapping $\mathbb{R}^k \to \mathbb{R}^m$. It is given as a sequence of layers $L_1, \ldots, L_n$, where L_1 and L_n are the input and output layers, respectively. We denote the size of layer L_i as s_i, and its individual neurons as $v_i^1, \ldots, v_i^{s_i}$. We use V_i to denote the column vector $[v_i^1, \ldots, v_i^{s_i}]^T$. During evaluation, the input values V_1 are given, and $V_2, \ldots, V_n$ are computed iteratively. The network also includes a mapping $T_N : \mathbb{N} \to \mathcal{T}$, such that $T(i)$ indicates the *type* of hidden layer i. For our purposes, we focus on layer types $\mathcal{T} = \{\text{weighted sum}, \text{ReLU}, \text{max}\}$, but of course other types could be included. If $T_n(i) = \text{weighted sum}$, then layer L_i has a weight matrix W_i of dimensions $s_i \times s_{i-1}$ and a bias vector B_i of size s_i, and its values are computed as $V_i = W_i \cdot V_{i-1} + B_i$. For $T_n(i) = \text{ReLU}$, the ReLU function is applied to each neuron, i.e. $v_i^j = \mathrm{ReLU}(v_{i-1}^j)$ (we required that $s_i = s_{i-1}$ in this case). If $T_n(i) = \text{max}$, then each neuron v_i^j in layer L_i has a list src of source indices, and its value is computed as $v_i^j = \max_{k \in src} v_{i-1}^k$.

A simple illustration appears in Fig. 1. This network has a weighted sum layer and a ReLU layer as its hidden layers, and a weighted sum layer as its output layer. For the weighted sum layers, the weights and biases are listed in the figure. On input $V_1 = [1, 2]^T$, the first

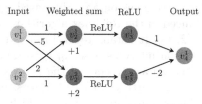

Fig. 1: A toy DNN.

layer's neurons evaluate to $V_2 = [6, -1]^T$. After ReLUs are applied, we get $V_3 = [6, 0]^T$, and finally the output is $V_4 = [6]$.

Binarized Neural Networks. In a *binarized neural network* (*BNN*), the layers are typically organized into binary *blocks*, regarded as units with binary inputs and outputs. Following the definitions of Hubara et al. [26] and Narodytska et al. [43], a

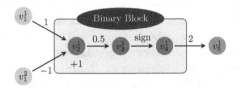

Fig. 2: A toy BNN with a single binary block composed of three layers: a weighted sum layer, a batch normalization layer, and a sign layer.

binary block is comprised of three layers: (i) a *weighted sum* layer, where each entry of the weight matrix W is either 1 or -1; (ii) a *batch normalization* layer, which normalizes the values from its preceding layer (this layer can be regarded as a weighted sum layer, where the weight matrix W has real-valued entries in its diagonal, and 0 for all other entries); and (iii) a *sign* layer, which applies the sign function to each neuron in the preceding layer. Because each block ends with a sign layer, its output is always a binary vector, i.e. a vector whose entries are ± 1. Thus, when several binary blocks are concatenated, the inputs and outputs of each block are always binary. Here, we call a network *strictly binarized* if it is composed solely of binary blocks (except for the output layer). If the network contains binary blocks but also additional layers (e.g., ReLU layers), we say that it is a *partially binarized* neural network. BNNs can be made to fit into our definitions by extending the set $\mathcal{T}$ to include the sign function. An example appears in Fig. 2; for input $V_1 = [-1, 3]^T$, the network's output is $V_5 = [-2]$.

SMT-Based Verification of Deep Neural Networks. Given a DNN N that transforms an input vector x into an output vector $y = N(x)$, a pre-condition P on x, and a post-condition Q on y, the *DNN verification problem* [33] is to determine whether there exists a concrete input x_0 such that $P(x_0) \wedge Q(N(x_0))$. Typically, Q represents an undesirable output of the DNN, and so the existence of such an x_0 constitutes a counterexample. A sound and complete verification engine should return a suitable x_0 if the problem is satisfiable (SAT), or reply that it is unsatisfiable (UNSAT). As in most DNN verification literature, we will restrict ourselves to the case where P and Q are conjunctions of linear constraints over the input and output neurons, respectively [16, 33, 52].

Here, we focus on an SMT-based approach for DNN verification, which was introduced in the Reluplex algorithm [33] and extended in the Marabou framework [2, 34]. It entails regarding the DNN's node values as variables, and the verification query as a set of constraints on these variables. The solver's goal is to find an assignment of the DNN's nodes that satisfies P and Q. The constraints are partitioned into two sets: *linear constraints*, i.e. equations and variable lower and upper bounds, which include the input constraints in P, the output constraints in Q, and the weighted sum layers within the network; and *piecewise-linear constraints*, which include the activation function constraints, such as ReLU or max constraints. The linear constraints are easier to solve (specifically, they can be phrased as a linear program [6], solvable in polynomial time); whereas the piecewise-linear constraints are more difficult, and render the problem NP-complete [33]. We observe that sign constraints are also piecewise-linear.

In Reluplex, the linear constraints are solved iteratively, using a variant of the Simplex algorithm [13]. Specifically, Reluplex maintains a variable assignment, and iteratively corrects the assignments of variables that violate a linear constraint. Once the linear constraints are satisfied, Reluplex attempts to correct any violated piecewise-linear constraints — again by making iterative adjustments to the assignment. If these steps re-introduce violations in the linear constraints, these constraints are addressed again. Often, this process converges; but if it does not, Reluplex performs a *case split*, which transforms one piecewise-linear constraint into a disjunction of linear constraints. Then, one of the disjuncts is applied and the others are stored, and the solving process continues; and if UNSAT is reached, Reluplex backtracks, removes the disjunct it has applied and applies a different disjunct instead. The process terminates either when one of the search paths returns SAT (the entire query is SAT), or when they all return UNSAT (the entire query is UNSAT). It is desirable to perform as few case splits as possible, as they significantly enlarge the search space to be explored.

The Reluplex algorithm is formally defined as a sound and complete calculus of derivation rules [33]. We omit here the derivation rules aimed at solving the linear constraints, and bring only the rules aimed at addressing the piecewise-linear constraints; specifically, ReLU constraints [33]. These derivation rules are given in Fig. 3, where: (i) $\mathcal{X}$ is the set of all variables in the query; (ii) R is the set of all ReLU pairs; i.e., $\langle b, f \rangle \in R$ implies that it should hold that $f = \text{ReLU}(b)$; (iii) α is the current assignment, mapping variables to real values; (iv) l and u map variables to their current lower and upper bounds, respectively; and (v) the $update(\alpha, x, v)$ procedure changes the current assignment α by setting the value of x to v. The ReluCorrect$_b$ and ReluCorrect$_f$ rules are used for correcting an assignment in which a ReLU constraint is currently violated, by adjusting either the value of b or f, respectively. The ReluSplit rule transforms a ReLU constraint into a disjunction, by forcing either b's lower bound to be non-negative, or its upper bound to be non-positive. This forces the constraint into either its active phase (the identity function) or its inactive phase (the zero function). In the case when we guess that a ReLU is active, we also apply the $addEq$ operation to add the equation $f = b$, in order to make sure the ReLU is satisfied in the active phase. The Success rule terminates the search procedure when all variable assignments are within their bounds (i.e., all linear constraints hold), and all ReLU constraints are satisfied. The rule for reaching an UNSAT conclusion is part of the linear constraint derivation rules which are not depicted; see [33] for additional details.

The aforementioned derivation rules describe a *search* procedure: the solver incrementally constructs a satisfying assignment, and performs case splitting

$$\text{ReluCorrect}_b \quad \frac{\langle b, f \rangle \in R, \quad \alpha(f) \neq \text{ReLU}(\alpha(b))}{\alpha := update(\alpha, b, \alpha(f))} \qquad \text{ReluCorrect}_f \quad \frac{\langle b, f \rangle \in R, \quad \alpha(f) \neq \text{ReLU}(\alpha(b))}{\alpha := update(\alpha, f, \text{ReLU}(\alpha(b)))}$$

$$\text{ReluSplit} \quad \frac{\langle b, f \rangle \in R}{\begin{array}{ll} u(b) := \min(u(b), 0), & \\ l(f) := \max(l(f), 0), & l(b) := \max(l(b), 0), \\ u(f) := \min(u(f), 0) & addEq(f = b) \end{array}}$$

$$\text{Success} \quad \frac{\forall x \in \mathcal{X}. \ l(x) \leq \alpha(x) \leq u(x), \quad \forall \langle b, f \rangle \in R. \ \alpha(f) = \text{ReLU}(\alpha(b))}{\text{SAT}}$$

Fig. 3: Derivation rules for the Reluplex algorithm (simplified; see [33] for more details).

when needed. Another key ingredient in modern SMT solvers is *deduction* steps, aimed at narrowing down the search space by ruling out possible case splits. In this context, deductions are aimed at obtaining tighter bounds for variables: i.e., finding greater values for $l(x)$ and smaller values for $u(x)$ for each variable $x \in \mathcal{X}$. These bounds can indeed remove case splits by fixing activation functions into one of their phases; for example, if $f = \text{ReLU}(b)$ and we deduce that $b \geq 3$, we know that the ReLU is in its active phase, and no case split is required. We provide additional details on some of these deduction steps in Section 4.

3   Extending Reluplex to Support Sign Constraints

In order to extend Reluplex to support sign constraints, we follow a similar approach to how ReLUs are handled. We encode every sign constraint $f = \text{sign}(b)$ as two separate variables, f and b. Variable b represents the input to the sign function, whereas f represents the sign's output. In the toy example from Fig. 2, b will represent the assignment for neuron v_3^1, and f will represent v_4^1.

Initially, a sign constraint poses no bound constraints over b, i.e. $l(b) = -\infty$ and $u(b) = \infty$. Because the values of f are always ± 1, we set $l(f) = -1$ and $u(f) = 1$. If, during the search and deduction process, tighter bounds are discovered that imply that $b \geq 0$ or $f > -1$, we say that the sign constraint has been fixed to the *positive* phase; in this case, it can be regarded as a linear constraint, namely $b \geq 0 \wedge f = 1$. Likewise, if it is discovered that $b < 0$ or $f < 1$, the constraint is fixed to the *negative* phase, and is regarded as $b < 0 \wedge f = -1$. If neither case applies, we say that the constraint's phase has not yet been fixed.

In each iteration of the search procedure, a violated constraint is selected and corrected, by altering the variable assignment. A violated sign constraint is corrected by assigning f the appropriate value: -1 if the current assignment of b is negative, and 1 otherwise. Case splits (which are needed to ensure completeness and termination) are handled similarly to the ReLU case: we allow the solver to assert that a sign constraint is in either the positive or negative phase, and then backtrack and flip that assertion if the search hits a dead-end.

More formally, we define this extension to Reluplex by modifying the derivation rules described in Fig. 3 as follows. The rules for handling linear con-

$$\text{SignCorrect}_- \ \frac{\langle b, f \rangle \in S, \ \ \alpha(b) < 0, \ \ \alpha(f) \neq -1}{\alpha := update(\alpha, f, -1)} \qquad \text{SignCorrect}_+ \ \frac{\langle b, f \rangle \in S, \ \ \alpha(b) \geq 0, \ \ \alpha(f) \neq 1}{\alpha := update(\alpha, f, 1)}$$

$$\text{SignSplit} \ \frac{\langle b, f \rangle \in S}{\begin{array}{ll} u(b) := \min(u(b), -\epsilon), & l(b) := \max(l(b), 0), \\ l(f) := \max(l(f), -1), & l(f) := \max(l(f), 1), \\ u(f) := \min(u(f), -1) & u(f) := \min(u(f), 1) \end{array}}$$

$$\text{Success} \ \frac{\forall x \in \mathcal{X}. \ l(x) \leq \alpha(x) \leq u(x),}{\forall \langle b, f \rangle \in S. \ \alpha(f) = \text{sign}(\alpha(b)), \quad \forall \langle b, f \rangle \in R. \ \alpha(f) = \text{ReLU}(\alpha(b))}{\text{SAT}}$$

Fig. 4: The extended Reluplex derivation rules, with support for sign constraints.

straints and ReLU constraints are unchanged — the approach is modular and extensible in that sense, as each type of constraint is addressed separately. In Fig. 4, we depict new derivation rules, capable of addressing sign constraints. The SignCorrect_ and SignCorrect_+ rules allow us to adjust the assignment of f to account for the current assignment of b — i.e., set f to -1 if b is negative, and to 1 otherwise. The SignSplit is used for performing a case split on a sign constraint, introducing a disjunction for enforcing that either b is non-negative ($l(b) \geq 0$) and $f = 1$, or b is negative ($u(b) \leq -\epsilon$; epsilon is a small positive constant, chosen to reflect the desired precision) and $f = -1$. Finally, the Success rule *replaces* the one from Fig. 3: it requires that all linear, ReLU and sign constraints be satisfied simultaneously.

We demonstrate this process with a simple example. Observe again the toy example for Fig. 2, the pre-condition $P = (1 \leq v_1^1 \leq 2) \wedge (-1 \leq v_1^2 \leq 1)$, and the post-condition $Q = (v_5^1 \leq 5)$. Our goal is to find an assignment to the variables $\{v_1^1, v_1^2, v_2^1, v_3^1, v_4^1, v_5^1\}$ that satisfies P, Q, and also the constraints imposed by the BNN itself, namely the weighted sums $v_2^1 = v_1^1 - v_1^2 + 1$, $v_3^1 = 0.5v_2^1$, and $v_5^1 = 2v_4^1$, and the sign constraint $v_4^1 = \text{sign}(v_3^1)$.

Initially, we invoke derivation rules that address the linear constraints (see [33]), and come up with an assignment that satisfies them, depicted as assignment 1 in Fig. 5. However, this assignment violates the sign constraint: $v_4^1 = -1 \neq \text{sign}(v_3^1) = \text{sign}(1) = 1$. We can thus invoke the SignCorrect_+ rule, which adjusts the assignment, leading to assignment 2

variable	v_1^1	v_1^2	v_2^1	v_3^1	v_4^1	v_5^1
assignment 1	1	0	2	1	-1	-2
assignment 2	1	0	2	1	1	-2
assignment 3	1	0	2	1	1	**2**

Fig. 5: An iterative solution for a BNN verification query.

in the figure. The sign constraint is now satisfied, but the linear constraint $v_5^1 = 2v_4^1$ is violated. We thus let the solver correct the linear constraints again, this time obtaining assignment 3 in the figure, which satisfies all constraints. The Success rule now applies, and we return SAT and the satisfying variable assignment.

The above-described calculus is sound and complete (assuming the ϵ used in the SignSplit rule is sufficiently small): when it answers SAT or UNSAT, that statement is correct, and for any input query there is a sequence of derivation steps that will lead to either SAT or UNSAT. The proof is quite similar to that of the original Reluplex procedure [33], and is omitted. A naive strategy that will always lead to termination is to apply the SignSplit rule to saturation; this effectively transforms the problem into an (exponentially long) sequence of linear programs. Then, each of these linear programs can be solved quickly (linear programming is known to be in P). However, this strategy is typically quite slow. In the next section we discuss how many of these case splits can be avoided by applying multiple optimizations.

4   Optimizations

Weighted Sum Layer Elimination. The SMT-based approach introduces a new variable for each node in a weighted sum layer, and an equation to express that node's value as a weighted sum of nodes from the preceding layer. In BNNs, we often encounter consecutive weighted sum layers — specifically because of the binary block structure, in which a weighted sum layer is followed by a batch normalization layer, which is also encoded as weighted sum layer. Thus, a straightforward way to reduce the number of variables and equations, and hence to expedite the solution process, is to combine two consecutive weighted sum layers into a single layer. Specifically, the original layers can be regarded as transforming input x into $y = W_2(W_1 \cdot x + B_1) + B_2$, and the simplification as computing $y = W_3 \cdot x + B_3$, where $W_3 = W_2 \cdot W_1$ and $B_3 = W_2 \cdot B_1 + B_2$. An illustration appears in Fig. 6 (for simplicity, all bias values are assumed to be 0).

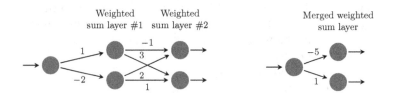

Fig. 6: On the left, a (partial) DNN with two consecutive weighted sum layers. On the right, an equivalent DNN with these two layers merged into one.

LP Relaxation. Given a constraint $f = \text{sign}(b)$, it is beneficial to deduce tighter bounds on the b and f variables — especially if these tighter bounds fix the constraints into one of its linear phases. We thus introduce a preprocessing phase, prior to the invocation of our enhanced Reluplex procedure, in which tighter bounds are computed by invoking a linear programming (LP) solver.

The idea, inspired by similar relaxations for ReLU nodes [14, 49], is to over-approximate each constraint in the network, including sign constraints, as a set of linear constraints. Then, for every variable v in the encoding, an LP solver is used to compute an upper bound u (by maximizing) and a lower bound l (by minimizing) for v. Because the LP encoding is an over-approximation, v is indeed within the range $[l, u]$ for any input to the network.

Let $f = \text{sign}(b)$, and suppose we initially know that $l \leq b \leq u$. The linear over-approximation that we introduce for f is a trapezoid (see Fig. 7), with the following edges: (i) $f \leq 1$; (ii) $f \geq -1$; (iii) $f \leq \frac{2}{-l} \cdot b + 1$; and (iv) $f \geq \frac{2}{u} \cdot b - 1$. It is straightforward to show that these four equations form the smallest convex polytope containing the values of f.

We demonstrate this process on the simple BNN depicted on the left-hand side of Fig. 7. Suppose we know that the input variable, x, is bounded in the range $-1 \leq x \leq 1$, and we wish to compute a lower bound for y. Simple, interval-arithmetic based bound propagation [33] shows that $b_1 = 3x + 1$ is bounded in the range $-2 \leq b_1 \leq 4$, and similarly that $b_2 = -4x + 2$ is in the range $-2 \leq b_2 \leq 6$. Because neither b_1 nor b_2 are strictly negative or positive, we only know that $-1 \leq f_1, f_2 \leq 1$, and so the best bound obtainable for y is $y \geq -2$. However, by formulating the LP relaxation of the problem (right-hand side of Fig. 7), we get the optimal solution $x = -\frac{1}{3}, b_1 = 0, b_2 = \frac{10}{3}, f_1 = -1, f_2 = \frac{1}{9}, y = -\frac{8}{9}$, implying the tighter bound $y \geq -\frac{8}{9}$.

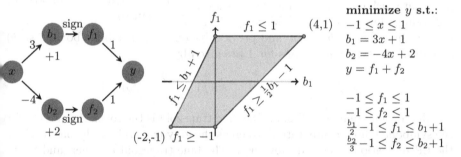

Fig. 7: A simple BNN (left), the trapezoid relaxation of $f_1 = \text{sign}(b_1)$ (center), and its LP encoding (right). The trapezoid relaxation of f_2 is not depicted.

The aforementioned linear relaxation technique is effective but expensive — because it entails invoking the LP solver twice for each neuron in the BNN encoding. Consequently, in our tool, the technique is applied only once per query, as a preprocessing step. Later, during the search procedure, we apply a related but more lightweight technique, called *symbolic bound tightening* [52], which we enhanced to support sign constraints.

Symbolic Bound Tightening. In symbolic bound tightening, we compute for each neuron v a symbolic lower bound $sl(x)$ and a symbolic upper bound $su(x)$, which are linear combinations of the input neurons. Upper and lower bounds can then be derived from their symbolic counterparts using simple interval arithmetic. For example, suppose the network's input nodes are x_1 and

x_2, and that for some neuron v we have:

$$sl(v) = 5x_1 - 2x_2 + 3, \quad su(v) = 3x_1 + 4x_2 - 1$$

and that the currently known bounds are $x_1 \in [-1, 2], x_2 \in [-1, 1]$ and $v \in [-2, 11]$. Using the symbolic bounds and the input bounds, we can derive that the upper bound of v is at most $6 + 4 - 1 = 9$, and that its lower bound is at least $-5 - 2 + 3 = -4$. In this case, the upper bound we have discovered for v is tighter than the previous one, and so we can update v's range to be $[-2, 9]$.

The symbolic bound expressions are propagated layer by layer [52]. Propagation through weighted sum layers is straightforward: the symbolic bounds are simply multiplied by the respective edge weights and summed up. Efficient approaches for propagations through ReLU layers have also been proposed [51]. Our contribution here is an extension of these techniques for propagating symbolic bounds also through sign layers. The approach again uses a trapezoid, although a more coarse one — so that we can approximate each neuron from above and below using a single linear expression. More specifically,

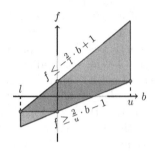

Fig. 8: Symbolic bounds for $f = \text{sign}(b)$.

for $f = \text{sign}(b)$ with $b \in [l, u]$ and previously-computed symbolic bounds $su(b)$ and $sl(b)$, the symbolic bounds for f are given by:

$$sl(f) = \frac{2}{u} \cdot sl(b) - 1, \quad su(f) = -\frac{2}{l} \cdot su(b) + 1$$

An illustration appears in Fig. 8. The blue trapezoid is the relaxation we use for the symbolic bound computation, whereas the gray trapezoid is the one used for the LP relaxation discussed previously. The blue trapezoid is larger, and hence leads to looser bounds than the gray trapezoid; but it is computationally cheaper to compute and use, and our evaluation demonstrates its usefulness.

Polarity-based Splitting. The Marabou framework supports a parallelized solving mode, using the Split-and-Conquer (S&C) algorithm [54]. At a high level, S&C partitions a verification query ϕ into a set of sub-queries $\Phi := \{\phi_1, ... \phi_n\}$, such that ϕ and $\bigvee_{\phi' \in \Phi} \phi'$ are equi-satisfiable, and handles each sub-query independently. Each sub-query is solved with a timeout value; and if that value is reached, the sub-query is again split into additional sub-queries, and each is solved with a greater timeout value. The process repeats until one of the sub-queries is determined to be SAT, or until all sub-queries are proven UNSAT.

One Marabou strategy for creating sub-queries is by splitting the ranges of input neurons. For example, if in query ϕ an input neuron x is bounded in the range $x \in [0, 4]$ and ϕ times out, it might be split into ϕ_1 and ϕ_2 such that $x \in [0, 2]$ in ϕ_1 and $x \in [2, 4]$ in ϕ_2. This strategy is effective when the neural network being verified has only a few input neurons.

Another way to create sub-queries is to perform case-splits on piecewise-linear constraints — sign constraints, in our case. For instance, given a verification query $\phi := \phi' \wedge f = \text{sign}(b)$, we can partition it into $\phi^- := \phi' \wedge b < 0 \wedge f = -1$ and $\phi^+ := \phi' \wedge b \geq 0 \wedge f = 1$. Note that ϕ and $\phi^+ \vee \phi^-$ are equi-satisfiable.

The heuristics for picking which sign constraint to split on have a significant impact on the difficulty of the resulting sub-problems [54]. Specifically, it is desirable that the sub-queries be *easier* than the original query, and also that they be *balanced* in terms of runtime — i.e., we wish to avoid the case where ϕ_1 is very easy and ϕ_2 is very hard, as that makes poor use of parallel computing resources. To create easier sub-problems, we propose to split on sign constraints that occur in the earlier layers of the BNN, as that leads to efficient bound propagation when combined with our symbolic bound tightening mechanism. To create balanced sub-problems, we use a metric called *polarity*, which was proposed in [54] for ReLUs and is extended here to support sign constraints.

Definition 1. *Given a sign constraint* $f = \text{sign}(b)$, *and the bounds* $l \leq b \leq u$, *where* $l < 0$, *and* $u > 0$, *the polarity of the sign constraint is defined as* $p = \frac{u+l}{u-l}$.

Intuitively, the closer the polarity is to 0, the more balanced the resulting queries will be if we perform a case-split on this constraint. For example, if $\phi = \phi' \wedge -10 \leq b \leq 10$ and we create $\phi_1 = \phi' \wedge -10 \leq b < 0$, $\phi_2 = \phi' \wedge 0 \leq b \leq 10$, then queries ϕ_1 and ϕ_2 are roughly balanced. However, if initially $-10 \leq b \leq 1$, we obtain $\phi_1 = \phi' \wedge -10 \leq b < 0$ and $\phi_2 = \phi' \wedge 0 \leq b \leq 1$. In this case, ϕ_2 might prove significantly easier than ϕ_1 because the smaller range of b in ϕ_2 could lead to very effective bound tightening. Consequently, we use a heuristic that picks the sign constraint with the smallest polarity among the first k candidates (in topological order), where k is a configurable parameter. In our experiments, we empirically selected $k = 5$.

5   Implementation

We implemented our approach as an extension to Marabou [34], which is an open-source, freely available SMT-based DNN verification framework [2]. Marabou implements the Reluplex algorithm, but with multiple extensions and optimizations — e.g., support for additional activation functions, deduction methods, and parallelization [54]. It has been used for a variety of verification tasks, such as network simplification [19] and optimization [47], verification of video streaming protocols [35], DNN modification [20], adversarial robustness evaluation [9,22,32] verification of recurrent networks [28], and others. However, to date Marabou could not support sign constraints, and thus, could not be used to verify BNNs. Below we describe our main contributions to the code base. Our complete code is available as an artifact accompanying this paper [1], and has also been merged into the main Marabou repository [2].

Basic Support for Sign Constraints (*SignConstraint.cpp*). During execution, Marabou maintains a set of piecewise-linear constraints that are part of the query being solved. To support various activation functions, these constraints are represented using classes that inherit from the abstract *Piecewise-LinearConstraint* class. Here, we added a new sub-class, *SignConstraint*, that inherits from *PiecewiseLinearConstraint*. The methods of this class check whether the piecewise-linear sign constraint is satisfied, and in case it is not — which possible changes to the current assignment could fix the violation. This class' methods also extend Marabou's deduction mechanism for bound tightening.

Input Interfaces for Sign Constraints (*MarabouNetworkTF.py*). Marabou supports various input interfaces, most notable of which is the TensorFlow interface, which automatically translates a DNN stored in TensorFlow *protobuf* or *savedModel* formats into a Marabou query. As part of our extensions, we enhanced this interface so that it can properly handle BNNs and sign constraints. Additionally, users can create queries using Marabou's native C++ interface, by instantiating the *SignConstraint* class discussed previously.

Network-Level Reasoner (*NetworkLevelReasoner.cpp, Layer.cpp, LP-Formulator.cpp*). The *Network-Level Reasoner* (*NLR*) is the part of Marabou that is aware of the topology of the neural network being verified, as opposed to just the individual constraints that comprise it. We extended Marabou's NLR to support sign constraints and implement the optimizations discussed in Section 4. Specifically, one extension that we added allows this class to identify consecutive weighted sum layers and merge them. Another extension creates a linear over-approximation of the network, including the trapezoid-shaped over-approximation of each sign constraint. As part of the symbolic bound propagation process, the NLR traverses the network, layer by layer, each time computing the symbolic bound expressions for each neuron in the current layer.

Polarity-Based Splitting (*DnCManager.cpp*). We extended the methods of this class, which is part of Marabou's S&C mechanism, to compute the polarity value of each sign constraint (see Definition 1), based on the current bounds.

6   Evaluation

All the benchmarks described in this section are included in our artifact, and are publicly available online [1].

Strictly Binarized Networks. We began by training a strictly binarized network over the MNIST digit recognition dataset.[4] This dataset includes 70,000 images of handwritten digits, each given as a 28×28 pixeled image, with normalized brightness values ranging from 0 to 1. The network that we trained has an input layer of size 784, followed by six binary blocks (four blocks of size 50,

---

[4] http://yann.lecun.com/exdb/mnist/

two blocks of size 10), and a final output layer with 10 neurons. Note that in the first block we omitted the sign layer in order to improve the network's accuracy.[5] The model was trained for 300 epochs using the *Larq* library [17] and the *Adam* optimizer [36], achieving 90% accuracy.

After training, we used Larq's export mechanism to save the trained network in a TensorFlow format, and then used our newly added Marabou interface to load it. For our verification queries, we first chose 500 samples from the test set which were classified correctly by the network. Then, we used these samples to formulate *adversarial robustness* queries [33,48]: queries that ask Marabou to find a slightly perturbed input which is misclassified by the network, i.e. is assigned a different label than the original. We formulated 500 queries, constructed from 50 queries for each of ten possible perturbation values $\delta \in \{0.1, 0.15, 0.2, 0.3, 0.5, 1, 3, 5, 10, 15\}$ in L_∞ norm, one query per input sample. An UNSAT answer from Marabou indicates that no adversarial perturbation exists (for the specified δ), whereas a SAT answer includes, as the counterexample, an actual perturbation that leads to misclassification. Such adversarial robustness queries are the most widespread verification benchmarks in the literature (e.g., [16,25,33,52]). An example appears in Fig. 9: the image on the left is the original, correctly classified as 1, and the image on the right is the perturbed image discovered by Marabou, misclassified as 3.

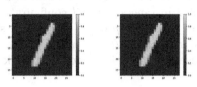

Fig. 9: An adversarial example for the MNIST network.

Through our experiments we set out to evaluate our tool's performance, and also measured the contribution of each of the features that we introduced: (i) weighted sum (ws) layer elimination; (ii) LP relaxation; (iii) symbolic bound tightening (sbt); and (iv) polarity-based splitting. We thus defined five configurations of the tool: the *all* category, in which all four features are enabled, and four *all-X* configurations for $X \in \{ws, lp, sbt, polarity\}$, indicating that feature X is turned off and the other features are enabled. All five configurations utilized Marabou's parallelization features, except for *all-polarity* — where instead of polarity-based splitting we used Marabou's default splitting strategy, which splits the input domain in half in each step.

Fig. 10 depicts Marabou's results using each of the five configurations. Each experiment was run on an Intel Xeon E5-2637 v4 CPUs machine, running Ubuntu 16.04 and using eight cores, with a wall-clock timeout of 5,000 seconds. Most notably, the results show the usefulness of polarity-based splitting when compared to Marabou's default splitting strategy: whereas the *all-polarity* configuration only solved 218 instances, the *all* configuration solved 458. It also shows that the weighted sum layer elimination feature significantly improves performance, from 436 solved instances in *all-ws* to 458 solved instances in *all*, and with significantly faster solving speed. With the remaining two features, namely LP

---

[5] This is standard practice; see **https://docs.larq.dev/larq/guides/bnn-architecture/**

relaxations and symbolic bound tightening, the results are less clear: although the *all-lp* and *all-sbt* configurations both slightly outperform the *all* configuration, indicating that these two features slowed down the solver, we observe that for many instances they do lead to an improvement; see Fig. 11. Specifically, on UNSAT instances, the *all* configuration was able to solve one more benchmark than either *all-lp* or *all-sbt*; and it strictly outperformed *all-lp* on 13% of the instances, and *all-sbt* on 21% of the instances. Gaining better insights into the causes for these differences is a work in progress.

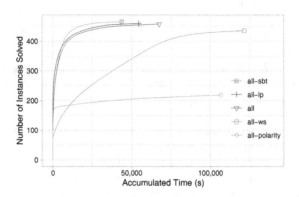

Fig. 10: Running the five configurations of Marabou on the MNIST BNN.

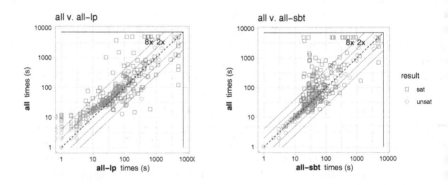

Fig. 11: Evaluating the LP relaxation and symbolic bound tightening features.

XNOR-Net. XNOR-Net [45] is a BNN architecture for image recognition networks. XNOR-Nets consist of a series of *binary convolution* blocks, each containing a sign layer, a convolution layer, and a max-pooling layer

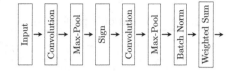

Fig. 12: The XNOR-Net architecture of our network.

(here, we regard convolution layers as a specific case of weighted sum layers). We constructed such a network with two binary convolution blocks: the first block has three layers, including a convolution layer with three filters, and the second block has four layers, including a convolution layer with two filters. The two binary convolution blocks are followed by a batch normalization layer and a fully-connected weighted sum layer (10 neurons) for the network's output, as depicted in Fig. 12. Our network was trained on the Fashion-MNIST dataset, which includes 70,000 images from ten different clothing categories [55], each given as a 28 × 28 pixeled image. The model was trained for 30 epochs, and achieved a modest accuracy of 70.97%.

For our verification queries, we chose 300 correctly classified samples from the test set, and used them to formulate adversarial robustness queries. Each query was formulated using one sample and a perturbation value $\delta \in \{0.05, 0.1, 0.15, 0.2, 0.25, 0.3\}$ in L_∞ norm. Fig. 13 depicts the adversarial image that Marabou produced for one

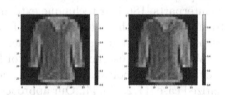

Fig. 13: An original image (left) and its perturbed, misclassified image (right).

of these queries. The image on the left is a correctly classified image of a shirt, and the image on the right is the perturbed image, now misclassified as a coat.

Based on the results from the previous set of experiments, we used Marabou with weighted sum layer elimination and polarity-based splitting turned on, but with symbolic bound tightening and LP relaxation turned off. Each experiment ran on an Intel Xeon E5-2637 v4 machine, using eight cores and a wall-clock timeout of 7,200 seconds. The results are depicted in Table 1. The results demonstrate that UNSAT queries tended to be solved significantly faster than SAT ones, indicating that Marabou's search procedure for these cases needs further optimization. Overall, Marabou was able to solve 203 out of 300 queries. To the best of our knowledge, this is the first effort to formally verify an XNOR-Net. We note that these results demonstrate the usefulness of an SMT-based approach for BNN verification, as it allows the verification of DNNs with multiple types of activation functions, such as a combination of sign and max-pooling.

7   Related Work

DNNs have become pervasive in recent years, and the discovery of various faults and errors has given rise to multiple approaches for verifying them. These in-

Table 1: Marabou's performance on the XNOR-Net queries.

δ	SAT		UNSAT		
	# Solved	Avg. Time (s)	# Solved	Avg. Time (s)	# Timeouts
0.05	15	909.13	23	4.96	12
0.1	15	1,627.67	20	12.15	15
0.15	9	1,113.33	29	5	12
0.2	10	1,387.7	24	4.96	16
0.25	9	1,426	22	4.91	19
0.3	7	1,550.86	20	26.75	23
Total	65	1,317.52	138	9.16	97

clude various SMT-based approaches (e.g., [25, 33, 34, 38]), approaches based on LP and MILP solvers (e.g., [8, 14, 41, 49]), approaches based on symbolic interval propagation or abstract interpretation (e.g., [16,50,52,53]), abstraction-refinement (e.g., [3, 15]), and many others. Most of these lines of work have focused on non-quantized DNNs. Verification of quantized DNNs is PSPACE-hard [24], and requires different tools than the ones used for their non-quantized counterparts [18]. Our technique extends an existing line of SMT-based verifiers to support also the sign activation functions needed for verifying BNNs; and these new activations can be combined with various other layers.

Work to date on the verification of BNNs has relied exclusively on reducing the problem to Boolean satisfiability, and has thus been limited to the strictly binarized case [11,29,43,44]. Our approach, in contrast, can be applied to binarized neural networks that include activation functions beyond the sign function, as we have demonstrated by verifying an XNOR-Net. Comparing the performance of Marabou and the SAT-based approaches is left for future work.

8 Conclusion

BNNs are a promising avenue for leveraging deep learning in devices with limited resources. However, it is highly desirable to verify their correctness prior to deployment. Here, we propose an SMT-based verification approach that enables the verification of BNNs. This approach, which we have implemented as part of the Marabou framework [2], seamlessly integrates with the other components of the SMT solver in a modular way. Using Marabou, we have verified, for the first time, a network that uses both binarized and non-binarized layers. In the future, we plan to improve the scalability of our approach, by enhancing it with stronger bound deduction capabilities, based on abstract interpretation [16].

Acknowledgements. We thank Nina Narodytska, Kyle Julian, Kai Jia, Leon Overweel and the Plumerai research team for their contributions to this project. The project was partially supported by the Israel Science Foundation (grant number 683/18), the Binational Science Foundation (grant number 2017662), the National Science Foundation (grant number 1814369), and the Center for Interdisciplinary Data Science Research at The Hebrew University of Jerusalem.

References

1. Artifact repository. https://github.com/guyam2/BNN_Verification_Artifact.
2. Marabou   repository.   https://github.com/NeuralNetworkVerification/
   Marabou.
3. P. Ashok, V. Hashemi, J. Kretinsky, and S. Mühlberger. DeepAbstract: Neural
   Network Abstraction for Accelerating Verification. In *Proc. 18th Int. Symposium
   on Automated Technology for Verification and Analysis (ATVA)*, 2020.
4. P. Bacchus, R. Stewart, and E. Komendantskaya. Accuracy, Training Time and
   Hardware Efficiency Trade-Offs for Quantized Neural Networks on FPGAs. In
   Proc. 16th Int. Symposium on Applied Reconfigurable Computing (ARC), pages
   121–135, 2020.
5. C. Barrett and C. Tinelli. *Satisfiability modulo theories.* Springer, 2018.
6. O. Bastani, Y. Ioannou, L. Lampropoulos, D. Vytiniotis, A. Nori, and A. Criminisi.
   Measuring Neural Net Robustness with Constraints. In *Proc. 30th Conf. on Neural
   Information Processing Systems (NIPS)*, 2016.
7. M. Bojarski, D. Del Testa, D. Dworakowski, B. Firner, B. Flepp, P. Goyal,
   L. Jackel, M. Monfort, U. Muller, J. Zhang, X. Zhang, J. Zhao, and K. Zieba.
   End to End Learning for Self-Driving Cars, 2016. Technical Report. http:
   //arxiv.org/abs/1604.07316.
8. R. Bunel, I. Turkaslan, P. Torr, P. Kohli, and P. Mudigonda. A Unified View
   of Piecewise Linear Neural Network Verification. In *Proc. 32nd Conf. on Neural
   Information Processing Systems (NeurIPS)*, pages 4795–4804, 2018.
9. N. Carlini, G. Katz, C. Barrett, and D. Dill. Provably Minimally-Distorted Adversarial Examples, 2017. Technical Report. https://arxiv.org/abs/1709.10207.
10. H. Chen, L. Zhuo, B. Zhang, X. Zheng, J. Liu, R. Ji, D. D., and G. Guo. Binarized Neural Architecture Search for Efficient Object Recognition, 2020. Technical
   Report. http://arxiv.org/abs/2009.04247.
11. C.-H. Cheng, G. Nührenberg, C.-H. Huang, and H. Ruess. Verification of Binarized
   Neural Networks via Inter-Neuron Factoring, 2017. Technical Report. http://
   arxiv.org/abs/1710.03107.
12. D. Ciregan, U. Meier, and J. Schmidhuber. Multi-Column Deep Neural Networks
   for Image Classification. In *Proc. IEEE Conf. on Computer Vision and Pattern
   Recognition (CVPR)*, pages 3642–3649, 2012.
13. G. Dantzig. *Linear Programming and Extensions.* Princeton University Press,
   1963.
14. R. Ehlers. Formal Verification of Piece-Wise Linear Feed-Forward Neural Networks. In *Proc. 15th Int. Symp. on Automated Technology for Verification and
   Analysis (ATVA)*, pages 269–286, 2017.
15. Y. Elboher, J. Gottschlich, and G. Katz. An Abstraction-Based Framework for
   Neural Network Verification. In *Proc. 32nd Int. Conf. on Computer Aided Verification (CAV)*, pages 43–65, 2020.
16. T. Gehr, M. Mirman, D. Drachsler-Cohen, E. Tsankov, S. Chaudhuri, and
   M. Vechev. AI2: Safety and Robustness Certification of Neural Networks with
   Abstract Interpretation. In *Proc. 39th IEEE Symposium on Security and Privacy
   (S&P)*, 2018.
17. L. Geiger and P. Team. Larq: An Open-Source Library for Training Binarized
   Neural Networks. *Journal of Open Source Software*, 5(45):1746, 2020.
18. M. Giacobbe, T. Henzinger, and M. Lechner. How Many Bits Does it Take to
   Quantize Your Neural Network? In *Proc. 26th Int. Conf. on Tools and Algorithms
   for the Construction and Analysis of Systems (TACAS)*, pages 79–97, 2020.

19. S. Gokulanathan, A. Feldsher, A. Malca, C. Barrett, and G. Katz. Simplifying Neural Networks using Formal Verification. In *Proc. 12th NASA Formal Methods Symposium (NFM)*, pages 85–93, 2020.

20. B. Goldberger, Y. Adi, J. Keshet, and G. Katz. Minimal Modifications of Deep Neural Networks using Verification. In *Proc. 23rd Int. Conf. on Logic for Programming, Artificial Intelligence and Reasoning (LPAR)*, pages 260–278, 2020.

21. I. Goodfellow, Y. Bengio, A. Courville, and Y. Bengio. *Deep learning*, volume 1. MIT press Cambridge, 2016.

22. D. Gopinath, G. Katz, C. Păsăreanu, and C. Barrett. DeepSafe: A Data-driven Approach for Assessing Robustness of Neural Networks. In *Proc. 16th. Int. Symposium on on Automated Technology for Verification and Analysis (ATVA)*, pages 3–19, 2018.

23. S. Han, H. Mao, and W. Dally. Deep Compression: Compressing Deep Neural Networks with Pruning, Trained Quantization and Huffman Coding. In *Proc. 4th Int. Conf. on Learning Representations (ICLR)*, 2016.

24. T. Henzinger, M. Lechner, and D. Zikelic. Scalable Verification of Quantized Neural Networks (Technical Report), 2020. Technical Report. https://arxiv.org/abs/2012.08185.

25. X. Huang, M. Kwiatkowska, S. Wang, and M. Wu. Safety Verification of Deep Neural Networks. In *Proc. 29th Int. Conf. on Computer Aided Verification (CAV)*, pages 3–29, 2017.

26. I. Hubara, M. Courbariaux, D. Soudry, R. El-Yaniv, and Y. Bengio. Binarized Neural Networks. In *Proc. 30th Conf. on Neural Information Processing Systems (NIPS)*, pages 4107–4115, 2016.

27. I. Hubara, M. Courbariaux, D. Soudry, R. El-Yaniv, and Y. Bengio. Quantized Neural Networks: Training Neural Networks with Low Precision Weights and Activations. *The Journal of Machine Learning Research*, 18(1):6869–6898, 2017.

28. Y. Jacoby, C. Barrett, and G. Katz. Verifying Recurrent Neural Networks using Invariant Inference. In *Proc. 18th Int. Symposium on Automated Technology for Verification and Analysis (ATVA)*, 2020.

29. K. Jia and M. Rinard. Efficient Exact Verification of Binarized Neural Networks, 2020. Technical Report. http://arxiv.org/abs/2005.03597.

30. K. Julian, J. Lopez, J. Brush, M. Owen, and M. Kochenderfer. Policy Compression for Aircraft Collision Avoidance Systems. In *Proc. 35th Digital Avionics Systems Conf. (DASC)*, pages 1–10, 2016.

31. G. Katz, C. Barrett, D. Dill, K. Julian, and M. Kochenderfer. Reluplex: An Efficient SMT Solver for Verifying Deep Neural Networks. In *Proc. 29th Int. Conf. on Computer Aided Verification (CAV)*, pages 97–117, 2017.

32. G. Katz, C. Barrett, D. Dill, K. Julian, and M. Kochenderfer. Towards Proving the Adversarial Robustness of Deep Neural Networks. In *Proc. 1st Workshop on Formal Verification of Autonomous Vehicles (FVAV)*, pages 19–26, 2017.

33. G. Katz, C. Barrett, D. Dill, K. Julian, and M. Kochenderfer. Reluplex: a Calculus for Reasoning about Deep Neural Networks, 2021. Submitted, preprint avaialble upon request.

34. G. Katz, D. Huang, D. Ibeling, K. Julian, C. Lazarus, R. Lim, P. Shah, S. Thakoor, H. Wu, A. Zeljić, D. Dill, M. Kochenderfer, and C. Barrett. The Marabou Framework for Verification and Analysis of Deep Neural Networks. In *Proc. 31st Int. Conf. on Computer Aided Verification (CAV)*, pages 443–452, 2019.

35. Y. Kazak, C. Barrett, G. Katz, and M. Schapira. Verifying Deep-RL-Driven Systems. In *Proc. 1st ACM SIGCOMM Workshop on Network Meets AI & ML (NetAI)*, pages 83–89, 2019.

36. D. Kingma and J. Ba. Adam: a Method for Stochastic Optimization, 2014. Technical Report. http://arxiv.org/abs/1412.6980.

37. A. Krizhevsky, I. Sutskever, and G. Hinton. Imagenet Classification with Deep Convolutional Neural Networks. In *Proc. 26th Conf. on Neural Information Processing Systems (NIPS)*, pages 1097–1105, 2012.

38. L. Kuper, G. Katz, J. Gottschlich, K. Julian, C. Barrett, and M. Kochenderfer. Toward Scalable Verification for Safety-Critical Deep Networks, 2018. Technical Report. https://arxiv.org/abs/1801.05950.

39. S. Lai, L. Xu, K. Liu, and J. Zhao. Recurrent Convolutional Neural Networks for Text Classification. In *Proc. 29th AAAI Conf. on Artificial Intelligence*, 2015.

40. D. Lin, S. Talathi, and S. Annapureddy. Fixed Point Quantization of Deep Convolutional Networks. In *Proc. 33rd Int. Conf. on Machine Learning (ICML)*, pages 2849–2858, 2016.

41. A. Lomuscio and L. Maganti. An Approach to Reachability Analysis for Feed-Forward ReLU Neural Networks, 2017. Technical Report. http://arxiv.org/abs/1706.07351.

42. P. Molchanov, S. Tyree, T. Karras, T. Aila, and J. Kautz. Pruning Convolutional Neural Networks for Resource Efficient Inference, 2016. Technical Report. http://arxiv.org/abs/1611.06440.

43. N. Narodytska, S. Kasiviswanathan, L. Ryzhyk, M. Sagiv, and T. Walsh. Verifying Properties of Binarized Deep Neural Networks, 2017. Technical Report. http://arxiv.org/abs/1709.06662.

44. N. Narodytska, H. Zhang, A. Gupta, and T. Walsh. In Search for a SAT-friendly Binarized Neural Network Architecture. In *Proc. 7th Int. Conf. on Learning Representations (ICLR)*, 2019.

45. M. Rastegari, V. Ordonez, J. Redmon, and A. Farhadi. XNOR-Net: Imagenet Classification using Binary Convolutional Neural Networks. In *Proc. 14th European Conf. on Computer Vision (ECCV)*, pages 525–542, 2016.

46. K. Simonyan and A. Zisserman. Very Deep Convolutional Networks for Large-Scale Image Recognition. In *Proc. 3rd Int. Conf. on Learning Representations (ICLR)*, 2015.

47. C. Strong, H. Wu, A. Zeljić, K. Julian, G. Katz, C. Barrett, and M. Kochenderfer. Global Optimization of Objective Functions Represented by ReLU networks, 2020. Technical Report. http://arxiv.org/abs/2010.03258.

48. C. Szegedy, W. Zaremba, I. Sutskever, J. Bruna, D. Erhan, I. Goodfellow, and R. Fergus. Intriguing Properties of Neural Networks, 2013. Technical Report. http://arxiv.org/abs/1312.6199.

49. V. Tjeng, K. Xiao, and R. Tedrake. Evaluating Robustness of Neural Networks with Mixed Integer Programming. In *Proc. 7th Int. Conf. on Learning Representations (ICLR)*, 2019.

50. H. Tran, S. Bak, and T. Johnson. Verification of Deep Convolutional Neural Networks Using ImageStars. In *Proc. 32nd Int. Conf. on Computer Aided Verification (CAV)*, pages 18–42, 2020.

51. S. Wang, K. Pei, J. Whitehouse, J. Yang, and S. Jana. Efficient Formal Safety Analysis of Neural Networks, 2018. Technical Report. https://arxiv.org/abs/1809.08098.

52. S. Wang, K. Pei, J. Whitehouse, J. Yang, and S. Jana. Formal Security Analysis of Neural Networks using Symbolic Intervals. In *Proc. 27th USENIX Security Symposium*, pages 1599–1614, 2018.

53. T.-W. Weng, H. Zhang, H. Chen, Z. Song, C.-J. Hsieh, D. Boning, I. Dhillon, and L. Daniel. Towards Fast Computation of Certified Robustness for ReLU Networks, 2018. Technical Report. http://arxiv.org/abs/1804.09699.
54. H. Wu, A. Ozdemir, A. Zeljić, A. Irfan, K. Julian, D. Gopinath, S. Fouladi, G. Katz, C. Păsăreanu, and C. Barrett. Parallelization Techniques for Verifying Neural Networks. In *Proc. 20th Int. Conf. on Formal Methods in Computer-Aided Design (FMCAD)*, pages 128–137, 2020.
55. H. Xiao, K. Rasul, and R. Vollgraf. Fashion-Mnist: a Novel Image Dataset for Benchmarking Machine Learning Algorithms, 2017. Technical Report. http://arxiv.org/abs/1708.07747.
56. J. Yang, X. Shen, J. Xing, X. Tian, H. Li, B. Deng, J. Huang, and X.-S. Hua. Quantization Networks. In *Proc. IEEE Conf. on Computer Vision and Pattern Recognition (CVPR)*, pages 7308–7316, 2019.
57. Y. Zhou, S.-M. Moosavi-Dezfooli, N.-M. Cheung, and P. Frossard. Adaptive Quantization for Deep Neural Network, 2017. Technical Report. http://arxiv.org/abs/1712.01048.

cake_lpr: Verified Propagation Redundancy Checking in CakeML

Yong Kiam Tan[1]($\boxtimes$) , Marijn J. H. Heule[1] , and Magnus O. Myreen[2]

[1] Computer Science Department, Carnegie Mellon University, Pittsburgh, USA
{yongkiat,mheule}@cs.cmu.edu
[2] Chalmers University of Technology, Gothenburg, Sweden
myreen@chalmers.se

Abstract. Modern SAT solvers can emit independently checkable proof certificates to validate their results. The state-of-the-art proof system that allows for compact proof certificates is *propagation redundancy* (PR). However, the only existing method to validate proofs in this system with a formally verified tool requires a transformation to a weaker proof system, which can result in a significant blowup in the size of the proof and increased proof validation time. This paper describes the first approach to formally verify PR proofs on a succinct representation; we present (i) a new *Linear PR* (LPR) proof format, (ii) a tool to efficiently convert PR proofs into LPR format, and (iii) cake_lpr, a verified LPR proof checker developed in CakeML. The LPR format is backwards compatible with the existing LRAT format, but extends the latter with support for the addition of PR clauses. Moreover, cake_lpr is verified using CakeML's binary code extraction toolchain, which yields correctness guarantees for its machine code (binary) implementation. This further distinguishes our clausal proof checker from existing ones because unverified extraction and compilation tools are removed from its trusted computing base. We experimentally show that LPR provides efficiency gains over existing proof formats and that the strong correctness guarantees are obtained without significant sacrifice in the performance of the verified executable.

Keywords: linear propagation redundancy · binary code extraction

1 Introduction

Given a formula of propositional logic, the task of a SAT solver is to decide if there exists an assignment that satisfies the formula. Such a *satisfying assignment*, if found by a SAT solver, is easily verifiable by independent checkers and so one does not need to trust the inner workings of the solver. The situation with *unsatisfiable* formulas, i.e., where no satisfying assignment exists, is not as straightforward. Here, SAT solvers must produce an *unsatisfiability proof*. Ideally, the proof system (and proof format) for such proofs should be sufficiently expressive, allowing SAT solvers to efficiently produce proofs that correspond to the SAT solving techniques they use at runtime. At the same time, the resulting proofs ought to be efficiently checkable by independent and trustworthy tools.

© The Author(s) 2021
J. F. Groote and K. G. Larsen (Eds.): TACAS 2021, LNCS 12652, pp. 223–241, 2021.
https://doi.org/10.1007/978-3-030-72013-1_12

The de facto standard proof system for propositional unsatisfiability proofs is known as Resolution Asymmetric Tautology (RAT) [24]. The associated DRAT format [36] combines clause addition based on RAT steps and clause deletion. Independent checking tools can validate proofs in the DRAT format; they have been used to check the results of the SAT competitions since 2014 [36] and in industry [15]. Enriching DRAT proofs with hints is the main technique for developing efficient verified proof checkers, e.g., existing verified checkers use the enriched proof formats LRAT [6] and GRAT [28].

A recently proposed proof system, called Propagation Redundancy (PR) [21], generalizes RAT. There exist short PR proofs without new variables for many problems that are hard for resolution, such as pigeonhole formulas, Tseitin problems, and mutilated chessboard problems [19]. Due to the absence of new variables it is easier to find PR proofs automatically [20], and it is considered unlikely that there exist short RAT proofs for these problems that do not introduce new variables nor reuse eliminated variables [21]. Such PR proofs can be checked directly [21], or they can first be transformed into DRAT proofs or even Extended Resolution proofs by introducing new variables [18,25]. In theory, the blowup is small, i.e., polynomial-sized. However, in practice, the transformed proofs can be significantly more expensive to validate compared to the original PR proofs [21].

A natural question arises: why should proof checkers be trusted to correctly check proofs if we do not likewise trust SAT solvers to correctly determine satisfiability? One answer is that proof checkers are much easier to implement so their code can be carefully audited. Another answer is that the algorithms underlying proof checkers have been *formally verified* in a proof assistant [6,15,28]. However, to get executable code for these verified checkers, some additional unverified steps are still required. Although unlikely, each of these steps can introduce bugs in the resulting executable: (1) the algorithms are extracted by unverified code generation tools into source code for a programming language; (2) unverified parsing, file I/O, and command-line interface code is added; (3) the combined code is then compiled by unverified compilers down to executable machine code.

The contributions of this paper are: (i) a new Linear PR (henceforth LPR) proof format that enriches PR proofs with hints and is backwards compatible with the LRAT format; (ii) a tool to efficiently enrich PR proofs with hints; and (iii) `cake_lpr`, an efficient verified LPR proof checker with correctness guarantees, including for steps (1)–(3) enumerated above. The `cake_lpr` tool is publicly available at https://github.com/tanyongkiam/cake_lpr and it was used to validate the unsatisfiability proofs in the 2020 SAT Competition because of its strong trust story combined with easy compilation and usage. Moreover, the stronger proof system could be supported in future competitions.

Section 3 shows how PR proofs can be enriched to obtain LPR proofs and presents the corresponding LPR proof checking algorithm (Contributions i & ii). Notably, existing LRAT proof checkers can be extended in a clean and minimal way to support LPR proofs. Section 4 explains the implementation of our checker in CakeML, as well as the correctness guarantees and high-level verification strategy behind the proofs (Contribution iii). Section 5 benchmarks our proof format

Table 1. A comparison of SAT proof checkers that have been verified in various proof assistants [6,15,28]. Green background (cells with +) indicates desirable properties, e.g., LPR is based on a stronger proof system than LRAT and GRAT, while red backgrounds (cells with ×) indicate less desirable properties. Yellow backgrounds (cells with −) are also undesirable but to a lesser extent.

Property	ACL2 checker [15]	Coq checker [6]	GRATchk [28]	cake_lpr
Proof System (Section 3)	− LRAT	− LRAT	− GRAT	+ LPR
Executable Code (Section 4)	− Directly Executed	× Unverified Extraction	× Unverified Extraction	+ Binary Code Extraction
Checking Speed (Section 5)	+ Fast	× Slow	+ Very Fast	+ Fast

and proof checker against existing implementations. A summary comparison of the new proof checker against existing verified proof checkers is in Table 1.

2   Background

This section provides background on CakeML and its related tools. It also recalls the standard problem format and clausal proof systems used by SAT solvers.

2.1   HOL4 and CakeML

HOL4 is a proof assistant implementing classical higher-order logic [34]. CakeML is a programming language *deeply embedded* in HOL4, i.e., its abstract syntax is represented as a HOL datatype and its semantics is formalized within HOL4. Several tools for developing verified CakeML software are used in this work to fill the verification gaps in the correspondingly enumerated items in Section 1:

(1) Two tools are used to produce (or extract) verified CakeML source code:
   - the CakeML proof-producing translator [32] automatically synthesizes verified source code from pure algorithmic specifications;
   - the CakeML characteristic formula (CF) framework [14] provides a separation logic which can be used to manually verify (more efficient) imperative code for performance-critical parts of the proof checker.

(2) CakeML provides a foreign function interface (FFI) and a corresponding formal FFI model [10]. These are used to verify system call interactions, e.g., file I/O and command-line interfaces, under carefully specified assumptions.

(3) Most importantly, CakeML has a compiler that is *verified* [35] to preserve the semantics of source CakeML programs down to their compiled machine code implementations. Hence, all guarantees obtained from the preceding steps can be carried down to the level of machine code.

The combination of these tools enables *binary code extraction* [27] where verified machine code is extracted directly in HOL4. Several other CakeML-based programs have been verified using these tools, including: certificate checkers for floating-point error bounds [3] and vote counting [13], and an OpenTheory article checker [1]. Œuf provides a similar toolchain in the Coq proof assistant [31].

2.2   SAT Problems and Clausal Proofs

Fix a set of boolean *variables* $x_1, \ldots, x_n$, where the negation of variable x_i is denoted $\overline{x}_i$, and the negation of $\overline{x}_i$ is identified with x_i. Variables and their negations are called *literals* and are denoted using l. The input for propositional SAT solvers is a formula F in *conjunctive normal form* (CNF) over the set of variables $x_1, \ldots, x_n$. Here, CNF means that F consists of an outer logical conjunction $F \equiv \bigwedge_{i=1}^m C_i$, where each *clause* C_i is a disjunction over some of the literals $C_i \equiv l_{i1} \vee l_{i2}, \cdots \vee l_{ik}$. Formulas in CNF can be represented directly as sets of clauses and clauses as sets of literals. The empty clause is denoted $\perp$. An *assignment* α assigns boolean values to each variable; α can be *partial*, i.e., it only assigns values to some of the variables. Like formulas and clauses, a (partial) assignment can be represented as the set of literals assigned the boolean value true by that assignment. The negation of an assignment, denoted $\overline{\alpha}$, assigns the negation of all literals in α. An assignment α *satisfies* a clause C iff their set intersection is nonempty. Additionally, we define $C|\alpha = \top$ if α satisfies C; otherwise, $C|\alpha$ denotes the result of removing from C all the literals falsified by α, i.e., $C|\alpha = C \setminus \overline{\alpha}$. For a formula F, we define $F|\alpha = \{C|\alpha \mid C \in F \text{ and } C|\alpha \neq \top\}$. Intuitively, $F|\alpha$ contains the remaining clauses in formula F after committing to the partial assignment α.

The task of a SAT solver is to determine whether F is *satisfiable*, i.e., whether there exists a (possibly partial) assignment α such that $F|\alpha$ is empty. Any satisfying assignment can be used as certificate of satisfiability. Formulas without a satisfying assignment are *unsatisfiable*. Certifying unsatisfiability is more difficult and typically uses a *clausal* proof system [21]. The idea behind these proof systems is briefly recalled next, using the key concept of clause redundancy.

Definition 1. *A clause C is redundant with respect to formula F iff $F \wedge C$ and F are both satisfiable or both unsatisfiable, i.e., they are satisfiability equivalent.*

A clause C that is redundant for F can be added to F without changing its satisfiability. Clausal proof systems work by successively adding redundant clauses to F until the empty clause $\perp$ is added, as illustrated below:

$$F \overset{+ \text{ redundant } C_1}{\Longrightarrow} F \wedge C_1 \overset{+ \text{ redundant } C_2}{\Longrightarrow} F \wedge C_1 \wedge C_2 \overset{+ \text{ redundant } C_3}{\Longrightarrow} \cdots \Longrightarrow F \wedge C_1 \wedge C_2 \wedge \cdots \wedge \perp$$

Satisfiability is preserved along each $\Longrightarrow$ step because of redundancy, e.g., satisfiability of F implies satisfiability of $F \wedge C_1$. Since the final formula is unsatisfiable, the sequence of redundant clause addition steps $C_1, C_2, \ldots, \perp$ corresponds to a proof of unsatisfiability for F. Deciding clause redundancy is as hard as solving the SAT problem itself because $\bot$ is always redundant for unsatisfiable formulas. The difference between clausal proof systems is how the redundancy of a (proposed) redundant clause C is efficiently certified at each proof step.

Many notions of redundancy are based on unit propagation. A *unit clause* is a clause with only one literal. The result of applying the *unit clause rule* to a formula F is the formula $F|l$ where (l) is a unit clause in F. The iterated application of the unit clause rule to a formula F until no unit clauses are left is called *unit propagation*. If unit propagation on F yields the empty clause $\bot$, denoted by $F \vdash_1 \bot$, we say that F implies $\bot$ by unit propagation. The notion of *implied by unit propagation* is also used for regular clauses as follows: $F \vdash_1 C$ iff $F \wedge \neg C \vdash_1 \bot$ with $\neg C = \bigwedge_{l \in C}(\bar{l})$. Observe that $\neg C$ can be viewed as a partial assignment that assigns the literals $\bar{l}$, for $l \in C$, to true. For a formula G, $F \vdash_1 G$ iff $F \vdash_1 C$ for all $C \in G$. The main clausal proof system used in this paper is based on propagation redundant clauses, which are defined as follows.

Definition 2. *Let F be a formula, C a nonempty clause, and α the smallest assignment that falsifies C. Then, C is* propagation redundant (PR) *with respect to F if there exists an assignment ω which satisfies C and such that $F|\alpha \vdash_1 F|\omega$.*

Intuitively, a PR clause C is redundant because any satisfying assignment for F that does not already satisfy C can be modified to a satisfying assignment for $F \wedge C$ by updating its literals assigned to true according to the (partial) witnessing assignment ω [21]. Propagation redundancy is efficiently checkable in polynomial time using the witnessing assignment and PR generalizes various other notions of clause redundancy, including the de facto standard Resolution Asymmetric Tautology (RAT) proof system (see [21, Theorem 2]) that is able to compactly express all current techniques used in state-of-the-art SAT solvers [24].

In practice, clausal proof formats also contain deletion information to speed up proof validation. Hence, unsatisfiability proofs for formula F are modeled as sequences $I_1, \ldots, I_n$ of *instructions* that either add or delete a clause. An *addition instruction* is a triple $\langle a, C, \omega \rangle$, where C is a clause and ω is a (possibly empty) *witnessing assignment*; a *deletion instruction* is a pair $\langle d, C \rangle$ where C is a clause. The sequence $I_1, \ldots, I_n$ gives rise to formulas $F_1, \ldots, F_n$ with $F_0 = F$ as follows, where F_j is the *accumulated formula* up to the j-th instruction:

$$F_j = \begin{cases} F_{j-1} \cup \{C\} & \text{if } I_j \text{ is of the form } \langle a, C, \omega \rangle \\ F_{j-1} \setminus \{C\} & \text{if } I_j \text{ is of the form } \langle d, C \rangle \end{cases}$$

A PR proof of unsatisfiability is *valid* if the last instruction adds the empty clause $I_n = \langle a, \bot, \emptyset \rangle$, and, for all addition instructions $I_j = \langle a, C_j, \omega_j \rangle$, it holds that C_j is PR with respect to F_{j-1} using witness ω_j. In case an empty witness is provided for I_j, then $F_{j-1} \vdash_1 C$ should hold.

3 Linear Propagation Redundancy

This section describes a new clausal proof format called LPR (short for Linear Propagation Redundancy). The format is designed to allow efficient validation

$$
\begin{aligned}
\langle proof \rangle &= \{\langle line \rangle\} \\
\langle line \rangle &= ((\langle lpr \rangle \mid \langle delete \rangle)), \text{``}\backslash n\text{''} \\
\langle lpr \rangle &= \langle id \rangle, \langle clause \rangle, \boldsymbol{\langle witness \rangle}, \text{``0''}, \langle idlist \rangle, \{\langle reduced \rangle\}, \text{``0''} \\
\langle delete \rangle &= \langle id \rangle, \text{``d''}, \langle idlist \rangle, \text{``0''} \\
\langle reduced \rangle &= \langle neg \rangle, \langle idlist \rangle \\
\langle idlist \rangle &= \{\langle id \rangle\} \\
\langle id \rangle &= \langle pos \rangle \\
\langle lit \rangle &= \langle pos \rangle \mid \langle neg \rangle \\
\langle pos \rangle &= \text{``1''} \mid \text{``2''} \mid \ldots \\
\langle neg \rangle &= \text{``--''}, \langle pos \rangle \\
\langle clause \rangle &= \{\langle lit \rangle\} \\
\boldsymbol{\langle witness \rangle} &= \boldsymbol{\{\langle lit \rangle\}}
\end{aligned}
$$

Fig. 1. The grammar for the LPR format. Additions compared to the LRAT grammar [6] are highlighted in bold.

of PR clauses using a (verified) proof checker. We also enhanced the DPR-trim tool[3] to efficiently add hints to PR proofs, thereby turning them into LPR proofs. Throughout the section, we emphasize how LPR can be viewed as a clean and minimal extension of the existing LRAT proof format, which thereby enables its straightforward implementation in existing LRAT tools.

The most commonly used proof format for SAT solvers is DRAT, which combines deletion with RAT redundancy [36]. DRAT proofs are easy for SAT solvers to emit and top-tier SAT solvers support it, but have some disadvantages for verified proof checking. In particular, checking whether a clause is RAT requires a significant amount of proof search to find the unit clauses necessary for showing the implied-by-unit-propagation property. This complicates verification of the proof checking algorithm and slows down the resulting verified proof checkers. The idea behind the Linear RAT (LRAT) [6,15] and GRAT [28] formats is to include these unit clauses as hints so that verified proof checkers can follow the hints directly without the need for proof search. The LPR format lifts this idea to allow fast validation of the PR property.

An assignment ω *reduces* a clause C if $C|_\omega \subset C$ and $C|_\omega \neq \top$. To check the PR property $F|_\alpha \vdash_1 F|_\omega$, it suffices to check, for each clause $C \in F$ reduced by ω, that $F|_\alpha \vdash_1 C|_\omega$. Hence, in practice, a smaller ω yields a cheaper PR check. The LPR format extends the PR format by adding, for each clause that is reduced by the witness, a list of all unit clause hints required for showing the implied-by-unit-propagation property. Additionally, in order to point to clauses, the LPR format includes an index for each clause at the beginning of each line. The grammar of the LPR format is shown in Fig. 1.

Our extension to DPR-trim enriches input PR proofs by finding and adding all required unit clause hints. It also shrinks the witness ω where possible: every literal in $\omega \cap \alpha$ is removed as well as any literal in ω that is implied by unit propagation from $F|_\alpha$. The shrinking was shown to be correct [21], but has

---

[3] LPR hint addition is now part of the public GitHub version available at https://github.com/marijnheule/dpr-trim using the command-line option -L.

DIMACS file   LPR proof file

p cnf 12 22	**23** -3 -10 -3 -10 1 12 0 -5 17 -8 20 -19 7 -22 10 0
1 2 3 0	**24** -3 -11 -3 -11 2 12 0 -6 18 -9 21 -19 7 -22 10 0
4 5 6 0	**25** -3 0 23 24 4 13 0
7 8 9 0	**26** -6 -10 -6 -10 4 12 0 -5 11 -13 7 -14 20 -22 16 0
10 11 12 0	**27** -6 -11 -6 -11 5 12 0 -6 12 -13 7 -15 21 -22 16 0
-1 -4 0	**28** -6 0 26 27 4 19 0
-2 -5 0	**29** -9 -10 -9 -10 7 12 0 -8 11 -13 10 -14 17 -19 16 0
-3 -6 0	**30** -9 -11 -9 -11 8 12 0 -9 12 -13 10 -15 18 -19 16 0
-1 -7 0	**31** -9 0 29 30 4 22 0
-2 -8 0	**32** -2 0 6 9 28 **31** 2 3 14 0
-3 -9 0	**33** -5 0 6 15 25 **31** 1 3 8 0
. . .	**34** 0 25 28 32 **33** 1 2 5 0

Fig. 2. (Left) The first ten clauses of pigeonhole formula (4 pigeons, 3 holes) in the DIMACS format used by SAT solvers. (Right) The LPR refutation consisting of clause-witness pairs and unit clause hints. The first bold integer in each line is the clause index while other bold integers are the unit clause hints. Dropping the bold integers yields a proof in the PR format. Redundant spaces have been added to improve readability.

not been implemented so far. We observed that the witnesses in the PR proofs produced by SaDiCaL [20] can be substantially compressed using this method.

Fig. 2 (left) shows an example formula in the standard DIMACS problem format. The DIMACS format includes a header line starting with "p cnf " followed by the number of variables and the number of clauses. The non-comment lines (not starting with "c ") represent clauses, and they end with "0". Positive integers denote positive literals, while negative integers denote negative literals. Fig. 2 (right) shows a corresponding proof in LPR format. Deletion lines in LPR are formatted identically to LRAT [6] (not shown here). For clause addition lines, the LPR format only differs from LRAT in case the clause to be added has PR but not RAT redundancy. A clause addition line in LPR format consists of three parts. The first part is the first integer on the line, which denotes the index of the new clause. The second part consists of the clause and the witness; the first group of literals is the clause. The (potentially empty) witness starts from the second occurrence of the first literal of the clause until the first 0 that separates the unit clause hints. The second part exactly matches the PR proof format [21]. The third part (after the first 0) are the unit clause hints, which exactly matches the LRAT format [6].

The checking algorithm for LPR, shown in Fig. 3, overlaps significantly with that for LRAT (see [6, Algorithm 1]). The only differences are Steps 4 and 5.1. In Step 4, the witness is used (if present) instead of always using the first literal in C_j. In Step 5.1, clauses are skipped if they are satisfied by the witness. Notice that a clause can only be both reduced and satisfied by a witness if the witness consists of at least two literals, while in the LRAT format witnesses always consist of exactly one literal. Note also that the algorithm does not check whether $C_j|\omega = \top$, which is a requirement for PR. This omission is allowed because the first literal in ω in the LPR (and PR) format is the same as the first literal in C_j.

Input: CNF $F = \{C_i\}_{i \in \mathcal{I}}$ and line ℓ an LPR step.
Output: YES if parsed clause C_j proved PR for F by ℓ,
    NO otherwise.

1. parse ℓ as $\left[j, C_j, \boldsymbol{\omega_j}, 0, \widetilde{i^0}, \{-i^k, \widetilde{i^k}\}_{k=1}^n \right]$
   instantiating variables with (vectors of) positive integers.

2. set $\alpha \leftarrow \neg C_j$

3. for $i \in \widetilde{i^0}$
   3.1. set $C_i' \leftarrow C_i|\alpha$
   3.2. if $C_i' = \bot$, return YES
   3.3. if $C_i' = \top$ or $|C_i'| \geq 2$, return NO
   3.4. set $\alpha \leftarrow \alpha \cup C_i'$

4. **if $\boldsymbol{\omega_j} \neq \emptyset$ then set $\boldsymbol{\omega} \leftarrow \boldsymbol{\omega_j}$ else set $\omega \leftarrow (C_j)_1$**
   (if $C_j = \bot$, return NO)

5. for $i \in \mathcal{I}$
   5.1. if C_i is **satisfied by** ω or is not reduced by ω,
        skip to next iteration of Step 5.
   5.2. find k such that $i^k = i$ (from ℓ)
        (return NO if no such k exists)
   5.3. if $C_i|(\alpha \setminus \overline{\omega}) = \top$, skip
   5.4. set $\alpha' \leftarrow \alpha \cup (\neg C_i \setminus \omega)$
   5.5. for $m \in \widetilde{i^k}$
        5.5.1. set $C_m' \leftarrow C_m|\alpha'$
        5.5.2. if $C_m' = \bot$, skip to next iteration of Step 5.
        5.5.3. if $C_m' = \top$ or $|C_m'| \geq 2$, return NO
        5.5.4. set $\alpha' \leftarrow \alpha' \cup C_m'$
   5.6. return NO

6. return YES

Fig. 3. Algorithm to check a single clause addition step in the LPR format. The bold parts show the additions compared to LRAT proof checking [6].

4   CakeML Proof Checking

This section explains the implementation and verification of `cake_lpr`, our verified CakeML LPR proof checker. Section 4.1 focuses on the high-level verification strategy which we used to reduce the verification task to mostly routine low-level proofs (the latter details are omitted). Section 4.2 highlights important verified performance optimizations used in the proof checker.

4.1   Verification Strategy

The development of `cake_lpr` proceeds in three refinement steps, where each step progressively produces a more concrete and performant implementation of the proof checker. These refinements are visualized in the three columns of Fig. 4.

Step 1 formalizes the definition of CNF formulas and their unsatisfiability, as well as the PR proof system described in Section 2.2. The inputs and outputs to

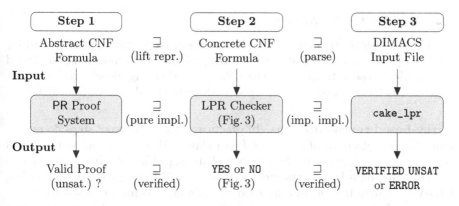

Fig. 4. The three step refinement used in the development of cake_lpr.

the proof system are abstract and not tied to any concrete representation at this step. For example, input variables are drawn from an arbitrary type α, clauses and CNFs are represented using sets. The correctness of the PR proof system is proved in this step, i.e., we show that a valid PR proof implies unsatisfiability of the input CNF. The proof essentially follows [21, Theorem 1].

Step 2 implements a purely functional version of the LPR proof checking algorithm from Fig. 3. Here, the inputs and outputs are given concrete representations with computable datatypes, e.g., literals are integers (similar to DIMACS), clauses are lists of integers, and CNFs are lists of clauses. These concrete representations lift naturally to the abstract, set-based representation from Step 1. The output is a YES or NO answer according to the algorithm from Fig. 3. The correctness theorem for Step 2 shows that LPR proof checking correctly refines the PR proof system, i.e., if it outputs YES, then there exists a valid PR proof for the input (lifted) CNF; by Step 1, this implies that the CNF is unsatisfiable.[4]

Step 3 uses imperative features available in the CakeML source language, e.g., (byte) arrays and exceptions, to improve code performance; these optimizations are detailed further in Section 4.2. This step also adds user interface features like parsing and file I/O so that the input CNF formula is read (and parsed) from a file, and the results are printed on the standard output and error streams. The verification of this step uses CakeML's proof-producing translator [32] and characteristic formula framework [14] to prove the correctness of the source code implementation of cake_lpr; this code is subsequently compiled with the verified CakeML compiler. Composing the correctness theorem for source cake_lpr with CakeML's compiler correctness theorem yields the corresponding correctness theorem for the cake_lpr binary. The final correctness theorem is given in Appendix A. Briefly, it shows that if the cake_lpr executable prints the string "s VERIFIED UNSAT\n" to the standard output stream (in CakeML's FFI model [10]), then the input (parsed) DIMACS file is an unsatisfiable CNF.

---

[4] If the output is NO, the input CNF could still be unsatisfiable, but the input LPR proof is not valid according to the algorithm in Fig. 3.

4.2   Verified Optimizations

To minimize verification effort, CakeML's imperative features are only used for the most performance-critical steps of `cake_lpr`. Our design decisions are based on empirical observations about the LPR proof checking algorithm. These are explained below with reference to specific steps in the algorithm from Fig. 3.

Array-based representations. In practice, many LPR proof steps do not require the full strength of a PR (or RAT) clause. Hence, a large part of proof checking time is spent in the Step 3 loop of the algorithm and it is important to compute the main loop bottleneck, $C_i|\alpha$ in Step 3.1, as efficiently as possible. CakeML's native byte arrays are used to maintain a compact bitset-like representation of the assignment α, so that $C_i|\alpha$ can be computed in one pass over C_i with constant time bitset lookup for each literal in C_i.

For proof steps requiring the full strength of PR clauses, Step 5 loops over all undeleted clauses in the formula. Formulas are represented as an array of clauses[5] together with a lazily updated list that tracks all indices of the array containing undeleted clauses. This enables both constant-time lookup of clauses throughout the algorithm and fast iteration over the undeleted clauses for Step 5. Deletion in the index list is done in (amortized) constant time by removing a deleted index only when the index is looked up in Step 5.1. Additionally, for each literal, the smallest clause index where that literal occurs (if any) is lazily tracked in a lookup array; for a given witness ω, all clauses occurring at indices below the index of any literal in $\overline{\omega}$ can be skipped in Step 5.1.

Proof checking exceptions. There are several steps in the proof checking algorithm that can fail (report NO) if the input proof is invalid, e.g., in Step 3.3. In a purely functional implementation, results are represented with an option: None indicating a failure and Some *res* indicating success with result *res*. While conceptually simple, this means that common case (successful) intermediate results are always boxed within an option and then immediately unboxed with pattern matching to be used again. In `cake_lpr`, failures instead raise exceptions which are directly handled at the top level. Thus, successful results can be passed directly, i.e., as *res*, without any boxing. Support for verifying the use of exceptions is a unique feature of CakeML's CF framework [14].

Buffered I/O streams. Proof files generated by SAT solvers can be large, e.g., ranging from 300 MB to 4 GB for the second benchmark suite in Section 5. These files are streamed into memory line by line because each proof step depends only on information contained in its corresponding line in the file. This streaming interaction is optimized using CakeML's verified buffered I/O library [29] which maintains an internal buffer of yet-to-be-read bytes from the read-only proof file to batch and minimize the number of expensive filesystem I/O calls.

---

[5] Deleted clauses are no longer referenced by the array and are automatically freed by CakeML's garbage collector.

5   Benchmarks

This section compares the verified CakeML LPR proof checker against other verified checkers on two benchmark suites and a RAT microbenchmark. The first suite is a collection of problems with PR proofs generated by the *satisfaction-driven clause learning* (SDCL) solver SaDiCaL [20], while the second suite consists of unsatisfiable problems from the SAT Race 2019 competition.[6] The RAT microbenchmark consists of proofs for large mutilated chessboards generated by a BDD-based SAT solver [5]. The CakeML checker is labeled cake_lpr (default 4GB heap and stack space), while other checkers used are labeled acl2-lrat (verified in ACL2 [15]), coq-lrat (verified in Coq [6]), and GRATchk (verified in Isabelle/HOL [28]) respectively. All experiments were run on identical nodes with Intel Xeon E5-2695 v3 CPUs (35M cache, 2.30GHz) and 128GB RAM. Configuration options specific to each benchmark suite are reported below.

5.1   SaDiCaL PR Benchmarks

The SaDiCaL solver produces PR proofs for hard SAT problems in its benchmark suite [20] and it is experimentally much faster than a plain DRAT-based CDCL solver on those problems [20, Section 7]. The PR proofs are directly checked by cake_lpr after conversion into LPR format with DPR-trim. For all other checkers, the PR proofs were first converted to DRAT format using pr2drat (as in the earlier approach [20]), and then into LRAT and GRAT formats using the DRAT-trim and GRATgen[7] tools respectively. All tools were ran with a timeout of 10000 seconds and all timings are reported in seconds (to one d.p.). Results are summarized in Tables 2 and 3.

All benchmarks were successfully solved by SaDiCaL except mchess19 which exceeded the time limit. For the remaining benchmarks, generating and checking LPR proofs required a comparable (1–2.5x) amount of time to solving the problems, except mchess, for which LPR generation and checking is much faster than solving (Table 2). Unsurprisingly, direct checking of LPR proofs is *much faster* than the circuitous route of converting into DRAT and then into either LRAT or GRAT (Table 3). Unlike LPR, checking PR proofs via the LRAT route is 5–60x slower than solving those problems; this is a significant drawback to using the route in practice for certifying solver results.

The backwards compatibility of cake_lpr is also shown in Table 3, where it is used to check the generated LRAT proofs. Among the LRAT checkers, acl2-lrat is fastest, followed by cake_lpr (LRAT checking), and coq-lrat. Although cake_lpr (LRAT checking) is on average 1.3x slower than acl2-lrat, it scales better on the mchess problems and is actually much faster than acl2-lrat on mchess18. We also observed that the GRAT toolchain (summing SaDiCaL, pr2drat, GRATgen and GRATchk times) is much slower than the LRAT toolchains

---

[6] The suites are available at http://fmv.jku.at/sadical/ and http://sat-race-2019.ciirc. cvut.cz/ respectively.

[7] GRATgen, the only tool that supports parallelism, was ran with 8 threads.

Table 2. Timings for PR benchmarks with conversion into LPR format. The "Total (LPR)" column sums the generation and checking times. The timing for `mchess19` is omitted because `SaDiCaL` timed out; timings for the Urquhart `U.-s3-*` benchmarks are omitted because they took a negligible amount of time (< 1.0s total).

Problem	SaDiCaL	DPR-trim	cake_lpr	Total (LPR)		Problem	SaDiCaL	DPR-trim	cake_lpr	Total (LPR)
hole20	1.0	0.5	0.7	2.2		U.-s4-b1	0.7	0.6	0.3	1.6
hole30	6.9	2.4	6.1	15.4		U.-s4-b2	0.3	0.4	0.2	0.8
hole40	31.3	10.0	25.1	66.3		U.-s4-b3	0.4	0.4	0.2	1.0
hole50	101.7	35.5	87.9	225.1		U.-s4-b4	0.3	0.5	0.3	1.1
mchess15	18.5	1.1	2.1	21.7		U.-s5-b1	2.5	0.9	1.3	4.7
mchess16	21.7	1.2	2.1	25.0		U.-s5-b2	1.2	0.6	0.7	2.4
mchess17	34.8	1.6	3.4	39.8		U.-s5-b3	3.2	1.5	2.0	6.8
mchess18	59.8	2.3	5.2	67.2		U.-s5-b4	5.5	1.5	3.2	10.1

Table 3. Timings for PR benchmarks, first converted to DRAT and subsequently converted into LRAT and GRAT formats. The "Total (LRAT)" and "Total (GRAT)" columns sum the fastest generation and checking times for the LRAT and GRAT formats respectively. The "Total (LPR)" column (in **bold**, fastest total time) is reproduced from Table 2 for ease of comparison. Fail(T) indicates a timeout. Timings for the `mchess19` and `U.-s3-*` benchmarks are omitted as in Table 2.

Prob.	pr2drat	DRAT-trim	cake_lpr (LRAT)	acl2-lrat	coq_lrat	GRATgen	GRATchk	Total (LPR)	Total (LRAT)	Total (GRAT)
hole20	0.8	4.4	18.5	7.9	966.7	4.6	18.2	**2.2**	14.2	24.6
hole30	6.8	61.4	180.4	105.9	Fail(T)	24.5	647.9	**15.4**	181.0	686.1
hole40	32.4	460.0	1039.5	711.8	Fail(T)	101.3	Fail(T)	**66.3**	1235.5	-
hole50	108.6	2663.0	4697.4	3292.2	Fail(T)	337.2	Fail(T)	**225.1**	6165.5	-
mchess15	7.7	48.2	49.3	36.2	Fail(T)	48.4	2023.1	**21.7**	110.6	2097.7
mchess16	9.0	62.0	59.8	53.2	Fail(T)	55.2	2903.8	**25.0**	145.9	2989.6
mchess17	14.5	105	97.3	88.5	Fail(T)	86.1	7050.9	**39.8**	242.7	7186.3
mchess18	25.1	195.0	152.7	296.8	Fail(T)	135.9	Fail(T)	**67.2**	432.5	-
U.-s4-b1	0.5	2.5	3.6	3.3	135.7	3.6	44.8	**1.6**	7.0	49.7
U.-s4-b2	0.2	0.8	1.4	1.0	23.2	1.7	8.2	**0.8**	2.3	10.4
U.-s4-b3	0.3	1.3	2.0	1.5	49.2	2.4	16.2	**1.0**	3.5	19.3
U.-s4-b4	0.3	1.1	1.8	1.4	38.3	2.0	10.3	**1.1**	3.1	12.9
U.-s5-b1	4.2	13.6	16.7	12.5	3048.7	17.4	933.2	**4.7**	32.8	957.3
U.-s5-b2	1.7	5.6	7.3	5.5	614.7	7.7	189.6	**2.4**	13.9	200.2
U.-s5-b3	5.0	18.4	26.3	22.2	8750.5	21.1	2316.3	**6.8**	48.8	2345.6
U.-s5-b4	11.3	34.2	36.9	30.1	Fail(T)	40.6	Fail(T)	**10.1**	81.0	-

(summing `SaDiCaL`, `pr2drat`, `DRAT-trim` and fastest LRAT checking times). This is in contrast to the SAT Race 2019 benchmarks below (Fig. 5), where we observed the opposite relationship. We believe that the difference in checking speed is due to the various checkers having different optimizations for checking the expensive RAT proof steps produced by conversion from PR proofs.

5.2 SAT Race 2019 Benchmarks

We further benchmarked the verified checkers on a suite of 117 unsatisfiable problems from the SAT Race 2019 competition. For all problems, DRAT proofs were generated using the state-of-the-art SAT solver `CaDiCaL` before conversion into the LRAT or GRAT formats. Notably, proofs generated by `CaDiCaL` on this

Table 4. A summary of the SAT Race 2019 benchmark results. The N/A row counts problems that timed out or failed in an earlier step of the respective toolchains.

Status	CaDiCaL	DRAT-trim	acl2-lrat	cake_lpr	coq-lrat	GRATgen	GRATchk
Success	102	97	96	97	36	100	100
Timeout	15	5	0	0	61	0	0
Failure	0	0	1	0	0	2	0
N/A	0	15	20	20	20	15	17

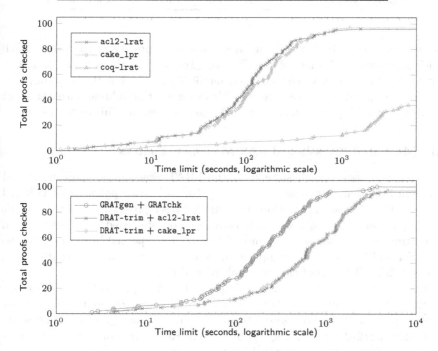

Fig. 5. (Top) Total SAT Race 2019 proofs checked within a given (per instance) time limit for the LRAT proof checkers. (Bottom) Total SAT Race 2019 proofs generated and checked within a given (per instance) time limit for the LRAT and GRAT toolchains.

suite rarely require RAT (or PR) steps, so the checkers are stress-tested on their implementation of file I/O, parsing, and Step 3.1 from Fig. 3; cake_lpr is the *only* tool with a formally verified implementation of the former two steps. All tools were ran with the SAT competition standard timeout of 5000 seconds.

A summary of the results is given in Table 4. All proofs generated by CaDiCaL were checked by at least one checker. The acl2-lrat checker fails with a parse error on one problem even though none of the other checkers reported such an error; GRATgen aborted on two problems for an unknown reason. Plots comparing LRAT proof checking time and overall proof generation and checking time (LRAT and GRAT) are shown in Fig. 5. From Fig. 5 (top), the relative order of LRAT checking speeds remains the same, where cake_lpr is on average 1.2x slower than acl2-lrat, although cake_lpr is faster on 28 bench-

Table 5. Timings for the RAT microbenchmark. The number of proof steps and file size of the proofs (in MB) are shown in the last two columns. Fail(T) indicates a timeout.

Problem	pgbdd	lrat-check	cake_lpr	acl2-lrat	coq-lrat	LRAT Steps	File Size
mchess20	3.9	0.5	0.5	19.6	3405.2	125752	5.1
mchess40	47.5	1.0	3.5	453.4	Fail(T)	769287	36
mchess60	311.7	2.7	10.6	4885.2	Fail(T)	2300522	114
mchess80	1164.1	4.8	22.6	Fail(T)	Fail(T)	5089457	259
mchess100	3599.0	9.3	44.2	Fail(T)	Fail(T)	9506092	499

marks. From Fig. 5 (bottom), both LRAT toolchains are slower than the GRAT toolchain (average 3.5 times slower for cake_lpr and 3.4 times for acl2-lrat). Part of the speedup for GRAT comes from GRATgen, which is the only tool that can be ran in parallel (with 8 threads). This suggests that adding native support for GRAT-based input to cake_lpr could be a worthwhile future extension.

5.3   Mutilated Chessboard RAT Microbenchmarks

The final microbenchmark suite tests the LRAT checkers on large mutilated chessboard problem instances (up to 100 by 100) solved by pgbdd, a BDD-based SAT solver [5]. Unlike the previous two suites, LRAT proofs are emitted *directly* by the solver so additional DRAT-trim conversion is not needed. All tools were ran with a timeout of 10000 seconds and all timings are reported in seconds (to one d.p.). For additional scaling comparison, we also report results for lrat-check, an *unverified* LRAT proof checker implemented in C.

The results in Table 5 show the impact of cake_lpr's RAT optimizations (Section 4.2). Notably, cake_lpr scales essentially *linearly* in the size of the proofs (up to ≈ 10 million proof steps). As a result, cake_lpr is significantly faster than acl2-lrat and coq-lrat on these RAT-heavy proofs and it comes within a 5x factor of the unverified lrat-check tool.

6   Related Work

Verified Proof Checking. There are several RAT-based verified proof checkers, in ACL2 [15], Coq [6], and Isabelle/HOL [28]. All three checkers are based on extensions of DRAT, which is itself an extension of the DRUP format [16]; the Coq checker is based on a predecessor for the GRIT [7] format. The ACL2 checker can be efficiently and *directly executed* (without extraction) using imperative primitives native to the ACL2 kernel [15]. However, the implementation of these features in ACL2 itself must be trusted to trust the proof checking results, hence the yellow background in Table 1. SMTCoq [2, 9] is another certificate-based checker for SAT and SMT problems in Coq. Its resolution-based proof certificates can be checked natively using native computation extensions of the Coq kernel.

Applications. SAT solving is a key technology underlying many software and hardware verification domains [4, 23]. Certifying SAT results adds a layer of trust and is clearly a worthwhile endeavor. Solver-aided mathematical results [17, 22, 26] are particularly interesting and challenging to certify because these often feature complicated SAT encodings, custom (hand-crafted) proof steps, and enormous resulting proofs [22]. Our cake_lpr checker can handle the latter two challenges effectively. For the first challenge, the SAT encoding of mathematical problems can also be verified within proof assistants. This was demonstrated for the Boolean Pythagorean Triples problem building on the Coq proof checker [8].

Verified SAT Solving. An alternative to proof checking is to verify the SAT solvers [11, 12, 30, 33]. This is a significant undertaking but it would allow the pipeline of generating and checking proofs to be entirely bypassed. Furthermore, such verification efforts can yield new insights about key invariants underlying SAT solving techniques compared to prior pen-and-paper presentations, e.g., the 2WL invariant [12]. However, the performance of verified SAT solvers are not yet competitive with modern (unverified) SAT solving technology [11, 12].

7 Conclusion

This work presents the new LPR proof format for verified checking of PR proofs. It demonstrates the feasibility of using binary code extraction to verify a performant LPR proof checker, cake_lpr, down to its machine code implementation.

Given the strength of the PR proof system, there is ongoing research into the design of *satisfaction-driven clause learning* techniques [20, 21] for SAT solvers based on PR clauses. Our proof checker opens up the possibility of using a verified checker to help check and debug the implementation of these new techniques. It also gives future SAT competitions the option of providing PR as the default (verified) proof system for participating solvers.

Acknowledgments. We thank Jasmin Blanchette and the anonymous reviewers for their helpful feedback on earlier drafts of this paper, Peter Lammich for help with GRATgen, and Stefan O'Rear for help with profiling CakeML programs.

The first author was supported by A*STAR, Singapore, the second author was supported by the National Science Foundation (NSF) under grant CCF-2010951, and the third author was supported by the Swedish Foundation for Strategic Research, Sweden. This work was also supported by NSF award number ACI-1445606 at the Pittsburgh Supercomputing Center (PSC).

A   Correctness Theorem for cake_lpr

The correctness theorem for cake_lpr verified in HOL4 is shown in Fig. 6. The assumptions (1) (in red) are routine for compiled CakeML programs that use its basis library. The first line assumes that the command-line *cl* and file system *fs* models are well-formed. The second line assumes that the compiled code is correctly placed into (code) memory according to CakeML's x64 machine model.

$$\vdash \text{wfcl } cl \wedge \text{wfFS } fs \wedge \text{std\_streams } fs \wedge \text{hasFreeFD } fs \Rightarrow \qquad (1)$$
$$\text{installed\_x64 cake\_lpr\_code (basis\_ffi } cl \ fs) \ mc \ ms \Rightarrow$$
$$\text{machine\_sem } mc \text{ (basis\_ffi } cl \ fs) \ ms \subseteq$$
$$\quad \text{extend\_with\_resource\_limit} \qquad (2)$$
$$\quad \{ \text{ Terminate Success (cake\_lpr\_io\_events } cl \ fs) \} \wedge$$
$$\exists \ out \ err.$$
$$\quad \text{extract\_fs } fs \text{ (cake\_lpr\_io\_events } cl \ fs) =$$
$$\quad \text{Some (add\_stdout (add\_stderr } fs \ err) \ out) \wedge$$
$$\quad \text{if } out = \text{«s VERIFIED UNSAT\textbackslash n» then} \qquad (3)$$
$$\quad \quad (\text{length } cl = 3 \vee \text{length } cl = 4) \wedge \text{inFS\_fname } fs \text{ (el 1 } cl) \wedge$$
$$\quad \quad \exists \ mv \ fml.$$
$$\quad \quad \quad \text{parse\_dimacs (all\_lines } fs \text{ (el 1 } cl)) = \text{Some } (mv, fml) \wedge$$
$$\quad \quad \quad \text{unsatisfiable (interp } fml)$$
$$\quad \text{else if length } cl = 2 \wedge \text{inFS\_fname } fs \text{ (el 1 } cl) \text{ then}$$
$$\quad \quad \text{case parse\_dimacs (all\_lines } fs \text{ (el 1 } cl)) \text{ of} \qquad (4)$$
$$\quad \quad \quad \text{None} \Rightarrow out = \text{«»}$$
$$\quad \quad | \text{ Some } (mv, fml) \Rightarrow out = \text{concat (print\_dimacs } fml)$$
$$\quad \text{else } out = \text{«»}$$

Fig. 6. The end-to-end correctness theorem for the CakeML LPR proof checker.

The first guarantee (2) (in blue) is that the machine code implementation always terminates normally according to CakeML's x64 machine code semantics. In particular, the code never crashes and may emit some I/O events when run; however, it possibly terminates with an out-of-memory error (extend_with_resource_limit) when CakeML runs out of stack or heap space.

The main correctness guarantee for **cake_lpr** is (3) (in green) and (4) (in black). Briefly, (3) says that the only observable change to the filesystem after executing **cake_lpr** are strings printed on standard output *out* and standard error *err*. According to (3), if the string "s VERIFIED UNSAT\n" is printed onto standard output, then **cake_lpr** was provided with a file (in its first command-line argument), and the file parses in DIMACS format to a formula *fml* which is unsatisfiable. The remaining else case (4), says that the only other possibilities for standard output are either (i) a printed version of the parsed DIMACS file (if no LPR proof file is provided), or (ii) the empty string. All other error messages are printed onto standard error.

In addition, the DIMACS parser (parse_dimacs) is proved to be left inverse to the DIMACS printer (print_dimacs) in the following sense:

$$\vdash \text{wf\_fml } fml \Rightarrow$$
$$\exists \ mv \ fml'.$$
$$\quad \text{parse\_dimacs (print\_dimacs } fml) = \text{Some } (mv, fml') \wedge \text{interp } fml = \text{interp } fml'$$

Briefly, this says that for any well-formed formula *fml*, printing that formula into DIMACS format then parsing it yields another formula *fml'* which is guaranteed to have the same interpretation according to the semantics of CNFs formalized in HOL4. All parsed formulas are well-formed (not shown here).

References

1. Abrahamsson, O.: A verified proof checker for higher-order logic. J. Log. Algebraic Methods Program. **112**, 100530 (2020). https://doi.org/10.1016/j.jlamp.2020.100530
2. Armand, M., Faure, G., Grégoire, B., Keller, C., Théry, L., Werner, B.: A modular integration of SAT/SMT solvers to Coq through proof witnesses. In: Jouannaud, J., Shao, Z. (eds.) CPP. LNCS, vol. 7086, pp. 135–150. Springer (2011). https://doi.org/10.1007/978-3-642-25379-9_12
3. Becker, H., Zyuzin, N., Monat, R., Darulova, E., Myreen, M.O., Fox, A.C.J.: A verified certificate checker for finite-precision error bounds in Coq and HOL4. In: Bjørner, N., Gurfinkel, A. (eds.) FMCAD. pp. 1–10. IEEE (2018). https://doi.org/10.23919/FMCAD.2018.8603019
4. Biere, A., Cimatti, A., Clarke, E.M., Zhu, Y.: Symbolic model checking without BDDs. In: Cleaveland, R. (ed.) TACAS. LNCS, vol. 1579, pp. 193–207. Springer (1999). https://doi.org/10.1007/3-540-49059-0_14
5. Bryant, R.E., Heule, M.J.H.: Generating extended resolution proofs with a BDD-based SAT solver. In: Groote, J.F., Larsen, K.G. (eds.) TACAS. LNCS, Springer (2021), to appear
6. Cruz-Filipe, L., Heule, M.J.H., Hunt Jr., W.A., Kaufmann, M., Schneider-Kamp, P.: Efficient certified RAT verification. In: de Moura, L. (ed.) CADE. LNCS, vol. 10395, pp. 220–236. Springer (2017). https://doi.org/10.1007/978-3-319-63046-5_14
7. Cruz-Filipe, L., Marques-Silva, J., Schneider-Kamp, P.: Efficient certified resolution proof checking. In: Legay, A., Margaria, T. (eds.) TACAS. LNCS, vol. 10205, pp. 118–135 (2017). https://doi.org/10.1007/978-3-662-54577-5_7
8. Cruz-Filipe, L., Marques-Silva, J., Schneider-Kamp, P.: Formally verifying the solution to the boolean Pythagorean triples problem. J. Autom. Reasoning **63**(3), 695–722 (2019). https://doi.org/10.1007/s10817-018-9490-4
9. Ekici, B., Mebsout, A., Tinelli, C., Keller, C., Katz, G., Reynolds, A., Barrett, C.W.: SMTCoq: A plug-in for integrating SMT solvers into Coq. In: Majumdar, R., Kuncak, V. (eds.) CAV. LNCS, vol. 10427, pp. 126–133. Springer (2017). https://doi.org/10.1007/978-3-319-63390-9_7
10. Férée, H., Pohjola, J.Å., Kumar, R., Owens, S., Myreen, M.O., Ho, S.: Program verification in the presence of I/O - semantics, verified library routines, and verified applications. In: Piskac, R., Rümmer, P. (eds.) VSTTE. LNCS, vol. 11294, pp. 88–111. Springer (2018). https://doi.org/10.1007/978-3-030-03592-1_6
11. Fleury, M.: Optimizing a verified SAT solver. In: Badger, J.M., Rozier, K.Y. (eds.) NFM. LNCS, vol. 11460, pp. 148–165. Springer (2019). https://doi.org/10.1007/978-3-030-20652-9_10
12. Fleury, M., Blanchette, J.C., Lammich, P.: A verified SAT solver with watched literals using imperative HOL. In: Andronick, J., Felty, A.P. (eds.) CPP. pp. 158–171. ACM (2018). https://doi.org/10.1145/3167080
13. Ghale, M.K., Pattinson, D., Kumar, R., Norrish, M.: Verified certificate checking for counting votes. In: Piskac, R., Rümmer, P. (eds.) VSTTE. LNCS, vol. 11294, pp. 69–87. Springer (2018). https://doi.org/10.1007/978-3-030-03592-1_5
14. Guéneau, A., Myreen, M.O., Kumar, R., Norrish, M.: Verified characteristic formulae for CakeML. In: Yang, H. (ed.) ESOP. LNCS, vol. 10201, pp. 584–610. Springer (2017). https://doi.org/10.1007/978-3-662-54434-1_22

15. Heule, M., Hunt Jr., W.A., Kaufmann, M., Wetzler, N.: Efficient, verified checking of propositional proofs. In: Ayala-Rincón, M., Muñoz, C.A. (eds.) ITP. LNCS, vol. 10499, pp. 269–284. Springer (2017). https://doi.org/10.1007/978-3-319-66107-0_-18

16. Heule, M., Hunt Jr., W.A., Wetzler, N.: Trimming while checking clausal proofs. In: FMCAD. pp. 181–188. IEEE (2013). https://doi.org/10.1109/FMCAD.2013.6679408

17. Heule, M.J.H.: Schur number five. In: McIlraith, S.A., Weinberger, K.Q. (eds.) AAAI. pp. 6598–6606. AAAI Press (2018)

18. Heule, M.J.H., Biere, A.: What a difference a variable makes. In: Beyer, D., Huisman, M. (eds.) TACAS. LNCS, vol. 10806, pp. 75–92. Springer (2018). https://doi.org/10.1007/978-3-319-89963-3_5

19. Heule, M.J.H., Kiesl, B., Biere, A.: Clausal proofs of mutilated chessboards. In: Badger, J.M., Rozier, K.Y. (eds.) NFM. LNCS, vol. 11460, pp. 204–210. Springer (2019). https://doi.org/10.1007/978-3-030-20652-9_13

20. Heule, M.J.H., Kiesl, B., Biere, A.: Encoding redundancy for satisfaction-driven clause learning. In: Vojnar, T., Zhang, L. (eds.) TACAS. LNCS, vol. 11427, pp. 41–58. Springer (2019). https://doi.org/10.1007/978-3-030-17462-0_3

21. Heule, M.J.H., Kiesl, B., Biere, A.: Strong extension-free proof systems. J. Autom. Reasoning **64**(3), 533–554 (2020). https://doi.org/10.1007/s10817-019-09516-0

22. Heule, M.J.H., Kullmann, O., Marek, V.W.: Solving and verifying the boolean Pythagorean triples problem via cube-and-conquer. In: Creignou, N., Berre, D.L. (eds.) SAT. LNCS, vol. 9710, pp. 228–245. Springer (2016). https://doi.org/10.1007/978-3-319-40970-2_15

23. Jackson, D., Schechter, I., Shlyakhter, I.: Alcoa: the alloy constraint analyzer. In: Ghezzi, C., Jazayeri, M., Wolf, A.L. (eds.) ICSE. pp. 730–733. ACM (2000). https://doi.org/10.1145/337180.337616

24. Järvisalo, M., Heule, M., Biere, A.: Inprocessing rules. In: Gramlich, B., Miller, D., Sattler, U. (eds.) IJCAR. LNCS, vol. 7364, pp. 355–370. Springer (2012). https://doi.org/10.1007/978-3-642-31365-3_28

25. Kiesl, B., Rebola-Pardo, A., Heule, M.J.H.: Extended resolution simulates DRAT. In: Galmiche, D., Schulz, S., Sebastiani, R. (eds.) IJCAR. LNCS, vol. 10900, pp. 516–531. Springer (2018). https://doi.org/10.1007/978-3-319-94205-6_34

26. Konev, B., Lisitsa, A.: Computer-aided proof of Erdős discrepancy properties. Artif. Intell. **224**, 103–118 (2015). https://doi.org/10.1016/j.artint.2015.03.004

27. Kumar, R., Mullen, E., Tatlock, Z., Myreen, M.O.: Software verification with ITPs should use binary code extraction to reduce the TCB - (short paper). In: Avigad, J., Mahboubi, A. (eds.) ITP. LNCS, vol. 10895, pp. 362–369. Springer (2018). https://doi.org/10.1007/978-3-319-94821-8_21

28. Lammich, P.: Efficient verified (UN)SAT certificate checking. J. Autom. Reasoning **64**(3), 513–532 (2020). https://doi.org/10.1007/s10817-019-09525-z

29. Lind, J., Mihajlovic, N., Myreen, M.O.: Verified hash map and buffered I/O libraries for CakeML. In: Trends in Functional Programming (TFP) (2021), accepted for presentation

30. Maric, F.: Formal verification of a modern SAT solver by shallow embedding into Isabelle/HOL. Theor. Comput. Sci. **411**(50), 4333–4356 (2010). https://doi.org/10.1016/j.tcs.2010.09.014

31. Mullen, E., Pernsteiner, S., Wilcox, J.R., Tatlock, Z., Grossman, D.: Œuf: minimizing the Coq extraction TCB. In: Andronick, J., Felty, A.P. (eds.) CPP. pp. 172–185. ACM (2018). https://doi.org/10.1145/3167089

32. Myreen, M.O., Owens, S.: Proof-producing translation of higher-order logic into pure and stateful ML. J. Funct. Program. **24**(2-3), 284–315 (2014). https://doi.org/10.1017/S0956796813000282

33. Oe, D., Stump, A., Oliver, C., Clancy, K.: versat: A verified modern SAT solver. In: Kuncak, V., Rybalchenko, A. (eds.) VMCAI. LNCS, vol. 7148, pp. 363–378. Springer (2012). https://doi.org/10.1007/978-3-642-27940-9_24

34. Slind, K., Norrish, M.: A brief overview of HOL4. In: Mohamed, O.A., Muñoz, C.A., Tahar, S. (eds.) TPHOLs. LNCS, vol. 5170, pp. 28–32. Springer (2008). https://doi.org/10.1007/978-3-540-71067-7_6

35. Tan, Y.K., Myreen, M.O., Kumar, R., Fox, A.C.J., Owens, S., Norrish, M.: The verified CakeML compiler backend. J. Funct. Program. **29**, e2 (2019). https://doi.org/10.1017/S0956796818000229

36. Wetzler, N., Heule, M., Hunt Jr., W.A.: DRAT-trim: Efficient checking and trimming using expressive clausal proofs. In: Sinz, C., Egly, U. (eds.) SAT. LNCS, vol. 8561, pp. 422–429. Springer (2014). https://doi.org/10.1007/978-3-319-09284-3_31

Deductive Verification of Floating-Point Java Programs in KeY

Rosa Abbasi[1] (✉), Jonas Schiffl[2], Eva Darulova[1],
Mattias Ulbrich[2], and Wolfgang Ahrendt[3]

[1] MPI-SWS, Kaiserslautern and Saarbrücken, Germany, {rosaabbasi,eva}@mpi-sws.org
[2] Karlsruhe Institute of Technology, Karlsruhe, Germany,
{jonas.schiffl,ulbrich}@kit.edu
[3] Chalmers University of Technology, Göteborg, Sweden, ahrendt@chalmers.se

Abstract. Deductive verification has been successful in verifying interesting properties of real-world programs. One notable gap is the limited support for floating-point reasoning. This is unfortunate, as floating-point arithmetic is particularly unintuitive to reason about due to rounding as well as the presence of the special values infinity and 'Not a Number' (NaN). In this paper, we present the first floating-point support in a deductive verification tool for the Java programming language. Our support in the KeY verifier handles arithmetic via floating-point decision procedures inside SMT solvers and transcendental functions via axiomatization. We evaluate this integration on new benchmarks, and show that this approach is powerful enough to prove the absence of floating-point special values—often a prerequisite for further reasoning about numerical computations—as well as certain functional properties for realistic benchmarks.

Keywords: Deductive Verification · Floating-point Arithmetic · Transcendental Functions.

1 Introduction

Deductive verification has been successful in providing functional verification for programs written in popular programming languages such as Java [4,23,41,49], Python [29], Rust [6], C [25,54], and Ada [19,50]. Deductive verifiers allow a user to annotate methods in a program with pre- and postconditions, from which they automatically generate verification conditions (VCs). These are then either proven directly by the verifier itself, or discharged with external tools such as automated (SMT) solvers or interactive proof assistants.

While deductive verifiers fully implement many sophisticated data representations (including heap data structures, objects, and ownership), support for floating-point numbers remains rather limited – solely Frama-C and SPARK offer automated support for floating-point arithmetic in C and Ada [32]. This state of affairs is at least partially a result of previous limitations in floating-point support in SMT solvers. Consequently, deductive verification has been used for

© The Author(s) 2021
J. F. Groote and K. G. Larsen (Eds.): TACAS 2021, LNCS 12652, pp. 242–261, 2021.
https://doi.org/10.1007/978-3-030-72013-1_13

floating-point programs only by experts with considerable manual effort [15, 32]. This is unfortunate as it makes deductive verification unavailable for a large number of programs across many domains including embedded systems, machine learning, and scientific computing. With the increasing need for parallelization in code, scientific computing specifically has recently experienced algorithmic challenges for which formal methods may contribute to a solution [10, 56].

One of the main challenges of floating-point arithmetic is its unintuitive behavior and the special values that the IEEE 754 standard [39] introduces. For instance, an overflow or a division by zero results in the special value (positive or negative) *infinity*, and not a runtime exception. Similarly, invalid operations like sqrt(-1.0) result in a *Not a Number* (NaN) value. These special values are problematic as seemingly straight-forward identities do not hold (x == x or x * 0.0 == 0.0). In addition, every operation on floating-point numbers potentially involves rounding, which compromises familiar rules like associativity and distributivity. Hence, reasoning support for writing correct floating-point programs is indispensable.

Abstract interpretation-based tools can prove the absence of runtime errors and special values [20, 43], and bound roundoff errors due to floating-point's finite precision [11, 21, 26, 36, 57]. SMT decision procedures [18] or SAT-based model-checking [24, 56], on the other hand, can prove intricate properties requiring bit-precise reasoning. However, these techniques and tools largely support only purely floating-point programs or program snippets, or analyze programs only up to a predefined depth of the call stack. General reasoning about real-world object-oriented programs, however, also requires support for features such as the (unbounded) heap, necessitating different analyses which need to be combined with floating-point reasoning.

Handling floating-points in a deductive verifier has unique advantages. First, the deductive verification approach already comes with the infrastructure for reasoning about complex control and data structures (like exception handling and heap). Second, it allows one to flexibly combine the verifier's symbolic execution reasoning with external decision procedures. Third, depending on the theory support, the verifier or external solver may also generate counterexamples of a property and thus help program debugging – something an abstract interpretation-based approach fundamentally cannot provide.

We report on adding floating-point support to the KeY deductive verifier, providing the first automated deductive floating-point support for the Java programming language. We focus mainly on proving the absence of the special values infinity and NaN. While these are helpful in certain circumstances, for most applications they signal an error. Hence, showing their absence is a prerequisite for further (functional) reasoning. That said, our extension also allows one to express and discharge arbitrary functional properties expressible in floating-point arithmetic, including bounds on roundoff errors for certain programs, and bounds on differences between two similar floating-point programs

We exploit both KeY's symbolic execution and external SMT support. On the one hand, we handle arithmetic operations by relying on a combination of

KeY's symbolic execution to handle the heap and SMT based decision procedures to handle the floating-point part of the VCs. On the other hand, we support transcendental functions via axiomatization in the KeY prover itself.

Transcendental functions such as sine are a common feature in numerical programs, but are not supported by floating-point decision procedures. We explore two ways of supporting them soundly but approximately, by encoding them as axiomatized uninterpreted function symbols once directly in the SMT queries, and once in additional calculus rules in KeY. Our evaluation shows that even though such reasoning is approximate, it is nonetheless sufficient to prove the absence of special values in many interesting programs.

We evaluate KeY's floating-point support on a number of real-world floating-point Java programs. Our benchmark set allows us to evaluate recent progress in SMT floating-point support in Z3 [28], CVC4 [8] and MathSAT [22] on yet unseen benchmarks. For instance, we observe that quantifiers are challenging even if they do not affect satisfiability of SMT queries. Our benchmarks are openly available, and we expect our insights to be useful for further solver development.

Contributions In summary, we make the following contributions:

- we implement and evaluate the first automated deductive verification of floating-point Java programs by combining the strength of rule based and SMT based deduction;
- we collect a new set of challenging real-world floating-point benchmarks in Java (available at https://gitlab.mpi-sws.org/AVA/key-float-benchmarks/);
- we compare different SMT solvers for discharging floating-point VCs on this new set of benchmarks;
- and we develop novel automated support for reasoning about transcendental functions in a deductive verifier.

2 Background

2.1 Introduction to KeY

KeY [4] is a platform for deductive verification of Java programs, working at a source code level. The input is a Java program annotated in the Java Modeling Language (JML) [45], encouraging a *Design by Contract* ([46,51]) approach to software development. The user specifies the expected behavior of Java classes with *class invariants* that the program has to maintain at critical points. Methods are specified with *method contracts*, consisting mainly of pre- and postconditions, with the understanding that if the precondition holds when the method is called, the postcondition has to hold after the method returns.

After loading an annotated program, KeY translates it to a formula in Java Dynamic Logic [4] (JavaDL), an instance of Dynamic Logic [37] which enables logical reasoning about Java programs. Logical rules are provided for the translation of programs into first-order logic, and for closing the resulting *goals*, or proof obligations. KeY is semi-interactive in that it allows manual rule application, while also offering powerful built-in automation and macros. In addition, it is also possible to translate an open goal into SMT-LIB format [9] and call an external SMT solver. For specific theories, SMT solvers can be much more efficient than KeY's own automation. This makes it possible to prove some goals, which depend on SMT supported theories, by using an SMT solver, while others are proved internally, using KeY's own automation.

2.2 Floating-Point Arithmetic in Java

In the following, we summarize some central characteristics of Java floating-point numbers, loosely following [53]. Each *normal* floating-point number x can be represented as a triplet (s, m, e), such that $x = (-1)^s * m * 2^e$, where $s \in \{0, 1\}$ is the *sign*, m (called *significand*) is a binary fixed-point number with one digit before the radix point and $p - 1$ digits after the radix point (note that $0 \le m < 2$), and e (*exponent*) is an integer such that $e_{min} \le e \le e_{max}$. Java supports two floating-point formats (both in base 2): float ('single') precision with $p = 24$, and minimal and maximal exponent $e_{min} = -126, e_{max} = 127$ and double precision with $p = 53, e_{min} = -1022, e_{max} = 1023$.

Whenever the result of a computation cannot be exactly represented with the given precision, it is rounded. IEEE 754 defines various rounding modes, of which Java only supports *round to nearest, ties to even*. Rounding is exact, as if one would first compute the ideal real number, and round afterwards.

The triple representation gives us two zeros, $+0$ and -0, represented by $(0, 0, 0)$ and $(1, 0, 0)$, respectively. If the absolute value of the ideal result of a computation is too small to be representable as a floating-point number of the given format, the resulting floating point number is $+0$ or -0. In addition, there are three special values, $+\infty$, $-\infty$, and NaN (Not a Number). If the absolute value of the ideal result of a computation is too big to be representable as a floating-point number of the given format, the result is $+\infty$ or $-\infty$. Also, division by zero will give an infinite result (e.g., $7.13 / +0 = +\infty$). Computing further with infinity may give an infinite result (e.g., $+\infty + +\infty = +\infty$), but may also result in the additional 'error value' NaN (e.g., $+\infty - +\infty = $ NaN). Due to the presence of infinities and NaN, floating-point operations do *not* throw Java exceptions.

By default, the Java virtual machine is allowed to make use of higher-precision formats provided by the hardware. This can make computation more accurate, but it also leads to platform dependent behaviour. This can be avoided by using the strictfp modifier, ensuring that only the single and double precision types are used. This modifier ensures portability.

3 Floating-Point Support in KeY

3.1 Arithmetics

In order to be able to specify and verify programs containing floating-point numbers, we made several extensions to the KeY tool. First, we added the float

Listing 1.1: The Rectangle.scale benchmark

```
/*@ public normal_behavior
  @   requires \fp_nice(arg0.x) && \fp_nice(arg0.y)
  @      && \fp_nice(arg1) && \fp_nice(arg2);
  @   ensures !\fp_nan(\result.x) && !\fp_nan(\result.y) &&
  @    !\fp_nan(\result.width) && !\fp_nan(\result.height);
  @ also
  @ public normal_behavior
  @   requires -5.53 <= arg0.x && arg0.x <= -3.38 &&
  @     -5.53 <= arg0.y && arg0.y <= -3.38 &&
  @     3.1 < arg0.width && arg0.width <= 3.7332 &&
  @     3.0000001 < arg0.height && arg0.height <=4.0004 &&
  @     3.0003001 < arg1 && arg1 <= 4.0024 &&
  @     -6.4000003 < arg2 && arg2 <= 3.0001;
  @   ensures !\fp_nan(\result.x) && !\fp_nan(\result.y)&&
  @    !\fp_nan(\result.width) &&!\fp_nan(\result.height);
  @*/
public Rectangle scale(Rectangle arg0, double arg1, double arg2){
    Area v1 = new Area(arg0);
    AffineTransform v2 = AffineTransform.getScaleInstance(arg1, arg2);
    Area v3 = v1.createTransformedArea(v2);
    Rectangle v4 = v3.getRectangle2D();
    return v4;
}
```

and `double` types to the KeY type system, together with an enum type for the different rounding modes of the IEEE 754 Standard.

We further introduced functions and predicate symbols to formalize operations $(+, *, \dots)$ and comparisons $(<, ==, \dots)$ on floating-point expressions. The translation supports both code with and without the `strictfp` modifier. However, since the actual precision of non-strictfp operations is not known, the function symbols remain uninterpreted. We extended KeY's parser to correctly handle programs and annotations containing floating-point numbers, and added logic rules for translating floating-point expressions from Java or JML to JavaDL.

As an example, Listing 1.1 shows JML specifications of our `Rectangle` benchmark that contains floating-point literals and makes use of the `fp_nan` and `fp_nice` predicates. `fp_nan` states that a floating-point expression is NaN and `fp_nice`, which is shorthand for "not infinity and not NaN", states that a floating-point expression is not NaN or infinity. The `scale` method contains two contracts that are checked separately, ensuring that the class fields of a scaled rectangle object are not NaN, considering different preconditions. For the first contract, the SMT solver produces a counterexample. In the second, we bound inputs by concrete ranges that we picked arbitrarily and get the valid result. In practice, such ranges would come from the context, e.g. from the kind of rectangles that appear in an application, or from known ranges of sensor values.

Concerning discharging the resulting proof obligations, there were two main ways to consider. One is to create a floating-point theory within KeY by adding axioms and deduction rules, so that the desired properties can be proven in KeY's sequent calculus. The other way is to translate the proof obligations from JavaDL to SMT-LIB and call an external SMT solver. While the KeY approach traditionally favors conducting proofs within KeY, for this work, we partially deviated from this way in order to harness the greater experience and efficiency of SMT solvers when it comes to floating-point arithmetic. Our approach attempts to get the best of both worlds by distinguishing between basic floating-point arithmetic, i. e., elementary operations and comparisons, and more complex functions which do not have an SMT-LIB equivalent (e. g., the transcendental functions), or where the SMT-LIB function is not usefully implemented by current SMT solvers (see Section 3.2.B).

Elementary operations and comparisons get translated to the corresponding SMT-LIB functions. In SMT-LIB, all floating-point computations conform to the IEEE 754 Standard. Therefore, only Java programs with the strictfp modifier can be directly translated to SMT-LIB without loss of correctness.

We developed a translation from KeY's floating-point theory to SMT-LIB. In order to integrate it into KeY, we also overhauled the existing translation from JavaDL to SMT-LIB to create a new, more modular framework, which now supports all the features of the original translation, e. g., heaps and integer arithmetic, but also floating-point expressions at the same time.

Floating-point intricacies sometimes require extra caution. For example, there are two different notions of equality for floats: bitwise equality and IEEE754 equality. Our implementation ensures these are distinguished correctly, and that the specification language remains intuitive for a developer to use.

Using the translation to SMT-LIB, we can specify and prove two classes of properties in KeY: The absence of special values is specified using the fp_nan and fp_infinite predicates (or the fp_nice equivalent). Furthermore, one can specify *functional* properties that are expressible in floating-point arithmetic, e.g. one can compare the result of a computation against the result of a different program which is known to produce a good result or a reference value.

3.2   Transcendental Functions

Floating-point decision procedures in SMT solvers successfully handle programs consisting of arithmetic and square root operations. Many numerical real-world programs, however, include transcendental functions such as sin and cos. In Java programs, these functions are implemented as static library functions in the class java.lang.Math.

Unlike arithmetic operations, transcendental functions are much more loosely specified by the IEEE 754 Standard—only an upper bound on the roundoff error is given. Libraries are thus free to provide different implementations, and even tighter error bounds. Exact reasoning in the same spirit as floating-point arithmetic would thus have to encode a specific implementation. Given that these implementations are highly optimized, this approach would be arguably complex.

We observe, however, that such exact reasoning about transcendental functions is often not necessary and a sound approximate approach is sufficient and efficient.

In this section, we introduce an axiomatic approach for reasoning about programs containing transcendental functions. We observe that with the flexibility of deductive verification and KeY itself, we can instantiate it in two different ways. We encode transcendental functions as uninterpreted functions and axiomatize them in the SMT queries. Alternatively, we encode these axioms in KeY as logical inference rules.

(A) Axiomatization in SMT We encode library functions as uninterpreted functions and include a set of axioms in the SMT-LIB translation for each method that is called in a benchmark. That is, we extended KeY such that when a transcendental function exists in the proof obligation, its definition alongside all the axioms for that function are added to the translation.

For the axiomatization of transcendentals, we did *not* add rules that expand to a definition or allow a repeated approximation of the function value (like expansion into a Taylor series). Instead, we added a number of lemmata encoding interesting properties related to special values. For instance, the following axiom states that if the input to the sin function is not a NaN or infinity, then the returned value of sin is between -1.0 and 1.0:

```
(assert (forall ((a Float64)) (=>
  (and (not (fp.isNaN a)) (not (fp.isInfinite a)))
  (and (fp.leq (sinDouble a) (fp #b0 #b01111111111 #b0000...000000))
       (fp.geq (sinDouble a) (fp #b1 #b01111111111 #b0000...000000))))))
```

Note that this implies that the result is not a NaN or infinity. The other axioms are similar in spirit, so we do not list them.

These axioms are expressed as quantified floating-point formulas and capture high-level properties of library functions complying with the specifications in the IEEE 754 Standard. Clearly, since we do not have the actual implementations of these functions, we are not able to prove arbitrary properties. However, such an axiomatization is often sufficient to check for the (absence of) special values, i.e. NaN and infinity, as our experiments in Section 4.4 show.

(B) Taclets in KeY Reasoning about quantified formulas in SMT is a long-lasting challenge [34]. We have also observed in our experiments with only arithmetic operations (Section 4.3) that SMT solvers struggle with quantifiers in combination with floating-points. We have therefore implemented an alternative approach encoding the axioms not in the SMT queries, but instead as deductive inference rules (so-called taclets) in KeY.

The rules encode the same logical information as the universally quantified assertions that we add in SMT-LIB (and where we leave the choice of instantiations entirely to the SMT/SAT solver). With our taclet approach, we instantiate a quantifier (only) to one's needs. We note that for proving a property correct, this results in a correct (under)approximation. However, the prize for achieving

benchmark	# classes	Benchmark Details			Automode Statistics			
		# method calls	# arith. ops	library functions	# goals closed by KeY	# goals to be closed externally	# rules applied	automode time (s)
Complex.add (2)	1	0	2	-	3 / 3	1 / 4	185 / 286	0.7 / 0.2
Complex.divide (2)	1	0	11	-	10 / 8	2 / 8	483 / 625	0.7 / 0.8
Complex.compare	1	0	2	-	3	2	216	0.2
Complex.reciprocal (2)	1	1	6	-	1 / 1	2 / 2	402 / 406	0.4 / 0.5
Circuit.impedance	2	1	3	-	1	4	360	0.5
Circuit.current (2)	2	3	14	-	11 / 11	4 / 1	1267 / 1238	4.0 / 4.1
Matrix2.transposedEq	1	3	3	-	3	1	735	0.9
Matrix3.transposedEq	1	4	34	-	3	1	1786	5.1
Matrix3.transposedEqV2	1	4	34	-	3	1	1796	5.4
Rectangle.scale (2)	3 + 1	23	22	-	32 / 32	32 / 16	5990 / 5617	18.4 / 14.5
Rotate.computeError	1 + 1	6	26	-	108	8	3693	74.2
Rotate.computeRelErr	1 + 1	6	28	-	120	8	3898	79.6
FPLoop.fploop	1	0	1	-	2	4	99	0.1
FPLoop.fploop2	1	0	1	-	2	4	99	0.1
FPLoop.fploop3	1	0	1	-	2	4	99	0.1
Cartesian.toPolar	2 + 1	3	6	sqrt, atan	1	4	438	0.5
Cartesian.distanceTo	1 + 1	1	5	sqrt	2	1	191	0.5
Polar.toCartesian	2 + 1	3	4	cos, sin	1	2	364	0.5
Circuit.instantCurrent	2 + 1	14	23	sqrt, atan, cos	17	2	1686	14.1
Circuit.instantVoltage	1 + 1	1	4	cos	0	2	138	0.1

Table 1: Benchmark details and KeY automode statistics, time is measured in seconds

more closed proofs and shorter running times is that for disproving a property, not considering all possible quantifier instantiations may lead to spurious counterexamples, i.e., false positives.

A heuristic strategy applies the rules automatically using the occurrences of transcendentals as instantiation triggers. However, instantiating the axioms too eagerly, considerably increases the number of open goals, which is why we assume that the user selects the axioms to apply manually (and did so in the experiments). After the application the proof obligation can either be closed, i.e proven, by KeY automatically, or be given to the SMT solver as before for final solving.

Currently, the set of axioms (in the SMT-LIB translation and as taclets in KeY) only contains axioms for the transcendental functions occurring in our benchmarks. So far we have 10 axioms; however, adding more axioms (also for further transcendentals like exponentiation or logarithm) is straightforward. The full set of axioms is included in the Appendix of the technical report [3].

4 Evaluation

4.1 Benchmark Programs

We collected a set of existing floating-point Java programs representing real-world applications in order to evaluate the feasibility and performance of KeY's floating-point support.

The left half of Table 1 provides an overview of our benchmarks. Each benchmark consists of one method, which is composed of arithmetic operations

Listing 1.2: The Circuit.instantCurrent benchmark

```
public class Circuit {
double maxVoltage, frequency, resistance, inductance;
// ...

/*@ public normal_behavior
 @ requires 1.0 < this.maxVoltage && this.maxVoltage < 12.0 &&
 @  1.0 < this.frequency && this.frequency < 100.0 &&
 @  1.0 < this.resistance && this.resistance < 50.0 &&
 @  0.001 < this.inductance && this.inductance < 0.004 &&
 @  0.0 < time && time < 300.0;
 @ ensures !\fp_nan(\result) && !\fp_infinite(\result);
 @*/
public double instantCurrent(double time) {
  Complex current = computeCurrent();
  double maxCurrent = Math.sqrt(current.getRealPart() * current.getRealPart() +
    current.getImaginaryPart() * current.getImaginaryPart());
  double theta = Math.atan(current.getImaginaryPart() / current.getRealPart());
  return maxCurrent * Math.cos((2.0 * Math.PI * frequency * time) + theta);
}}
```

and method calls to potentially other classes. The invocations of methods from java.lang.Math (e.g. Math.abs) are marked by "+1" in Table 1; these are resolved by inlining the method implementation. For benchmarks that contain calls to transcendental functions and square root, the called functions are listed; these are handled by our axiomatization. We include sqrt in this list, as we have observed that exact support can be expensive, so it may be advantageous to handle sqrt axiomatically. Benchmarks Rectangle, Circuit, Matrix3 and Rotation are partially shown in Listings 1.1, 1.2, 1.3 and 1.4 respectively.

Each benchmark also includes a JML contract that is to be checked. For some methods, we specify two contracts (marked by "(2)" in the first column of Table 1), each serving as an independent benchmark. The contracts for most of these benchmarks check that the methods do not return a special value i.e infinity and/or NaN, the preconditions being that the variables are not themselves special values and possibly are bounded in a given range. For the Matrix, FPLoop and Rotate benchmarks, we check a *functional* property (see Section 4.3). FPLoop, which has three contracts, additionally shows how to specify floating-point loop behavior using loop invariants.

4.2   Proof Obligation Generation

To reason about the contract of a selected benchmark, we apply KeY, which generates proof obligations or 'goals'. Some of these goals (heap-related) are closed by KeY automatically. The remaining open goals are closed by either SMT solvers with floating-point support directly (Section 3.1 and Section 3.2.A), or with a combination of transcendental KeY taclets and floating-point SMT solving (Section 3.2.B).

Columns 6 and 7 in Table 1 show the number of proof obligations closed by KeY directly and to be discharged by external solvers, respectively. The next two columns show the number of taclet rules that KeY applied in order to close its goals, and the time this takes. For benchmarks with two contracts we show the respective values separated by '/'.

We run our experiments on a server with 1.5 TB memory and 4x12 CPU cores at 3 GHz. However, KeY runs single-threadedly and does not use more than 8GB of memory.

For our set of benchmarks, the symbolic execution process is fully automated. Note that the machinery can deal with loop invariants, if they are provided. Loop invariant generation is, however, particularly challenging for floating-points due to roundoff errors [27,40], and a research topic in itself.

4.3   Evaluation of SMT Floating-Point Support

Previous work [32] reported that SMT support for floating-point arithmetic is rather limited. However, with recent advances [18], we evaluate the situation again. Most benchmarks used to evaluate SMT solvers' decision procedures [1] aim to check (individual) specialized (corner case) properties of floating-point arithmetic. The proof obligations generated from our set of benchmarks are complementary in that they are more arithmetic heavy, while nonetheless relying on accurate reasoning about special values and functional properties.

For each open goal not automatically closed, KeY generates one SMT-LIB file that is fed to the solvers for validation. We compare the performance of the three major SMT solvers with floating-point support CVC4 [8] (version 1.8, with the SymFPU library [18] enabled), Z3 (4.8.9) [28] and MathSAT (5.6.3) [22]. For this we set a timeout of 300s for each proof obligation. While KeY is able to discharge proof obligations in parallel, for our experiments, we do so sequentially to maintain comparability.

KeY's default translation to SMT includes quantifiers. These quantifications are not related to floating-point arithmetic, but are used to logically encode important properties of the Java memory model, like the type hierarchy and the absence of dangling references on any valid Java heap. If we reason about floating-point problems in isolation, they are not needed, but if we want to consider Java verification more holistically with questions combining aspects of heap and floating point reasoning, they become essential. We manually inspected that the proof obligations without our axiomatized treatment of transcendental functions do not depend on these properties and investigate the quantifier support by including or removing them from the SMT translations. We do not report results with quantifiers for MathSAT, since it does not support them.

Table 2 summarizes the results of our experiments. Column 4 shows the number of expected valid or invalid goals for all benchmarks. For each solver we show the number of goals that each solver can validate or invalidate, together with the average time (in seconds) needed. The goals resulting in timeout were

index experiment	quantified axioms	# goals	CVC4		Z3		MathSAT	
			# goals decided	avg.	# goals decided	avg.	# goals decided	avg.
1 valid	✓	80	79	4.1	25	18.4	-	-
2 contracts	✗	80	79	4.0	52	35.0	80	8.8
3 invalid	✓	9	0	3.4	0	3.4	-	-
4 contracts	✗	9	8	36.7	7	27.6	9	3.9
5 axioms in SMT	✓	10	9	33.2	4	63.4	-	-
6 axioms as taclets	✗	10	10	33.4	5	74.2	8	0.9
7 fp.sqrt	✗	7	7	46.2	1	23.5	5	0.4
8 axiomatized sqrt	✗	7	5	2.4	5	282.8	5	5.7

Table 2: Summary of valid / invalid goals correctly decided and average running times of each solver for the SMT translations with and without quantified axioms

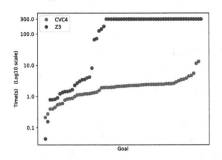
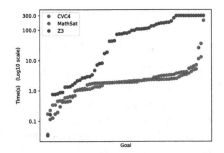

Fig. 1: Runtimes for valid goals with SMT translations *with* quantifiers

Fig. 2: Runtimes for valid goals with SMT translations *without* quantifiers

excluded from the computation of the average time. Column 3 shows whether the SMT queries include quantifiers or not.

Rows 1 and 2 of Table 2 show the results for benchmarks with valid contracts. This experiment thus represents the common behavior of KeY, whose main goal is to *prove* contracts correct. Rows 3 and 4 of Table 2 demonstrate the results for benchmarks with invalid contracts, i.e. for those we expect a counterexample for at least one of the goals. The Appendix of the technical report [3] contains the detailed results for each experiment separated by benchmark. Figure 1 and Figure 2 show a more detailed view of the solvers' running time for the valid benchmarks. The x-axis shows the number of open goals that are discharged by the SMT solvers, sorted by running time for each solver individually. The k-th point of one graph shows the minimum running time needed by the solver to close each of the k fastest goals. Note that each solver may have different goals which are its k fastest. The y-axis shows the time on a logarithmic scale.

We conclude that in the presence of quantified axioms and floating-point arithmetic solvers' performance deteriorate for both valid and invalid goals. In particular, none of the solvers is able to find counterexamples for any of the invalid goals. However, when the quantified axioms are removed from the

SMT translations, their performance improves. For valid contracts, CVC4 and MathSAT perform better than Z3, in terms of both number of goals validated and the running time per goal. In particular, MathSAT is able to prove all goals. However, the running time performance of CVC4 is better than MathSAT's. For invalid contracts, solvers are able to produce the expected counterexamples at least partially. Particularly, MathSAT has a better performance than CVC4 and Z3 in terms of both running time and the number of proof obligations for which it can produce counterexamples.

We conducted another experiment on our Rectangle.scale benchmark to assess the solvers' sensitivity to various changes, applied to the benchmark's contract or its implementation. We considered modifications such as reducing the number of classes while keeping the same functionality, having tighter and larger bounds for variables, reducing the number of arithmetic operations etc. The details of this experiment can be found in the Appendix of the technical report [3]. In summary, solvers' performance seems to be sensitive to slight innocuous looking changes such as the number of classes involved and variable bounds. For example, constraining arg2 in the original benchmark more tightly allows CVC4 to validate all goals (1 more). This behavior could be potentially exploited by e.g. relaxing a variable's bounds.

Proving Functional Properties Listings 1.3 and 1.4 show examples of functional properties that are expressible in floating-point arithmetic and that KeY can handle. The verification results are included in rows 1 and 2 of Table 2, for more details see the Appendix of the technical report [3].

For Matrix, we check that the determinants of a matrix and its transpose are equal. Note that this property holds trivially under real arithmetic, but not necessarily under floating-points. After feeding transposedEq (which uses the determinant method) and its contract to KeY, increasing the default timeout sufficiently and discharging the created goal, CVC4 generates a counterexample in 170.2s seconds and MathSAT in 16.2s. Z3 times out after 30 minutes. By feeding transposedEqV2 (which uses the determinantNew method) to KeY, CVC4 validates the contract in 1.1s, MathSAT in 3.9s and Z3 times out again. One thing worth noting is that the way programs are written can greatly influence the computational complexity needed to reject or verify the contract. This is evident from the fact that slightly modifying the order of operations (using determinantNew instead) substantially reduces verification time and changes the verification result for MathSAT and CVC4.

For Rotate, we check that the difference between an original vector and the one that is rotated four times by 90 degrees, must not be larger than 1.0E-15. We also verified the same bound for the relative difference (by exploiting another method and contract) for this benchmark. The constant cos90 in Listing 1.4 is not precisely 0.0 to account for rounding effects in the computation of the cosine. FPLoop includes three loops, for which the contracts check that the return value is bigger than a given constant.

Though not always very fast, these examples show that verification of functional floating-point properties is viable.

Listing 1.3: The Matrix3 benchmark

```java
public class Matrix3 {
  double a, b, c, d, e, f, g, h, i; //The matrix: [[a b c],[d e f],[g h i]]
  double det;
  // method transpose not shown

  double determinant() {
    return (a * e * i + b * f * g + c * d * h) -
    (c * e * g + b * d * i + a * f * h);
  }
  double determinantNew() {
    return (a * (e * i) + (g * (b * f) + c * (d * h))) -
    (e * (c * g) + (i * (b * d) + a * (f * h)));
  }
  /*@ ensures \fp_normal(\result) ==> (\result == det); @*/
  double transposedEq() {
    det = determinant();
    return transpose().determinant();
  }
  /*@ ensures \fp_normal(\result) ==> (\result == det); @*/
  double transposedEqV2() {
    det = determinantNew();
    return transpose().determinantNew();
  }
}
```

Listing 1.4: The Rotation benchmark

```java
public class Rotation {
  final static double cos90 = 6.123233995736766E-17;
  final static double sin90 = 1.0;

  // rotates a 2D vector by 90 degrees
  public static double[] rotate(double[] vec) {
    double x = vec[0] * cos90 - vec[1] * sin90;
    double y = vec[0] * sin90 + vec[1] * cos90;
    return new double[]{x, y};
  }
  /*@ requires (\forall int i; 0 <= i && i < vec.length;
    @    \fp_nice(vec[i]) && vec[i] > 1.0 && vec[i] < 2.0) && vec.length == 2;
    @ ensures \result[0] < 1.0E-15 && \result[1] < 1.0E-15;
    */
  public static double[] computeError(double[] vec) {
    double[] temp = rotate(rotate(rotate(rotate(vec))));
    return new double[]{Math.abs(temp[0] - vec[0]), Math.abs(temp[1] - vec[1])};
  }
}
```

4.4   Evaluation of Support for Transcendental Functions in KeY

We evaluated the two approaches from Section 3.2.A on our set of benchmarks; rows 5 and 6 in Table 2 summarize the results. (The detailed results of these experiments are included in the Appendix of the technical report [3].) Note that both approaches are fully automated.

We conclude that the SMT solvers perform better when the axiomatization is applied at the KeY level. When axioms for transcendental functions are added to the SMT-LIB translation directly Z3 validates 4 out of 10 goals. With the axiomatization at the KeY level, solvers are able to validate more goals (with quantified formulas removed from the SMT translations), e.g. Z3 is able to validate 5 goals and CVC4 can validate all. Therefore, it is preferable to apply them on the KeY side via taclet rules.

All the solvers we have used in this work comply with the IEEE 754 standard and therefore have bit-precise support for the square root function. They provide bit-precise reasoning by effectively encoding the behavior of floating-point circuits over bitvectors (which is naturally expensive), together with different heuristics and abstractions to speed up solving time. However, depending on the property, we do not always need bit-precise reasoning, so we propose handling the square root function with the same taclet-based axiomatization as introduced in Section 3.2.B.

To this end, we conducted an experiment on the benchmarks containing sqrt, comparing the approach from Section 3.2.B (adding the necessary axioms, resp. taclet rules) to using the square root implemented in SMT solvers (fp.sqrt). We chose to include only axioms specified in or inferred from the IEEE 754 standard (e.g. if the argument of the square root function is NaN or less than zero, then the square root results in NaN). The full set of axioms that we used is included in the Appendix of the technical report [3].

Rows 7 and 8 in Table 2 summarize the results for this experiment; the detailed results are included in the Appendix of the technical report [3]. We observed that for two out of the three benchmarks, the average running time of all solvers decreases using the axiomatized square root. Furthermore, Z3 is able to reason about more proof obligations with the axiomatized version. However, the success of this approach depends on the axioms added to KeY and may not always work if we do not have suitable axioms. For example, for the Circuit.instantCurrent benchmark (Listing 1.2), using the axiomatized square root, CVC4 is not able to validate the contract, but with fp.sqrt the contract is validated.

In summary, treating sqrt axiomatically can result in shorter solving times than performing bit-precise reasoning, but the approach may not always succeed when the axioms are not sufficient to prove a particular property.

4.5   Discussion and insights

The experiments show that highly automated floating point program verification is viable for relevant properties (handling of special values and some functional properties), up to a certain level of complexity (given by the SMT solvers). The choices of which parts of a proof obligation are delegated to SMT, and how they are translated to SMT, are crucial for achieving effective and efficient program verification. Arithmetic operations proved to be more efficiently dealt with by delegation to SMT, whereas for transcendental functions, axiomatization and rule based treatment in the theorem prover, outside the SMT solver, performs clearly better.

5 Related Work

Our implementation uses the floating-point SMT-LIB theory [17], which however does not handle transcendental functions, as their semantics is (library) implementation dependent. Some real-valued automated solvers do handle transcendental functions [5,33], but to the best of our knowledge, the combination of floating-points and reals in SMT solvers is still severely limited.

None of the existing deductive verifiers support floating-point transcendental functions automatically. The Why3 deductive verification framework [30] has support for floating-point arithmetic, with front-ends for the C and Ada programming languages through Frama-C [25] and SPARK [19,32], respectively. Why3 has back-end support for different SMT solvers, as well as interactive proof assistants like Coq. Until recently, Why3 would discharge still many interesting floating-point problems with help of Coq, relying on significant user interaction. In later work [32] (in the context with floating-point verification for Ada programs), Why3 can achieve a higher degree of automation. Note, however, that the user is still required to add code assertions as well as 'ghost code' to a significant extent.

The Boogie intermediate verification language [47] also supports floating-point expressions, and targets Z3 for discharging proof obligations. In the Boogie community, it was observed that writing a specification in Boogie leads to decreases in SMT solver performance when compared to writing the goal in SMT-LIB directly, probably due to an inherent mixing of theories when using Boogie [2]. This matches our own experiences, and separation of theories should be considered an important task for the further development of floating-point verification.

Other deductive verifiers for Java have only rudimentary support for floating-points. Verifast [41] treats floating-point operations as if they were real values, and OpenJML [23] parses programs with floating-point operations, but essentially treats `float` and `double` as uninterpreted sorts.

The Java category of verification competition SV-COMP [12] contains a number of benchmarks that make use of floating-point variables. However, the focus of these benchmarks is usually not on arithmetical properties of expressions, but on the completeness of the Java language support. Amongst the participants of SV-COMP 2020, the Symbolic (Java) Pathfinder (SPF) [55] (and various extensions) and the Java Bounded Model Checker (JBMC) [24] support floating-point arithmetic. Besides being limited to exploring the state space up to a bounded depth, their constraint languages do not support quantifiers and abstracting of method calls—which are features that we have used in this work.

Floating-point arithmetic has also been formalized in several interactive theorem provers [16, 31, 42]. While one can prove intricate properties about floating-point programs [14, 15, 38], proofs using interactive provers are to a large part manual and require significant expertise.

Abstract interpretation based techniques can show the absence of special values in floating-point code fully automatically, and several abstract domains which are sound with respect to floating-point arithmetic exist [20, 43]. While the analysis itself is fully automated, applying it successfully to real-world programs in general requires adaptation to each program analyzed by end-users, e.g. the selection of suitable abstract domains or widening thresholds [13].

Besides showing the absence of special values, recent research has developed static analyses to bound floating-point roundoff errors [26, 35, 48, 52, 57]. These analyses currently work only for small arithmetic kernels and the tools in particular do not accept programs with objects.

Dynamic analyses generally scale well on real-world programs, but can only identify bugs (when given failure-triggering input), rather than proving correctness for *all* possible inputs. Executing a floating-point program together with a higher-precision one allows one to find inputs which cause large roundoff errors [11, 21, 44]. Ariadne [7] uses a combination of symbolic execution, real-valued SMT solving and testing to find inputs that trigger floating-point exceptions, including overflow and invalid operations. Our work subsumes this approach as the SMT solvers that we use can directly generate counterexamples, but more importantly, KeY is able to prove the absence of such exceptions.

6   Conclusion

By joining the forces of rule-based deduction and SAT-based SMT solving, we presented the first working floating-point support in a deductive verification tool for Java and by that close a remaining gap in KeY to now support full sequential Java. Our evaluation shows that for specifications dealing with value ranges and absence of NaN and infinity, our approach can verify realistic programs within a reasonable time frame. We observe that the MathSAT and CVC4 solver's floating-point support scales sufficiently for our benchmarks, as long as the queries do not include any quantifiers, and that our axiomatized approach for handling transcendental functions is best realized using calculus rules in KeY's internal reasoning engine. While our work is implemented within the KeY verifier, we expect our approach to be portable to other verifiers.

Acknowledgements

This research was partially funded by the Deutsche Forschungsgemeinschaft (DFG, German Research Foundation) project 387674182. The authors would like to thank Daniel Eddeland, who together with co-author W. Ahrendt performed prestudies which impacted the current work.

References

1. QF_FP   SMT   benchmarks.   https://clc-gitlab.cs.uiowa.edu:2443/ SMT-LIB-benchmarks/QF_FP (2019)
2. Slow verification of programs combining multiple floating point values (Github issue) (2019 (accessed May 11, 2020)), https://github.com/boogie-org/boogie/issues/109
3. Abbasi, R., Schiffl, J., Darulova, E., Ulbrich, M., Ahrendt, W.: Deductive Verification of Floating-Point Java Programs in KeY. CoRR **abs/2101.08733** (2021)
4. Ahrendt, W., Beckert, B., Bubel, R., Hähnle, R., Schmitt, P.H., Ulbrich, M. (eds.): Deductive Software Verification - The KeY Book - From Theory to Practice, LNCS, vol. 10001. Springer (2016)
5. Akbarpour, B., Paulson, L.C.: MetiTarski: An Automatic Theorem Prover for Real-Valued Special Functions. Journal of Automated Reasoning **44**(3) (2010)
6. Astrauskas, V., Müller, P., Poli, F., Summers, A.J.: Leveraging Rust Types for Modular Specification and Verification. In: Object-Oriented Programming Systems, Languages, and Applications (OOPSLA) (2019)
7. Barr, E.T., Vo, T., Le, V., Su, Z.: Automatic Detection of Floating-point Exceptions. In: Principles of Programming Languages (POPL) (2013)
8. Barrett, C., Conway, C.L., Deters, M., Hadarean, L., Jovanovi'c, D., King, T., Reynolds, A., Tinelli, C.: CVC4. In: Computer Aided Verification (CAV) (2011), snowbird, Utah
9. Barrett, C., Stump, A., Tinelli, C., et al.: The SMT-LIB Standard: Version 2.0. In: Proceedings of the 8th International Workshop on Satisfiability Modulo Theories (2010)
10. Beckert, B., Nestler, B., Kiefer, M., Selzer, M., Ulbrich, M.: Experience Report: Formal Methods in Material Science. CoRR **abs/1802.02374** (2018)
11. Benz, F., Hildebrandt, A., Hack, S.: A Dynamic Program Analysis to Find Floating-Point Accuracy Problems. In: Programming Language Design and Implementation (PLDI) (2012)
12. Beyer, D.: Advances in automatic software verification: Sv-comp 2020. In: Tools and Algorithms for the Construction and Analysis of Systems (TACAS) (2020)
13. Blanchet, B., Cousot, P., Cousot, R., Feret, J., Mauborgne, L., Miné, A., Monniaux, D., Rival, X.: A Static Analyzer for Large Safety-Critical Software. In: Programming Language Design and Implementation (PLDI) (2003)
14. Boldo, S., Clément, F., Filliâtre, J.C., Mayero, M., Melquiond, G., Weis, P.: Wave Equation Numerical Resolution: A Comprehensive Mechanized Proof of a C Program. Journal of Automated Reasoning **50**(4) (2013)
15. Boldo, S., Filliâtre, J.C., Melquiond, G.: Combining Coq and Gappa for Certifying Floating-Point Programs. In: Intelligent Computer Mathematics (2009)
16. Boldo, S., Melquiond, G.: Flocq: A Unified Library for Proving Floating-Point Algorithms in Coq. In: IEEE Symposium on Computer Arithmetic (ARITH) (2011)
17. Brain, M., Tinelli, C., Rümmer, P., Wahl, T.: An Automatable Formal Semantics for IEEE-754 Floating-Point Arithmetic. In: IEEE Symposium on Computer Arithmetic (ARITH) (2015)
18. Brain, M., Schanda, F., Sun, Y.: Building Better Bit-Blasting for Floating-Point Problems. In: Tools and Algorithms for the Construction and Analysis of Systems (TACAS) (2019)
19. Chapman, R., Schanda, F.: Are We There Yet? 20 Years of Industrial Theorem Proving with SPARK. In: Interactive Theorem Proving (ITP) (2014)

20. Chen, L., Miné, A., Cousot, P.: A Sound Floating-Point Polyhedra Abstract Domain. In: Asian Symposium on Programming Languages and Systems (APLAS) (2008)
21. Chiang, W.F., Gopalakrishnan, G., Rakamaric, Z., Solovyev, A.: Efficient Search for Inputs Causing High Floating-point Errors. In: Principles and Practice of Parallel Programming (PPoPP) (2014)
22. Cimatti, A., Griggio, A., Schaafsma, B., Sebastiani, R.: The MathSAT5 SMT Solver. In: Proceedings of Tools and Algorithms for the Construction and Analysis of Systems (TACAS) (2013)
23. Cok, D.R.: OpenJML: JML for Java 7 by extending OpenJDK. In: NASA Formal Methods (2011)
24. Cordeiro, L.C., Kesseli, P., Kroening, D., Schrammel, P., Trtík, M.: JBMC: A Bounded Model Checking Tool for Verifying Java Bytecode. In: Computer Aided Verification (CAV) (2018)
25. Cuoq, P., Kirchner, F., Kosmatov, N., Prevosto, V., Signoles, J., Yakobowski, B.: Frama-C. In: Software Engineering and Formal Methods (SEFM) (2012)
26. Darulova, E., Izycheva, A., Nasir, F., Ritter, F., Becker, H., Bastian, R.: Daisy - Framework for Analysis and Optimization of Numerical Programs. In: Tools and Algorithms for the Construction and Analysis of Systems (TACAS) (2018)
27. Darulova, E., Kuncak, V.: Towards a Compiler for Reals. TOPLAS **39**(2) (2017)
28. De Moura, L., Bjørner, N.: Z3: An Efficient SMT Solver. In: Tools and Algorithms for the Construction and Analysis of Systems (TACAS) (2008)
29. Eilers, M., Müller, P.: Nagini: A Static Verifier for Python. In: Computer Aided Verification (CAV) (2018)
30. Filliâtre, J.C., Paskevich, A.: Why3 — Where Programs Meet Provers. In: European Symposium on Programming (ESOP) (2013)
31. Fox, A., Harrison, J., Akbarpour, B.: A Formal Model of IEEE Floating Point Arithmetic. HOL4 Theorem Prover Library (2017), https://github.com/HOL-Theorem-Prover/HOL/tree/master/src/floating-point
32. Fumex, C., Marché, C., Moy, Y.: Automating the Verification of Floating-Point Programs. In: Verified Software: Theories, Tools, and Experiments (VSTTE) (2017)
33. Gao, S., Kong, S., Clarke, E.M.: dReal: An SMT Solver for Nonlinear Theories over the Reals. In: Automated Deduction – CADE-24 (2013)
34. Ge, Y., de Moura, L.: Complete Instantiation for Quantified Formulas in Satisfiabiliby Modulo Theories. In: Computer Aided Verification (CAV) (2009)
35. Goubault, E., Putot, S.: Static Analysis of Finite Precision Computations. In: Verification, Model Checking, and Abstract Interpretation (VMCAI) (2011)
36. Goubault, E., Putot, S.: Robustness Analysis of Finite Precision Implementations. In: Asian Symposium on Programming Languages and Systems (APLAS) (2013)
37. Harel, D., Kozen, D., Tiuryn, J.: Dynamic Logic. In: Handbook of Philosophical Logic, pp. 99–217. Springer (2001)
38. Harrison, J.: Floating Point Verification in HOL Light: The Exponential Function. Formal Methods in System Design **16**(3) (2000)
39. IEEE, C.S.: IEEE Standard for Floating-Point Arithmetic. IEEE Std 754-2008 (2008)
40. Izycheva, A., Darulova, E., Seidl, H.: Counterexample and Simulation-Guided Floating-Point Loop Invariant Synthesis. In: Static Analysis Symposium (SAS) (2020)
41. Jacobs, B., Smans, J., Philippaerts, P., Vogels, F., Penninckx, W., Piessens, F.: VeriFast: A Powerful, Sound, Predictable, Fast Verifier for C and Java. In: NASA Formal Methods (NFM) (2011)

42. Jacobsen, C., Solovyev, A., Gopalakrishnan, G.: A Parameterized Floating-Point Formalizaton in HOL Light. Electronic Notes in Theoretical Computer Science **317** (2015)
43. Jeannet, B., Miné, A.: Apron: A Library of Numerical Abstract Domains for Static Analysis. In: Computer Aided Verification (CAV) (2009)
44. Lam, M.O., Hollingsworth, J.K., Stewart, G.W.: Dynamic Floating-point Cancellation Detection. Parallel Comput. **39**(3) (2013)
45. Leavens, G.T., Baker, A.L., Ruby, C.: Preliminary design of JML: A behavioral interface specification language for Java. ACM SIGSOFT Software Engineering Notes **31**(3) (2006)
46. Leavens, G.T., Cheon, Y.: Design by Contract with JML (2006), http://www.jmlspecs.org/jmldbc.pdf
47. Leino, K.R.M.: This is Boogie 2 (June 2008), https://www.microsoft.com/en-us/research/publication/this-is-boogie-2-2/
48. Magron, V., Constantinides, G., Donaldson, A.: Certified Roundoff Error Bounds Using Semidefinite Programming. ACM Trans. Math. Softw. **43**(4) (2017)
49. Marché, C., Paulin-Mohring, C., Urbain, X.: The KRAKATOA tool for certification of Java/JavaCard programs annotated in JML. The Journal of Logic and Algebraic Programming **58**(1) (2004)
50. McCormick, J.W., Chapin, P.C.: Building High Integrity Applications with SPARK. Cambridge University Press (2015)
51. Meyer, B.: Applying "Design by Contract". Computer **25**(10) (1992)
52. Moscato, M., Titolo, L., Dutle, A., Muñoz, C.: Automatic Estimation of Verified Floating-Point Round-Off Errors via Static Analysis. In: SAFECOMP (2017)
53. Muller, J., Brisebarre, N., de Dinechin, F., Jeannerod, C., Lefèvre, V., Melquiond, G., Revol, N., Stehlé, D., Torres, S.: Handbook of Floating-Point Arithmetic. Birkhäuser (2010)
54. Müller, P., Schwerhoff, M., Summers, A.J.: Viper: A Verification Infrastructure for Permission-Based Reasoning. In: Verification, Model Checking, and Abstract Interpretation (VMCAI) (2016)
55. Pasareanu, C.S., Mehlitz, P.C., Bushnell, D.H., Gundy-Burlet, K., Lowry, M.R., Person, S., Pape, M.: Combining unit-level symbolic execution and system-level concrete execution for testing NASA software. In: International Symposium on Software Testing and Analysis (ISSTA) (2008)
56. Siegel, S.F., Mironova, A., Avrunin, G.S., Clarke, L.A.: Using Model Checking with Symbolic Execution to Verify Parallel Numerical Programs. In: International Symposium on Software Testing and Analysis (ISSTA) (2006)
57. Solovyev, A., Jacobsen, C., Rakamaric, Z., Gopalakrishnan, G.: Rigorous Estimation of Floating-Point Round-off Errors with Symbolic Taylor Expansions. In: Formal Methods (FM) (2015)

Helmholtz: A Verifier for Tezos Smart Contracts Based on Refinement Types

Yuki Nishida[1]([✉])[ID], Hiromasa Saito[1], Ran Chen[1],
Akira Kawata[1]*, Jun Furuse[2],
Kohei Suenaga[1][ID], and Atsushi Igarashi[1][ID]

[1] Kyoto University, Kyoto, Japan
{nishida,hsaito,aran,akira,ksuenaga,igarashi}@fos.kuis.kyoto-u.ac.jp
[2] DaiLambda, Inc., Kyoto, Japan
jun.furuse@dailambda.jp

Abstract. A *smart contract* is a program executed on a blockchain, based on which many cryptocurrencies are implemented, and is being used for automating transactions. Due to the large amount of money that smart contracts deal with, there is a surging demand for a method that can statically and formally verify them.

This tool paper describes our type-based static verification tool HELMHOLTZ for Michelson, which is a statically typed stack-based language for writing smart contracts that are executed on the blockchain platform Tezos. HELMHOLTZ is designed on top of our extension of Michelson's type system with refinement types. HELMHOLTZ takes a Michelson program annotated with a user-defined specification written in the form of a refinement type as input; it then typechecks the program against the specification based on the refinement type system, discharging the generated verification conditions with the SMT solver Z3. We briefly introduce our refinement type system for the core calculus Mini-Michelson of Michelson, which incorporates the characteristic features such as compound datatypes (e.g., lists and pairs), higher-order functions, and invocation of another contract. HELMHOLTZ successfully verifies several practical Michelson programs, including one that transfers money to an account and that checks a digital signature.

1 Introduction

A *blockchain* is a data structure to implement a distributed ledger in a trustless yet secure way. The idea of blockchains is initially devised for the Bitcoin cryptocurrency [12] platform. Many cryptocurrencies are implemented using blockchains, in which value equivalent to a significant amount of money is exchanged.

Recently, many cryptocurrency platforms allow programs to be executed on a blockchain. Such programs are called *smart contracts* [19] (or, simply a *contract* in this paper) since they work as a device to enable automated execution of a contract. In general, a smart contract is a program P_a associated with an account

---

* Current affiliation: Preferred Networks, Inc.

© The Author(s) 2021
J. F. Groote and K. G. Larsen (Eds.): TACAS 2021, LNCS 12652, pp. 262–280, 2021.
https://doi.org/10.1007/978-3-030-72013-1_14

a on a blockchain. When the account a receives money from another account b with a parameter v, the computation defined in P_a is conducted, during which the state of the account a (e.g., the balance of the account and values that are stored by the previous invocations of P_a) which is recorded on the blockchain may be updated. The contract P_a may execute money transactions to another account (say c), which results in invocations of other contracts (say P_c) during or after the computation; therefore, contract invocations may be chained.

Although smart contracts' original motivation was handling simple transactions (e.g., money transfer) among the accounts on a blockchain, recent contracts are being used for more complicated purposes (e.g., establishing a fund involving multiple accounts). Following this trend, the languages for writing smart contracts also evolve from those that allow a contract to execute relatively simple transactions (e.g., Script for Bitcoin) to those that allow a program that is as complex as one written in standard programming languages (e.g., EVM for Ethereum and Michelson [1] for Tezos [4]).

Due to a large amount of money they deal with, verification of smart contracts is imperative. *Static* verification is especially needed since a smart contract cannot be fixed once deployed on a blockchain. Attack on a vulnerable contract indeed happened. For example, the DAO attack, in which the vulnerability of a fundraising contract was exploited, resulted in the loss of cryptocurrency equivalent to approximately 150M USD [18].

In this paper, we describe our type-based static verifier HELMHOLTZ[3] for smart contracts written in Michelson. The Michelson language is a statically- and simply typed stack-based language equipped with rich data types (e.g., lists, maps, and higher-order functions) and primitives to manipulate them. Although several high-level languages that compile to Michelson are being developed, Michelson is most widely used to write a smart contract for Tezos as of writing.

A Michelson program expresses the above computation in a purely functional style, in which the Michelson program corresponding to P_a is defined as a function. The function takes a pair of the parameter v and a value s that represents the current state of the account (called *storage*) and returns a pair of a list of *operations* and the updated storage s'. Here, an operation is a Michelson value that expresses the computation (e.g., transferring money to an account and invoking the contract associated with the account) that is to be conducted after the current computation (i.e., P_a) terminates. After the computation specified by P_a finishes with a pair of a storage value and an operation list, a blockchain system invokes the computation specified in the operation list. This purely functional style admits static verification methods for Michelson programs similar to those for standard functional languages.

As the theoretical foundation of HELMHOLTZ, we design a refinement type system for Michelson as an extension of the original simple type system. In contrast to standard refinement types that refine the types of values, our type

---

[3] Hermann von Helmholtz (1821–1894), a German physicist and physician, was a doctoral advisor of Albert A. Michelson (1852–1931), whom the Michelson language is apparently named after.

system refines the type of *stacks*. We briefly describe our type system in Section 3; a detailed explanation is deferred to a future paper.

We show that our tool can verify several practical smart contracts. In addition to the contracts we wrote ourselves, we apply our tool to the sample Michelson programs used in Mi-cho-coq [3], a formalization of Michelson in Coq proof assistant [21]. These contracts consist of practical contracts such as one that checks a digital signature and one that transfers money.

We note that HELMHOLTZ currently supports approximately 80% of the whole instructions of the Michelson language. Another limitation of the current HELMHOLTZ is that it can verify only a single contract, although one often uses multiple contracts for an application, in which a contract may call another by a money transfer operation, and their behavior as a whole is of interest. We are currently extending HELMHOLTZ so that it can deal with more programs.

Our contribution is summarized as follows: (1) Definition of the core calculus Mini-Michelson and its refinement type system; (2) Automated verification tool HELMHOLTZ for Michelson contracts implemented based on the type system of Mini-Michelson; the interface to the implementation can be found at https: //www.fos.kuis.kyoto-u.ac.jp/trylang/Helmholtz; and (3) Evaluation of HELM-HOLTZ with various Michelson contracts, including practical ones.

The rest of this paper is organized as follows. Before introducing the technical details, we present an overview of the verifier HELMHOLTZ in Section 2 using a simple example of a Michelson contract. Section 3 introduces the core calculus Mini-Michelson and its refinement type system. Section 4 describes the verifier HELMHOLTZ, a case study, and experimental results. After discussing related work in Section 5, we conclude in Section 6.

2   Overview of Helmholtz and Michelson

We overview our tool HELMHOLTZ in this section before presenting its technical details. We also explain Michelson by example (Section 2.2) and user-written annotation added to a Michelson program for verification purposes (Section 2.3).

2.1   Helmholtz

As input, HELMHOLTZ takes a Michelson program annotated with (1) its specification expressed in a refinement type and (2) additional user annotations such as loop invariants. It typechecks the annotated program against the specification using our refinement type system; the verification conditions generated during the typechecking is discharged by the SMT solver Z3 [11]. If the code successfully typechecks, then the program is guaranteed to satisfy the specification.

HELMHOLTZ is implemented as a subcommand of `tezos-client`, the client program of the Tezos blockchain. For example, to verify `boomerang.tz` in Figure 1, we run `tezos-client refinement boomerang.tz`. If the verification succeeds, the command outputs `VERIFIED` to the terminal screen (with a few log messages); otherwise, it outputs `UNVERIFIED`.

```
1    parameter unit;
2    storage unit;
3    << ContractAnnot { (param, st) | True } ->
4       { (ops, st') | amount = 0 && ops = [] ||
5          amount <> 0 && ops = [Transfer Unit amount (Contract source)]}
6       & { _ | False } >>
7    code                    /* (param,st) */
8    { CDR;                   /* st */
9      NIL operation;         /* [] ▷ st */
10     AMOUNT;                /* amount ▷ [] ▷ st */
11     PUSH mutez 0;          /* 0 ▷ amount ▷ [] ▷ st */
12     IFCMPEQ
13       {                    /* [] ▷ st   (amount ≤ 0) */ }
14       {                    /* [] ▷ st   (amount > 0) */
15         SOURCE;            /* src ▷ [] ▷ st */
16         CONTRACT unit;     /* Some (Contract src) ▷ [] ▷ st */
17         ASSERT_SOME;       /* (Contract src) ▷ [] ▷ st */
18         AMOUNT; UNIT;      /* Unit ▷ amount ▷ (Contract src) ▷ [] ▷ st */
19         TRANSFER_TOKENS;   /* Transfer Unit amount (Contract src) ▷ [] ▷ st */
20         CONS               /* [Transfer Unit amount (Contract src)] ▷ st */
21       };
22              /* ops ▷ st, where ops is the top element at the end of each branch, namely,
23                 [Transfer Unit amount (Contract src)] if amount > 0; or [] otherwise */
24     PAIR    /* (ops, st) */
25   }
```

Fig. 1. boomerang.tz. The comment inside /* */ describes the stack at the program point.

2.2   An Example Contract in Michelson

Figure 1 shows an example of a Michelson program called boomerang. A Michelson program is associated with an account on the Tezos blockchain; the program is invoked by transferring money to this account. This artificial program in Figure 1, when it is invoked, is supposed to transfer the received money back to the account that initiated the transaction.

A Michelson program starts with type declarations of its parameter, whose value is given by contract invocation, and storage, which is the state that the contract account stores. Lines 1–2 declare that the types of both are unit, the type inhabited by the only value Unit. Lines 3–6 surrounded by << and >> are a user-written annotation used by HELMHOLTZ for verification; we will explain this annotation later. The code section in Lines 8–24 is the body of this program.

Let us take a look at the code section of the program. In the following explanation of each instruction, we describe the state of the stack after each instruction as comments; stack elements are delimited by ▷.

- Execution of a Michelson program starts with a stack with one value, which is a pair (param, st) of a parameter param and a storage value storage.
- CDR pops the pair at the top of the stack and pushes the second value of the popped pair; therefore, after executing the instruction, the stack contains the single value st.
- NIL pushes the empty list [] to the stack; the instruction is accompanied by the type operation of the list elements for typechecking purposes.

- AMOUNT pushes the nonnegative **amount** of the money sent to the account to which this program is associated.
- PUSH mutez 0 pushes the value 0. The type **mutez** represents a unit of money used in Tezos.
- IFCMPEQ b1 b2, if the state of the stack before executing the instruction is v1 ▷ v2 ▷ tl, (1) pops v1 and v2 and (2) executes the then-branch b1 (resp., the else-branch b2) if v2 = v1 (resp., v2 ≠ v1). In boomerang, this instruction does nothing if amount = 0; otherwise, the instructions in the else-branch are executed.
- SOURCE at the beginning of the else-branch pushes the address **src** of the source account, which initiated the chain of contract invocations that the current contract belongs to, resulting in the stack src ▷ [] ▷ st.
- CONTRACT T pops an address **addr** from the stack and typechecks whether the contract associated with addr takes an argument of type T. If the typechecking succeeds, then Some (Contract addr) is pushed; otherwise, None is pushed. The constructor Contract creates an object that represents a typechecked contract at the given address. In Tezos, the source account is always a contract that takes the value Unit as a parameter; thus, Some (Contract src) will always be pushed onto the stack.
- ASSERT_SOME pops a value v from the stack and pushes v' if v is Some v'; otherwise, it raises an exception.
- UNIT pushes the unit value Unit to the stack.
- TRANSFER_TOKENS, if the stack is of the shape varg ▷ vamt ▷ vcontr ▷ tl, pops varg, vamt, and vcontr from the stack and pushes (Transfer varg vamt vcontr) onto tl. The value Transfer varg vamt vcontr is an *operation object* expressing that money (of amount vamt) shall be sent to the account vcontr with the argument varg after this program finishes without raising an exception. Therefore, the program associated with vcontr is invoked after this program finishes.
- CONS with the stack v1 ▷ v2 ▷ tl pops v1 and v2, and pushes a cons list v1::v2 onto the stack. (We use the list notation in OCaml here.)
- After executing one of the branches associated with IFCMPEQ in this program, the shape of the stack should be ops ▷ storage, where ops is [] if amount = 0 or [Transfer varg vamt vcontr] if amount > 0. The instruction PAIR pops ops and storage, and pushes (ops,storage).

A Michelson program is supposed to finish its execution with a singleton stack whose unique element is a pair of (1) a list of operations to be executed after the current execution of the contract finishes and (2) the new value for the storage.

Michelson is a statically typed language. Each instruction is associated with a typing rule that specifies the shapes of stacks before and after it by a sequence of simple types such as int and int list. For example, CONS requires the type of top element to be T and that of the second to be T list (for any T); it ensures the top element after it has type T list.

Other notable features of Michelson include first-class functions, hashing, instructions related to cryptography such as signature verification, and manipulation of a blockchain using operations.

2.3 Specification

A user can specify the behavior of a program by a `ContractAnnot` annotation, which is a part of the augmented syntax of our verification tool. A `ContractAnnot` annotation gives a specification of a Michelson program by the following notation inspired by the refinement types: {(param,st) | pre} -> {(ops,st') | post} & {exc | abpost} where pre, post, and abpost are predicates. This specification reads as follows: if this program is invoked with a parameter param and storage st that satisfies the property pre, then (1) if the execution of this program succeeds, then it returns a list of operations ops and new storage `storage'` that satisfy the property post; (2) if this program raises an exception with value exc, then exc satisfies abpost. The specification language is expressive enough to cover the specifications for practical contracts, including the ones we used in the experiments in Section 4.3. In the predicates, one can use several keywords such as amount for the amount of the money sent to this program when it is invoked and source for the source account's address.

The `ContractAnnot` annotation in Figure 1 (Lines 3–6) formalizes this program's specification as follows. This program can take any parameter and storage (Line 3). Successful execution of this program results in a pair (ops,st') that satisfies the condition in Lines 4–5 that expresses (1) if amount = 0, then ops is empty, that is, no operation will be issued; (2) if amount > 0, then ops is a list of a single element `Transfer Unit amount (Contract source)`, which expresses transfer of money of the amount amount to the account at source with the unit argument.[4] In the specification language, source and amount are keywords that stand for the source account and the amount of money sent to this program, respectively. The part & { _ | False } expresses that this program does not raise an exception. This specification correctly formalizes the intended behavior of this program.

3 Refinement Type System for Mini-Michelson

In this section, we formalize Mini-Michelson, a core subset of Michelson with its syntax, operational semantics, and refinement type system. We also state that the type system is sound. We omit many features from the full language in favor of conciseness but includes language constructs—such as higher-order functions and iterations—that make verification difficult.

Figure 2 shows the syntax of Mini-Michelson. *Values*, ranged over by V, consist of integers i; addresses a; operations $\text{transaction}(V, i, a)$ to invoke a contract at a by sending money of amount i and an argument V; pairs (V_1, V_2) of values; the empty list $[\,]$; cons $V_1 :: V_2$; and code $\langle IS \rangle$ of first-class functions.[5]

---

[4] As we mentioned in Section 1, HELMHOLTZ can currently verify the behavior of a single contract, although there will be an invocation of the contract associated with **source** after the termination of **boomerang**. An operation is treated as an opaque data structure, from which one cannot extract values.

[5] Closures are not needed because functions in Michelson can access only arguments.

$$V ::= i \mid a \mid \mathtt{transaction}\,(V, i, a) \mid (V_1, V_2) \mid [\,] \mid V_1 :: V_2 \mid \langle IS \rangle$$
$$T ::= \mathtt{int} \mid \mathtt{address} \mid \mathtt{operation} \mid T_1 \times T_2 \mid T\,\mathtt{list} \mid T_1 \to T_2$$
$$IS ::= \{I_1; \ldots; I_n\}$$
$$I ::= IS \mid \mathtt{DIP}\,IS \mid \mathtt{DROP} \mid \mathtt{DUP} \mid \mathtt{SWAP} \mid \mathtt{PUSH}\,T\,V \mid \mathtt{NOT} \mid \mathtt{ADD} \mid \mathtt{IF}\,IS_1\,IS_2 \mid$$
$$\quad\quad \mathtt{LOOP}\,IS \mid \mathtt{PAIR} \mid \mathtt{CAR} \mid \mathtt{CDR} \mid \mathtt{NIL}\,T \mid \mathtt{CONS} \mid \mathtt{IF\_CONS}\,IS_1\,IS_2 \mid \mathtt{ITER}\,IS \mid$$
$$\quad\quad \mathtt{LAMBDA}\,T_1\,T_2\,IS \mid \mathtt{EXEC} \mid \mathtt{TRANSFER\_TOKENS}\,T$$

Fig. 2. Syntax of Mini-Michelson

Unlike Michelson, we use integers as a substitute for Boolean values so that 0 means *false* and the others mean *true*. *Simple types*, ranged over by T, consist of base types (int, address, and operation, which are self-explanatory), pair types $T_1 \times T_2$, list types $T\,\mathtt{list}$, and function types $T_1 \to T_2$. *Instruction sequences*, ranged over by IS, are a sequence of *instructions*, ranged over by I, enclosed by curly braces. A Mini-Michelson *program* is an instruction sequence.

Instructions include those for stack manipulation (to DROP, DUPlicate, SWAP, and PUSH values); NOT and ADD for manipulating integers; PAIR, CAR, and CDR for pairs; NIL and CONS for constructing lists; and TRANSFER_TOKENS to create an operation that expresses a money transfer after the current contract execution. The instruction IF branches depending on whether the stack top is 0 or not; IF_CONS branches on whether the stack top is a cons or not. The instruction LOOP IS repeats IS as long as the stack top is a nonzero integer at the loop entry; ITER IS is for iterating the list at the stack top. LAMBDA pushes a function (described by its operand IS) onto the stack, and EXEC calls a function. Perhaps unfamiliar is DIP IS, which pops and saves the stack top somewhere else, executes IS, and then pushes the saved value back.

We also use a few kinds of stacks in the following definitions: value stacks, ranged over by S, type stacks, ranged over by $\bar{T}$, and type binding stacks, ranged over by Υ, of the form $x_1 : T_1 \triangleright .. \triangleright x_n : T_n$. The empty stack is denoted by $\ddagger$, and push is by $\triangleright$. We often omit the empty stack and write, for example, $V_1 \triangleright V_2$ for $V_1 \triangleright V_2 \triangleright \ddagger$. Intuitively, $T_1 \triangleright .. \triangleright T_n$ and $x_1 : T_1 \triangleright .. \triangleright x_n : T_n$ describe stacks $V_1 \triangleright .. \triangleright V_n$ where each value V_i is of type T_i. We will use variables to name stack elements in the refinement type system.

Mini-Michelson (as well as Michelson) is equipped with a simple type system. The type judgment for instructions is written $\bar{T} \vdash I \Rightarrow \bar{T}'$, which means that instruction I transforms a stack of type $\bar{T}$ into another stack of type $\bar{T}'$. The type judgment for values is written $V : T$, which means that V is given simple type T. We omit typing rules as they are fairly straightforward.

3.1 Operational Semantics

We give a big-step operational semantics of Mini-Michelson by defining the judgment $S \vdash I \Downarrow S'$, which means that executing the instruction I under the stack S results in the stack S', (and also $S \vdash IS \Downarrow S'$). Most rules for $S \vdash I \Downarrow S'$ are straightforward. We show rules for DIP and LOOP below and omit other rules.

$$\frac{S \vdash IS \Downarrow S'}{V \rhd S \vdash \text{DIP } IS \Downarrow V \rhd S'} \qquad \frac{S \vdash IS \Downarrow S' \qquad S' \vdash \text{LOOP } IS \Downarrow S'' \qquad (i \neq 0)}{i \rhd S \vdash \text{LOOP } IS \Downarrow S''} \qquad \frac{}{0 \rhd S \vdash \text{LOOP } IS \Downarrow S}$$

The first rule means that the body IS is executed with the stack S obtained by removing the top element V, which is pushed back onto the resulting stack S'. There are two rules for LOOP: the first rule means that if the stack top is nonzero, then the body is executed, and then the execution of LOOP IS is repeated; the second rule means that, if the stack top is zero, then the loop acts as a no-op.

3.2 Refinement Type System

In the refinement type system, a simple stack type $T_1 \rhd .. \rhd T_n$ is augmented with a formula φ of first-order logic to describe the relationship among stack elements. We introduce *refinement stack types*, ranged over by Φ, of the form $\{x_1 : T_1 \rhd ... \rhd x_n : T_n \mid \varphi(x_1, ..., x_n)\}$, which denotes stacks $V_1 \rhd .. \rhd V_n$ such that $V_1 : T_1, ..., V_n : T_n$ and $\varphi(V_1, ..., V_n)$ hold.

We show (part of) the syntax of terms and formulae of the first-order logic:

$$t ::= x \mid V \mid \text{transaction}\,(t_1, t_2, t_3) \mid t_1 :: t_2 \mid (t_1, t_2) \mid t_1 + t_2 \mid \cdots$$
$$\varphi ::= t_1 = t_2 \mid \text{call}\,(t_1, t_2) = t_3 \mid \varphi_1 \vee \varphi_2 \mid \neg \varphi \mid \exists x : T.\varphi \mid \cdots$$

The language for predicates is multi-sorted, where a sort is a simple type of Michelson. The sorting rules for term constructors and relation symbols are standard. For example, in $t_1 + t_2$, both t_1 and t_2 have to be of sorts int; and in $t_1 = t_2$, the sorts of t_1 and t_2 must be the same, and so on. The only relation symbol worth explaining is call $(t_1, t_2) = t_3$, which informally means that calling function t_1 with argument t_2 (as the only element of the input stack) yields a stack consisting only of t_3 as a result. We use other predicates, connectives, and quantifiers such as $t_1 \neq t_2$, $\varphi_1 \wedge \varphi_{12}$, $\varphi_1 \implies \varphi_2$, and $\forall x : T.\varphi$, which can be considered as derived forms.

We define the semantics of the formulae in a standard manner. Let σ be a *value assignment*, i.e., a sort-respecting finite map from variables to values. We define the interpretation $[\![t]\!]_\sigma$ of t under σ and *valid* formulae under a value assignment, denoted by $\sigma \models \varphi$; for call $(t_1, t_2) = t_3$, we define $\sigma \models$ call $(t_1, t_2) = t_3$ iff $[\![t_2]\!]_\sigma \rhd \ddagger \vdash [\![t_1]\!]_\sigma \Downarrow [\![t_3]\!]_\sigma \rhd \ddagger$. Equality on instruction sequences is intensional: formula $\langle IS \rangle = \langle IS' \rangle$ is valid only if IS and IS' are syntactically equal.

For a finite mapping Γ (called a type environment) from variables to sorts, $\Gamma \models \sigma$ and $\Gamma \models \varphi$ are defined as usual: $\Gamma \models \sigma$ iff $\text{dom}\,(\sigma) = \text{dom}\,(\Gamma)$ and $\sigma(x) : \Gamma(x)$ for any $x \in \text{dom}\,(\sigma)$; $\Gamma \models \varphi$ iff $\sigma \models \varphi$ for any value assignment σ such that $\Gamma \models \sigma$.

The type system is equipped with subtyping whose judgment is of the form $\Gamma \vdash \Phi_1 <: \Phi_2$, which means stack type Φ_1 is a subtype of Φ_2 under Γ. The type judgment for instructions (resp. instruction sequences) is of the form $\Gamma \vdash \Phi_1 \, I \, \Phi_2$ (resp. $\Gamma \vdash \Phi_1 \, IS \, \Phi_2$), which means that, under Γ, if I (resp. IS) is executed under a stack satisfying Φ_1, the resulting stack (if the execution terminates) satisfies Φ_2. We often call Φ_1 *pre-condition* and Φ_2 *post-condition*.

We show representative typing rules in Figure 3.

$$\frac{\Gamma, x : T \vdash \{\Upsilon \mid \varphi\} \; IS \; \{\Upsilon' \mid \varphi'\}}{\Gamma \vdash \{x : T \triangleright \Upsilon \mid \varphi\} \; \mathtt{DIP} \; IS \; \{x : T \triangleright \Upsilon' \mid \varphi'\}} \quad \text{(RT-Dip)}$$

$$\frac{\Gamma \vdash \{\Upsilon \mid \exists x : \mathtt{int}.\varphi \, \wedge \, x \neq 0\} \; IS_1 \; \Phi \qquad \Gamma \vdash \{\Upsilon \mid \exists x : \mathtt{int}.\varphi \, \wedge \, x = 0\} \; IS_2 \; \Phi}{\Gamma \vdash \{x : \mathtt{int} \triangleright \Upsilon \mid \varphi\} \; \mathtt{IF} \; IS_1 \; IS_2 \; \Phi} \quad \text{(RT-If)}$$

$$\frac{\Gamma \vdash \{\Upsilon \mid \exists x : \mathtt{int}.\varphi \, \wedge \, x \neq 0\} \; IS \; \{x : \mathtt{int} \triangleright \Upsilon \mid \varphi\}}{\Gamma \vdash \{x : \mathtt{int} \triangleright \Upsilon \mid \varphi\} \; \mathtt{LOOP} \; IS \; \{\Upsilon \mid \exists x : \mathtt{int}.\varphi \, \wedge \, x = 0\}} \quad \text{(RT-Loop)}$$

$$\frac{y_1' : T_1 \vdash \{y_1 : T_1 \mid y_1' = y_1 \, \wedge \, \varphi_1\} \; IS \; \{y_2 : T_2 \mid \varphi_2\}}{\Gamma \vdash \{\Upsilon \mid \varphi\} \; \mathtt{LAMBDA} \; T_1 \; T_2 \; IS}$$
$$\{x : T_1 \to T_2 \triangleright \Upsilon \mid \varphi \, \wedge \, \forall y_1' : T_1, y_2 : T_2.\varphi_1[y_1 := y_1'] \, \wedge \, \mathtt{call}\,(x, y_1') = y_2 \implies \varphi_2\} \quad \text{(RT-Lambda)}$$

$$\overline{\Gamma \vdash \{x_1 : T_1 \triangleright x_2 : T_1 \to T_2 \triangleright \Upsilon \mid \varphi\} \; \mathtt{EXEC} \; \{x_3 : T_2 \triangleright \Upsilon \mid \exists x_1 : T_1, x_2 : T_1 \to T_2.\varphi \wedge \mathtt{call}\,(x_2, x_1) = x_3\}} \quad \text{(RT-Exec)}$$

$$\frac{\Gamma \vdash \Phi_1 <: \Phi_1' \qquad \Gamma \vdash \Phi_1' \; I \; \Phi_2' \qquad \Gamma \vdash \Phi_2' <: \Phi_2}{\Gamma \vdash \Phi_1 \; I \; \Phi_2} \quad \text{(RT-Sub)}$$

Fig. 3. Typing rules (excerpt)

- (RT-Dip) means that DIP IS is well typed if the body IS is typed under the stack type obtained by removing the top element. The popped value named x is moved to the type environment part so that it can be referred to in the refinement predicate φ in the pre-condition.
- (RT-If) means that the instruction is well typed if both branches have the same post-condition; the pre-conditions of the branches are strengthened by the assumptions that the top of the input stack is true ($x \neq 0$) and false ($x = 0$). The variable x is existentially quantified because the top element will be removed before the execution of either branch.
- (RT-Loop) is similar to the proof rule for while-loops in Hoare logic. The formula φ is a loop invariant. Since the body of LOOP is executed while the stack top is nonzero, the pre-condition for the body IS is strengthened by $x \neq 0$, whereas the post-condition of LOOP IS is strengthened by $x = 0$.
- (RT-Lambda) is for the instruction to push a first-class function onto the operand stack. The premise of the rule means that the body IS takes a value (named y_1) of type T_1 that satisfies φ_1 and outputs a value (named y_2) of type T_2 that satisfies φ_2 (if it terminates). The post-condition in the conclusion expresses, by using $\mathtt{call}$, that the function x has the property above. The extra variable y_1' in the type environment of the premise is an alias of y_1; being a variable declared in the type environment y_1' can appear in both φ_1 and φ_2[6] and can describe the relationship between the input and output of the function.
- (RT-Exec) adds $\mathtt{call}\,(x_2, x_1) = x_3$ to the post-condition, meaning that the result of a call to the function x_2 with x_1 as an argument yields x_3. It may look simpler than expected; the crux here is that φ is expected to imply $\forall x_1 : T_1, x_3 : T_2.\varphi_1 \wedge \mathtt{call}\,(x_2, x_1) = x_3 \implies \varphi_2$, where φ_1 and φ_2 represent

---

[6] The scope of a variable in a refinement stack type is its predicate part and so y_1 cannot appear in the post-condition.

the pre- and post-conditions, respectively, of function x_2. If x_1 satisfies φ_1, then we can derive that φ_2 holds.

- (RT-SUB) is the rule for subsumption to strengthening the pre-condition and weakening the post-condition. In our type system, subtyping is defined semantically: A *subtyping* judgment $\Gamma \vdash \{\Upsilon \mid \varphi_1\} <: \{\Upsilon \mid \varphi_2\}$ holds if for any σ such that $\forall x \in \text{dom}\,(\Gamma, \Upsilon).\sigma(x) : (\Gamma, \Upsilon)(x)$, $\sigma \models \varphi_1 \implies \varphi_2$ is valid. (Here, by abuse of notation, the type binding stack Υ is regarded as a mapping from variables to sorts.)

We state that our type system is *sound*: For a well-typed instruction, if we execute the instruction under a stack that satisfies the pre-condition of the typing, then (if the execution halts) the resulting stack satisfies the post-condition of the typing. To state the soundness theorem, we define an auxiliary relation $\Gamma \models S : \Phi$, which means "stack S satisfies stack refinement type Φ under environment Γ", by: $\Gamma \models V_1 \rhd .. \rhd V_m : \{y_1 : T_1' \rhd .. \rhd y_m : T_m' \mid \varphi\} \iff V_1 : T_1', \ldots, V_m : T_m'$ and $\sigma[y_1 \mapsto V_1, .., y_m \mapsto V_m] \models \varphi$ for any σ such that $\Gamma \models \sigma$.

Then, the soundness theorem, whose proof will appear in a forthcoming full version, is stated as follows:

Theorem 1 (Soundness). *If* $\Gamma \vdash \Phi_1$ *IS* Φ_2, $\Gamma \models S : \Phi_1$, *and* $S \vdash$ *IS* $\Downarrow S'$, *then* $\Gamma \models S' : \Phi_2$.

Sketch of Typechecking We implement a typechecking algorithm as follows. Given a type environment, a pre-condition, and a post-condition, our algorithm computes the strongest post-condition of the code starting from the given pre-condition. This computation is conducted according to the syntax-directed version of the typing rules created essentially in the same way as a type system with subtyping (e.g., one described in [15]). An application of the subtyping generates verification conditions. The accumulated verification conditions are fed to Z3; the typechecking succeeds if they are successfully discharged.

3.3   Extensions

The implementation supports a few extensions of the formalization explained above, which are explained below.

The type system implemented in HELMHOLTZ is extended with refinements for values thrown by raising exceptions. For example, the typing rule for instruction FAILWITH, which raises an exception with the value at the stack top, is given as follows:

$$\Gamma \vdash \{x : T \rhd \Upsilon \mid \varphi\} \text{ FAILWITH } \{\Upsilon \mid \bot\}\&\{\text{err} \mid \exists x : T, \Upsilon.\varphi \wedge x = \text{err}\}.$$

The rule expresses that, if FAILWITH is executed under a non-empty stack that satisfies φ, then the program point just after the instruction is not reachable (hence, $\{\Upsilon \mid \bot\}$). The refinement $\exists x : T, \Upsilon.\varphi \wedge x = \text{err}$ for the exception case states that φ in the pre-condition with the top element x is equal to the raised value **err**; since x is not in the scope in the exception refinement, x is bound by an existential quantifier. The typing rules for the other instructions can be extended with the "&" part easily.

HELMHOLTZ deals with measure functions introduced by Kawaguchi et al. [9] and supported by Liquid Haskell [23]. If a measure function is defined by a **Measure** annotation, HELMHOLTZ "weaves" the function definition into relevant typing rules. For instance, given the annotation **Measure len : list int -> int where [] = 0 | h :: t = (1 + len t)**, HELMHOLTZ assumes an uninterpreted function symbol **len** and augments (RT-NIL) and (RT-CONS) as follows, where the last equality in each post-condition comes from the definition of **len**.

$$\Gamma \vdash \{\Upsilon \mid \varphi\} \, \text{NIL} \, T \, \{x : T \, \text{list} \triangleright \Upsilon \mid \varphi \land x = [\,] \land \text{len}\,[\,] = 0\}$$

$$\Gamma \vdash \{x_1 : T \triangleright x_2 : T \, \text{list} \triangleright \Upsilon \mid \varphi\} \, \text{CONS} \, \{x_3 : T \, \text{list} \triangleright \Upsilon \mid \exists x_1 : T, x_2 : T \, \text{list}.\varphi \land x_1 :: \\ x_2 = x_3 \land \text{len}\,(x_1 :: x_2) = 1 + \text{len}\,x_2\}$$

4   Tool Implementation

In this section, we discuss annotations in detail, show a case study of contract verification, and present verification experiments.

4.1   Annotations

HELMHOLTZ supports several forms of annotations (surrounded by << and >> in the source code), other than **ContractAnnot** explained in Section 2.

Assert Φ and **Assume** Φ can appear before or after an instruction. The former asserts that the stack at the annotated program location satisfies the type Φ; the assertion is verified by HELMHOLTZ. If there is an annotation **Assume** Φ, HELMHOLTZ assumes that the stack satisfies the type Φ at the annotated program location. A user can give a hint to HELMHOLTZ by using **Assume** Φ. The user has to make sure that it is correct; if an **Assume** annotation is incorrect, the verification result may be incorrect.

LoopInv Φ asserts the loop invariant of a loop instruction (e.g., **LOOP** and **ITER**). In the current implementation, annotating a loop invariant using **LoopInv** Φ is mandatory. HELMHOLTZ checks that Φ is indeed a loop invariant and uses it to verify the rest of the program.

In the current implementation, a **LAMBDA** instruction, which pushes a function on the top of the stack, must be accompanied by the **LambdaAnnot** annotation, where $\Phi_{\text{pre}} \to \Phi_{\text{post}}$ & Φ_{abpost} is a specification of the pushed function and the bindings $(x_1 : T_1, \ldots, x_n : T_n)$ introduce the ghost variables that can be used in the annotations in the body of the annotated **LAMBDA** instruction;[7] one can omit the declaration of ghost variables if it is empty. The first contract in Figure 4, which pushes a function that takes a pair of integers and returns the sum of them, presents an example of **LambdaAnnot**. The annotated type of the function (Line 5)

---

[7] **ContractAnnot** also allows declarations of ghost variable used in the **code** section.

```
1    parameter unit ;
2    storage int;
3    << ContractAnnot { _ | True } -> { _ | True } & { _ | False } >>
4    code { DROP;
5         << LambdaAnnot { p | p = (3, 1) } -> { x | x = 4 } & { _ | False }
6            (a:int, b:int) >>
7         LAMBDA (pair int int) int
8         { << Assume { p | p = (a, b) } >>
9           UNPAIR; ADD
10          << Assert { p | p = a + b } >>
11        };
12        PUSH int 1; PUSH int 3; PAIR; EXEC;
13        << Assert { x | x = 4 } >>
14        NIL operation; PAIR
15     }
```

```
1    parameter (list int);
2    storage int;
3    << Measure len : list int -> int where [] = 0 | h :: t = (1 + len t) >>
4    << ContractAnnot
5       { (p, _) | True } -> { (_, ret) | len p = ret } & { _ | False } >>
6    code { CAR; PUSH int 0; SWAP;
7         << LoopInv { l : n | len l + n = len p } >>
8         ITER { DROP; PUSH int 1; ADD };
9         NIL operation;
10        PAIR
11     }
```

Fig. 4. `lambda.tz`, which uses higher-order functions, and `length.tz`, which uses a measure function in the contract annotation.

expresses that it returns 4 if it is fed with a pair $(3, 1)$. The ghost variables a and b are used in the annotations Assume (Line 8) and Assert (Line 10) in the body to denote the first and the second arguments of the pair passed to this function.

HELMHOLTZ allows user-defined (recursive) functions to be used in annotations; these functions are called *measure functions* following the terminology of Liquid-Haskell [9]. The annotation Measure $x : T_1 \to T_2$ where $p_1 = e_1 | \cdots | p_n = e_n$ defines a recursive function x that takes a value of type T_1, destructs it by the pattern matching, and returns a value of type T_2. Metavariables p and e represent ML-like patterns and expressions. The second contract in Figure 4, which computes the length of the list passed as a parameter, exemplifies the usage of the Measure annotation. This contract defines a measure function len that takes a list of integers and returns its type; it is used in ContractAnnot and LoopInv.

4.2 Case Study: Contract with Signature Verification

Figure 5 presents the code of the contract `checksig.tz`, which verifies that a sender indeed signed certain data using her private key. This contract uses instruction CHECK_SIGNATURE, which is supposed to be executed under a stack of the form key ▷ sig ▷ bytes ▷ tl, where key is a public key, sig is a signature, and bytes is some data. CHECK_SIGNATURE pops these three values from the

```
1    parameter (pair signature string);
2    storage (pair address key);
3    << ContractAnnot
4       { (param, store) | match Contract store.first with
5                            Contract<string> _ -> True | _ -> False } ->
6       { (ops, new_store) | store = new_store &&
7            sig store.second param.first (Pack param.second) &&
8            ops = [ Transfer param.second 1 (Contract store.first) ] }
9       & { _ | not (sig store.second param.first (Pack param.second)) } >>
10   code  { DUP; DUP; DUP;
11          DIP { CAR; UNPAIR; DIP { PACK } }; CDDR;
12          CHECK_SIGNATURE; ASSERT;
13
14          UNPAIR; CDR; SWAP; CAR;
15          CONTRACT string; ASSERT_SOME; SWAP;
16          PUSH mutez 1; SWAP;
17          TRANSFER_TOKENS;
18
19          NIL operation; SWAP;
20          CONS; DIP { CDR };
21          PAIR
22        }
```

Fig. 5. checksig.tz, which involves signature verification.

stack and pushes **true** if **sig** is the valid signature for **bytes** with the private key corresponding to **key**.

The intended behavior of **checksig.tz** is as follows. It stores a pair of an address **addr**, which is the address of a contract that takes a **string** parameter, and a public key **key** in its storage. It takes a pair (sig,s) of type **pair signature string** as a parameter where **signature** is the primitive Michelson type for signatures. This contract terminates without exception if **sig** is created from the serialized (packed) representation of **s** and signed by the private key corresponding to **key**. In a normal termination, this contract transfers 1 **mutez** to the contract with address **addr**. If this signature verification fails, then an exception is raised.

This behavior is expressed as a specification in the **ContractAnnot** annotation in **checksig.tz** as follows.

- The refinement of its pre-condition part expresses that the address stored in the first element **store.first** of the storage **store** is an address of a contract that takes a value of type **string** as a parameter. This is expressed by the pattern-matching of **Contract store.first**, which represents the contract stored at the address **store.first**, to the pattern expression **Contract<string> _**, which matches a contract that takes a **string** value.
- The refinement of the post-condition forces the following three conditions: (1) the store is not updated by this contract (**store = new_store**); (2) **param.first** is the signature created from the packed string **Pack param. second** of the string in the second element of the parameter and signed by the private key corresponding to the second element **store.second** of the store (**sig store.second param.first (Pack param.second)**); and (3) the operations **ops** returned by this contract is [**Transfer param.second 1**

(Contract store.first)], which represents an operation of transferring 1 mutez to the contract Contract store.first with the parameter param. second. The predicate sig and the constructor Pack are primitives of HELM-HOLTZ that can be used in an annotation.

- The refinement in the exception part expresses that if an exception is raised, then the signature verification should have failed (not (sig store.second param.first (Pack param.second))).

HELMHOLTZ successfully verifies checksig.tz without any additional annotation in the code section. If we change the instruction ASSERT in Line 12 to DROP to let the contract drop the result of the signature verification (hence, an exception is not raised even if the signature verification fails), the verification fails as intended.

4.3   Experiments

We applied HELMHOLTZ to various contracts; Table 1 is an excerpt of the result, in which we show (1) the number of the instructions in each contract (column #instr.) and (2) time (ms) spent to verify each contract. The experiments are conducted on MacOS Catalina 10.15.7 with Dual-Core Intel Core i5 (1.8 GHz), 8 GB RAM. We used Z3 version 4.8.8. The contracts boomerang.tz, deposit.tz, manager.tz, vote.tz, and reservoir.tz are taken from the benchmark of Mi-cho-coq [3]. checksig.tz is derived from weather_insurance.tz of the official Tezos test suite.[8] vote_for_delegate.tz and xcat.tz are taken from the official test suite; xcat.tz is simplified from the original. triangular_num.tz is a simple test case that we made as an example of using LOOP. The source code of these contracts can be found at the Web interface of HELMHOLTZ. Each contract is supposed to work as follows.

- boomerang.tz: Transfers the received amount of money to the source account.
- deposit.tz: Transfers money to the sender if the address of the sender is identical to that is stored in the storage.
- manager.tz: Calls the passed function if the address of the caller matches the address stored in the storage.
- vote.tz: Accepts a vote to a candidate if the voter transfers enough voting fee, and stores the tally.
- checksig.tz: The one explained in Section 4.2.
- vote_for_delegate.tz: Delegates one's ballot in voting by stakeholders, which is one of the fundamental features of Tezos, to another using a primitive operation of Tezos.
- xcat.tz: Transfers all stored money to one of the two accounts specified beforehand if called with the correct password. The account that gets money is decided based on whether the contract is called before or after a deadline.

---

[8] https://gitlab.com/tezos/tezos/-/tree/ee2f75bb941522acbcf6d5065a9f3b2/tests_python/contracts/mini_scenarios

- `reservoir.tz`: Sends a certain amount of money to either a contract or another depending on whether the contract is executed before or after the deadline.
- `triangular_num.tz`: Calculates the sum from 1 to n, which is the passed parameter.

In the experiments, we verified that each contract indeed works according to the intention explained above. `triangular_num.tz` was the only contract that required a manual annotation for verification in the `code` section; we needed to specify a loop invariant in this contract.

Table 1. Benchmark result

Filename	#instr.	time (ms)	Filename	#instr.	time (ms)
boomerang.tz	17	35	checksig_unverified.tz	36	62
deposit.tz	24	54	vote_for_delegate.tz	87	143
manager.tz	29	60	xcat.tz	64	188
vote.tz	24	62	reservoir.tz	45	87
checksig.tz	38	65	triangular_num.tz	16	35

Although the numbers of instructions in these contracts are not large, they capture essential features of smart contracts; everyone except `triangular_num.tz` executes transactions; `deposit.tz` and `manager.tz` check the identity of the caller; and `checksig.tz` conducts signature verification. The time spent on verification is small.

5   Related Work

There are several publications on the formalization of programming languages for writing smart contracts. Hirai [7] formalizes EVM, a low-level smart contract language of Ethereum and its implementation, using Lem [13], a language to specify semantic definitions; definitions written in Lem can be compiled into definitions in Coq, HOL4, and Isabelle/HOL. Based on the generated definition, he verifies several properties of Ethereum smart contracts using Isabelle/HOL. Bernardo et al. [3] implemented Mi-Cho-Coq, a formalization of the semantics of Michelson using the Coq proof assistant. They also verified several Michelson contracts. Compared to their approach, we aim to develop an automated verification tool for smart contracts. Park et al. [14] developed a formal verification tool for EVM by using the K-framework [17], which can be used to derive a symbolic model checker from a formally specified language semantics (in this case, formalized EVM semantics [6]), and successfully applied the derived model checker to a few EVM contracts. It would be interesting to formalize the semantics of Michelson in the K-framework to compare HELMHOLTZ with the derived model checker.

The DAO attack [18], mentioned in Section 1, is one of the notorious attacks on a smart contract. It exploits a vulnerability of a smart contract that is related to a callback. Grossman et al. [5] proposed a type-based technique to verify that execution of a smart contract that may contain callbacks is equivalent to another execution without any callback. This property, called *effectively callback freedom*, can be seen as one of the criteria for execution of a smart contract not to be vulnerable to the DAO-like attack. Their type system focuses on verifying the ECF property of *execution* of a smart contract, whereas ours concerns the verification of generic functional properties of a smart contract.

Benton proposes a program logic for a minimal stack-based programming language [2]. His program logic can give an assertion to a stack as our stack refinement types do. However, his language does not support first-class functions nor instructions for dealing with smart contracts (e.g., signature verification).

Our type system is an extension of the Michelson type system with refinement types, which have been successfully applied to various programming languages [16,22,9,10,20,26,23,24,25]. DTAL [25] is a notable example of an application of refinement types to an assembly language, a low-level language like Michelson. A DTAL program defines a computation using registers; we are not aware of refinement types for stack-based languages like Michelson.

We notice the resemblance between our type system and a program logic for PCF proposed by Honda and Yoshida [8], although the targets of verification are different. Their logic supports a judgment of the form $A \vdash e :_u B$, where e is a PCF program, A is a pre-condition assertion, B is a post-condition assertion, and u represents the value that e evaluates to and can be used in B, which resembles our type judgment in the formalization in Section 3. Their assertion language also incorporates a term expression $f \bullet x$, which expresses the value resulting from the application of f to x; this expression resembles the formula $\texttt{call}\,(t_1, t_2) = t_3$ used in a refinement predicate. We have not noticed an automated verifier implemented based on their logic. Further comparison is interesting future work.

6   Conclusion

We described our automated verification tool HELMHOLTZ for the smart contract language Michelson based on the refinement type system for Mini-Michelson. HELMHOLTZ verifies whether a Michelson program follows a specification given in the form of a refinement type. We also demonstrated that HELMHOLTZ successfully verifies various practical Michelson contracts.

Currently, HELMHOLTZ supports approximately 80% of the whole instructions of the Michelson language. The definition of a measure function is limited in the sense that, for example, it can define only a function with one argument. We are currently extending HELMHOLTZ so that it can deal with more programs.

HELMHOLTZ currently verifies the behavior of a single contract, although a blockchain application often consists of multiple contracts in which contract calls are chained. To verify such an application as a whole, we plan to extend HELMHOLTZ so that it can verify an inter-contract behavior compositionally by combining the verification results of each contract.

References

1. Michelson: the language of smart contracts in Tezos. https://tezos.gitlab.io/whitedoc/michelson.html, retrieved Oct. 14, 2020.
2. Benton, N.: A Typed, Compositional Logic for a Stack-Based Abstract Machine. In: Proceedings of Asian Sympoisum on Programming Languages and Systems (APLAS). pp. 364–380. Springer Berlin Heidelberg (2005). https://doi.org/10.1007/11575467_24
3. Bernardo, B., Cauderlier, R., Hu, Z., Pesin, B., Tesson, J.: Mi-Cho-Coq, a framework for certifying Tezos smart contracts. In: Formal Methods. FM 2019 International Workshops - Porto, Portugal, October 7-11, 2019, Revised Selected Papers, Part I. Lecture Notes in Computer Science, vol. 12232, pp. 368–379. Springer (2019). https://doi.org/10.1007/978-3-030-54994-7_28
4. Goodman, L.: Tezos — a self-amending crypto-ledger. white paper. https://tezos.com/static/white_paper-2dc8c02267a8fb86bd67a108199441bf.pdf (2014), retrieved Oct. 14, 2020.
5. Grossman, S., Abraham, I., Golan-Gueta, G., Michalevsky, Y., Rinetzky, N., Sagiv, M., Zohar, Y.: Online detection of effectively callback free objects with applications to smart contracts. Proc. ACM Program. Lang. 2(POPL) (Dec 2017). https://doi.org/10.1145/3158136
6. Hildenbrandt, E., Saxena, M., Rodrigues, N., Zhu, X., Daian, P., Guth, D., Moore, B., Park, D., Zhang, Y., Stefanescu, A., Rosu, G.: KEVM: A Complete Formal Semantics of the Ethereum Virtual Machine. In: 2018 IEEE 31st Computer Security Foundations Symposium (CSF). pp. 204–217 (Jul 2018). https://doi.org/10.1109/CSF.2018.00022
7. Hirai, Y.: Defining the Ethereum virtual machine for interactive theorem provers. In: Financial Cryptography and Data Security. pp. 520–535. Springer International Publishing (2017)
8. Honda, K., Yoshida, N.: A compositional logic for polymorphic higher-order functions. In: Proceedings of the 6th International ACM SIGPLAN Conference on Principles and Practice of Declarative Programming, 24-26 August 2004, Verona, Italy. pp. 191–202. ACM (2004). https://doi.org/10.1145/1013963.1013985
9. Kawaguchi, M., Rondon, P.M., Jhala, R.: Type-based data structure verification. In: Proceedings of the 2009 ACM SIGPLAN Conference on Programming Language Design and Implementation, PLDI 2009, Dublin, Ireland, June 15-21, 2009. pp. 304–315. ACM (2009). https://doi.org/10.1145/1542476.1542510
10. Kobayashi, N., Sato, R., Unno, H.: Predicate abstraction and CEGAR for higher-order model checking. In: Proceedings of the 32nd ACM SIGPLAN Conference on Programming Language Design and Implementation, PLDI 2011, San Jose, CA, USA, June 4-8, 2011. pp. 222–233 (2011). https://doi.org/10.1145/1993498.1993525
11. de Moura, L.M., Bjørner, N.: Z3: an efficient SMT solver. In: Tools and Algorithms for the Construction and Analysis of Systems, 14th International Conference, TACAS 2008, Held as Part of the Joint European Conferences on Theory and Practice of Software, ETAPS 2008, Budapest, Hungary, March 29-April 6, 2008. Proceedings. pp. 337–340 (2008). https://doi.org/10.1007/978-3-540-78800-3_24
12. Nakamoto, S.: Bitcoin: A peer-to-peer electronic cash system. https://bitcoin.org/bitcoin.pdf (2008), retrieved Oct. 12, 2020.
13. Owens, S., Böhm, P., Zappa Nardelli, F., Sewell, P.: Lem: A lightweight tool for heavyweight semantics. In: Interactive Theorem Proving. pp. 363–369. Springer Berlin Heidelberg (2011)

14. Park, D., Zhang, Y., Saxena, M., Daian, P., Roşu, G.: A formal verification tool for Ethereum VM bytecode. In: Proceedings of the 2018 26th ACM Joint Meeting on European Software Engineering Conference and Symposium on the Foundations of Software Engineering. pp. 912–915. ACM (Oct 2018). https://doi.org/10.1145/3236024.3264591
15. Pierce, B.C.: Types and Programming Languages. MIT Press (2002)
16. Rondon, P.M., Kawaguchi, M., Jhala, R.: Liquid types. In: Proceedings of the ACM SIGPLAN 2008 Conference on Programming Language Design and Implementation, Tucson, AZ, USA, June 7-13, 2008. pp. 159–169 (2008). https://doi.org/10.1145/1375581.1375602
17. Roşu, G., Şerbănută, T.F.: An overview of the K semantic framework. The Journal of Logic and Algebraic Programming 79(6), 397–434 (Aug 2010). https://doi.org/10.1016/j.jlap.2010.03.012
18. Siegel, D.: Understanding the DAO attack. CoinDesk (2016), https://www.coindesk.com/understanding-dao-hack-journalists, retrieved Oct. 13, 2020.
19. Szabo, N.: Formalizing and securing relationships on public networks. First Monday 2(9) (Sep 1997). https://doi.org/10.5210/fm.v2i9.548
20. Terauchi, T.: Dependent types from counterexamples. In: Proceedings of the 37th ACM SIGPLAN-SIGACT Symposium on Principles of Programming Languages, POPL 2010, Madrid, Spain, January 17-23, 2010. pp. 119–130 (2010). https://doi.org/10.1145/1706299.1706315
21. The Coq development team: The coq proof assistant reference manual (2020), http://coq.inria.fr, version 8.12.0
22. Unno, H., Kobayashi, N.: Dependent type inference with interpolants. In: Proceedings of the 11th International ACM SIGPLAN Conference on Principles and Practice of Declarative Programming, September 7-9, 2009, Coimbra, Portugal. pp. 277–288 (2009). https://doi.org/10.1145/1599410.1599445
23. Vazou, N., Seidel, E.L., Jhala, R., Vytiniotis, D., Jones, S.L.P.: Refinement types for Haskell. In: Proceedings of the 19th ACM SIGPLAN international conference on Functional programming, Gothenburg, Sweden, September 1-3, 2014. pp. 269–282. ACM (2014). https://doi.org/10.1145/2628136.2628161
24. Xi, H.: Dependent ML an approach to practical programming with dependent types. J. Funct. Program. 17(2), 215–286 (2007). https://doi.org/10.1017/S0956796806006216
25. Xi, H., Harper, R.: A dependently typed assembly language. In: Proceedings of the Sixth ACM SIGPLAN International Conference on Functional Programming (ICFP '01), Firenze (Florence), Italy, September 3-5, 2001. pp. 169–180. ACM (2001). https://doi.org/10.1145/507635.507657
26. Zhu, H., Jagannathan, S.: Compositional and lightweight dependent type inference for ML. In: Verification, Model Checking, and Abstract Interpretation, 14th International Conference, VMCAI 2013, Rome, Italy, January 20-22, 2013. Proceedings. pp. 295–314 (2013). https://doi.org/10.1007/978-3-642-35873-9_19

SyReNN: A Tool for Analyzing Deep Neural Networks *

Matthew Sotoudeh ⓘ (✉) and Aditya V. Thakur ⓘ (✉)

University of California, Davis CA 95616, USA
{masotoudeh,avthakur}@ucdavis.edu

Abstract. Deep Neural Networks (DNNs) are rapidly gaining popularity in a variety of important domains. Formally, DNNs are complicated vector-valued functions which come in a variety of sizes and applications. Unfortunately, modern DNNs have been shown to be vulnerable to a variety of attacks and buggy behavior. This has motivated recent work in formally analyzing the properties of such DNNs. This paper introduces SyReNN, a tool for understanding and analyzing a DNN by computing its *symbolic representation*. The key insight is to decompose the DNN into linear functions. Our tool is designed for analyses using *low-dimensional subsets* of the input space, a unique design point in the space of DNN analysis tools. We describe the tool and the underlying theory, then evaluate its use and performance on three case studies: computing Integrated Gradients, visualizing a DNN's decision boundaries, and patching a DNN.

Keywords: Deep Neural Networks · Symbolic representation · Integrated Gradients

1 Introduction

Deep Neural Networks (DNNs) [18] have become the state-of-the-art in a variety of applications including image recognition [53,33] and natural language processing [12]. Moreover, they are increasingly used in safety- and security-critical applications such as autonomous vehicles [31] and medical diagnosis [10,38,28,37]. These advances have been accelerated by improved hardware and algorithms.

DNNs (Section 2) are programs that compute a vector-valued function, i.e., from $\mathbb{R}^n$ to $\mathbb{R}^m$. They are straight-line programs written as a concatenation of alternating linear and non-linear *layers*. The coefficients of the linear layers are learned from data via *gradient descent* during a training process. A number of different non-linear layers (called *activation functions*) are commonly used, including the *rectified linear* and *maximum pooling* functions.

Owing to the variety of application domains and deployment constraints, DNNs come in many different sizes. For instance, large image-recognition and

---

* Artifact available at https://zenodo.org/record/4124489. Extended paper available at https://arxiv.org/abs/2101.03263.

ⓒ The Author(s) 2021
J. F. Groote and K. G. Larsen (Eds.): TACAS 2021, LNCS 12652, pp. 281–302, 2021.
https://doi.org/10.1007/978-3-030-72013-1_15

natural-language processing models are trained and deployed using cloud resources [33,12], medium-size models could be trained in the cloud but deployed on hardware with limited resources [31], and finally small models could be trained and deployed directly on edge devices [47,9,22,34,35]. There has also been a recent push to compress trained models to reduce their size [24]. Such smaller models play an especially important role in privacy-critical applications, such as wake word detection for voice assistants, because they allow sensitive user data to stay on the user's own device instead of needing to be sent to a remote computer for processing.

Although DNNs are very popular, they are not perfect. One particularly concerning development is that modern DNNs have been shown to be extremely vulnerable to *adversarial examples,* inputs which are intentionally manipulated to appear unmodified to humans but become misclassified by the DNN [54,19,40,8]. Similarly, *fooling examples* are inputs that look like random noise to humans, but are classified with high confidence by DNNs [41]. Mistakes made by DNNs have led to loss of life [36,17] and wrongful arrests [26,27]. For this reason, it is important to develop techniques for analyzing, understanding, and repairing DNNs.

This paper introduces SyReNN, a tool for understanding and analyzing DNNs. SyReNN implements state-of-the-art algorithms for computing precise symbolic representations of piecewise-linear DNNs (Section 3). Given an input subspace of a DNN, SyReNN computes a symbolic representation that decomposes the behavior of the DNN into finitely-many linear functions. SyReNN implements the one-dimensional analysis algorithm of Sotoudeh and Thakur [50] and extends it to the two-dimensional setting as described in Section 4.

Key insights. There are two key insights enabling this approach, first identified in Sotoudeh and Thakur [50]. First, most popular DNN architectures today are *piecewise-linear*, meaning they can be precisely decomposed into finitely-many linear functions. This allows us to reduce their analysis to equivalent questions in linear algebra, one of the most well-understood fields of modern mathematics. Second, many applications only require analyzing the behavior of the DNN on a *low-dimensional subset* of the input space. Hence, whereas prior work has attempted to give up precision for efficiency in analyzing high-dimensional input regions [48,49,16], our work has focused on algorithms that are *both efficient and precise* in analyzing lower-dimensional regions (Section 4).

Tool design. The SyReNN tool is designed to be easy to use and extend, as well as efficient (Section 5). The core of SyReNN is written as a highly-optimized, parallel C++ server using Intel TBB for parallelization [45] and Eigen for matrix operations [23]. A user-friendly Python front-end interfaces with the PyTorch deep learning framework [44].

Use cases. We demonstrate the utility of SyReNN using three applications. The first computes *Integrated Gradients* (IG), a state-of-the-art measure used to determine which input dimensions (e.g., pixels for an image-recognition network) were most important in the final classification produced by the network (Section 6.1). The second precisely visualizes the decision boundaries of a DNN (Section 6.2). The last *patches* (repairs) a DNN to satisfy some desired specification involving infinitely-many points (Section 6.3). Thus, SyReNN is an interesting and useful tool in the toolbox for understanding and analyzing DNNs.

Contributions. The contributions of this paper are:

- A definition of symbolic representation of DNNs (Section 3).
- An efficient algorithm for computing symbolic representations for DNNs over low-dimensional input subspaces (Section 4).
- A design of a usable and well-engineered tool implementing these ideas called SyReNN (Section 5).
- Three applications of SyReNN (Section 6).

Section 2 presents preliminaries about DNNs; Section 7 presents related work; Section 8 concludes. SyReNN is available on GitHub at https://github.com/95616ARG/SyReNN.

2   Preliminaries

We now formally define the notion of *DNN* we will use in this paper.

Definition 1. *A* Deep Neural Network *(DNN) is a function* $f : \mathbb{R}^n \to \mathbb{R}^m$ *which can be written* $f = f_1 \circ f_2 \cdots \circ f_n$ *for a sequence of* layer functions f_1, f_2, ..., f_n.

Our work is primarily concerned with the popular class of *piecewise-linear* DNNs, defined below. In this definition and the rest of this paper, we will use the term "polytope" to mean a *convex and bounded* polytope except where specified.

Definition 2. *A function* $f : \mathbb{R}^n \to \mathbb{R}^m$ *is* piecewise-linear *(PWL) if its input domain* $\mathbb{R}^n$ *can be partitioned into finitely-many possibly-unbounded polytopes* $X_1, X_2, \ldots, X_k$ *such that* $f_{\restriction X_i}$ *is linear for every* X_i.

The most common activation function used today is the ReLU function, a PWL activation function which is defined below.

Definition 3. *The* rectified linear function *(ReLU) is a function* $\mathrm{RELU} : \mathbb{R}^n \to \mathbb{R}^m$ *defined component-wise by*

$$\mathrm{RELU}(\vec{v})_i := \begin{cases} 0 & \text{if } v_i < 0 \\ v_i & \text{otherwise,} \end{cases}$$

where $\mathrm{RELU}(\vec{v})_i$ *is the ith component of the vector* $\mathrm{RELU}(\vec{v})$ *and* v_i *is the ith component of the vector* $\vec{v}$.

In order to see that RELU is PWL, we must show that its input domain $\mathbb{R}^n$ can be partitioned such that, in each partition, RELU is linear. In this case, we can use the orthants of $\mathbb{R}^n$ as our partitioning: within each orthant, the signs of the components do not change hence RELU is the linear function that just zeros out the negative components.

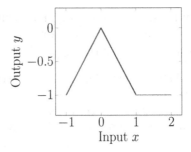

Fig. 1: Example function for which $\widehat{f_{\restriction[-1,2]}} = \{[-1,0],[0,1],[1,2]\}$.

Although we focus on RELU due to its popularity and expository power, SyReNN works with a number of other popular PWL layers include MaxPool, Leaky ReLU, Hard Tanh, Fully-Connected, and Convolutional layers, as defined in [18]. PWL layers have become exceedingly common. In fact, nearly all of the state-of-the-art image recognition models bundled with Pytorch [43] are PWL.

Example 1. The DNN $f : \mathbb{R}^1 \to \mathbb{R}^1$ defined by

$$f(x) := \begin{bmatrix} 1 & -1 & -1 \end{bmatrix} \text{RELU} \left(\begin{bmatrix} 1 & -1 \\ 1 & 0 \\ -1 & 0 \end{bmatrix} \begin{bmatrix} x \\ 1 \end{bmatrix} \right)$$

can be broken into layers $f = f_1 \circ f_2 \circ f_3$ where

$$f_1(x) := \begin{bmatrix} 1 & -1 \\ 1 & 0 \\ -1 & 0 \end{bmatrix} \begin{bmatrix} x \\ 1 \end{bmatrix}, \quad f_2 = \text{RELU}, \quad \text{and} \quad f_3(\vec{v}) = \begin{bmatrix} 1 & -1 & -1 \end{bmatrix} \vec{v}.$$

The DNN's input-output behavior on the domain $[-1,2]$ is shown in Figure 1.

3   A Symbolic Representation of DNNs

We formalize the symbolic representation according to the following definition:

Definition 4. *Given a PWL function* $f : \mathbb{R}^n \to \mathbb{R}^m$ *and a bounded convex polytope* $X \subseteq \mathbb{R}^n$, *we define the symbolic representation of* f *on* X, *written* $\widehat{f_{\restriction X}}$, *to be a finite set of polytopes* $\widehat{f_{\restriction X}} = \{P_1, \ldots, P_n\}$, *such that:*

1. *The set* $\{P_1, P_2, \ldots, P_n\}$ *partitions* X, *except possibly for overlapping boundaries.*
2. *Each* P_i *is a bounded convex polytope.*
3. *Within each* P_i, *the function* $f_{\restriction P_i}$ *is linear.*

Notably, if f is a DNN using only PWL layers, then f is PWL and so we can define $\widehat{f_{\restriction X}}$. This symbolic representation allows one to reduce questions about the DNN f to questions about finitely-many linear functions F_i. For example, because linear functions are convex, to verify that $\forall x \in X.\ f(x) \in Y$ for some polytope Y, it suffices to verify $\forall P_i \in \widehat{f_{\restriction X}}.\forall \vec{v} \in \mathtt{Vert}(P_i).\ f(\vec{v}) \in Y$, where $\mathtt{Vert}(P_i)$ is the (finite) set of vertices for the bounded convex polytope P_i; thus, here both of the quantifiers are over finite sets. The symbolic representation described above can be seen as a generalization of the EXACTLINE representation [50], which considered only *one-dimensional* restriction domains of interest.

Example 2. Consider again the DNN $f : \mathbb{R}^1 \to \mathbb{R}^1$ given by

$$f(x) := \begin{bmatrix} 1 & -1 & -1 \end{bmatrix} \mathrm{ReLU}\left(\begin{bmatrix} 1 & -1 \\ 1 & 0 \\ -1 & 0 \end{bmatrix} \begin{bmatrix} x \\ 1 \end{bmatrix} \right)$$

and the region of interest $X = [-1, 2]$. The input-output behavior of f on X is shown in Figure 1. From this, we can see that

$$\widehat{f_{\restriction X}} = \{[-1, 0], [0, 1], [1, 2]\}.$$

Within each of these partitions, the input-output behavior is *linear*, which for $\mathbb{R}^1 \to \mathbb{R}^1$ we can see visually as just a line segment. As this set fully partitions X, then, this is a valid $\widehat{f_{\restriction X}}$.

4   Computing the Symbolic Representation

This section presents an efficient algorithm for computing $\widehat{f_{\restriction X}}$ for a DNN f composed of PWL layers. To retain both scalability and precision, we will *require the input region X be two-dimensional.* This design choice is relatively unexplored in the neural-network analysis literature (most analyses strike a balance between precision and scalability, ignoring dimensionality). We show that, for two-dimensional X, we can use an efficient polytope representation to produce an algorithm that demonstrates good best-case and in-practice efficiency while retaining full precision. This algorithm represents a direct generalization of the approach of [50].

The difficulties our algorithm addresses arise from three areas. First, when computing $\widehat{f_{\restriction X}}$ there may be exponentially many such partitions on all of $\mathbb{R}^n$ but only a small number of them may intersect with X. Consequently, the algorithm needs to be able to find those partitions that intersect with X efficiently without explicitly listing all of the partitions on $\mathbb{R}^n$. Second, it is often more convenient to specify the partitioning via *hyperplanes separating the partitions* than explicit polytopes. For example, for the one-dimensional RELU function we may simply state that the line $x = 0$ separates the two partitions, because RELU is linear both in the region $x \leq 0$ and $x \geq 0$. Finally, neural networks are typically composed of sequences of linear and piecewise-linear layers, where the partitioning imposed by each layer individually may be well-understood but their composition is more complex. For example, identifying the linear partitions of $y = \text{RELU}(4 \cdot \text{RELU}(-3x - 1) + 2)$ is non-trivial, even though we know the linear partitions of each composed function individually.

Our algorithm only requires the user to specify the hyperplanes defining the partitioning for the activation function used in each layer; our current implementation comes with support for common PWL activation functions. For example, if a RELU layer is used for an n-dimensional input vector, then the hyperplanes would be defined by the equations $x_1 = 0, x_2 = 0, \ldots, x_n = 0$. It then computes the symbolic representation for a *single layer at a time*, composing them sequentially to compute the symbolic representation across the entire network.

To allow such compositions of layers, instead of directly computing $\widehat{f}_{\restriction X}$, we will define another primitive, denoted by the operator $\otimes$ and sometimes referred to as EXTEND, such that

$$\text{EXTEND}(h, \widehat{g}) = h \otimes \widehat{g} = \widehat{h \circ g}. \tag{1}$$

Consider $f = f_n \circ f_{n-1} \circ \cdots \circ f_1$, and let $I : x \mapsto x$ be the identity map. I is linear across its entire input space, and, thus, $\widehat{I}_{\restriction X} = \{X\}$. By the definition of EXTEND$(f_1, \cdot)$, we have $f_1 \otimes \widehat{I}_{\restriction X} = \widehat{(f_1 \circ I)}_{\restriction X} = \widehat{f_1}_{\restriction X}$, where the final equality holds by the definition of the identity map I. We can then iteratively apply this procedure to inductively compute $\widehat{(f_i \circ \cdots \circ f_1)}_{\restriction X}$ from $\widehat{(f_{i-1} \circ \cdots f_1)}_{\restriction X}$ like so:

$$f_i \otimes \widehat{(f_{i-1} \circ \cdots \circ f_1)}_{\restriction X} = \widehat{(f_i \circ f_{i-1} \circ \cdots \circ f_1)}_{\restriction X}$$

until we have computed $\widehat{(f_n \circ f_{n-1} \circ \cdots \circ f_1)}_{\restriction X} = \widehat{f}_{\restriction X}$, which is the required symbolic representation.

4.1   Algorithm for Extend

Algorithm 1 present an algorithm for computing EXTEND for arbitrary PWL functions, where $\text{EXTEND}(h, \widehat{g}) = h \otimes \widehat{g} = \widehat{h \circ g}$.

Geometric intuition for the algorithm.   Consider the RELU function (Definition 3). It can be shown that, within any orthant (i.e., when the signs of all coefficients are held constant), $\text{RELU}(\vec{x})$ is equivalent to some linear function, in particular the element-wise product of $\vec{x}$ with a vector that zeroes out the negative-signed components. However, for our algorithm, all we need to know is that the linear partitions of RELU (in this case the orthants) are separated by hyperplanes $x_1 = 0, x_2 = 0, \ldots, x_n = 0$.

Given a two-dimensional convex bounded polytope X, the execution of the algorithm for $f = \text{RELU}$ can be visualized as follows. We pick some vertex v of X, and begin traversing the boundary of the polytope in counter-clockwise order. If we hit an orthant boundary (corresponding to some hyperplane $x_i = 0$), it implies that the behavior of the function behaves differently at the points of the polytope to one side of the boundary from those at the other side of the boundary. Thus, we *partition X into X_1 and X_2*, where X_1 lies to one side of the hyperplane and X_2 lies to the other side. We recursively apply this procedure to X_1 and X_2 until the resulting polytopes all lie on exactly one side of every hyperplane (orthant boundary). But lying on exactly one side of every hyperplane (orthant boundary) implies each polytope lies entirely within a linear partition of the function (a single orthant), hence the application of the function on that polytope is linear, and hence we have our partitioning.

Functions used in algorithm. Given a two-dimensional bounded convex polytope X, $\texttt{Vert}(X)$ returns a list of its vertices in counter-clockwise order, repeating the initial vertex at the end. Given a set of points X, $\texttt{ConvexHull}(X)$ represents their convex hull (the smallest bounded polytope containing every point in X). Given a scalar value x, $\texttt{Sign}(x)$ computes the sign of that value (i.e., -1 if $x < 0$, $+1$ if $x > 0$, and 0 if $x = 0$).

Algorithm description. The key insight of the algorithm is to recursively partition the polytopes until such a partition lies entirely within a linear region of the function f. Algorithm 1 begins by constructing a queue containing the polytopes of $\widehat{g_{\restriction X}}$. Each iteration either removes a polytope from the queue that lies entirely in one linear region (placing it in Y), or splits (partitions) some polytope into two smaller polytopes that get put back into the queue. When we pop a polytope P from the queue, Line 6 iterates over all hyperplanes $N_k \cdot x = b_k$ defining the piecewise-linear partitioning of f, looking for any for which some vertex V_i lies on the positive side of the hyperplane and another vertex V_j lies on the negative side of the hyperplane. If none exist (Line 7), by convexity we are guaranteed that the entire polytope lies entirely on one side with respect to every hyperplane, meaning it lies entirely within a linear partition of f. Thus, we can add it to Y and continue. If two such vertices are found (starting Line 10), then we can find "extreme" i and j indices such that V_i is the last vertex in a counter-clockwise traversal to lie on the same side of the hyperplane as V_1 and V_j is the last vertex lying on the opposite side of the hyperplane. We then call $\texttt{SplitPlane}()$ (Algorithm 2) to actually partition the polytope on opposite sides of the hyperplane, adding both to our worklist.

In the best case, each partition is in a single orthant: the algorithm never calls $\texttt{SplitPlane}()$ at all — it merely iterates over all of the n input partitions, checks their v vertices, and appends to the resulting set (for a best-case complexity of $O(nv)$). In the worst case, it splits each polytope in the queue on each face, resulting in exponential time complexity. As we will show in Section 6, this exponential worst-case behavior is not encountered in practice, thus making SyReNN a practical tool for DNN analysis.

Please see the extended version of this paper for a worked example of the algorithm's execution.

4.2 Representing Polytopes

We close this section with a discussion of implementation concerns when representing the convex polytopes that make up the partitioning of $\widehat{f_{\restriction X}}$. In standard computational geometry, bounded polytopes can be represented in two equivalent forms:

M. Sotoudeh and A. V. Thakur

Algorithm 1: $f \otimes \widehat{g_{\restriction X}}$ for two-dimensional X. f is defined by hyper-planes $N_1 \cdot x = b_1$ through $N_m \cdot x = b_m$ such that, within any partition imposed by the hyperplanes f is equivalent to some affine function.

Input: $\widehat{g_{\restriction X}} = \{P_1, \ldots, P_n\}$.

Output: $\widehat{f \circ g_{\restriction X}}$

1   $W \leftarrow \texttt{ConstructQueue}(\widehat{g_{\restriction X}})$
2   $Y \leftarrow \emptyset$
3   **while** W *not empty* **do**
4      $P \leftarrow \texttt{Pop}(W)$
5      $V \leftarrow \texttt{Vert}(P)$
6      $K \leftarrow \{N_k \mid \exists i, j : \texttt{Sign}(N_k \cdot g(V_i) - b_k) > 0 \wedge \texttt{Sign}(N_k \cdot g(V_j) - b_k) < 0\}$
7   **if** $K = \emptyset$ **then**
8          $Y \leftarrow Y \cup \{P\}$
9   **continue**
10     $N, b \leftarrow$ any element from K
11     $i \leftarrow \arg\max_i \{\texttt{Sign}(N \cdot g(V_i) - b) = \texttt{Sign}(N \cdot g(V_1) - b)\}$
12     $j \leftarrow \arg\max_j \{\texttt{Sign}(N \cdot g(V_j) - b) \neq \texttt{Sign}(N \cdot g(V_i) - b)\}$
13   **for** $V' \in \texttt{SplitPlane}(V, g, i, j, N, b)$ **do**
14         $W \leftarrow \texttt{Push}(W, \texttt{ConvexHull}(V'))$

15 **return** Y

---

1. The *half-space* or *H-representation*, which encodes the polytope as an intersection of finitely-many half-spaces. (Each half-space being defined as a halfspace defined by an affine inequality $Ax \leq b$.)
2. The *vertex* or *V-representation*, which encodes the polytope as a set of finitely many points; the polytope is then taken to be the convex hull of the points (i.e., smallest convex shape containing all of the points).

Certain operations are more efficient when using one representation compared to the other. For example, finding the intersection of two polytopes in an H-representation can be done in linear time by concatenating their representative half-spaces, but the same is not possible in V-representation.

There are two main operations on polytopes we need perform in our algorithms: (i) splitting a polytope with a hyperplane, and (ii) applying an affine map to all points in the polytope. In general, the first is more efficient in an H-representation, while the latter is more efficient in a V-representation. However, when restricted to two-dimensional polygons, the former is also efficient in a V-representation, as demonstrated by Algorithm 2, helping to motivate our use of the V-representation in our algorithm.

Furthermore, the two polytope representations have different resiliency to floating-point operations. In particular, H-representations for polytopes in $\mathbb{R}^n$ are notoriously difficult to achieve high-precision with, because the error introduced from using floating point numbers gets arbitrarily large as one goes in a particular direction along any hyperplane face. Ideally, we would like the

---

Algorithm 2: SplitPlane(V, g, i, j, N, b)

Input: V, the vertices of the polytope in the input space of g. A function g. i is the index of the last vertex lying on the same side of the orthant face as V_1. j is the index of the last vertex lying on the opposite side of the orthant face as V_1. N and b define the hyperplane $N \cdot x = b$ to split on.

Output: $\{P_1, P_2\}$, two sets of vertices whose convex hulls form a partitioning of V such that each lies on only one side of the $N \cdot x = b$ hyperplane.

1 $p_i \leftarrow V_i + \frac{b - N \cdot g(V_i)}{N \cdot (g(V_{i+1}) - g(V_i))}(V_{i+1} - V_i)$

2 $p_j \leftarrow V_j + \frac{b - N \cdot g(V_j)}{N \cdot (g(V_{j+1}) - g(V_j))}(V_{j+1} - V_j)$

3 $A \leftarrow \{p_i, p_j\} \cup \{v \in V \mid \mathtt{Sign}(N \cdot v - b) = \mathtt{Sign}(N \cdot V_i - b)\}$

4 $B \leftarrow \{p_i, p_j\} \cup \{v \in V \mid \mathtt{Sign}(N \cdot v - b) = \mathtt{Sign}(N \cdot V_j - b)\}$

5 **return** $\{A, B\}$

---

hyperplane to be most accurate in the region of the polytope itself, which corresponds to choosing the magnitude of the norm vector correctly. Unfortunately, to our knowledge, there is no efficient algorithm for computing the ideal floating point H-representation of a polytope, although libraries such as APRON [30] are able to provide reasonable results for low-dimensional spaces. However, because neural networks utilize extremely high-dimensional spaces (often hundreds or thousands of dimensions) and we wish to iteratively apply our analysis, we find that errors from using floating-point H-representations can quickly multiply and compound to become infeasible. By contrast, floating-point inaccuracies in a V-representation are directly interpretable as slightly misplacing the vertices of the polytope; no "localization" process is necessary to penalize inaccuracies close to the polytope more than those far away from it.

Another difference is in the space complexity of the representation. In general, H-representations can be more space-efficient for common shapes than V-representations. However, when the polytope lies in a low-dimensional subspace of a larger space, the V-representation is usually significantly more efficient.

Thus, V-representations are a good choice for low-dimensionality polytopes embedded in high-dimensional space, which is exactly what we need for analyzing neural networks with two-dimensional restriction domains of interest. This is why we designed our algorithms to rely on $\mathtt{Vert}(X)$, so that they could be directly computed on a V-representation.

The 2D algorithm described above can be seen as implementing the recursive case of a more general, n-dimensional version of the algorithm that recurses on each of the $(n - 1)$-dimensional facets. Please see the extended version of this paper for more details.

5   SyReNN tool

This section provides more details about the design and implementation of our tool, SyReNN (Symbolic Representations of Neural Networks), which computes

$\widehat{f_{\restriction X}}$, where f is a DNN using only piecewise-linear layers and X is a union of one- or two-dimensional polytopes. The tool is available under the MIT license at https://github.com/95616ARG/SyReNN and in the PyPI package pysyrenn.

Input and output format. SyReNN supports reading DNNs from two standard formats: ERAN (a textual format used by the ERAN project [1]) as well as ONNX (an industry-standard format supporting a wide variety of different models) [42]. Internally, the input DNN is described as an instance of the Network class, which is itself a list of sequential Layers. A number of layer types are provided by SyReNN, including FullyConnectedLayer, ConvolutionalLayer, and ReLULayer. To support more complicated DNN architectures, we have implemented a ConcatLayer, which represents a concatenation of the output of two different layers. The input region of interest, X, is defined as a polytope described by a list of its vertices in counter-clockwise order. The output of the tool is the symbolic representation $\widehat{f_{\restriction X}}$.

Overall Architecture. We designed SyReNN in a client-server architecture using gRPC [20] and protocol buffers [21] as a standard method of communication between the two. This architecture allows the bulk of the heavy computation to be done in efficient C++ code, while allowing user-friendly interfaces in a variety of languages. It also allows practitioners to run the server remotely on a more powerful machine if necessary. The C++ server implementation uses the Intel TBB library for parallelization. Our official front-end library is written in Python, and available as a package on PyPI so installation is as simple as `pip install pysyrenn`. The entire project can be built using the Bazel build system, which manages dependencies using checksums.

Server Architecture. The major algorithms are implemented as a gRPC server written in C++. When a connection is first made, the server initializes the state with an empty DNN $f(x) = x$. During the session, three operations are permitted: (i) append a layer g so that the current session's DNN is updated from f_0 to $f_1(x) := g(f_0(x))$, (ii) compute $\widehat{f_{\restriction X}}$ for a one-dimensional X, or (iii) compute $\widehat{f_{\restriction X}}$ for a two-dimensional X. We have separate methods for one- and two-dimensional X, because the one-dimensional case has specific optimizations for controlling memory usage. The SegmentedLine and UPolytope types are used to represent one- and two-dimensional partitions of X, respectively. When operation (1) is performed, a new instance of the LayerTransformer class is initialized with the relevant parameters and added to a running vector of the current layers. When operation (2) is performed, a new queue of SegmentedLines is constructed, corresponding to X, and the before-allocated LayerTransformers are applied sequentially to compute $\widehat{f_{\restriction X}}$. In this case, extra control is provided to automatically gauge memory usage and pause computation for portions of X until more memory is made available. Finally, when operation (3) is a performed, a new instance of UPolytope is initialized with the vertices of X and the LayerTransformers are again applied sequentially to compute $\widehat{f_{\restriction X}}$.

Client Architecture. Our Python client exposes an interface for defining DNNs similar to the popular Sequential-Network Keras API [11]. Objects represent individual layers in the network, and they can be combined sequentially into a `Network` instance. The key addition of our library is that this `Network` exposes methods for computing $\widehat{f_{\restriction X}}$ given a V-representation description of X. To do this, it invokes the server and passes a layer-by-layer description of f followed by the polytope X, then parses the response $\widehat{f_{\restriction X}}$.

Extending to support different layer types. Different layer types are supported by sub-classing the `LayerTransformer` class. Instances of this class expose a method for computing EXTEND($h, \cdot$) for the corresponding layer h. To simplify implementation, two sub-classes of `LayerTransformer` are provided: one for entirely-linear layers (such as fully-connected and convolutional layers), and one for piecewise-linear layers. For fully-linear layers, all that needs to be provided is a method computing the layer function itself. For piecewise-linear layers, two methods need to be provided: (1) computing the layer function itself, and (2) one describing the hyperplanes which separate the linear regions. The base class then directly implements Algorithm 1 for that layer. This architecture makes supporting new layers a straight-forward process.

Float Safety. Like Reluplex [32], SyReNN uses floating-point arithmetic to compute $\widehat{f_{\restriction X}}$ efficiently. Unfortunately, this means that in some cases its results will not be entirely precise when compared to a real-valued or multiple-precision version of the algorithm. Approaches for addressing this are discussed in the extended version of this paper.

6 Applications of SyReNN

This section presents the use of SyReNN in three example case studies.

6.1 Integrated Gradients

A common problem in the field of *explainable machine learning* is understanding *why* a DNN made the prediction it did. For example, given an image classified by a DNN as a 'cat,' why did the DNN decide it was a cat instead of, say, a dog? Were there particular pixels which were particularly important in deciding this? Integrated Gradients (IG) [52] is the state-of-the-art method for computing such *model attributions*.

Definition 5. *Given a DNN f, the integrated gradients along dimension i for input x and baseline x' is defined to be:*

$$IG_i(x) \stackrel{def}{=} (x_i - x'_i) \times \int_{\alpha=0}^{1} \frac{\partial f(x' + \alpha \times (x - x'))}{\partial x_i} d\alpha. \tag{2}$$

The computed value $IG_i(x)$ determines relatively how important the ith input (e.g., pixel) was to the classification.

However, exactly computing this integral requires a symbolic, closed form for the gradient of the network. Until [50], it was not known how to compute such a closed-form and so IGs were always only *approximated* using a sampling-based approach. Unfortunately, because it was unknown how to compute the true value, there was no way for practitioners to determine how accurate their approximations were. This is particularly concerning in fairness applications where an accurate attribution is exceedingly important.

In [50], it was recognized that, when $X = \texttt{ConvexHull}(\{x, x'\})$, $\widehat{f_{\upharpoonright X}}$ can be used to *exactly* compute $IG_i(x)$. This is because within each partition of $\widehat{f_{\upharpoonright X}}$ the gradient of the network is *constant* because it behaves as a linear function, and hence the integral can be written as the weighted sum of such finitely-many gradients.[1] Using our symbolic representation, the exact IG can thus be computed as follows:

$$\sum_{\texttt{ConvexHull}(\{y_i, y_i'\}) \in \widehat{f_{\upharpoonright \texttt{ConvexHull}(\{x, x'\})}}} (y_i' - y_i) \times \frac{\partial f(0.5 \times (y_i + y_i'))}{\partial x_i} \tag{3}$$

Where here y_i, y_i' are the endpoints of the segment with y_i closer to x and y_i' closest to x'.

Implementation. The helper class `IntegratedGradientsHelper` is provided by our Python client library. It takes as input a DNN f and a set of (x, x') input-baseline pairs and then computes IG for each pair.

Empirical Results. In [50] SyReNN was used to show conclusively that existing sampling-based methods were insufficient to adequately approximate the true IG. This realization led to changes in the official IG implementation to use the more-precise trapezoidal sampling method we argued for.

Timing Numbers. In those experiments, we used SyReNN to compute $\widehat{f_{\upharpoonright X}}$ for three different DNNs f, namely the small, medium, and large convolutional models from [1]. For each DNN, we ran SyReNN on 100 one-dimensional lines. The 100 calls to SyReNN completed in 20.8 seconds for the small model, 183.3 for the medium model, and 615.5 for the big model. Tests were performed on an Intel Core i7-7820X CPU at 3.60GHz with 32GB of memory.

6.2 Visualization of DNN Decision Boundaries

Whereas IG helps understand why a DNN made a particular prediction about a single input point, another major task is *visualizing* the decision boundaries of a DNN on *infinitely-many* input points. Figure 2 shows a visualization of an ACAS Xu DNN [31] which takes as input the position of an airplane and an approaching attacker, then produces as output one of five advisories instructing the plane, such as "clear of conflict" or to move "weak left." Every point in the diagram represents the relative position of the approaching plane, while the color indicates the advisory.

---

[1] As noted in [50], this technically requires a slight strengthening of the definition of $\widehat{f_{\upharpoonright X}}$ which is satisfied by our algorithms as defined above.

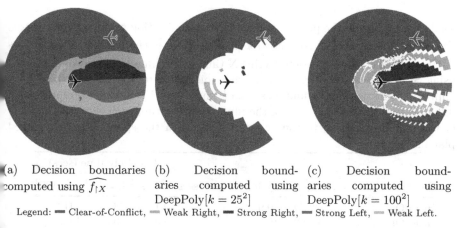

(a) Decision boundaries computed using $\widehat{f_{\restriction X}}$

(b) Decision boundaries computed using DeepPoly[$k = 25^2$]

(c) Decision boundaries computed using DeepPoly[$k = 100^2$]

Legend: ▬ Clear-of-Conflict, ▬ Weak Right, ▬ Strong Right, ▬ Strong Left, ▬ Weak Left.

Fig. 2: Visualization of decision boundaries for the ACAS Xu network. Using SyReNN (left) quickly produces the exact decision boundaries. Using abstract interpretation-based tools like DeepPoly (middle and right) are slower and produce only imprecise approximations of the decision boundaries.

One approach to such visualizations is to simply sample finitely-many points and extrapolate the behavior on the entire domain from those finitely-many points. However, this approach is imprecise and risks missing vital information because there is no way to know the correct sampling density to use to identify all important features.

Another approach is to use a tool such as DeepPoly [49] to over-approximate the output range of the DNN. However, because DeepPoly is a relatively coarse over-approximation, there may be regions of the input space for which it cannot state with confidence the decision made by the network. In fact, the approximations used by DeepPoly are extremely coarse. A naïve application of DeepPoly to this problem results in it being unable to make claims about *any* of the input space of interest. In order to utilize it, we must *partition* the space and run DeepPoly within each partition, which significantly slows down the analysis. Even when using 25^2 partitions, Figure 2b shows that most of the interesting region is still unclassifiable with DeepPoly (shown in white). Only with 100^2 partitions can DeepPoly effectively approximate the decision boundaries, although it is still quite imprecise.

By contrast, $\widehat{f_{\restriction X}}$ can be used to *exactly* determine the decision boundaries on any 2D polytope subset of the input space, which can then be plotted. This is shown in Figure 2a. Furthermore, as shown in Table 1, the approach using $\widehat{f_{\restriction X}}$ is *significantly* faster than that using ERAN, even as we get the *precise* answer instead of an approximation. Such visualizations can be particularly helpful in identifying issues to be fixed using techniques such as those in Section 6.3.

Table 1: Comparing the performance of DNN visualization using SyReNN versus DeepPoly for the ACAS Xu network [31]. $\widehat{f_{\restriction X}}$ size is the number of partitions in the symbolic representation. SyReNN time is the time taken to compute $\widehat{f_{\restriction X}}$ using SyReNN. DeepPoly[k] time is the time taken to compute DeepPoly for approximating decision boundaries with k partitions. Each scenario represents a different two-dimensional slice of the input space; within each slice, the heading of the intruder relative to the ownship along with the speed of each involved plane is fixed.

Scenario	$\widehat{f_{\restriction X}}$ size	SyReNN time (secs)	DeepPoly time (secs)		
			$k = 25^2$	$k = 55^2$	$k = 100^2$
Head-On, Slow	33200	10.9	9.1	43.2	141.3
Head-On, Fast	30769	10.2	8.2	39.0	128.0
Perpendicular, Slow	37251	12.5	9.2	42.9	141.7
Perpendicular, Fast	33931	11.4	8.2	39.2	127.5
Opposite, Slow	36743	12.1	9.8	46.7	152.5
Opposite, Fast	38965	13.0	9.5	45.2	147.3
-Perpendicular, Slow	36037	11.9	9.5	45.0	146.4
-Perpendicular, Fast	33208	10.9	8.3	39.5	130.2

Implementation. The helper class `PlanesClassifier` is provided by our Python client library. It takes as input a DNN f and an input region X, then computes the decision boundaries of f on X.

Timing Numbers. Timing comparisons are given in Table 1. We see that SyReNN is quite performant, and the exact SyReNN can be computed more quickly than even a mediocre approximation from DeepPoly using 55^2 partitions. Tests were performed on a dedicated Amazon EC2 c5.metal instance, using BenchExec [5] to limit the number of CPU cores to 16 and RAM to 16GB.

6.3   Patching of DNNs

We have now seen how SyReNN can be used to visualize the behavior of a DNN. This can be particularly useful for identifying buggy behavior. For example, in Figure 2a we can see that the decision boundary between "strong right" and "strong left" is not symmetrical.

The final application we consider for SyReNN is *patching DNNs* to correct undesired behavior. Patching is described formally in [51]. Given an initial network N and a *specification* ϕ describing desired constraints on the input/output, the goal of patching is to find a small modification to the parameters of N producing a new DNN N' that satisfies the constraints in ϕ.

The key theory behind DNN patching we will use was developed in [51]. The key realization of that work is that, for a certain DNN architecture, correcting the network behavior on an infinite, 2D region X is exactly equivalent to correcting

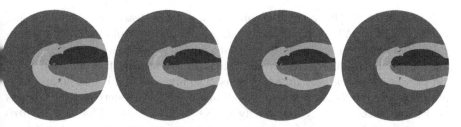

(a) Before patching. (b) Patched pockets. (c) Patched bands. (d) Patched symmetry.

Legend: ▬ Clear-of-Conflict, ▬ Weak Right, ▬ Strong Right, ▬ Strong Left, ▬ Weak Left.

Fig. 3: Network patching.

ts behavior on *the finitely-many vertices* $\text{Vert}(P_i)$ for each of the finitely-many
$P_i \in \widehat{f_{\restriction X}}$. Hence, SyReNN plays a key role in enabling efficient DNN patching.

For this case study, we patched the same aircraft collision-avoidance DNN
visualized in Section 6.2. We patched the DNN three times to correct three different buggy behaviors of the network: (i) remove "Pockets" of strong left/strong
right in regions that are otherwise weak left/weak right; (ii) remove the "Bands"
of weak-left advisory behind and to the left of the plane; and (iii) enforce "Symmetry" across the horizontal. The DNNs before and after patching with different
specifications are shown in Figure 3.

Implementation The helper class NetPatcher is provided by our Python
client library. It takes as input a DNN f and pairs of input region, output label
X_i, Y_i, then computes a new DNN f' which maps all points in each X_i into Y_i.

Timing Numbers. As in Section 6.2, computing $\widehat{f_{\restriction X}}$ for use in patching took
approximately 10 seconds.

7 Related Work

The related problem of exact reach set analysis for DNNs was investigated in
[58]. However, the authors use an algorithm that relies on explicitly enumerating
all exponentially-many (2^n) possible signs at each RELU layer. By contrast,
our algorithm adapts to the actual input polytopes, efficiently restricting its
consideration to activations that are actually possible.

Hanin and Rolnick [25] prove theoretical properties about the cardinality of
$\widehat{f_{\restriction X}}$ for RELU networks, showing that $|\widehat{f_{\restriction X}}|$ is expected to grow polynomially
with the number of nodes in the network for randomly-initialized networks.

Thrun [55] and Bastani et al.[4] extract symbolic rules meant to approximate
DNNs, which can approximate the symbolic representation $\widehat{f_{\restriction X}}$.

In particular, the ERAN [1] tool and underlying DeepPoly [49] domain were
designed to verify the non-existence of adversarial examples. Breutel et al. [6]
give an iterative refinement algorithm for an overapproximation of the weakest
precondition as a polytope where the required output is also a polytope.

Scheibler et al. [46] verify the safety of a machine-learning controller using the SMT-solver iSAT3, but support small unrolling depths and basic safety properties. Zhu et al. [60] use a synthesis procedure to generate a safe deterministic program that can enforce safety conditions by monitoring the deployed DNN and preventing potentially unsafe actions. The presence of adversarial and fooling inputs for DNNs as well as applications of DNNs in safety-critical systems has led to efforts to verify and certify DNNs [3,32,14,29,16,7,57,49,2]. *Approximate reachability analysis* for neural networks safely overapproximates the set of possible outputs [16,58,59,57,13,56].

Prior work in the area of network patching focuses on enforcing constraints on the network during training. DiffAI [39] is an approach to train neural networks that are certifiably robust to adversarial perturbations. DL2 [15] allows for training and querying neural networks with logical constraints.

8   Conclusion and Future Work

We presented SyReNN, a tool for understanding and analyzing DNNs. Given a piecewise-linear network and a low-dimensional polytope subspace of the input subspace, SyReNN computes a symbolic representation that decomposes the behavior of the DNN into finitely-many linear functions. We showed how to efficiently compute this representation, and presented the design of the corresponding tool. We illustrated the utility of SyReNN on three applications: computing exact IG, visualizing the behavior of DNNs, and patching (repairing) DNNs.

In contrast to prior work, SyReNN explores a unique point in the design space of DNN analysis tools. Instead of trading off precision of the analysis for efficiency, SyReNN focuses on analyzing DNN behavior on *low-dimensional subspaces* of the domain, for which we can provide *both* efficiency and precision.

We plan on extending SyReNN to make use of GPUs and other massively-parallel hardware to more quickly compute $\widehat{f_{\restriction X}}$ for large f or X. Techniques to support input polytopes that are greater than two dimensional is also a ripe area of future work. We may also be able to take advantage of the fact that non-convex polytopes can be represented efficiently in 2D. Extending algorithms for $\widehat{f_{\restriction X}}$ to handle architectures such as Recurrent Neural Networks (RNNs) will open up new application areas for SyReNN.

Acknowledgements. We thank the anonymous reviewers for their feedback and suggestions on this work. This material is based upon work supported by a Facebook Probability and Programming award.

References

1. ETH robustness analyzer for neural networks (ERAN). https://github.com/eth-sri/eran (2019), accessed: 2019-05-01

2. Anderson, G., Pailoor, S., Dillig, I., Chaudhuri, S.: Optimization and abstraction: a synergistic approach for analyzing neural network robustness. In: McKinley, K.S., Fisher, K. (eds.) Proceedings of the 40th ACM SIGPLAN Conference on Programming Language Design and Implementation, PLDI 2019, Phoenix, AZ, USA, June 22-26, 2019. pp. 731–744. ACM (2019). https://doi.org/10.1145/3314221.3314614, https://doi.org/10.1145/3314221.3314614

3. Bastani, O., Ioannou, Y., Lampropoulos, L., Vytiniotis, D., Nori, A.V., Criminisi, A.: Measuring neural net robustness with constraints. In: Lee, D.D., Sugiyama, M., von Luxburg, U., Guyon, I., Garnett, R. (eds.) Advances in Neural Information Processing Systems 29: Annual Conference on Neural Information Processing Systems 2016, December 5-10, 2016, Barcelona, Spain. pp. 2613–2621 (2016), http://papers.nips.cc/paper/6339-measuring-neural-net-robustness-with-constraints

4. Bastani, O., Pu, Y., Solar-Lezama, A.: Verifiable reinforcement learning via policy extraction. In: Bengio, S., Wallach, H.M., Larochelle, H., Grauman, K., Cesa-Bianchi, N., Garnett, R. (eds.) Advances in Neural Information Processing Systems 31: Annual Conference on Neural Information Processing Systems 2018, NeurIPS 2018, December 3-8, 2018, Montréal, Canada. pp. 2499–2509 (2018), http://papers.nips.cc/paper/7516-verifiable-reinforcement-learning-via-policy-extraction

5. Beyer, D.: Reliable and reproducible competition results with benchexec and witnesses (report on SV-COMP 2016). In: Chechik, M., Raskin, J. (eds.) Tools and Algorithms for the Construction and Analysis of Systems - 22nd International Conference, TACAS 2016, Held as Part of the European Joint Conferences on Theory and Practice of Software, ETAPS 2016, Eindhoven, The Netherlands, April 2-8, 2016, Proceedings. Lecture Notes in Computer Science, vol. 9636, pp. 887–904. Springer (2016). https://doi.org/10.1007/978-3-662-49674-9_55, https://doi.org/10.1007/978-3-662-49674-9_55

6. Breutel, S., Maire, F., Hayward, R.: Extracting interface assertions from neural networks in polyhedral format. In: ESANN 2003, 11th European Symposium on Artificial Neural Networks, Bruges, Belgium, April 23-25, 2003, Proceedings. pp. 463–468 (2003), https://www.elen.ucl.ac.be/Proceedings/esann/esannpdf/es2003-72.pdf

7. Bunel, R., Turkaslan, I., Torr, P.H.S., Kohli, P., Mudigonda, P.K.: A unified view of piecewise linear neural network verification. In: Bengio, S., Wallach, H.M., Larochelle, H., Grauman, K., Cesa-Bianchi, N., Garnett, R. (eds.) Advances in Neural Information Processing Systems 31: Annual Conference on Neural Information Processing Systems 2018, NeurIPS 2018, December 3-8, 2018, Montréal, Canada. pp. 4795–4804 (2018), http://papers.nips.cc/paper/7728-a-unified-view-of-piecewise-linear-neural-network-verification

8. Carlini, N., Wagner, D.A.: Audio adversarial examples: Targeted attacks on speech-to-text. In: 2018 IEEE Security and Privacy Workshops, SP Workshops 2018, San Francisco, CA, USA, May 24, 2018. pp. 1–7. IEEE Computer Society (2018). https://doi.org/10.1109/SPW.2018.00009, https://doi.org/10.1109/SPW.2018.00009

9. Chen, J., Ran, X.: Deep learning with edge computing: A review. Proc. IEEE **107**(8), 1655–1674 (2019). https://doi.org/10.1109/JPROC.2019.2921977, https://doi.org/10.1109/JPROC.2019.2921977

10. Ching, T., Himmelstein, D.S., Beaulieu-Jones, B.K., Kalinin, A.A., Do, B.T., Way, G.P., Ferrero, E., Agapow, P.M., Zietz, M., Hoffman, M.M., Xie, W., Rosen, G.L., Lengerich, B.J., Israeli, J., Lanchantin, J., Woloszynek, S., Carpenter, A.E., Shrikumar, A., Xu, J., Cofer, E.M., Lavender, C.A., Turaga, S.C., Alexandari, A.M., Lu, Z., Harris, D.J., DeCaprio, D., Qi, Y., Kundaje, A., Peng, Y., Wiley, L.K., Segler,

M.H.S., Boca, S.M., Swamidass, S.J., Huang, A., Gitter, A., Greene, C.S.: Opportunities and obstacles for deep learning in biology and medicine. Journal of The Royal Society Interface **15**(141), 20170387 (2018). https://doi.org/10.1098/rsif.2017.0387

11. Chollet, F., et al.: Keras. https://keras.io (2015)

12. Devlin, J., Chang, M., Lee, K., Toutanova, K.: BERT: pre-training of deep bidirectional transformers for language understanding. In: Burstein, J., Doran, C., Solorio, T. (eds.) Proceedings of the 2019 Conference of the North American Chapter of the Association for Computational Linguistics: Human Language Technologies, NAACL-HLT 2019, Minneapolis, MN, USA, June 2-7, 2019, Volume 1 (Long and Short Papers). pp. 4171–4186. Association for Computational Linguistics (2019). https://doi.org/10.18653/v1/n19-1423, https://doi.org/10.18653/v1/n19-1423

13. Dutta, S., Jha, S., Sankaranarayanan, S., Tiwari, A.: Output range analysis for deep feedforward neural networks. In: Dutle, A., Muñoz, C.A., Narkawicz, A. (eds.) NASA Formal Methods - 10th International Symposium, NFM 2018, Newport News, VA, USA, April 17-19, 2018, Proceedings. Lecture Notes in Computer Science, vol. 10811, pp. 121–138. Springer (2018). https://doi.org/10.1007/978-3-319-77935-5_9, https://doi.org/10.1007/978-3-319-77935-5_9

14. Ehlers, R.: Formal verification of piece-wise linear feed-forward neural networks. In: D'Souza, D., Kumar, K.N. (eds.) Automated Technology for Verification and Analysis - 15th International Symposium, ATVA 2017, Pune, India, October 3-6, 2017, Proceedings. Lecture Notes in Computer Science, vol. 10482, pp. 269–286. Springer (2017). https://doi.org/10.1007/978-3-319-68167-2_19, https://doi.org/10.1007/978-3-319-68167-2_19

15. Fischer, M., Balunovic, M., Drachsler-Cohen, D., Gehr, T., Zhang, C., Vechev, M.T.: DL2: training and querying neural networks with logic. In: Chaudhuri, K., Salakhutdinov, R. (eds.) Proceedings of the 36th International Conference on Machine Learning, ICML 2019, 9-15 June 2019, Long Beach, California, USA. Proceedings of Machine Learning Research, vol. 97, pp. 1931–1941. PMLR (2019), http://proceedings.mlr.press/v97/fischer19a.html

16. Gehr, T., Mirman, M., Drachsler-Cohen, D., Tsankov, P., Chaudhuri, S., Vechev, M.T.: AI2: safety and robustness certification of neural networks with abstract interpretation. In: 2018 IEEE Symposium on Security and Privacy, SP 2018, Proceedings, 21-23 May 2018, San Francisco, California, USA. pp. 3–18. IEEE Computer Society (2018). https://doi.org/10.1109/SP.2018.00058, https://doi.org/10.1109/SP.2018.00058

17. Gonzales, R.: Feds say self-driving uber suv did not recognize jaywalking pedestrian in fatal crash. NPR https://www.npr.org/2019/11/07/777438412/feds-say-self-driving-uber-suv-did-not-recognize-jaywalking-pedestrian-in-fatal- (Nov 2019), accessed: 2020-06-06

18. Goodfellow, I., Bengio, Y., Courville, A.: Deep Learning. MIT Press (2016), http://www.deeplearningbook.org

19. Goodfellow, I.J., Shlens, J., Szegedy, C.: Explaining and harnessing adversarial examples. In: Bengio, Y., LeCun, Y. (eds.) 3rd International Conference on Learning Representations, ICLR 2015, San Diego, CA, USA, May 7-9, 2015, Conference Track Proceedings (2015), http://arxiv.org/abs/1412.6572

20. Google: grpc: A high-performance, open source universal rpc framework. "https://grpc.io/ (2020)

21. Google: Protocol buffers - google's data interchange format. https://developers.google.com/protocol-buffers/ (2020)

22. Gopinath, S., Ghanathe, N., Seshadri, V., Sharma, R.: Compiling kb-sized machine learning models to tiny iot devices. In: McKinley, K.S., Fisher, K. (eds.) Proceedings of the 40th ACM SIGPLAN Conference on Programming Language Design and Implementation, PLDI 2019, Phoenix, AZ, USA, June 22-26, 2019. pp. 79–95. ACM (2019). https://doi.org/10.1145/3314221.3314597, https://doi.org/10.1145/3314221.3314597

23. Guennebaud, G., Jacob, B., et al.: Eigen v3. http://eigen.tuxfamily.org (2010)

24. Han, S., Mao, H., Dally, W.J.: Deep compression: Compressing deep neural network with pruning, trained quantization and huffman coding. In: Bengio, Y., LeCun, Y. (eds.) 4th International Conference on Learning Representations, ICLR 2016, San Juan, Puerto Rico, May 2-4, 2016, Conference Track Proceedings (2016), http://arxiv.org/abs/1510.00149

25. Hanin, B., Rolnick, D.: Complexity of linear regions in deep networks. In: Chaudhuri, K., Salakhutdinov, R. (eds.) Proceedings of the 36th International Conference on Machine Learning, ICML 2019, 9-15 June 2019, Long Beach, California, USA. Proceedings of Machine Learning Research, vol. 97, pp. 2596–2604. PMLR (2019), http://proceedings.mlr.press/v97/hanin19a.html

26. Hern, A.: Facebook translates 'good morning' into 'attack them', leading to arrest. https://www.theguardian.com/technology/2017/oct/24/facebook-palestine-israel-translates-good-morning-attack-them-arrest (Jun 2017), accessed: 2020-06-06

27. Hill, K.: Wrongfully accused by an algorithm. New York Times. https://www.nytimes.com/2020/06/24/technology/facial-recognition-arrest.html (Jun 2020), accessed: 2020-06-06

28. Hosny, A., Parmar, C., Quackenbush, J., Schwartz, L.H., Aerts, H.J.: Artificial intelligence in radiology. Nature Reviews Cancer p. 1 (2018)

29. Huang, X., Kwiatkowska, M., Wang, S., Wu, M.: Safety verification of deep neural networks. In: Majumdar, R., Kuncak, V. (eds.) Computer Aided Verification - 29th International Conference, CAV 2017, Heidelberg, Germany, July 24-28, 2017, Proceedings, Part I. Lecture Notes in Computer Science, vol. 10426, pp. 3–29. Springer (2017). https://doi.org/10.1007/978-3-319-63387-9_1, https://doi.org/10.1007/978-3-319-63387-9_1

30. Jeannet, B., Miné, A.: Apron: A library of numerical abstract domains for static analysis. In: Bouajjani, A., Maler, O. (eds.) Computer Aided Verification, 21st International Conference, CAV 2009, Grenoble, France, June 26 - July 2, 2009. Proceedings. Lecture Notes in Computer Science, vol. 5643, pp. 661–667. Springer (2009). https://doi.org/10.1007/978-3-642-02658-4_52, https://doi.org/10.1007/978-3-642-02658-4_52

31. Julian, K.D., Kochenderfer, M.J., Owen, M.P.: Deep neural network compression for aircraft collision avoidance systems. CoRR **abs/1810.04240** (2018), http://arxiv.org/abs/1810.04240

32. Katz, G., Barrett, C.W., Dill, D.L., Julian, K., Kochenderfer, M.J.: Reluplex: An efficient SMT solver for verifying deep neural networks. In: Majumdar, R., Kuncak, V. (eds.) Computer Aided Verification - 29th International Conference, CAV 2017, Heidelberg, Germany, July 24-28, 2017, Proceedings, Part I. Lecture Notes in Computer Science, vol. 10426, pp. 97–117. Springer (2017). https://doi.org/10.1007/978-3-319-63387-9_5, https://doi.org/10.1007/978-3-319-63387-9_5

33. Krizhevsky, A., Sutskever, I., Hinton, G.E.: Imagenet classification with deep convolutional neural networks. In: Bartlett, P.L., Pereira, F.C.N., Burges, C.J.C.,

Bottou, L., Weinberger, K.Q. (eds.) Advances in Neural Information Processing Systems 25: 26th Annual Conference on Neural Information Processing Systems 2012. Proceedings of a meeting held December 3-6, 2012, Lake Tahoe, Nevada, United States. pp. 1106–1114 (2012), http://papers.nips.cc/paper/4824-imagenet-classification-with-deep-convolutional-neural-networks

34. Kumar, A., Seshadri, V., Sharma, R.: Shiftry: RNN inference in 2kb of RAM. Proc. ACM Program. Lang. 4(OOPSLA), 182:1–182:30 (2020). https://doi.org/10.1145/3428250, https://doi.org/10.1145/3428250

35. Kusupati, A., Singh, M., Bhatia, K., Kumar, A., Jain, P., Varma, M.: Fastgrnn: A fast, accurate, stable and tiny kilobyte sized gated recurrent neural network. In: Bengio, S., Wallach, H.M., Larochelle, H., Grauman, K., Cesa-Bianchi, N., Garnett, R. (eds.) Advances in Neural Information Processing Systems 31: Annual Conference on Neural Information Processing Systems 2018, NeurIPS 2018, December 3-8, 2018, Montréal, Canada. pp. 9031–9042 (2018)

36. Lee, D.: US opens investigation into Tesla after fatal crash. BBC. https://www.bbc.co.uk/news/technology-36680043 (Jul 2016), accessed: 2020-06-06

37. Mendelson, E.B.: Artificial intelligence in breast imaging: potentials and limitations. American Journal of Roentgenology 212(2), 293–299 (2019)

38. Miotto, R., Wang, F., Wang, S., Jiang, X., Dudley, J.T.: Deep learning for healthcare: review, opportunities and challenges. Briefings Bioinform. 19(6), 1236–1246 (2018). https://doi.org/10.1093/bib/bbx044, https://doi.org/10.1093/bib/bbx044

39. Mirman, M., Gehr, T., Vechev, M.T.: Differentiable abstract interpretation for provably robust neural networks. In: Dy, J.G., Krause, A. (eds.) Proceedings of the 35th International Conference on Machine Learning, ICML 2018, Stockholmsmässan, Stockholm, Sweden, July 10-15, 2018. Proceedings of Machine Learning Research, vol. 80, pp. 3575–3583. PMLR (2018), http://proceedings.mlr.press/v80/mirman18b.html

40. Moosavi-Dezfooli, S., Fawzi, A., Frossard, P.: Deepfool: A simple and accurate method to fool deep neural networks. In: 2016 IEEE Conference on Computer Vision and Pattern Recognition, CVPR 2016, Las Vegas, NV, USA, June 27-30, 2016. pp. 2574–2582. IEEE Computer Society (2016). https://doi.org/10.1109/CVPR.2016.282, https://doi.org/10.1109/CVPR.2016.282

41. Nguyen, A.M., Yosinski, J., Clune, J.: Deep neural networks are easily fooled: High confidence predictions for unrecognizable images. In: IEEE Conference on Computer Vision and Pattern Recognition, CVPR 2015, Boston, MA, USA, June 7-12, 2015. pp. 427–436. IEEE Computer Society (2015). https://doi.org/10.1109/CVPR.2015.7298640, https://doi.org/10.1109/CVPR.2015.7298640

42. ONNX: Open neural network exchange. https://onnx.ai/ (2020)

43. Paszke, A., Gross, S., Chintala, S., Chanan, G., Yang, E., DeVito, Z., Lin, Z., Desmaison, A., Antiga, L., Lerer, A.: Automatic differentiation in pytorch (2017)

44. Paszke, A., Gross, S., Massa, F., Lerer, A., Bradbury, J., Chanan, G., Killeen, T., Lin, Z., Gimelshein, N., Antiga, L., Desmaison, A., Köpf, A., Yang, E., DeVito, Z., Raison, M., Tejani, A., Chilamkurthy, S., Steiner, B., Fang, L., Bai, J., Chintala, S.: Pytorch: An imperative style, high-performance deep learning library. In: Wallach, H.M., Larochelle, H., Beygelzimer, A., d'Alché-Buc, F., Fox, E.B., Garnett, R. (eds.) Advances in Neural Information Processing Systems 32: Annual Conference on Neural Information Processing Systems 2019, NeurIPS 2019, December 8-14, 2019, Vancouver, BC, Canada. pp. 8024–8035 (2019), http://papers.nips.cc/paper/9015-pytorch-an-imperative-style-high-performance-deep-learning-library

45. Reinders, J.: Intel threading building blocks: outfitting C++ for multi-core processor parallelism. " O'Reilly Media, Inc." (2007)
46. Scheibler, K., Winterer, L., Wimmer, R., Becker, B.: Towards verification of artificial neural networks. In: Heinkel, U., Kriesten, D., Rößler, M. (eds.) Methoden und Beschreibungssprachen zur Modellierung und Verifikation von Schaltungen und Systemen, MBMV 2015, Chemnitz, Germany, March 3-4, 2015. pp. 30–40. Sächsische Landesbibliothek (2015)
47. Sharma, H., Park, J., Mahajan, D., Amaro, E., Kim, J.K., Shao, C., Mishra, A., Esmaeilzadeh, H.: From high-level deep neural models to fpgas. In: 49th Annual IEEE/ACM International Symposium on Microarchitecture, MICRO 2016, Taipei, Taiwan, October 15-19, 2016. pp. 17:1–17:12. IEEE Computer Society (2016). https://doi.org/10.1109/MICRO.2016.7783720, https://doi.org/10.1109/MICRO.2016.7783720
48. Singh, G., Gehr, T., Mirman, M., Püschel, M., Vechev, M.T.: Fast and effective robustness certification. In: Bengio, S., Wallach, H.M., Larochelle, H., Grauman, K., Cesa-Bianchi, N., Garnett, R. (eds.) Advances in Neural Information Processing Systems 31: Annual Conference on Neural Information Processing Systems 2018, NeurIPS 2018, December 3-8, 2018, Montréal, Canada. pp. 10825–10836 (2018), http://papers.nips.cc/paper/8278-fast-and-effective-robustness-certification
49. Singh, G., Gehr, T., Püschel, M., Vechev, M.T.: An abstract domain for certifying neural networks. Proc. ACM Program. Lang. 3(POPL), 41:1–41:30 (2019). https://doi.org/10.1145/3290354, https://doi.org/10.1145/3290354
50. Sotoudeh, M., Thakur, A.V.: Computing linear restrictions of neural networks. In: Wallach, H.M., Larochelle, H., Beygelzimer, A., d'Alché-Buc, F., Fox, E.B., Garnett, R. (eds.) Advances in Neural Information Processing Systems 32: Annual Conference on Neural Information Processing Systems 2019, NeurIPS 2019, December 8-14, 2019, Vancouver, BC, Canada. pp. 14132–14143 (2019), http://papers.nips.cc/paper/9562-computing-linear-restrictions-of-neural-networks
51. Sotoudeh, M., Thakur, A.V.: Correcting deep neural networks with small, generalizing patches. In: Workshop on Safety and Robustness in Decision Making (2019)
52. Sundararajan, M., Taly, A., Yan, Q.: Axiomatic attribution for deep networks. In: Precup, D., Teh, Y.W. (eds.) Proceedings of the 34th International Conference on Machine Learning, ICML 2017, Sydney, NSW, Australia, 6-11 August 2017. Proceedings of Machine Learning Research, vol. 70, pp. 3319–3328. PMLR (2017), http://proceedings.mlr.press/v70/sundararajan17a.html
53. Szegedy, C., Vanhoucke, V., Ioffe, S., Shlens, J., Wojna, Z.: Rethinking the inception architecture for computer vision. In: 2016 IEEE Conference on Computer Vision and Pattern Recognition, CVPR 2016, Las Vegas, NV, USA, June 27-30, 2016. pp. 2818–2826. IEEE Computer Society (2016). https://doi.org/10.1109/CVPR.2016.308, https://doi.org/10.1109/CVPR.2016.308
54. Szegedy, C., Zaremba, W., Sutskever, I., Bruna, J., Erhan, D., Goodfellow, I.J., Fergus, R.: Intriguing properties of neural networks. In: Bengio, Y., LeCun, Y. (eds.) 2nd International Conference on Learning Representations, ICLR 2014, Banff, AB, Canada, April 14-16, 2014, Conference Track Proceedings (2014), http://arxiv.org/abs/1312.6199
55. Thrun, S.: Extracting rules from artifical neural networks with distributed representations. In: Tesauro, G., Touretzky, D.S., Leen, T.K. (eds.) Advances in Neural Information Processing Systems 7, [NIPS Conference, Denver, Colorado, USA, 1994]. pp. 505–512. MIT Press (1994)

56. Wang, S., Pei, K., Whitehouse, J., Yang, J., Jana, S.: Formal security analysis of neural networks using symbolic intervals. In: Enck, W., Felt, A.P. (eds.) 27th USENIX Security Symposium, USENIX Security 2018, Baltimore, MD, USA, August 15-17, 2018. pp. 1599–1614. USENIX Association (2018), https://www.usenix.org/conference/usenixsecurity18/presentation/wang-shiqi

57. Weng, T., Zhang, H., Chen, H., Song, Z., Hsieh, C., Daniel, L., Boning, D.S., Dhillon, I.S.: Towards fast computation of certified robustness for relu networks. In: Dy, J.G., Krause, A. (eds.) Proceedings of the 35th International Conference on Machine Learning, ICML 2018, Stockholmsmässan, Stockholm, Sweden, July 10-15, 2018. Proceedings of Machine Learning Research, vol. 80, pp. 5273–5282. PMLR (2018), http://proceedings.mlr.press/v80/weng18a.html

58. Xiang, W., Tran, H., Johnson, T.T.: Reachable set computation and safety verification for neural networks with relu activations. CoRR **abs/1712.08163** (2017), http://arxiv.org/abs/1712.08163

59. Xiang, W., Tran, H., Rosenfeld, J.A., Johnson, T.T.: Reachable set estimation and safety verification for piecewise linear systems with neural network controllers. In: 2018 Annual American Control Conference, ACC 2018, Milwaukee, WI, USA, June 27-29, 2018. pp. 1574–1579. IEEE (2018). https://doi.org/10.23919/ACC.2018.8431048, https://doi.org/10.23919/ACC.2018.8431048

60. Zhu, H., Xiong, Z., Magill, S., Jagannathan, S.: An inductive synthesis framework for verifiable reinforcement learning. In: McKinley, K.S., Fisher, K. (eds.) Proceedings of the 40th ACM SIGPLAN Conference on Programming Language Design and Implementation, PLDI 2019, Phoenix, AZ, USA, June 22-26, 2019. pp. 686–701. ACM (2019). https://doi.org/10.1145/3314221.3314638, https://doi.org/10.1145/3314221.3314638

MachSMT: A Machine Learning-based Algorithm Selector for SMT Solvers*

Joseph Scott[1](✉) , Aina Niemetz[2] , Mathias Preiner[2] ,
Saeed Nejati[1] , and Vijay Ganesh[1]

[1] University of Waterloo, Waterloo, Ontario, Canada
{joseph.scott, snejati, vijay.ganesh}@uwaterloo.ca
[2] Stanford University, Stanford, USA
{niemetz,preiner}@cs.stanford.edu

Abstract. In this paper, we present MachSMT, an algorithm selection tool for Satisfiability Modulo Theories (SMT) solvers. MachSMT supports the entirety of the SMT-LIB language. It employs machine learning (ML) methods to construct both empirical hardness models (EHMs) and pairwise ranking comparators (PWCs) over state-of-the-art SMT solvers. Given an SMT formula $\mathcal{I}$ as input, MachSMT leverages these learnt models to output a ranking of solvers based on predicted run time on the formula $\mathcal{I}$. We evaluate MachSMT on the solvers, benchmarks, and data obtained from SMT-COMP 2019 and 2020. We observe MachSMT frequently improves on competition winners, winning 54 divisions outright and up to a 198.4% improvement in PAR-2 score, notably in logics that have broad applications (e.g., BV, LIA, NRA, etc.) in verification, program analysis, and software engineering. The MachSMT tool is designed to be easily tuned and extended to any suitable solver application by users. MachSMT is not a replacement for SMT solvers by any means. Instead, it is a tool that enables users to leverage the collective strength of the diverse set of algorithms implemented as part of these sophisticated solvers.

Keywords: SMT Solvers · Machine Learning · Algorithm Selection

1 Introduction

Satisfiability Modulo Theories (SMT) solvers are tools to decide the satisfiability of formulas over first-order theories such as bit-vectors, floating-point arithmetic, integers, reals, strings, arrays, and their combinations [44,9,24,18,47,20,46]. In recent years, SMT solvers have had a revolutionary impact on applications in software engineering (broadly construed), such as software testing [17,48] and verification [23,15,27,39], as well as in sub-fields of AI [53,35,30]. This impact is a driver for an insatiable demand for evermore efficient solvers, not only to scale to larger instances obtained from existing applications (e.g., automatic bug-finding

---

* This work was supported in part by DARPA (award no. FA8650-18-2-7861) and ONR (award no. N68335-17-C-0558).

J. F. Groote and K. G. Larsen (Eds.): TACAS 2021, LNCS 12652, pp. 303–325, 2021.
https://doi.org/10.1007/978-3-030-72013-1_16

in commercial software [26,4]), but also to solve problems from new application domains (e.g., verification and synthesis of cryptographic primitives [13]).

Motivation for Algorithm Selection for SMT Solvers. In response to this high demand, the SMT community has developed a plethora of solver heuristics and configurations. For example, in the 2019 edition of the annual SMT-COMP competition [10,31], more than 50 solvers and their configurations were submitted. Many of these solvers implement very different algorithms to tackle the satisfiability problem for (a combination of) first-order theories, with significantly varying performance profiles. For example, in the quantifier-free theory of floating-point arithmetic (QF_FP), there exist several substantially different decision procedures, e.g., bit-blasting [16], abstract CDCL [14], inter-reduction methods [55], and reduction to global optimization [22,11]. In this specific setting of floating-point solvers, input instances may be derived from a variety of applications, such as software verification or analysis of machine learning (ML) models [56]. In such a scenario, a very natural question arises: which solver or configuration is best for a given input instance?

Another well-known issue with many SMT solvers (even state-of-the-art ones) is that users may not know a priori which formula features or encoding would make an instance easy to solve. This can be very frustrating for users as they have to try a large number of different encodings with different solver configurations before they can figure out which combination works best for their specific scenario, which may result in a combinatorial explosion. Users have also noted that as their applications change, what was once a great solver configuration in an earlier setting is suddenly not very good in the newer one. One possible approach to address this problem is to use a portfolio of solvers, just as has been successfully done in the context of SAT solvers. Unfortunately, given the plethora of solvers (more than 50 in SMT-COMP 2019 and 2020) and configurations (CVC4 [9] alone utilizes 23 different configurations in a sequential portfolio setting for quantified logics) such an approach becomes quickly infeasible in the SMT solver setting.

Brief Overview of MachSMT. One way to address the above-mentioned problems is to use an automated algorithm-selection tool that can automatically and with high accuracy predict the best algorithm from a given set of algorithms for a specific input. Such a tool selects the best SMT solver from a set of solvers for a given SMT formula. To this end, we introduce MachSMT, a machine learning-based algorithm-selection tool. MachSMT supports the entirety of the SMT-LIB language [8]. It takes as input an instance for a specified theory of interest, and outputs a ranking of solvers predicted to have the lowest runtime. Internally, MachSMT is a set of machine learnt models constructed by analyzing the runtimes of solver configurations on benchmarks with respect to the frequencies of grammatical constructs (e.g., predicates, functions, rounding modes, etc.). Additionally, it defines other syntactical properties that can have influence in performance (e.g., quantifier nesting levels).

At a high-level, MachSMT works as follows. At its core, MachSMT uses two techniques to perform algorithm selection: empirical hardness models (EHMs) and pairwise ranking comparators (PWCs). MachSMT uses frequencies of grammatical constructs from the SMT-LIB language [8], in addition to several other syntactical metrics for features pipelined with Principal Component Analysis (PCA) and AdaBoosting to construct its empirical hardness models and comparators.

An EHM for a given solver $\mathcal{S}$ is a mapping from an input instance $\mathcal{I}$ to a predicted runtime of $\mathcal{S}$ on $\mathcal{I}$. At runtime, given $\mathcal{I}$, MachSMT queries all EHMs for all solvers (that were considered during training) over $\mathcal{I}$, and outputs a ranking of solvers based on their predicted runtimes (top-ranked solver is predicted to solve the input problem the fastest). By contrast, a learnt pairwise ranking comparator (PWC) is a mapping that takes as input pair $(\mathcal{S}_1, \mathcal{S}_2)$ of solvers and an input instance $\mathcal{I}$, and outputs a ranking over the input solvers based on which one of them is predicted to have a lower runtime on $\mathcal{I}$ (denoted as $\mathcal{S}_1 \leq \mathcal{S}_2$ or $\mathcal{S}_1 \geq \mathcal{S}_2$). During evaluation, given an input instance $\mathcal{I}$, MachSMT uses the learnt PWC as a comparator to rank the set of solvers.

While algorithm selection has been considered in the broad setting of solvers (e.g., QBF solvers [50] and SAT solvers [67]) as well as certain specific SMT theories [57,5,64], we are not aware of previous work on algorithm selection aimed at the entirety of SMT-LIB [7]. Our results demonstrate that the MachSMT algorithm selector is highly effective, in that it outperforms the competition winners on the majority of tracks from the SMT-COMP in 2019 and 2020.

Perhaps the first algorithm selection tool in the context of logic solvers was SATZilla [67]. Since its introduction, SATZilla has had a tremendous impact on SAT solver research, winning multiple gold medals in the SAT competitions. Having said that, there are several significant differences between MachSMT and SATZilla. Briefly, SATZilla deploys a feature selection scheme to avoid the curse of dimensionality, while MachSMT leverages a learnt dimensionality reduction scheme, namely, Principal Component Analysis (PCA). In fact, a feature selection scheme would simply not scale in the context of SMT solvers given the very large number of learnt models that are incorporated into MachSMT. We discuss additional differences between SATZilla and MachSMT at length in Section 6.

It goes without saying that MachSMT is only as powerful as the underlying solvers that it has access to. MachSMT is clearly not a replacement for any particular SMT solver, but rather a tool that enables users to leverage the collective strength of the diverse set of algorithms and configurations implemented as part of these sophisticated solvers.

Contributions.

We make the following contributions in this paper.

1. **The MachSMT Algorithm Selection Tool.** We present the MachSMT tool, an algorithm selection tool for the entirety of SMT-LIB. MachSMT uses machine learning (ML) to construct EHMs and PWCs of solvers for algorithm selection. A key feature of MachSMT tool is that it is designed to be easily tuned and extended by SMT solver users (Section 3).

2. **Analysis of MachSMT over SMT-COMP 2019 and 2020 Benchmarks and Solvers**. We perform an extensive experimental analysis of MachSMT across all divisions from SMT-COMP 2019 and 2020. We observe that MachSMT improves on competition winners in 54 divisions, with up to 198.4% improvement in performance for the QF_BVFPLRA SQ '20 and up to 191.1% for the QF_BVFP SQ '20 division. We provide our learnt models, used in our experimentation, for ease of use and transparency. While building learnt models for MachSMT can be computationally expensive (a one time cost), installing, downloading, and using our models is easy (Section 4). All source code and learnt models from our experience can be found at: https://github.com/j29scott/MachSMT. The artifact is available at: https://zenodo.org/record/4458699.

The rest of this paper is structured as follows. Section 2 provides the necessary background, Section 3 gives a technical description of MachSMT, Section 4 gives an experimental evaluation of MachSMT over SMT-COMP 2019 and 2020, Section 5 provides an analysis of the experimental results, Section 6 describes related work, and Section 7 concludes the paper and discusses future work.

2 Background

In this section, we provide some background on algorithm selection via EHMs and PWCs, and the machine learning methods we use, such as principal component analysis (PCA) and k-fold cross validation.

2.1 A Brief Overview of Algorithm Selection

The idea of algorithm selection was first proposed and formalized by Rice et. al. [51] in 1976. Researchers have long known that given a set of different algorithms and implementations for the same specification or problem, it is often the case that one of these implementations may perform poorly on a given class of inputs while another might perform very well. This is especially true for problems believed to be computationally hard (e.g., NP-hard). The reasons for this phenomenon could be as diverse as choice of data structures, fundamental differences between algorithms, or the fact that heuristics implemented as part of one algorithm can exploit the input problem structure or the underlying hardware better than the others.

It is natural to want to exploit the diversity in algorithmic approaches to minimize the cumulative runtimes. However, in practice users often deploy *greedy* algorithm selection – picking the best observed algorithm based on empirical analysis and testing. However, greedy algorithm selection can be sub-optimal when the best empirical algorithm has deficiencies relative to other algorithms on certain families of inputs.

With the recent advances in AI and ML, researchers are beginning to leverage these new technologies to advance algorithm selection. To the best of our knowledge, there are two key approaches for ML-driven algorithm selection in the context of constraint solvers: through the use of Empirical Hardness Models (EHMs), and through Pairwise Ranking Comparators (PWCs).

Algorithm Selection via Empirical Hardness Models (EHMs): Let $\mathcal{I}$ be an input in the language of $\mathcal{S}$ with a corresponding feature vector $\vec{x} \in \mathbb{R}^n$. For an algorithm $s \in \mathcal{S}$, an EHM is a learnt function $f_s : \mathbb{R}^n \to \mathbb{R}$ that predicts the runtime of s on $\mathcal{I}$. An EHM is constructed with an ML regression model trained on collected runtime data. The algorithm is then selected by computing:

$$\underset{s \in \mathcal{S}}{\mathrm{argmin}}\, f_s(\vec{x})$$

Algorithm Selection via Pairwise Ranking Comparators (PWCs). Let P be the set of all unique pair sets (sets of size two). For each $p = (\mathcal{S}_i, \mathcal{S}_j) \in P$, construct a learnt comparator $f_p : \mathbb{R}^n \to \{0, 1\}$, that returns 0 if algorithm $\mathcal{S}_i$ solves $\mathcal{I}$ faster than $\mathcal{S}_j$, and 1 otherwise. For an input $\mathcal{I}$ with a feature vector $\vec{x}$, we compute a ranking of algorithms as a map r over $\mathcal{S}$, where for $s \in \mathcal{S}$, $r[s]$ is the ranking of solver s that represents: "how many solvers in $\mathcal{S}$ are faster than s in solving the input $\mathcal{S}$", or more formally: $r[s] = \Sigma_{p:s \in p} f_s(\vec{x})$. The selected solver is then the minimum ranked solver, i.e.,

$$\underset{s \in \mathcal{S}}{\mathrm{argmin}}\, r[s]$$

2.2 Supervised Learning, Adaptive Boosting, Curse of Dimensionality, and K-Fold Cross-Validation

Supervised learning is one of the most predominant areas of ML. Supervised learning takes as input a dataset of features X and labels Y, and each datapoint $\vec{x} \in X$ has a label $y \in Y$. A datapoint is a real valued vector $\vec{x} \in \mathbb{R}^n$ describing a sample. The learning problem is said to be a *classification* problem if the labels $y \in Y$ come from a fixed and finite set of classes $\mathcal{C}$ (e.g., a set of algorithms). Alternatively, the learning problem is a *regression* problem if the labels are real valued (e.g., runtimes).

One efficient and effective approach to supervised learning is *Adaptive Boosting (AdaBoost)*. AdaBoost is an *ensemble* approach to machine learning invented by Freund and Schapire et. al. [21], which won the Gödel Prize in 2003. In ensemble learning, a set of learning algorithms (e.g., weak learners) are trained, and predictions are made diplomatically across the set. In this paper, we exclusively consider AdaBoost to solve both the classification and regression problems for algorithm selection. We use an ensemble of 200 decision trees in the AdaBoost algorithm. For more, we refer to Drucker et al. [19].

While supervised learning has had tremendous impacts in several areas of research, there are pitfalls, such as the *curse of dimensionality* (CoD). Consider the convex polytope P formed around the convex hull of X. The volume of P

increases exponentially with the dimensionality of X requiring an exponential amount of datapoints to avoid extreme sparsity in X. Sparsity in datasets is one of the leading causes of poor performances in learnt models [28]. There is a large literature on managing the CoD. In this paper, we discuss *feature selection* and deploy *dimensionality reduction* solutions. In feature selection, a new dataset X' is computed from X by selecting the subset of features that are the most performant on a validation dataset. Feature selection was deployed in the successful SATZilla algorithm selection tool for Boolean satisfiability.

Despite the success of feature selection in SATZilla, feature selection does have some flaws. First, there is a significant loss of information. In the case of SATZilla, a feature vector composed of more than a hundred values describing an input is reduced to just five values. Second, the total number of feature subsets is exponential in the number of features. While there has been a great deal of research in reducing the time spent searching for high performing subsets [65,36], in our experiments, we found it to be the most computationally taxing component of the SATZilla framework.

When evaluating the performance of a supervised learning model, a training set is used to construct the learnt model and a testing set is set aside to evaluate. However, this method alone can be prone to overfitting and selection bias [54,43]. Instead, researchers often use $k-$fold cross-validation to evaluate their learnt models. In $k-$fold cross validation, the dataset is split into k sets, and the learnt model is trained on $k-1$ sets and is evaluated on the set that is left out. This process is repeated k times so each set gets evaluated.

2.3   Unsupervised Learning and Principal Component Analysis

Unsupervised learning, in contrast to supervised learning, is the study of detecting patterns in an unlabelled dataset X. Applications of unsupervised learning include dimensionality reduction [66,63], clustering [29,72], and anomaly detection [38,1]. Principal Component Analysis (PCA) is an unsupervised learning dimensionality reduction technique. PCA computes an orthogonal transformation of a dataset X composed of points in $\mathbb{R}^n$ to a new data set X' composed of points in $\mathbb{R}^{n'}$ where $n' < n$. PCA is an incremental algorithm, wherein, each iteration a new component (or dimension) is computed. On the first iteration, a hyperplane is fit around the dataset X and its corresponding spanning vector is the first element of the basis around the transformation onto X'. On each subsequent iteration, a new hyperplane is computed under the additional constraint of it being orthogonal to its predecessors. This process is repeated until the desired number of iterations is achieved [32,66].

3   An overview of MachSMT

In this section, we provide an overview of the MachSMT tool. The architecture diagram of MachSMT is presented in Figure 1.

Feature ID	Description
1–4	Frequency of problem description grammatical constructs (e.g., assert, check-sat, etc.)
5–13	Frequency of declaration/definition grammatical constructs (e.g., declare-const, define-fun, declare-sort, etc.)
14–15	Frequency of the echo/exit grammatical constructs
16–27	Frequency of the get-* grammatical constructs (e.g., get-model, get-unsat-core, etc.)
28–29	Frequency of the push/pop incremental benchmark grammatical constructs
30–31	Frequency of the reset/reset-assertions grammatical constructs
32–35	Frequency of the set-* grammatical constructs (e.g., set-logic)
36–37	Frequency of the forall/exists quantifiers
38	Frequency of let bindings
39–49	Frequency of core/Boolean constructs, sorts, and literals (e.g., true, Bool, and, =>, ite, distinct, etc.)
50–52	Frequency of grammatical constructs of the theory of arrays (e.g., select, store, etc.)
53–88	Frequency of grammatical constructs of the theory of bit-vectors (e.g., BitVec, bvor, bvuge, bvsge, bvult, etc.)
89–135	Frequency of grammatical constructs of the theory of floating-point (e.g., fp.add, Float32, RNE, fp.eq, fp.isNaN, fp.to_real, etc.)
135–150	Frequency of grammatical constructs of the theory of integers and reals (e.g., Int, Real, *, +, to_real, is_int)
151	Average number of selects per array
152	Average store chain depth per array
153–155	Average/Median/Deviation of BV adder chains
156–158	Number of forall/exists variables and their ratio
159	Average quantifier nesting level
160–161	Average arity and applications of uninterpreted functions
162	Size of the smt2 file in bytes

Table 1: Complete list of the 162 features used in MachSMT

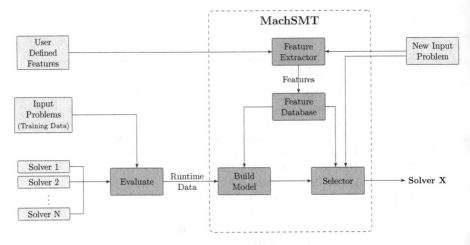

Fig. 1 *Architecture of MachSMT.*

3.1 Features, Preprocessing, and Learning

MachSMT uses a feature vector with 162 entries (i.e., dimensions). A complete description of each feature is provided in Table 1. We deploy two strategies to mitigate taxing feature calculation times, which can severely impair algorithm selection solutions. First, all features are entirely syntactical properties of the input. This is a major difference between MachSMT and other algorithm selection solutions, such as SATZilla. Second, all features are calculated within a strict and user-adjustable timeout (default 10s). On a timeout, the feature value is recorded as -1.0.

MachSMT performs three key preprocessing steps before constructing any learnt models over a given dataset. We describe each subsequently. First, all feature values are scaled to zero mean and unit variance[3]. This data normalization technique is common in ML research and applications to improve both model efficiency and numerical robustness. The second step in the preprocessing pipeline is computing the polynomial interaction terms of degree two on the resultant normalized feature vector. These polynomial features make interacting correlations of features explicit. These first two preprocessing steps are included in the SATZilla preprocessing pipeline [71].

As discussed in Section 2, ML in a high dimensional space is prone to the curse of dimensionality. While other algorithm selection solutions (e.g., SATZilla) commonly implement feature selection solutions, we propose the use of learnt dimensionality, namely PCA. As discussed above, feature selection can be a proactive solution to the curse of dimensionality but presents many challenges when applying to SMT. Internally MachSMT manages more than a thousand learnt models, and calculating optimal feature subsets for each one is infeasible.

---

[3] $\frac{x-\mu}{\sigma}$, where x is a feature sample, μ is the mean across the specific feature on the training set, and σ is the deviation across the specific feature on the training set.

The third and final preprocessing step is applying PCA on the resultant polynomial features. The final feature vector is composed of the first 35 principal components. PCA is the final step in the MachSMT preprocessing pipeline. The resultant feature set is used when constructing the learnt models with AdaBoost. We use AdaBoost for both regression in the EHMs and classifications in the PWCs. We configure AdaBoost with 200 decision tree estimators and linear loss. MachSMT uses scikit-learn and numpy as its ML backend and the entire tool is written in Python [49]. MachSMT is easily extensible and supports any ML model/pipeline under scikit-learn syntax.

3.2 Variants of MachSMT

MachSMT implements the following algorithm selection solutions.

1. **MachSMT-SolverEHM** – This variant of MachSMT is analogous to the algorithm selection approach taken by SATZilla. As described in Section 2, an EHM is constructed for each solver, and the selected solver is computed by taking an argmin over all predictions.

2. **MachSMT-SolverLogicEHM** – This approach is similar to MachSMT-SolverEHM, with the key difference being an EHM is constructed for every solver, logic pair. As state-of-the-art SMT solvers implement significantly different algorithms depending on the logic of the input problem, datapoints from different logics could negatively skew predictions.

3. **MachSMT-SolverPWC** – This variant of MachSMT deploys the PairWise comparator approach as described in Section 2. In this variant of the PWC, comparators are trained for every pair of solvers across all provided data.

4. **MachSMT-SolverLogicPWC** – This variant of MachSMT is analogous to MachSMT-SolverPWC, with the key difference that solver-wise comparators are constructed by only training on the benchmarks of a common logic.

MachSMT by default creates models for all aforementioned approaches to algorithm selection. In evaluation, MachSMT evaluates each approach's performance on each logic. In deployment, MachSMT uses the approach that had the best-observed performance in evaluation.

3.3 Using MachSMT

MachSMT consists of three core tools, which are used to build, evaluate, and deploy MachSMT, respectively.

1. `machsmt_build` – This tool is the interface for building MachSMT's database around the solvers and benchmarks provided by the user. It takes as input a csv data file denoting the columns 'solver', 'benchmark', and 'score'. The output is a library directory containing the resultant database, and learnt models under default settings.

```
machsmt_build -f data.csv -l /path/to/lib/dir
```

Logic, Track, Year	Winner	Improvement over Random [%]	Winner [%]	Distance from VBS [%]
QF_BVFP, SQ'20	Bitwuzla	195.1	191.1	86.2
QF_BVFPLRA, SQ'20	MathSAT5	199.1	198.4	34.0
QF_UFBV, SQ'19	Yices	153.5	113.3	95.3
NRA, SQ'19	Vampire	169.6	114.0	99.2
QF_NRA, SQ'19	Yices	101.3	71.5	52.1
QF_UFNRA, SQ'19	Yices	148.1	77.1	36.1
QF_LIA, SQ'20	MathSAT5	132.6	71.5	46.4
QF_UFBV, SQ'20	Yices	137.8	67.4	109.4
QF_UFNRA, SQ'20	Yices	151.3	47.9	42.6
QF_ABV, INC'20	Yices	169.4	50.8	114.6
QF_NRA, SQ'20	Yices	82.5	41.2	46.5
QF_AUFLIA, SQ'20	Yices	200.0	37.2	27.9
BV, SQ'20	CVC4	112.1	30.6	117.8
QF_LRA, SQ'19	SPASS-SATT	89.3	28.4	59.5
QF_UFLRA, INC'20	Z3	133.3	26.2	19.9
QF_ANIA, SQ'20	MathSAT5	199.0	26.1	61.6
QF_LIA, SQ'19	SPASS-SATT	161.5	29.8	66.3
BV, SQ'19	Q3B	91.8	25.0	83.7
LIA, SQ'20	CVC4	172.5	22.3	19.6
QF_UFNIA, SQ'20	CVC4	125.6	21.9	105.0
UFDTNIRA, SQ'20	Vampire	123.9	24.0	92.6
QF_UFLRA, INC'19	Z3	110.0	19.6	22.0
QF_FP, SQ'19	COLIBRI	41.6	18.4	62.8
QF_AUFBV, SQ'20	Yices	82.0	20.4	3.6

Table 2: Selected results of MachSMT on data from SMT-COMP 2019 and 2020. All numbers are percent differences of PAR-2 scores across all benchmarks. Columns 3 and 4 show the improvement over random selection and competition winners (higher is better). Column 5 shows the PAR-2 difference to the VBS (lower is better).

2. `machsmt_eval` – This tool takes as input the library directory generated by `machsmt_build` and evaluates it under k-fold cross validation and provides a summary of results. It further tunes MachSMT to use the best empirically observed variant based on the logic and track of the input benchmark.

```
machsmt_eval -l /path/to/lib/dir
```

3. `machsmt` – This tool is the primary interface to MachSMT' algorithm selection. Provided an input benchmark and its library files, it will output a ranking of solvers that are predicted to solve the benchmark the fastest.

```
machsmt benchmark.smt2 -l /path/to/lib/dir
```

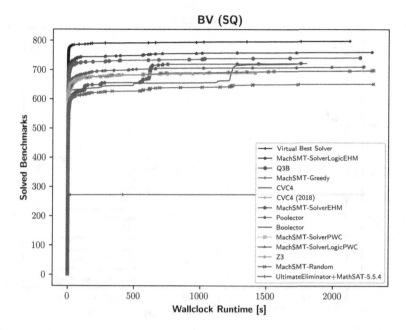

Fig. 2 *Plot for BV in the Single Query (SQ) Track in SMT-COMP '19.*

3.4 User-defined Features

We include a simple interface for users to extend the considered features in MachSMT's algorithm selection. All that is required is to create a Python method that returns a single floating-point number (or an iterable object thereof) representing the feature. As input, the user enters the path of the SMT-LIB input, as well as its logic and track. If a user feature is to be considered by MachSMT, the user-defined procedure should return its floating-point representation; otherwise, it returns none. All user-defined features are automatically included in building MachSMT. These custom features in principal can significantly affect the accuracy of MachSMT when engineered to target a specific class of benchmarks.

4 Experimental Evaluation of MachSMT on SMT-COMP 2019 and 2020 Data

In this section, we present the evaluation of our MachSMT tool (refer to Table 2 and CDF plots in Figures 2–6), specifically with the benchmarks, solvers, and solver runtime analysis from SMT-COMP 2019 and 2020. The artifact is available at: https://zenodo.org/record/4458699.

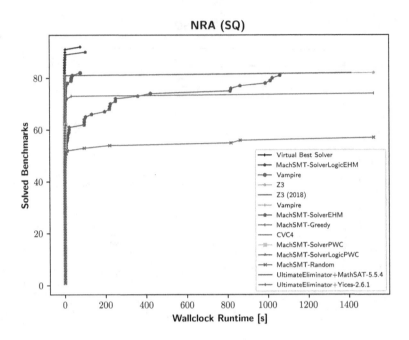

Fig. 3   *Plot for NRA in the Single Query (SQ) Track in SMT-COMP '19.*

4.1   Experimental Setup and Methodology

In this experiment, we used the benchmarks, timing analysis, and solvers provided by the organizers of the SMT-COMP 2019 and 2020 competitions [31,6]. In both years, all solver input queries were performed on the StarExec computing service [58], which consists of a cluster of 2.4 GHz Intel Xeon machines running Red Hat Enterprise Linux 7.2. Each solver/benchmark pair was configured to have 4 cores and 60GB of memory available. The time limit for each pair was 2400 seconds in 2019, and 1200 seconds in 2020.

We evaluate MachSMT and all of its variants using k-fold cross validation (with $k = 5$). In cross validation, the dataset is randomly partitioned into k subsets per division. A model is then trained over $k - 1$ subsets and makes predictions over the subset that is excluded from training. This process is repeated to obtain fair predictions for each subset. Cross validation is commonly deployed to analyze machine learning models. For more details, please see Section 2.

4.2   Experimental Results

For every division, we evaluated MachSMT by checking whether we beat the competition winner from each division. For the sequential tracks, we evaluate solvers across, according to PAR-2 scores (i.e., the wallclock runtime on success-

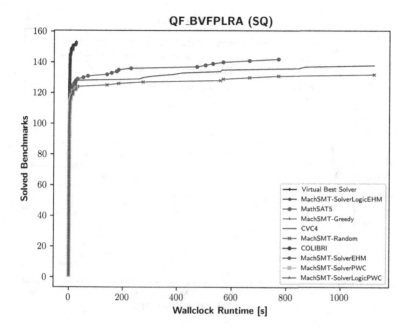

Fig. 4 *Division QF_BVFPLRA in the Single Query Track in SMT-COMP 2020.*

ful termination, otherwise twice the wallclock timeout)[4] [42]. For incremental tracks, we use the following formula:

$$w + (2 * t/n) * (n - m)$$

where w is the wall clock runtime, t is the wallclock timeout, n is the total number of check-sats in the benchmark, and m is the total number of check-sats successfully solved.

We present select results in Table 2. We consider three baselines when evaluating MachSMT, namely: random algorithm selection, the competition winner, and the virtual best solver (VBS) (note, VBS is perfect algorithm selection and cannot be beaten). We consider all divisions of at least 25 benchmarks and observe MachSMT to improve on the competition winner in 54 out of 85. We report the results for MachSMT-SolverLogicEHM in the table as it is by far the most performant, dominating in all divisions except for 4.

We present select CDF plots in Figures 2-6. A CDF plot is a visualization of how a solver performs on a database of inputs. A point (X,Y) denotes that a solver S solves Y inputs within X seconds each.

---

[4] In case of an incorrect answer, the score is recorded as 10 times the wallclock timeout.

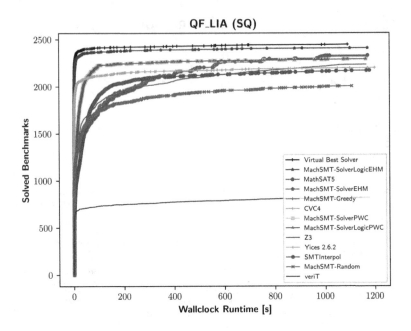

Fig. 5 *Division QF_LIA in the Single Query Track in SMT-COMP 2020.*

5   Analysis and Discussion of Results

In Section 3.2, we describe four formulations of MachSMT. In our evaluation (see Table 2), we observe MachSMT-SolverLogicEHM to be significantly more performant than all other formulations. When evaluating over SMT-COMP, in all divisions that MachSMT improved over the competition winner, MachSMT-SolverLogicEHM was the most performant in all except for three (which were won by MachSMT-SolverLogicPWC).

Our experimental results validate the idea that algorithm selection (in particular through the use of EHMs) can be a powerful way to address the combinatorial explosion that solver users face when trying to decide which solver-configuration pair is best suited for their application. We note that MachSMT is particularly powerful in the context of logics, such as QF_UFBV, that are derived from a diverse set of applications and a wide variety of algorithms have been designed to solve them. As has been noted in previous work, algorithm selection methods work well for non-homogeneous benchmarks, especially where there is no single algorithm (solver) that performs the best across the board. EHMs are an effective way to distinguish between such algorithms given a problem instance and predict which one might perform the best on said instance.

One major threat to the validity of any ML solution is the generalizability of the learnt models on unseen data. It has been noted in previous work that a practical way to address this issue is to use k-fold cross validation scheme [54,43], thus motivating our use of this approach in our experiments. We further note

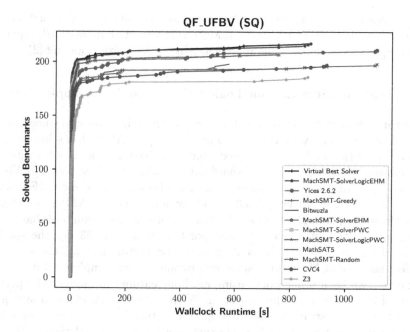

Fig. 6 *Division QF_UFBV in the Single Query Track in SMT-COMP 2020.*

that our evaluation of MachSMT includes decades of runtime analysis and more than 100 GB of benchmarks spanning numerous applications, giving us greater confidence in the robustness of our results.

6 Related Work

In this section we provide an overview of previous work on algorithm selection in the context of constraint solvers and contrast it with MachSMT.

6.1 Key differences between SATZilla and MachSMT

As mentioned above, SATZilla was the first algorithm selection method in the context of logic solvers [67]. While our work is inspired by SATZilla, MachSMT differs from SATZilla in several key ways. First, SATZilla deploys a feature selection scheme to avoid the curse of dimensionality. While good in practice for the SAT setting, feature selection does lose significant amounts of information. Further, it can be very expensive to compute optimal feature subsets.

By contrast, MachSMT leverages a learnt dimensionality reduction scheme, namely, Principal Component Analysis (PCA). The key advantage of PCA is that it does not perform a search for optimal feature subset (like one has to do in the context of feature selection), and hence is significantly more efficient. In fact, a feature selection method is unlikely to scale for SMT solvers, unlike SAT, simply because of the significantly larger number of features, logics, and solvers that one has to contend with. Second, MachSMT deploys a modern ML pipeline, including an ensemble learning approach, namely Adaptive Boosting [21].

6.2   Algorithm Selection for Logic Solvers and Their Applications

Algorithm selection tools have a rich history and have been around since at least 1976 when Rice et al. were the first to propose it [51]. Algorithm selectors have been extensively used in many contexts, e.g., classifiers for machine learning [2], combinatorics [37], and other NP-hard optimization problems [60,62]. Within the context of solvers, algorithm selectors have been proposed for QBF [50,41], SAT [67,68,69], CSP solvers [25,3,34], and recommenders for ATP tools [59,61].

In the setting of SMT solver applications, symbolic execution tools have used algorithm selection strategies [64] and portfolio strategies [33] for the specific classes of instances within the context of the bit-vector theory. This would be an ideal use case of MachSMT, since we provide a more complete solution.

There have been other works using machine learning to improve the performance of SMT solvers. Balunovic et al. [5] use neural networks and synthesis to find tactics and strategies for three SMT-LIB theories. A previous version of our work proposed an algorithm selection tool for the QF_FP theory [57]. To the best of our knowledge, MachSMT is the first publicly available tool for the entirety of SMT-LIB. Other works have leverage machine learning to improve internal heuristics in solvers [12,52,40]

Pairwise ranking has been used in algorithm selection in the latest versions of SATZilla [70], as well as in other settings such as variable selection in the context of splitting heuristics in divide-and-conquer parallel SAT solvers [45].

7   Conclusions and Future Work

In this paper, we presented MachSMT, the first algorithm selection tool that spans the entirety of the SMT-LIB logics. MachSMT is designed to be user-friendly and easily modifiable by users for their specific application and SMT solvers of interest.

Using MachSMT, we observe improvement in 54 out of 85 divisions in all tracks from the SMT-COMP 2019 and 2020, with up to a 198.4% improvement for the QF_BVFPLRA SQ '20 division in PAR-2 score. Most of the logics on which we don't see improvement are ones for which we have very few benchmarks.

For future work, we plan to extend our scoring scheme to take into account model validation and unsat core divisions. We further plan to extend our feature set with more (theory-)specific features based on feedback from the SMT community. It is very likely that users may have domain-specific knowledge about certain features that might be most predictive of solver runtime for their particular application. Hence, we have provided an interface to easily extend and specialize MachSMT to a user's specific setting.

References

1. Agrawal, S., Agrawal, J.: Survey on anomaly detection using data mining techniques. Procedia Computer Science **60**, 708–713 (2015). https://doi.org/10.1016/j.procs.2015.08.220
2. Ali, S., Smith, K.A.: On learning algorithm selection for classification. Appl. Soft Comput. **6**(2), 119–138 (2006). https://doi.org/10.1016/j.asoc.2004.12.002
3. Amadini, R., Gabbrielli, M., Mauro, J.: SUNNY: a lazy portfolio approach for constraint solving. Theory Pract. Log. Program. **14**(4-5), 509–524 (2014). https://doi.org/10.1017/S1471068414000179
4. Backes, J., Bolignano, P., Cook, B., Dodge, C., Gacek, A., Luckow, K.S., Rungta, N., Tkachuk, O., Varming, C.: Semantic-based automated reasoning for AWS access policies using SMT. In: Bjørner, N., Gurfinkel, A. (eds.) 2018 Formal Methods in Computer Aided Design, FMCAD 2018, Austin, TX, USA, October 30 - November 2, 2018. pp. 1–9. IEEE (2018). https://doi.org/10.23919/FMCAD.2018.8602994
5. Balunovic, M., Bielik, P., Vechev, M.T.: Learning to solve SMT formulas. In: Bengio, S., Wallach, H.M., Larochelle, H., Grauman, K., Cesa-Bianchi, N., Garnett, R. (eds.) Advances in Neural Information Processing Systems 31: Annual Conference on Neural Information Processing Systems 2018, NeurIPS 2018, December 3-8, 2018, Montréal, Canada. pp. 10338–10349 (2018), http://papers.nips.cc/paper/8233-learning-to-solve-smt-formulas
6. Barbosa, H., Hyvärinen, A., Hoenecke, J.: Smt-comp 2020. https://www.smt-comp.org/2020 (2020)
7. Barrett, C., Fontaine, P., Tinelli, C.: The Satisfiability Modulo Theories Library (SMT-LIB). www.SMT-LIB.org (2020)
8. Barrett, C., Stump, A., Tinelli, C.: The SMT-LIB Standard: Version 2.0. In: Gupta, A., Kroening, D. (eds.) Proceedings of the 8th International Workshop on Satisfiability Modulo Theories (Edinburgh, UK) (2010)
9. Barrett, C.W., Conway, C.L., Deters, M., Hadarean, L., Jovanovic, D., King, T., Reynolds, A., Tinelli, C.: CVC4. In: Gopalakrishnan, G., Qadeer, S. (eds.) Computer Aided Verification - 23rd International Conference, CAV 2011, Snowbird, UT, USA, July 14-20, 2011. Proceedings. Lecture Notes in Computer Science, vol. 6806, pp. 171–177. Springer (2011). https://doi.org/10.1007/978-3-642-22110-1_14
10. Barrett, C.W., de Moura, L.M., Stump, A.: SMT-COMP: satisfiability modulo theories competition. In: Etessami, K., Rajamani, S.K. (eds.) Computer Aided Verification, 17th International Conference, CAV 2005, Edinburgh, Scotland, UK, July 6-10, 2005, Proceedings. Lecture Notes in Computer Science, vol. 3576, pp. 20–23. Springer (2005). https://doi.org/10.1007/11513988_4
11. Ben Khadra, M.A., Stoffel, D., Kunz, W.: gosat: Floating-point satisfiability as global optimization. In: Stewart, D., Weissenbacher, G. (eds.) 2017 Formal Methods in Computer Aided Design, FMCAD 2017, Vienna, Austria, October 2-6, 2017. pp. 11–14. IEEE (2017). https://doi.org/10.23919/FMCAD.2017.8102235
12. Beyer, D., Dangl, M.: Strategy selection for software verification based on boolean features - A simple but effective approach **11245**, 144–159 (2018). https://doi.org/10.1007/978-3-030-03421-4_11
13. Bhargavan, K., Bond, B., Delignat-Lavaud, A., Fournet, C., Hawblitzel, C., Hritcu, C., Ishtiaq, S., Kohlweiss, M., Leino, R., Lorch, J.R., Maillard, K., Pan, J., Parno, B., Protzenko, J., Ramananandro, T., Rane, A., Rastogi, A., Swamy, N., Thompson, L., Wang, P., Béguelin, S.Z., Zinzindohoue, J.K.:

Everest: Towards a verified, drop-in replacement of HTTPS. In: Lerner, B.S., Bodík, R., Krishnamurthi, S. (eds.) 2nd Summit on Advances in Programming Languages, SNAPL 2017, May 7-10, 2017, Asilomar, CA, USA. LIPIcs, vol. 71, pp. 1:1–1:12. Schloss Dagstuhl - Leibniz-Zentrum für Informatik (2017). https://doi.org/10.4230/LIPIcs.SNAPL.2017.1, https://doi.org/10.4230/LIPIcs.SNAPL.2017.1

14. Brain, M., D'Silva, V., Griggio, A., Haller, L., Kroening, D.: Deciding floating-point logic with abstract conflict driven clause learning. Formal Methods Syst. Des. **45**(2), 213–245 (2014). https://doi.org/10.1007/s10703-013-0203-7

15. Brain, M., Schanda, F., Sun, Y.: Building better bit-blasting for floating-point problems. In: Vojnar, T., Zhang, L. (eds.) Tools and Algorithms for the Construction and Analysis of Systems - 25th International Conference, TACAS 2019, Held as Part of the European Joint Conferences on Theory and Practice of Software, ETAPS 2019, Prague, Czech Republic, April 6-11, 2019, Proceedings, Part I. Lecture Notes in Computer Science, vol. 11427, pp. 79–98. Springer (2019). https://doi.org/10.1007/978-3-030-17462-0_5

16. Brain, M., Schanda, F., Sun, Y.: Building better bit-blasting for floating-point problems. In: Vojnar, T., Zhang, L. (eds.) Tools and Algorithms for the Construction and Analysis of Systems - 25th International Conference, TACAS 2019, Held as Part of the European Joint Conferences on Theory and Practice of Software, ETAPS 2019, Prague, Czech Republic, April 6-11, 2019, Proceedings, Part I. Lecture Notes in Computer Science, vol. 11427, pp. 79–98. Springer (2019). https://doi.org/10.1007/978-3-030-17462-0_5

17. Cadar, C., Ganesh, V., Pawlowski, P.M., Dill, D.L., Engler, D.R.: EXE: automatically generating inputs of death. ACM Trans. Inf. Syst. Secur. **12**(2), 10:1–10:38 (2008). https://doi.org/10.1145/1455518.1455522

18. Cimatti, A., Griggio, A., Schaafsma, B.J., Sebastiani, R.: The mathsat5 SMT solver. In: Piterman, N., Smolka, S.A. (eds.) Tools and Algorithms for the Construction and Analysis of Systems - 19th International Conference, TACAS 2013, Held as Part of the European Joint Conferences on Theory and Practice of Software, ETAPS 2013, Rome, Italy, March 16-24, 2013. Proceedings. Lecture Notes in Computer Science, vol. 7795, pp. 93–107. Springer (2013). https://doi.org/10.1007/978-3-642-36742-7_7

19. Drucker, H.: Improving regressors using boosting techniques. In: Fisher, D.H. (ed.) Proceedings of the Fourteenth International Conference on Machine Learning (ICML 1997), Nashville, Tennessee, USA, July 8-12, 1997. pp. 107–115. Morgan Kaufmann (1997)

20. Dutertre, B.: Yices 2.2. In: Biere, A., Bloem, R. (eds.) Computer Aided Verification - 26th International Conference, CAV 2014, Held as Part of the Vienna Summer of Logic, VSL 2014, Vienna, Austria, July 18-22, 2014. Proceedings. Lecture Notes in Computer Science, vol. 8559, pp. 737–744. Springer (2014). https://doi.org/10.1007/978-3-319-08867-9_49

21. Freund, Y., Schapire, R., Abe, N.: A short introduction to boosting. Journal-Japanese Society For Artificial Intelligence **14**(771-780), 1612 (1999)

22. Fu, Z., Su, Z.: Xsat: A fast floating-point satisfiability solver. In: Chaudhuri, S., Farzan, A. (eds.) Computer Aided Verification - 28th International Conference, CAV 2016, Toronto, ON, Canada, July 17-23, 2016, Proceedings, Part II. Lecture Notes in Computer Science, vol. 9780, pp. 187–209. Springer (2016). https://doi.org/10.1007/978-3-319-41540-6_11

23. Gadelha, M.Y.R., Monteiro, F.R., Cordeiro, L.C., Nicole, D.A.: ESBMC v6.0: Verifying C programs using k-induction and invariant inference - (competition contribution). In: Beyer, D., Huisman, M., Kordon, F., Steffen, B. (eds.) Tools and Algorithms for the Construction and Analysis of Systems - 25 Years of TACAS: TOOLympics, Held as Part of ETAPS 2019, Prague, Czech Republic, April 6-11, 2019, Proceedings, Part III. Lecture Notes in Computer Science, vol. 11429, pp. 209–213. Springer (2019). https://doi.org/10.1007/978-3-030-17502-3_15

24. Ganesh, V., Dill, D.L.: A decision procedure for bit-vectors and arrays. In: Damm, W., Hermanns, H. (eds.) Computer Aided Verification, 19th International Conference, CAV 2007, Berlin, Germany, July 3-7, 2007, Proceedings. Lecture Notes in Computer Science, vol. 4590, pp. 519–531. Springer (2007). https://doi.org/10.1007/978-3-540-73368-3_52

25. Gent, I.P., Jefferson, C., Kotthoff, L., Miguel, I., Moore, N.C.A., Nightingale, P., Petrie, K.E.: Learning when to use lazy learning in constraint solving. In: Coelho, H., Studer, R., Wooldridge, M.J. (eds.) ECAI 2010 - 19th European Conference on Artificial Intelligence, Lisbon, Portugal, August 16-20, 2010, Proceedings. Frontiers in Artificial Intelligence and Applications, vol. 215, pp. 873–878. IOS Press (2010). https://doi.org/10.3233/978-1-60750-606-5-873

26. Godefroid, P., Levin, M.Y., Molnar, D.A.: SAGE: whitebox fuzzing for security testing. Commun. ACM 55(3), 40–44 (2012). https://doi.org/10.1145/2093548.2093564

27. Goues, C.L., Leino, K.R.M., Moskal, M.: The boogie verification debugger (tool paper). In: Barthe, G., Pardo, A., Schneider, G. (eds.) Software Engineering and Formal Methods - 9th International Conference, SEFM 2011, Montevideo, Uruguay, November 14-18, 2011. Proceedings. Lecture Notes in Computer Science, vol. 7041, pp. 407–414. Springer (2011). https://doi.org/10.1007/978-3-642-24690-6_28

28. Greenland, S., Mansournia, M.A., Altman, D.G.: Sparse data bias: a problem hiding in plain sight. bmj 352, i1981 (2016). https://doi.org/10.1136/bmj.i1981

29. Grira, N., Crucianu, M., Boujemaa, N.: Unsupervised and semi-supervised clustering: a brief survey. A review of machine learning techniques for processing multimedia content 1, 9–16 (2004)

30. Guidotti, D., Barrett, C., Katz, G., Pulina, L., Narodyska, N., Tacchella, A.: The VNN-LIB standard, http://www.vnnlib.org/wp-content/uploads/2020/07/main-1.pdf

31. Hadarean, L., Hyvärinen, A., Niemetz, A., Reger, G.: Smt-comp 2019. https://www.smt-comp.org/2019 (2019)

32. Halko, N., Martinsson, P., Tropp, J.A.: Finding structure with randomness: Probabilistic algorithms for constructing approximate matrix decompositions. SIAM Rev. 53(2), 217–288 (2011). https://doi.org/10.1137/090771806

33. Healy, A., Monahan, R., Power, J.F.: Predicting SMT solver performance for software verification. In: Dubois, C., Masci, P., Méry, D. (eds.) Proceedings of the Third Workshop on Formal Integrated Development Environment, F-IDE@FM 2016, Limassol, Cyprus, November 8, 2016. EPTCS, vol. 240, pp. 20–37 (2016). https://doi.org/10.4204/EPTCS.240.2

34. Hurley, B., Kotthoff, L., Malitsky, Y., O'Sullivan, B.: Proteus: A hierarchical portfolio of solvers and transformations. In: Simonis, H. (ed.) Integration of AI and OR Techniques in Constraint Programming - 11th International Conference, CPAIOR 2014, Cork, Ireland, May 19-23, 2014. Proceedings. Lecture Notes in Computer Science, vol. 8451, pp. 301–317. Springer (2014). https://doi.org/10.1007/978-3-319-07046-9_22

35. Katz, G., Barrett, C.W., Dill, D.L., Julian, K., Kochenderfer, M.J.: Reluplex: An efficient SMT solver for verifying deep neural networks. In: Majumdar, R., Kuncak, V. (eds.) Computer Aided Verification - 29th International Conference, CAV 2017, Heidelberg, Germany, July 24-28, 2017, Proceedings, Part I. Lecture Notes in Computer Science, vol. 10426, pp. 97–117. Springer (2017). https://doi.org/10.1007/978-3-319-63387-9_5

36. Kira, K., Rendell, L.A.: A practical approach to feature selection. In: Sleeman, D.H., Edwards, P. (eds.) Proceedings of the Ninth International Workshop on Machine Learning (ML 1992), Aberdeen, Scotland, UK, July 1-3, 1992, pp. 249–256. Morgan Kaufmann (1992). https://doi.org/10.1016/b978-1-55860-247-2.50037-1

37. Kotthoff, L.: Algorithm selection for combinatorial search problems: A survey. In: Bessiere, C., Raedt, L.D., Kotthoff, L., Nijssen, S., O'Sullivan, B., Pedreschi, D. (eds.) Data Mining and Constraint Programming - Foundations of a Cross-Disciplinary Approach, Lecture Notes in Computer Science, vol. 10101, pp. 149–190. Springer (2016). https://doi.org/10.1007/978-3-319-50137-6_7

38. Kwon, D., Kim, H., Kim, J., Suh, S.C., Kim, I., Kim, K.J.: A survey of deep learning-based network anomaly detection. Clust. Comput. **22**(Suppl 1), 949–961 (2019). https://doi.org/10.1007/s10586-017-1117-8

39. Leino, K.R.M.: Automating theorem proving with SMT. In: Blazy, S., Paulin-Mohring, C., Pichardie, D. (eds.) Interactive Theorem Proving - 4th International Conference, ITP 2013, Rennes, France, July 22-26, 2013. Proceedings. Lecture Notes in Computer Science, vol. 7998, pp. 2–16. Springer (2013). https://doi.org/10.1007/978-3-642-39634-2_2

40. Liang, J.H., Ganesh, V., Poupart, P., Czarnecki, K.: Learning rate based branching heuristic for SAT solvers. In: Creignou, N., Berre, D.L. (eds.) Theory and Applications of Satisfiability Testing - SAT 2016 - 19th International Conference, Bordeaux, France, July 5-8, 2016, Proceedings. Lecture Notes in Computer Science, vol. 9710, pp. 123–140. Springer (2016). https://doi.org/10.1007/978-3-319-40970-2_9

41. Malitsky, Y.: Evolving instance-specific algorithm configuration. In: Instance-Specific Algorithm Configuration, pp. 93–105. Springer (2014). https://doi.org/10.1007/978-3-319-11230-5, https://doi.org/10.1007/978-3-319-11230-5

42. Marijn Heule, Matti Järvisalo, M.S.: Sat race 2019 (2019), http://sat-race-2019.ciirc.cvut.cz/

43. Moore, A.W.: Cross-validation for detecting and preventing overfitting. School of Computer Science Carneigie Mellon University (2001)

44. de Moura, L.M., Bjørner, N.: Z3: an efficient SMT solver. In: Ramakrishnan, C.R., Rehof, J. (eds.) Tools and Algorithms for the Construction and Analysis of Systems, 14th International Conference, TACAS 2008, Held as Part of the Joint European Conferences on Theory and Practice of Software, ETAPS 2008, Budapest, Hungary, March 29-April 6, 2008. Proceedings. Lecture Notes in Computer Science, vol. 4963, pp. 337–340. Springer (2008). https://doi.org/10.1007/978-3-540-78800-3_24

45. Nejati, S., Frioux, L.L., Ganesh, V.: A machine learning based splitting heuristic for divide-and-conquer solvers. In: Simonis, H. (ed.) Principles and Practice of Constraint Programming - 26th International Conference, CP 2020, Louvain-la-Neuve, Belgium, September 7-11, 2020, Proceedings. Lecture Notes in Computer Science, vol. 12333, pp. 899–916. Springer (2020). https://doi.org/10.1007/978-3-030-58475-7_52

46. Niemetz, A., Preiner, M.: Bitwuzla at the SMT-COMP 2020. CoRR **abs/2006.01621** (2020), https://arxiv.org/abs/2006.01621
47. Niemetz, A., Preiner, M., Biere, A.: Boolector 2.0. J. Satisf. Boolean Model. Comput. **9**(1), 53–58 (2014). https://doi.org/10.3233/sat190101
48. Pasareanu, C.S., Visser, W.: A survey of new trends in symbolic execution for software testing and analysis. Int. J. Softw. Tools Technol. Transf. **11**(4), 339–353 (2009). https://doi.org/10.1007/s10009-009-0118-1
49. Pedregosa, F., Varoquaux, G., Gramfort, A., Michel, V., Thirion, B., Grisel, O., Blondel, M., Prettenhofer, P., Weiss, R., Dubourg, V., Vanderplas, J., Passos, A., Cournapeau, D., Brucher, M., Perrot, M., Duchesnay, E.: Scikit-learn: Machine learning in Python. Journal of Machine Learning Research **12**, 2825–2830 (2011)
50. Pulina, L., Tacchella, A.: A multi-engine solver for quantified boolean formulas. In: Bessiere, C. (ed.) Principles and Practice of Constraint Programming - CP 2007, 13th International Conference, CP 2007, Providence, RI, USA, September 23-27, 2007, Proceedings. Lecture Notes in Computer Science, vol. 4741, pp. 574–589. Springer (2007). https://doi.org/10.1007/978-3-540-74970-7_41
51. Rice, J.R.: The algorithm selection problem. Adv. Comput. **15**, 65–118 (1976). https://doi.org/10.1016/S0065-2458(08)60520-3
52. Richter, C., Wehrheim, H.: Pesco: Predicting sequential combinations of verifiers - (competition contribution). In: Beyer, D., Huisman, M., Kordon, F., Steffen, B. (eds.) Tools and Algorithms for the Construction and Analysis of Systems - 25 Years of TACAS: TOOLympics, Held as Part of ETAPS 2019, Prague, Czech Republic, April 6-11, 2019, Proceedings, Part III. Lecture Notes in Computer Science, vol. 11429, pp. 229–233. Springer (2019). https://doi.org/10.1007/978-3-030-17502-3_19
53. Rintanen, J.: Madagascar: Scalable planning with sat. Proceedings of the 8th International Planning Competition (IPC-2014) **21** (2014)
54. Rodríguez, J.D., Martínez, A.P., Lozano, J.A.: Sensitivity analysis of k-fold cross validation in prediction error estimation. IEEE Trans. Pattern Anal. Mach. Intell. **32**(3), 569–575 (2010). https://doi.org/10.1109/TPAMI.2009.187
55. Salvia, R., Titolo, L., Feliú, M.A., Moscato, M.M., Muñoz, C.A., Rakamaric, Z.: A mixed real and floating-point solver. In: Badger, J.M., Rozier, K.Y. (eds.) NASA Formal Methods - 11th International Symposium, NFM 2019, Houston, TX, USA, May 7-9, 2019, Proceedings. Lecture Notes in Computer Science, vol. 11460, pp. 363–370. Springer (2019). https://doi.org/10.1007/978-3-030-20652-9_25
56. Scott, J., Panju, M., Ganesh, V.: LGML: logic guided machine learning (student abstract). In: The Thirty-Fourth AAAI Conference on Artificial Intelligence, AAAI 2020, The Thirty-Second Innovative Applications of Artificial Intelligence Conference, IAAI 2020, The Tenth AAAI Symposium on Educational Advances in Artificial Intelligence, EAAI 2020, New York, NY, USA, February 7-12, 2020. pp. 13909–13910. AAAI Press (2020), https://aaai.org/ojs/index.php/AAAI/article/view/7227
57. Scott, J., Poupart, P., Ganesh, V.: An algorithm selection approach for QF_FP solvers. In: 17th International Workshop on Satisfiability Modulo Theories (2019)
58. Stump, A., Sutcliffe, G., Tinelli, C.: Starexec: A cross-community infrastructure for logic solving. In: Demri, S., Kapur, D., Weidenbach, C. (eds.) Automated Reasoning - 7th International Joint Conference, IJCAR 2014, Held as Part of the Vienna Summer of Logic, VSL 2014, Vienna, Austria, July 19-22, 2014. Proceedings. Lecture Notes in Computer Science, vol. 8562, pp. 367–373. Springer (2014). https://doi.org/10.1007/978-3-319-08587-6_28

59. Sutcliffe, G.: The TPTP problem library and associated infrastructure - from CNF to th0, TPTP v6.4.0. J. Autom. Reason. **59**(4), 483–502 (2017). https://doi.org/10.1007/s10817-017-9407-7

60. Tierney, K., Malitsky, Y.: An algorithm selection benchmark of the container pre-marshalling problem. In: Dhaenens, C., Jourdan, L., Marmion, M. (eds.) Learning and Intelligent Optimization - 9th International Conference, LION 9, Lille, France, January 12-15, 2015. Revised Selected Papers. Lecture Notes in Computer Science, vol. 8994, pp. 17–22. Springer (2015). https://doi.org/10.1007/978-3-319-19084-6_2

61. Urban, J., Sutcliffe, G., Pudlák, P., Vyskocil, J.: Malarea SG1- machine learner for automated reasoning with semantic guidance. In: Armando, A., Baumgartner, P., Dowek, G. (eds.) Automated Reasoning, 4th International Joint Conference, IJCAR 2008, Sydney, Australia, August 12-15, 2008, Proceedings. Lecture Notes in Computer Science, vol. 5195, pp. 441–456. Springer (2008). https://doi.org/10.1007/978-3-540-71070-7_37

62. Vallati, M., Chrpa, L., Kitchin, D.E.: Portfolio-based planning: State of the art, common practice and open challenges. AI Commun. **28**(4), 717–733 (2015). https://doi.org/10.3233/AIC-150671

63. Van Der Maaten, L., Postma, E., Van den Herik, J.: Dimensionality reduction: a comparative. J Mach Learn Res **10**(66-71), 13 (2009)

64. Wen, S.H., Mow, W.L., Chen, W.N., Wang, C.Y., Hsiao, H.C.: Enhancing symbolic execution by machine learning based solver selection (01 2019). https://doi.org/10.14722/bar.2019.23080

65. Weston, J., Mukherjee, S., Chapelle, O., Pontil, M., Poggio, T.A., Vapnik, V.: Feature selection for svms. In: Leen, T.K., Dietterich, T.G., Tresp, V. (eds.) Advances in Neural Information Processing Systems 13, Papers from Neural Information Processing Systems (NIPS) 2000, Denver, CO, USA. pp. 668–674. MIT Press (2000), https://proceedings.neurips.cc/paper/2000/hash/8c3039bd5842dca3d944faab91447818-Abstract.html

66. Wold, S., Esbensen, K., Geladi, P.: Principal component analysis. Chemometrics and intelligent laboratory systems **2**(1-3), 37–52 (1987)

67. Xu, L., Hutter, F., Hoos, H.H., Leyton-Brown, K.: Satzilla-07: The design and analysis of an algorithm portfolio for SAT. In: Bessiere, C. (ed.) Principles and Practice of Constraint Programming - CP 2007, 13th International Conference, CP 2007, Providence, RI, USA, September 23-27, 2007, Proceedings. Lecture Notes in Computer Science, vol. 4741, pp. 712–727. Springer (2007). https://doi.org/10.1007/978-3-540-74970-7_50

68. Xu, L., Hutter, F., Hoos, H.H., Leyton-Brown, K.: Satzilla: Portfolio-based algorithm selection for SAT. J. Artif. Intell. Res. **32**, 565–606 (2008). https://doi.org/10.1613/jair.2490

69. Xu, L., Hutter, F., Hoos, H.H., Leyton-Brown, K.: Satzilla2009: an automatic algorithm portfolio for sat. SAT **4**, 53–55 (2009)

70. Xu, L., Hutter, F., Hoos, H.H., Leyton-Brown, K.: Evaluating component solver contributions to portfolio-based algorithm selectors. In: Cimatti, A., Sebastiani, R. (eds.) Theory and Applications of Satisfiability Testing - SAT 2012 - 15th International Conference, Trento, Italy, June 17-20, 2012. Proceedings. Lecture Notes in Computer Science, vol. 7317, pp. 228–241. Springer (2012). https://doi.org/10.1007/978-3-642-31612-8_18

71. Xu, L., Hutter, F., Shen, J., Hoos, H.H., Leyton-Brown, K.: Satzilla2012: Improved algorithm selection based on cost-sensitive classification models. Proceedings of SAT Challenge pp. 57–58 (2012)

72. Xu, R., II, D.C.W.: Survey of clustering algorithms. IEEE Trans. Neural Networks **16**(3), 645–678 (2005). https://doi.org/10.1109/TNN.2005.845141, https://doi.org/10.1109/TNN.2005.845141

dtControl 2.0: Explainable Strategy Representation via Decision Tree Learning Steered by Experts *

Pranav Ashok[1], Mathias Jackermeier[1], Jan Křetínský[1],
Christoph Weinhuber[1](✉), Maximilian Weininger[1], and Mayank Yadav[2]

[1] Technical University of Munich, Munich, Germany
firstname.lastname@tum.de
[2] Department of Computer Science and Engineering, I.I.T. Delhi,
New Delhi, India
cs1180356@iitd.ac.in

Abstract. Recent advances have shown how decision trees are apt data structures for concisely representing strategies (or controllers) satisfying various objectives. Moreover, they also make the strategy more explainable. The recent tool `dtControl` had provided pipelines with tools supporting strategy synthesis for hybrid systems, such as `SCOTS` and `Uppaal Stratego`. We present `dtControl 2.0`, a new version with several fundamentally novel features. Most importantly, the user can now provide domain knowledge to be exploited in the decision tree learning process and can also interactively steer the process based on the dynamically provided information. To this end, we also provide a graphical user interface. It allows for inspection and re-computation of parts of the result, suggesting as well as receiving advice on predicates, and visual simulation of the decision-making process. Besides, we interface model checkers of probabilistic systems, namely `STORM` and `PRISM` and provide dedicated support for categorical enumeration-type state variables. Consequently, the controllers are more explainable and smaller.

Keywords: Strategy representation · Controller representation · Decision Tree · Explainable Learning · Hybrid systems · Probabilistic Model Checking · Markov Decision Process

1 Introduction

A *controller* (also known as strategy, policy or scheduler) of a system assigns to each state of the system a set of actions that should be taken in order to achieve a certain goal. For example, one may want to satisfy a given specification of a robot's

---

* This work has been partially supported by the German Research Foundation (DFG) project No. 383882557 *SUV* (KR 4890/2-1), No. 427755713 *GOPro* (KR 4890/3-1) and the TUM International Graduate School of Science and Engineering (IGSSE) grant 10.06 *PARSEC*. We thank Tim Quatman for implementing JSON-export of strategies in `STORM` and Pushpak Jagtap for his support with the `SCOTS` models.

J. F. Groote and K. G. Larsen (Eds.): TACAS 2021, LNCS 12652, pp. 326–345, 2021.
https://doi.org/10.1007/978-3-030-72013-1_17

behaviour or exhibit a concurrency bug appearing only in some interleaving. It is desirable that the controllers possess several additional properties, besides achieving the goal, in order to be usable in practice. Firstly, controllers should be *explainable*. Only then can they be understood, trusted and implemented by the engineers, certified by the authorities, or used in the debugging process [11]. Secondly, they should be *small* in size and efficient to run. Only then they can be deployed on embedded devices with limited memory of a few kilobytes, while the automatically synthesized ones are orders of magnitude larger [49]. Thirdly, whenever the primary goal, e.g. functional correctness, is accompanied by a secondary criterion, e.g. energy efficiency, they should be *performant* with respect to this criterion.

Automatic controller synthesis is able to provide controllers for a given goal in various domains, such as probabilistic systems [32, 17], hybrid systems [45, 16, 30, 19] or reactive systems [35]. In some cases, even the performance can be reflected [16]. However, despite recent interest in explainability in connection to AI-based controllers [2] and despite typically small memories of embedded devices, automatic techniques for controller synthesis mostly fall short of producing small explainable results. A typical outcome is a controller in the form of a look-up table, listing the actions for each possible state, or a binary decision diagram (BDD) [14] representation thereof. While the latter reduces the size to some extent, none of the two representations is explainable: the former due to its size, the latter due to the bit-level representation with all high-level structure lost. Instead, learning representations in the form of decision trees (DT) [38] has been recently explored to this end [7, 3]. DTs turn out to be usually smaller than BDD but do not drown to the bit level and are generally well known for their interpretability and explainability due to their simple structure. However, despite showing significant potential, the state-of-the-art tool dtControl [4] uses predicates without natural interpretation, and moreover, the best size reductions are achieved using *determinization*, i.e. making the controller less permissive, which negatively affects performance [7].

Example 1 (Motivating example). Consider the cruise control model of [34], where we want to control the speed of our car so that it never crashes into the car in front while, as a secondary performance objective, keeping the distance between the two cars small.

A safe controller for the this model as returned by Uppaal Stratego, is a lookup table of size 418 MB with 300,000 lines. The respective BDD has 1,448 nodes with all information bit-blasted. Using adaptations of standard DT-construction algorithms, as implemented in dtControl, we can get a DT with 987 nodes, which is still too large to be explained. Using determinization techniques, the controller can be compressed to 3 nodes! However, then the DT allows only to decelerate until the minimum velocity. This is safe, as we cannot crash into the car in front, but it does not even attempt at getting close to the front car, and thus has a very bad performance.

One can find a strategy with optimal performance, retaining the maximal permissiveness, not determinizing at all, which can be represented by a DT with 11 nodes. A picture of this DT as well as reasoning how to derive the predicates from the kinematic equations is in the extended version of this paper [5, Appendix A].

However, exactly because the predicates are based on the *domain knowledge*, namely the kinematic equations, they take the form of *algebraic predicates* and not simply linear predicates, which are the only ones in dtControl and commonly in the machine-learning literature on DTs.   △

This motivating example shows that using domain knowledge and algebraic predicates, available now in dtControl 2.0, one can get smaller representation than when using existing heuristics. Further, it improves the performance of the DT, and it is easily explainable, as it is based on domain knowledge. In fact, the discussed controller is so explainable that it allowed us to find a bug in the original model. In general, using dtControl 2.0 a domain expert can try to compress the controller, thus gain more insight and validate that it is correct. Another example of this has been reported from the use of dtControl in the manufacturing domain [31].

While automatic synthesis of good predicates from the domain knowledge may seem as distant as automatic synthesis of program invariants or automatic theorem provers, we adopt the philosophy of those domains and offer *semi-automatic techniques*.

Additionally, if not performance but only safety of a controller is relevant, we can still benefit from determinization without drawbacks. To this end, we also provide a new determinization procedure that generalizes the extremely successful MaxFreq technique of [4] and is as good or better on all our examples.

To incorporate the changes just discussed, namely algebraic predicates, semi-automatic approach, and better determinization, we have also reworked the tool and its interfaces. To begin with, the software architecture of dtControl 2.0 is now very modular and allows for easy further modifications, as well as adding support for new synthesis tools. In fact, we have already added parsers for the tools STORM [17] and PRISM [32], and thus we support probabilistic models as well. Since these models also contain categorical (or enumeration-type) variables, e.g. protocol states, we have also added support for categorical predicates. Furthermore, we added a graphical user interface that not only is easier to use than the command-line interface, but also allows to inspect the DT, modify and retrain parts of it, and simulate runs of the model under its control, further increasing the possibilities to explain the DT and validate the controller.

Summing up, the main improvements of dtControl 2.0 over the previous version [4] are the following:

- Support of algebraic predicates and categorical predicates
- Semi-automatic interface and GUI with several interactive modes
- New determinization procedure
- Interfaces for model checkers PRISM and Storm and experimental evidence of improvements on probabilistic models compared to BDD

The paper is structured as follows. After recalling necessary background in Section 2, we give an overview of the improvements over the previous version of the tool from the global perspective in Section 3. We detail on the algorithmic contribution in Sections 4 (predicate domains), 5 (predicate selection) and 6 (determinization). Section 7 provides experimental evaluation and Section 8 concludes.

Related work. DTs have been suggested for representing controllers of and counterexamples in probabilistic systems in [11], however, the authors only discuss approximate representations. The ideas have been extended to other setting, such as reactive synthesis [12] and hybrid systems [7]. More general linear predicates have been considered in leaves of the trees in [3]. dtControl 2.0 contains the DT induction algorithms from [7, 3]. The differences to the previous version of the tool dtControl [4] are summarized above and schematically depicted in Figure 2.

Besides, DTs have been used to represent and learn strategies for safety objectives in [40] and to learn program invariants in [21]. Further, DTs were used for representing the strategies during the model checking process, namely in strategy iteration [10] or in simulation-based algorithms [42]. Representing controllers exactly using a structure similar to DT (mistakenly claimed to be an algebraic decision diagram) was first suggested by [22], however, no automatic construction algorithm was provided.

The idea of non-linear predicates has been explored in [28]. In that work, however, it is not based on domain knowledge, but rather on projecting the state-space to higher dimensions.

BDDs [14] have been commonly used to represent strategies in planning [15], symbolic model checking [32] as well as to represent hybrid system controllers [45, 30]. While BDD [14] operate only on Boolean variables, they have the advantage of being diagrams and not trees. Moreover, they correspond to Boolean functions that can be implemented on hardware easily. [18] proposes an automatic compression technique for numerical controllers using BDDs. Similar to our work, [49] considers the problem of obtaining concise BDD representation of controllers and presents a technique to obtain smaller BDDs via determinization. However, BDDs are difficult to explain due to variables being bit-blasted and their size is very sensitive to the chosen variable ordering. An extension of BDDs, algebraic or multi-terminal decision diagrams (ADD/MTBDD) [8, 20], have been used in reinforcement learning for strategy synthesis [26, 47]. ADDs extend BDDs with the possibility to have multiple values in the terminal nodes, but the predicates still work only on boolean variables, retaining the disadvantages of BDDs.

2   Decision tree learning for controller representation

In this section, we briefly describe how controllers can be represented as decision trees as in [4]. We give an exemplified overview of the method, pinpointing the role of our algorithmic contributions.

A (non-deterministic, also called permissive) *controller* is a map $C : S \mapsto 2^A$ from states to non-empty sets of actions. This notion of a controller is fairly general; the only requirement is that it has to be memoryless and non-randomized. These kind of controllers are optimal for many tasks such as expected (discounted) reward, reachability or parity objectives. Moreover, even finite-memory controllers can be written in this form by considering the product of the state space with the finite memory as the domain, for example, like in LTL model checking.

Decision trees (DT), e.g. [38], are trees where every leaf node is labelled with a non-empty set of actions and every inner node is labelled with a *predicate* $\rho : S \mapsto \{true, false\}$.

v_o	v_f	d	actions
0	0	5	$\{neu\}$
2	6	10	$\{dec, neu, acc\}$
2	6	15	$\{dec, neu, acc\}$
4	4	15	$\{dec, neu\}$

(a)

(b)

Fig. 1: An example controller based on the cruise-control model in the form of a lookup table (left), and the corresponding decision tree (right).

Example 2 (Decision tree representation). As an example, consider the controller given in Figure 1a. It is a subset of the real cruise-control case study from the motivating Example 1. A state is a 3-tuple of the variables v_o, v_f and d, which denote the velocity of our car, the front car and the distance between the cars respectively. In each state, our car may be allowed to perform a subset of the following set of actions: decelerate (*dec*), stay in neutral (*neu*) or accelerate (*acc*). A DT representing this lookup table is depicted in Figure 1b.

Given a state, for example $v_o = v_f = 4, d = 10$, the DT is evaluated as follows: We start at the root and, since it is an inner node, we evaluate its predicate $v_o > 0$. As this is true, we follow the true branch and reach the inner node labelled with the predicate $v_f > 4$. This is false, so we follow the false branch and reach the leaf node labelled $\{dec, neu\}$. Hence, we know that all three possibilities of decelerating, staying neutral and accelerating are allowed by the controller. △

To construct a DT representation of a given controller, the following recursive algorithm may be used. Note that it is heuristic since constructing an optimal binary decision tree is an NP-complete problem [27].

Base case: If all states in the the controller agree on their set of actions B (i.e. for all states s we have $C(s) = B$), return a leaf node with label B.

Recursive case: Otherwise, we split the controller. For this, we select a predicate ρ and construct an inner node with label ρ. Then we partition the controller by evaluating the predicate on the state space, and recursively construct one DT for the sub-controller on states $\{s \in S \mid \rho(s)\}$ where the predicate is true, and one for the sub-controller where it is false. These controllers are the children of the inner node with label ρ and we proceed recursively.

For selecting the predicate, we consider two hyper-parameters: The *domain* of the predicates (see Section 4) and the way to *select* predicates (see Section 5). The selection is typically performed by selecting the predicate with the lowest *impurity*; this is a measure for how homogenous (or "pure") the controller is after the split, in other words the degree to which all the states agree on their actions.

We also consider a third hyper-parameter of the algorithm, namely *determinization* by *safe early stopping* (see Section 6). This modifies the base case as follows: if all states in the controller agree on at least one action a (i.e. for all states s we have $a \in C(s)$), then we return a leaf node with label $\{a\}$. This variant of early stopping ensures that, even though the controller is not represented exactly, still for every state a safe action is allowed.

Hence, if the original controller satisfies some property, e.g. that a safe set of states is never left, the DT construction algorithm ensures that this property is retained. This is because our algorithm represents the strategy exactly (or a safe subset, in case of determinization) and does not generalize as DTs typically do in machine learning. DTs are suitable for both tasks, as both rely on the strength of DTs exploiting underlying structure.

Remark 1. Note that for some types of objectives such as reachability, determinization of permissive strategies might lead to a violation of the original guarantees. For example, consider a strategy that allows both a self-looping and a non-self-looping action at a particular state. If the determinizer decides to restrict to the self-looping action, the reachability property may be violated in the determinized strategy. However, this problem can be addressed when synthesizing the strategy by ensuring that every action makes progress towards the target.

3   Tool

dtControl 2.0 is an easy-to-use open-source tool for representing memoryless symbolic controllers as more compact and more interpretable DTs, while retaining safety guarantees of the original controllers. Our website dtcontrol.model.in.tum.de offers hyperlinks to the easy-to-install pip package[3], the documentation and the source code. Additionally, the artifact that has passed the TACAS 21 artifact evaluation is available here [6].

The schema in Figure 2 illustrates the workflow of using dtControl, highlighting new features in red. Considering dtControl as a black box, it shows that given a controller, it returns a DT representing the controller and also offers the possibility to simulate a run of the system under the control of the DT, visualizing

---

[3] pip is a standard package-management system used to install and manage software packages written in Python.

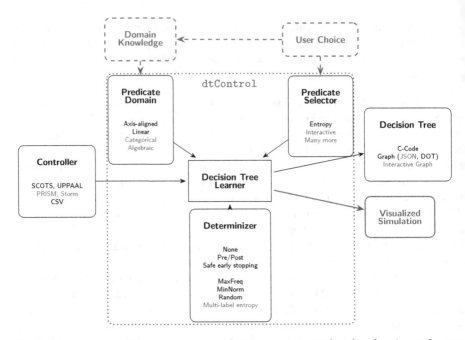

Fig. 2: An overview of the components of dtControl 2.0, thereby showing software architecture and workflow. Contributions of this paper are highlighted in red.

the decisions made. The controller can be input in various formats, including the newly supported strategy representations of the well-known probabilistic model checkers PRISM [32] and STORM [17]. The DT is output in several machine readable formats, and as C-code that can be directly used for executing the controller on embedded devices. Note that this C-code consists only of nested if-else-statements. The new graphical user interface also offers the possibility to inspect the graph in an interactive web user interface, which even allows to edit the DT. This means that parts of the DT can be retrained with a different set of hyper-parameters and directly replaced. This way, one can for example first train a determinized DT and then retrain important parts of it to be more permissive and hence more performant for a secondary criterion. Figure 3 shows a screenshot of the newly integrated graphical user interface.

Looking at the inner workings of dtControl, we see the three important hyper-parameters that were already introduced in Section 2: predicate domain, predicate selector, and determinizer. For each of these, dtControl offers various choices, some of which were newly added for version 2.0. Most prominently, the user now has the possibility to directly influence both the predicate domain and the predicate selector, by providing domain knowledge and thus also additional predicates, or by directly using the interactive predicate selection. More details on the predicate domain and how domain knowledge is specified can be found in Section 4. The different ways to select predicates, especially the new interactive mode, are the topic of Section 5. Our new insights into determinization are

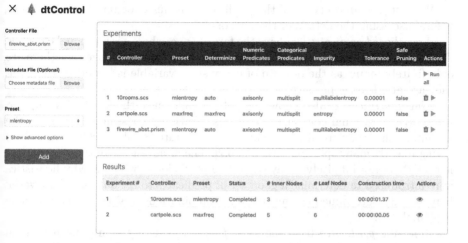

Fig. 3: Screenshot of the new web-based graphical user interface. It offers a sidebar for easy selection of the controller file and hyper-parameters, an experiments table where benchmarks can be queued, and a results table in which some statistics of the run are provided. Moreover, users can click on the 'eye' icon in the results table to inspect the built decision tree.

described in Section 6. To support the user in finding a good set of hyper-parameters, dtControl also offers extensive benchmarking functionality, allowing to specify multiple variants and reporting several statistics.

Technical notes. dtControl 2.0 is written in Python 3 following an architecture closely resembling the schema in Figure 2. The modularity, along with our technical documentation, allows users to easily extend the tool. For example, supporting another input format is only a matter of adding a parser.

dtControl 2.0 works with Python version 3.7.9 or higher. The core of the tool which runs the learning algorithms requires numpy [23], pandas [36] and scikit-learn [41] and optionally the library for the heuristic OC1 [39]. The algebraic predicates rely on SymPy [37] and SciPy [48]. The web user interface is powered by Flask [1] and D3.js [9].

4   Predicate domain

The domain of the predicates that we allow in the inner nodes of the DT is of key importance. As we saw in the motivating Example 1, allowing for more expressive predicates can dramatically reduce the size of the DT.

We assume that our state space is structured, i.e. it is a Cartesian product of the domain of the variables ($S = S_1 \times \ldots \times S_n$). We use s_i to refer to the i-th state-variable of a state $s \in S$. In Example 2, the three state-variables are the velocity of our car, the velocity of the front car, and the distance.

We first give an overview of the predicate domains dtControl 2.0 supports, before discussing the details of the new ones.

Axis-aligned predicates [38] have the form $s_i \leq c$, where c is a rational constant. This is the easiest form of predicates, and they have the advantage that there are only finitely many, as the domain of every state-variable is bounded. However, they are also least expressive.

Linear predicates (also known as oblique [39]) have the form $\sum_i s_i \cdot a_i \leq c$, where a_i are rational coefficients and c is a rational constant. They have the advantage that they are able to combine several state-variables which can lead to saving linearly many splits, cf. [29, Fig. 5.2]. The disadvantage of these predicates is that there are infinitely many choices of coefficients, which is why heuristics were introduced to determine a good set of predicates to try out [39, 4]. However, heuristically determined coefficients and combinations of variables can impede explainability.

Algebraic predicates have the form $f(s) \leq c$, where f is any mathematical function over the state-variables and c is a rational constant. It can use elementary functions such as exponentiation, log, or even trigonometric functions. Example 1 illustrated how this can reduce the size and improve explainability. More discussion of these predicates follows in Section 4.2.

Categorical predicates are special predicates for categorical (enumeration-type) state-variables such as colour or protocol state, and they are discussed in Section 4.1.

4.1   Categorical predicates

Categorical state-variables do not have a numeric domain, but instead are unordered and qualitative. They commonly occur in the models coming from the tools PRISM and STORM.

Example 3. Let one state-variable be 'colour' with the domain {red, blue, green}. A simple approach is to assign numbers to every value, e.g. red $= 0$, blue $= 1$, green $= 2$, and treat this variable as numeric. However, a resulting predicate such as colour ≤ 2 is hardly explainable and additionally depends on the assignment of numbers. For example, it would not be possible to single out colour $\in$ {red, green} using a single predicate, given the aforementioned numeric assignment. Using linear predicates, for example adding half of the colour to some other state-variable, is even more confusing and dependent on the numeric assignment. △

Instead of treating the categorical variables using their numeric encodings, dtControl 2.0 supports specialized algorithms from literature, see e.g. [43, 44]. They work by labelling an inner node with a categorical variable and performing a (possibly non-binary) split according to the value of the categorical variable. The node can have at most one child for every possible value of the categorical variable, but it can also group together similarly behaving values, see Figure 4 for an example. For the grouping, dtControl 2.0 uses the greedy algorithm from [44,

Chapter 7] called attribute-value grouping. It proceeds by first considering to have a branch for every single possible value of the categorical variable, and then merging branches as long as it improves the predicate; see [5, Appendix C] for the full pseudocode of the algorithm.

In our experiments we found that the grouping algorithm sometimes did not merge branches in cases where it would actually have made the DT smaller or more explainable. This is because the resulting impurity, the goodness of a predicate, could be marginally worse due to floating-point inaccuracies. Thus, we introduce *tolerance*, a bias parameter in favour of larger value groups. When checking whether to merge branches, we do not require the impurity to improve, but we allow it to become worse up to our tolerance. Setting tolerance to 0 corresponds exactly to the algorithm from [44], while setting tolerance to ∞ results in merging branches until only two remain, thus producing binary predicates.

To allow dtControl 2.0 to use categorical predicates, the user has to provide a metadata file, which tells the tool which variables are categorical and which are numeric; see [5, Appendix B.1] for an example.

4.2 Algebraic predicates

It is impossible to try out every mathematical expression over the state-variables, and it would also not necessarily result in an explainable DT. Instead, we allow the user to enter *domain knowledge* to suggest templates of predicates that dtControl 2.0 should try. See [5, Appendix B.2] for a discussion of the format in which domain knowledge can be entered.

Providing the basic equations that govern the model behaviour can already help in finding a good predicate, and is easy to do for a domain expert. Additionally, dtControl 2.0 offers several possibilities to further exploit the provided domain knowledge:

Firstly, the given predicates need not be exact, but may contain coefficients. These coefficients can be both completely arbitrary or may come from a finite set suggested by the user. For coefficients with finite domain, dtControl 2.0 tries all possibilities; for arbitrary coefficients, it uses curve fitting to find a good

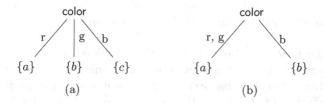

Fig. 4: Two examples of a categorical split. On the left, all possible values of the state-variable colour lead to a different child in a non-binary split. On the right, red and green lead to the same child, which is a result of grouping similar values together.

value. For example, the user can specify a predicate such as $d + (v_o - v_f) \cdot c_0 > c_1$ with c_0 being an arbitrary rational number and $c_1 \in \{0, 5, 10\}$.

Secondly, the interactive predicate selection (see Section 5) allows the user to try out various predicates at once and observe their respective impurity in the current node. The user can then choose among them as well as iteratively suggest further predicates, inspired by those where the most promising results were observed.

Thirdly, the decisions given by a DT can be visualized in the simulator, possibly leading to better understanding the controller. Upon gaining any further insight, the user can directly edit any subtree of the result, possibly utilizing the interactive predicate selection again.

5   Predicate selection

The tool offers a range of options to affect the selection of the most appropriate predicate from a given domain.

Impurity measures: As mentioned in Section 2, the predicate selection is typically based on the lowest *impurity* induced. The most commonly used impurity measure (and the only one the first version of dtControl supported) is Shannon's entropy [46]. In dtControl 2.0, a number of other impurity measures from the literature [43, 13, 25, 39, 3] are available. However, our results indicate that entropy typically performs the best, and therefore it is used as the default option unless the user specifies otherwise. Due to lack of space, we delegate the details and experimental comparison between the impurity measures to [5, Appendix D].

Priorities: dtControl 2.0 also has the new functionality to assign *priorities* to the predicate generating algorithms. Priorities are rational numbers between 0 and 1. The impurity of every predicate is divided by the priority of the algorithm that generated it. For example, a user can use axis-aligned splits with priority 1 and a linear heuristic with priority 1/2. Then the more complicated linear predicate is only chosen if it is at least twice as good (in terms of impurity) as the easier-to-understand axis-aligned split. A predicate with priority 0 is only considered after all predicates with non-zero priority have failed to split the data. This allows the user to give just a few predicates from domain knowledge, which are then strictly preferred to the automatically generated ones, but which need not suffice to construct a complete DT for the controller.

Interactive predicate selection: dtControl 2.0 offers the user the possibility to manually select the predicate in every split. This way, the user can prefer predicates that are explainable over those that optimize the impurity.

The screenshot of the interactive interface in [5, Appendix F] shows the information that dtControl 2.0 provides. The user is given some statistics and metadata, e.g. minimum, maximum and step size of the state-variables in the current node, a few automatically generated predicates for reference and all predicates generated from domain knowledge. The user can specify new predicates and is immediately informed about their impurity. Upon selecting a predicate, the split is performed and the user continues in the next node.

The user can also first construct a DT using some automatic algorithm and then restart the construction from an arbitrary node using the interactive predicate selection to handcraft an optimized representation, or at any point decide that the rest of the DT should be constructed automatically.

6 New insights about determinization

In our context, *determinization* denotes a procedure that, for some or all states, picks a subset of the allowed actions. Formally, a determinization function δ transforms a controller C into a "more determinized" C', such that for all states $s \in C$ we have $\emptyset \subsetneq C'(s) \subseteq C(s)$. This reduces the permissiveness, but often also reduces the size. Note that, for safety controllers, this always preserves the original guarantees of the controller. For other (non-safety) controllers, see Remark 1.

dtControl 2.0 supports three different general approaches to determinizing a controller: pre-processing, post-processing and safe early stopping. Pre-processing commits to a single determinization before constructing the DT. Post-processing prunes the DT after its construction, e.g. safe pruning in [7]. The basic idea of safe early stopping is already described in Section 2: if all states agree on at least one action, then instead of continuing to split the controller, stop early and return a leaf node with that common action. Alternatively, to preserve more permissiveness, one can return not only a single common action, but all common actions; formally, return the maximum set B such that for all states s in the node $B \subseteq C(s)$.

The results of [4] show that both pre-processing and post-processing are outperformed by an on-the-fly approach based on safe early stopping. This is because pre-processing discards a lot of information that could have been useful in the DT construction and post-processing can only affect the bottom-most nodes of the resulting DT, but usually not those close to the root.

We now give a new view on safe early stopping approaches for determinizing a controller that allows us to generalize the techniques of [4], reducing the size of the resulting DTs even more.

Example 4. Consider the following controller: $C(s_1) = \{a, b, c\}$, $C(s_2) = \{a, b, d\}$, $C(s_3) = \{x, y\}$. All three states map to different sets of actions, and thus an impurity measure like entropy penalizes grouping s_1 and s_2 the same as grouping s_1 and s_3. However, if determinization is allowed, grouping s_1 and s_2 need not be penalized at all, as these states agree on some actions, namely a and b. Grouping s_1 and s_2 into the same child node thus allows the algorithm to stop early at that point and return a leaf node with $\{a, b\}$, in contrast to grouping s_1 and s_3. $\triangle$

Knowing that we want to determinize by safe early stopping affects the predicate selection process. Intuitively, sets of states are more homogeneous the more actions they share. We want to take this into account when calculating the impurity of predicates. One way to do this would be to calculate the impurity of all possible determinization functions and pick the best one. This, however, is infeasible, hence we propose the heuristic of *multi-label impurity measures*. These impurity measures do not only consider the full set of allowed actions in their calculation, but instead they depend on the individual actions occurring in the set. This allows the DT construction to pick better predicates, namely those whose resulting children are more likely to be determinizable. In [5, Appendix E] we formally derive the multi-label variants of entropy and Gini-index.

To conclude this section, we point out the key difference between the new approach of multi-label impurity measures and the previous idea that was intro- duced in [4]. The approach from [4] does not evaluate the impurity of all possible determinization functions, but rather picks a smart one – that of maximum frequency (MaxFreq) – and evaluates according to that. MaxFreq determinizes in the following way: for every state, it selects from the allowed actions that action occurring most frequently throughout the whole controller. This way, many states share common actions. This is already better than pre-processing, as it does not determinize the controller a priori, but rather considers a different determinization function at every node. However, in every node we calculate the impurity for several different predicates, and the optimal choice of determinization function depends on the predicate. Thus, choosing a single determinization function for a whole node is still too coarse, as it is fixed independent of the considered predicate. We illustrate the arising problem in the following Example 5.

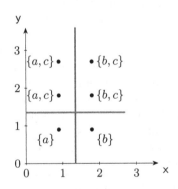

Fig. 5: A simple example of a dataset that is split suboptimally by the MaxFreq approach from [4], but optimally by the new multi-label entropy approach.

Example 5. Figure 5 shows a simple controller with a two-dimensional state space. Every point is labeled with its set of allowed actions.

As c is the most frequent action, MaxFreq determinizes the states $(1, 2)$, $(1, 3)$, $(2, 2)$ and $(2, 3)$ to action c. Hence the red split (predicate $y < 1.5$) is considered optimal, as it groups together all four states that map to c. The blue split (predicate $x < 1.5$) is considered suboptimal, as then the data still looks very heterogeneous. So, using MaxFreq, we need two splits for this controller; one to split of all the c's and one to split the two remaining states.

However, it is better to first choose a predicate and then determine a fitting determinization function. When calculating the impurity of the blue split, we can choose to determinize all states with $x = 1$ to $\{a\}$ and all states with $x = 2$ to $\{b\}$. Thus, in both resulting sub-controllers the impurity is 0 as all states agree on at least one action. This way, one split suffices to get a complete DT. Multi-label impurity measures notice when labels are shared between many (or all) states in a sub-controller, and thus they allow to prefer the optimal blue split.   △

7 Experiments

Experimental setup. We compare three approaches: BDDs, the first version of dtControl from [4] and dtControl 2.0. For BDDs[4] the variable ordering is important, so we report the smallest of 20 BDDs that we constructed by starting with a random initial variable ordering and reordering until convergence. To determinize BDDs, we used the pre-processing approach, 10 times with the minimum norm and 10 times with MaxFreq. For the previous version of dtControl, we picked the smaller of either a DT with only axis-aligned predicates or a DT with linear predicates using the logistic regression heuristic that was typically best in [4]. Determinization uses safe early stopping with the MaxFreq approach. For dtControl 2.0, we use the multi-label entropy based determinization and utilize the categorical predicates for the case studies from probabilistic model checking. We ran all experiments on a server with operating system Ubuntu 19.10, a 2.2GHz Intel(R) Xeon(R) CPU E5-2630 v4 and 250 GB RAM.

Comparing determinization techniques on cyber-physical systems. Table 1 shows the sizes of determinized BDDs and DTs on the permissive controllers of the tools SCOTS and Uppaal Stratego that were already used in [4]. We see that the new determinization approach is strictly better than the previous one, with only two DTs being of equal size, as the result of the previous method was already optimal. With the exception of the case studies helicopter and truck_trailer where BDDs are comparable or slightly better, both approaches using DTs are orders of magnitude smaller than BDDs or an explicit representation of the state-action mapping.

Case studies from probabilistic model checking. For Table 2, we used case studies from the quantitative verification benchmark set [24], which includes models from the PRISM benchmark suite [33]. Note that these case studies contain unordered enumeration-type state-variables for which we utilize the new categorical predicates. To get the controllers, we solved the case study with STORM and exported the resulting controller. This export already eliminates unreachable states. The

---

[4] Our implementation of BDDs is based on the dd python library https://github.com/tulip-control/dd.

Table 1: Controller sizes of different determinized representations of the controllers from SCOTS and Uppaal Stratego. "States" is the number of states in the controller, "BDD" the number of nodes of the smallest BDD from 20 tries, dtControl 1.0 [4] the smallest DT the previous version of dtControl could generate and dtControl 2.0 the smallest DT the new version can construct. "TO" denotes a failure to produce a result in 3 hours. The smallest numbers in each row are highlighted.

Case study	States	BDD	dtControl 1.0	dtControl 2.0
cartpole	271	127	11	**7**
10rooms	26,244	128	**7**	**7**
helicopter	280,539	870	221	**123**
cruise-latest	295,615	1,448	**3**	3
dcdc	593,089	381	9	**5**
truck_trailer	1,386,211	**18,186**	42,561	31,499
traffic_30m	16,639,662	TO	127	**97**

previous version of dtControl was not able to handle these case studies, so we only compare dtControl 2.0 to BDDs.

Table 2 shows that also for case studies from probabilistic model checking, DTs are a good way of representing controllers. The DT is the smallest representation on 13 out of 19 case studies, often reducing the size by an order of magnitude compared to BDDs or the explicit representation. On 3 case studies, BDDs are smallest, and on 2 case studies, both the DT and the BDD fail to reduce the size compared to the explicit representation. This happens if there are many different actions and thus states cannot be grouped together. A worst case example of this is a model where every state has a different action; then, a DT would have as many leaf nodes as there are states, and hence twice as many nodes in total.

Remark 2. Note that the controllers exported by STORM are deterministic, so no determinization approach can be utilized in the DT construction. We conjecture that if a permissive strategy was exported, dtControl 2.0 would benefit from the additional information and be able to reduce the controller size further as for the cyber-physical systems.

8   Conclusion

We have presented a radically new version of the tool dtControl for representing controllers by decision trees. The tool now features a graphical user interface, allowing both experts and non-experts to conveniently interact with the decision tree learning process as well as the resulting tree. There is now a range of possibilities on how the user can provide additional information. The algebraic predicates provide the means to capture the (often non-linear) relationships from the domain knowledge. The categorical predicates together with the interface to probabilistic model checkers allow for efficient representation of strategies for Markov decision processes, too. Finally, the more efficient determinization yields

Table 2: Controller sizes of different representations of controllers from the quantitative verification benchmark set [24], i.e. from the tools STORM and PRISM. "States" is the number of states in the controller, "BDD" the number of nodes of the smallest BDD of 20 tries and dtControl 2.0 the smallest DT we could construct. The smallest numbers in each row are highlighted.

Case study	States	BDD	dtControl 2.0
triangle-tireworld.9	48	51	**23**
pacman.5	232	330	**33**
rectangle-tireworld.11	**241**	498	373
philosophers-mdp.3	344	295	**181**
firewire_abst.3.rounds	610	61	**25**
rabin.3	704	303	**27**
ij.10	1,013	**436**	753
zeroconf.1000.4.true.correct_max	1,068	386	**63**
blocksworld.5	1,124	3,985	**855**
cdrive.10	**1,921**	5,134	2,401
consensus.2.disagree	2,064	138	**67**
beb.3-4.LineSeized	4,173	913	**59**
csma.2-4.some_before	7,472	1,059	**103**
eajs.2.100.5.ExpUtil	12,627	1,315	**153**
elevators.a-11-9	14,742	**6,750**	9,883
exploding-blocksworld.5	76,741	34,447	**1,777**
echoring.MaxOffline1	104,892	43,165	**1,543**
wlan_dl.0.80.deadline	189,641	5,738	**2,563**
pnueli-zuck.5	303,427	**50,128**	150,341

very small (possibly non-performant) controllers, which are particularly useful for debugging the model.

We see at least two major promising future directions. Firstly, synthesis of predicates could be made more automatic using mathematical reasoning on the domain knowledge, such as substituting expressions with a certain unit of measurement into other domain equations in the places with the same unit of measurement, e.g. to plug difference of two velocities into an equation for velocity. Secondly, one could transform the controllers into possibly entirely different controllers (not just less permissive) so that they still preserve optimality (or yield ε-optimality) but are smaller or simpler. Here, a closer interaction loop with the model checkers might lead to efficient heuristics.

References

1. Flask web development: developing web applications with python. `https://pypi.org/project/Flask/`, accessed: 14.10.2020
2. Adadi, A., Berrada, M.: Peeking inside the black-box: A survey on explainable artificial intelligence (XAI). IEEE Access **6**, 52138–52160 (2018)
3. Ashok, P., Brázdil, T., Chatterjee, K., Křetínský, J., Lampert, C.H., Toman, V.: Strategy representation by decision trees with linear classifiers. In: QEST. Lecture Notes in Computer Science, vol. 11785, pp. 109–128. Springer (2019)
4. Ashok, P., Jackermeier, M., Jagtap, P., Křetínský, J., Weininger, M., Zamani, M.: dtcontrol: decision tree learning algorithms for controller representation. In: HSCC. pp. 17:1–17:7. ACM (2020)
5. Ashok, P., Jackermeier, M., Křetínský, J., Weinhuber, C., Weininger, M., Yadav, M.: dtControl 2.0: Explainable strategy representation via decision tree learning steered by experts. CoRR **abs/2101.07202** (2021)
6. Ashok, P., Jackermeier, M., Křetínský, J., Weinhuber, C., Weininger, M., Yadav, M.: dtControl 2.0: Explainable strategy representation via decision tree learning steered by experts (TACAS 21 artifact) (Jan 2021). https://doi.org/10.5281/zenodo.4437169
7. Ashok, P., Křetínský, J., Larsen, K.G., Coënt, A.L., Taankvist, J.H., Weininger, M.: SOS: safe, optimal and small strategies for hybrid Markov decision processes. In: QEST. Lecture Notes in Computer Science, vol. 11785, pp. 147–164. Springer (2019)
8. Bahar, R.I., Frohm, E.A., Gaona, C.M., Hachtel, G.D., Macii, E., Pardo, A., Somenzi, F.: Algebraic decision diagrams and their applications. Formal Methods Syst. Des. **10**(2/3), 171–206 (1997)
9. Bostock, M., Ogievetsky, V., Heer, J.: D^3 data-driven documents. IEEE transactions on visualization and computer graphics **17**(12), 2301–2309 (2011)
10. Boutilier, C., Dearden, R., Goldszmidt, M.: Exploiting structure in policy construction. In: IJCAI. pp. 1104–1113. Morgan Kaufmann (1995)
11. Brázdil, T., Chatterjee, K., Chmelik, M., Fellner, A., Křetínský, J.: Counterexample explanation by learning small strategies in Markov decision processes. In: CAV (1). Lecture Notes in Computer Science, vol. 9206, pp. 158–177. Springer (2015)
12. Brázdil, T., Chatterjee, K., Křetínský, J., Toman, V.: Strategy representation by decision trees in reactive synthesis. In: TACAS (1). Lecture Notes in Computer Science, vol. 10805, pp. 385–407. Springer (2018)
13. Breiman, L., Friedman, J.H., Olshen, R.A., Stone, C.J.: Classification and Regression Trees. Wadsworth (1984)
14. Bryant, R.E.: Graph-based algorithms for boolean function manipulation. IEEE Trans. Computers **35**(8), 677–691 (1986)
15. Cimatti, A., Roveri, M., Traverso, P.: Automatic obdd-based generation of universal plans in non-deterministic domains. In: AAAI/IAAI. pp. 875–881. AAAI Press / The MIT Press (1998)
16. David, A., Jensen, P.G., Larsen, K.G., Mikucionis, M., Taankvist, J.H.: Uppaal stratego. In: TACAS. Lecture Notes in Computer Science, vol. 9035, pp. 206–211. Springer (2015)
17. Dehnert, C., Junges, S., Katoen, J., Volk, M.: A storm is coming: A modern probabilistic model checker. In: CAV (2). Lecture Notes in Computer Science, vol. 10427, pp. 592–600. Springer (2017)
18. Della Penna, G., Intrigila, B., Lauri, N., Magazzeni, D.: Fast and compact encoding of numerical controllers using obdds. In: Cetto, J.A., Ferrier, J.L., Filipe, J. (eds.)

Informatics in Control, Automation and Robotics: Selcted Papers from the International Conference on Informatics in Control, Automation and Robotics 2008, pp. 75–87. Springer Berlin Heidelberg, Berlin, Heidelberg (2009)

19. Frehse, G., Guernic, C.L., Donzé, A., Cotton, S., Ray, R., Lebeltel, O., Ripado, R., Girard, A., Dang, T., Maler, O.: Spaceex: Scalable verification of hybrid systems. In: CAV. Lecture Notes in Computer Science, vol. 6806, pp. 379–395. Springer (2011)

20. Fujita, M., McGeer, P.C., Yang, J.C.: Multi-terminal binary decision diagrams: An efficient data structure for matrix representation. Formal Methods Syst. Des. **10**(2/3), 149–169 (1997)

21. Garg, P., Neider, D., Madhusudan, P., Roth, D.: Learning invariants using decision trees and implication counterexamples. In: POPL. pp. 499–512. ACM (2016)

22. Girard, A.: Low-complexity quantized switching controllers using approximate bisimulation. CoRR **abs/1209.4576** (2012)

23. Harris, C.R., Millman, K.J., van der Walt, S., Gommers, R., Virtanen, P., Cournapeau, D., Wieser, E., Taylor, J., Berg, S., Smith, N.J., Kern, R., Picus, M., Hoyer, S., van Kerkwijk, M.H., Brett, M., Haldane, A., del Río, J.F., Wiebe, M., Peterson, P., Gérard-Marchant, P., Sheppard, K., Reddy, T., Weckesser, W., Abbasi, H., Gohlke, C., Oliphant, T.E.: Array programming with numpy. CoRR **abs/2006.10256** (2020)

24. Hartmanns, A., Klauck, M., Parker, D., Quatmann, T., Ruijters, E.: The quantitative verification benchmark set. In: TACAS (1). Lecture Notes in Computer Science, vol. 11427, pp. 344–350. Springer (2019)

25. Heath, D.G., Kasif, S., Salzberg, S.: Induction of oblique decision trees. In: Proceedings of the 13th International Joint Conference on Artificial Intelligence. Chambéry, France, August 28 - September 3, 1993. pp. 1002–1007 (1993)

26. Hoey, J., St-Aubin, R., Hu, A.J., Boutilier, C.: SPUDD: stochastic planning using decision diagrams. In: UAI. pp. 279–288. Morgan Kaufmann (1999)

27. Hyafil, L., Rivest, R.L.: Constructing optimal binary decision trees is NP-complete. Inf. Process. Lett. **5**(1), 15–17 (1976)

28. Ittner, A., Schlosser, M.: Non-linear decision trees - NDT. In: ICML. pp. 252–257. Morgan Kaufmann (1996)

29. Jackermeier, M.: dtControl: Decision Tree Learning for Explainable Controller Representation. Bachelor's thesis, Technische Universität München (2020)

30. Jr., M.M., Davitian, A., Tabuada, P.: PESSOA: A tool for embedded controller synthesis. In: CAV. Lecture Notes in Computer Science, vol. 6174, pp. 566–569. Springer (2010)

31. Kiesbye, J.: Private Communication (2020)

32. Kwiatkowska, M.Z., Norman, G., Parker, D.: PRISM 4.0: Verification of probabilistic real-time systems. In: CAV. Lecture Notes in Computer Science, vol. 6806, pp. 585–591. Springer (2011)

33. Kwiatkowska, M.Z., Norman, G., Parker, D.: The PRISM benchmark suite. In: QEST. pp. 203–204. IEEE Computer Society (2012)

34. Larsen, K.G., Mikucionis, M., Taankvist, J.H.: Safe and optimal adaptive cruise control. In: Correct System Design. Lecture Notes in Computer Science, vol. 9360, pp. 260–277. Springer (2015)

35. Luttenberger, M., Meyer, P.J., Sickert, S.: Practical synthesis of reactive systems from LTL specifications via parity games. Acta Informatica **57**(1-2), 3–36 (2020)

36. Wes McKinney: Data Structures for Statistical Computing in Python. In: Stéfan van der Walt, Jarrod Millman (eds.) Proceedings of the 9th Python in Science Conference. pp. 56 – 61 (2010). https://doi.org/10.25080/Majora-92bf1922-00a

37. Meurer, A., Smith, C.P., Paprocki, M., Certík, O., Kirpichev, S.B., Rocklin, M., Kumar, A., Ivanov, S., Moore, J.K., Singh, S., Rathnayake, T., Vig, S., Granger, B.E., Muller, R.P., Bonazzi, F., Gupta, H., Vats, S., Johansson, F., Pedregosa, F., Curry, M.J., Terrel, A.R., Roucka, S., Saboo, A., Fernando, I., Kulal, S., Cimrman, R., Scopatz, A.M.: Sympy: symbolic computing in python. PeerJ Comput. Sci. **3**, e103 (2017)
38. Mitchell, T.M.: Machine learning. McGraw Hill series in computer science, McGraw-Hill (1997)
39. Murthy, S.K., Kasif, S., Salzberg, S., Beigel, R.: OC1: A randomized induction of oblique decision trees. In: AAAI. pp. 322–327. AAAI Press / The MIT Press (1993)
40. Neider, D., Markgraf, O.: Learning-based synthesis of safety controllers. In: FMCAD. pp. 120–128. IEEE (2019)
41. Pedregosa, F., Varoquaux, G., Gramfort, A., Michel, V., Thirion, B., Grisel, O., Blondel, M., Prettenhofer, P., Weiss, R., Dubourg, V., Vanderplas, J., Passos, A., Cournapeau, D., Brucher, M., Perrot, M., Duchesnay, E.: Scikit-learn: Machine learning in Python. Journal of Machine Learning Research **12**, 2825–2830 (2011)
42. Pyeatt, L.D., Howe, A.E., et al.: Decision tree function approximation in reinforcement learning. In: Proceedings of the third international symposium on adaptive systems: evolutionary computation and probabilistic graphical models. vol. 2, pp. 70–77. Cuba (2001)
43. Quinlan, J.R.: Induction of decision trees. Mach. Learn. **1**(1), 81–106 (1986)
44. Quinlan, J.R.: C4.5: Programs for Machine Learning. Morgan Kaufmann (1993)
45. Rungger, M., Zamani, M.: SCOTS: A tool for the synthesis of symbolic controllers. In: HSCC. pp. 99–104. ACM (2016)
46. Shannon, C.E.: A mathematical theory of communication. Bell Syst. Tech. J. **27**(4), 623–656 (1948)
47. St-Aubin, R., Hoey, J., Boutilier, C.: APRICODD: approximate policy construction using decision diagrams. In: NIPS. pp. 1089–1095. MIT Press (2000)
48. Virtanen, P., Gommers, R., Oliphant, T.E., Haberland, M., Reddy, T., Cournapeau, D., Burovski, E., Peterson, P., Weckesser, W., Bright, J., van der Walt, S., Brett, M., Wilson, J., Millman, K.J., Mayorov, N., Nelson, A.R.J., Jones, E., Kern, R., Larson, E., Carey, C.J., Polat, I., Feng, Y., Moore, E.W., VanderPlas, J., Laxalde, D., Perktold, J., Cimrman, R., Henriksen, I., Quintero, E.A., Harris, C.R., Archibald, A.M., Ribeiro, A.H., Pedregosa, F., van Mulbregt, P., SciPy: Scipy 1.0-fundamental algorithms for scientific computing in python. CoRR **abs/1907.10121** (2019)
49. Zapreev, I.S., Verdier, C., Jr., M.M.: Optimal symbolic controllers determinization for BDD storage. In: ADHS 2018. IFAC-PapersOnLine, vol. 51, pp. 1–6. Elsevier (2018). https://doi.org/10.1016/j.ifacol.2018.08.001

Tool Demo Papers

HLola: a Very Functional Tool for Extensible Stream Runtime Verification*

Felipe Gorostiaga[1,2,3](✉) and César Sánchez[1]

[1] IMDEA Software Institute, Madrid, Spain
[2] Universidad Politécnica de Madrid, Madrid, Spain
[3] CIFASIS, Rosario, Argentina
{felipe.gorostiaga,cesar.sanchez}@imdea.org

Abstract. We present HLola, an extensible Stream Runtime Verification (SRV) tool, that borrows from the functional language Haskell (1) rich types for data in events and verdicts; and (2) functional features for parametrization, libraries, high-order specification transformations, etc.
SRV is a formal dynamic analysis technique that generalizes Runtime Verification (RV) algorithms from temporal logics like LTL to stream monitoring, allowing the computation of verdicts richer than Booleans (quantitative values and beyond). The keystone of SRV is the clean separation between temporal dependencies and data computations. However, in spite of this theoretical separation previous engines include hardwired implementations of just a few datatypes, requiring complex changes in the tool chain to incorporate new data types. Additionally, when previous tools implement features like parametrization these are implemented in an ad-hoc way. In contrast, HLola is implemented as a Haskell embedded DSL, borrowing datatypes and functional aspects from Haskell, resulting in an extensible engine[4]. We illustrate HLola through several examples, including a UAV monitoring infrastructure with predictive characteristics that has been validated in online runtime verification in real mission planning.

1 Introduction

Runtime Verification [4, 14, 18] is a dynamic technique that studies (1) how to generate monitors from formal specifications, and (2) algorithms to monitor the system under analysis, one trace at a time. Early RV specification languages were based on logics like past LTL [19] adapted to finite traces [5, 10, 15], regular expressions [23], fix-point logics [1], rule based languages [3], or rewriting [21]. Verdicts and many times observations in most of these specification logics are restricted to Booleans, often because most early logics in RV were borrowed from static verification—where decidability is crucial. SRV [9, 22] attempts to generalize these monitoring algorithms to richer datatypes, including in observations and verdicts. SRV offers declarative specifications where off-set expressions allow accessing streams at different moments in time, including future instants. Most previous SRV developments [9, 11] and their extensions to event-based

---

* This work was funded in part by the Madrid Regional Government under project "S2018/TCS-4339 (BLOQUES-CM)", by Spanish National Project "BOSCO (PGC2018-102210-B-100)".
[4] The tool is available open-source at http://github.com/imdea-software/hlola

J. F. Groote and K. G. Larsen (Eds.): TACAS 2021, LNCS 12652, pp. 349–356, 2021.
https://doi.org/10.1007/978-3-030-72013-1_18

systems [8,11,12,17] focus on efficiently implementing the temporal engine, promising that new datatypes can be incorporated easily. However, in practice, adding a datatype requires modifying the parser, the internal representation and the runtime system. Consequently, existing tools only support a limited hardwired collection of datatypes (typically Booleans and numeric types for quantitative monitoring).

In this paper we demonstrate the tool HLola, whose core language is Lola [9], but that enables arbitrary datatypes. HLola is implemented as an embedded DSL in Haskell. Other RV tools implemented as eDSLs include [2, 13] (in Scala), and [24] which implements LTL as an eDSL in Haskell. The main theoretical novelty of HLola is a technique called *lift deep embedding*, that consists in borrowing types transparently from Haskell and embedding the resulting language back into Haskell (see [7] for an introduction to HLola with details of the theoretical underpinnings). In fact, most HLola datatypes were introduced after the temporal engine was completed without requiring any re-implementation. An eDSL enables higher-order functions to describe transformations that produce stream declarations from stream declarations, enabling stream parametrization for free. HLola libraries collect these transformers so new logics like LTL, MTL, etc with Boolean and quantitative semantics can be implemented in a few lines (see Section 2). Haskell type-classes enable *simplifiers*, which can anticipate the value of an expression without requiring the computation of all its sub-expressions. Implementing these in previous systems requires to re-invent and implement features manually (like macro expansions, etc). HLola even allows specifications as data to implement "specifications within specifications" (a feature that allows computing a full auxiliary specification at every instant, useful in simulation and for nested properties). This is used in an UAV scenario to implement Kalman filters [16] as monitors that predict the trajectory of the unmanned aircraft. The output of this monitor is used to anticipate problems (using another monitor) and take preventive planning actions.

Stream Runtime Verification in a nutshell SRV generalizes monitoring algorithms to arbitrary data, where datatypes are abstracted using multi-sorted first-order interpreted signatures (called data theories in the Lola terminology). The signatures are interpreted in the sense that every functional symbol f used to build terms of a given type is accompanied with an evaluation function f (the interpretation) that allows the computation of values (given values of the arguments). A Lola specification $\langle I, O, E \rangle$ consists of (1) a set of typed input stream variables I, which correspond to the inputs observed by the monitor; (2) a set of typed output stream variables O which represent the outputs of the monitor as well as intermediate observations; and (3) defining equations, which associate every output $y \in O$ with a stream expression E_y that describes declaratively the intended values of y. The set of *stream expressions* of a given type is built from constants and function symbols as constructors (as usual), and also from *offset expressions* of the form $s[k, d]$ where s is a stream variable, k is an integer number and d is a value of the type of s used as default. For example, altitude[-1, 0.0m] represents the value of stream altitude in the previous step of time, with 0.0m as default value to be used at the initial instant. Online efficient algorithms can be synthesized for specifications with (bounded) future accesses [9, 22], where efficiency means that resources (time and space) are independent of the length of the trace and can be calculated statically. HLola can be efficiently monitored in a trace-length independent sense [7].

2 The HLola Tool

Fig. 1 shows the software architecture of HLola. We start from an HLola specification, which can borrow datatypes, notation and features from the Haskell language (represented by the red dashed arrow in Fig. 1). A simple translator processes the specification and generates code in the Haskell eDSL. The translator does not fully parse the spec and only preforms simple rewrites, leaving most of the specification unchanged. The resulting code is combined with the HLola engine (developed in Haskell) and compiled into a binary in the target platform. A well-known downside of this approach is that during the second compilation stage, error reports may be rather cryptic. On the other hand, a Haskell expert can write specifications directly in the embedded DSL, which still resembles Lola, to finely tune an HLola specification.

The enhanced capabilities of HLola with respect to Lola (streams as data, stream type polymorphism and parametric streams) impact the syntax of the language, which diverges slightly from the syntax of the original Lola. HLola files can either be libraries or specifications: *Libraries* include HLola code that define streams and facilities to create streams, and must be declared using **library** <Name> (where <Name> is the name of the library) on the first line of the HLola file. *Specifications* first state the format for input and output events as **format JSON** or **format CSV**. Source files then can import libraries and stream data manipulation facilities (called theories) with the statements **use library** <Name> and **use theory** <Name> respectively. HLola files can also import arbitrary Haskell libraries using the statement **use haskell** <Name>, and include Haskell code directly anywhere within the blocks delimited between #HASKELL and #ENDOFHASKELL. Specifications then define the input and output streams. An *Input stream* is declared by its type and name in a line of the form **input** <Type> <name>, just like in the original Lola language. The syntax of <Type> follows the Haskell notation. An *Output stream* is specified by its type, name and parameters on the left hand side of **=**, and its defining expression on the right hand side of **=**:

```
output <TypeConstraints>? <Type> <name> <args>* = <Expr>,
```

where <TypeConstraints> is an optional set of constraints over the polymorphic types handled by the stream (expressed in Haskell notation), and <args> is an optional list of arguments of the form <Type> **<name>**. We can use **define** instead of **output** to define intermediate streams, whose values are not reported by the monitor but can be used by other streams. The defining <Expr> of an output stream allows the use of

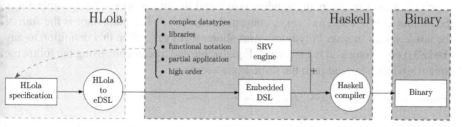

Fig. 1. Software Architecture of HLola.

`let` clauses, `where` blocks, type annotation, `do` notation, etc. The access to the *value* of a stream s at the current instant uses the term `s[now]` to distinguish it from s, the stream itself (whose type is *stream of values*). The offset expression that accesses a stream s at a shift of i with default value d is written as `s[i|d]`, as in classic Lola. The symbol `'` is used to lift an object o from the theory as in `'o`. We sometimes indicate the arity of the object o being lifted for clarity or to aid the type inference as in `2'o`. To improve readability, some operators have been overridden by their lifted version, such as `if-then-else`.

Libraries. The following HLola file defines a library of Past-LTL operators, called `LTL`, as part of the HLola distribution[5].

```
library LTL
use library Utils
output Bool historically <Stream Bool p> = p[now] && historically p [-1|'True]
output Bool once <Stream Bool p> = p[now] || once p[-1|'False]
output Bool since <Stream Bool p> <Stream Bool q> = q[now] ||
                                      (p[now] && p `since` q [-1|'False])
output Int nFalses <Stream Bool p> = nFalses p[-1|0] + if p[now] then 0 else 1
output Double percFalses <Stream Bool p> = nFalses p[now] `intdiv` (instantN[now])
```

The auxiliary library `Utils` includes `instantN`, which stores the current instant number. Stream `historically` is parametrized by `Boolean` stream **p**. Once instantiated, `historically p` will be *true* until p becomes *false* for the first time, and will be *false* thereafter. This definition uses offsets to define the unrolling, using the constant value *true* in the first instant, lifted from Haskell as `'True`. This library also contains quantitative operators like `nFalses`, that counts the total number of falsifications up to an instant, and `percFalses` that calculates the ratio of falsifications. A similar library for MTL includes the parametrized definition of $\varphi \, \mathcal{U}_{(a,b)} \psi$:

```
output Bool until <(Int,Int) (a,b)> <Stream Bool phi> <Stream Bool psi> = from a
  where from a | a == b   = psi[a|'False]
               | otherwise = psi[a|'False] || (phi[a|'True] && from (a+1))
```

Here the parametrized stream `until` takes the interval (a, b) and the streams φ and ψ as parameters. Similarly, the library for Quantitative MTL introduces a parametrized stream to calculate the arithmetic mean of the last k values of a given stream:

```
output Double meanLast <Int k> <Stream Double str> = numr / denom
  where denom=1'fromIntegral (2'min 'k (instantN[now])) ; numr=sumLast k str [now]
```

which takes as parameters the window size `k` and the stream **str**. The denominator is the minimum of k and `instantN`, converted to `Double`. The numerator is the sum of the last k values in `str`. Polymorphosim allows us to generalize this definition to any Haskell type as long as it is Fractional, Equalizable and Streamable, using the following stream signature instead (and the same expression):

```
output (Eq a, Fractional a, Streamable a) => a meanLast <Int k> <Stream a str>
```

---

[5] All libraries, definitions and examples are available open-source in the GitHub repository and at https://software.imdea.org/hlola/specs.html.

3 Example Specifications

In this section we show a collection of HLola specifications to demonstrate the capabilities of HLola to define stream based monitors.

Temporal Logics. HLola allows us to easily define, in a declarative way, many specifications written in temporal logic. The HLola distribution contains many LTL examples, including a sender/receiver model from [6], and other temporal logics. Consider the following MTL property from [20]: $\Box(alarm \rightarrow (\Diamond_{[0,10]} allClear \lor \Diamond_{[10,10]} shutdown))$, which includes deadlines between environment events and the corresponding system responses, stating that that an *alarm* is followed by a *shutdown* event in exactly 10 time units unless *allClear* is received. This is defined in HLola as follows:

```
format JSON
use library MTL
#HASKELL
data Event = Alarm | AllClear | ShutDown deriving (Generic,Read,FromJSON,Eq)
#ENDOFHASKELL
input Event event
define Bool allClear = event [now] === 'AllClear
define Bool shutdown = event [now] === 'Shutdown
define Bool alarm    = event [now] === 'Alarm
output Bool property = alarm [now] `implies` (willClear[now] || willShutdown[now])
   where willClear     = eventually (0,10) allClear
         willShutdown = eventually (10,10) shutdown
```

Pinescript example. TradingView is an online charting platform for stock exchange, which offers the Pinescript language to query stock time series. Pinescript queries are then run in the company's servers. We have implemented the indicators of Pinescript in HLola as a library, and we have implementated a trading strategy[6] using the HLola Pinescript library. Compared to Pinescript, HLola offers formal semantics, runtime resource guarantees (time and space) and is much more expressive, for example allowing relational queries that involve multiple stocks (their averages, etc).

UAV specifications. We have used HLola also for the online monitoring of several properties of UAVs missions. For example: (1) That the UAV does not fly over forbidden regions, and (2) that the UAV is in good position when it takes a picture. The input streams of these two specifications consist of the state of the UAV at every instant and the onboard camera events to detect when a picture is being captured. This specification imports geometric facilities from **theory** Geometry2D, and Haskell libraries Data.Maybe and Data.List. It then defines custom datatypes to retrieve data from the UAV, which are enclosed in a verbatim HASKELL block. The output stream all_ok_capturing assesses that, whenever the vehicle is taking a picture, the height, roll and pitch are acceptable and the vehicle is near the target location. The output stream flying_in_safe_zones reports if the UAV is flying outside every forbidden region. The output stream depth_into_poly takes the minimum of the distances between the vehicle position and every side of the forbidden region inside which the vehicle is.

---

[6] Available at www.tradingview.com/script/DushajXt-MACD-Strategy

```
format JSON
use theory Geometry2D
use library Utils
use haskell Data.Maybe
use haskell Data.List

#HASKELL
data Attitude = Attitude {yaw :: Double, roll :: Double, pitch :: Double}
                        deriving (Show,Generic,Read,FromJSON,ToJSON)
data Target   = Target {x :: Double, y :: Double, num_wp :: Double} ...
data Position = Position {x :: Double, y :: Double, alt :: Double} ...
#ENDOFHASKELL

input     Attitude attitude
input      Vector2 velocity
input     Position position
input       Double altitude
input       Target target
input [[[Double]]] nofly
input     [String] events_within

output Bool all_ok_capturing = capturing [now] `implies`
  (height_ok [now] && near [now] && roll_ok [now] && pitch_ok [now])

output Bool flying_in_safe_zones = 'isNothing (flying_in_poly [now])

output (Maybe Double) depth_into_poly = let
  mSides = '(fmap polygonSides) (flying_in_poly [now])
  distance_from_pos = 'shortestDist (filtered_pos [now])
  in    2'fmap distance_from_pos mSides
  where shortestDist x = minimum.map (distancePointSegment x)

define Bool capturing = ...

define Double filtered_pos_component <(Position->Double) field> <String nm> = ...

define Double filtered_pos_x   = filtered_pos_component x "x" [now]

define Double filtered_pos_y   = filtered_pos_component y "y" [now]

define Double filtered_pos_alt = filtered_pos_component alt "alt" [now]

define Point2 filtered_pos = 'P (filtered_pos_x [now]) (filtered_pos_y [now])

define Bool near = let target_pos = 'targetToPoint (target [now])
  in    2'distance (filtered_pos [now]) target_pos < 1
  where targetToPoint (Target x y _) = P x y

define Bool height_ok = filtered_pos_alt [now] > 0

define Bool roll_ok   = '(abs.roll) (attitude [now]) < 0.0523

define Bool pitch_ok  = '(abs.pitch) (attitude [now]) < 0.0523

define [Polygon] no_fly_polys = ...

define (Maybe Polygon) flying_in_poly = let
  position_in_poly = 'pointInPoly (filtered_pos [now])
  in 2'find position_in_poly (no_fly_polys [now])
```

Intermediate stream `capturing` captures whether the UAV is taking a picture (omitted for brevity). The streams `filtered_pos_alt` and `filtered_pos` represent the location and altitude of the UAV filtered to reduce noise from the sensors. We omit the definition of the filter, which is implemented in `filtered_pos_component` The streams `height_ok`, `roll_ok`, and `pitch_ok`, calculate that the corresponding attitude of the vehicle is within certain boundaries. Finally, the intermediate stream `no_fly_polys` obtains a set of Polygons from the input forbidden regions (its definition has been omitted), and the stream `flying_in_poly` returns the forbidden region in which the vehicle is flying, if any. The artifact attached to this paper includes more UAV specifications, which have been validated in real missions [25].

References

1. Howard Barringer, Allen Goldberg, Klaus Havelund, and Koushik Sen. Rule-based runtime verification. In *Proc. of the 5th Int'l Conf. on Verification, Model Checking and Abstract Interpretation (VMCAI'04)*, volume 2937 of *LNCS*, pages 44–57. Springer, 2004.
2. Howard Barringer and Klaus Havelund. Tracecontract: A scala DSL for trace analysis. In Michael J. Butler and Wolfram Schulte, editors, *FM 2011: Formal Methods - 17th International Symposium on Formal Methods, Limerick, Ireland, June 20-24, 2011. Proceedings*, volume 6664 of *Lecture Notes in Computer Science*, pages 57–72. Springer, 2011.
3. Howard Barringer, David Rydeheard, and Klaus Havelund. Rule systems for run-time monitoring: From eagle to ruler. In Oleg Sokolsky and Serdar Taşıran, editors, *Runtime Verification*, pages 111–125, Berlin, Heidelberg, 2007. Springer Berlin Heidelberg.
4. Ezio Bartocci and Yliès Falcone, editors. *Lectures on Runtime Verification - Introductory and Advanced Topics*, volume 10457 of *LNCS*. Springer, 2018.
5. Andreas Bauer, Martin Leucker, and Chrisitan Schallhart. Runtime verification for LTL and TLTL. *ACM Transactions on Software Engineering and Methodology*, 20(4):14, 2011.
6. Marco Benedetti and Alessandro Cimatti. Bounded model checking for past LTL. In *Proc. of TACAS'03*, volume 2619 of *LNCS*, pages 18–33. Springer, 2003.
7. Martín Ceresa, Felipe Gorostiaga, and César Sánchez. Declarative stream runtime verification (hlola). In Bruno C. d. S. Oliveira, editor, *Programming Languages and Systems*, pages 25–43, Cham, 2020. Springer International Publishing.
8. Lukas Convent, Sebastian Hungerecker, Martin Leucker, Torben Scheffel, Malte Schmitz, and Daniel Thoma. TeSSLa: Temporal stream-based specification language. In *Proc. of SBMF'18*, volume 11254 of *LNCS*. Springer, 2018.
9. Ben D'Angelo, Sriram Sankaranarayanan, César Sánchez, Will Robinson, Bernd Finkbeiner, Henny B. Sipma, Sandeep Mehrotra, and Zohar Manna. LOLA: Runtime monitoring of synchronous systems. In *Proc. of the 12th Int'l Symp. of Temporal Representation and Reasoning (TIME'05)*, pages 166–174. IEEE CS Press, 2005.
10. Cindy Eisner, Dana Fisman, John Havlicek, Yoad Lustig, Anthony McIsaac, and David Van Campenhout. Reasoning with temporal logic on truncated paths. In *Proc. of the 15th Int'l Conf. on Computer Aided Verification (CAV'03)*, volume 2725 of *LNCS*, pages 27–39. Springer, 2003.
11. Peter Faymonville, Bernd Finkbeiner, Malte Schledjewski, Maximilian Schwenger, Marvin Stenger, Leander Tentrup, and Torfah Hazem. StreamLAB: Stream-based monitoring of cyber-physical systems. In *Proc. of the 31st Int'l Conf. on Computer-Aided Verification (CAV'19)*, volume 11561 of *LNCS*, pages 421–431. Springer, 2019.
12. Felipe Gorostiaga and César Sánchez. Striver: Stream runtime verification for real-time event-streams. In *Proc. of the 18th Int'l Conf. on Runtime Verification (RV'18)*, volume 11237 of *LNCS*, pages 282–298. Springer, 2018.
13. Klaus Havelund. Rule-based runtime verification revisited. *Int. J. Softw. Tools Technol. Transf.*, 17(2):143–170, 2015.
14. Klaus Havelund and Allen Goldberg. Verify your runs. In *Proc. of VSTTE'05*, LNCS 4171, pages 374–383. Springer, 2005.
15. Klaus Havelund and Grigore Roşu. Synthesizing monitors for safety properties. In *Proc. of the 8th Int'l Conf. on Tools and Algorithms for the Construction and Analysis of Systems (TACAS'02)*, volume 2280 of *LNCS*, pages 342–356. Springer-Verlag, 2002.
16. Rudolph Emil Kalman. A new approach to linear filtering and prediction problems. *Transactions of the ASME–Journal of Basic Engineering*, 82(Series D):35–45, 1960.
17. Martin Leucker, César Sánchez, Torben Scheffel, Malte Schmitz, and Alexander Schramm. TeSSLa: Runtime verification of non-synchronized real-time streams. In *Proc. of the 33rd Symposium on Applied Computing (SAC'18)*. ACM, 2018.

18. Martin Leucker and Christian Schallhart. A brief account of runtime verification. *J. Logic Algebr. Progr.*, 78(5):293–303, 2009.
19. Zohar Manna and Amir Pnueli. *Temporal Verification of Reactive Systems*. Springer-Verlag, 1995.
20. Joël Ouaknine and James Worrell. Some recent results in metric temporal logic. In *Proc. of FORMATS'08*, volume 5215 of *LNCS*, pages 1–13. Springer, 2008.
21. Grigore Roşu and Klaus Havelund. Rewriting-based techniques for runtime verification. *Automated Software Engineering*, 12(2):151–197, 2005.
22. César Sánchez. Online and offline stream runtime verification of synchronous systems. In *Proc. of the 18th Int'l Conf. on Runtime Verification (RV'18)*, volume 11237 of *LNCS*, pages 138–163. Springer, 2018.
23. Koushik Sen and Grigore Roşu. Generating optimal monitors for extended regular expressions. In Oleg Sokolsky and Mahesh Viswanathan, editors, *Electronic Notes in Theoretical Computer Science*, volume 89. Elsevier, 2003.
24. Volker Stolz and Frank Huch. Runtime verification of concurrent haskell programs. *Electron. Notes Theor. Comput. Sci.*, 113:201–216, 2005.
25. Sebastián Zudaire, Felipe Gorostiaga, César Sánchez, Gerardo Schneider, and Sebastián Uchitel. Assumption monitoring using runtime verification for UAV temporal task plan executions. Under submission, 2020.

AMulet 2.0 for Verifying Multiplier Circuits*

Daniela Kaufmann, Armin Biere

Johannes Kepler University, Linz, Austria
{daniela.kaufmann,biere}@jku.at

Abstract. AMULET 2.0 is a fully automatic tool for the verification of
integer multipliers using computer algebra. Our tool models multiplier
circuits given as and-inverter graphs as a set of polynomials and applies
preprocessing techniques based on elimination theory of Gröbner bases.
Finally it uses a polynomial reduction algorithm to verify the correctness
of the given circuit. AMULET 2.0 is a re-factorization and improved re-
implementation of our previous multiplier verification tool AMULET 1.0.

1 Introduction

Formal verification of arithmetic circuits is important to prevent issues like the
famous Pentium FDIV bug [28]. Up to now there have been many attempts to
verify these circuits, but even today the problem of fully automatic verification
of arithmetic circuits, and especially multipliers, is still considered to be hard.

Methods based on decision diagrams [6] rely on manual structural decomposition of the multiplier. Approaches based on satisfiability checking (SAT) are not
scalable [3]. Recently progress has been made using theorem provers [29]. However, the multipliers have to be given as SVL netlists, which relies on preservation
of hierarchical information.For flattened gate-level multipliers the currently most
successful technique uses algebraic reasoning [7, 15, 17, 25, 26]. In this line of
work the circuit is modeled as a set of polynomials and the specification is then
checked to be implied by the circuit polynomials. For non-experts Chap. 2 of [15]
might serve as introduction to bit-level verification using computer algebra.

In our approach [17] we apply a combination of SAT solving and computer
algebra. Certain parts of the multiplier, i.e., complex final stage adders that
are generate-and-propagate (GP) adders [27], are hard to verify using computer
algebra, but are easy to verify using SAT solvers [21]. Therefore we apply adder
substitution [17] and replace complex final stage adders by simple ripple-carry
(RC) adders. The equivalence of the adders is verified using SAT solvers. The
correctness of the simplified multiplier is shown using computer algebra [17].

This tool paper presents AMULET 2.0, a successor of AMULET 1.0 [17,19].
AMULET 2.0 reads multipliers given as and-inverter graphs (AIG) [22] and
fully automatically applies adder substitution and verifies the (simplified) circuit.
Furthermore, certificates can be generated in the Nullstellensatz proof format [16]
or in the practical algebraic calculus (PAC) [20] to validate the verification results.

---

* This work is supported by the LIT AI Lab funded by the State of Upper Austria.

J. F. Groote and K. G. Larsen (Eds.): TACAS 2021, LNCS 12652, pp. 357–364, 2021.
https://doi.org/10.1007/978-3-030-72013-1_19

AMULET 2.0 is a modular C++ re-implementation of AMULET 1.0 (while AMULET 1.0 consists of a single C file). AMULET 2.0 is not only a standalone tool but also serves as a polynomial reasoning framework, i.e., parts can easily be integrated into different workflows, cf. Sect. 4. AMULET 2.0 still provides the same functionality as AMULET 1.0, but with improved algorithms, cf. Sect 5, based on the same theory [15,17]. In this paper we focus on novelties of AMULET 2.0 and refer the reader to [19] for an introduction to AMULET 1.0.

2   Circuit Verification using Computer Algebra

AMULET 2.0 takes as input signed or unsigned integer multipliers C, given as AIGs, with $2n$ input bits $a_0, \ldots, a_{n-1}, b_0, \ldots, b_{n-1} \in \{0,1\}$ and output bits $s_0, \ldots, s_{2n-1} \in \{0,1\}$. We denote the internal AIG nodes by $l_1, \ldots, l_k \in \{0,1\}$. Let $\mathbb{Z}[X] = \mathbb{Z}[a_0, \ldots, a_{n-1}, b_0, \ldots, b_{n-1}, l_1, \ldots, l_k, s_0, \ldots, s_{2n-1}]$. The multiplier C is correct iff for all possible inputs $a_i, b_i \in \{0,1\}$ the specification $\mathcal{L} = 0$ holds:

$$\mathcal{L} = -\sum_{i=0}^{2n-1} 2^i s_i + \left(\sum_{i=0}^{n-1} 2^i a_i\right)\left(\sum_{i=0}^{n-1} 2^i b_i\right) \tag{1}$$

For signed multipliers the most significant bits s_{2n-1}, a_{n-1}, and b_{n-1} determine the sign and the weights have to be negated, i.e., 2^{2n-1} becomes -2^{2n-1}.

The semantics of each AIG node implies a polynomial relation, e.g., $u = v \wedge \neg w$ implies $-u + v - vw = 0$. Let $G(C) \subseteq \mathbb{Z}[X]$ be the set of polynomials that contains for each AIG node the corresponding polynomial relation. Additionally, all variables $x \in X$ are Boolean and we enforce this property by the set of *Boolean value constraints* $B(X) = \{x(1-x) \mid x \in X\} \subseteq \mathbb{Z}[X]$. The polynomials in $G(C) \cup B(X)$ are ordered according to a lexicographic order, such that the output variable of a gate is always greater than the inputs of the gate [23].

Let $J(C) = \langle G(C) \cup B(X)\rangle \subseteq \mathbb{Z}[X]$ be the ideal generated by $G(C) \cup B(X)$. The circuit fulfills its specification if and only if we can derive that $\mathcal{L} \in J(C)$ [17]. We showed in [17] that $G(C) \cup B(X)$ is a D-Gröbner basis [2] for $J(C) \subseteq \mathbb{Z}[X]$. Thus, the correctness of the circuit can be established by reducing $\mathcal{L}$ by the polynomials $G(C) \cup B(X)$ and checking whether the result is zero.

However, simply reducing the specification by $G(C) \cup B(X)$ leads to large intermediate results [24]. Hence, we eliminate variables in $G(C) \cup B(X)$ prior to reduction to yield a more compact D-Gröbner basis [17], which boils down to simple substitutions, but relies on the elimination theorem of Gröbner bases [9].

3   Usage

AMULET 2.0 is available at http://fmv.jku.at/amulet2 and is published as open source under the MIT license. AMULET 2.0 relies on the AIGER library [5] and the GMP library [10]. The AIGER library is provided together with the source code of AMULET 2.0, the GMP library needs to be pre-installed by the user. AMULET 2.0 is compiled executing "./configure.sh && make".

In a complete workflow one should first apply adder substitution, using the *substitution mode* of AMULET 2.0, to make sure that a potential complex final stage adder is replaced by a simple RC adder. Afterwards, one of the two modes, the *verification mode* or *certification mode*, can be applied to verify the (simplified) multiplier, which we will call in the following *rewritten* multiplier. If it is known that the final stage adder is not a complex GP adder, the substitution step can be omitted. We present a complete demonstration for the unsigned 64-bit multiplier <bpwtcl.aig>, which is included in the complementary material [14]. The output of AMULET 2.0 can be seen in the corresponding log-files that are also included in the artifact.

Adder Substitution. First we apply adder substitution by running

```
./amulet -substitute bpwtcl.aig miter.cnf rewritten.aig [options]
```

If the multiplier computes multiplication of signed integers the option "-signed" has to be involved, because the signedness is part of the circuit specification.

If adder substitution can be applied successfully, the generated miter is written to <miter.cnf> and the rewritten multiplier to <rewritten.aig>. Otherwise, the input multiplier will be written to <rewritten.aig> and a trivially unsatisfiable CNF is written to <miter.cnf>. The file <miter.cnf> has to be given to a SAT solver, e.g. KISSAT [4], which is then expected to return *unsatisfiable*. The rewritten multiplier can be verified or certified using AMULET 2.0.

Verification. Verification is executed by

```
./amulet -verify rewritten.aig [options]
```

As for adder substitution, one has to invoke the option "-signed" for signed multipliers. Furthermore, the option "-no-counter-examples" is available, which turns off generation and saving of counter examples in <rewritten.cex>, in the case when the multiplier in <rewritten.aig> is incorrect.

Certification. Certification is applied using

```
./amulet -certify rewritten.aig out.pol out.prf out.spc [options]
```

In this mode, AMULET 2.0 verifies the multiplier and automatically generates proof certificates, which can be checked by corresponding proof checkers. AMULET 2.0 supports two proof formats, Nullstellensatz proofs [1,16] and PAC proofs [20] based on the polynomial calculus [8]. The default proof format is the Nullstellensatz proof, because it generates smaller proof files and is faster to check. Proofs in the PAC format can be generated using the option "-pac". All options of the verification mode are available too.

The proofs are stored in the provided files <out.pol>, <out.prf>, and <out.spc>. The file <out.pol> contains the gate constraints, the second file <out.prf> the core proof in the selected proof format and the third file <out.spc> the specification of the multiplier. The generated proofs can be given to the proof checkers NUSS-CHECKER [16] for Nullstellensatz proofs or to the proof checkers PACHECK [20], or PASTÈQUE [20] for PAC proofs.

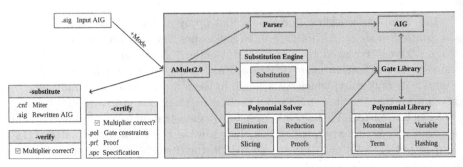

Fig. 1. Architecture of AMULET 2.0.

4   AMulet 2.0

In this section we present the architecture of AMULET 2.0 and discuss novel optimizations. The design of AMULET 2.0 is shown in Fig. 1. In contrast to AMULET 1.0, which consists of one single C file, AMULET 2.0 is split into components, which also allows to integrate only parts, e.g., the polynomial library or the polynomial solver, in different workflows, cf. the provided demos in the artifact [14]. AMULET 2.0 is implemented in C++11 and consists of around 6 000 lines of code. It relies on the AIGER library [5] to process the given AIG and the GMP library [10] to represent large integers.

The mode of AMULET 2.0 is triggered by the command line input, cf. Sect. 3. In substitution mode, AMULET 2.0 parses the AIG, allocates the internal gate structure, and invokes the substitution engine for adder substitution. In verification mode, AMULET 2.0 reads the AIG and initializes the gate structure. Afterwards, the circuit is verified in the polynomial solver using polynomial operations of the polynomial library. In certification mode proofs are generated in addition. In the following we present the individual components of AMULET 2.0.

Parser Module   AMULET 2.0 checks whether the given AIG circuit fulfills the requirements described in Sect. 2, i.e., the AIG circuit has an even number of inputs and an equal number of outputs. The AIG module wraps functions of the external AIGER library that are needed to process the input file.

Gate Library   After parsing we allocate a gate for each AIG node, which includes structural information, such as dependencies, or whether the gate represents an input/output or an XOR-gate. Furthermore, each gate is linked to a unique variable. If the given AIG is verified or certified, AMULET 2.0 also initializes the gate constraints and creates the specification polynomial $\mathcal{L} \in \mathbb{Z}[X]$.

Substitution Engine   In substitution mode, AMULET 2.0 applies heuristic pattern matching to identify GP adders [17]. In AMULET 2.0 we enhanced the identification heuristics and cover special cases that are not considered in AMULET 1.0. Thus, AMULET 2.0 is able to detect more GP adders than AMULET 1.0. After a positive GP pattern match, AMULET 2.0 generates an equivalent RC adder and replaces the GP adder by the RC adder. A bit-level miter is generated in CNF to verify the equivalence of the adders. The rewritten multiplier and the CNF miter are printed to the provided output files.

Polynomial Solver   The polynomial solver is based on the solving engine of AMULET 1.0 [19] and is used to verify or certify the given multiplier. In a nutshell, the polynomial solver first applies preprocessing by eliminating selected variables. Afterwards, the remaining variables are ordered into column-wise slices, such that we can apply our incremental verification algorithm [18], where we split the specification $\mathcal{L}$ into multiple polynomials and verify the multiplier by deriving the correctness of each slice using polynomial reduction. The necessary polynomial operations are implemented in the **Polynomial Library**.

In AMULET 2.0 we eliminate variables before ordering them, while in AMULET 1.0 it is the other way around. We eliminate all internal gates of the XOR-structures and all single-parent nodes in the AIG. Thus, fewer variables are considered for ordering, which improves computation time of AMULET 2.0.

Furthermore, we include a novel XOR-based slicing approach in AMULET 2.0, which relies on the fact that many multiplier architectures use XOR-skeletons to compute the output bits. We identify these skeletons and assign all nodes of a skeleton to the same slice. Gates occurring between XOR-skeletons are assigned to the smaller (less significant) slice. Hence, after two iterations all slices are fixed, which improves slicing compared to AMULET 1.0. All variables that are not assigned to slices, e.g., gates used to compute the partial products in Booth encoding [27], are eliminated from the gate structure.

In few cases, where we cannot identify XOR-skeletons, e.g., in multipliers containing a carry-select adder, we fall back on the slicing approach of AMULET 1.0: We slice based on input cones and eagerly move gates between slices to reduce the number of carries, by iterating multiple times over the variables.

After assigning gates to slices, AMULET 2.0 reduces the slice-wise specifications incrementally by the sliced gate constraints and checks whether the final result is zero, following the implementation of AMULET 1.0. If the final remainder is not zero, AMULET 2.0 detects counter examples, i.e., input assignments for which the multiplier circuit computes an incorrect result.

In certification mode, AMULET 2.0 tracks polynomial operations in the selected proof format, i.e., Nullstellensatz or PAC, and prints gate constraints, the generated proof, and the specification $\mathcal{L}$ to the provided files.

Polynomial Library   The polynomial library implements the arithmetic operations for addition and multiplication of polynomials (by constants), and division by terms. Since all variables represent Boolean values, we always reduce exponents greater than one automatically to one, i.e., we assume $x \cdot x = x$.

Polynomials are represented as linked lists of monomials. Each monomial consists of a coefficient, represented using the GMP library, and a term. Terms are linked lists of variables, which are internally shared using a hash table.

In AMULET 1.0 we do not share monomials and make hard copies in the few occasions when a monomial needs to be copied. This has the benefit that we can simply modify coefficients of the monomials, e.g., during addition. In our experiments we observed that allocating new GMP objects is actually quite time consuming, and therefore we now share monomials in AMULET 2.0, using reference counting, which decreases verification time by a factor of two.

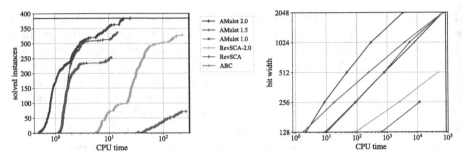

Fig. 2. Verification of AOKI multipliers (left) and of large multipliers (right), in seconds.

5   Evaluation

In our experiments we use an Intel Xeon E5-2620 v4 CPU at 2.10 GHz (with turbo-mode disabled) with a memory limit of 128 GB. The time is listed in seconds (wall-clock time). We compare AMULET 2.0 to our previous tool AMULET 1.0 and to the most recent related work RevSCA, RevSCA-2.0 [25] and ABC-based work of [7] on multiplier verification using computer algebra, where circuits are given as AIGs. The tool of [26] is not yet available. We consider two versions of AMULET 1.0: (i) AMULET 1.0 as published in [17], (ii) AMULET 1.5 a slightly improved version [13] with new heuristics for detecting GP adders. The experimental data is included in the artifact [14].

In our first experiment we consider the comprehensive AOKI benchmark set [12], which provides 384 signed and unsigned integer multiplier architectures up to input bit-width 64, also covering Booth encoding. We consider all 384 architectures of bit-width 64. The time limit is set to 300 seconds. The results are shown on the left side of Fig. 2, where it can be seen that AMULET 2.0 is the only tool that is able to verify the complete benchmark set. RevSCA only supports verification of unsigned integers. ABC-based work of [7] uses an optimization, which only works for simple multiplier architectures. Enabling this optimization on the more involved AOKI benchmarks leads to incompleteness. Without enabling it [7] either produces a segmentation fault or exceeds the time limit. Thus there are no results for [7] on the left side of Fig. 2.

In our second experiment we generate benchmarks of simple multipliers up to input size 2 048, using scripts by Arist Kojevnikov [11]. The time limit is set to 86 400 seconds (24 h) and the results are shown on the right side of Fig. 2. It can be seen that AMULET 2.0 outperforms all competitor tools and is an order of magnitude faster on large multiplier circuits.

6   Conclusion

We presented AMULET 2.0, a fully automatic tool for verifying multiplier circuits given as AIGs. AMULET 2.0 is a re-factorization and re-implementation of our previous verification tool AMULET 1.0 [17,19] and successfully verifies a large set of multiplier architectures. In the future we want to directly integrate a SAT solver into AMULET 2.0 and provide language bindings, e.g. for Python.

References

1. P. Beame, R. Impagliazzo, J. Krajíček, T. Pitassi, and P. Pudlák. Lower Bounds on Hilbert's Nullstellensatz and Propositional Proofs. In *Proc. London Math. Society*, volume s3-73, pages 1–26, 1996.
2. T. Becker, V. Weispfenning, and H. Kredel. *Gröbner Bases*, volume 141 of *Graduate texts in mathematics*. Springer, 1993.
3. A. Biere. Collection of Combinational Arithmetic Miters Submitted to the SAT Competition 2016. In *SAT Competition 2016*, volume B-2016-1 of *Dep. of Computer Science Report Series B*, pages 65–66. University of Helsinki, 2016.
4. A. Biere, K. Fazekas, M. Fleury, and M. Heisinger. CaDiCaL, Kissat, Paracooba, Plingeling and Treengeling entering the SAT Competition 2020. In *Proc. of SAT Competition 2020 – Solver and Benchmark Descriptions*, volume B-2020-1 of *Dep. of Computer Science Report Series B*, pages 51–53. University of Helsinki, 2020.
5. A. Biere, K. Heljanko, and S. Wieringa. AIGER 1.9 And Beyond. Technical report, FMV Reports Series, JKU Linz, Austria, 2011.
6. R. E. Bryant and Y. Chen. Verification of arithmetic circuits using binary moment diagrams. *STTT*, 3(2):137–155, 2001.
7. M. J. Ciesielski, T. Su, A. Yasin, and C. Yu. Understanding Algebraic Rewriting for Arithmetic Circuit Verification: a Bit-Flow Model. *IEEE TCAD*, pages 1–1, 2019. Early acces.
8. M. Clegg, J. Edmonds, and R. Impagliazzo. Using the Groebner Basis Algorithm to Find Proofs of Unsatisfiability. In *STOC 1996*, pages 174–183. ACM, 1996.
9. D. Cox, J. Little, and D. O'Shea. *Ideals, Varieties, and Algorithms*. Springer-Verlag New York, 1997.
10. T. Granlund and the GMP development team. GNU MP: The GNU Multiple Precision Arithmetic Library, 2016. Version 6.1.2.
11. E. Hirsch, D. Itsykson, A. Kojevnikov, E. Kulikov, and S. Nikolenko. Report on the Mixed Boolean-Algebraic Solver. Technical report, Laboratory of Mathematical Logic of St. Petersburg Dep. of Steklov Institute of Mathematics, 2005.
12. N. Homma, Y. Watanabe, T. Aoki, and T. Higuchi. Formal Design of Arithmetic Circuits Based on Arithmetic Description Language. *IEICE Transactions*, 89-A(12):3500–3509, 2006.
13. D. Kaufmann. Amulet 1.5. https://github.com/d-kfmnn/amulet, 2020.
14. D. Kaufmann. Artifact for AMulet2.0 for verifying multiplier circuits. http://fmv.jku.at/amulet2_artifact, 2020.
15. D. Kaufmann. *Formal Verification of Multiplier Circuits using Computer Algebra*. PhD thesis, Informatik, Johannes Kepler University Linz, 2020.
16. D. Kaufmann and A. Biere. Nullstellensatz-proofs for multiplier verification. In *Computer Algebra in Scientific Computing*, volume 12291 of *LNCS*, pages 368–389. Springer, 2020.
17. D. Kaufmann, A. Biere, and M. Kauers. Verifying Large Multipliers by Combining SAT and Computer Algebra. In *FMCAD 2019*, pages 28–36. IEEE, 2019.
18. D. Kaufmann, A. Biere, and M. Kauers. Incremental Column-wise verification of arithmetic circuits using computer algebra. *Formal Methods Syst. Des.*, 56(1):22–54, 2020.
19. D. Kaufmann, A. Biere, and M. Kauers. SAT, Computer Algebra, Multipliers. In *Vampire 2018 and Vampire 2019*, volume 71 of *EPiC Series in Computing*, pages 1–18. EasyChair, 2020.

20. D. Kaufmann, M. Fleury, and A. Biere. Pacheck and Pastèque, Checking Practical Algebraic Calculus Proofs. In *FMCAD 2020*, volume 1 of *FMCAD*, pages 264–269. TU Vienna Academic Press, 2020.

21. D. Kaufmann, M. Kauers, A. Biere, and D. Cok. Arithmetic Verification Problems Submitted to the SAT Race 2019. In *SAT Race 2019*, volume B-2019-1 of *Dep. of Computer Science Report Series B*, page 49. University of Helsinki, 2019.

22. A. Kuehlmann, V. Paruthi, F. Krohm, and M. Ganai. Robust Boolean reasoning for equivalence checking and functional property verification. *IEEE TCAD*, 21(12):1377–1394, 2002.

23. J. Lv, P. Kalla, and F. Enescu. Efficient Gröbner Basis Reductions for Formal Verification of Galois Field Arithmetic Circuits. *IEEE TCAD*, 32(9):1409–1420, 2013.

24. A. Mahzoon, D. Große, and R. Drechsler. PolyCleaner: Clean your Polynomials before Backward Rewriting to verify Million-gate Multipliers. In *ICCAD 2018*, pages 129:1 – 129:8. ACM, 2018.

25. A. Mahzoon, D. Große, and R. Drechsler. RevSCA: Using Reverse Engineering to Bring Light into Backward Rewriting for Big and Dirty Multipliers. In *DAC 2019*, pages 185:1–185:6. ACM, 2019.

26. A. Mahzoon, D. Große, C. Scholl, and R. Drechsler. Towards formal verification of optimized and industrial multipliers. In *DATE*, pages 544–549. IEEE, 2020.

27. B. Parhami. *Computer Arithmetic - Algorithms and Hardware designs*. Oxford University Press, 2000.

28. H. Sharangpani and M. L. Barton. Statistical analysis of floating point flaw in the pentium processor. 1994.

29. M. Temel, A. Slobodová, and W. A. Hunt. Automated and scalable verification of integer multipliers. In *CAV (1)*, volume 12224 of *Lecture Notes in Computer Science*, pages 485–507. Springer, 2020.

RTLola on Board: Testing Real Driving Emissions on your Phone*

Sebastian Biewer[1]([✉]) [iD], Bernd Finkbeiner[2] [iD],
Holger Hermanns[1,3] [iD], Maximilian A. Köhl[1] [iD],
Yannik Schnitzer[1] [iD], and Maximilian Schwenger[2] [iD]

[1] Saarland University, Saarland Informatics Campus, Saarbrücken, Germany
biewer@depend.uni-saarland.de
[2] CISPA Helmholtz Center for Information Security, Saarbrücken, Germany
[3] Institute of Intelligent Software, Guangzhou, China

Abstract. This paper is about shipping runtime verification to the masses. It presents the crucial technology enabling everyday car owners to monitor the behaviour of their cars in-the-wild. Concretely, we present an Android app that deploys RTLOLA runtime monitors for the purpose of diagnosing automotive exhaust emissions. For this, it harvests the availability of cheap bluetooth adapters to the On-Board-Diagnostics (OBD) ports, which are ubiquitous in cars nowadays. We detail its use in the context of Real Driving Emissions (RDE) tests and report on sample runs that helped identify violations of the regulatory framework currently valid in the European Union.

1 Introduction

In the last decade, far more than 600 million cars have entered the streets worldwide [10]. With very few exceptions, each of these cars is equipped with a standardized On-Board-Diagnostics (OBD [16]) interface. Five years ago it surfaced that many of the cars out there do not adhere to the regulatory framework with which they are supposed to comply. For example, a number of undeniable proofs of tampered emission cleaning systems in passenger cars [5,3,14] are known by now. When this scandal first surfaced, the regulations imposed by the authorities were related to isolated tests carried out under lab-like conditions on chassis dynamometers [20,4]. Since then, there has been a growing understanding that emission and fuel or battery consumption measurements should best take place in a realistic context. Hence, the first test framework for testing on public roads, the *Real Driving Emissions* (RDE) test has been developed [19,17] and is being rolled out for car model approval in Europe and other entities of jurisdiction.

The RDE regulation specifies the conditions under which a car trip qualifies as a valid RDE test. These conditions refer to the trajectory driven, duration,

* This work is partly supported by DFG grant 389792660 as part of TRR 248 – CPEC, by the European Research Council (ERC) grants 683300 (OSARES), 695614 (POWVER), and 966770 (LEOpowver), and by the Key-Area Research and Development Program Grant 2018B010107004 of Guangdong Province.

J. F. Groote and K. G. Larsen (Eds.): TACAS 2021, LNCS 12652, pp. 365–372, 2021.
https://doi.org/10.1007/978-3-030-72013-1_20

altitudes, speeds, and on the dynamics of the driving profile [17]. By combining the information available at the OBD port and the position of the car, it is possible to cast RDE testing into a runtime monitoring [21,13,12] problem. Indeed we have shown in earlier work [9] how to formalize the RDE regulations in RTLOLA [7,8], a real-time extension of the stream-based specification language Lola [6]. Lola combines the ease-of-use of rule-based specification languages with the expressive power of heavy-weight scripting languages or temporal logics. The eponymous framework generates runtime monitors for such specifications, which were successfully deployed, for instance, on unmanned aircraft [18,2].

An official RDE test requires a calibrated *portable emissions measurement system* (PEMS) to be connected to the car's exhaust pipe while driving the test, so as to correctly quantify the amount of exhaust emissions induced. The purchasing costs of a PEMS are in the order of €250,000 which is close to unaffordable even in a research context. However, many car models expose a variety of diagnosis data through OBD and an OBD-to-Bluetooth adapter can be purchased for around €10. The data exposed depends on the type of engine, emission cleaning system, and other components in use. There are several minimal combinations of OBD data giving good approximations of emitted gases. In particular, various car models expose the sensor readings of their after-treatment NO_x sensor deployed at the rear of the exhaust pipe.

Contribution. This paper presents LOLADRIVES, an Android app enabling car owners to carry out real driving emission tests with little investment. Prerequisites are (i) an Android phone, (ii) an OBD-to-Bluetooth adapter, and (iii) a car model that does indeed expose the needed values via OBD. If the latter is not the case, the app can still serve the user as a convenient personal monitoring and logging device for the many quantities exposed while driving.

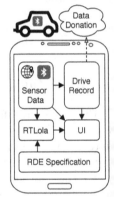

Fig. 1: LOLADRIVES

A structural overview of LOLADRIVES is depicted in Figure 1. At the core of the app is an Android version of the RTLOLA engine [7]. The engine is strictly separated from the data acquisition and the RTLOLA RDE specification. This separation will make it possible to reuse the approach in other runtime monitoring contexts, be it of espresso machines via USB, or drones via Wi-Fi. In both cases, it would especially be the specification in RTLOLA that needs to change, not the engine. Car sensor data is acquired via Bluetooth from the OBD device, and combined with location data provided by Android's GPS service. The data streams are recorded for later diagnosis. Anticipating future application scenarios involving crowd sourcing car data, we advertise the app as part of a *car data platform* (CDP), which includes an upload facility for donating drive records. While driving, the app's user interface (UI) displays diagnostic information to the user, both regarding the correct execution of an RDE test drive and the car's emission data. We will detail the separate components of the app next.

Notably, the lack of any calibration and the unknown precision of the data exposed by the car manufacturer via OBD make it impossible to consider the RDE test results reported by LOLADRIVES as anything more than indicators of the car's RDE behaviour in a legal sense.

2   RDE Monitoring on Android

The primary feature of LOLADRIVES is to monitor the progress of an RDE test drive. For this, it uses the RTLOLA monitoring framework. This bridges the gap between formally sound concepts and every-day use cases. While RTLOLA does target a broad audience, that audience is still intended to be expert users rather than the general public. It requires users to execute three tasks: provide a formal specification of the intended behaviour, supply input data, and interpret the monitor's output. LOLADRIVES reduces these tasks to minimal action points for end-users.

Specification. No end-user input is required with respect to the RTLOLA specification. The definition of what is a valid RDE test is fixed [9] and strictly follows the constraints imposed by the regulation issued by the European Commission [17]. These constraints concern the driving behaviour and layout of the route. Some of them apply universally, e.g., the ambient temperature must range between 273 K and 303 K. For others, the RDE regulation differentiates three environments: urban, rural, and motorway with different environments imposing different restrictions on the car, such as an average velocity between 15 and 40 km/h in an urban environment. A *segment* refers to all parts of the test drive in which the car operates in a certain environment. While segments may be interrupted, each one needs to occupy a specific share of the total distance travelled.

Input Data Provision. LOLADRIVES uses sensor readings provided over the OBD interface as input data. The user only has to plug the OBD-to-Bluetooth adapter in the respective port at (or close to) the dashboard of her car and pair it with her phone. The car then automatically transmits data to the phone while driving.

Interpretation of Output. While driving, LOLADRIVES assists the user in the critical task of satisfying all the constraints that make up a valid RDE. It provides feedback on the driving behaviour indicating which requirements on the test are satisfied to what extent, and which still need attention. Furthermore, it evaluates the measured exhaust data and informs the user of whether or not the car violates emission regulations. Both of these tasks require an online analysis of driving data. For this analysis, LOLADRIVES uses the RTLOLA monitoring framework.

Foundational Underpinning. RTLOLA [8,7] is a stream-based runtime verification framework. The RTLOLA monitor analyses sequences of input data to assess whether or not the system complies with the specification. The specification language has a formal semantics which enables devising provably correct monitoring algorithms [15].

An RTLOLA specification consists of input stream declarations where each input stream corresponds to a source of input data such as the NO_x sensor of the car. Output stream declarations then spell out how to filter and refine the input data. For this, RTLOLA provides primitives for complex analyses such as sliding window aggregation for common aggregation functions. Further, the specification contains binary trigger conditions. The satisfaction of such a condition constitutes a violation of the specification and prompts the monitor to immediately relay a warning to the user. The following snippet is an extract of an RTLOLA specification for RDE test drives [11]:

```
input velo_kmph, accel_mpss: Float64
output is_rural := ... output rural_avg_velo := ...
output rural_dyn : Float64 @1Hz filter: is_rural := velo_kmph *
    accel_mpss / 3.6
output rural_pctl_dyn : Float64 @1Hz :=
    rural_dyn.aggregate(over: 7200, using: pctl(95)).defaults(to: 0.0)
trigger rural_pctl_dyn > (0.136 * rural_avg_velo + 14.44)
    ∧ rural_avg_velo <= 74.6
```

This specification fragment checks whether the car complies with the RDE regulations regarding the driving dynamics in the rural segment[4]. The first line declares two input streams representing the velocity in $km\,h^{-1}$ and acceleration in $m\,s^{-2}$ supplied by the car. The third line computes the dynamics in $m^2\,s^{-3}$, by multiplying the velocity and acceleration. The regulations then demand that the 95th percentile of the dynamics are no greater than $0.136 \cdot v_{avg} + 14.44$ where v_{avg} is the average velocity of the vehicle. The computation of the velocity and the dynamics only consider sensor readings obtained while in the rural segment. The full specifications are publicly available [1]. Note that while the specification is relatively easy to design and understand for computer scientists and engineers, it exceeds the expertise expectable of laymen users. However, it is not necessary for them to be confronted with the full potential of the language because LOLADRIVES comes preconfigured with a set of RDE-specific specifications.

As can be seen, the requirements on the end-user are minimal. Thus, the setup enables users to conduct RDE test drives and assess the emission-behaviour of their cars without requiring them to understand the underlying technology.

3   User Experience

This section discusses the user perspective on LOLADRIVES. After a general overview, we report on the use of LOLADRIVES for conducting RDE test drives with a rented vehicle (the precise car model being unknown upfront).

Overview. The preparation of the test requires the user to plug the OBD-adapter into the OBD-port of the car. After starting car and app, LOLADRIVES receives data packets and determines the sensor profile of the car, assuming phone and adapter are paired via Bluetooth. Some sensor profiles provide insufficient data to conduct an RDE test drive. In this case, the app is still convenient to use for real-time displaying and logging the available data regardless of RDE regulations,

---

[4] See Annex IIIA, Appendix 7a, 3.1.3 in the EU regulations [17].

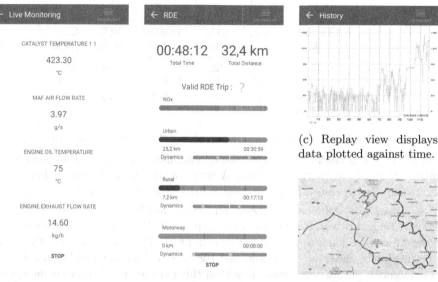

(a) Diagnostics view displays the most recent diagnostics information.

(b) RDE progress view displays current state parameters of the test drive.

(c) Replay view displays data plotted against time.

(d) Map of the second RDE test drive.

Fig. 2: UI of LOLADRIVES displaying different views and a map of a test route.

see Figure 2a. If the data suffices, the app selects an appropriate specification and initializes the RTLOLA monitor. LOLADRIVES then starts filtering and visualising the data output and trigger notifications provided by the monitor.

After successful setup, the UI switches to an RDE guiding view (Figure 2b). From top to bottom, it shows the total time, which must be between 90 and 120 min to finish the test, and the total distance travelled. The next line indicates the current state of the conditions for a valid RDE test drive disregarding emission data. In the screenshot, the drive is still in progress and inconclusive, indicated by the question mark. Instead, the UI can also indicate success or failure. The latter verdict can occur far before the time limit is reached, caused by an irrecoverable situation such as transgression of the $160 \, \text{km} \, \text{h}^{-1}$ speed limit. Note that the indicator reports the *current* status if the test drive were to end in this moment. Together with the regulatory constraints, this implies that the current verdict can alternate between success and failure from minute 90 to 120. As there is no specific point in time when the test ends, the app continues to compute statistics until the tester manually stops it or the 120 min mark is reached. Beneath the status indicator is the green NO_x bar displaying the total NO_x emissions. The vertical red bar denotes the permitted threshold of $168 \, \text{mg} \, \text{km}^{-1}$.

The next three UI groups represent the progress in each of the distinct segments: urban, rural, and motorway. Each group consists of two horizontal bars. The gray progress bar displays the distance covered in the respective segment. The vertical blue indicators denote lower and upper bounds as per official regulation, for an expected trip length of 83 km. The blue bar below the gray one

	Drive 1			Drive 2		
	Distance [km]	NO$_x$ [mg/km]	CO$_2$ [g/km]	Distance [km]	NO$_x$ [mg/km]	CO$_2$ [g/km]
Urban	35.45	137	222	37.46	102	251
Rural	22.33	305	154	27.40	90	172
Motorway	26.10	241	153	25.37	105	175
Total	83.88	214	183	90.22	99	205

Table 1: Aggregation of the emission data based on the CDP.

illustrates two different metrics for the driving dynamics. Both dots need to remain below/above their thresholds. A more aggressive acceleration behaviour shifts the dots to the right and a passive driving style to the left.

Test Drive. The technical framework and visual feedback of the app were tested in two RDE test drives. Both tests were conducted with an Audi A6 Avant 45-TDI hybrid diesel, which is approved as Euro 6d-TEMP (DG) with an NO$_x$ threshold of $80 \, \mathrm{mg \, km^{-1}}$ under lab conditions and $168 \, \mathrm{mg \, km^{-1}}$ for RDE conditions. Among the diagnosis parameters available within this car are vehicle and engine speed, ambient temperature, engine fuel rate, mass air flow, and two NO$_x$-sensors—one in front and one behind the emission cleaning system in the exhaust pipe. With this data, exhaust mass flow and fuel consumption can be computed, from which the total amounts of NO$_x$ and CO$_2$ can be derived [11]. In both drives, the driving dynamics were close to the allowed maximum, in the first test below and in the second test above the threshold, so the second test drive did not result in a valid RDE test. In both cases, the app correctly confirmed the satisfaction and violation of the RDE criteria. In the first drive, the app reported an average NO$_x$ emission of $214 \, \mathrm{mg \, km^{-1}}$. This constitutes a violation of the regulation.

The app also allows for inspection of the driving data in a plotted form (Figure 2c). Figure 2d shows the route of an RDE test drive. The first half of the time constituted the urban segment (green). The next 30-40% of the test mainly consisted of the rural segment (purple) followed by the motorway segment (red).

Data Harvesting. For further analysis, data can be uploaded to a cloud storage which is part of the car data platform (CDP). This platform provides a uniform way to harvest data by specifying a format for collection, analysis, and exchange of this data. CDP builds upon a JSON format (`https://json-schema.org/`) containing timestamped events such as an OBD response, including its raw payload. As an example, the data presented in Table 1 is an aggregation of the RDE test drives mentioned above obtained by post-processing the data.

4   Conclusion

LOLADRIVES pushes runtime verification technology into cars and phones of everyday users. The app is available in *Google Play* [1]; a version for iOS is already initiated. Moreover, the car data platform constitutes a crowd-sourcing initiative for car data with the intention to enable large scale analyses of emission data beyond a single trip and a single car model.

References

1. LolaDrives web page, `https://loladrives.app`
2. Baumeister, J., Finkbeiner, B., Schirmer, S., Schwenger, M., Torens, C.: RTLola cleared for take-off: Monitoring autonomous aircraft. In: CAV 2020. LNCS, vol. 12225, pp. 28–39. Springer (2020). https://doi.org/10.1007/978-3-030-53291-8_3
3. BBC: Audi chief Rupert Stadler arrested in diesel emissions probe. BBC, https://www.bbc.com/news/business-44517753 (2018), `https://www.bbc.com/news/business-44517753`, Online; accessed: 2020-10-15
4. Biewer, S., D'Argenio, P., Hermanns, H.: Doping tests for cyber-physical systems. In: Parker, D., Wolf, V. (eds.) Quantitative Evaluation of Systems, 16th International Conference, QEST 2019, Glasgow, UK, September 10-12, 2019, Proceedings. Lecture Notes in Computer Science, vol. 11785, pp. 313–331. Springer (2019). https://doi.org/10.1007/978-3-030-30281-8_18
5. Contag, M., Li, G., Pawlowski, A., Domke, F., Levchenko, K., Holz, T., Savage, S.: How they did it: An analysis of emission defeat devices in modern automobiles. In: 2017 IEEE Symposium on Security and Privacy, SP 2017, San Jose, CA, USA, May 22-26, 2017. pp. 231–250. IEEE Computer Society (2017). https://doi.org/10.1109/SP.2017.66
6. D'Angelo, B., Sankaranarayanan, S., Sánchez, C., Robinson, W., Finkbeiner, B., Sipma, H.B., Mehrotra, S., Manna, Z.: Lola: Runtime monitoring of synchronous systems. In: TIME 2005. pp. 166–174. IEEE Computer Society Press (June). https://doi.org/10.1109/TIME.2005.26
7. Faymonville, P., Finkbeiner, B., Schledjewski, M., Schwenger, M., Stenger, M., Tentrup, L., Torfah, H.: StreamLAB: Stream-based Monitoring of Cyber-Physical Systems. In: CAV 2019. LNCS, vol. 11561, pp. 421–431. Springer (2019). https://doi.org/10.1007/978-3-030-25540-4_24
8. Faymonville, P., Finkbeiner, B., Schwenger, M., Torfah, H.: Real-time Stream-based Monitoring. CoRR **abs/1711.03829** (2017), `http://arxiv.org/abs/1711.03829`
9. Hermanns, H., Biewer, S., D'Argenio, P.R., Köhl, M.A.: Verification, testing, and runtime monitoring of automotive exhaust emissions. In: LPAR. pp. 1–17 (2018). https://doi.org/10.29007/6zxt
10. International Organization of Motor Vehicle Manufacturers: 2005-2019 sales statistics `http://www.oica.net/category/sales-statistics`
11. Köhl, M.A., Hermanns, H., Biewer, S.: Efficient monitoring of real driving emissions. In: Colombo, C., Leucker, M. (eds.) Runtime Verification - 18th International Conference, RV 2018, Limassol, Cyprus, November 10-13, 2018, Proceedings. Lecture Notes in Computer Science, vol. 11237, pp. 299–315. Springer (2018). https://doi.org/10.1007/978-3-030-03769-7_17
12. Lee, I., Kannan, S., Kim, M., Sokolsky, O., Viswanathan, M.: Runtime assurance based on formal specifications. In: Arabnia, H.R. (ed.) Proceedings of the International Conference on Parallel and Distributed Processing Techniques and Applications, PDPTA 1999, June 28 - Junlly 1, 1999, Las Vegas, Nevada, USA. pp. 279–287. CSREA Press (1999)
13. Moosbrugger, P., Rozier, K.Y., Schumann, J.: R2U2: Monitoring and Diagnosis of Security Threats for Unmanned Aerial Systems. Formal Methods Syst. Des. **51**(1), 31–61 (2017). https://doi.org/10.1007/s10703-017-0275-x
14. Riley, C.: Volkswagen's diesel scandal costs hit $30 billion. CNN Business (2018), `https://money.cnn.com/2017/09/29/investing/`

volkswagen-diesel-cost-30-billion/index.html, Online; accessed: 2020-
10-15

15. Schwenger, M.: Let's not Trust Experience Blindly: Formal Monitoring of Humans
    and other CPS. Master thesis, Saarland University (2019)
16. The European Parliament and the Council of the European Union: Direc-
    tive 98/69/ec of the european parliament and of the council. Official Journal
    of the European Communities (1998), http://eur-lex.europa.eu/LexUriServ/
    LexUriServ.do?uri=CELEX:31998L0069:EN:HTML
17. The European Parliament and the Council of the European Union: Commission
    Regulation (EU) 2017/1151 (June 2017), http://data.europa.eu/eli/reg/2017/
    1151/oj
18. Torens, C., Adolf, F., Faymonville, P., Schirmer, S.: Towards intelligent system
    health management using runtime monitoring. In: AIAA Information Systems-
    AIAA Infotech @ Aerospace. American Institute of Aeronautics and Astronautics
    (AIAA) (jan 2017). https://doi.org/10.2514/6.2017-0419
19. Tutuianu, M., Bonnel, P., Ciuffo, B., Haniu, T., Ichikawa, N., Marotta, A., Pavlovic,
    J., Steven, H.: Development of the world-wide harmonized light duty test cycle
    (wltc) and a possible pathway for its introduction in the european legislation.
    Transportation Research Part D: Transport and Environment **40**(Supplement C),
    61 – 75 (2015). https://doi.org/10.1016/j.trd.2015.07.011
20. United Nations: UN Vehicle Regulations - 1958 Agreement, Revision 2, Addendum
    100, Regulation No. 101, Revision 3 — E/ECE/324/Rev.2/Add.100/Rev.3 (2013),
    http://www.unece.org/trans/main/wp29/wp29regs101-120.html
21. Watanabe, K., Kang, E., Lin, C., Shiraishi, S.: Runtime monitoring for safety of
    intelligent vehicles. In: Proceedings of the 55th Annual Design Automation Confer-
    ence, DAC 2018, San Francisco, CA, USA, June 24-29, 2018. pp. 31:1–31:6. ACM
    (2018). https://doi.org/10.1145/3195970.3199856

Replicating RESTART with Prolonged Retrials: An Experimental Report*

Carlos E. Budde [✉] [ID] and Arnd Hartmanns [✉] [ID]

University of Twente, Enschede, The Netherlands
{c.e.budde,a.hartmanns}@utwente.nl

Abstract Statistical model checking uses Monte Carlo simulation to analyse stochastic formal models. It avoids state space explosion, but requires rare event simulation techniques to efficiently estimate very low probabilities. One such technique is RESTART. Villén-Altamirano recently showed—by way of a theoretical study and ad-hoc implementation—that a generalisation of RESTART to *prolonged retrials* offers improved performance. In this paper, we demonstrate our independent replication of the original experimental results. We implemented RESTART with prolonged retrials in the FIG and modes tools, and apply them to the models used originally. To do so, we had to resolve ambiguities in the original work, and refine our setup multiple times. We ultimately confirm the previous results, but our experience also highlights the need for precise documentation of experiments to enable replicability in computer science.

1 Introduction

In stochastic timed systems, the time between faults, customer interarrival times, transmission delays, or exponential backoff wait times follow (continuous) probability distributions. Probabilistic model checking [3] can compute dependability metrics like reliability and availability in the Markovian case. To evade state space explosion and evaluate non-Markovian systems, statistical model checking (SMC [2]) has become a popular alternative. At its core, SMC is Monte Carlo simulation for formal models. It faces a runtime explosion when estimating the probability p of a *rare event* with a sufficiently low error, e.g. an error of $\pm 10^{-10}$ for $p \approx 10^{-9}$ (i.e. a *relative* error of 0.1). *Rare event simulation* (RES) techniques [17] address this problem. They can broadly be categorised into *importance sampling* and *importance splitting*. The former changes the probability distributions while the latter changes the simulation algorithm to make the rare event more likely. Both techniques then compensate for these changes in the statistical evaluation. RES has garnered the interest of mathematicians and computer scientists alike. The scientific outcomes range from theoretical studies of a RES technique's limit behaviour and optimality [8,14,16] over experimental validation on Matlab studies or ad-hoc implementations [10,11,19] to application

---

* Authors are listed alphabetically. This work was supported by NWO via project no. 15474 (SEQUOIA) and VENI grant no. 639.021.754.

J. F. Groote and K. G. Larsen (Eds.): TACAS 2021, LNCS 12652, pp. 373–380, 2021.
https://doi.org/10.1007/978-3-030-72013-1_21

reports using larger case studies [5,12,18] as well as automated tools [4,6,15,18] that accept a loss of optimality in exchange for practicality.

Two recent papers showed theoretically [21] and empirically [19] that *prolonging retrials* in the RESTART importance splitting technique [22] reduces the required number of samples for the same error, with optimal runtime around prolonging by 1 to 2 levels. The models and parameters used in [19] are described in supplementary material [20], but the implementation is not publicly available. In this paper, we demonstrate our *replication* of the results of [19,21], where replication "means that an independent group can obtain the same result using artifacts which they develop completely independently" in the ACM terminology [1]. To this end, we implemented RESTART with prolonged retrials (RESTART-P) in the FIG rare event simulator [4] and the modes statistical model checker [7] of the MODEST TOOLSET [13]. We recreated the models in the IOSA and MODEST languages, and ran experiments following the original setup.

Our experiments confirm the behaviour and performance improvements of RESTART-P reported in [19,21]. However, we encountered ambiguities in the textual and pictorial descriptions of RESTART-P and the experimental setup in the original papers, some of which we could only resolve with input from the author of [19,21]. Different parts of our work thus reside on different levels between replication and *reproduction* (which "means that an independent group can obtain the same result using the author's own artifacts" [1]). Throughout the paper, we document where we achieved fully independent replication, where information from private communication was needed, and where we had to ultimately resort to requesting and inspecting the source code for the original implementation.

The contribution of this paper is thus threefold: (1) We provide pseudocode for RESTART-P in Sect. 2 that clarifies the technical details w.r.t. [19,21]. (2) We demonstrate the new RESTART-P capabilities of FIG and modes by replicating the original experiments in Sect. 3. (3) We reflect on our experience (as practical computer scientists) in independently replicating existing (theoretically-flavoured) work.

2   RESTART with Prolonged Retrials

Let a stochastic timed discrete-event model be given as a tuple $\langle S, s_0, step, F \rangle$ of a set of states S, an initial state $s_0 \in S$, a function $step \colon S \to [0, \infty) \times S$ where $step(s)$ samples a random path from s to the next event and returns a pair $\langle t, s' \rangle$ of its duration and next state, and a subset of rare event states $F \subseteq S$. A simulation *run* is a sequence of states obtained by repeatedly applying $step$. Models with general probability distributions encode their memory in the states.

Importance splitting uses an *importance function* $f_I \colon S \to [0, \infty)$ indicating "how close" a state is to the rare event. Partition the range of f_I into $k+1$ nonempty intervals to obtain a *level function* $f_L \colon S \to \{0, \dots, k\}$ with $f_L(s_1) < f_L(s_2) \Rightarrow f_I(s_1) < f_I(s_2)$. For simplicity, assume $f_I(s_0) = 0$ and $step(s) = \langle t, s' \rangle \Rightarrow f_L(s') \le f_L(s)+1$ (a step moves up by at most one level). Let $C_i \stackrel{\text{def}}{=} \{s \mid f_L(s) \ge i\}$. Then "thresholds T_i of f_I are defined so that each set C_i is associated

Input: model $\langle S, s_0, step, F \rangle$, f_L, f_S, prolongation depth j, max. sim. time T_{max}

$t_F := 0$, list $\xi := \{| \langle s_0, 0, 0, 0 \rangle |\}$ // $\langle$state, time, creation level, last-split level$\rangle$
while $\xi \neq \varnothing$ **do**   // run all trials to end
    $\langle s, t, \ell_{create}, \ell_{split} \rangle := \xi.\text{get-remove}()$ // data of current trial
    while $t < T_{max}$ **do**
        $\langle t', s' \rangle := step(s)$ // simulate to next change in state
        $t' := \min\{t', T_{max} - t\}$, $t := t + t'$ // advance time, at most to T_{max}
        if $s \in F$ **then** $t_F := t_F + t' / \prod_{i=1}^{\ell_{split}} f_S(i)$ // accumulate weighted rare time
        $\langle \ell, \ell' \rangle := \langle f_L(s), f_L(s') \rangle$, $s := s'$
        if $\ell' < \ell$ **then**   // trial went **down**:
            if $\ell' = 0 = \ell_{create}$ **then** $\ell_{split} := 0$ // reset main trial at level 0
            else if $\ell' = 0 \vee \ell' < \ell_{create} - j$ **then break**   // end retrial if 0 or j down
            else $\ell_{split} := \min(\ell_{split}, \ell' + j)$ // else update last-split level
        else if $\ell' > \ell_{split}$ **then**   // trial went **up** far enough:
            $\ell_{split} := \ell'$ // update last-split level
            foreach $i \in \{1, \ldots, f_S(\ell') - 1\}$ **do** $\xi.\text{add}(\langle s', t, \ell', \ell_{split} \rangle)$ // split off retrials

return t_F // return accumulated weighted time spent in rare states

Algorithm 1: RESTART with prolonged retrials of depth j (RESTART-P$_j$)

---

with $f_I \geq T_i$." [21]. Function $f_S \colon \{1, \ldots, k\} \to \mathbb{N} \setminus \{0\}$ defines *splitting factors*. f_I, f_L, and f_S are specified by experts or derived automatically [6]. Importance splitting with RESTART starts a run (the *main trial*) from s_0 that, whenever it moves up from s in current level $l - 1$ to s' in level l, spawns $f_S(l) - 1$ new child runs (*retrials of level l*) from s'. Retrials end when they move down below their creation level. The trials' weights in probability estimation are appropriately reduced to compensate. RESTART with prolonged retrials of depth j, denoted RESTART-P$_j$, is defined as follows in [21] (shortened and adapted to our notation):

> In RESTART-P$_j$, each of the retrials of level i finishes when it leaves set C_{i-j}; that is, it continues until it down-crosses the threshold $i - j$. If one of these trials again up-crosses the threshold where it was generated (or any other between $i - j + 1$ and i), a new set of retrials is not performed. If $j \geq i$, the retrials are cut when they reach the threshold 0. The main trial, which continues after leaving set C_{i-j}, potentially leads to new sets of retrials if it up-crosses threshold T_i after having left set C_{i-j}. If the main trial reaches the threshold 0, it collects the weight of all the retrials (which has been cut at that threshold) and thus, new sets of retrials of level 1 are performed next time the main trial up-crosses threshold T_1.

In addition, [21, Fig. 1] graphically illustrates the behaviour of RESTART-P$_1$. The original RESTART [22] is RESTART-P$_0$. The above textual description clearly conveys the core idea of RESTART-P, but we found it to omit three technical details:

- The condition for when an up-going retrial spawns new retrials is more complex than with RESTART. We became aware of this when comparing the textual description with the graphical depiction in [21, Fig. 1]. In fact, we need

to keep track of the last level at which a retrial will split, and decrement that value when it moves more than j levels down. (Independent replication.)
- The definitions in [19,21] do not include 0 in the range of values for i in C_i and T_i. Our definitions would associate T_0 with states s where $f_I(s) = 0$. Implemented in FIG, this lead to increasing underestimation as the prolongation depth j increased. Only once we interpreted threshold 0 to refer to *level* 0 (i.e. states s where $f_L(s) = 0$) did we obtain consistent estimations across different j. The correctness of this interpretation was confirmed by the author of [19,21] in private communication. (Semi-independent replication.)
- When a trial reaches, or spends time in, a state in F, we must weight this event's influence on the statistical estimate by a factor of $1/\prod_{i=1}^{f_L(s)} f_S(i)$ in the original RESTART. With this weight calculation, FIG produced subtle underestimations on some of the models from [20] when $j > 0$. We finally requested the source code for the original experiments and found that $f_L(s)$ must be replaced by *the level on which the current trial was last split*, i.e. the value must not change when moving down $\leq j$ levels. (Resembles a reproduction.)

We make these details explicit in Algorithm 1, for the case of estimating the long-run average time spent in F (i.e. steady-state simulation). FIG evolved as described above and is thus mostly a replication. modes was extended with prolongations later, using a recursive formulation of the algorithm gleaned from the original code. It thus lacks the complete independence of a replication as per [1].

3   Experiments

Table 2 in [21] provides steady-state estimates, numbers of samples, and runtimes obtained using RESTART-P$_j$ on a Jackson (i.e. Markov) 2-tandem queueing network for $j \in \{0, \dots, 4\}$. The same data is given in [19] for $j \in \{0, \dots, 2\}$ on a similar system with three queues and a seven-node network, in Jackson and non-Jackson (using Erlang and hyperexponential distributions) variants. The original articles and extra material [20] describe the models, and the experimental setup:
- The set F is characterised. E.g. for the 3-tandem network, it contains the states where the third queue has $\geq L = 30$ (Jackson) or 14 packets (non-Jackson).
- All probability distributions and the f_I, f_L, and f_S functions are characterised.
- T_{max} time values for the steady-state simulations are specified for all models.
- The statistical evaluation aims for a relative error of 0.1 with 95 % confidence (except for the tandem queue, where the error is 0.005); RESTART-P runs are performed sequentially until the half-width of the 95 % confidence interval is below 10 % (resp. 0.5 %) of the current estimate. (Note that this guarantees the requested confidence only asymptotically for decreasing width [9].)

In our replication attempt, we had to resolve the following unspecified aspects:
- The queue capacities $C > L$ are not documented, but influence the estimate: for C close to L, the steady-state probability is underestimated. We settled for $C = 20 \cdot L$ in FIG's IOSA models (replication); the influence of $C - L$ rapidly diminishes beyond small values. Later, from inspecting the original source

Table 1. Experimental results for the examples considered in [19,21]

model (type) p	j	original [19,21]			adapted orig. code			modes			FIG		
		$\hat{p}$	n	time	$\hat{p}$	n	time	$\hat{p}$	n	time	$\hat{p}$	n	time
2-tandem (Jackson) 4.86E-15	0	4.85E-15	3909	2906	4.84E-15	2731	1930	4.88E-15	2542	988	4.85E-15	2537	4202
	1	4.86E-15	3032	2107	4.93E-15	1905	1654	4.87E-15	1859	939	4.82E-15	1969	4000
	2	4.86E-15	2660	2091	4.80E-15	1831	1959	4.85E-15	1845	1175	4.86E-15	1700	4379
	3	4.87E-15	2476	2287	4.86E-15	1691	2319	4.83E-15	1626	1322	4.84E-15	1656	5448
	4	4.85E-15	2458	3188	4.88E-15	1562	2638	4.85E-15	1610	1626	4.86E-15	1580	6402
3-tandem (Jackson) 4.86E-15	0	4.66E-15	120	54	4.90E-15	89	28	4.24E-15	116	9	4.58E-15	122	43
	1	4.61E-15	88	35	4.84E-15	44	20	4.90E-15	97	10	5.63E-15	80	36
	2	4.66E-15	78	38	4.84E-15	49	19	4.83E-15	79	11	5.23E-15	65	39
3-tandem (non-J.)	0	7.08E-15	95	137	8.38E-15	728	180	8.87E-15	1002	256	8.28E-15	1293	715
	1	7.03E-15	65	90	8.50E-15	661	181	8.10E-15	650	182	8.65E-15	618	436
	2	7.03E-15	55	90	8.34E-15	388	191	8.53E-15	386	157	9.59E-15	386	402
7-nodes (Jackson) 2.54E-15	0	2.53E-15	42	16	2.33E-15	44	18	2.59E-15	36	10	2.34E-15	52	277
	1	2.46E-15	28	12	2.50E-15	34	14	2.34E-15	26	11	2.47E-15	32	248
	2	2.46E-15	27	12	2.41E-15	20	13	2.63E-15	25	15	2.42E-15	32	332
7-nodes (non-J.)	0	7.57E-15	54	56	7.96E-15	149	52	8.98E-15	135	88	8.55E-15	202	1305
	1	7.40E-15	44	52	7.37E-15	92	45	7.46E-15	103	84	8.03E-15	142	1323
	2	7.64E-15	30	32	7.29E-15	79	52	8.31E-15	91	119	7.45E-15	126	1495

code, we found that the queues are practically unbounded (implemented as 32-bit integer counters), which we reproduce in the MODEST models for modes.
- FIG by default uses the *batch means* technique for steady-state simulation, where a single run is partitioned into equal-duration batches, each of which provides one sample value. In communication with the original author, we found that each of their samples results from an independent run. We adapted FIG to do the same. It is the default in modes. (Semi-independent replication.)
- We also found in this communication that the original runs perform no splitting for the first 40 clients served; this part of the run is ignored as an initial transient phase. We confirmed this in the source code. We measured the average time to serve 40 clients for each model and use the result as transient phase *duration* with FIG and modes since neither tool supports a transient phase based on clients served. (Semi-independent replication.)

The original experiments were realised in a single file of C code that represents both the algorithm and the models, specialised to queueing models with transition probabilities and service rates specified in constant arrays. In fact, the code we received implemented the 2-tandem queueing network only. We extended this code with a compile-time choice among the models described in [20], and fixed few small bugs. We thus have four sets of results to compare, shown in Table 1: the original numbers given in [19,21], plus those from our new executions of the adapted code, modes, and FIG. In the table, time is in seconds, $\hat{p}$ is the estimate, p is the true steady-state probability where it can be derived, and n is the number of samples needed by the statistical evaluation. The adapted code and FIG ran on an Intel Xeon E5-2630 v3 (2.4-3.2 GHz), and modes ran on a Core i7-4790

(3.6-4.0 GHz, 4 physical/8 logical cores) system. The adapted code and FIG are single-threaded whereas modes used 7 simulation threads. The adapted code is tailor-mode for these models, while FIG has to encode them in the more general IOSA framework, making it slower; modes in turn profits from a special-case implementation for CTMC to speed up the Markovian cases. Comparing runtimes *between tools* is thus of limited use. The estimates are the centers of confidence intervals returned by the tools with confidence and relative width as described above. Each ⟨estimate, n, time⟩ triple was selected from 5 tool executions by picking the one with the median runtime. We underline the best runtimes among values for j. However, the wide confidence intervals (except for 2-tandem), few executions, and in principle unsound stopping criterion that we reproduce from the original experiments mean that results, including best values of j, vary a lot for different random seeds. The original experimental setup is thus insufficient for drawing conclusions about the precise tradeoffs between specific values of j, but may at most expose an overall trend.

Nevertheless, our estimates are mostly within the margin of error around the original or true results. We confirm the main experimental conclusion of [19,21]: as j increases, n decreases, but from some point—mostly $j > 1$ or 2—runtime increases, due to the overhead of more retrials surviving longer. For the non-Jackson triple tandem network, none of our results matches the numbers of [19]. Since *the original code*, albeit adapted, agrees with FIG and modes rather than with the original results, we suspect an error in [19] or [20] w.r.t. this one model.

4   Conclusion

We demonstrated the extension of the FIG and modes rare event simulation tools to support prolonged retrials in rare event simulation using RESTART importance splitting. These implementations and experiments were the outcome of an exercise in independently *replicating* experimental research originally performed in mathematics, from a computer science perspective. We confirm the key findings of the earlier work. At the same time, we document several issues—small but critical technical details of the algorithm and experimental setup—where the publicly available information was insufficient for a completely independent replication. We in particular noticed that replicating randomised/statistical algorithms poses a particular challenge since small errors may result in subtle mis-estimations that are often drowned in the overall statistical error. In the end, however, all issues could be resolved due to the exceptional support, responsiveness, and openness of the original author, José Villén-Altamirano, whom we thank earnestly. However, such support cannot be expected for experimental work in general, in particular where temporary staff like Ph.D. students—who eventually graduate and move to new institutions or industry—perform the bulk of the experiments. This paper thus also highlights the need for computer science and the formal verification community to continue their push for artifact evaluation and archived, publicly available *reproduction* packages. A reproduction package for our experiments is archived at DOI 10.6084/m9.figshare.12269462.

References

1. ACM: Artifact review and badging (2020), https://www.acm.org/publications/policies/artifact-review-and-badging-current, version 1.1.
2. Agha, G., Palmskog, K.: A survey of statistical model checking. ACM Trans. Model. Comput. Simul. **28**(1), 6:1–6:39 (2018). https://doi.org/10.1145/3158668
3. Baier, C., de Alfaro, L., Forejt, V., Kwiatkowska, M.: Model checking probabilistic systems. In: Handbook of Model Checking, pp. 963–999. Springer (2018). https://doi.org/10.1007/978-3-319-10575-8_28
4. Budde, C.E.: FIG: The finite improbability generator. In: TACAS. LNCS, vol. 12078, pp. 483–491. Springer (2020). https://doi.org/10.1007/978-3-030-45190-5_27
5. Budde, C.E., Biagi, M., Monti, R.E., D'Argenio, P.R., Stoelinga, M.: Rare event simulation for non-Markovian repairable fault trees. In: TACAS. LNCS, vol. 12078, pp. 463–482. Springer (2020). https://doi.org/10.1007/978-3-030-45190-5_26
6. Budde, C.E., D'Argenio, P.R., Hartmanns, A.: Automated compositional importance splitting. Sci. Comput. Program. **174**, 90–108 (2019). https://doi.org/10.1016/j.scico.2019.01.006
7. Budde, C.E., D'Argenio, P.R., Hartmanns, A., Sedwards, S.: A statistical model checker for nondeterminism and rare events. In: TACAS. LNCS, vol. 10806, pp. 340–358. Springer (2018). https://doi.org/10.1007/978-3-319-89963-3_20
8. Buijsrogge, A., de Boer, P.T., Scheinhardt, W.R.W.: Importance sampling for non-Markovian tandem queues using subsolutions. Queueing Systems **93**, 31–65 (2019). https://doi.org/10.1007/s11134-019-09623-0
9. Chow, Y.S., Robbins, H.: On the asymptotic theory of fixed-width sequential confidence intervals for the mean. Ann. Math. Statist. **36**(2), 457–462 (1965). https://doi.org/10.1214/aoms/1177700156
10. Dean, T., Dupuis, P.: Splitting for rare event simulation: A large deviation approach to design and analysis. Stochastic Processes and their Applications **119**(2), 562–587 (2009). https://doi.org/10.1016/j.spa.2008.02.017
11. Garvels, M.J.J., van Ommeren, J.K.C.W., Kroese, D.P.: On the importance function in splitting simulation. Eur. Trans. Telecommun. **13**(4), 363–371 (2002). https://doi.org/10.1002/ett.4460130408
12. Hartmanns, A., Hensel, C., Klauck, M., Klein, J., Kretínský, J., Parker, D., Quatmann, T., Ruijters, E., Steinmetz, M.: The 2019 comparison of tools for the analysis of quantitative formal models. In: TACAS. LNCS, vol. 11429. Springer (2019). https://doi.org/10.1007/978-3-030-17502-3_5
13. Hartmanns, A., Hermanns, H.: The Modest Toolset: An integrated environment for quantitative modelling and verification. In: TACAS. LNCS, vol. 8413, pp. 593–598. Springer (2014). https://doi.org/10.1007/978-3-642-54862-8_51
14. Hult, H., Nyquist, P.: Large deviations for weighted empirical measures arising in importance sampling. Stochastic Processes and their Applications **126**(1), 138–170 (2016). https://doi.org/10.1016/j.spa.2015.08.002
15. Legay, A., Sedwards, S., Traonouez, L.M.: Plasma Lab: A modular statistical model checking platform. In: ISoLA. LNCS, vol. 9952, pp. 77–93 (2016). https://doi.org/10.1007/978-3-319-47166-2_6
16. Reijsbergen, D., Boer, P.T.D., Scheinhardt, W., Juneja, S.: Path-ZVA: General, efficient, and automated importance sampling for highly reliable Markovian systems. ACM Trans. Model. Comput. Simul. **28**(3) (2018). https://doi.org/10.1145/3161569

17. Rubino, G., Tuffin, B.: Introduction to rare event simulation. pp. 1–13. Wiley (2009). https://doi.org/10.1002/9780470745403.ch1
18. Ruijters, E., Reijsbergen, D., de Boer, P.T., Stoelinga, M.: Rare event simulation for dynamic fault trees. Reliability Engineering & System Safety **186**, 220–231 (2019). https://doi.org/10.1016/j.ress.2019.02.004
19. Villén-Altamirano, J.: RESTART vs Splitting: A comparative study. Performance Evaluation **121–122**, 38–47 (2018). https://doi.org/10.1016/j.peva.2018.02.002
20. Villén-Altamirano, J.: Simulation details of the paper "RESTART vs Splitting: a comparative study". [19]. https://doi.org/10.1016/j.peva.2018.02.002, Appendix A. Supplementary data
21. Villén-Altamirano, J.: An improved variant of the rare event simulation method RESTART using prolonged retrials. Operations Research Perspectives **6**, 100–108 (2019). https://doi.org/10.1016/j.orp.2019.100108
22. Villén-Altamirano, M., Villén-Altamirano, J.: RESTART: a method for accelerating rare event simulations. In: Queueing, Performance and Control in ATM (ITC-13). pp. 71–76. Elsevier (1991)

A Web Interface for Petri Nets with Transits and Petri Games *

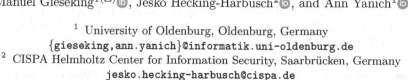

Manuel Gieseking[1]([✉]) [ID], Jesko Hecking-Harbusch[2] [ID], and Ann Yanich[1] [ID]

[1] University of Oldenburg, Oldenburg, Germany
{gieseking,ann.yanich}@informatik.uni-oldenburg.de
[2] CISPA Helmholtz Center for Information Security, Saarbrücken, Germany
jesko.hecking-harbusch@cispa.de

Abstract. Developing algorithms for distributed systems is an error-prone task. Formal models like Petri nets with transits and Petri games can prevent errors when developing such algorithms. Petri nets with transits allow us to follow the data flow between components in a distributed system. They can be model checked against specifications in LTL on both the local data flow and the global behavior. Petri games allow the synthesis of local controllers for distributed systems from safety specifications. Modeling problems in these formalisms requires defining extended Petri nets which can be cumbersome when performed textually.
In this paper, we present a web interface[1] that allows an intuitive, visual definition of Petri nets with transits and Petri games. The corresponding model checking and synthesis problems are solved directly on a server. In the interface, implementations, counterexamples, and all intermediate steps can be analyzed and simulated. Stepwise simulations and interactive state space generation support the user in detecting modeling errors.

1 Introduction

Distributed systems consist of several individual components. Each component has incomplete information about the other components. Asynchronous distributed systems have no fixed rate at which components progress but rather each component progresses at its individual rate between synchronizations with other components. Implementing correct algorithms for asynchronous distributed systems is difficult because they have to both work with the incomplete information of the components and for every possible scheduling between the components.

Petri nets [22,21] are a natural model for asynchronous distributed systems. Tokens represent components and transitions with more than one token correspond to synchronizations between the components. *Petri nets with transits* [9] extend Petri nets with a transit relation to model the data flow in asynchronous

* This work has been supported by the German Research Foundation (DFG) through Grant Petri Games (392735815) and through the Collaborative Research Center "Foundations of Perspicuous Software Systems" (TRR 248, 389792660), and by the European Research Council (ERC) through Grant OSARES (683300).
[1] The web interface is deployed at http://adam.informatik.uni-oldenburg.de.

J. F. Groote and K. G. Larsen (Eds.): TACAS 2021, LNCS 12652, pp. 381–388, 2021.
https://doi.org/10.1007/978-3-030-72013-1_22

distributed systems. *Flow-LTL* [9] is a specification language for Petri nets with transits and allows us to specify linear properties on both the global and the local view of the system. In particular, it is possible to globally select desired runs of the system with LTL (e.g., only fair and maximal runs) and check the local data flow of only those runs again with LTL. A model checker for Petri nets with transits against Flow-LTL is implemented in the tool ADAMMC [10].

Petri games [14] define the synthesis of asynchronous distributed systems based on Petri nets and causal memory. With causal memory, players exchange their entire causal past only upon synchronization. Without synchronization, players have no information of each other. For safety winning conditions, the synthesis algorithm for Petri games with a bounded number of controllable components and one uncontrollable component is implemented in ADAMSYNT [12][2]. Both tools are command-line tools lacking visual support to model Petri nets with transits or Petri games and the possibility to simulate or interactively explore implementations, counterexamples, and parts of the created state space.

In this paper, we present a web interface[3] for model checking asynchronous distributed systems with data flows and for the synthesis of asynchronous distributed systems with causal memory from safety specification. The web interface offers an input for Petri nets with transits and Petri games where the user interactively creates places, transitions, and their connections with a few inputs.

As a back-end, the algorithms of ADAMMC are used to model check Petri nets with transits against a given Flow-LTL formula as specification. Internally, the problem is reduced to the model checking problem of Petri nets against LTL. Both, the input Petri net with transits and the constructed Petri net can be visualized and simulated in the web interface. For a positive result, the web interface lets the user follow the control flow of the combined system and the data flow of the components. For a negative result, the web interface simulates the counterexample with a visual separation of the global and each local behavior.

The algorithms of ADAMSYNT solve the given Petri game with safety specification. Internally, the problem is reduced to solving a finite two-player game with complete information. For a positive result, a winning strategy for the Petri game and the two-player game can be visualized and the former can be simulated. For a negative result, the web interface lets the user interactively construct strategies of the two-player game and highlights why they violate the specification. These new intuitive construction methods, interactive features, and visualizations are of great impact when developing asynchronous distributed systems.

2   Web Interface for Petri Nets with Transits

The web interface can model check Petri nets with transits against Flow-LTL. We use an example from software-defined networks to showcase the workflow.

---

[2] ADAMSYNT was previously called ADAM. From now on, ADAMMC and ADAMSYNT are combined in the tool ADAM (https://github.com/adamtool/adam).

[3] The web interface is open source (https://github.com/adamtool/webinterface) and a corresponding artifact to set it all up locally in a virtual machine is available [16].

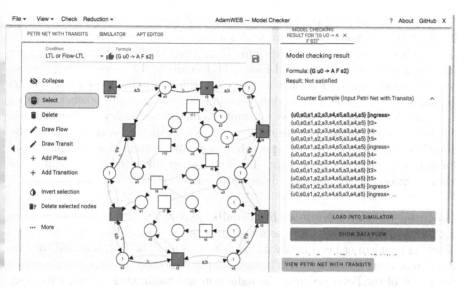

Fig. 1. Screenshot from the web interface for the model checking workflow.

Workflow for Petri Nets With Transits One application domain for Petri nets with transits are *software-defined networks (SDNs)* [20,4]. The nodes of the network are *switches* which forward *packets* along the edges of the network according to the *routing configuration*. Packets enter the network at *ingress switches* and leave it at *egress switches*. SDNs separate the packet forwarding process, called the *data plane*, from the routing process, called the *control plane*. *Concurrent updates* to the routing configuration are difficult to get right [15].

The separation of data and control plane and updates to the routing configuration can be encoded into Petri nets with transits [9]. Using this encoding, we demonstrate the workflow of the web interface for model checking an asynchronous distributed system with data flows. The packets of the SDN are modeled by the data flow in the Petri net with transits. The data flow relation as an extension from Petri nets to Petri nets with transits is depicted as colored and labeled arcs. In Fig. 1, the web interface presents the resulting Petri net with transits $\mathcal{N}$. First, we use the tools on the left to create for each switch a place si with $i \in \{0, \ldots, 5\}$ and add a token (cf. outer parts of $\mathcal{N}$). Then, we create transitions for the connections between the switches and for the origin of packets in the SDN (cf. transition *ingress* in the top-left corner) and link them with flows in both directions. Additionally, we create local transits between the switches corresponding to the forwarding of packets. They are displayed in light blue and red and are identified by the letters. This constitutes the *data plane*.

Next, we define the *control plane*, i.e., which forwarding is activated. Each transition to forward packets is connected to a place ai with $i \in \{0, \ldots, 5\}$ which has a token when the forwarding is configured initially (cf. places $a3$, $a4$, and $a5$) and no token otherwise (cf. places $a0$, $a1$, and $a2$). For the concurrent update, we create places ui with $i \in \{0, \ldots, 7\}$ and transitions ti with $i \in \{6, \ldots, 11\}$ with corresponding flows (cf. inner parts of $\mathcal{N}$).

Transitions for the forwarding are set as weak fair, i.e., whenever a transition is infinitely long enabled in a run, it also has to fire infinitely often, indicated by the purple color of the outer transitions. Transitions for the update do not require fairness assumptions. A satisfied Flow-LTL formula is $A F\, s5$ specifying that all packets eventually reach switch $s5$. An unsatisfied formula is $(G\, u0 \Rightarrow A F\, s2)$ requiring for runs, where the update is never executed, that all packets are taking the lower-left route. The fairness assumptions and a maximality assumption, i.e., whenever some transition can fire in a run some transition fires, are automatically added to the formula. In the screenshot, a counterexample for the unsatisfied formula is displayed on the right. The first packet takes the upper-right route via transitions $t3$, $t4$, and $t5$ and the update never starts.

Features for Petri Nets with Transits. ADAMMC [10] is a command-line model checking tool for Petri nets with transits and Flow-LTL [9]. The model checking problem of Petri nets with transits against Flow-LTL is solved by a reduction to Petri nets and LTL. The web interface allows displaying and arranging the nodes of the Petri net from the reduction and the input Petri net with transits. Automatic layout techniques are applied to avoid the overlapping of nodes. A physics control, which modifies the repulsion, link, and gravity strength of nodes, can be used to minimize the overlapping of edges. Heuristics generate coordinates for the constructed Petri net by using the coordinates of the input Petri net with transits to obtain a similar layout of corresponding parts.

For a positive result, the web interface allows visualizing the data flow trees for given firing sequences of the nets. For a negative result, the counterexample can be simulated both in the Petri net with transits and in the Petri net from the reduction. The witness of the counterexample for each flow subformula and the run violating the global behavior can be displayed by the web interface. This functionality is helpful when developing an encoding of a problem into Petri net with transits to ensure that a counterexample is not an error in the encoding. The constructed Petri net can be exported into a standard format for Petri net model checking (PNML) and the constructed LTL formula can be displayed.

3   Web Interface for Petri Games

The web interface can synthesize local controllers from safety specifications. The workflow is showcased for a distributed alarm system given as a Petri game.

Workflow for Petri Games We demonstrate the workflow of the web interface for the synthesis of asynchronous distributed systems with causal memory from safety specifications. Petri games separate the places of an underlying Petri net into *system places* and *environment places*. Tokens on system places are *system players* and tokens on environment places are *environment players*. Each player has *causal memory*: only upon synchronization with other players, they exchange their entire causal past. For safety specifications, the system players have to avoid that a bad place is reached for all behaviors of the environment players.

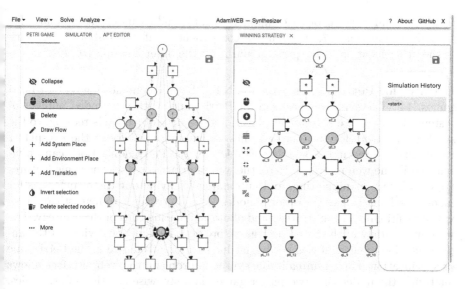

Fig. 2. Screenshot from the web interface for the synthesis workflow.

We want to obtain two local controllers of a distributed alarm system that should indicate the location of a burglary at both controllers. In Fig. 2, the web interface presents the resulting Petri game on the left and the winning strategy for the alarm system on the right. The burglar is modeled by an environment player and each component of the distributed alarm system by a system player. Environment players are on white places and system players on gray ones. We create five environment places $e0$, $e1$, $e2$, eL, and eR. The place $e0$ has a token, $e1$ and $e2$ serve for the decision to burgle a location, and eL and eR for actually burgling the location. Each component $x \in \{p, q\}$ of the alarm system has one system place $x0$ with a token, two system places $x1$ and $x2$ to detect a burglary and inform the other component, and two system places xL and xR to sound an alarm with the position of a burglary. We create rows of transitions for the environment player deciding where to burgle (first row), for the components detecting a burglary (second row), for the communication between the components (third row), and for sounding the alarm at each location (fourth row).

At last, we use transitions fai with $i \in \{0, \ldots, 3\}$ and frj with $j \in \{0, \ldots, 7\}$ connected to the bad place bad to define that the implementation of the distributed alarm system should avoid false alarms and false reports. A *false alarm* occurs if the burglar did not burgle any location but an alarm occurred, i.e., in every pair of places $\{e0\} \times \{pL, pR, qL, qR\}$. A *false report* occurs if a burglary happened at a location but a component of the alarm system indicates a burglary at the other location, i.e., in every pair of places $\{e1, eL\} \times \{pR, qR\}$ and $\{e2, eR\} \times \{pL, qL\}$. We add transitions and flows to bad for these cases.

The web interface finds a winning strategy (depicted on the right in Fig. 2) for the Petri game described above. Each component locally monitors its location ($t2$, $t3$) and simultaneously waits for information about a burglary at the other location ($t4$, $t5$). When a burglary is detected at the location of the component then it first informs the other component (*t*4, *t*5) and then outputs an alarm for the current location (*t*7, *t*8). When a component is informed about a burglary at the other location, it outputs an alarm for the other location (*t*6, *t*9).

Features for Petri Games ADAMSYNT [12] is a command-line tool for Petri games [14]. The synthesis problem for Petri games with a bounded number of system players, one environment player, and a safety objective is reduced to the synthesis problem for two-player games. A winning strategy in the two-player game is translated into a winning strategy for the Petri game. Both can be visualized in the web interface. Here, the web interface provides the same features for visualizing, manipulating, and automatically laying out the elements as for model checking. It uses the order of nodes of the Petri game to heuristically provide a positioning of the strategy and allows simulating runs of the strategy. The winning strategy of the two-player game provides an additional view on the implementation to check if it is not bogus due to a forgotten case in the Petri game or specification. For an unrealizable synthesis problem, the web interface allows analyzing the underlying two-player game via a stepwise creation of strategies. This guides the user towards changes to make the problem realizable.

4   Implementation Details

The server is implemented using the Sparkjava micro-framework [23] for incoming HTTP and WebSocket connections. The client is a single-page application written in Javascript using Vue.js [25], D3 [5], and the Vuetify component library [26]. We constructed libraries out of the tools ADAMMC and ADAMSYNT and implemented one interface handling both libraries. Common features like the physics control of nodes share the same implementation. All components of the libraries and the web interface [2] are open source and available on GitHub [1].

5   Conclusion

We presented a web interface for two tools: ADAMMC, a model checker for data flows in asynchronous distributed systems represented by Petri nets with transits, and ADAMSYNT, a synthesis tool for local controllers from safety specifications in asynchronous distributed systems with causal memory represented by Petri games. The web interface makes the modeling and debugging of Petri nets with transits and Petri games user-friendly as it presents visual representations of the input, all intermediate steps, and the output of the tools. The interactive features are a great assistance for correctly modeling distributed systems.

We plan to extend the web interface and tool support to model checking Petri nets with transits against Flow-CTL* [11], to other classes of Petri games with a decidable synthesis problem [13,3], to the bounded synthesis approach for Petri games [7,8,19,18], and to high-level Petri games [17]. As our web interface is open source and easy to extend, we also plan to connect it to other tools for Petri nets like APT [24], LoLA [27], or TAPAAL [6].

References

1. ADAM: https://github.com/adamtool/ (2020)
2. ADAMWEB: https://github.com/adamtool/webinterface (2020)
3. Beutner, R., Finkbeiner, B., Hecking-Harbusch, J.: Translating asynchronous games for distributed synthesis. In: 30th International Conference on Concurrency Theory, CONCUR. LIPIcs, vol. 140, pp. 26:1–26:16. Schloss Dagstuhl - Leibniz-Zentrum für Informatik (2019), https://doi.org/10.4230/LIPIcs.CONCUR.2019.26
4. Casado, M., Foster, N., Guha, A.: Abstractions for software-defined networks. Commun. ACM **57**(10), 86–95 (2014), https://doi.org/10.1145/2661061.2661063
5. D3: https://d3js.org/ (2020)
6. David, A., Jacobsen, L., Jacobsen, M., Jørgensen, K.Y., Møller, M.H., Srba, J.: TAPAAL 2.0: Integrated development environment for timed-arc Petri nets. In: Tools and Algorithms for the Construction and Analysis of Systems - 18th International Conference, TACAS. Lecture Notes in Computer Science, vol. 7214, pp. 492–497. Springer (2012), https://doi.org/10.1007/978-3-642-28756-5_36
7. Finkbeiner, B.: Bounded synthesis for Petri games. In: Correct System Design - Symposium in Honor of Ernst-Rüdiger Olderog on the Occasion of His 60th Birthday. Lecture Notes in Computer Science, vol. 9360, pp. 223–237. Springer (2015), https://doi.org/10.1007/978-3-319-23506-6_15
8. Finkbeiner, B., Gieseking, M., Hecking-Harbusch, J., Olderog, E.: Symbolic vs. bounded synthesis for Petri games. In: Sixth Workshop on Synthesis, SYNT@CAV. EPTCS, vol. 260, pp. 23–43 (2017), https://doi.org/10.4204/EPTCS.260.5
9. Finkbeiner, B., Gieseking, M., Hecking-Harbusch, J., Olderog, E.: Model checking data flows in concurrent network updates. In: Automated Technology for Verification and Analysis - 17th International Symposium, ATVA. Lecture Notes in Computer Science, vol. 11781, pp. 515–533. Springer (2019), https://doi.org/10.1007/978-3-030-31784-3_30
10. Finkbeiner, B., Gieseking, M., Hecking-Harbusch, J., Olderog, E.: AdamMC: A model checker for Petri nets with transits against Flow-LTL. In: Computer Aided Verification - 32nd International Conference, CAV. Lecture Notes in Computer Science, vol. 12225, pp. 64–76. Springer (2020), https://doi.org/10.1007/978-3-030-53291-8_5
11. Finkbeiner, B., Gieseking, M., Hecking-Harbusch, J., Olderog, E.: Model checking branching properties on Petri nets with transits. In: Automated Technology for Verification and Analysis - 18th International Symposium, ATVA. Lecture Notes in Computer Science, vol. 12302, pp. 394–410. Springer (2020), https://doi.org/10.1007/978-3-030-59152-6_22
12. Finkbeiner, B., Gieseking, M., Olderog, E.: Adam: Causality-based synthesis of distributed systems. In: Computer Aided Verification - 27th International Conference, CAV. Lecture Notes in Computer Science, vol. 9206, pp. 433–439. Springer (2015), https://doi.org/10.1007/978-3-319-21690-4_25
13. Finkbeiner, B., Gölz, P.: Synthesis in distributed environments. In: 37th IARCS Annual Conference on Foundations of Software Technology and Theoretical Computer Science, FSTTCS. LIPIcs, vol. 93, pp. 28:1–28:14. Schloss Dagstuhl - Leibniz-Zentrum für Informatik (2017), https://doi.org/10.4230/LIPIcs.FSTTCS.2017.28
14. Finkbeiner, B., Olderog, E.: Petri games: Synthesis of distributed systems with causal memory. Inf. Comput. **253**, 181–203 (2017), https://doi.org/10.1016/j.ic.2016.07.006

15. Förster, K., Mahajan, R., Wattenhofer, R.: Consistent updates in software defined networks: On dependencies, loop freedom, and blackholes. In: IFIP Networking Conference. pp. 1–9. IEEE Computer Society (2016), https://doi.org/10.1109/IFIPNetworking.2016.7497232
16. Gieseking, M., Hecking-Harbusch, J., Yanich, A.: AdamWEB: A Web Interface for Petri Nets with Transits and Petri Games (2020). https://doi.org/10.6084/m9.figshare.13089800
17. Gieseking, M., Olderog, E., Würdemann, N.: Solving high-level Petri games. Acta Informatica **57**(3-5), 591–626 (2020), https://doi.org/10.1007/s00236-020-00368-5
18. Hecking-Harbusch, J., Metzger, N.O.: Efficient trace encodings of bounded synthesis for asynchronous distributed systems. In: Automated Technology for Verification and Analysis - 17th International Symposium, ATVA. Lecture Notes in Computer Science, vol. 11781, pp. 369–386. Springer (2019), https://doi.org/10.1007/978-3-030-31784-3_22
19. Hecking-Harbusch, J., Tentrup, L.: Solving QBF by abstraction. In: Ninth International Symposium on Games, Automata, Logics, and Formal Verification, GandALF. EPTCS, vol. 277, pp. 88–102 (2018), https://doi.org/10.4204/EPTCS.277.7
20. McKeown, N., Anderson, T.E., Balakrishnan, H., Parulkar, G.M., Peterson, L.L., Rexford, J., Shenker, S., Turner, J.S.: Openflow: enabling innovation in campus networks. Comput. Commun. Rev. **38**(2), 69–74 (2008), https://doi.org/10.1145/1355734.1355746
21. Nielsen, M., Plotkin, G.D., Winskel, G.: Petri nets, event structures and domains, part I. Theor. Comput. Sci. **13**, 85–108 (1981), https://doi.org/10.1016/0304-3975(81)90112-2
22. Reisig, W.: Petri Nets: An Introduction, EATCS Monographs on Theoretical Computer Science, vol. 4. Springer (1985), https://doi.org/10.1007/978-3-642-69968-9
23. Sparkjava: http://sparkjava.com/ (2020)
24. University of Oldenburg: APT – Analyse von Petri-Netzen und Transitionssystemen. https://github.com/CvO-Theory/apt (2012)
25. Vue.js: https://vuejs.org/ (2020)
26. Vuetify: https://vuetifyjs.com/ (2020)
27. Wolf, K.: Petri net model checking with LoLA 2. In: Application and Theory of Petri Nets and Concurrency - 39th International Conference, PETRI NETS. Lecture Notes in Computer Science, vol. 10877, pp. 351–362. Springer (2018), https://doi.org/10.1007/978-3-319-91268-4_18

Momba: JANI Meets Python*

Maximilian A. Köhl[1] (✉), Michaela Klauck[1], and Holger Hermanns[1,2]

[1]Saarland University, Saarland Informatics Campus, Saarbrücken, Germany
[2]Institute of Intelligent Software, Guangzhou, China
{koehl,klauck,hermanns}@cs.uni-saarland.de

Abstract. JANI-model [6] is a model interchange format for networks of interacting automata. It is well-entrenched in the quantitative model checking community and allows modeling a variety of systems involving concurrency, probabilistic and real-time aspects, as well as continuous dynamics. Python is a general purpose programming language preferred by many for its ease of use and vast ecosystem. In this paper, we present *Momba*, a flexible Python framework for dealing with formal models centered around the JANI-model format and formalism. Momba strives to deliver an integrated and intuitive experience for experimenting with formal models making them accessible to a broader audience. To this end, it provides a pythonic interface for model construction, validation, and analysis. Here, we demonstrate these capabilities.

1 Introduction

Dealing with formal models encompasses a variety of tasks which can be challenging from time to time—especially for newcomers. Everything starts with the *construction* of a model or a family thereof. Often a textual or other, more formal, description of the scenario to be modeled is already existing, such as a rough sketch of the desired behavior or a circuit diagram. Then, after a formal model has finally been conceived, one has to *validate* that the model actually adequately models what should be modeled. In this regard models are just like any other human artifact, inadequate initially but over time it gets better. Only after confidence in the model has been established, one is able to harvest the benefits by handing over the model to *analysis* tools, e. g., a model checker.

In this paper, we present *Momba*, a flexible Python framework for dealing with formal models. Momba strives to deliver an integrated and intuitive experience to aid the process of model construction, validation, and analysis. It provides convenience functions for the constructions of models effectively turning Python into a syntax-aware macro language enabling the construction of models in a modular fashion. Momba's built-in simulation engine allows gaining

---

* This work was partially supported by the ERC Advanced Investigators Grant 695614 (POWVER), by the German Research Foundation (DFG) under grant No. 389792660, as part of TRR 248, see https://perspicuous-computing.science, and by the Key-Area Research and Development Program Grant 2018B010107004 of Guangdong Province.

J. F. Groote and K. G. Larsen (Eds.): TACAS 2021, LNCS 12652, pp. 389–398, 2021.
https://doi.org/10.1007/978-3-030-72013-1_23

confidence in a model, for instance, by rapidly prototyping a tool for interactive model exploration and visualization, or by connecting it to a testing framework. Finally, thanks to the JANI-model [6] interchange format, several state-of-the-art model checkers and other tools are readily available for analysis. The latest version of Momba is always available on GitHub [1] and the evaluated artifact of this tool demo paper can be found on Zenodo [27].

Why Momba? The idea to harvest a general purpose programming environment for formal modelling is not new at all. For instance, the SVL language combines the power of process algebraic modelling with the power of the bourne shell. As part of many CADP installations [12,13], it is in daily use since its inception [11]. Many formal modeling tools also already provide Python bindings [23,10]. Momba tries not to be yet another incarnation of these ideas.

While the construction of formal models clearly is an integral part of Momba, Momba is more than just a framework for constructing models with the help of Python. Most importantly, it also provides features to work with these models such as a simulator or an interface to different model checking tools. At the same time, it is not just a binding to an API developed for another language, say C++. Momba is *tool-agnostic* and aims to provide a pythonic interface for dealing with formal models while leveraging existing tools. Momba covers the whole process from model creation through validation to analysis. To this end, it is centered around the well-entrenched JANI-model interchange format.

Why JANI? Traditionally, most analysis tools for formal models came with their own modeling languages and formats. The resulting fragmentation hindered interoperability between and comparability across different tools. JANI-model [6] has been conceived with the vision to put an end to this fragmentation. It has since been adopted by many quantitative model checkers [20,21,9] while for others translators have been developed [20,9] enabling cross-tool comparability and fostering competition within the community [22,19,7]. Recently, JANI has also been discovered by the planning community [24,25].

Momba supports all features of the JANI-model specification and some of its optional extensions. JANI is the natural foundation for a project like Momba. It provides a solid, well-established, and powerful modeling formalism for a variety of different kinds of systems involving concurrency, probabilistic and real-time aspects, as well as continuous dynamics. A JANI model is a network of interacting automata with variables. Attached to a model one can also specify various kinds of probabilistic and timed properties which can then be checked by several model checkers, e. g., ePMC [20], The Modest Toolset [21], and Storm [23]. The broad tool support for JANI models enables us to build upon existing research and to outsource computation-intensive tasks via unified interfaces.

Why Python? Python is a popular high-level programming language, preferred by many for its ease of use and ecosystem. Especially within the data-science community, Python is the go-to language for data analysis and machine learning leaveraging tools such as TensorFlow [2] and scikit-learn [29]. Around these tools, scientific general purpose tools such as Jupyter [26] have emerged. Jupyter provides a platform for documenting scientific experiments and their results in a reproducible way combining code, data, and documentation.

Our vision is to harvest Python's ecosystem and the tools developed by the scientific community for dealing with formal models. Imagine, a Jupyter notebook documenting a model, including the code to construct it, with interactive visualizations of the model itself and various analysis results.

By basing our efforts on a popular language that is appreciated by scientists and established in the scientific community, we hope to lower the entry barrier, especially for those outside the formal methods community.

The User Perspective. In what follows, we demonstrate multiple facets of Momba using a variant of Racetrack, a well-known benchmark in autonomous AI decision making [4,31] which has recently found its use in several model checking contexts [16,3,15]. too. We go through the entire process from the construction of a family of models through their validation to their analysis. For each step, we highlight what Momba has to offer in terms of effectively supporting the process.

Originally Racetrack has been a pen-and-paper game [14]. A *track* is a two-dimensional grid comprising *start, goal, wall,* and *blank* cells (cf. Fig. 1) [4]. A vehicle starts off with some initial velocity from a start cell, with the objective to reach a goal cell as fast as possible without crashing into a wall. The vehicle is controlled by nine possible actions modifying the current velocity vector. Racetrack naturally lends itself as a benchmark for sequential decision making in risky scenarios, in particular, when extended with probabilistic noise. In a variety of such noisy forms, it has been adopted as a benchmark for *Markov Decision Process* (MDP) algorithms in the AI community [4,5,28,30,31].

For our demonstration, we consider multiple *variants* of Racetrack giving rise to a family of MDPs, studied recently [3] from a feature-oriented perspective [8]. For example, there are different tank options and fuel is consumed according to various consumption models. In addition, there are different undergrounds inducing probabilistic noise modeling slippery road conditions. Clearly, this modeling scenario is beyond what is possible with mere model parametrization, especially so because we are interested in the car's performance on different tracks each inducing its own MDP [4].

2   Scenario-Based Model Construction

Usually, formal models are not constructed out of thin air but based on some kind of scenario description existing upfront. Such descriptions usually comprise an operational characterization of the behavior to model together with additional and sometimes more formal information about the specific case. Our use case is no exemption, here a textual description of the behavior of the car is provided together with a specific track and a specification of the variant.

Naturally, Python can be used to nicely capture the formal parts of a scenario description in various data structures. Combined with a domain-specific parser for configuration files, scenario descriptions are interchangeable and easy to interface with the code for model construction. In our case, a textual representation of the track (cf. Fig. 1) [4] is provided and parsed together with additional

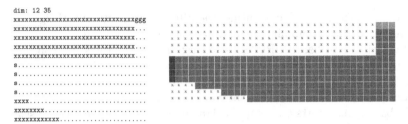

```
dim: 12 35
xxxxxxxxxxxxxxxxxxxxxxxxxxxxxxxxxggg
xxxxxxxxxxxxxxxxxxxxxxxxxxxxxxxx...
xxxxxxxxxxxxxxxxxxxxxxxxxxxxxxxx...
xxxxxxxxxxxxxxxxxxxxxxxxxxxxxxxx...
xxxxxxxxxxxxxxxxxxxxxxxxxxxxxxxx...
s.................................
s.................................
s.................................
s.................................
xxxx..............................
xxxxxxxx..........................
xxxxxxxxxxx.......................
```

Fig. 1. Textual representation (left) and picture of a track (right): start cells in blue (s), goal cells in green (g), and wall cells marked with x.

parameters, like the size of the tank and the type of the underground, into a data structure tailored to that purpose.

Now, how does Momba support the construction of models from such data structures? A distinguishing feature of Momba is that it effectively turns Python into a syntax-aware macro language enabling the modular construction of models. For our Racetrack use case different fuel consumption models can be captured as macros from JANI expressions to JANI expressions:

```
linear = lambda dx, dy: expr("abs($dx) + abs($dy)", dx=dx, dy=dy)
quadratic = lambda dx, dy: expr("$linear ** 2", linear=linear(dx, dy))
```

A macro is simply a Python function. Upon execution, these macros construct JANI expressions using a straightforward syntax inspired by Python expressions. In this case, both functions take expressions for the current velocity of the vehicle in x and y dimension and return an expression for the resulting fuel consumption which is either *linear* or *quadratic* in the velocity. In contrast to how macros work in languages like C, syntax-aware macros using Momba's expr function prevent surprises from mere text-based expansion. Being Python functions, macros can be easily passed around and used elsewhere:

```
assignments = {
    "fuel": expr(
        "min(TANK_SIZE, max(0, fuel - floor($consumption)))",
        consumption=fuel_model(car_dx, car_dy),
    )
}
```

Here, we update the fuel level by taking whatever macro has been provided for computing the fuel consumption. This code is part of constructing an edge for the tank automaton in a modular fashion in the sense that the consumption model is exchangeable. Momba provides further functions, for instance, for declaring variables, like fuel, and constructing automata, networks, as well as other model objects. Most of these functions provide all kinds of comforts, for instance, directly checking the types of the involved expressions.

Using syntax-aware macros and Momba's other convenience functions, we arrive at a Python script racetrack.py [27] generating a collection of JANI models from scenario descriptions comprising a track and specifying a variant. Iterating over possible scenario descriptions, hundreds of JANI models can be generated fully automatically and consequently be analyzed.

3 Validation by Simulation

Having our models ready, we have to somehow gain confidence that they actually model what we want them to, before handing them over to analysis tools. One way of gaining confidence into a model is by simulating its behavior and manually checking it for consistency with the own understanding of what the model should do. Just like any kind of debugging, this can be a tedious and frustrating process, especially with text-based traces generated by some generic simulator. Momba instead comprises a built-in simulation engine, enabling rapid development of interactive visualizations. This effectively allows us to steer a vehicle through a track thereby exploring a model's behavior, testing edge cases as in a racing game, and ultimately gaining confidence in the model.

Momba's built-in simulation engine supports the simulation of a variety of different JANI models including timed models. It has been written completely from scratch with easy accessibility from Python in mind. Non-determinism can be resolved by uniform random sampling or by querying an external oracle such as, in the case of our interactive visualization, the user, a testing framework, or even a neural network as done for DSMC [16]. For each step, the simulator provides all the necessary information like the binding of variables to values, the locations the various automata of a network are in, and the possible actions (and time delays for timed models) that can be taken. This information can then be extracted and used to display whatever is of interest for understanding and investigating the behavior of the model under scrutiny.

Fig. 2 shows a simple interactive visualization of the Racetrack example based on Momba's simulation engine where the user can steer the vehicle (indicated by the yellow asterisk) through the track by entering acceleration values. Certainly, there is ample room for beautification of this simulator (see TraceVis [15] for example) but for rapid model development this is not needed. After playing around with the interactive simulation for a while and testing various edge cases, we are confident that the model is adequate.

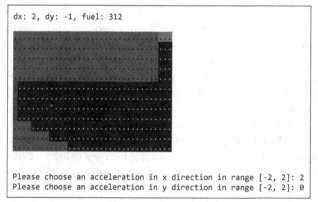

Fig. 2. Interactive visualization using Momba's simulation engine.

4   Harvesting the Benefits

Having constructed the models and gained confidence in their adequacy, we are now ready to harvest the benefits of formal modeling and to apply various state-of-the-art analysis tools, exploiting the JANI-model interchange. Again, Momba provides the necessary functions to define properties and hand our models, with the respective properties attached to them, over to common analysis tools.

Imagine that we are interested in the property $P_{max}(\lozenge \text{ on\_goal} \wedge \textit{fuel} > 0)$, i. e., the maximal probability of reaching a goal cell with a non-empty tank from a given start cell. Using Momba's syntax-aware macros, we first construct a disjunction over all goal cells and then define the property using the concise syntax provided by Momba's `prop` function:

```
on_goal = reduce(lor, (expr("car_pos == $g", g=g) for g in goal_cells), False)
define_property(
    prop("min({ Pmax(F($on_goal and fuel > 0)) | initial })", on_goal=on_goal),
    name="goalProbabilityFuel",
)
```

After generating a model with the vehicle starting from position $(0, 7)$ on the track depicted in Fig. 1 and with sand as underground, the value iteration engine mcsta [18] of The Modest Toolset calculates a probability of 87.5 % taking 153 s when invoked by Momba with the model. Momba also cross-checks the results for us, by invoking Storm's dd engine [9] (the fastest engine for this model) and obtains the same result in 107 s. These experiments have been carried out on a standard laptop with an Intel Core i7 at 2.7 GHz.

5   Conclusion

We presented Momba, a Python framework for dealing with quantitative models covering the whole process of model creation, validation, and analysis providing an integrated and intuitive experience. In a user story on Racetrack, we demonstrated how Momba's capabilities can be used throughout all stages of the development process of cyber-physical models.

We demonstrated how Momba enables scenario-based model construction with Python code in a concise and modular way with syntax-aware macros. Using Momba's simulation engine, we were able to rapidly prototype an interactive visualization thereby gaining confidence in our models and, finally, thanks to JANI-model, we demonstrated how to analyse our models with state-of-the-art model checkers directly invoked and cross-checked by Momba.

By basing Momba on Python, we aim to harvest the tools developed by the data-science community. Especially, when combined with Jupyter [26], Momba enables literate programming [32] combining code, data, and documentation for reproducible experiments and process documentation.

We hope that Momba helps to open up the world of formal modeling towards a broader community by lowering or removing barriers otherwise obstructing the application of formal models. Momba's infrastructure is implemented in such a way that it can easily be extended into other directions and for connections to other research areas, e. g., model checking policies machine learned with Python libraries [16,17].

References

1. Momba on GitHub, https://github.com/koehlma/momba
2. Abadi, M., Barham, P., Chen, J., Chen, Z., Davis, A., Dean, J., Devin, M., Ghemawat, S., Irving, G., Isard, M., Kudlur, M., Levenberg, J., Monga, R., Moore, S., Murray, D.G., Steiner, B., Tucker, P., Vasudevan, V., Warden, P., Wicke, M., Yu, Y., Zheng, X.: Tensorflow: A system for large-scale machine learning. In: Proceedings of the 12th USENIX Conference on Operating Systems Design and Implementation. p. 265283. OSDI'16, USENIX Association, USA (2016)
3. Baier, C., Dubslaff, C., Hermanns, H., Klauck, M., Klüppelholz, S., Köhl, M.A.: Components in probabilistic systems: Suitable by construction. In: Proceedings of the 9th International Symposium On Leveraging Applications of Formal Methods, Verification and Validation. X by Construction. (2020)
4. Barto, A.G., Bradtke, S.J., Singh, S.P.: Learning to act using real-time dynamic programming. Artificial Intelligence **72**(1), 81 – 138 (1995). https://doi.org/10.1016/0004-3702(94)00011-O
5. Bonet, B., Geffner, H.: Labeled RTDP: improving the convergence of real-time dynamic programming. In: ICAPS. pp. 12–21 (2003)
6. Budde, C.E., Dehnert, C., Hahn, E.M., Hartmanns, A., Junges, S., Turrini, A.: JANI: Quantitative model and tool interaction. In: Legay, A., Margaria, T. (eds.) Tools and Algorithms for the Construction and Analysis of Systems - 23rd International Conference, TACAS 2017, Held as Part of the European Joint Conferences on Theory and Practice of Software, ETAPS 2017, Uppsala, Sweden, April 22-29, 2017, Proceedings, Part II. Lecture Notes in Computer Science, vol. 10206, pp. 151–168 (2017). https://doi.org/10.1007/978-3-662-54580-5_9
7. Budde, C.E., Hartmanns, A., Klauck, M., Kretinsky, J., Parker, D., Quatmann, T., Turrini, A., Zhang, Z.: On Correctness, Precision, and Performance in Quantitative Verification (QComp 2020 Competition Report). In: Proceedings of the 9th International Symposium On Leveraging Applications of Formal Methods, Verification and Validation. Software Verification Tools. (2020)
8. Chrszon, P., Dubslaff, C., Klüppelholz, S., Baier, C.: Profeat: feature-oriented engineering for family-based probabilistic model checking. Formal Aspects Comput. **30**(1), 45–75 (2018). https://doi.org/10.1007/s00165-017-0432-4, https://doi.org/10.1007/s00165-017-0432-4
9. Dehnert, C., Junges, S., Katoen, J., Volk, M.: A storm is coming: A modern probabilistic model checker. In: Majumdar, R., Kuncak, V. (eds.) Computer Aided Verification - 29th International Conference, CAV 2017, Heidelberg, Germany, July 24-28, 2017, Proceedings, Part II. Lecture Notes in Computer Science, vol. 10427, pp. 592–600. Springer (2017). https://doi.org/10.1007/978-3-319-63390-9_31
10. Duret-Lutz, A., Lewkowicz, A., Fauchille, A., Michaud, T., Renault, E., Xu, L.: Spot 2.0a framework for ltl and ω-automata manipulation. In: International Symposium on Automated Technology for Verification and Analysis. pp. 122–129. Springer (2016)
11. Fernandez, J., Garavel, H., Kerbrat, A., Mounier, L., Mateescu, R., Sighireanu, M.: CADP - A protocol validation and verification toolbox. In: Alur, R., Henzinger, T.A. (eds.) Computer Aided Verification, 8th International Conference, CAV '96, New Brunswick, NJ, USA, July 31 - August 3, 1996, Proceedings. Lecture Notes in Computer Science, vol. 1102, pp. 437–440. Springer (1996). https://doi.org/10.1007/3-540-61474-5_97

12. Garavel, H., Lang, F., Mateescu, R., Serwe, W.: CADP 2011: a toolbox for the construction and analysis of distributed processes. Int. J. Softw. Tools Technol. Transf. **15**(2), 89–107 (2013). https://doi.org/10.1007/s10009-012-0244-z

13. Garavel, H., Lang, F., Mounier, L.: Compositional verification in action. In: Howar, F., Barnat, J. (eds.) Formal Methods for Industrial Critical Systems - 23rd International Conference, FMICS 2018, Maynooth, Ireland, September 3-4, 2018, Proceedings. Lecture Notes in Computer Science, vol. 11119, pp. 189–210. Springer (2018). https://doi.org/10.1007/978-3-030-00244-2_13

14. Gardner, M.: Mathematical games. Scientific American **229**, 118–121 (1973)

15. Gros, T.P., Groß, D., Gumhold, S., Hoffmann, J., Klauck, M., Steinmetz, M.: TraceVis: Towards Visualization for Deep Statistical Model Checking. In: Proceedings of the 9th International Symposium On Leveraging Applications of Formal Methods, Verification and Validation. From Verification to Explanation. (2020)

16. Gros, T.P., Hermanns, H., Hoffmann, J., Klauck, M., Steinmetz, M.: Deep statistical model checking. In: Gotsman, A., Sokolova, A. (eds.) Formal Techniques for Distributed Objects, Components, and Systems - 40th IFIP WG 6.1 International Conference, FORTE 2020, Held as Part of the 15th International Federated Conference on Distributed Computing Techniques, DisCoTec 2020, Valletta, Malta, June 15-19, 2020, Proceedings. Lecture Notes in Computer Science, vol. 12136, pp. 96–114. Springer (2020). https://doi.org/10.1007/978-3-030-50086-3_6

17. Gros, T.P., Höller, D., Hoffmann, J., Wolf, V.: Tracking the race between deep reinforcement learning and imitation learning. In: Gribaudo, M., Jansen, D.N., Remke, A. (eds.) Quantitative Evaluation of Systems - 17th International Conference, QEST 2020, Vienna, Austria, August 31 - September 3, 2020, Proceedings. Lecture Notes in Computer Science, vol. 12289, pp. 11–17. Springer (2020). https://doi.org/10.1007/978-3-030-59854-9_2

18. Hahn, E.M., Hartmanns, A.: A comparison of time- and reward-bounded probabilistic model checking techniques. In: Fränzle, M., Kapur, D., Zhan, N. (eds.) Dependable Software Engineering: Theories, Tools, and Applications - Second International Symposium, SETTA 2016, Beijing, China, November 9-11, 2016, Proceedings. Lecture Notes in Computer Science, vol. 9984, pp. 85–100 (2016). https://doi.org/10.1007/978-3-319-47677-3_6

19. Hahn, E.M., Hartmanns, A., Hensel, C., Klauck, M., Klein, J., Kretínský, J., Parker, D., Quatmann, T., Ruijters, E., Steinmetz, M.: The 2019 comparison of tools for the analysis of quantitative formal models - (QComp 2019 competition report). In: Beyer, D., Huisman, M., Kordon, F., Steffen, B. (eds.) Tools and Algorithms for the Construction and Analysis of Systems - 25 Years of TACAS: TOOLympics, Held as Part of ETAPS 2019, Prague, Czech Republic, April 6-11, 2019, Proceedings, Part III. Lecture Notes in Computer Science, vol. 11429, pp. 69–92. Springer (2019). https://doi.org/10.1007/978-3-030-17502-3_5

20. Hahn, E.M., Li, Y., Schewe, S., Turrini, A., Zhang, L.: iscasmc: A web-based probabilistic model checker. In: Jones, C.B., Pihlajasaari, P., Sun, J. (eds.) FM 2014: Formal Methods - 19th International Symposium, Singapore, May 12-16, 2014. Proceedings. Lecture Notes in Computer Science, vol. 8442, pp. 312–317. Springer (2014). https://doi.org/10.1007/978-3-319-06410-9_22

21. Hartmanns, A., Hermanns, H.: The Modest Toolset: An integrated environment for quantitative modelling and verification. In: Ábrahám, E., Havelund, K. (eds.) Tools and Algorithms for the Construction and Analysis of Systems - 20th International Conference, TACAS 2014, Held as Part of the European Joint Conferences on Theory and Practice of Software, ETAPS 2014, Grenoble, France, April 5-13, 2014,

Proceedings. Lecture Notes in Computer Science, vol. 8413, pp. 593–598. Springer (2014). https://doi.org/10.1007/978-3-642-54862-8_51

22. Hartmanns, A., Klauck, M., Parker, D., Quatmann, T., Ruijters, E.: The Quantitative Verification Benchmark Set. In: Vojnar, T., Zhang, L. (eds.) Tools and Algorithms for the Construction and Analysis of Systems - 25th International Conference, TACAS 2019, Held as Part of the European Joint Conferences on Theory and Practice of Software, ETAPS 2019, Prague, Czech Republic, April 6-11, 2019, Proceedings, Part I. Lecture Notes in Computer Science, vol. 11427, pp. 344–350. Springer (2019). https://doi.org/10.1007/978-3-030-17462-0_20

23. Hensel, C., Junges, S., Katoen, J., Quatmann, T., Volk, M.: The probabilistic model checker storm. CoRR **abs/2002.07080** (2020), https://arxiv.org/abs/2002.07080

24. Hoffmann, J., Hermanns, H., Klauck, M., Steinmetz, M., Karpas, E., Magazzeni, D.: Let's learn their language? A case for planning with automata-network languages from model checking. In: The Thirty-Fourth AAAI Conference on Artificial Intelligence, AAAI 2020, The Thirty-Second Innovative Applications of Artificial Intelligence Conference, IAAI 2020, The Tenth AAAI Symposium on Educational Advances in Artificial Intelligence, EAAI 2020, New York, NY, USA, February 7-12, 2020. pp. 13569–13575. AAAI Press (2020)

25. Klauck, M., Steinmetz, M., Hoffmann, J., Hermanns, H.: Bridging the gap between probabilistic model checking and probabilistic planning: Survey, compilations, and empirical comparison. J. Artif. Intell. Res. **68**, 247–310 (2020). https://doi.org/10.1613/jair.1.11595

26. Kluyver, T., Ragan-Kelley, B., Pérez, F., Granger, B.E., Bussonnier, M., Frederic, J., Kelley, K., Hamrick, J.B., Grout, J., Corlay, S., et al.: Jupyter notebooks-a publishing format for reproducible computational workflows. In: ELPUB. pp. 87–90 (2016)

27. Köhl, M.A., Klauck, M., Hermanns, H.: (TACAS21 Artifact) Momba: JANI Meets Python. https://doi.org/10.5281/zenodo.4431780

28. McMahan, H.B., Gordon, G.J.: Fast exact planning in Markov decision processes. In: ICAPS. pp. 151–160 (2005)

29. Pedregosa, F., Varoquaux, G., Gramfort, A., Michel, V., Thirion, B., Grisel, O., Blondel, M., Prettenhofer, P., Weiss, R., Dubourg, V., et al.: Scikit-learn: Machine learning in python. the Journal of machine Learning research **12**, 2825–2830 (2011)

30. Pineda, L.E., Lu, Y., Zilberstein, S., Goldman, C.V.: Fault-tolerant planning under uncertainty. In: IJCAI. pp. 2350–2356 (2013)

31. Pineda, L.E., Zilberstein, S.: Planning under uncertainty using reduced models: Revisiting determinization. In: Chien, S.A., Do, M.B., Fern, A., Ruml, W. (eds.) Proceedings of the Twenty-Fourth International Conference on Automated Planning and Scheduling, ICAPS 2014, Portsmouth, New Hampshire, USA, June 21-26, 2014. AAAI (2014)

32. Ruys, T.C., Brinksma, E.: Experience with literate programming in the modelling and validation of systems. In: Steffen, B. (ed.) Tools and Algorithms for Construction and Analysis of Systems, 4th International Conference, TACAS '98, Held as Part of the European Joint Conferences on the Theory and Practice of Software, ETAPS'98, Lisbon, Portugal, March 28 - April 4, 1998, Proceedings. Lecture Notes in Computer Science, vol. 1384, pp. 393–408. Springer (1998). https://doi.org/10.1007/BFb0054185

SV-Comp Tool Competition Papers

Software Verification: 10th Comparative Evaluation (SV-COMP 2021)

Dirk Beyer [ID][✉]

LMU Munich, Munich, Germany

Abstract. SV-COMP 2021 is the 10th edition of the Competition on Software Verification (SV-COMP), which is an annual comparative evaluation of fully automatic software verifiers for C and Java programs. The competition provides a snapshot of the current state of the art in the area, and has a strong focus on reproducibility of its results. The competition was based on 15 201 verification tasks for C programs and 473 verification tasks for Java programs. Each verification task consisted of a program and a property (reachability, memory safety, overflows, termination). SV-COMP 2021 had 30 participating verification systems from 27 teams from 11 countries.

Keywords: Formal Verification · Program Analysis · Competition · Software Verification · Verification Tasks · Benchmark · C Language · Java Language · SV-Benchmarks

1 Introduction

Among several other objectives, the Competition on Software Verification (SV-COMP, https://sv-comp.sosy-lab.org/2021) showcases the state of the art in the area of automatic software verification. This edition of SV-COMP is already the 10th edition of the competition and presents again an overview of the currently achieved results by tool implementations that are based on the most recent ideas, concepts, and algorithms for fully automatic verification. This competition report describes the (updated) rules and definitions, presents the competition results, and discusses some interesting facts about the execution of the competition experiments. The objectives of the competitions were discussed earlier (1-4 [16]) and extended over the years (5-6 [17]):

1. provide an overview of the state of the art in software-verification technology and increase visibility of the most recent software verifiers,
2. establish a repository of software-verification tasks that is publicly available for free use as standard benchmark suite for evaluating verification software,

---

This report extends previous reports on SV-COMP [10, 11, 12, 13, 14, 15, 16, 17].
Reproduction packages are available on Zenodo (see Table 4).
Funded in part by the Deutsche Forschungsgemeinschaft (DFG) – 378803395 (ConVeY).
[✉] dirk.beyer@sosy-lab.org

J. F. Groote and K. G. Larsen (Eds.): TACAS 2021, LNCS 12652, pp. 401–422, 2021.
https://doi.org/10.1007/978-3-030-72013-1_24

3. establish standards that make it possible to compare different verification tools, including a property language and formats for the results,
4. accelerate the transfer of new verification technology to industrial practice by identifying the strengths of the various verifiers on a diverse set of tasks,
5. educate PhD students and others on performing reproducible benchmarking, packaging tools, and running robust and accurate research experiments, and
6. provide research teams that do not have sufficient computing resources with the opportunity to obtain experimental results on large benchmark sets.

The previous report [17] discusses the outcome of the SV-COMP competition so far with respect to these objectives.

Related Competitions. Competitions are an important evaluation method and there are many competitions in the field of formal methods. We refer to the previous report [17] for a more detailed discussion and give here only the references to the most related competitions [9, 19, 55, 56].

Quick Summary of Changes. We strive to continuously improve the competition, and this report describes the changes of the last year. In the following we list a brief summary of new items in SV-COMP 2021:

- SPDX identification of licenses in SV-Benchmarks collection
- WitnessLint: New checker for syntactical validity of verification witnesses
- Upgrade of the task-definition format to version 2.0
- Addition of several verification tasks and whole new sub-categories to the SV-Benchmarks collection
- Elimination of competition-specific functions `__VERIFIER_error` and `__VERIFIER_assume` from the verification tasks (and rules)
- Change in scoring schema: Unconfirmed results not counted anymore (when validation was applied)
- CoVeriTeam: New tool that can be used to remotely execute verification runs on the competition machines
- Automatic participation of previous verifiers

2   Organization, Definitions, Formats, and Rules

Procedure. The overall organization of the competition did not change in comparison to the earlier editions [10, 11, 12, 13, 14, 15, 16, 17]. SV-COMP is an open competition (also known as comparative evaluation), where all verification tasks are known before the submission of the participating verifiers, which is necessary due to the complexity of the C language. The procedure is partitioned into the *benchmark submission* phase, the *training* phase, and the *evaluation* phase. The participants received the results of their verifier continuously via e-mail (for pre-runs and the final competition run), and the results were publicly announced on the competition web site after the teams inspected them. The *Competition Jury* oversees the process and consists of the competition chair and one member of each participating team. Team representatives of the jury are listed in Table 5.

Table 1: Tools for witness-based result validation (validators) and witness linter

Validator	References	Represent./Developer	Affiliation
CPACHECKER	[22, 23, 25]	Martin Spiessl	LMU Munich, Germany
UAUTOMIZER	[22, 23]	Daniel Dietsch	Uni Freiburg, Germany
CPA-W2T	[24]	Thomas Lemberger	LMU Munich, Germany
FSHELL-W2T	[24]	Michael Tautschnig	Queen Mary U. of London, UK
NITWIT	[78]	Philipp Berger	RWTH Aachen, Germany
METAVAL	[29]	Martin Spiessl	LMU Munich, Germany
WITNESSLINT		Sven Umbricht	LMU Munich, Germany

License Requirements. Starting 2018, SV-COMP required that the verifier must be publicly available for download and has a license that

(i) allows reproduction and evaluation by anybody (incl. results publication),
(ii) does not restrict the usage of the verifier output (log files, witnesses), and
iii) allows any kind of (re-)distribution of the unmodified verifier archive.

During the qualification phase, when the jury members inspect the verifier archives, several issues with licenses (missing licenses, incompatibilities) were detected that the developers were able to address the issues on time.

With SV-COMP 2021, the community started the process of making the benchmark collection REUSE compliant (https://reuse.software) by adding SPDX license identifiers (https://spdx.dev). A few directories are properly labeled already, and continuous-integration checks with REUSE ensure that new contributions adhere to the standard.

Validation of Results. This time, the validation of the verification results was done by seven validation tools, which are listed in Table 1, including references to literature. The validators CPACHECKER and UAUTOMIZER support the competition since the beginning of its result validation in 2015. Execution-based validation was added in 2018 using CPA-W2T and FSHELL-W2T. Two new validators participated since the previous SV-COMP in 2020: NITWIT and METAVAL. A few categories were still excluded from validation because no validators were available for some types of programs or properties.

For SV-COMP 2021, the new validator WITNESSLINT was added for validating witnesses regarding their syntax. It checks the witnesses produced by the verification tools against the specification of the format for verification witnesses (https://github.com/sosy-lab/sv-witnesses/tree/svcomp21). For example, WITNESSLINT ensures that a verification witness is a proper XML/GraphML file and contains the required meta data. This means that the validators can focus on the validation of the verification result, assuming that the verification witness is syntactically valid. If the witness linter deems a verification witness as syntactically invalid, then the answers of the result validators are ignored and the result is not counted as confirmed.

Task-Definition Format 2.0. The format for the task definitions in the SV-Benchmarks repository was recently extended to include a set of options that can carry information from the verification task to the verification tool. SV-COMP 2021 used the task-definition format in version 2.0 (`https://gitlab.com/sosy-lab/benchmarking/task-definition-format/-/tree/2.0`). More details can be found in the report for Test-Comp 2021 [19].

Properties. Please see the 2015 competition report [13] for the definition of the properties and the property format. All specifications are available in the directory `c/properties/` of the benchmark repository.

Categories. The updated category structure is illustrated by Fig. 1. The categories are also listed in Tables 7 and 8, and described in detail on the competition web site (`https://sv-comp.sosy-lab.org/2021/benchmarks.php`). Compared to the category structure for SV-COMP 2020, we added the sub-categories *XCSP* and *Combinations* to category *ReachSafety*, and the sub-categories *DeviceDriversLinux64Large ReachSafety*, *uthash MemSafety*, *uthash NoOverflows*, and *uthash ReachSafety* to category *SoftwareSystems*.

Another effort was to integrate some of the Juliet benchmark tasks [31] into the SV-Benchmarks collection. We requested a license for the Juliet programs that properly clarifies the license terms also outside the USA. We thank our colleagues from NIST for releasing their Juliet benchmark (which is declared as public domain) under the Creative Commons license CC0-1.0 (`https://github.com/sosy-lab/sv-benchmarks/blob/svcomp21/LICENSES/CC0-1.0.txt`). SV-COMP 2021 used many verification tasks from Juliet, in particular for the memory-safety properties CWE121 (stack-based buffer overflow), CWE401 (memory leak), CWE415 (double free), CWE476 (null-pointer dereference), and CWE590 (free memory that is not on the heap) (see `https://github.com/sosy-lab/sv-benchmarks/blob/svcomp21/c/MemSafety-Juliet.set`). All those new contributions to the benchmark collection lead to the growth of the number of verification tasks from 11 052 in SV-COMP 2020 to 15 201 in SV-COMP 2021.

Verification Tasks. The previous verification tasks and competition rules used special definitions for the functions `__VERIFIER_error` and `__VERIFIER_assume`. These special definitions were found to be unintuitive and inconsistent with expectations in the verification community, and repeatedly caused confusion among participants. A call of function `__VERIFIER_error()` was defined to never return. A call of function `__VERIFIER_assume(p)` was defined such that if expression p evaluates to false, then the function loops forever, otherwise the function returns without any side effects. This led to unintended interactions with other properties.

We eliminated these two functions in two steps. In the first step, each function call was replaced by a C-code implementation of the intended behavior. In most of the cases, `__VERIFIER_error();` was replaced by the C code `reach_error(); abort();`, where `reach_error` is a 'normal' function, i.e., one whose interpretation follows the C standard [3].

Eliminating `__VERIFIER_assume` was more complicated: In some tasks for property *memory-cleanup*, `__VERIFIER_assume(p);` was replaced by the C code `assume_cycle_if_not(p);`, which is implemented

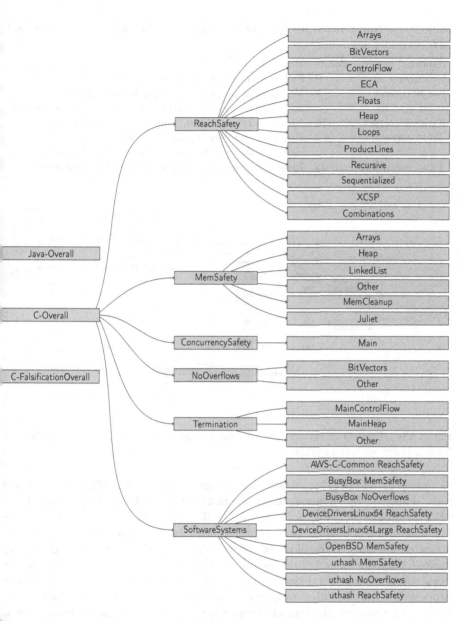

Fig. 1: Category structure for SV-COMP 2021; category *C-FalsificationOverall* contains all verification tasks of *C-Overall* without *Termination*; *Java-Overall* contains all Java verification tasks; compared to SV-COMP 2020, there are two new sub-categories in *ReachSafety* and four new sub-categories in *SoftwareSystems*

Table 2: Scoring schema for SV-COMP 2021 (new: no point for unconfirmed correct results anymore)

Reported result	Points	Description
UNKNOWN	0	Failure to compute verification result
FALSE correct	+1	Violation of property in program was correctly found and a validator confirmed the result based on a witness
FALSE incorrect	−16	Violation reported but property holds (false alarm)
TRUE correct	+2	Program correctly reported to satisfy property and a validator confirmed the result based on a witness
TRUE incorrect	−32	Incorrect program reported as correct (wrong proof)

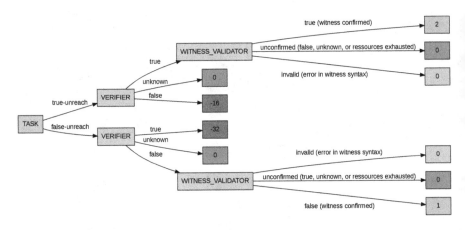

Fig. 2: Visualization of the scoring schema for the reachability property (adjusted from a previous report [15])

as if (!p) while(1);, while for other tasks, __VERIFIER_assume(p); was replaced by assume_abort_if_not(p);, which is implemented as if (!p) abort();. The solution nicely illustrates the problem of the special semantics: Consider property *memory-cleanup*, which requires that all allocated memory is deallocated before the program terminates. Here, the desired behavior of a failing assume statement would be that the program does not terminate (and does not unintendedly violate the *memory-cleanup* property). Now consider property *termination*, which requires that every path finally reaches the end of the program. Here, the desired behavior of a failing assume statement would be that the program terminates (and does not unintendedly violate the *termination* property).

In the second step, the specifications for functions __VERIFIER_error and __VERIFIER_assume were removed from the competition rules (because no such functions exist anymore in the SV-Benchmarks collection).

Scoring Schema and Ranking. Table 2 provides an overview and Fig. 2 visually illustrates the score assignment for the reachability property as an example.

The scoring schema was changed regarding the special rule for unconfirmed correct results for expected result TRUE. There was a rule during the transitioning phase to assign one point if the answer matches the expected result but the witness was not confirmed. Now score points are only assigned if the results got validated (or no validator was available).

As in the last years, the rank of a verifier was decided based on the sum of points (normalized for meta categories). In case of a tie, the rank was decided based on success run time, which is the total CPU time over all verification tasks for which the verifier reported a correct verification result. *Opt-out from Categories* and *Score Normalization for Meta Categories* was done as described previously [11] (page 597).

3   Reproducibility

To allow independent reproduction of the SV-COMP results, we made all major components that were used in the competition available in public version-control repositories. An overview of the components that contribute to the reproducible setup of SV-COMP is provided in Fig. 3, and the details are given in Table 3. We refer to the SV-COMP 2016 report [14] for a description of all components of the SV-COMP organization.

We have published the competition artifacts at Zenodo (see Table 4) to guarantee their long-term availability and immutability. These artifacts comprise the verification tasks, the competition results, the produced verification witnesses, and the BENCHEXEC package. The archive for the competition results includes the raw results in BENCHEXEC's XML exchange format, the log output of the verifiers and validators, and a mapping from file names to SHA-256 hashes. The hashes of the files are useful for validating the exact contents of a file, and accessing the files inside the archive that contains the verification witnesses.

Competition Workflow. The workflow of the competition is described in the report for Test-Comp 2021 [19].

CoVeriTeam. The competition was for the first time supported by CoVeriTeam [26] (https://gitlab.com/sosy-lab/software/coveriteam/), which is a tool for cooperative verification. Among its many capabilities, it enables remote execution of verification runs directly on the competition machines, which was found to be a valuable service for trouble shooting.

4   Results and Discussion

The results of the competition experiments represent the state of the art in fully automatic software-verification tools. The report shows the results, in terms of effectiveness (number of verification tasks that can be solved and correctness of the results, as accumulated in the score) and efficiency (resource consumption in terms of CPU time and CPU energy). The results are presented in the same way as in last years, such that the improvements compared to last year are easy

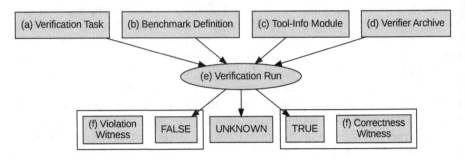

Fig. 3: Benchmarking components of SV-COMP and competition's execution flow (same as for SV-COMP 2020)

Table 3: Publicly available components for reproducing SV-COMP 2021

Component	Fig. 3	Repository	Version
Verification Tasks	(a)	`github.com/sosy-lab/sv-benchmarks`	svcomp21
Benchmark Definitions	(b)	`gitlab.com/sosy-lab/sv-comp/bench-defs`	svcomp21
Tool-Info Modules	(c)	`github.com/sosy-lab/benchexec`	3.6
Verifier Archives	(d)	`gitlab.com/sosy-lab/sv-comp/archives-2021`	svcomp21
Benchmarking	(e)	`github.com/sosy-lab/benchexec`	3.6
Witness Format	(f)	`github.com/sosy-lab/sv-witnesses`	svcomp21

Table 4: Artifacts published for SV-COMP 2021

Content	DOI	Reference
Verification Tasks	`10.5281/zenodo.4459126`	[20]
Competition Results	`10.5281/zenodo.4458215`	[18]
Verification Witnesses	`10.5281/zenodo.4459196`	[21]
BenchExec	`10.5281/zenodo.4317433`	[82]

to identify. The results presented in this report were inspected and approved by the participating teams. We now discuss the highlights of the results.

Participating Verifiers. Table 5 provides an overview of the participating verification systems (see also the listing on the competition web site at `https://sv-comp.sosy-lab.org/2021/systems.php`). Table 6 lists the algorithms and techniques that are used by the verification tools.

Automatic Participation. To ensure that the comparative evaluation continues to give an overview of the state of the art that is as broad as possible, a rule was introduced before SV-COMP 2020 which enables the option for the organizer to reuse systems that participated in previous years for the comparative evaluation. This option was used three times in SV-COMP 2021: for COASTAL, PREDATORHP, and SPF. Those participations are marked as 'hors concours' in Table 5.

Table 5: Competition candidates with tool references and representing jury members

Participant	Ref.	Jury member	Affiliation
2LS	[32, 63]	Viktor Malík	BUT, Brno, Czechia
BRICK		Lei Bu	Nanjing U., China
CBMC	[60]	Michael Tautschnig	Queen Mary U. of London, UK
COASTAL	[79]	(hors concours)	–
CPA-BAM-BNB	[4, 81]	Vadim Mutilin	ISP RAS, Russia
CPALOCKATOR	[5, 6]	Pavel Andrianov	ISP RAS, Russia
CPACHECKER	[27, 41]	Stephan Holzner	LMU Munich, Germany
DARTAGNAN	[48, 68]	Hernán Ponce de León	U. Bundeswehr Munich, Germany
DIVINE	[8, 61]	Henrich Lauko	Masaryk U., Brno, Czechia
ESBMC-INCR	[36, 39]	Felipe R. Monteiro	Amazon Web Services, USA
ESBMC-KIND	[46, 47]	Lucas Cordeiro	U. of Manchester, UK
FRAMA-C	[40]	Martin Spiessl	LMU Munich, Germany
GAZER-THETA	[1, 74]	Ákos Hajdu	BME, Hungary
GOBLINT	[73, 80]	Simmo Saan	U. of Tartu, Estonia
JAVA RANGER	[76, 77]	Soha Hussein	U. of Minnesota, USA
JAYHORN	[59, 75]	Hossein Hojjat	U. of Tehran, Iran
JBMC	[37, 38]	Peter Schrammel	U. of Sussex / Diffblue, UK
JDART	[62, 64]	Falk Howar	TU Dortmund, Germany
KORN	[45]	Gidon Ernst	LMU Munich, Germany
LAZY-CSEQ	[57, 58]	Omar Inverso	Gran Sasso Science Institute, Italy
PESCO	[71, 72]	Cedric Richter	Paderborn U., Germany
PINAKA	[35]	Saurabh Joshi	IIT Hyderabad, India
PREDATORHP	[54, 67]	(hors concours)	–
SMACK	[51, 70]	Zvonimir Rakamaric	U. of Utah, USA
SPF	[65, 69]	(hors concours)	–
SYMBIOTIC	[33, 34]	Marek Chalupa	Masaryk U., Brno, Czechia
UAUTOMIZER	[52, 53]	Matthias Heizmann	U. of Freiburg, Germany
UKOJAK	[44, 66]	Dominik Klumpp	U. of Freiburg, Germany
UTAIPAN	[43, 49]	Daniel Dietsch	U. of Freiburg, Germany
VERIABS	[2, 42]	Priyanka Darke	Tata Consultancy Services, India

Computing Resources. The resource limits were the same as in the previous competitions [14]: Each verification run was limited to 8 processing units (cores), 15 GB of memory, and 15 min of CPU time. Witness validation was limited to 2 processing units, 7 GB of memory, and 1.5 min of CPU time for violation witnesses and 15 min of CPU time for correctness witnesses. The machines for running the experiments are part of a compute cluster that consists of 168 machines; each verification run was executed on an otherwise completely unloaded, dedicated machine, in order to achieve precise measurements. Each machine had one Intel Xeon E3-1230 v5 CPU, with 8 processing units each, a frequency of 3.4 GHz, 33 GB of RAM, and a GNU/Linux operating system (x86_64-linux, Ubuntu 20.04 with Linux kernel 5.4). We used BENCHEXEC [28] to measure and control computing resources (CPU time, memory, CPU energy) and VERIFIERCLOUD (https://vcloud.sosy-lab.org) to distribute, install, run, and clean-up verification runs, and to collect the results. The values for time and

Table 6: Algorithms and techniques that the competition candidates used

Participant	CEGAR	Predicate Abstraction	Symbolic Execution	Bounded Model Checking	k-Induction	Property-Directed Reach.	Explicit-Value Analysis	Numeric. Interval Analysis	Shape Analysis	Separation Logic	Bit-Precise Analysis	ARG-Based Analysis	Lazy Abstraction	Interpolation	Automata-Based Analysis	Concurrency Support	Ranking Functions	Evolutionary Algorithms	Algorithm Selection	Portfolio
2LS				✓	✓		✓	✓			✓						✓			
BRICK	✓		✓	✓			✓									✓				
CBMC				✓							✓					✓				
COASTAL			✓																	
CPA-BAM-BnB	✓	✓					✓				✓	✓	✓	✓						
CPALockator	✓	✓					✓				✓	✓	✓	✓		✓				
CPAchecker	✓	✓		✓	✓		✓	✓	✓		✓	✓	✓	✓		✓	✓		✓	✓
Dartagnan				✓							✓					✓				
Divine			✓				✓				✓					✓			✓	✓
ESBMC-incr				✓	✓						✓					✓				
ESBMC-kind				✓	✓			✓			✓					✓				
FRAMA-C								✓												
GAZER-THETA	✓	✓		✓			✓				✓	✓	✓	✓						✓
GOBLINT								✓			✓					✓				
JAVA RANGER			✓								✓									
JAYHORN	✓	✓				✓	✓						✓	✓						
JBMC				✓							✓					✓				
JDART			✓								✓									✓
KORN		✓	✓				✓													✓
LAZY-CSEQ				✓							✓					✓				
PeSCo	✓	✓		✓	✓		✓	✓	✓		✓	✓	✓	✓		✓	✓		✓	✓
PINAKA				✓	✓						✓									
PREDATORHP									✓											
SMACK				✓							✓		✓			✓				
SPF			✓						✓							✓				
SYMBIOTIC			✓		✓				✓	✓	✓									✓
UAUTOMIZER	✓	✓									✓		✓	✓	✓	✓	✓		✓	✓
UKOJAK	✓	✓									✓		✓	✓						
UTAIPAN	✓	✓					✓	✓			✓		✓	✓	✓	✓			✓	✓
VERIABS	✓			✓	✓		✓	✓										✓	✓	✓

energy are accumulated over all cores of the CPU. To measure the CPU energy, we used CPU ENERGY METER [30] (integrated in BENCHEXEC [28]).

One complete verification execution of the competition consisted of 163 177 verification runs (each verifier on each verification task of the selected categories according to the opt-outs), consuming 470 days of CPU time and 126 kWh of CPU energy (without validation). Witness-based result validation required 961 919 validation runs (each validator on each verification task for categories with witness validation, and for each verifier), consuming 274 days of CPU time. Each tool was executed several times, in order to make sure no installation issues occur during the execution. Including preruns, the infrastructure managed a total of 1.33 million verification runs consuming 4.16 years of CPU time, and 7.31 million validation runs consuming 3.84 years of CPU time.

Quantitative Results. Table 7 presents the quantitative overview of all tools and all categories. The head row mentions the category, the maximal score for the category, and the number of verification tasks. The tools are listed in alphabetical order; every table row lists the scores of one verifier. We indicate the top three candidates by formatting their scores in bold face and in larger font size. An empty table cell means that the verifier opted-out from the respective main category (perhaps participating in subcategories only, restricting the evaluation to a specific topic). More information (including interactive tables, quantile plots for every category, and also the raw data in XML format) is available on the competition web site (https://sv-comp.sosy-lab.org/2021/results) and in the results artifact (see Table 4).

Table 8 reports the top three verifiers for each category. The run time (column 'CPU Time') and energy (column 'CPU Energy') refer to successfully solved verification tasks (column 'Solved Tasks'). We also report the number of tasks for which no witness validator was able to confirm the result (column 'Unconf. Tasks'). The columns 'False Alarms' and 'Wrong Proofs' report the number of verification tasks for which the verifier reported wrong results, i.e., reporting a counterexample when the property holds (incorrect FALSE) and claiming that the program fulfills the property although it actually contains a bug (incorrect TRUE), respectively.

Score-Based Quantile Functions for Quality Assessment. We use score-based quantile functions [11, 28] because these visualizations make it easier to understand the results of the comparative evaluation. The web site (https://sv-comp.sosy-lab.org/2021/results) and the results archive (see Table 4) include such a plot for each (sub-)category. As an example, we show the plot for category *C-Overall* (all verification tasks) in Fig. 4. A total of 10 verifiers participated in category *C-Overall*, for which the quantile plot shows the overall performance over all categories (scores for meta categories are normalized [11]). A more detailed discussion of score-based quantile plots, including examples of what insights one can obtain from the plots, is provided in previous competition reports [11, 14].

Alternative Rankings. The community suggested to report a couple of alternative rankings that honor different aspects of the verification process as complement to the official SV-COMP ranking. Table 9 is similar to Table 8, but

Table 7: Quantitative overview over all results; empty cells represent opt-outs; an asterisk after the tool name marks hors-concours participation

Participant	ReachSafety 7844 points 4927 tasks	MemSafety 4981 points 3296 tasks	ConcurrencySafety 1413 points 1130 tasks	NoOverflows 682 points 452 tasks	Termination 3897 points 2212 tasks	SoftwareSystems 5608 points 3184 tasks	FalsificationOverall 6173 points 12989 tasks	Overall 23778 points 15201 tasks	JavaOverall 693 points 473 tasks
2LS	3021	1100	0	414	**1315**	-7	1436	6219	
BRICK									
CBMC	3395	-725	486	279	872	565	2609	5289	
CPA-BAM-BNE						491			
CPALOCKATOR			-819						
CPACHECKER	**4764**	**2992**	**1050**	**531**	1356	736	**4356**	**12217**	
DARTAGNAN			309						
DIVINE	2012	95	391	0	0	124	306	2083	
ESBMC-INCR			-134						
ESBMC-KIND	4486	1281	37	317	832	694	2002	6656	
FRAMA-C				172					
GAZER-THETA									
GOBLINT	777		46	156		331			
KORN									
LAZY-CSEQ			**1206**						
PESCO	**4526**					878	4329	12208	
PINAKA	3408			-200	669				
PREDATORHP*		2187							
SMACK						**894**			
SYMBIOTIC	3864	**3125**	0	373	1043	**2001**	2947	9268	
UAUTOMIZER	3502	**1615**	**943**	**512**	**3019**	359	**3432**	**11769**	
UKOJAK	1768	925	0	441	0	298	1800	4332	
UTAIPAN	2743	1436	937	**506**	0	282	3336	7676	
VERIABS	**5771**								
COASTAL*									298
JAVA RANGER									**630**
JAYHORN									369
JBMC									603
JDART									623
SPF*									409

Table 8: Overview of the top-three verifiers for each category (measurement values for CPU time and energy rounded to two significant digits)

Rank	Verifier	Score	CPU Time (in h)	CPU Energy (in kWh)	Solved Tasks	Unconf. Tasks	False Alarms	Wrong Proofs
ReachSafety								
1	VeriAbs	**5771**	130	1.5	3 526	725		
2	CPAchecker	4764	100	1.2	2 922	251	6	
3	PeSCo	4526	53	0.48	2 820	272	7	
MemSafety								
1	Symbiotic	**3125**	1.6	0.021	370	8		
2	CPAchecker	2992	7.8	0.069	3 092	0		
3	UAutomizer	1615	4.1	0.046	160	2		
ConcurrencySafety								
1	Lazy-CSeq	**1206**	4.0	0.051	985	34		
2	CPAchecker	1050	16	0.13	903	0	1	
3	UAutomizer	943	9.6	0.087	775	176		
NoOverflows								
1	CPAchecker	**531**	1.2	0.012	366	3		
2	UAutomizer	512	1.7	0.015	358	0		
3	UTaipan	506	1.9	0.018	355	0		
Termination								
1	UAutomizer	**3019**	22	0.24	1 581	9		
2	CPAchecker	1356	17	0.20	1 078	70	10	
3	2LS	1315	2.5	0.021	977	363	3	
SoftwareSystems								
1	Symbiotic	**2001**	0.55	0.0075	1 024	128		
2	Smack	894	14	0.14	1 362	58		2
3	PeSCo	878	27	0.27	1 484	234	1	
FalsificationOverall								
1	CPAchecker	**4356**	71	0.76	3 814	98	8	
2	PeSCo	4329	47	0.41	3 798	106	9	
3	UAutomizer	3432	30	0.30	1 585	215	1	
Overall								
1	CPAchecker	**12217**	190	2.1	9 835	514	18	
2	PeSCo	12208	120	1.2	9 743	579	19	
3	UAutomizer	11769	99	1.0	5 980	489	1	1
JavaOverall								
1	Java Ranger	**630**	4.9	0.056	427	0		
2	JDart	623	0.93	0.0093	437	0		
3	Jbmc	603	0.22	0.0022	423	0		

contains the alternative ranking categories *Correct* and *Green Verifiers*. Column 'Quality' gives the score in score points, column 'CPU Time' the CPU usage of successful runs in hours, column 'CPU Energy' the CPU usage of successful runs in kWh, column 'Solved Tasks' the number of correct results, column 'Wrong Re-

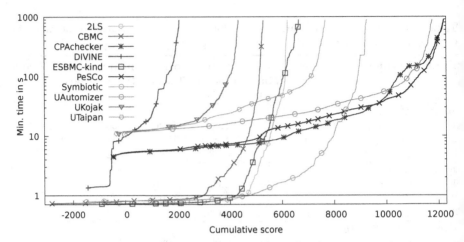

Fig. 4: Quantile functions for category *C-Overall*. Each quantile function illustrates the quantile (*x*-coordinate) of the scores obtained by correct verification runs below a certain run time (*y*-coordinate). More details were given previously [11]. A logarithmic scale is used for the time range from 1 s to 1000 s, and a linear scale is used for the time range between 0 s and 1 s.

Table 9: Alternative rankings for catagory *Overall*; quality is given in score points (sp), CPU time in hours (h), kilo-watt-hours (kWh), wrong results in errors (E), rank measures in errors per score point (E/sp), joule per score point (J/sp), and score points (sp)

Rank	Verifier	Quality (sp)	CPU Time (h)	CPU Energy (kWh)	Solved Tasks	Wrong Results (E)	Rank Measure
Correct Verifiers							(E/sp)
1	UAUTOMIZER	11 769	99	1.0	5 980	2	.00017
2	UKOJAK	4 332	46	0.48	2 476	1	.00023
3	CPACHECKER	12 217	190	2.1	9 835	18	.0015
worst						48	.023
Green Verifiers							(J/sp)
1	SYMBIOTIC	9 268	21	0.26	4 999	16	100
2	2LS	6 219	26	0.24	3 372	12	140
3	CBMC	5 289	26	0.31	5 596	52	210
worst							630

sults' the sum of false alarms and wrong proofs in number of errors, and column 'Rank Measure' gives the measure to determine the alternative rank.

Correct Verifiers — Low Failure Rate. The right-most columns of Table 8 report that the verifiers achieve a high degree of correctness (all top three verifiers in the *C-Overall* have less than 2 ‰ wrong results). The winners of category *Java-Overall* produced not a single wrong answer. The first category in

Table 10: New verifiers in SV-COMP 2020 and SV-COMP 2021

Verifier	Language	First Year	Sub-categories
Frama-C	C	2021	4
Gazer-Theta	C	2021	9
Goblint	C	2021	25
Korn	C	2021	13
Brick	C	2020	1
Dartagnan	C	2020	5
Gacal	C	2020	1
Coastal	Java	2020	1
Java Ranger	Java	2020	1
JDart	Java	2020	1

Table 11: Confirmation rate of verification witnesses in SV-COMP 2021

Result	True			False		
	Total	Confirmed	Unconf.	Total	Confirmed	Unconf.
2ls	2 252	2 245 99.7 %	7	1 591	1 127 70.8 %	464
Cbmc	3 875	3 498 90.3 %	377	3 772	2 098 55.6 %	1 674
CPachecker	5 992	5 646 94.2 %	346	4 357	4 189 96.1 %	168
Divine	1 673	1 649 98.6 %	24	1 317	986 74.9 %	331
ESBMC-kind	4 954	4 901 98.9 %	53	1 736	1 625 93.6 %	111
PeSCo	5 973	5 570 93.3 %	403	4 349	4 173 96.0 %	176
Symbiotic	3 351	3 149 94.0 %	202	2 166	1 850 85.4 %	316
UAutomizer	4 121	3 856 93.6 %	265	2 348	2 124 90.5 %	224
UKojak	1 816	1 796 98.9 %	20	690	680 98.6 %	10
UTaipan	2 602	2 542 97.7 %	60	1 637	1 417 86.6 %	220

Table 9 uses a failure rate as rank measure: $\frac{\text{number of incorrect results}}{\text{total score}}$, the number of errors per score point (E/sp). We use E as unit for number of incorrect results and sp as unit for total score. The worst result was $0.032\,E/sp$ in SV-COMP 2020 and is now improved to $0.023\,E/sp$.

Green Verifiers — Low Energy Consumption. Since a large part of the cost of verification is given by the energy consumption, it might be important to also consider the energy efficiency. The second category in Table 9 uses the energy consumption per score point as rank measure: $\frac{\text{total CPU energy}}{\text{total score}}$, with the unit J/sp. The worst result from SV-COMP 2020 was $2\,200\,J/sp$, now improved to $630\,J/sp$.

New Verifiers. To acknowledge the verification systems that participate for the first or second time in SV-COMP, Table 10 lists the new verifiers (in SV-COMP 2020 or SV-COMP 2021).

Verifiable Witnesses. Results validation is of primary importance in the competition. All SV-COMP verifiers are required to justify the result (True or False) by producing a verification witness (except for those categories for which no witness validator is available). We used six independently developed witness-based result validators and one witness linter (see Table 1).

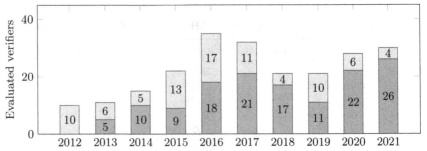

Fig. 5: Number of evaluated verifiers for each year (first-time participants on top)

Table 11 shows the confirmed versus unconfirmed results: the first column lists the verifiers of category *C-Overall*, the three columns for result TRUE reports the total, confirmed, and unconfirmed number of verification tasks for which the verifier answered with TRUE, respectively, and the three columns for result FALSE reports the total, confirmed, and unconfirmed number of verification tasks for which the verifier answered with FALSE, respectively. More information (for all verifiers) is given in the detailed tables on the competition web site and in the results artifact; all verification witnesses are also contained in the witnesses artifact (see Table 4). The verifiers 2LS and UKOJAK are the winners in terms of confirmed results for expected results TRUE and FALSE, respectively. The overall interpretation is similar to SV-COMP 2020 [17].

5   Conclusion

The 10th edition of the Competition on Software Verification (SV-COMP 2021) had 30 participating verification systems from 11 countries (see Fig. 5 for the participation numbers and Table 5 for the details). The competition does not only execute the verifiers and collect results, but also validates the verification results using verification witnesses. We used six independent validators to check the results and a witness linter to check if the verification witnesses are syntactically valid (Table 1). The number of verification tasks was increased to 15 201 in the C category and to 473 in the Java category. The high quality standards of the TACAS conference, in particular with respect to the important principles of fairness, community support, and transparency are ensured by a competition jury in which each participating team had a member. The results of our comparative evaluation provide a broad overview of the state of the art in automatic software verification. SV-COMP is instrumental in developing more reliable tools, as well as identifying and propagating successful techniques for software verification.

Data Availability Statement. The verification tasks and results of the competition are published at Zenodo, as described in Table 4. All components and data that are necessary for reproducing the competition are available in public version repositories, as specified in Table 3. Furthermore, the results are presented online on the competition web site for easy access: https://sv-comp.sosy-lab.org/2021/results/.

References

1. Ádám, Zs., Sallai, Gy., Hajdu, Á.: GAZER-THETA: LLVM-based verifier portfolio with BMC/CEGAR (competition contribution). In: Proc. TACAS (2). LNCS 12652, Springer (2021). https://doi.org/10.1007/978-3-030-72013-1_27
2. Afzal, M., Asia, A., Chauhan, A., Chimdyalwar, B., Darke, P., Datar, A., Kumar, S., Venkatesh, R.: VERIABS: Verification by abstraction and test generation. In: Proc. ASE. pp. 1138–1141 (2019). https://doi.org/10.1109/ASE.2019.00121
3. American National Standards Institute: ANSI/ISO/IEC 9899-1999: Programming Languages — C. American National Standards Institute, 1430 Broadway, New York, NY 10018, USA (1999)
4. Andrianov, P., Friedberger, K., Mandrykin, M.U., Mutilin, V.S., Volkov, A.: CPA-BAM-BNB: Block-abstraction memoization and region-based memory models for predicate abstractions (competition contribution). In: Proc. TACAS. pp. 355–359. LNCS 10206, Springer (2017). https://doi.org/10.1007/978-3-662-54580-5_22
5. Andrianov, P., Mutilin, V., Khoroshilov, A.: CPALOCKATOR: Thread-modular approach with projections (competition contribution). In: Proc. TACAS (2). LNCS 12652, Springer (2021). https://doi.org/10.1007/978-3-030-72013-1_25
6. Andrianov, P.S.: Analysis of correct synchronization of operating system components. Program. Comput. Softw. **46**, 712–730 (2020). https://doi.org/10.1134/S0361768820080022
7. Balyo, T., Heule, M.J.H., Järvisalo, M.: SAT Competition 2016: Recent developments. In: Proc. AAAI. pp. 5061–5063. AAAI Press (2017)
8. Baranová, Z., Barnat, J., Kejstová, K., Kučera, T., Lauko, H., Mrázek, J., Ročkai, P., Štill, V.: Model checking of C and C++ with DIVINE 4. In: Proc. ATVA. pp. 201–207. LNCS 10482, Springer (2017). https://doi.org/10.1007/978-3-319-68167-2_14
9. Bartocci, E., Beyer, D., Black, P.E., Fedyukovich, G., Garavel, H., Hartmanns, A., Huisman, M., Kordon, F., Nagele, J., Sighireanu, M., Steffen, B., Suda, M., Sutcliffe, G., Weber, T., Yamada, A.: TOOLympics 2019: An overview of competitions in formal methods. In: Proc. TACAS (3). pp. 3–24. LNCS 11429, Springer (2019). https://doi.org/10.1007/978-3-030-17502-3_1
10. Beyer, D.: Competition on software verification (SV-COMP). In: Proc. TACAS. pp. 504–524. LNCS 7214, Springer (2012). https://doi.org/10.1007/978-3-642-28756-5_38
11. Beyer, D.: Second competition on software verification (Summary of SV-COMP 2013). In: Proc. TACAS. pp. 594–609. LNCS 7795, Springer (2013). https://doi.org/10.1007/978-3-642-36742-7_43
12. Beyer, D.: Status report on software verification (Competition summary SV-COMP 2014). In: Proc. TACAS. pp. 373–388. LNCS 8413, Springer (2014). https://doi.org/10.1007/978-3-642-54862-8_25
13. Beyer, D.: Software verification and verifiable witnesses (Report on SV-COMP 2015). In: Proc. TACAS. pp. 401–416. LNCS 9035, Springer (2015). https://doi.org/10.1007/978-3-662-46681-0_31
14. Beyer, D.: Reliable and reproducible competition results with BENCHEXEC and witnesses (Report on SV-COMP 2016). In: Proc. TACAS. pp. 887–904. LNCS 9636, Springer (2016). https://doi.org/10.1007/978-3-662-49674-9_55
15. Beyer, D.: Software verification with validation of results (Report on SV-COMP 2017). In: Proc. TACAS. pp. 331–349. LNCS 10206, Springer (2017). https://doi.org/10.1007/978-3-662-54580-5_20

16. Beyer, D.: Automatic verification of C and Java programs: SV-COMP 2019. In: Proc. TACAS (3). pp. 133–155. LNCS 11429, Springer (2019). https://doi.org/10.1007/978-3-030-17502-3_9

17. Beyer, D.: Advances in automatic software verification: SV-COMP 2020. In: Proc. TACAS (2). pp. 347–367. LNCS 12079, Springer (2020). https://doi.org/10.1007/978-3-030-45237-7_21

18. Beyer, D.: Results of the 10th Intl. Competition on Software Verification (SV-COMP 2021). Zenodo (2021). https://doi.org/10.5281/zenodo.4458215

19. Beyer, D.: Status report on software testing: Test-Comp 2021. In: Proc. FASE. LNCS 12649, Springer (2021). https://doi.org/10.1007/978-3-030-71500-7_17

20. Beyer, D.: SV-Benchmarks: Benchmark set of 10th Intl. Competition on Software Verification (SV-COMP 2021). Zenodo (2021). https://doi.org/10.5281/zenodo.4459126

21. Beyer, D.: Verification witnesses from SV-COMP 2021 verification tools. Zenodo (2021). https://doi.org/10.5281/zenodo.4459196

22. Beyer, D., Dangl, M., Dietsch, D., Heizmann, M.: Correctness witnesses: Exchanging verification results between verifiers. In: Proc. FSE. pp. 326–337. ACM (2016). https://doi.org/10.1145/2950290.2950351

23. Beyer, D., Dangl, M., Dietsch, D., Heizmann, M., Stahlbauer, A.: Witness validation and stepwise testification across software verifiers. In: Proc. FSE. pp. 721–733. ACM (2015). https://doi.org/10.1145/2786805.2786867

24. Beyer, D., Dangl, M., Lemberger, T., Tautschnig, M.: Tests from witnesses: Execution-based validation of verification results. In: Proc. TAP. pp. 3–23. LNCS 10889, Springer (2018). https://doi.org/10.1007/978-3-319-92994-1_1

25. Beyer, D., Friedberger, K.: Violation witnesses and result validation for multi-threaded programs. In: Proc. ISoLA (1). pp. 449–470. LNCS 12476, Springer (2020). https://doi.org/10.1007/978-3-030-61362-4_26

26. Beyer, D., Kanav, S.: COVERITEAM: On-demand composition of cooperative verification systems. unpublished manuscript (2021)

27. Beyer, D., Keremoglu, M.E.: CPACHECKER: A tool for configurable software verification. In: Proc. CAV. pp. 184–190. LNCS 6806, Springer (2011). https://doi.org/10.1007/978-3-642-22110-1_16

28. Beyer, D., Löwe, S., Wendler, P.: Reliable benchmarking: Requirements and solutions. Int. J. Softw. Tools Technol. Transfer $21(1)$, 1–29 (2019). https://doi.org/10.1007/s10009-017-0469-y

29. Beyer, D., Spiessl, M.: METAVAL: Witness validation via verification. In: Proc. CAV. pp. 165–177. LNCS 12225, Springer (2020). https://doi.org/10.1007/978-3-030-53291-8_10

30. Beyer, D., Wendler, P.: CPU ENERGY METER: A tool for energy-aware algorithms engineering. In: Proc. TACAS (2). pp. 126–133. LNCS 12079, Springer (2020). https://doi.org/10.1007/978-3-030-45237-7_8

31. Black, P.E.: JULIET 1.3 TEST SUITE: Changes from 1.2. Tech. Rep. NIST TN - 1995, NIST (June 2018). https://doi.org/10.6028/NIST.TN.1995

32. Brain, M., Joshi, S., Kröning, D., Schrammel, P.: Safety verification and refutation by k-invariants and k-induction. In: Proc. SAS. pp. 145–161. LNCS 9291, Springer (2015). https://doi.org/10.1007/978-3-662-48288-9_9

33. Chalupa, M., Jašek, T., Novák, J., Řechtáčková, A., Šoková, V., Strejček, J.: SYMBIOTIC 8: Beyond symbolic execution (competition contribution). In: Proc. TACAS (2). LNCS 12652, Springer (2021). https://doi.org/10.1007/978-3-030-72013-1_31

34. Chalupa, M., Strejček, J., Vitovská, M.: Joint forces for memory safety checking. In: Proc. SPIN. pp. 115–132. Springer (2018). https://doi.org/10.1007/978-3-319-94111-0_7
35. Chaudhary, E., Joshi, S.: PINAKA: Symbolic execution meets incremental solving (competition contribution). In: Proc. TACAS (3). pp. 234–238. LNCS 11429, Springer (2019). https://doi.org/10.1007/978-3-030-17502-3_20
36. Cordeiro, L.C., Fischer, B.: Verifying multi-threaded software using SMT-based context-bounded model checking. In: Proc. ICSE. pp. 331–340. ACM (2011). https://doi.org/10.1145/1985793.1985839
37. Cordeiro, L.C., Kesseli, P., Kröning, D., Schrammel, P., Trtík, M.: JBMC: A bounded model checking tool for verifying Java bytecode. In: Proc. CAV. pp. 183–190. LNCS 10981, Springer (2018). https://doi.org/10.1007/978-3-319-96145-3_10
38. Cordeiro, L.C., Kröning, D., Schrammel, P.: JBMC: Bounded model checking for Java bytecode (competition contribution). In: Proc. TACAS (3). pp. 219–223. LNCS 11429, Springer (2019). https://doi.org/10.1007/978-3-030-17502-3_17
39. Cordeiro, L.C., Morse, J., Nicole, D., Fischer, B.: Context-bounded model checking with ESBMC 1.17 (competition contribution). In: Proc. TACAS. pp. 534–537. LNCS 7214, Springer (2012). https://doi.org/10.1007/978-3-642-28756-5_42
40. Cuoq, P., Kirchner, F., Kosmatov, N., Prevosto, V., Signoles, J., Yakobowski, B.: Frama-C. In: Proc. SEFM. pp. 233–247. Springer (2012). https://doi.org/10.1007/978-3-642-33826-7_16
41. Dangl, M., Löwe, S., Wendler, P.: CPACHECKER with support for recursive programs and floating-point arithmetic (competition contribution). In: Proc. TACAS. pp. 423–425. LNCS 9035, Springer (2015). https://doi.org/10.1007/978-3-662-46681-0_34
42. Darke, P., Agrawal, S., Venkatesh, R.: VERIABS: A tool for scalable verification by abstraction (competition contribution). In: Proc. TACAS (2). LNCS 12652, Springer (2021). https://doi.org/10.1007/978-3-030-72013-1_32
43. Dietsch, D., Heizmann, M., Nutz, A., Schätzle, C., Schüssele, F.: ULTIMATE TAIPAN with symbolic interpretation and fluid abstractions (competition contribution). In: Proc. TACAS (2). pp. 418–422. LNCS 12079, Springer (2020). https://doi.org/10.1007/978-3-030-45237-7_32
44. Ermis, E., Hoenicke, J., Podelski, A.: Splitting via interpolants. In: Proc. VMCAI. pp. 186–201. LNCS 7148, Springer (2012). https://doi.org/10.1007/978-3-642-27940-9_13
45. Ernst, G.: A complete approach to loop verification with invariants and summaries. Tech. Rep. arXiv:2010.05812v2, arXiv (January 2020)
46. Gadelha, M.Y.R., Monteiro, F.R., Cordeiro, L.C., Nicole, D.A.: ESBMC v6.0: Verifying C programs using k-induction and invariant inference (competition contribution). In: Proc. TACAS (3). pp. 209–213. LNCS 11429, Springer (2019). https://doi.org/10.1007/978-3-030-17502-3_15
47. Gadelha, M.Y., Ismail, H.I., Cordeiro, L.C.: Handling loops in bounded model checking of C programs via k-induction. Int. J. Softw. Tools Technol. Transf. 19(1), 97–114 (Feb 2017). https://doi.org/10.1007/s10009-015-0407-9
48. Gavrilenko, N., Ponce de León, H., Furbach, F., Heljanko, K., Meyer, R.: BMC for weak memory models: Relation analysis for compact SMT encodings. In: Proc. CAV. pp. 355–365. LNCS 11561, Springer (2019). https://doi.org/10.1007/978-3-030-25540-4_19
49. Greitschus, M., Dietsch, D., Podelski, A.: Loop invariants from counterexamples. In: Proc. SAS. pp. 128–147. LNCS 10422, Springer (2017). https://doi.org/10.1007/978-3-319-66706-5_7

50. Hajdu, Á., Micskei, Z.: Efficient strategies for CEGAR-based model checking. J. Autom. Reasoning **64**(6), 1051–1091 (2020). https://doi.org/10.1007/s10817-019-09535-x

51. Haran, A., Carter, M., Emmi, M., Lal, A., Qadeer, S., Rakamarić, Z.: SMACK+Corral: A modular verifier (competition contribution). In: Proc. TACAS. pp. 451–454. LNCS 9035, Springer (2015). https://doi.org/10.1007/978-3-662-46681-0_42

52. Heizmann, M., Chen, Y.F., Dietsch, D., Greitschus, M., Hoenicke, J., Li, Y., Nutz, A., Musa, B., Schilling, C., Schindler, T., Podelski, A.: ULTIMATE AUTOMIZER and the search for perfect interpolants (competition contribution). In: Proc. TACAS (2). pp. 447–451. LNCS 10806, Springer (2018). https://doi.org/10.1007/978-3-319-89963-3_30

53. Heizmann, M., Hoenicke, J., Podelski, A.: Software model checking for people who love automata. In: Proc. CAV. pp. 36–52. LNCS 8044, Springer (2013). https://doi.org/10.1007/978-3-642-39799-8_2

54. Holík, L., Kotoun, M., Peringer, P., Šoková, V., Trtík, M., Vojnar, T.: PREDATOR shape analysis tool suite. In: Hardware and Software: Verification and Testing. pp. 202–209. LNCS 10028, Springer (2016). https://doi.org/10.1007/978-3-319-49052-6

55. Howar, F., Isberner, M., Merten, M., Steffen, B., Beyer, D.: The RERS grey-box challenge 2012: Analysis of event-condition-action systems. In: Proc. ISoLA. pp. 608–614. LNCS 7609, Springer (2012). https://doi.org/10.1007/978-3-642-34026-0_45

56. Huisman, M., Klebanov, V., Monahan, R.: VerifyThis 2012: A program verification competition. STTT **17**(6), 647–657 (2015). https://doi.org/10.1007/s10009-015-0396-8

57. Inverso, O., Tomasco, E., Fischer, B., La Torre, S., Parlato, G.: Lazy-CSeq: A lazy sequentialization tool for C (competition contribution). In: Proc. TACAS. pp. 398–401. LNCS 8413, Springer (2014). https://doi.org/10.1007/978-3-642-54862-8_29

58. Inverso, O., Tomasco, E., Fischer, B., La Torre, S., Parlato, G.: Bounded model checking of multi-threaded C programs via lazy sequentialization. In: Proc. CAV. pp. 585–602. LNCS 8559, Springer (2014). https://doi.org/10.1007/978-3-319-08867-9_39

59. Kahsai, T., Rümmer, P., Sanchez, H., Schäf, M.: JAYHORN: A framework for verifying Java programs. In: Proc. CAV. pp. 352–358. LNCS 9779, Springer (2016). https://doi.org/10.1007/978-3-319-41528-4_19

60. Kröning, D., Tautschnig, M.: CBMC: C bounded model checker (competition contribution). In: Proc. TACAS. pp. 389–391. LNCS 8413, Springer (2014). https://doi.org/10.1007/978-3-642-54862-8_26

61. Lauko, H., Ročkai, P., Barnat, J.: Symbolic computation via program transformation. In: Proc. ICTAC. pp. 313–332. Springer (2018). https://doi.org/10.1007/978-3-030-02508-3_17

62. Luckow, K.S., Dimjasevic, M., Giannakopoulou, D., Howar, F., Isberner, M., Kahsai, T., Rakamaric, Z., Raman, V.: JDART: A dynamic symbolic analysis framework. In: Proc. TACAS. pp. 442–459. LNCSS 9636, Springer (2016). https://doi.org/10.1007/978-3-662-49674-9_26

63. Malík, V., Schrammel, P., Vojnar, T.: 2LS: Heap analysis and memory safety (competition contribution). In: Proc. TACAS (2). pp. 368–372. LNCS 12079, Springer (2020). https://doi.org/10.1007/978-3-030-45237-7_22

64. Mues, M., Howar, F.: JDART: Portfolio solving, breadth-first search and smt-lib strings (competition contribution). In: Proc. TACAS (2). LNCS 12652, Springer (2021). https://doi.org/10.1007/978-3-030-72013-1_30

65. Noller, Y., Păsăreanu, C.S., Le, X.B.D., Visser, W., Fromherz, A.: Symbolic PATHFINDER for SV-COMP (competition contribution). In: Proc. TACAS (3). pp. 239–243. LNCS 11429, Springer (2019). https://doi.org/10.1007/978-3-030-17502-3_21

66. Nutz, A., Dietsch, D., Mohamed, M.M., Podelski, A.: ULTIMATE KOJAK with memory safety checks (competition contribution). In: Proc. TACAS. pp. 458–460. LNCS 9035, Springer (2015). https://doi.org/10.1007/978-3-662-46681-0_44

67. Peringer, P., Šoková, V., Vojnar, T.: PREDATORHP revamped (not only) for interval-sized memory regions and memory reallocation (competition contribution). In: Proc. TACAS (2). pp. 408–412. LNCS 12079, Springer (2020). https://doi.org/10.1007/978-3-030-45237-7_30

68. Ponce-De-Leon, H., Haas, T., Meyer, R.: DARTAGNAN: Leveraging compiler optimizations and the price of precision (competition contribution). In: Proc. TACAS (2). LNCS 12652, Springer (2021). https://doi.org/10.1007/978-3-030-72013-1_26

69. Păsăreanu, C.S., Visser, W., Bushnell, D.H., Geldenhuys, J., Mehlitz, P.C., Rungta, N.: Symbolic PATHFINDER: integrating symbolic execution with model checking for Java bytecode analysis. Autom. Software Eng. 20(3), 391–425 (2013). https://doi.org/10.1007/s10515-013-0122-2

70. Rakamarić, Z., Emmi, M.: SMACK: Decoupling source language details from verifier implementations. In: Proc. CAV. pp. 106–113. LNCS 8559, Springer (2014). https://doi.org/10.1007/978-3-319-08867-9_7

71. Richter, C., Hüllermeier, E., Jakobs, M.C., Wehrheim, H.: Algorithm selection for software validation based on graph kernels. Autom. Softw. Eng. 27(1), 153–186 (2020). https://doi.org/10.1007/s10515-020-00270-x

72. Richter, C., Wehrheim, H.: PESCO: Predicting sequential combinations of verifiers (competition contribution). In: Proc. TACAS (3). pp. 229–233. LNCS 11429, Springer (2019). https://doi.org/10.1007/978-3-030-17502-3_19

73. Saan, S., Schwarz, M., Apinis, K., Erhard, J., Seidl, H., Vogler, R., Vojdani, V.: GOBLINT: Thread-modular abstract interpretation using side-effecting constraints (competition contribution). In: Proc. TACAS (2). LNCS 12652, Springer (2021). https://doi.org/10.1007/978-3-030-72013-1_28

74. Sallai, Gy.: LLVM IR-based Transformations for Software Model Checking. Master's thesis, Budapest University of Technology and Economics (2019)

75. Shamakhi, A., Hojjat, H., Rümmer, P.: Towards string support in JAYHORN (competition contribution). In: Proc. TACAS (2). LNCS 12652, Springer (2021). https://doi.org/10.1007/978-3-030-72013-1_29

76. Sharma, V., Hussein, S., Whalen, M.W., McCamant, S.A., Visser, W.: JAVA RANGER at SV-COMP 2020 (competition contribution). In: Proc. TACAS (2). pp. 393–397. LNCS 12079, Springer (2020). https://doi.org/10.1007/978-3-030-45237-7_27

77. Sharma, V., Hussein, S., Whalen, M.W., McCamant, S.A., Visser, W.: JAVA RANGER: Statically summarizing regions for efficient symbolic execution of Java. In: Proc. ESEC/FSE. pp. 123–134. ACM (2020). https://doi.org/10.1145/3368089.3409734

78. Svejda, J., Berger, P., Katoen, J.P.: Interpretation-based violation witness validation for C: NITWIT. In: Proc. TACAS. pp. 40–57. LNCS 12078, Springer (2020). https://doi.org/10.1007/978-3-030-45190-5_3

79. Visser, W., Geldenhuys, J.: COASTAL: Combining concolic and fuzzing for Java (competition contribution). In: Proc. TACAS (2). pp. 373–377. LNCS 12079, Springer (2020). https://doi.org/10.1007/978-3-030-45237-7_23

80. Vojdani, V., Apinis, K., Rõtov, V., Seidl, H., Vene, V., Vogler, R.: Static race detection for device drivers: The Goblint approach. In: Proc. ASE. pp. 391–402. ACM (2016). https://doi.org/10.1145/2970276.2970337

81. Volkov, A.R., Mandrykin, M.U.: Predicate abstractions memory modeling method with separation into disjoint regions. Proceedings of the Institute for System Programming (ISPRAS) **29**, 203–216 (2017). https://doi.org/10.15514/ISPRAS-2017-29(4)-13

82. Wendler, P., Beyer, D.: sosy-lab/benchexec: Release 3.6. Zenodo (2021). https://doi.org/10.5281/zenodo.4317433

83. Wetzler, N., Heule, M.J.H., Jr., W.A.H.: DRAT-TRIM: Efficient checking and trimming using expressive clausal proofs. In: Proc. SAT. pp. 422–429. LNCS 8561, Springer (2014). https://doi.org/10.1007/978-3-319-09284-3_31

CPALockator: **Thread-Modular Analysis with Projections**

(Competition Contribution)

Pavel Andrianov ✉*[1] ⓘ, Vadim Mutilin[1,3] ⓘ, and Alexey Khoroshilov[1,2,3,4] ⓘ

[1] Ivannikov Institute for System Programming of RAS, Moscow, Russia
[2] Lomonosov Moscow State University, Moscow, Russia
[3] Moscow Institute of Physics and Technology, Moscow, Russia
[4] Higher School of Economics, Moscow, Russia

Abstract. Our submission to SV-COMP'21 is based on the software verification framework CPACHECKER and implements the extension to the thread-modular approach. It considers every thread separately, but in a special environment which models thread interactions. The environment is expressed by projections of normal transitions in each thread. A projection contains a description of possible effects over shared data and synchronization primitives, as well as conditions of its application. Adjusting the precision of the projections, one can find a balance between the speed and the precision of the whole analysis.
Implementation on the top of the CPACHECKER framework allows combining our approach with existing algorithms and analyses. Evaluation on the sv-benchmarks confirms the scalability and soundness of the approach.

Keywords: Multithreading · Projection · Thread-modular approach

1 Verification Approach

The main challenge for verification of industrial multithreaded software is to consider a potential thread interaction efficiently. Our verification approach is based on the thread-modular technique [4,5]. The approach allows avoiding a cartesian product of thread states by considering each thread state separately. Thus, an abstract state is not a complete one anymore and represents only one thread in a partial abstract state. However, due to this, the analysis has no information about transitions in other threads, which are strongly required for the soundness of the analysis. Thus, to not lose soundness we have to take into account the influence of other threads to the considered thread. For that purpose, we compute a special representation of the environment, which consists of a set of thread transitions, so-called projected transitions, or *projections*. The projections may be more or less precise, which strongly affects the precision and speed of the whole analysis. Note, the projections are independent and thus, a correct

---

* Representing jury member, corresponding author: andrianov@ispras.ru

J. F. Groote and K. G. Larsen (Eds.): TACAS 2021, LNCS 12652, pp. 423–427, 2021.
https://doi.org/10.1007/978-3-030-72013-1_25

sequence is missed. Potentially, all projections may affect the other thread in any time. It is an overapproximation, leading to an imprecise analysis.

Let us explain, how we increase precision considering only *compatible* projections.

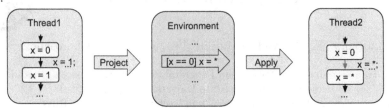

Fig. 1. Computation of a thread environment and its application

The figure 1 shows one step of the analysis. After computation of an abstract state in the first thread, we should spread the effect (x is a shared variable) to the other threads. Thus, we compute a *projection* of the operation. The projection is a part of the environment and affects the other threads through it. Then we *apply* a new effect to the other threads.

In the example, we lose the precision of the effect, abstracting from the assigned value ($x = *$). One of the key ideas of the proposed approach is to extend abstraction not only to states but also to operations, i.e. transitions. Thus, the projection may look like $x = 1$ and $* = *$ in other configurations. That allows adjusting the level of abstraction of the environment for a specific task. By adjusting the configuration it is possible to vary not only an abstraction level but also to construct an algorithm that may be closer either to data-flow analysis or to software model checking.

To be able to construct precise analysis we suggest to encode not only abstract operations but also some conditions of its application, so-called *guards*. The guards are related to a predecessor abstract state, but they are not required to be equal to it. The guards store some information about variable values, locks, threads, or even abstract predicates. In the figure 1 the guard contains information about the initial value of the modified variable x ($x == 0$). A projection may be applied to a particular state if the guards allow it. We say, that the projection is *compatible* to an abstract state of the other thread. In our example the effect $x = *$ may be applied to the other thread only if the corresponding state does not contradict the condition $x == 0$.

More information about the approach and theoretical preliminaries can be found in [1]. Practical application of the theory to the Linux kernel drivers can be found in [2].

2   Software Architecture

CPALOCKATOR is based on the CPACHECKER framework and has the same software architecture. Its key concept is CPA [3]. Each abstract domain is implemented in its own CPA. CPAs in the framework, i.e. value analysis or predicate analysis, can be combined to build an efficient and more precise approach. A configurable algorithm, CEGAR in case of CPALOCKATOR, uses CPAs to construct a set of reachable states. In the figure 2 current configuration is presented. The highlighted components are implemented and used only in CPALockator. Lock analysis tracks acquired locks. It helps to compute thread effects that can be applied to a particular thread. Thread analysis determines whether two code blocks may be executed in parallel. Predicate analysis is extended to handle environment actions. It allows constructing a predicate abstraction in a thread-modular case. More information about CPALOCKATOR may be found in [1,2].

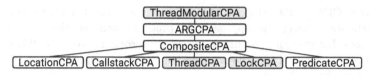

Fig. 2. Different CPAs in CPALockator configuration

3   Strengths and Weaknesses

First, we need to emphasize that the tool is targeted and used in practice for finding bugs in large industrial software systems, for example, operating system cores. We applied the tool to the Linux kernel and a number of private kernels of real-time OS. The main challenge is scalability there. And results on small but tricky sv-benchmarks look poor, just because of trade-off scalability vs. precision. Our tool is not so precise as other participants, but we show our scalability on a small set of complicated sv-benchmarks. However, it is useful for the community to have such comparison.

The thread-modular approach cannot solve tasks that contain control dependencies in the environment, as we consider all projections independently from each other and thus we lose their order. This is also a problem for witness validation, as the tool provides a path only in a single thread. It is a limitation of the approach, not only the tool itself. In practice we use more user-friendly format to analyze, visualize and evaluate error traces than witness validation [6]. However, the approach allows to simplify thread interaction, and the benefit is considerable for large complicated tasks, which cannot be analyzed with precise model checkers.

As the approach shows benefit for complicated tasks, like in *ldv-linux-3.14-races* directory. CPALOCKATOR correctly solves 4 of 7 those benchmarks and for one more obtains an imprecise counterexample. The rest of two tasks may be solved in the other, more faster, CPALOCKATOR configuration. The other tools mostly have problems with the benchmarks due to their complexity and size. The explanation of the results is rather evident. Most of the tools try to consider precise interaction between threads, while CPALOCKATOR abstracts from it and considers each thread separately. Note, the benchmarks have a strong hint for verifiers: there is only one assert to check while in the real world nobody knows where the bug may be located.

Overall results are not so good because of problems related both to the approach itself and its implementation. The majority of unknowns are related to unsupported atomic operations, like _atomic_ functions, *compare_and_swap* and so on. Currently, our tool supports only synchronization operations based on locks, as the industrial software mostly contains them. Another problem is related to predicate analysis and interpolation. The current implementation of an interpolation procedure cannot produce interpolants for other threads, which limits the power of predicate analysis. Other problems are also present, but they are not so significant.

Anyway, CPALOCKATOR does not produce incorrect **true** verdicts, which confirms the soundness of the approach. All produced **true** verdicts are confirmed by validators, however, its amount is not so numerous, as we skip all tasks with unsupported functions. Thus, the presented approach may be used in combination with more precise techniques.

4   Tool Setup and Configuration

We submitted CPALOCKATOR[5] built from svn revision **36155** for participation in the category *Concurrency*. The tool requires a Java 11 runtime environment. CPACHECKER has to be executed with the following command line:

```
scripts/cpa.sh -svcomp21-lockator -spec reach.prp program.i
```

or via **BenchExec** tool.

5   Project and Contributors

The CPACHECKER project is mainly developed by an international research group from the Ludwig-Maximilian University of Munich. CPALOCKATOR is based on CPACHECKER and is developed and supported by researchers from Ivannikov Institute for System Programming of the Russian Academy of Sciences. We thank Dirk Beyer and the CPACHECKER team for their work and fruitful discussions.

References

1. Andrianov, P.: Analysis of correct synchronization of operating system components. Programming and Computer Software **46**, 712–730 (2020)
2. Andrianov, P., Mutilin, V.: Scalable thread-modular approach for data race detection. In: Bruel, J.M., et al. (eds.) Frontiers in Software Engineering Education. pp. 371–385. Springer, Cham (2020)
3. Beyer, D., Henzinger, T.A., Théoduloz, G.: Configurable software verification: concretizing the convergence of model checking and program analysis. In: Proceedings of CAV. pp. 504–518. Springer (2007)
4. Gupta, A., Popeea, C., Rybalchenko, A.: Threader: A constraint-based verifier for multi-threaded programs. In: Proceedings of CAV. pp. 412–417. Springer (2011)

---

[5] https://doi.org/10.5281/zenodo.4486117

5. Henzinger, T.A., Jhala, R., Majumdar, R., Qadeer, S.: Thread-modular abstraction refinement. In: Proceedings of CAV. pp. 262–274. Springer (2003)
6. Novikov, E., Zakharov, I.: Verification of operating system monolithic kernels without extensions. In: Margaria, T., Steffen, B. (eds.) Leveraging Applications of Formal Methods, Verification and Validation. Industrial Practice. pp. 230–248 (2018)

DARTAGNAN: Leveraging Compiler Optimizations and the Price of Precision (Competition Contribution)

Hernán Ponce-de-León[1]*✉, Thomas Haas[2], and Roland Meyer[2]

[1]Bundeswehr University Munich, Munich, Germany
[2]TU Braunschweig, Braunschweig, Germany
hernan.ponce@unibw.de, t.haas@tu-braunschweig.de, roland.meyer@tu-bs.de

Abstract. We describe the new features of the bounded model checker DARTAGNAN for SV-COMP'21. We participate, for the first time, in the *ReachSafety* category on the verification of sequential programs. In some of these verification tasks, bugs only show up after many loop iterations, which is a challenge for bounded model checking. We address the challenge by simplifying the structure of the input program while preserving its semantics. For simplification, we leverage common compiler optimizations, which we get for free by using LLVM. Yet, there is a price to pay. Compiler optimizations may introduce bitwise operations, which require bit-precise reasoning. We evaluated an SMT encoding based on the theory of integers + bit conversions against one based on the theory of bit-vectors and found that the latter yields better performance. Compared to the unoptimized version of DARTAGNAN, the combination of compiler optimizations and bit-vectors yields a speed-up of an order of magnitude on average.

1 Overview

DARTAGNAN is a bounded model checking (BMC) tool for reachability analysis. It takes a program and converts it to an SMT formula representing all its executions up to a given bound. This formula, together with a reachability condition representing assertions, is passed to an SMT solver (we use Z3 as a backend). If the formula is satisfiable, an execution violating an assertion exists.

DARTAGNAN was initially developed to verify small concurrent programs (written in the .litmus format) under weak memory models. Since 2020, it also supports Boogie *intermediate verification language* as its input language. For C programs, we use SMACK [8] to compile to LLVM and transform the compiled code to Boogie. DARTAGNAN's architecture, and main verification techniques (in particular how to efficiently handle different memory models) are described in [3,4,7]. Version 2.0.7 participating in SV-COMP'21 [1] can be downloaded from https://github.com/hernanponcedeleon/Dat3M directly as a java archive (.jar) or built from source code using the Maven build system. DARTAGNAN's

---

* Jury member.

J. F. Groote and K. G. Larsen (Eds.): TACAS 2021, LNCS 12652, pp. 428–432, 2021.
https://doi.org/10.1007/978-3-030-72013-1_26

```
int main(void) {
  unsigned int x = 1;
  unsigned int y = 0;

  while (y < 1024) {
    x = 0;
    y++;
  }

  __VERIFIER_assert(x == 0);
}
```

Fig. 1. Benchmark `const_1-1.c` from the *ReachSafety-Loop* category.

verifier archive to reproduce the results of SV-COMP'21 is published at Zenodo under DOI 10.5281/zenodo.4483224.

Last year DARTAGNAN only participated in the *ConcurrencySafety* category. What is new for SV-COMP'21 is that DARTAGNAN also participates in (part of) the *ReachSafety* category for single threaded programs. Many tasks in that category contain loops of large bounds which impacts DARTAGNAN's performance. To address the problem, we propose to leverage compiler optimizations.

2 Leveraging Compiler Optimizations

BMC techniques are very sensitive to the program syntax. The loop structure and the number of variables directly impact the size of the SMT formula (which tends to relate to solving times). Our approach is to simplify the structure of the program (while preserving its semantics) before performing the verification. We do this by using compiler optimizations.

Consider the program in Fig. 1 from the *ReachSafety-Loop* category. A BMC tool has to unroll the program 1024 times to prove the program correct. However, since the value of x is constant at every loop iteration, the assignment can be moved outside the loop. Since the value of y is never read, the instruction y++ can be removed (using dead store elimination) leading to an empty loop which can also be removed. Finally, using constant propagation, the assertion can be re-written as `__VERIFIER_assert(0 == 0)` which is trivially true.

All these optimizations are implemented in most optimizing compilers. Since we perform the verification after compiling to LLVM, we get them for free. Due to the high number of loop iterations, DARTAGNAN needs more than 15 minutes to verify the program above. However, by using the -O3 optimization flag in the C-to-Boogie transformation, the verification task can be solved within seconds.

Using an optimizing compiler has its risks. Most optimizations are unsound for concurrent programs [9] and we do not use any for *ConcurrencySafety*. Even for sequential programs, there is a price to pay. Some optimizations introduce bitwise operations (e.g. multiplications tend to be compiled to shift operations) which were not present in the original program. We thus have to encode the semantics of such operations precisely.

3   The Price of Precision

To guarantee soundness when using the aforementioned compiler optimizations in the *ReachSafety* category, we use two precise encodings of integers. The first is a new implementation based on the theory of bit-vectors, where we get bit-precise reasoning for free. The second was our original implementation and it is based on the theory of integers. It does an *on-demand* conversion to bit-vectors and back (`Int2Bv` and `Bv2Int`). We are able to solve more benchmarks with the theory of bit-vectors than with the theory of integers plus conversion, which suggests that converting between the theories is expensive. For concurrent programs, the combination of bit-vectors with DARTAGNAN's memory-model-dependent encoding significantly degrades performance, and we use the theory of integers throughout the *ConcurrencySafety* category.

The trade-off between the efficiency of a theory and the precision in modeling semantics is well-known. In the context of symbolic execution, it was explored in [6]. SMACK implements an approach to diagnose spurious counterexamples caused by over-approximations and gradually refines the precision of reasoning about bitwise operations [5].

4   Evaluation

We evaluated how compiler optimizations and different integer encodings affect DARTAGNAN's verification capabilities for some benchmarks in the *ReachSafety* category. We support two levels of optimization: -O0 (no optimization) and -O3 (enables most optimizations). For integer encodings we use two different approaches: theory of integers + bit conversions (`QF_LIA` + `QF_BV` logics) and pure theory of bit-vectors (`QF_BV` logic).

The results are given in Fig. 2. We use BENCHEXEC [2] for reliable benchmarking. The graph shows the verification time w.r.t the verification score. Following the competition scheme, correct counter-examples and proofs give +1 and +2 points respectively. Wrong counter-examples and proofs give -16 and -32 points. The absolute score values for incorrect results are higher because a single correct answer should not compensate for a wrong answer.

It can be seen that, regardless of the chosen integer encoding, using compiler optimizations allows us to verify many more benchmarks, thus obtaining a higher score. The total number of solved tasks with no optimizations (`O0+Bit-vectors` and `O0+Int-exact` configurations from Fig. 2) is 89 with 77 correct and 12 incorrect results. When using optimizations (`O3+Bit-vectors` and `O3+Int-exact` configurations), we solved 336 tasks with 326 correct and 10 incorrect results.

The experiments show that combining theories to achieve precision is more expensive than using pure bit-vectors. The total number of solved tasks when using `QF_LIA` + `QF_BV` (configurations `O0+Int-exact` and `O3+Int-exact`) is 201

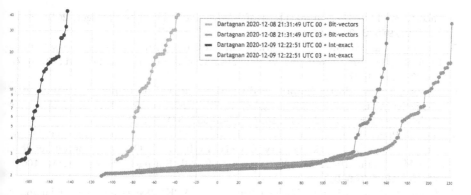

Fig. 2. Comparing the performance of DARTAGNAN with different optimization flags and integer encodings.

with 187 correct and 14 incorrect results. When using `QF_BV` (configurations `O0+Bit-vectors` and `O3+Bit-vectors`) we solved 224 tasks with 216 correct and 8 incorrect results. All encodings are guaranteed to be sound, the incorrect results are due to bugs in the verifier.

We used the evaluation described above to decide the configuration for SV-COMP'21. For category *ConcurrencySafety*, we use the integer encoding and no compiler optimizations. For categories *ReachSafety-Loop*, *ReachSafety-BitVectors* and *ReachSafety-Arrays*, DARTAGNAN uses the theory of bit-vectors and -O3 optimizations. These configurations are internally decided by the tool based on the use of the pthreads library. Compared with SV-COMP'20, we solved 60 more tasks in *ConcurrencySafety* (55% increase) and 474 more tasks overall (582% increase).

Acknowledgement: We thank the SMACK developers for their constant support with the C-to-Boogie transformation. We also thank Yun Zhang for her contributions to the development of the witness generation.

References

1. D. Beyer. Software verification: 10th comparative evaluation (SV-COMP 2021). In *Proc. TACAS (2)*, LNCS 12652. Springer, 2021.
2. Dirk Beyer, Stefan Löwe, and Philipp Wendler. Reliable benchmarking: requirements and solutions. *STTT*, 21(1):1–29, 2019. doi:10.1007/s10009-017-0469-y.
3. Hernán Ponce de León, Florian Furbach, Keijo Heljanko, and Roland Meyer. Dartagnan: Bounded model checking for weak memory models (competition contribution). In *TACAS (2)*, volume 12079 of *LNCS*, pages 378–382. Springer, 2020. doi:10.1007/978-3-030-45237-7_24.
4. Natalia Gavrilenko, Hernán Ponce de León, Florian Furbach, Keijo Heljanko, and Roland Meyer. BMC for weak memory models: Relation analysis for compact SMT

encodings. In *CAV*, volume 11561 of *LNCS*, pages 355–365. Springer, 2019. `doi: 10.1007/978-3-030-25540-4_19`.

5. Shaobo He and Zvonimir Rakamaric. Counterexample-guided bit-precision selection. In *APLAS*, volume 10695 of *LNCS*, pages 534–553. Springer, 2017. `doi:10.1007/978-3-319-71237-6_26`.

6. Timotej Kapus, Martin Nowack, and Cristian Cadar. Constraints in dynamic symbolic execution: Bitvectors or integers? In *TAP@FM*, volume 11823 of *LNCS*, pages 41–54. Springer, 2019. `doi:10.1007/978-3-030-31157-5_3`.

7. Hernán Ponce de León, Florian Furbach, Keijo Heljanko, and Roland Meyer. Portability analysis for weak memory models. PORTHOS: One tool for all models. In *SAS*, volume 10422 of *LNCS*, pages 299–320. Springer, 2017. `doi:10.1007/978-3-319-66706-5_15`.

8. Zvonimir Rakamaric and Michael Emmi. SMACK: Decoupling source language details from verifier implementations. In *CAV*, volume 8559 of *LNCS*, pages 106–113. Springer, 2014. `doi:10.1007/978-3-319-08867-9_7`.

9. Viktor Vafeiadis, Thibaut Balabonski, Soham Chakraborty, Robin Morisset, and Francesco Zappa Nardelli. Common compiler optimisations are invalid in the C11 memory model and what we can do about it. In *POPL*, pages 209–220. ACM, 2015. `doi:10.1145/2676726.2676995`.

Gazer-Theta: LLVM-based Verifier Portfolio with BMC/CEGAR (Competition Contribution)

Zsófia Ádám[1], Gyula Sallai[2], and Ákos Hajdu[1]*(✉)

[1] Budapest University of Technology and Economics, Budapest, Hungary
hajdua@mit.bme.hu
[2] SonarSource S.A., Geneva, Switzerland

Abstract. GAZER-THETA is a software model checking toolchain including various analyses for state reachability. The frontend, namely GAZER, supports C programs through an LLVM-based transformation and optimization pipeline. GAZER includes an integrated bounded model checker (BMC) and can also employ the THETA backend, a generic verification framework based on abstraction-refinement (CEGAR). On SV-COMP 2021, a portfolio of BMC, explicit-value analysis, and predicate abstraction is applied sequentially in this order.

1 Verification Approach and Software Architecture

GAZER-THETA is a software model checking toolchain with two main components: GAZER, an LLVM-based frontend and THETA, a generic model checking framework. An overview of the architecture and the verification approach can be seen in Figure 1.

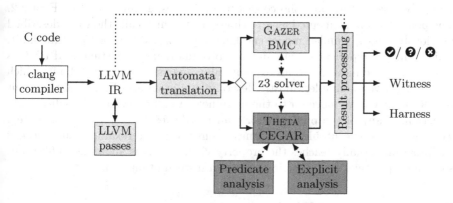

Fig. 1. Overview of the architecture. Solid arrows represent the workflow, dashed arrows indicate dependency. GAZER and THETA components are denoted by lighter and darker backgrounds, respectively.

---

* Jury member representing GAZER-THETA at SV-COMP 2021.

© The Author(s) 2021
J. F. Groote and K. G. Larsen (Eds.): TACAS 2021, LNCS 12652, pp. 433–437, 2021.
https://doi.org/10.1007/978-3-030-72013-1_27

Gazer. GAZER [7] is a verification frontend for C programs written in C++17, using the LLVM compiler infrastructure.[3] The input is a C program (possibly consisting of multiple source files) that is first translated to the LLVM IR (intermediate representation) using the *clang* compiler. Next, various built-in and custom *LLVM passes* are executed to perform optimizations (e.g., inlining, constant propagation, assertion lifting) and transformations (e.g., adding traceability information) on the IR. The LLVM IR is then transformed into different variants of *control flow automata* (CFA), depending on the backend to be used. GAZER includes a built-in variant [5,7] of *bounded model checking* [2], relying on the Z3 SMT solver [6]. The other supported backend is THETA (to be presented below). Currently, both backends provide analysis for *reachability properties*.

In the final step, the "raw" results of the backends are processed to produce a verdict (safe, unsafe, unknown) and a witness. Currently, GAZER only supports violation witnesses, both in a user-friendly syntax and in the format of SV-COMP. Furthermore, GAZER is also capable of generating executable test harnesses that can be used, e.g., in a debugger to reach the property violation.

Theta. THETA [8] is a generic and modular model checking framework written in Java 11, providing abstraction- and CEGAR-based analyses [4] for various formalisms, including CFA. THETA is highly configurable, supporting different abstract domains (such as *explicit-value analysis* [1] or *predicate abstraction* [3]) and refinement strategies, mostly based on interpolation (using SMT solvers such as Z3 [6]). In the explicit-value analysis, only a subset of program variables is tracked, while predicate abstraction keeps track of logical facts and relationships instead of concrete values.

Verification portfolio. Based on our preliminary experiments, at SV-COMP 2021, we apply a sequential portfolio consisting of 3 steps, as illustrated by Figure 2. The portfolio is implemented as a Python script, which calls the tools described previously. First, bounded model checking is performed with a 150s time limit, which – in our experience – can already solve many unsafe instances. If BMC is inconclusive, we move on to an explicit-value analysis with a 100s limit, which can be effective for simpler, mostly deterministic programs. Finally, if the result is still unknown, we move on to the more heavyweight method of predicate abstraction. If any of the phases reports an unsafe result, as an additional step, we generate an executable test harness from the counterexample and check if the program actually reaches the property violation. This allows us to filter out some false positives (by reporting unknown instead of unsafe).

2   Strengths and Weaknesses

GAZER-THETA currently targets reachability analysis so we participate in the *ReachSafety* category, excluding subcategories *Arrays*, *Heap* and *Sequentialized*, due to features with limited support (e.g., pointers). The strength of the tool is

---

[3] https://llvm.org/

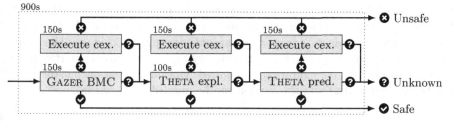

Fig. 2. Overview of the portfolio approach. Symbols ✔, ❓, ✖ indicate safe, inconclusive and unsafe results, respectively. Numbers indicate the time limit of each phase.

its modularity and configurability, combining the advantages of different analyses into a diverse portfolio. Out of the 3679 tasks, there are 1722 confirmed correct (1079 safe, 643 unsafe), 4 unconfirmed correct, and 13 incorrect (false positive) results. A majority of the solved tasks (86% of 1722) come from the BMC phase; with a few exceptions, the CEGAR analyses need to be utilized only for safe instances (though they could also handle most of the tasks solved by BMC based on our experiments). The explicit-value analysis handles further 100 tasks in the *ECA* subcategory, while predicate abstraction solves 130 additional instances from *Loops* and *ProductLines*. Surprisingly, BMC can actually solve a significant amount (857) of safe instances as well, which can be attributed to LLVM optimizations and enhancements in the algorithm [7]. Furthermore, we also observed that executable harnesses could rule out many (142) false positives.

The weakness of GAZER-THETA is its limited support for certain features, such as arrays, bit-precise reasoning (only available for BMC), and pointers. We also observed that the LLVM IR representation often results in large CFA (e.g., many temporary variables due to SSA form), which makes reasoning harder via CEGAR (as witnessed, e.g., by the *ECA* subcategory). Currently, the tool gives empty correctness witnesses only meeting syntactical requirements, but surprisingly most of them were accepted. Furthermore, our violation witnesses are quite "sparse" due to heavy usage of optimization passes, but some validators can still prove their correctness. The 13 false positive results are caused by unsupported library functions (related to floats) treated as external calls with undefined (arbitrary) behavior.

3 Tool Setup and Configuration

The competition contribution is based on GAZER v1.2.1[4] and THETA v2.5.0.[5] Additionally, the BMC backend of GAZER uses z3 version 4.8.6, while THETA is based on z3 version 4.5.0. The projects' repositories contain instructions on building the tools, but an archive can be found on Zenodo[6] with pre-built binaries

---

[4] https://github.com/ftsrg/gazer/releases/tag/v1.2.1
[5] https://github.com/ftsrg/theta/releases/tag/v2.5.0
[6] http://doi.org/10.5281/zenodo.4483627

for Ubuntu 18.04 or 20.04. The toolchain requires packages clang-9, libgomp1, llvm-9, openjdk-11-jre-headless and python3 to be installed. The entry point of the toolchain is scripts/gazer_starter.py, which takes the verification task (C program) as its only mandatory input and runs the portfolio. No other parameters or configuration is required. Optionally, the output directory can be set (--output) and the version can be queried (--version).

4   Software Project

GAZER and THETA are maintained by the Critical Systems Research Group[7] of the Budapest University of Technology and Economics with various contributors. The projects are available open-source on GitHub[8] under an Apache 2.0 license.

Acknowledgment. The authors would like to thank Tamás Tóth, László Radnai, Mihály Dobos-Kovács, István Majzik, Zoltán Micskei, András Vörös and Vince Molnár for their contributions to the projects; and the competition organizers, especially Dirk Beyer for their help during the preparation for SV-COMP.

This research has received funding from the EU ECSEL JU under the H2020 Framework Programme, JU grant nr. 826452 (Arrowhead Tools project) and from the partners' national funding authorities.

References

1. Beyer, D., Löwe, S.: Explicit-state software model checking based on CEGAR and interpolation. In: FASE 2013, LNCS, vol. 7793, pp. 146–162. Springer (2013). https://doi.org/10.1007/978-3-642-37057-1_11
2. Biere, A., Cimatti, A., Clarke, E.M., Zhu, Y.: Symbolic model checking without BDDs. In: TACAS 1999, LNCS, vol. 1579, pp. 193–207. Springer (1999). https://doi.org/10.1007/3-540-49059-0_14
3. Graf, S., Saidi, H.: Construction of abstract state graphs with PVS. In: CAV 1997, LNCS, vol. 1254, pp. 72–83. Springer (1997). https://doi.org/10.1007/3-540-63166-6_10
4. Hajdu, Á., Micskei, Z.: Efficient strategies for CEGAR-based model checking. Journal of Automated Reasoning **64**(6), 1051–1091 (2020). https://doi.org/10.1007/s10817-019-09535-x
5. Lal, A., Qadeer, S., Lahiri, S.: Corral: A solver for reachability modulo theories. In: CAV 2012. LNCS, vol. 7358, pp. 427–443. Springer (2012). https://doi.org/10.1007/978-3-642-31424-7_32
6. de Moura, L., Bjørner, N.: Z3: An efficient SMT solver. In: TACAS 2008, LNCS, vol. 4963, pp. 337–340. Springer (2008). https://doi.org/10.1007/978-3-540-78800-3_24
7. Sallai, Gy.: LLVM IR-based Transformations for Software Model Checking. Master's thesis, Budapest University of Technology and Economics (2019)
8. Tóth, T., Hajdu, Á., Vörös, A., Micskei, Z., Majzik, I.: Theta: a framework for abstraction refinement-based model checking. In: FMCAD 2017. pp. 176–179 (2017). https://doi.org/10.23919/FMCAD.2017.8102257

---

[7] https://ftsrg.mit.bme.hu
[8] https://github.com/ftsrg/gazer and https://github.com/ftsrg/theta

GOBLINT: Thread-Modular Abstract Interpretation Using Side-Effecting Constraints
(Competition Contribution)

Simmo Saan[1]([✉])*, Michael Schwarz[2]([✉]),
Kalmer Apinis[1], Julian Erhard[2], Helmut Seidl[2],
Ralf Vogler[2], and Vesal Vojdani[1]

[1] University of Tartu, Tartu, Estonia
{simmo.saan, kalmer.apinis, vesal.vojdani}@ut.ee
[2] Technische Universität München, Garching, Germany
{m.schwarz, julian.erhard, helmut.seidl, ralf.vogler}@tum.de

Abstract. GOBLINT is a static analysis framework for C programs specializing in data race analysis. It relies on thread-modular abstract interpretation where thread interferences are accounted for by means of flow-insensitive global invariants.

1 Verification Approach

GOBLINT is a static analyzer for C programs based on the framework of abstract interpretation [5]. It performs flow- and context-sensitive interprocedural analysis, using partial tabulation to handle procedure calls. The analysis of concurrent programs is thread-modular: analyzing each thread in isolation, as opposed to analyzing their interleavings. This scales well to larger programs with many threads. Interferences between threads happen through global variables, which are abstracted by a context- and flow-insensitive global invariant. When no other thread can interfere, copies of global variables are *privatized* within the local state. Their values may deviate from the global invariant due to local updates, thereby improving precision [11].

The analysis is specified using a side-effecting constraint system [3], in which right-hand sides of constraints can, during their evaluation, make additional contributions (*side effects*) to other constraint system variables. These side effects can be conveniently used both to express partial context-sensitivity of function calls and to add contributions to the global invariant. Such a constraint system is solved using a *local* generic solver, which yields a (post-)solution for just the reachable program points and contexts [1,8]. Solving is not strictly separated into widening and narrowing phases, but these may be intertwined instead [1]. Results of the analysis are reported only at the end based on the computed solution, as widening during the fixpoint computation might lead to spurious property violations, which later disappear due to narrowing.

---

* Jury member

J. F. Groote and K. G. Larsen (Eds.): TACAS 2021, LNCS 12652, pp. 438–442, 2021.
https://doi.org/10.1007/978-3-030-72013-1_28

Reachability Safety. Reachability is mainly determined using value analysis, which, for integers, employs abstract domains based on intervals and exclusion sets. The value analysis also handles pointers (computing points-to information), heap memory (using allocation-site abstraction), structs, unions and arrays. The abstraction of arrays employs partitioning by the symbolic expression that is used to index into the array. On top of that, both global variables and heap-allocated memory are partitioned into disjoint regions [9].

No Overflows. The sound interval analysis is implemented using arbitrary precision integers. If the interval for an expression lies completely in the value range of its signed integer type, no overflow can occur at this location.

No Data Race. The main goal of GOBLINT is data race detection and its analyses have been optimized for this purpose. Mutexes may be handled both path-sensitively and symbolically. Memory accesses are partitioned (e.g., by heap region [9]), while locking expressions and access expressions are correlated using address equalities (e.g., a domain of affine and Herbrand equalities [10]) in order to analyze more sophisticated locking patterns [11].

2 Software Architecture

GOBLINT is implemented in OCAML and uses an updated fork of CIL [6] as its parser frontend for the C language. Since the latter requires preprocessed code, GCC is executed for preprocessing the input, although this step should be unnecessary on the SV-COMP benchmarks. No other major libraries or external tools are required.

The architecture of GOBLINT [2] is designed to be modular. Analyses, which are defined by their abstract domains and transfer functions, can be activated via runtime configuration options. A flexible query system allows for communication between analyses. Together, the combined analyses and the control-flow graphs of the functions in the program provide the side-effecting constraint system, which is solved by some local generic solver. While a number of solvers are available, the improved top-down solver TD3 [8] was employed for SV-COMP 2021. Post-processing the solution yields results for the analysis.

3 Strengths and Weaknesses

Due to over-approximation, abstract interpretation as employed by GOBLINT can only determine whether the correctness specification *must hold* or *may be violated*, but not whether a concrete violating execution exists. Therefore, to avoid a large number of false alarms due to imprecision in SV-COMP, GOBLINT only reports results "true" and "unknown" respectively. This is a clear limitation of our approach, as all competing tools do report definite violations. The strength of our approach, on the other hand, is that it aims to be sound by design (up to out-of-scope features of the input program as, e.g., inline assembler). This is evidenced by the fact that GOBLINT does not produce any incorrect results in the competition.

GOBLINT performs best in the *SoftwareSystems* and *ReachSafety-Product-Lines* categories that consist of larger real-world programs, for which our approach is well suited. On the downside, our verifier performs poorly in reachability safety categories that contain smaller programs with intricate correctness conditions which our abstract domains cannot express.

Even though the support for checking overflows is very new in GOBLINT, it has some success in the *NoOverflows* category. Unfortunately, the tool has no success in *SoftwareSystems-*-NoOverflows*.

Although GOBLINT specializes in concurrency, it performs quite poorly in the *ConcurrencySafety* category. We believe this is because most benchmarks in the category require rather precise analysis of thread interleavings, which is not done in our thread-modular approach.

As GOBLINT has been optimized for data race detection, it unsurprisingly performs better in the *NoDataRace* demo category. It must be noted that the majority of benchmarks in the category were submitted from our own test suite, consisting of racy and race-free programs.

While the analyses can be fine-tuned via configuration options, the parameters are static and do not currently depend on the property nor the input program. A more granular and dynamic configuration system would allow increased precision, by enabling more expensive analyses where necessary, or decreased resource usage, by disabling unnecessary analyses, e.g., concurrency analyses on single-threaded programs. Furthermore, integrating counterexample-guided abstraction refinement (CEGAR) into our framework might allow GOBLINT to also report violations, while avoiding false alarms and gaining more precision.

4   Tool Setup and Configuration

GOBLINT version `svcomp21-0-g82e03b87` participated in SV-COMP 2021 [4,7]. It is available in both binary (Ubuntu 20.04) and source code form at our GitHub repository under the `svcomp21` tag.[3] The only runtime dependency is GCC. Instructions for building from source can be found in the README.

Both the tool-info module and the benchmark definition for SV-COMP are named `goblint`. They correspond to running the tool as follows:

```
./goblint --conf conf/svcomp21.json --sets ana.specification
property.prp input.c
```

GOBLINT participated in the following categories: *ReachSafety, ConcurrencySafety, NoOverflows, SoftwareSystems* (while opting-out from *SoftwareSystems-*-MemSafety*) and *NoDataRace* (demo category).

---

[3] https://github.com/goblint/analyzer/releases/tag/svcomp21

5   Software Project and Contributors

GOBLINT development takes place on GitHub,[4] while related publications are listed on its website.[5] It is an MIT-licensed joint project of the Technische Universität München (Chair of Formal Languages, Compiler Construction, Software Construction) and University of Tartu (Laboratory for Software Science).

Acknowledgements. This work was supported by Deutsche Forschungsgemeinschaft (DFG) – 378803395/2428 CONVEY and the Estonian Research Council grant PSG61. We would like to thank everyone who has contributed to GOBLINT over the years.

References

1. Amato, G., Scozzari, F., Seidl, H., Apinis, K., Vojdani, V.: Efficiently intertwining widening and narrowing. Science of Computer Programming **120**, 1–24 (May 2016). DOI: 10.1016/j.scico.2015.12.005
2. Apinis, K.: Frameworks for analyzing multi-threaded C. Ph.D. thesis, Technische Universität München (2014)
3. Apinis, K., Seidl, H., Vojdani, V.: Side-Effecting Constraint Systems: A Swiss Army Knife for Program Analysis. In: APLAS '12. pp. 157–172. Springer (2012). DOI: 10.1007/978-3-642-35182-2_12
4. Beyer, D.: Software Verification: 10th Comparative Evaluation (SV-COMP 2021). In: Proc. TACAS (2). LNCS 12652, Springer (2021)
5. Cousot, P., Cousot, R.: Abstract interpretation: a unified lattice model for static analysis of programs by construction or approximation of fixpoints. In: POPL '77. pp. 238–252 (1977). DOI: 10.1145/512950.512973
6. Necula, G.C., McPeak, S., Rahul, S.P., Weimer, W.: CIL: Intermediate language and tools for analysis and transformation of C programs. In: CC '02. pp. 213–228. Springer (2002). DOI: 10.1007/3-540-45937-5_16
7. Saan, S., Schwarz, M., Apinis, K., Erhard, J., Seidl, H., Vogler, R., Vojdani, V.: Goblint at SV-COMP 2021 (Dec 2020). DOI: 10.5281/zenodo.4485853
8. Seidl, H., Vogler, R.: Three improvements to the top-down solver. In: PPDP '18. pp. 1–14 (2018). DOI: 10.1145/3236950.3236967
9. Seidl, H., Vojdani, V.: Region Analysis for Race Detection. In: SAS '09. pp. 171–187. Springer (2009). DOI: 10.1007/978-3-642-03237-0_13
10. Seidl, H., Vojdani, V., Vene, V.: A Smooth Combination of Linear and Herbrand Equalities for Polynomial Time Must-Alias Analysis. In: FM '09. pp. 644–659. Springer (2009). DOI: 10.1007/978-3-642-05089-3_41
11. Vojdani, V., Apinis, K., Rõtov, V., Seidl, H., Vene, V., Vogler, R.: Static Race Detection for Device Drivers: The Goblint Approach. In: ASE 2016. pp. 391–402. ACM (2016). DOI: 10.1145/2970276.2970337

---

[4] https://github.com/goblint/analyzer
[5] https://goblint.in.tum.de

Towards String Support in **JayHorn**
(Competition Contribution)

Ali Shamakhi[1] (✉), Hossein Hojjat[1,2], and Philipp Rümmer[3]

[1] University of Tehran, Tehran, Iran
{ali.shamakhi,hojjat}@ut.ac.ir
[2] Tehran Institute for Advanced Studies, Tehran, Iran
[3] Uppsala University, Uppsala, Sweden
philipp.ruemmer@it.uu.se

Abstract. JayHorn is a Horn clause-based model checker for Java programs that has been competing at SV-COMP since 2019. An ongoing research and implementation effort is to add support for `String` data-type to JayHorn. Since current Horn solvers do not support strings natively, we consider a representation of (unbounded) strings using algebraic datatypes, more precisely as lists. This paper discusses Horn clause encodings of different string operations, and presents preliminary results.

1 The **JayHorn** Approach and Architecture

We start by summarising the approach used in JayHorn, and refer to earlier papers [5,6,7] for more details. JayHorn is a verification tool that encodes sequential Java programs as sets of Constrained Horn Clauses (CHCs) in order to check for possible assertion violations. The main CHC encoding in JayHorn is inspired by refinement types [2] and liquid types [8], and characterises programs in terms of *method contracts, state invariants,* and *instance invariants* of classes [5]. This encoding is over-approximate, and can prove absence of assertion violations. In order to find counterexamples, i.e., prove existence of violations, JayHorn also offers a bounded, under-approximate program encoding.

JayHorn is entirely implemented in Java, and uses the Soot framework [10] to process Java bytecode, and the CHC solver Eldarica [3] to solve Horn clauses.

2 Encoding of String Operations

In this paper, we focus on the handling of `Strings` and their operations, a feature of Java that was not previously supported by JayHorn. Since JayHorn verifies programs without imposing bounds on the number of execution steps or the size of input data, our goal is to handle also unbounded strings. Unfortunately, while there has been significant progress in SMT solving for strings, current CHC solvers do not yet support strings natively. We therefore use recursive algebraic data types to model strings, and follow the approach proposed in [4]: strings are represented using lists, with a binary constructor `cons` and the constant `nil`.

J. F. Groote and K. G. Larsen (Eds.): TACAS 2021, LNCS 12652, pp. 443–447, 2021.
https://doi.org/10.1007/978-3-030-72013-1_29

There are two ways to encode a string using cons and nil. The Left-To-Right (LTR) encoding starts with the leftmost character of the string. For example, "Jay" = cons('J', cons('a', cons('y', nil))). The Right-to-Left (RTL) encoding starts with the rightmost character. Each encoding has its own benefits and drawbacks in modeling various operations, an aspect we evaluate in this paper.

Three different LTR encodings of the concatenation operation are described in [4], and equivalent RTL encodings are easy to define. Moving beyond concatenation, in this paper we show models of some of the more involved operations.

2.1   The CompareTo Operation

The String.compareTo method in Java returns an integer, which is the difference of the length of strings if one of the strings is a prefix of the other (e.g., "cat".compareTo("c") == 2), or the difference of their leftmost same-index different characters otherwise (e.g., "card".compareTo("cash") == -1, since their leftmost same-index different characters are 'r' and 's', respectively).

The method is modeled using predicate $P_{rec}(left, right, comparison\_result)$ under LTR encoding, which allows us to recursively remove leftmost characters from both strings to reach a state which the $comparison\_result$ is known.

$$
\begin{aligned}
P_{rec}(x, \mathsf{nil}, \mathsf{len}(x)) &\leftarrow true \\
P_{rec}(\mathsf{nil}, y, -\mathsf{len}(y)) &\leftarrow true \\
P_{rec}(x, x, 0) &\leftarrow true \\
P_{rec}(\mathsf{cons}(j, x), \mathsf{cons}(k, y), j - k) &\leftarrow j \neq k \\
P_{rec}(\mathsf{cons}(h, x), \mathsf{cons}(h, y), d) &\leftarrow P_{rec}(x, y, d)
\end{aligned}
$$

The predicate under RTL encoding needs an extra argument to keep track of whether the $comparison\_result$ is based on character difference or not, so the predicate is $P'_{rec}(left, right, comparison\_result, char\_diff)$. The clauses use the len function to compute the length of a string, which is a built-in function in Eldarica.

$$
\begin{aligned}
P'_{rec}(x, \mathsf{nil}, \mathsf{len}(x), false) &\leftarrow true \\
P'_{rec}(\mathsf{nil}, y, -\mathsf{len}(y), false) &\leftarrow true \\
P'_{rec}(x, x, 0, false) &\leftarrow true \\
P'_{rec}(\mathsf{cons}(h, x), y, d + 1, false) &\leftarrow P'_{rec}(x, y, d, false) \wedge \mathsf{len}(x) \geq \mathsf{len}(y) \\
P'_{rec}(x, \mathsf{cons}(h, y), d - 1, false) &\leftarrow P'_{rec}(x, y, d, false) \wedge \mathsf{len}(x) \leq \mathsf{len}(y) \\
P'_{rec}(\mathsf{cons}(j, x), \mathsf{cons}(k, x), j - k, true) &\leftarrow j \neq k \\
P'_{rec}(\mathsf{cons}(h, x), y, d, true) &\leftarrow P'_{rec}(x, y, d, true) \\
P'_{rec}(x, \mathsf{cons}(h, y), d, true) &\leftarrow P'_{rec}(x, y, d, true)
\end{aligned}
$$

2.2   Integer to String conversion

The integer to string conversion relies on extracting digits one by one, which is done using integer arithmetic. Under LTR encoding, during the conversion process, the pre-condition stores the rest of the input after removing the converted digits so far starting from the lowest position. For example, if the number is

$i = \overline{d_{n-1}\cdots d_0}$ and the converted string so far is $s = \text{``}d_{k-1}\cdots d_0\text{''}$, the rest of the number will be $r = \overline{d_{n-1}\cdots d_k}$ which is stored at the pre-condition.

The pre-condition in RTL encoding stores the offset of the next digit that needs to be extracted, since extracting digits from highest place values requires knowing their positions.

2.3   StartsWith and EndsWith

The encoding of `String.startsWith` method needs to consider different states of both strings and their relation, which leads to multiple recursive relations.

For example, if x starts with y, we can prepend c to both strings under LTR encoding (to get x' and y') and the condition holds on the resulting strings (i.e. x' starts with y'). For another example, if x does not start with y and $\text{len}(x) \geq \text{len}(y)$ we can append c to x under RTL encoding (to get x') and the condition holds on the resulting string (i.e. x' does not start with y).

$$
\begin{aligned}
&& S_{rec}(x, \text{nil}, true) &\leftarrow true \\
&& S_{rec}(x, x, true) &\leftarrow true \\
&& S_{rec}(\text{nil}, y, false) &\leftarrow \text{len}(y) > 0 \\
&& S_{rec}(\text{cons}(j, x), \text{cons}(k, y), false) &\leftarrow S_{rec}(x, y, false) \\
\text{(LTR)} && S_{rec}(\text{cons}(h, x), \text{cons}(h, y), true) &\leftarrow S_{rec}(x, y, true) \\
\text{(LTR)} && S_{rec}(\text{cons}(j, x), \text{cons}(k, y), false) &\leftarrow j \neq k \\
\text{(RTL)} && S_{rec}(\text{cons}(h, x), y, true) &\leftarrow S_{rec}(x, y, true) \\
\text{(RTL)} && S_{rec}(\text{cons}(j, x), \text{cons}(k, x), false) &\leftarrow j \neq k \\
\text{(RTL)} && S_{rec}(\text{cons}(h, x), y, false) &\leftarrow S_{rec}(x, y, false) \wedge \text{len}(x) \geq \text{len}(y) \\
\text{(RTL)} && S_{rec}(x, \text{cons}(h, y), false) &\leftarrow S_{rec}(x, y, false)
\end{aligned}
$$

The RTL encoding of `endsWith` is the same as LTR encoding of `startsWith`, and the LTR encoding of `endsWith` is the same as RTL encoding of `startsWith`.

2.4   CharAt

The encoding definition of `String.charAt` relies on the fact that prepending a character to a string under LTR encoding increases indices of all previous characters by one, while appending a character to a string under RTL encoding does not change those indices.

$$
\begin{aligned}
\text{(LTR)} && ChAt_{rec}(\text{cons}(h, t), 0, h) &\leftarrow true \\
\text{(LTR)} && ChAt_{rec}(\text{cons}(h, t), i + 1, c) &\leftarrow ChAt_{rec}(t, i, c) \wedge 0 \leq i < \text{len}(t) \\
\text{(RTL)} && ChAt_{rec}(\text{cons}(h, t), \text{len}(t), h) &\leftarrow true \\
\text{(RTL)} && ChAt_{rec}(\text{cons}(h, t), i, c) &\leftarrow ChAt_{rec}(t, i, c) \wedge 0 \leq i < \text{len}(t)
\end{aligned}
$$

3   Performance of the String Encoding

The following table shows the results of JayHorn on the 53 problems in the SV-COMP Java track that involve strings. Many of the programs contain string operations that are not yet handled in JayHorn, but the results already make it possible to compare encoding choices. Uniformly, RTL performs better than LTR (probably because appending characters to strings is more common than adding characters in the beginning), and the under-approximating CHC encoding of JayHorn performs better than the over-approximate encoding (probably because over-approximation too often loses information about string contents). The choice between Iterative, Recursive, or Recursive-with-precondition [4] for string concatenation surprisingly had no effect on the results.

Encoding Choices	Iterative				Recursive				RecursiveWithPrec			
	U-Approx		O-Approx		U-Approx		O-Approx		U-Approx		O-Approx	
	LTR	RTL	LTR	RTL	LTR	RTL	LTR	RTL	LTR	RTL	LTR	RTL
# Solved	4	6	1	3	4	6	1	3	4	6	1	3
Avg. Time (s)	81	79	7.5	16	79	78	7.6	16	77	78	7.7	16

In other respects, JayHorn performed similarly in SV-COMP 2021 [1] as in the two previous years. JayHorn gave one incorrect answer, for the problem `UnsatAddition02` and due to the use of unbounded integer arithmetic instead of correct Java machine arithmetic semantics. JayHorn could correctly prove 125 benchmarks safe, and 151 benchmarks unsafe. Changes compared to 2020 include 59 of the 64 `MinePump` benchmarks (by encoding `enums`, see Section 4) and 6 of the 53 string benchmarks that JayHorn solves now.

The biggest factor influencing the performance of JayHorn in SV-COMP is still the incomplete model of the Java API in JayHorn, given the large number of API tests among the SV-COMP Java benchmarks. Our work on supporting `Strings`, described in this paper, is one of the efforts to address the situation.

4   Tool Setup

The version submitted to SV-COMP 2021 is JayHorn version 0.7.5-strings,[4] which is also available on Zenodo [9]. In the configuration used in the competition,[5] JayHorn only applies the Horn solver Eldarica. The Benchexec tool info module is called `jayhorn.py` and the benchmark definition file `jayhorn.xml`. JayHorn competes in the Java category.

Since JayHorn only has incomplete support for Java `enums`, in this year we added a small source transformation tool[6] to JayHorn that has the purpose of replacing `enums` with simple integer variables. The script used in the competition applies the transformation tool to the benchmark source code prior to compilation to bytecode.

---

[4] https://github.com/jayhorn/jayhorn/releases/tag/v0.7.5-strings
[5] Java options: `-Xss40000k -Xmx12g`
JayHorn options: `-inline-size 50 -conservative -specs -string-encoding recursiveWithPrec -string-direction rtl`
[6] https://github.com/jayhorn/jayhorn/tree/devel/enum-eliminator

5 Software Project and Contributors

JayHorn was initially developed by Temesghen Kahsai, Philipp Rümmer, and Martin Schäf, with contributions by Daniel Dietsch, Rody Kersten, Huascar Sanchez, and Valentin Wüstholz [6,7]. Further development of the tool is at the moment mainly carried out by the authors of this paper. JayHorn is open source, and distributed under MIT license on https://github.com/jayhorn/jayhorn.

Acknowledgements. The work on JayHorn has been supported by the Swedish Research Council (VR) under grant 2018-04727, by the Swedish Foundation for Strategic Research (SSF) under the project WebSec (Ref. RIT17-0011), and by grants from Microsoft and Amazon Web Services.

References

1. D. Beyer. Software verification: 10th comparative evaluation (SV-COMP 2021). In *Proc. TACAS (2)*, LNCS 12652. Springer, 2021.
2. T. Freeman and F. Pfenning. Refinement types for ML. In *PLDI*, pages 268–277, New York, NY, USA, 1991. ACM.
3. H. Hojjat and P. Rümmer. The ELDARICA Horn solver. In *FMCAD*. IEEE, 2018.
4. H. Hojjat, P. Rümmer, and A. Shamakhi. On strings in software model checking. In *APLAS*. Springer, 2019.
5. T. Kahsai, R. Kersten, P. Rümmer, and M. Schäf. Quantified heap invariants for object-oriented programs. In *LPAR*. EasyChair, 2017.
6. T. Kahsai, P. Rümmer, H. Sanchez, and M. Schäf. JayHorn: A framework for verifying Java programs. In *CAV*. Springer, 2016.
7. T. Kahsai, P. Rümmer, and M. Schäf. JayHorn: A Java model checker — (competition contribution). In D. Beyer, M. Huisman, F. Kordon, and B. Steffen, editors, *TACAS: TOOLympics*, volume 11429 of *LNCS*, pages 214–218. Springer, 2019.
8. P. M. Rondon, M. Kawaguchi, and R. Jhala. Liquid types. In R. Gupta and S. P. Amarasinghe, editors, *PLDI*, pages 159–169. ACM, 2008.
9. A. Shamakhi, H. Hojjat, and P. Rümmer. JayHorn artifact at SV-COMP 2021. Zenodo: https://doi.org/10.5281/zenodo.4485702.
10. R. Vallée-Rai, L. Hendren, V. Sundaresan, P. Lam, E. Gagnon, and P. Co. Soot - a Java Optimization Framework. In *CASCON*, 1999.

JDART: Portfolio Solving, Breadth-First Search and SMT-Lib Strings (Competition Contribution)

Malte Mues (✉) and Falk Howar

TU Dortmund University, Dortmund, Germany
{malte.mues, falk.howar}@tu-dortmund.de

Abstract. JDART performs dynamic symbolic execution of JAVA programs: it executes programs with concrete inputs while recording symbolic constraints on executed program paths. A portfolio of constraint solvers is then used for generating new concrete values from recorded constraints that drive execution along previously unexplored paths. For SV-COMP 2021, we improved JDART by implementing exploration strategies, bounded analysis, and path-specific constraint solving strategies, as well as by enabling the use of SMT-Lib string theory for encoding of string operations.

1 Overview

JDART is a dynamic symbolic execution engine for the JAVA virtual machine (JVM) built on top of Java PathFinder (JPF) [12]. We first entered SV-COMP 2020 with JDART. Our corresponding report gives a short overview of JDART's architecture and internals [9]. In this paper, we focus on the description of the following three improvements that were explicitly motivated by SV-COMP 2021 [2].

1. The re-implementation of the internal constraints-tree enables bounded analysis and exploration strategies (e.g., breadth first search instead of depth first search),
2. A new CVC4 backend in JCONSTRAINTS is the basis for path-based selection of constraint solvers and sequential portfolio solving (using Z3 and CVC4).
3. We integrate recent advances in string constraint solving [3,10] by modeling string operations as SMT-Lib string constraints instead of bit vectors.

While all three changes contribute to an improved performance of JDART, portfolio solving has by far the biggest impact on the number of analyzed benchmark instances of SV-COMP 2021. In this paper, we focus on the description of the changes for (1) and (2).

2 Tool Improvements for SV-COMP 2021

JDART runs as an extension of the JPF software model checker [12], using the JAVA virtual machine implemented by JPF and its capabilities for annotating

J. F. Groote and K. G. Larsen (Eds.): TACAS 2021, LNCS 12652, pp. 448–452, 2021.
https://doi.org/10.1007/978-3-030-72013-1_30

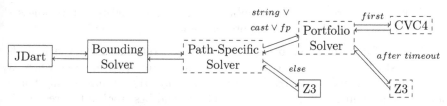

Fig. 1: The architecture and call hierarchy in the constraint solving backend.

values on the stack and the heap with symbolic information. The tool itself is written in JAVA and uses JCONSTRAINTS [6] for encoding SMT problems. Moreover, JCONSTRAINTS acts as a frontend to the Z3 [5] or CVC4 [1] SMT solver used for finding concrete values that drive the analysis.

Exploration Strategies. JDART has two main components: the *Executor* and the *Explorer*. While the *Executor* runs the concrete analysis and records symbolic constraints during concrete execution, the *Explorer* is responsible for exploration strategies and management of constraints. We re-designed the central data structure of the *Explorer*, the constraints tree, for SV-COMP 2021: The new tree supports different exploration strategies (e.g., breadth-first search) and bounds on the depth of exploration. In the past, JDART relied on unbounded depth-first exploration which would often 'get trapped' unrolling unbounded loops or recursion. Breadth-first search prevents this behavior and is more effective on the SV-COMP benchmark set.

Portfolio-Solving. Figure 1 demonstrates the architecture of the constraint solving backend used by JDART and JCONSTRAINTS for SV-COMP; dashed components and control-flow have been added for SV-COMP 2021: The *bounding solver* (developed for SV-COMP 2020) calls subsequent solvers with successively weaker bounds on numeric variables. For SV-COMP 2021, we use upper bounds 2, 8, 13, 21, 200, 600, ∞ and symmetric negative lower bounds. The new *path-specific solver* selects the most promising solving approach for every concrete path constraint: Currently, constraints involving string operations, type casts, or floating-point numbers are handed to the portfolio solver as we expect better performance. The *portfolio solver* wraps the CVC4 solver, starting repeated solving attempts in the case of (fairly frequent and random) segmentation faults as well as invocation of Z3 after a fixed timeout of 60 seconds. All other path constraints are passed directly to the Z3 solver as JDART used to do with all constraints at SV-COMP 2020.

3 Strengths and Weaknesses

JDART scored 623 points (max. of 693) in the JAVA track and was declared second winner for JAVA, after JAVA RANGER (630 points) [11]. Next best is JBMC [4] with 603 points. As JAVA RANGER and JBMC, JDART did not report a single incorrect verdict. JDART exhibits the general strengths and weaknesses of dynamic and symbolic analysis approaches for JAVA programs:

Fast search for counterexamples. Driven by concrete execution, the analysis is fairly fast. JDART $(950s)$ is overall the second fastest tool in cases where it can provide an answer after JBMC $(650s)$. Notably, JDART successfully found counterexamples in 251 of 253 instances. The second-best tool in this respect is JBMC with 243 correct *false* verdicts. Of the two instances for which JDART did not produce counterexamples one uses the `split` operation for strings that JDART does not yet model, leading to an *unknown* result. For the other instance, stack unrolling triggers an out of memory exception during the concolic execution of one path through the recursive Ackermann function.

Path Explosion. JDART is affected by path explosion in programs with long sequences of branching instructions with mutually unrelated conditions. Such sequences are common in code generated from models in the realm of embedded systems, e.g., by the *Alarm* benchmark instances in SV-COMP 2021. For these instances, JDART does not manage to explore all paths in the given time limit.

Unbounded Behavior. Based on principles of symbolic execution, JDART will only terminate on unbounded loops or in case of unbounded recursion when using manually configured bounds. In addition, the concolic execution might be configured to stop on property violations. As a consequence, assertion errors might be used as analysis bounds. For SV-COMP 2021, we used a search depth of 270 recorded decisions on paths in the constraints tree which we deemed conservative after initial experiments on the benchmark set: While in 13 instances *true* verdicts were given after exploring exhaustively up to the depth bound, there remain 30 problem instances for which JDART timed out exploring the search space up to the depth bound and 6 instances raising *unknown* verdicts (including the two mentioned above).

4   Tool Setup

The source code of JDART used for the competition artifact [8] is available on GitHub[1]. JDART is designed as a plug-in for JPF and relies on ant as a build system. One of its dependencies is the `jpf-core` project [12]. The other dependency is the JCONSTRAINTS library, which was configured to use Z3 [5] and CVC4 [1] for SV-COMP 2021. For the competition, JDART is wrapped by the `run-jdart.sh` shell script which generates `.jpf` configuration files, specifying which benchmark to analyze and the global configuration options of JDART. For SV-COMP 2021, we choose termination on the first assertion error, a depth bound of 270 (decisions on paths in the constraints tree) for exploration, breadth first search as exploration strategy, and the described path-specific solver together with iterative weakening of bounds on values in models as described in Section 2. Z3 is configured to run with the sequence solver for strings. The shell script records and interprets the output of JDART and can also report the version of JDART.

---

[1] https://github.com/tudo-aqua/jdart, Commit `4a9cc43`

5 Software Project

JDART, as used in SV-COMP 2021, is maintained by the Automated Quality Assurance Group at TU Dortmund University (in particular by the authors of this paper) and is available under the Apache License, version 2.0, on GitHub[1]. An initial version of JDART was developed by the authors of [7] at NASA Ames Research Center and Carnegie Mellon University. The original version of JDART is available on GitHub[2].

References

1. Barrett, C., Conway, C.L., Deters, M., Hadarean, L., Jovanović, D., King, T., Reynolds, A., Tinelli, C.: CVC4. In: Gopalakrishnan, G., Qadeer, S. (eds.) Computer Aided Verification. pp. 171–177. Springer (2011). https://doi.org/10.1007/978-3-642-22110-1_14
2. Beyer, D.: Software verification: 10th comparative evaluation (SV-COMP 2021). In: International Conference on Tools and Algorithms for the Construction and Analysis of Systems. Springer (2021)
3. Bjørner, N., Tillmann, N., Voronkov, A.: Path feasibility analysis for string-manipulating programs. In: International Conference on Tools and Algorithms for the Construction and Analysis of Systems. pp. 307–321. Springer (2009). https://doi.org/10.1007/978-3-642-00768-2_27
4. Cordeiro, L., Kroening, D., Schrammel, P.: JBMC: Bounded model checking for Java bytecode. In: Beyer, D., Huisman, M., Kordon, F., Steffen, B. (eds.) Tools and Algorithms for the Construction and Analysis of Systems. pp. 219–223. Springer International Publishing, Cham (2019). https://doi.org/10.1007/978-3-030-17502-3_17
5. De Moura, L., Bjørner, N.: Z3: An efficient SMT solver. In: International conference on Tools and Algorithms for the Construction and Analysis of Systems. pp. 337–340. Springer (2008). https://doi.org/10.1007/978-3-540-78800-3_24
6. Howar, F., Jabbour, F., Mues, M.: JConstraints: A library for working with logic expressions in Java. In: Models, Mindsets, Meta: The What, the How, and the Why Not?, pp. 310–325. Springer (2019). https://doi.org/10.1007/978-3-030-22348-9_19
7. Luckow, K.S., Dimjasevic, M., Giannakopoulou, D., Howar, F., Isberner, M., Kahsai, T., Rakamaric, Z., Raman, V.: JDart: A dynamic symbolic analysis framework. In: Proceedings of TACAS 2016. pp. 442–459 (2016). https://doi.org/10.1007/978-3-662-49674-9_26
8. Mues, M., Howar, F.: JDart artifact used in SV-COMP 2021 (Dec 2020). https://doi.org/10.5281/zenodo.4327551
9. Mues, M., Howar, F.: JDart: Dynamic symbolic execution for Java bytecode (competition contribution). In: International Conference on Tools and Algorithms for the Construction and Analysis of Systems. pp. 398–402. Springer (2020). https://doi.org/10.1007/978-3-030-45237-7_28
10. Reynolds, A., Woo, M., Barrett, C., Brumley, D., Liang, T., Tinelli, C.: Scaling up DPLL(T) string solvers using context-dependent simplification. In: International Conference on Computer Aided Verification. pp. 453–474. Springer (2017). https://doi.org/10.1007/978-3-319-63390-9_24

[2] https://github.com/psycopaths/jdart

11. Sharma, V., Hussein, S., Whalen, M., McCamant, S., Visser, W.: Java Ranger at SV-COMP 2020 (competition contribution). In: Tools and Algorithms for the Construction and Analysis of Systems. LNCS 12079, Springer (2020). https://doi.org/10.1007/978-3-030-45237-7_27
12. Visser, W., Havelund, K., Brat, G., Park, S., Lerda, F.: Model checking programs. Automated Software Engineering **10**(2), 203–232 (Apr 2003). https://doi.org/10.1023/A:1022920129859

Symbiotic 8: Beyond Symbolic Execution*
(Competition Contribution)

Marek Chalupa[1] ✉, Tomáš Jašek[1], Jakub Novák[1],
Anna Řechtáčková[1], Veronika Šoková[2], and
Jan Strejček[1]

[1] Masaryk University, Brno, Czech Republic
[2] Brno University of Technology, FIT, Brno, Czech Republic

Abstract. SYMBIOTIC 8 extends the traditional combination of static analyses, instrumentation, program slicing, and symbolic execution with one substantial novelty, namely a technique mixing symbolic execution with k-induction. This technique can prove the correctness of programs with possibly unbounded loops, which cannot be done by classic symbolic execution. SYMBIOTIC 8 delivers also several other improvements. In particular, we have modified our fork of the symbolic executor KLEE to support the comparison of symbolic pointers. Further, we have tuned the shape analysis tool PREDATOR (integrated already in SYMBIOTIC 7) to perform better on LLVM bitcode. We have also developed a light-weight analysis of relations between variables that can prove the absence of out-of-bound accesses to arrays.

1 Verification Approach

SYMBIOTIC is a program analysis framework that combines fast static analyses with code instrumentation and program slicing to speed up the code verification which is then performed by symbolic executor KLEE [3] (or, alternatively, by another supported verification tool). The main improvement in SYMBIOTIC 8 is a new verification technique combining symbolic execution with k-induction [8] that we call *KindSE*.

Symbolic execution with k-induction (KindSE) *KindSE* applies the idea of k-induction [8] to paths of the control flow graph. The approach can be roughly described by the following three steps.

1. Set k to 1. Let P be the set of all paths in the control flow graph of length k that end in an error location.
2. Use symbolic execution to execute every path $\pi \in P$. If the symbolic execution says that π is infeasible, remove π from P. If π is feasible and it starts in the initial location, report that the program is incorrect.

---

* This work has been supported by the Czech Science Foundation grant GA20-07487S.
✉ Jury member and the corresponding author: chalupa@fi.muni.cz.

J. F. Groote and K. G. Larsen (Eds.): TACAS 2021, LNCS 12652, pp. 453–457, 2021.
https://doi.org/10.1007/978-3-030-72013-1_31

3. If P is empty, the control flow graph contains no feasible path of length k (or more) leading to an error location and thus we report that the program is correct. If P is not empty, we replace each path $\pi \in P$ by paths of length $k+1$ that have π as its suffix, increase k by one, and go to step 2.

To improve the performance, we further extended the algorithm to summarize loop iterations. If we process a program location that is a loop header, we start unwinding the loop backwards. We over-approximate the states that we get in every loop iteration to cover more than one iteration if possible. If we are successful, the summarized loop states form an inductive invariant, which can help to prove that no error location is reachable from the loop header in k steps. Our loop summarization does not handle nested loops (in this case we fall-back to the algorithm without loop summarization) and calls of functions. To fix the latter restriction, we inline all procedures (if possible) before running KindSE.

KindSE is implemented in our prototype tool SLOWBEAST [1] which we integrated into SYMBIOTIC 8. The tool now supports only the `unreach-call` property. SLOWBEAST can also work as a standard symbolic executor (without k-induction), but it is noticeably slower than KLEE and it has some limitations. However, it supports symbolic floating point arithmetics, which KLEE does not.

Workflow of Symbiotic 8 As the first step, a given program is translated to LLVM [6]. If the program contains a call to `pthread_create`, SYMBIOTIC returns `unknown` as it cannot handle parallel programs. The rest of the workflow then depends on the verified property, as indicated in Figure 1.

For `unreach-call` property, we call slicer to remove instructions that have no influence on the property and run KLEE. If KLEE does not decide in 222 seconds, we run KindSE in SLOWBEAST. If it fails, we run KLEE again and if it also fails, we run SLOWBEAST as a standard symbolic executor. If some tool says

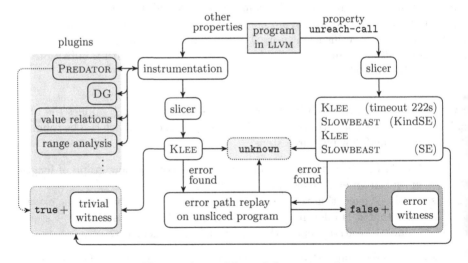

Fig. 1. The workflow of SYMBIOTIC 8

that the specified call is unreachable, we return **true** with the trivial witness. If we detect that the specified call is reachable, we try replaying the error path on the unsliced program. If the replay confirms that the call is reachable, we return **false** with the error witness generated from the replay.

For other properties, we instrument the program with the help of various analyses. For example, when checking memory safety, we use PREDATOR [5], DG [4], and a values-relations analysis to detect potentially unsafe instructions. If PREDATOR says that all instructions are safe, we directly return **true**. Otherwise, we slice the program with respect to potentially unsafe instructions and call KLEE. The rest of the process is identical to the previous case.

2   Software Architecture

All components of SYMBIOTIC 8 use LLVM 10 [6]. Scripts that call and control the components according to a given configuration are written in Python.

Instrumentation module is written in C++. In SYMBIOTIC 8, we have newly integrated a values-relations analysis as a plugin into instrumentation. This analysis is able to prove valid some accesses into arrays. We have also improved LLVM frontend of PREDATOR [5] to perform similarly well as the GCC frontend.

Program slicing module is written in C++ and is build around the library DG [4]. This year, we sped up the slicer by using more efficient data structures in pointer analysis and by using function summaries in data dependence analysis.

We use our own fork of KLEE [3] that differs from the upstream KLEE mainly in using segment-offset pointer representation which allows for better handling of symbolic pointers and symbolic-sized allocations. This year, we mended handling of symbolic pointers and added support for comparison of symbolic addresses.

Tool SLOWBEAST [1] is written in Python. Both, KLEE and SLOWBEAST use Z3 [7] as the SMT solver.

3   Strengths and Weaknesses

Symbolic execution may be very efficient in finding bugs but suffers from the *path explosion problem* which may prevent it from fully analyzing programs with high level of branching. We alleviate this problem by using program slicing. However, in the presence of unbounded loops or infinite execution paths, program slicing does not help unless it removes the unbounded computation from the program. Indeed, classical symbolic execution is unable to verify such programs at all.

To fight the inability of symbolic execution to verify unbounded programs, we use *KindSE*. However, its implementation in SLOWBEAST is still not fully matured and it handles only a very restricted set of programs.

Results of Symbiotic 8 in SV-COMP 2021 SYMBIOTIC 8 won *MemSafety* and *SoftwareSystems* categories [2]. In the *MemSafety* category, we lost many points in the new *MemSafety-Juliet* subcategory. These benchmarks contain threads and SYMBIOTIC immediately answered *unknown* due to the syntactic check mentioned in Section 1. However, most of these benchmarks actually do not spawn any thread and thus SYMBIOTIC could analyze them. The victory in *SoftwareSystems* category is mainly due to the dominance on the new *uthash* benchmarks.

This year, over 500 correct answers produced by SYMBIOTIC were not confirmed. Some of these cases must be accounted to the fact that SYMBIOTIC generates only trivial correctness witnesses. However, there are also unconfirmed answers because of missing witnesses, which turned out to be a bug in SLOW-BEAST integration. Unfortunately, these include all 99 benchmarks that were newly proved correct by KindSE, from which 85 were in the *ReachSafety-Loops* subcategory. We had also many unconfirmed witnesses for non-termination violation that still need to be investigated.

SYMBIOTIC had 16 incorrect answers: 14 incorrect *true* in *Termination* category and 2 incorrect *false* in *ReachSafety-Floats*. All of them were caused by last-minute commits that were fixed shortly after the submission deadline. Because of these mistakes, SYMBIOTIC ended up on the 4th place instead of on the 2nd in the *Termination* category.

In the *Overall* meta-category, SYMBIOTIC traditionally took the 4th place as every year since 2018.

4   Tool Setup and Project Contributors

The archive is available at https://doi.org/10.5281/zenodo.4483882. Run SYMBIOTIC as:

```
bin/symbiotic --sv-comp --prp <prpfile> [--32] <source>
```

The option --prp sets the verified property and --32 tells SYMBIOTIC to assume 32-bit architecture (64-bit architecture is assumed by default).

5   Software Project and Contributors

SYMBIOTIC 8 for SV-COMP 2021 has been developed by Marek Chalupa, Tomáš Jašek, Jan Novák, and Anna Řechtáčková under the supervision of Jan Strejček. Veronika Šoková provided a valuable help with adjusting PREDATOR modifications. SYMBIOTIC is available under the MIT license. All the external components that the tool uses are also available under open-source licenses that comply with SV-COMP's policy for the reproduction of results. The source code of SYMBIOTIC can be found at:

https://github.com/staticafi/symbiotic

References

1. SLOWBEAST. https://gitlab.fi.muni.cz/xchalup4/slowbeast/ (2020)
2. Beyer, D.: Software verification: 10th comparative evaluation (SV-COMP 2021). In: TACAS 2021. LNCS 12652, Springer (2021)
3. Cadar, C., Dunbar, D., Engler, D.R.: KLEE: Unassisted and automatic generation of high-coverage tests for complex systems programs. In: OSDI. pp. 209–224. USENIX Association (2008), http://www.usenix.org/events/osdi08/tech/full_papers/cadar/cadar.pdf
4. Chalupa, M.: DG: analysis and slicing of LLVM bitcode. In: ATVA 2020. LNCS, vol. 12302, pp. 557–563. Springer (2020), https://doi.org/10.1007/978-3-030-59152-6_33
5. Dudka, K., Peringer, P., Vojnar, T.: Predator: A practical tool for checking manipulation of dynamic data structures using separation logic. In: CAV 2011. LNCS, vol. 6806, pp. 372–378. Springer (2011), https://doi.org/10.1007/978-3-642-36742-7_49
6. Lattner, C., Adve, V.S.: LLVM: A compilation framework for lifelong program analysis & transformation. In: CGO 2004. pp. 75–88. IEEE Computer Society (2004), https://doi.org/10.1109/CGO.2004.1281665
7. de Moura, L.M., Bjørner, N.: Z3: an efficient SMT solver. In: TACAS 2008. LNCS, vol. 4963, pp. 337–340. Springer (2008), https://doi.org/10.1007/978-3-540-78800-3_24
8. Sheeran, M., Singh, S., Stålmarck, G.: Checking safety properties using induction and a SAT-solver. In: FMCAD 2000. LNCS, vol. 1954, pp. 108–125. Springer (2000), https://doi.org/10.1007/3-540-40922-X_8

VeriAbs: A Tool for Scalable Verification by Abstraction (Competition Contribution)

Priyanka Darke*⬚(✉), Sakshi Agrawal, and R. Venkatesh

TCS Research, Pune, India
{priyanka.darke, agrawal.sakshi4, r.venky}@tcs.com

Abstract. VeriAbs is a strategy selection-based reachability verifier for C programs. The selection of a suitable strategy is from a pre-defined set of strategies and by taking into account the syntax and semantics of the code to be verified. This year we present VeriAbs version 1.4.1 in which a novel preprocessor to strategy selection is introduced. The preprocessor checks for the feasibility of performing a lightweight slicing of the input code using function call graph and variable reference information. By this if the program is found to be *sliceable*, sub-programs or slices are generated, and the known strategy selection algorithm of VeriAbs is applied to each slice. The verification results of each slice are then composed to derive that of the entire program. This compositional verification has improved the scalability of VeriAbs and presented in this paper.

1 Verification Approach

VeriAbs is a C program verifier using a portfolio of twelve verification techniques [2]. These techniques are organized into four strategies as shown in Figure 1. Each of the strategies is defined such that it benefits verification of a specific type of programs. A program type is identified by a strategy selector based on the following code-structural and variable-data properties: (1) unstructured control flow, (2) loops with arrays, (3) short input ranges, and (4) numerical loops in code. The strategy selector looks for these properties in the given order and assigns a verification strategy to the code. For this it uses code-structure and interval analyses [2]. If the assigned strategy is unable to verify the program, it exits unless if the program contains arrays. In that case it selects the *default* strategy corresponding to numerical loops. Kindly refer to [2,3] for details on each verification technique implemented in VeriAbs.

The colored blocks in Figure 1 indicate the enhancements to the tool made this year and are explained next. The colored block with a dashed outline indicates that the component has been added for the first time in VeriAbs, and that with a solid outline indicates that a block that existed in older versions has been modified. The dashed arrows indicate information flow added this year. This information is the verification result of the respective strategy passed back to the slicer-analyzer explained in the next section. Besides these, there are changes in witness generation strategies and explained in the next section.

---

* Jury member

J. F. Groote and K. G. Larsen (Eds.): TACAS 2021, LNCS 12652, pp. 458–462, 2021.
https://doi.org/10.1007/978-3-030-72013-1_32

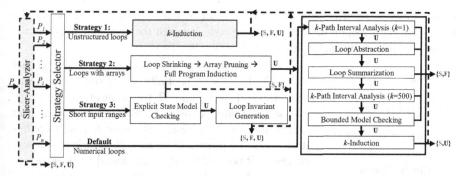

Fig. 1. VeriAbs Architecture (S: Program Safe, F: Property Fails, U: Unknown)

1.1 Tool Enhancements

Slicer-Analyzer. It has the following responsibilities: (1) checking the *sliceability* of input program P, (2) generating slices $P_1, P_2, ..., P_r$ if P is sliceable, and (3) computing the verification result R of P. Accordingly, the slicer-analyzer comprises of three parts. The first part checks for *sliceability*. Let *main* be the entry function of P. We define P to be sliceable with respect to *main* if all distinct functions $f_1, f_2, ..., f_r$ directly called from *main* are defined in P, and are independent of each other. We define the functions called from *main* independent iff *main* is non-recursive; contains no loops or unstructured control flow [2]; there is no transitive dependence (made up control and data dependence) between calls to $f_1, ..., f_r$ in *main*; no two functions in $f_1, f_2, ..., f_r$ transitively call the same function; and if $F(f_i)$ is the union of f_i and functions transitively called by f_i, then no two sets in $F(f_1), F(f_2), ..., F(f_r)$ refer to the same global variable in the program. That is, if $V(F(f_i))$ is the set of global variables referred by functions in $F(f_i)$ then $\forall m, n \mid 1 \leq m \leq r, 1 \leq n \leq r, m \neq n \implies V(F(f_m)) \cap V(F(f_n)) = \emptyset$. The call graph and referred variables information is computed using call-trees, and a light-weight flow insensitive pointer analysis.

```
void main() {
  b=30,c=10;
  if(!a) f1();
  else if(b) f2();
  ...
}
f1(){c++;}
f2(){b=0;assert(b);}
```

Fig. 2. Input Code

If above stated conditions are satisfied then using concepts presented in [10], the body of *main* is sliced with respect to call(s) to f_i to create the entry function $main^i$ of the executable slice P_i. Since *main* is sliced with respect to calls to f_i, P_i will only have functions in $F(f_i)$ and $main^i$. That is, the set of functions in slice P_i is given by $F(f_i) \cup main^i$. This way the set of all slices are generated by the second part of the slicer-analyzer. The proposed technique of slicing has the potential to greatly reduce the state space of the input program. This hypothesis is supported by experimental results presented later. The proposed slicing function uses control- and data-flow information local to *main*, hence it is lightweight.

Consider the example in Figure 2. One slice from this code is given in Figure 3. As seen, function *main* has been sliced with respect to the call to *f2* in Figure 3 which contains the error. Function $f1$ need not be analyzed to find the error. This type of slicing is helpful in analyzing large code in which the verifier may run out of resources while analyzing an irrelevant function like $f1$.

Next, VeriAbs applies its strategy selection to each slice $P_i, \forall i, 1 \leq i \leq r$ sequentially. The results of each slice are composed to compute R, the verification result of P, by the third part of the slicer-analyzer as follows: if an error trace is realized for any slice then R is set to *failure*; if all slices are proved to be safe, then R is set to *safe*; otherwise if none of the slices are found to be erroneous and there exists a slice that could not be verified, then R is set to *unknown*.

```
void main() {
  b=30,c=10;
  if(!a) ;
  else if(b) f2();
  ...
}
f2(){b=0;assert(b);}
```

Fig. 3. One Slice

This idea of slicing based on function call and variable reference information has been proposed for the first time. It is similar to a concept of clustering presented in [12]. Both these techniques partition a given application into independently executable slices. But [12] forms clusters with respect to un-called functions in the code base. The proposed sliceability criterion on the other hand focuses only on functions called from a given (entry) function *main*. It uses control- and data-flow analyses local only to the given function to slice it with respect to calls in its body. This in turn removes all functions not called from *main*. Another technique generates multiple backward slices at every calling context with respect to a property to be verified [8]. The proposed slicing technique however produces slices with respect to functions defined in P and called from *main*.

Witness Generation From Slices: VeriAbs stores slices in the form of separate C programs. To generate a valid witness from a slice it is critical to report the correct line numbers in the witness [5]. The slicer-analyzer maintains correct line numbers in the slice with respect to the original code by adding #line directives to it. The directives are added at every point in the slice which reads values from the environment, starts a block of code, or contains a branching condition. The witness generated from such a slice in VeriAbs is valid with respect to the original program.

Experimental results: The proposed slicing led to VeriAbs successfully analyzing 120 additional programs in ReachSafety in SV-COMP'21. On the other hand it runs out of time while verifying eighteen programs that it could successfully analyze earlier. This is due to the additional time required to slice. Overall these values demonstrate the feasibility of this approach.

Next we present modifications made to existing components of VeriAbs.

Strategy 1: Unstructured Control Flow. The first strategy meant for programs with unstructured control flow, thus far executed two verification techniques in parallel. The two techniques were evolutionary test generation algorithms using grey box fuzzing [13], and k-induction with continuously refined invariants [6]. This year we do not use the first algorithm in strategy 1. The reason being that the time taken by it to generate useful error traces is very large. We observe that as the program complexity increases with the number of constraints, branching conditions, and/or non-determinism, so does the time to reach the error by the test evolution algorithm. This leads to the effect of no apparent advantage of the algorithm when applied in parallel with k-induction. We present our experimental observations of the given algorithm in [2]. On the other hand, not using this algorithm led to time savings and verification of a few additional programs. We continue to use this algorithm for non-reactive loops and for programs with inputs of short ranges (strategy 3) [2]. Here we allocate it an independent thread with no time limits, while results are obtained quickly for non-reactive loops.

Witness Generation. This year VeriAbs uses the same strategies as last year to generate violation witnesses [3]. For correctness witnesses VeriAbs derives invariants from the over-approximation techniques in its portfolio. To save time this year VeriAbs does not extract invariants from k-induction [6] and interpolation [11] to generate correctness witnesses. From amongst the impacted witnesses, this led to 12 fewer witnesses being validated than last year.

2   Software Architecture

VeriAbs uses Vajra to perform full program induction [7], American Fuzzy Lop [13] to perform test evolution with fuzzing, and CPAchecker v1.8 [6] in the first strategy for k-induction. For bounded model checking VeriAbs uses the C Bounded Model Checker (CBMC) v5.10 [9] with the Glucose Syrup SAT solver v4.0 [4]. All remaining program analyses are implemented in the TCS Research group's program analysis framework called Prism [12]. The slicer-analyzer and the strategy selector are partly implemented in perl.

3   Strengths and Weaknesses

The main strengths of VeriAbs lie in its (1) portfolio of sound verification techniques, and its ability to (2) perform a lightweight slicing, (3) classify programs based on structural and variable data properties of code, and (4) match these code properties with suitable verification techniques. The main weakness of VeriAbs lies in its lack of an integrated implementation of witness generation that can utilize invariants derived across all strategies or techniques. This is because the invariants are to be derived from various abstractions, some of which are generated by off-the-shelf tools, and not yet extracted.

4   Tool Setup and Configuration

The VeriAbs SV-COMP 2021 executable is available for download at https://gitlab.com/sosy-lab/sv-comp/archives-2021/-/tree/master/2021/veriabs.zip. To install the tool, download the archive, extract its contents, and then follow the installation instructions in `VeriAbs/INSTALL.txt`. To execute VeriAbs, the user needs to specify the property file using the `--property-file` option. The witness is generated in the current working directory as `witness.graphml`. VeriAbs participated in the ReachSafety category of SV-COMP 2021. The BenchExec wrapper script for the tool is `veriabs.py` and the benchmark description file is `veriabs.xml`. A sample command is as follows:

```
VeriAbs/scripts/veriabs --property-file reach-safety.prp a.c
```

5   Software Project and Contributors

Few members of the Foundations of Computing group at TCS Research [1] maintain VeriAbs. They can be contacted at veriabs.tool@tcs.com. We thank past developers of VeriAbs, creators of Prism [12], Vajra, CPAchecker and CBMC. We specially thank Bharti Chimdyalwar, Shrawan Kumar and Ulka Shrotri for their insightful reviews.

References

1. Foundations of Computing Group at TCS Research.   https://www.tcs.com/designing-complex-intelligent-systems.
2. M. Afzal, A. Asia, A. Chauhan, B. Chimdyalwar, P. Darke, A. Datar, S. Kumar, and R Venkatesh. VeriAbs: Verification by Abstraction and Test Generation. In *ASE*, pages 1138–1141, 2019.
3. M. Afzal, S. Chakraborty, A. Chauhan, B. Chimdyalwar, P. Darke, A. Gupta, S. Kumar, C. Babu M, D. Unadkat, and R. Venkatesh. Veriabs : Verification by abstraction and test generation (competition contribution). In *TACAS (2)*, pages 383–387, 2020.
4. G. Audemard and L. Simon. On the glucose sat solver. *IJAIT*, 27(01), 2018.
5. D. Beyer. Software verification: 10th comparative evaluation (SV-COMP 2021). In *Proc. TACAS (2)*, LNCS 12652. Springer, 2021.
6. D. Beyer, M. Dangl, and P. Wendler. Boosting k-induction with continuously-refined invariants. In *CAV*, pages 622–640, 2015.
7. S. Chakraborty, A. Gupta, and D. Unadkat. Verifying array manipulating programs with full-program induction. In *Proc. TACAS (1)*, pages 22–39, 2020.
8. B. Chimdyalwar, P. Darke, A. Chavda, S. Vaghani, and A. Chauhan. Eliminating static analysis false positives using loop abstraction and bounded model checking. In *FM*, pages 573–576, 2015.
9. E. Clarke, D. Kroening, and F. Lerda. A Tool for Checking ANSI-C Programs. In *TACAS*, pages 168–176, 2004.
10. Mark Harman and Robert M. Hierons. An overview of program slicing. *Software Focus*, 2(3):85–92, 2001.
11. M. Heizmann, Y. Chen, D. Dietsch, M. Greitschus, J. Hoenicke, Y. Li, A. Nutz, B. Musa, C. Schilling, T. Schindler, and A. Podelski. Ultimate automizer and the search for perfect interpolants - (competition contribution). In *TACAS (2)*, pages 447–451, 2018.
12. S. Khare, S. Saraswat, and S. Kumar. Static program analysis of large embedded code base: an experience. In *ISEC*, pages 99–102, 2011.
13. M. Zalewski. American fuzzy lop. http://lcamtuf.coredump.cx/afl/.

Author Index

Printed in the United States
by Baker & Taylor Publisher Services